PATHWAYS

CIVILIZATIONS THROUGH TIME

Michael Cranny

With Contributions by
Graham Jarvis

Prentice
Hall

To my mother and father

Canadian Cataloguing in Publication Data

Cranny, Michael William, 1947–
　　Pathways : civilizations through time

Includes index.
ISBN 0-13-675463-5

1. Civilization - History. I. Title.

CB69.C72 1997　　909.07　　C97-931560-3

Prentice-Hall, Inc., Englewood Cliffs, New Jersey
Prentice-Hall International, Inc., London
Prentice-Hall of Australia, Pty., Ltd., Sydney
Prentice-Hall of India Pvt., Ltd., New Delhi
Prentice-Hall of Japan, Inc., Tokyo
Prentice-Hall of Southeast Asia (PTE) Ltd., Singapore
Editora Prentice-Hall do Brasil Ltda., Rio de Janeiro
Prentice-Hall Hispanoamericana. S.A., Mexico

ISBN 0-13-675463-5

Publisher: Anita Borovilos
Series Editor: Jessica Pegis
Editor and Writing Contributor: Margaret Hoogeveen
Assisting Editors: Carol Stokes (Managing Editor), Ed O'Connor (Editor)
Permissions/Photo Researchers: Karen Taylor, Alene McNeill
Proofreader: Dayne Ogilvie
Indexer: Chris Blackburn
Production: Sharon Houston
Art Director: Alex Li
Cover Design: Anne Goodes
Interior Design: Rob McPhail, Alex Li
Formatter: Anne Goodes
Illustrations: Alan Barnard, Wes Lowe, Kevin Cheng, Don Kilby, Eric Colquhoun, Henry Van Der
　　Linde, Karen Taylor
Technical Art: Anne Goodes, David Cheung, Carole Giguere
Maps: Deborah Crowle, Rob McPhail, Anne Goodes

Front Cover Images: Broadway tower (left): David Hiser/Tony Stone Images; Rinno-Ji temple, Japan
(right): Joel Rogers/Tony Stone Images; Camel caravan (bottom): Nicholas DeVore/Tony Stone Images
Back Cover Images: Roman cemetery figure (left): Erich Lessing/Art Resource, NY; Astrolabe (top,
right): Scala/Art Resource, NY; Ashanti gold head (middle): Werner Forman/Art Resource, NY; Camel
caravan (bottom): Nicholas DeVore/Tony Stone Images

Printed and bound in the United States of America by RR Donnelley & Sons Company

6 7 8 9　　RRD　　06 05 04 03

Note From the Publisher
The Publisher of *Pathways: Civilizations Through Time* has made every reasonable effort to trace the
ownership of data and visuals and to make full acknowledgment for their use. If any errors or
omissions have occurred, they will be corrected in future editions, providing written notification has
been received by the publisher.

PATHWAYS:
CIVILIZATIONS THROUGH TIME

PREFACE

Pathways: Civilizations Through Time brings a global perspective to the discipline of Social Studies by encouraging teachers and students to investigate the history and geography of many regions of the world. Moreover, the book incorporates skills and ideas from many disciplines, including literature, anthropology, and demography, just to name a few. A unique feature is the Window on the Past—an inviting chapter opener, often in the form of an illustrated fictional story based on actual historical occurrences. The windows are designed to catch the interest of students, and to give them the perspective necessary for an understanding of important periods and places.

In every chapter, *Pathways* asks students to consider a number of primary sources from a variety of genres, and to apply themselves to understanding the uses and limitations of each. The feature Viewpoints in Conflict helps students compare various perspectives. Equally important are the Link-Up features, which help students see the present-day relevance of their studies, and explore connections between cultures, time periods, and disciplines. Such studies are enhanced by colourful maps, tables, and graphs, which occur in every chapter. How-To features provide opportunities for skill development; time lines assist students in placing the events of each period; vocabulary definitions provide assistance with unfamiliar words; and Did You Know boxes alert students to interesting tidbits of information. A variety of activities at the end of features, sections, and chapters require recall, critical thinking, analysis, and evaluation of the raw materials of Social Studies, and the synthesis and extension of knowledge and skills.

ACKNOWLEDGMENTS

I would like to thank Anita Borovilos and Bob Kirk, for their commitment to this project, and for their help and encouragement throughout. I would also like to thank Jessica Pegis, Margaret Hoogeveen, and Ed O'Connor for their creativity, time, and energy.

The editorial team would like to thank the many reviewers of *Pathways: Civilizations Through Time* for offering their analyses and thoughtful advice; Judith Dawson, Greg Galbraith, and especially Graham Jarvis for writing contributions for *Pathways*; and Jessica Pegis for conceptualizing the feature boxes. We would like to extend a special thanks to everyone in production who worked so hard to make *Pathways* such a beautiful book.

AUTHOR BIOGRAPHY

Michael Cranny has been a Social Studies educator for over twenty years. He has been head of secondary Social Studies and Humanities departments in high schools in School District 91, Nechako Lakes, British Columbia; and was British Columbia's provincial Pacific Rim and Social Studies Coordinator for three years. Cranny earned his Master's degree in Archaeology and Anthropology from the University of British Columbia.

MAJOR EVENTS IN THE HISTORY OF CIVILIZATIONS

MAJOR EVENTS BEFORE 500 CE

8000 BCE Japan	JOMON AND AINU CULTURES EMERGE
6000 BCE Africa	FIRST ROCK PAINTINGS IN WHAT IS NOW THE SAHARA DESERT
3000 BCE Middle East Africa	MESOPOTAMIAN AND EGYPTIAN CIVILIZATIONS EMERGE
2500 BCE India	THE INDUS VALLEY CIVILIZATION BEGINS
1027 BCE China	FIRST BOOKS WRITTEN DURING THE ZHOU DYNASTY
1000 BCE Africa	FIRST KNOWN CARAVAN CROSSINGS OF THE SAHARA DESERT
900 BCE Africa	THE NOK PEOPLE DEVELOP TERRA COTTA SCULPTURE
500 BCE China	FOUNDING OF CONFUCIANISM
300 BCE Africa	THE AXUM KINGDOM RULES IN ETHIOPIA
206 BCE China	THE SILK ROAD OPENS
150 BCE Western Europe	GREECE FALLS TO ROME
70 BCE Western Europe	ROME DESTROYS JERUSALEM
0 Middle East	JESUS CHRIST IS BORN
311 CE Western Europe	ROMAN EMPEROR CONSTANTINE LEGALIZES CHRISTIANITY
410 CE Western Europe	THE GOTHS SACK ROME

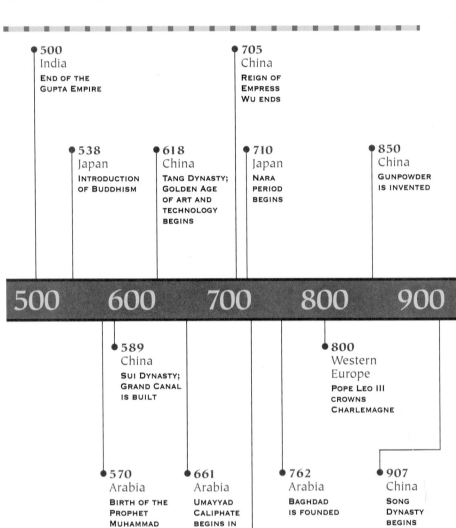

500
India
END OF THE GUPTA EMPIRE

705
China
REIGN OF EMPRESS WU ENDS

538
Japan
INTRODUCTION OF BUDDHISM

618
China
TANG DYNASTY; GOLDEN AGE OF ART AND TECHNOLOGY BEGINS

710
Japan
NARA PERIOD BEGINS

850
China
GUNPOWDER IS INVENTED

500   600   700   800   900

589
China
SUI DYNASTY; GRAND CANAL IS BUILT

800
Western Europe
POPE LEO III CROWNS CHARLEMAGNE

570
Arabia
BIRTH OF THE PROPHET MUHAMMAD

661
Arabia
UMAYYAD CALIPHATE BEGINS IN DAMASCUS

762
Arabia
BAGHDAD IS FOUNDED

907
China
SONG DYNASTY BEGINS

711
Western Europe
THE ARABS ARRIVE

950
India
CHOLA DYNASTY CONTROLS SOUTHERN INDIA

A mountain town in ancient Arabia. Towns develop in areas with conditions favourable to human survival. Then, because people want to live in peace together, they develop laws and common cultural ties—and so emerge the arts, music, and literature. Religion can play a particularly important role in helping people agree on acceptable behaviour within society.

Vikings attacking a monastery. Chaos gripped western Europe for centuries after the fall of Rome. Viking raids like the one pictured here, as well as a lack of education, leadership, communication, and government all contributed to the uncertainties of life in medieval Europe.

A section of the Silk Road, 1940. This ancient trading route linked China with trading partners throughout Asia and as far away as Africa and Europe. All the world desired the fine products of the oldest civilization in the world.

1 EUROPE'S EARLY MIDDLE AGES

CHAPTER OUTCOMES

In this chapter you will focus on the struggle between civilization and chaos that took place in Europe during the early Middle Ages. By the end of the chapter, you will

- describe the environmental factors that encouraged the emergence of Mediterranean civilizations

- explain how the Roman Empire succeeded, how it collapsed, and the consequences

- demonstrate an understanding of the origins and beliefs of the Jewish, Islamic, and Christian religions

- explain how Anglo-Saxon story tellers and Irish monks both preserved a cultural legacy

- analyze the impact of population and resources on Viking society

- assess the effects of conflict between Vikings and other Europeans

- make a bar graph

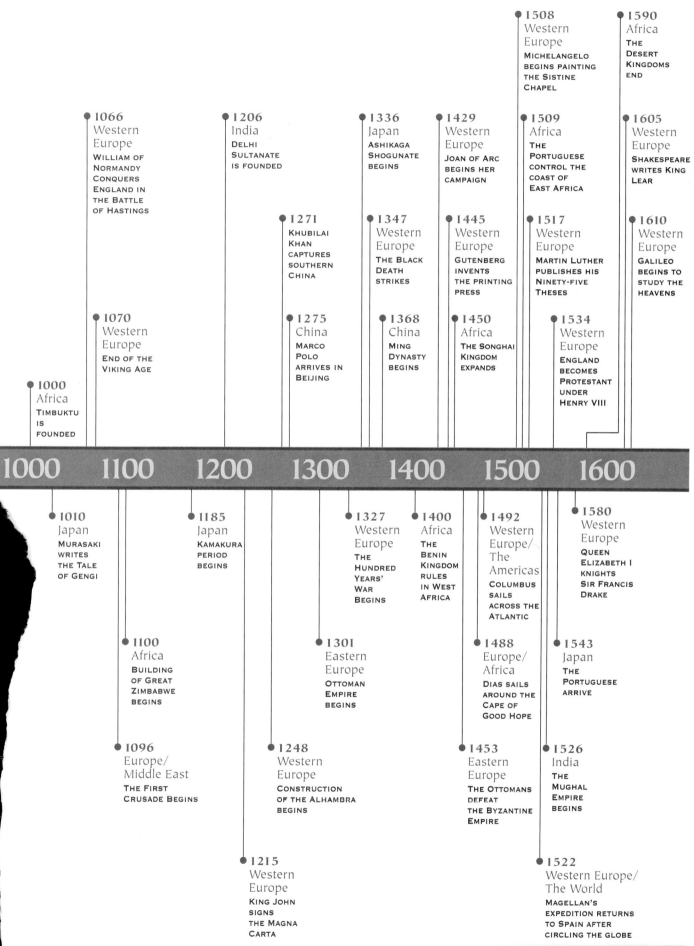

1508
Western Europe
MICHELANGELO BEGINS PAINTING THE SISTINE CHAPEL

1590
Africa
THE DESERT KINGDOMS END

1066
Western Europe
WILLIAM OF NORMANDY CONQUERS ENGLAND IN THE BATTLE OF HASTINGS

1206
India
DELHI SULTANATE IS FOUNDED

1336
Japan
ASHIKAGA SHOGUNATE BEGINS

1429
Western Europe
JOAN OF ARC BEGINS HER CAMPAIGN

1509
Africa
THE PORTUGUESE CONTROL THE COAST OF EAST AFRICA

1605
Western Europe
SHAKESPEARE WRITES KING LEAR

1271
KHUBILAI KHAN CAPTURES SOUTHERN CHINA

1347
Western Europe
THE BLACK DEATH STRIKES

1445
Western Europe
GUTENBERG INVENTS THE PRINTING PRESS

1517
Western Europe
MARTIN LUTHER PUBLISHES HIS NINETY-FIVE THESES

1610
Western Europe
GALILEO BEGINS TO STUDY THE HEAVENS

1070
Western Europe
END OF THE VIKING AGE

1275
China
MARCO POLO ARRIVES IN BEIJING

1368
China
MING DYNASTY BEGINS

1450
Africa
THE SONGHAI KINGDOM EXPANDS

1534
Western Europe
ENGLAND BECOMES PROTESTANT UNDER HENRY VIII

1000
Africa
TIMBUKTU IS FOUNDED

1000   1100   1200   1300   1400   1500   1600

1010
Japan
MURASAKI WRITES THE TALE OF GENGI

1185
Japan
KAMAKURA PERIOD BEGINS

1327
Western Europe
THE HUNDRED YEARS' WAR BEGINS

1400
Africa
THE BENIN KINGDOM RULES IN WEST AFRICA

1492
Western Europe/ The Americas
COLUMBUS SAILS ACROSS THE ATLANTIC

1580
Western Europe
QUEEN ELIZABETH I KNIGHTS SIR FRANCIS DRAKE

1100
Africa
BUILDING OF GREAT ZIMBABWE BEGINS

1301
Eastern Europe
OTTOMAN EMPIRE BEGINS

1488
Europe/ Africa
DIAS SAILS AROUND THE CAPE OF GOOD HOPE

1543
Japan
THE PORTUGUESE ARRIVE

1096
Europe/ Middle East
THE FIRST CRUSADE BEGINS

1248
Western Europe
CONSTRUCTION OF THE ALHAMBRA BEGINS

1453
Eastern Europe
THE OTTOMANS DEFEAT THE BYZANTINE EMPIRE

1526
India
THE MUGHAL EMPIRE BEGINS

1215
Western Europe
KING JOHN SIGNS THE MAGNA CARTA

1522
Western Europe/ The World
MAGELLAN'S EXPEDITION RETURNS TO SPAIN AFTER CIRCLING THE GLOBE

UNIT 1
FORGING CIVILIZATIONS, 500–1200

A struggle between civilization and chaos has dominated human society ever since human beings began gathering together to live in villages. Chaos is easy to define: confusion and disorder. War, lawlessness, and persecution are all signs of chaos in human society.

Civilization is a little more difficult to describe. It takes shape when people try to bring order and peace to their lives. Laws, education, politics, and religion are all examples of ways people do this. These organizing systems came about all over the world in isolated or scattered communities, but more commonly in big cities, which drew many people together in one place. To make these cities work, people had to organize themselves in an orderly fashion for their common good.

When organizing systems affect many people and last for many years, the society is usually known as a civilization. For example, as the Roman civilization developed, flourished, and then declined, it affected the lives of many people throughout the Roman Empire and left a remarkable legacy.

In this unit you will explore the emergence of society in the Mediterranean region, and how Europe struggled towards civilization after the fall of Rome. You also investigate the foundations of early Chinese civilization, and the environmental conditions that allowed this society to flourish. By 900, China had a 2000-year-old written history. Finally, you examine the early Arab world. By 1200, the Arab world had developed into a major world civilization, largely because of the influence of Islam.

Peasant farmers ploughing the land.
By 1200, much of western Europe was ruled by means of feudalism. Nobles controlled the land, on which 90 percent of the population toiled to make a meagre living.

The Viking Raid

The following fictional story is based on events that really happened. Similar events were recorded by people who were either present when they happened or were told about them by reliable sources. As you read this story, write down any questions the story raises for you, and try to answer them after reading Chapter 1.

At dawn, the Viking ship approaches the monastery unheard and unseen.

Pippin threw himself into the clump of tall ferns, pressing his body against the ground. He was still bleeding from a deep gash behind one ear, and he feared that the trail of blood he was leaving would make it easy for his pursuers to track him. He could hear the hoarse voices coming closer. If he could just lie quietly, he thought, perhaps he could avoid death. As he lay hugging the ground, Pippin's thoughts drifted back to the events of the past few hours.

•••••••

The Vikings had struck the **monastery** first thing in the morning, just as the monks were filing out of chapel. No one had seen the long dragon ship as it made its way silently down the wide river, or the raiding party as it stole through the monastery's orchards and gardens.

Pippin, a **novice**, watched in horror from behind the treasury door as the monks were slaughtered in the courtyard. The first victim was beheaded with one blow from the Viking chieftain's battle-axe. Others were run through by long spears or cut down by swords. Within minutes the massacre was over—all the monks were dead—and the looting began.

First the Vikings stripped gold vessels and embroidered cloths from the altar of the chapel and ripped the jewel-encrusted covers off the books in the library. Then, blazing torches in hand, they began to set fires. Before long the whole monastery was in flames.

The only item Pippin had time to save was the jewelled box in the treasury. The box contained the monastery's most prized possession: a finger bone from St. Sergius. **Pilgrims** came from all over the kingdom to be blessed with this **relic** and to pray to St. Sergius.

As Pippin crept out of the monastery grounds clutching the relic, he surprised a group of Vikings drinking wine from an oak cask behind the dining hall. He stared at them, too frightened to move. The men

Pippin loses the jewelled box containing the monastery's holy relic.

Pippin and Gisla are held captive in the bow of the Viking ship.

had rough beards and wore helmets of iron and leather. Their hands and faces were splattered with the blood of the murdered monks and blackened by smoke. They laughed aloud when they saw the young monk, and one threw a spear at Pippin as he turned to flee, catching him a **glancing** blow behind the ear.

·······

Now, hiding in the ferns with his face pressed to the ground, Pippin prayed to God for deliverance. Finally he felt sure the Vikings had gone and slowly raised his head. Pippin found himself looking directly into the hard blue eyes of the Viking chieftain. The man patted the battle-axe lying across his knee and laughed. As he rose to his feet, Pippin saw Vikings all around. One of them swung a club at Pippin's head while another ripped the

jewelled box out of his hand.

When Pippin came to, he was bound hand and foot, lying in the bow of the Viking ship. The Vikings were rowing furiously back to the mouth of the river, where the river emptied into the North Sea. From there the Vikings would raise the ship's sail and head for their home in Denmark.

Pippin groaned. The leather thongs bit into his wrists and ankles, and his head ached. A man wearing a helmet that hid most of his face laughed when he saw Pippin was awake.

"You should be happy, little priest," he said, speaking Frankish with a thick accent. "You will be my **thrall**. My name is Guthrum Bloodaxe. Now say your prayers and thank your god you are still alive."

Pippin, too stunned to pray, let his tears roll freely down his face. Everyone he loved was

gone; the life he had known for most of his fourteen years was completely ruined. This small group of thirty Vikings had killed dozens of monks, burned the monastery to the ground, and destroyed countless works of art. The precious books alone had taken years to copy out by hand. Pippin could only assume the Vikings had ravaged the nearby village as well. He wondered, was this a punishment sent by God for the sins of the people?

Then Pippin noticed he was not alone. Beside him on the wooden boards of the hull was a girl about his own age. She had been beaten and her shirt was bloody. Her arms and legs were bound with leather thongs. She stared at him with reddened eyes.

"See how fast they row," she said. Her voice was low and bitter but held a hint of hope.

"Now the hunters have become the hunted."

"What do you mean?" asked Pippin.

"They know the soldiers have been warned and are coming after us. Our people will try to cut the Northmen off at the dam the king built near the river's mouth. The Northmen will have to land there and push their boat past the dam. But if they can get back into the water before the soldiers arrive, we'll never see our people again."

Pippin examined the girl's face. "I know you. You're Gisla, from the village, aren't you? How do you know all this?"

"My father serves in the king's army," Gisla replied. "When the Vikings came to the village this morning, my brother managed to escape. He must have raised the alarm."

Sooner than Gisla had hoped, the Viking ship reached the dam, a wall of sharpened wooden stakes built across the river at its narrowest point. By building these structures on several rivers, the emperor Charlemagne intended to discourage Viking raiders, whose savage attacks had been growing more numerous. No settlement near the sea was safe.

The Vikings brought their ship to the river bank, where they hauled the vessel onto a platform of tree trunks they had cut down the night before. Pippin and Gisla were left in the ship while the men pushed it along the ground using the logs as rollers. The Vikings heaved their ship forward with a ferocious sense of purpose.

All at once, Pippin and Gisla heard the drumming of horses' hooves, and then a sound like hammers pounding on iron. As they huddled on the floor of the ship, they heard warlike cries and shrill screams of agony. The exhausted Vikings fought bravely but were overwhelmed by the well-organized and much larger band of Franks. The battle continued until the last Viking was dead.

Soon after, Pippin and Gisla found themselves standing in a clearing freed of their bonds and surrounded by Frankish soldiers. An older man with a thick, grey mustache and a weather-beaten face walked his horse towards them. A soldier motioned with his spear for them to kneel.

A Frankish war party attacks the fleeing invaders.

"Bow down," he commanded, "to Charles, Emperor of the Romans and King of the Franks!"

Charlemagne ordered the bodies of the Vikings to be taken to the river mouth, where they were hung from trees, in plain view of the sea, as a warning to other pirates. That night, the army camped farther down the coast. They built a bonfire on the seashore and held a feast to celebrate their victory over the raiding Northmen. Everyone seemed happy except Charlemagne himself, who walked up and down the shore staring out to sea.

Gisla and Pippin sat with Gisla's father, one of Charlemagne's commanders.

"What does the king look for in the dark sea?" Pippin asked.

"The king is an old man now," Gisla's father replied. "He has won many battles and was crowned emperor by the pope himself. But he worries about the future and what it will bring. Until now he has been able to hold the Northmen in check. But who will stop the Northmen after death has stopped the king?"

monastery: a self-contained community for people, such as monks or nuns, who have taken religious vows

novice: a person training to become a nun or monk

pilgrim: a person who travels to a holy place for religious reasons

relic: an item associated with a saint; thought to have great powers

glancing: indirect, not solid

thrall: the Viking word for "slave"

pope: the head of the Catholic Church

technology: anything made by humans to extend our abilities

Charlemagne walks the beach, wondering what dangers the future will bring.

ACTIVITIES

1. List three reasons why Vikings would want to attack a monastery.

2. **Technology** consists of anything we make to extend our abilities. Examples include the fork, the wheelbarrow, and computer software. A defensive technology is something we make to protect ourselves. What technologies did the Franks use to defend themselves against the Vikings? Were these defences effective? Explain.

3. **a)** Do you sympathize with one character in particular in the story of the Viking raid? Which one? Why?

   b) Because this story is written from Pippin's point of view, our sympathies tend to lie with him. Write a point-form version of this story from Guthrum Bloodaxe's point of view. Do you still sympathize with the same characters? Why or why not?

4. Do you know someone who has experienced armed conflict? Perhaps that person—maybe you, a family member, or another student—would share the story with the rest of the class. Where did the events take place? How has violence affected this person's life?

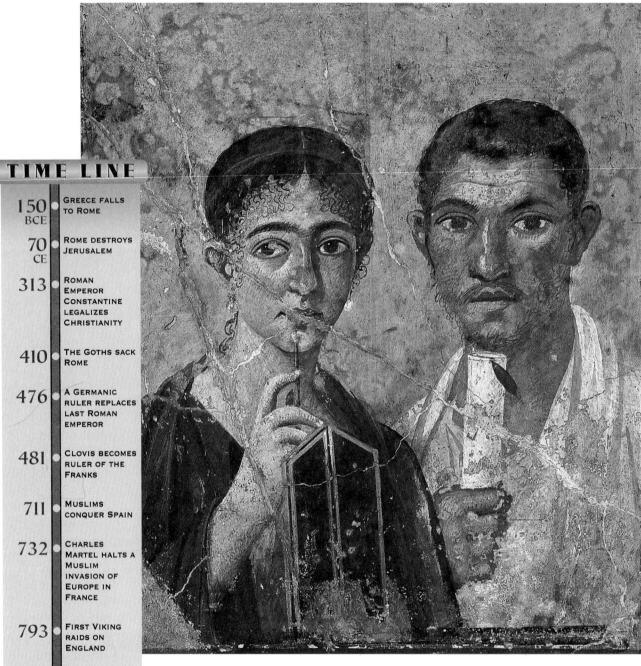

TIME LINE

150 BCE	GREECE FALLS TO ROME
70 CE	ROME DESTROYS JERUSALEM
313	ROMAN EMPEROR CONSTANTINE LEGALIZES CHRISTIANITY
410	THE GOTHS SACK ROME
476	A GERMANIC RULER REPLACES LAST ROMAN EMPEROR
481	CLOVIS BECOMES RULER OF THE FRANKS
711	MUSLIMS CONQUER SPAIN
732	CHARLES MARTEL HALTS A MUSLIM INVASION OF EUROPE IN FRANCE
793	FIRST VIKING RAIDS ON ENGLAND
800	POPE LEO III CROWNS CHARLEMAGNE
855	THE VIKING LEADER RAGNAR ATTACKS PARIS
912	THE VIKING LEADER ROLLO SETTLES IN NORMANDY
1070	END OF THE VIKING AGE

Who would believe that Rome, built upon the conquest of the whole world, would fall to the ground? That the mother herself would become the tomb of her peoples?

—SAINT JEROME

Saint Jerome was a Roman citizen and Christian leader who translated the Bible into Latin. He saw Rome sacked in 410 C.E. by Alaric and the Goths. Like many people of the time, he could hardly believe that the "whole world"—the world he knew—was gone forever. What event could disturb you in the same way?

INTRODUCTION

Despite Europe's relatively small size, the people of this region have had an enormous impact on world culture. Much of what we see around us today—the world's art, architecture, literature, forms of government, and even the way many of us think—has been strongly affected by the **legacy** of western Europe. For example, many modern sports arenas use domes and look like the Colosseum, a stadium built by the Romans.

Europe was shaped not just by the Greeks and Romans in ancient times, however. During the early Middle Ages, the Germanic peoples had much more influence. Their gradual conversion to Christianity, for example, utterly changed medieval European society. Three of these peoples—the Franks, the Anglo-Saxons, and the Vikings—as well as the Celtic people of Ireland, each made a unique contribution to the development of western European civilization.

legacy: knowledge and culture passed down from one generation or civilization to another

THE MEDITERRANEAN WORLD

The history of western European civilization began thousands of years ago on the shores of the Mediterranean Sea. The Mediterranean environment had everything necessary to sustain large numbers of people: fertile soil, plenty of rainfall and sunshine, and a climate that was moderate, neither too hot nor too cold. This meant that plants had a long growing season and that a surplus of food could be produced. The population grew rapidly and towns formed.

The Mediterranean Sea itself formed a transportation route that encouraged people to travel widely to trade and to learn from each other. Ideas from the Middle East, Asia, Africa, and Europe spread easily. All civilizations flourish and grow stronger through fresh ideas.

The two most important early European civilizations were those of Greece and Rome. The Greeks eagerly studied **philosophy**, which is usually defined as the pursuit of ideas. They also made great advances in art, architecture, drama, literature, medicine, and science. In the fourth century B.C.E., Alexander the Great conquered many lands and spread Greek culture as far east as India.

The Greek Empire weakened and fell to the Romans about 150 B.C.E. Because they admired the accomplishments of the Greeks, the Romans borrowed Greek attitudes and learning and made them their own. They gathered thinkers and builders from Asia, eastern Europe, and the Middle East. In addition, they became superb organizers, developing such systems as aqueducts to deliver running water, road networks, and military organizations. The **Roman Legions** were so powerful that the Roman Empire at its peak controlled most of Europe, southeast Asia, and northern Africa. For more than six centuries, the Mediterranean world and the Roman Empire were really one and the same.

philosophy: the search for ideas, wisdom, knowledge

B.C.E.: before the common era

Roman Legions: Roman armed forces

DID YOU KNOW?

The roots of European civilization go deep. Herodotus, for example, a famous Greek historian, repeatedly indicates Greece's debt to ancient Egypt.

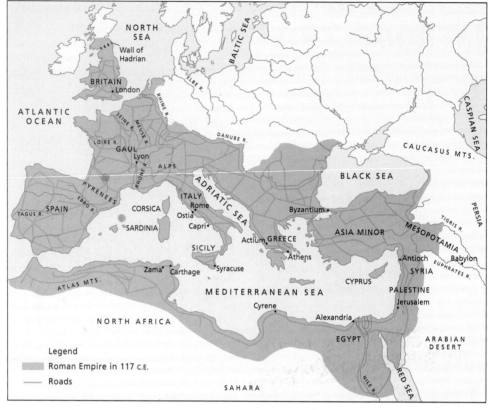

Figure 1–1 The shaded area in this map shows the extent of the Roman Empire about 150 C.E. How would the extensive network of roads have helped the empire stay united? What would have been involved in designing this system of roads? Think about materials, organizational techniques, labour, and time.

c.e.: of the common era

architecture: the art and science of designing buildings

Latin: the language of the Romans. During the Middle Ages, Latin served as a common language for educated people throughout Europe.

gladiator: a fighter who battled at public shows; most were slaves

THE ROMANS

Under the Romans, western European culture flourished like never before. The Romans admired the achievements of the ancient Greeks, so they copied and developed Greek arts and **architecture**. They also built great cities decorated with works of art, magnificent gardens, arenas, public baths, and theatres. The Romans were a highly literate people. Roman scholars and poets wrote thousands of books, and great libraries were filled with ancient works from Greece and Egypt. **Latin** provided a common language for the whole empire.

The Romans developed a code of laws for all the peoples they ruled. Some Canadian laws and rules of justice are based on these Roman laws. For example, all Roman citizens had the right to a fair trial and to rescue

Figure 1–2 The Roman Colosseum (at left) could seat 50 000 spectators, only slightly fewer than the 60 000 that fit into Vancouver's BC Place (at right). The Colosseum was the scene of executions, mock naval battles, and combats between **gladiators**. People were eaten alive by wild animals. Were these "entertainments" examples of civilization? Why or why not?

from poverty. Within the borders of the empire, Roman law protected all peoples from war and from violent outlaws on land and pirates at sea. The *Pax Romana*, or Roman peace, encouraged trade and the exchange of ideas. Of course, a price was paid: Rome demanded taxes, slaves, and submission from all the lands it controlled. Further, not everyone benefited under Roman law. Women, non-Romans, and slaves were all denied the rights of Roman citizenship.

The Fall of Rome

In the year 410 C.E., the Mediterranean world was shocked by news that the city of Rome, the centre of European civilization, had been conquered by the Goths, a **Germanic** people. The impossible had happened. The Roman Empire, which had once stretched from Iran to Scotland and from Upper Egypt to the North Sea, had collapsed. Only the Eastern Roman Empire, with its capital in Constantinople, remained strong.

Historians often disagree about why Rome fell. Some believe that all civilizations have a life span and that they eventually grow old and die, almost like living things.

After the Fall

Though the accomplishments of Greek and Roman civilizations were great, they were to be lost for centuries after the fall of Rome. Only through the foresight and determination of individuals did Roman culture survive in isolated monasteries and distant lands. Ages later, Greek and Roman art, architecture, drama, literature, sports, mythology, philosophy, laws, and systems of government would all be reborn in various forms to inspire and enrich modern civilizations. But first, Europe experienced a period the Romans would have called "barbarous."

For centuries Rome had been in contact with Germanic peoples to the north and east. These peoples were known to the Greeks and Romans as

Germanic people: one of the European peoples that spoke a Germanic language; for example, the Teutones, Visigoths, Angles, Saxons, Jutes, Franks, and Ostrogoths

Why Did Rome Fall?

The death of an empire is usually caused by a combination of internal forces (those coming from inside) and external forces (those coming from outside). Historians think that the following forces contributed to Rome's fall. Classify each as an internal or external force.

- Small businesses suffered when Romans began using slaves to supply goods and services.

- Romans spent more money than they should have on entertainment and expensive luxuries.

- Contagious diseases, brought to Rome by soldiers in the Roman Legions, killed thousands.

- After the Roman republic ended in 30 B.C.E., Rome was ruled by emperors rather than a government that respected individual freedom.

- Because the empire was so large and contained such a wide variety of terrain, the empire became impossible to defend.

- New religions weakened the will of the Roman people to defend their empire, because many chose their new religion over Rome.

- The empire grew weak because of repeated attacks by the Germanic peoples.

Barbarians, meaning "people who speak an unfamiliar language." In other words, a Barbarian was anyone not Greek or Roman. As the Western Roman Empire collapsed and the Roman Legions withdrew to Rome, Germanic peoples moved into Roman provinces such as Gaul (France), Britain, and Spain. These peoples— Angles, Saxons, Jutes, Goths, Vandals, Lombards, and Franks—were attracted to the riches of the Roman Empire. They pushed out the original populations of Celtish peoples and other native peoples and lived by their own laws, customs, and religions.

Civilization in western Europe began to wither away. Roads fell into disrepair; travel became dangerous; cities decayed and were deserted.

Soon few people could read or write except monks in isolated monasteries. Western Europe slipped into an age of chaos and savagery, torn by violence and ignorance. A kind of gang warfare prevailed.

The glory of Rome became a memory, and, strangely, a dream for the future. Local rulers tried again and again to rekindle the fire of civilization, the fire that they themselves had helped put out. This time of turmoil lasted from approximately 476 C.E., when the last Roman emperor lost his power, to 800. In that year, Pope Leo III crowned Charlemagne Emperor of the Romans, and the slow crawl back to organized, widespread civilization began.

ACTIVITIES

1. Create a brochure for the Mediterranean region in 150 C.E. that describes its climate and physical features and tells why many people live there. By consulting an encyclopedia or atlas, find out the average summer and winter temperatures and rainfall in the region. What features of the region support farming? And trade? Illustrate your brochure with drawings, cartoons, or charts. If possible, create your brochure using desktop publishing software.

2. Compare the map of the Roman Empire (Figure 1–1) with a modern map of the same area. What modern countries and major cities exist within the former boundaries of the Roman Empire?

3. Give three reasons why Rome succeeded as a civilization.

4. The Roman city of Pompeii was buried by the eruption of Mt. Vesuvius in 79 C.E. The painting shown on page 8 was discovered during archaeological digs at the site. Look carefully at the picture. What do you think these two people were like? Why do we value ancient works of art?

5. Describe Rome's legacy to future generations, giving at least five examples.

6. Assume you are the editor of your community newspaper. In the previous issue, you asked readers to write in with suggestions for events that could be held at the local sports stadium, which needs to make money or it will close.

   a) You receive a letter that calls for a revival of the "entertainments" ancient Romans watched in the Roman Colosseum. Write a one-page response to this letter explaining why you agree or disagree. In your arguments, you could refer to Canadian laws, what you feel would be the response of most members of your community, and your own personal beliefs.

   b) The following week, you receive a letter that proposes weekly boxing and wrestling matches in the cash-strapped stadium. How do you respond?

7. Identify four possible symptoms of a declining civilization. The Roman Empire was not the only civilization to rise, flourish, and then decline. Identify a present-day civilization that shows symptoms of decline.

8. Describe what happened to Europe after Rome fell.

RELIGION: A FORCE OF CHANGE

Religion was crucial in reshaping Europe after the fall of Rome. Religions influence the values and behaviour of individual people and society as a whole. The Romans, like the Germanic peoples, had believed in many gods. Each god had specific powers and responsibilities. Roman religion was a fantastic mix of Greek gods, Roman gods, and emperors who had become gods. To a certain degree, the Romans had allowed conquered peoples to practise their own religions as long as they paid their taxes and did not rebel against Roman rule.

After the fall of Rome, a few religions grew beyond anyone's expectations. Throughout the Middle Ages, most of the people of North Africa, the Middle East, and Europe believed in Judaism, Christianity, or Islam. These three religions are closely related. Christianity grew out of Judaism, and Islam confirmed the message of both. Christians, Jews, and Muslims all believe in only one god.

Christianity, through the Roman Catholic Church, had the greatest effect on the people of western Europe. The Church was important politically because it supported various monarchs, and important socially because it had such a strong influence on people's values. Finally the wars and persecutions that were carried out in the name of religion caused death and suffering and affected the history of the whole Mediterranean world.

JUDAISM

Judaism took shape in Israel over 3000 years ago, and is still a vital religion today. Central to the Jewish faith is a conviction that the Jewish people have a special relationship with God as His chosen people. To protect this relationship, Jews keep

Judaism: the religion of the Jews

Qur'ân: the holy book of Islam; *qur'ân,* in Arabic, means "reading"

DID YOU KNOW?
The Jewish holy book, the Torah, is part of the Christian Bible and is mentioned in the holy book of Islam, the **Qur'ân***.*

Figure 1–3 This section of a triumphal arch in Rome records the destruction of the Jewish Temple by Roman soldiers. The soldiers take away booty. How did the sculptor indicate that the soldiers were sacking a Jewish building?

The Jewish Covenant

In this passage from the book of Exodus, God explains the close relationship that will exist between God and the Jewish people. The relationship is to be protected by a covenant, a kind of contract between God and the people. What do the Jewish people have to do to keep their end of the bargain?

> The Lord called to [Moses] from the mountain, saying, "Thus shall you say to the House of Jacob and declare to the Children of Israel: You have seen what I did to the Egyptians, how I bore you on eagles' wings and brought you to Me. Now then, if you will obey Me faithfully and keep my covenant, you shall be my treasured possessions above all the peoples. Indeed, all the earth is Mine, but you shall be to Me a kingdom of priests and a holy nation."
>
> —*Exodus 19*

PRIMARY SOURCE

to persecute: to attack or harass someone for a specific reason, for example, race, religion, or politics

creed: the official belief of a religion

God's laws. These include the Ten Commandments, which Jews believe God gave to Moses as part of the Torah, the most important of the Jewish Holy Books.

The Torah has existed for many centuries. Over time, Jewish teachers and prophets have added comments and interpretations that form the Talmud, a guide for life and belief.

On several occasions in Roman times, the whole Jewish population was forced to move to distant lands far from their homes. In Jewish tradition, the final scattering of the Jewish people from Palestine was known as the Diaspora, or scattering. The Diaspora caused active Jewish communities to develop in most of the major

cities of the Mediterranean world. Often **persecuted**, even in their new communities, Jews held on to their traditions and their belief in their covenant with God.

ISLAM

Islam, which comes from the Arabic word for "submission," began in the seventh century. This religion is based on the Qur'ân, which Muslims (believers of Islam) know as the word of God revealed to the Prophet Mohammed. All Muslims try to follow the rules for worship and living that have been laid out in the Qur'ân. Islam spread rapidly into Asia, Africa, and finally Europe, when the Muslims conquered Spain in 711. Today a major population of Muslims live in the Balkan region of Eastern Europe. (For more information on Islam, see Chapters 4 and 10.)

Figure 1–4 These Canadian Muslims pray facing Mecca, just as their ancestors did over 1400 years ago.

Manage Your Time

Have you ever left a research assignment till the last minute, only to find that the reference book you simply *must* have has been signed out of the library? Or has it happened that, despite your good intentions, you don't have time to polish a report and add illustrations?

If you really want to get things done on time, make a plan and follow it. For example, let's assume you've been assigned the following research assignment:

1. Visit your school or local library to research the history of the Jewish people. Include a list of things Jews have done

to maintain their sense of community and identity. (You may wish to interview a Jewish friend or family member.)

As for any research assignment, draw up a list of the steps you need to take.

Making a timetable is the key to getting your project done on time. Make a chart with a box for every date from now to the due date. Then jot in any times you cannot work on the assignment because of classes, extra-curricular activities, a job, volunteer work, homework, or other assignments. Now decide how much time you need for each step listed above and

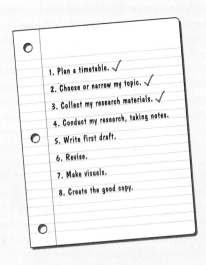

1. Plan a timetable. ✓
2. Choose or narrow my topic. ✓
3. Collect my research materials. ✓
4. Conduct my research, taking notes.
5. Write first draft.
6. Revise.
7. Make visuals.
8. Create the good copy.

block off time for each on your timetable. Be sure to leave time for illustrations, graphs, a table of contents, and so on. Always be generous with your time. Research tasks almost always take longer than we expect.

CHRISTIANITY

Christianity was founded in Palestine by the **apostles** of Jesus Christ. Jesus taught that the two greatest commandments were to love God with your whole being and to love your neighbour as yourself. Jesus and his apostles were Jews who felt that their religious leaders paid too much attention to the letter rather than the spirit of the Jewish Law. To the Jewish authorities of the time, much of what Jesus taught seemed to go against their traditions and the Law. At the same time, the Romans were very nervous about anyone who might lead an uprising against them. They killed Jesus by nailing him to a cross, which was the method of execution reserved for common criminals.

The followers of Jesus believed that Jesus died and was raised from the dead so that all people could share in eternal life. The story of Jesus is told in the **Gospels** of Matthew, Mark, Luke, and John in the New Testament of the Christian Bible. In the beginning, Christianity was an extension of Judaism. Jesus' disciples, all of whom were Jews, believed that he was the Jewish Messiah: the Son of God and the Saviour of the Jewish people.

The new religion spread quickly, following the trade routes of the Roman Empire. The man most

Figure 1–5 The death of Jesus Christ has inspired artists throughout the ages. This is a painting from the late Middle Ages by the Italian artist Duccio di Buoninsegna. What aspects of the Crucifixion did Duccio emphasize? Why?

apostles: the first twelve disciples, or followers, of Jesus

gospels: the first four books of the New Testament of the Christian Bible

Blessed Are...

In the Sermon on the Mount, Jesus told his disciples what human qualities God especially loved. These teachings are called the Beatitudes and are very important to Christians. Summarize the main message of the passage given here.

And he opened his mouth and taught them, saying:
"Blessed are the pure in spirit, for theirs is the kingdom of heaven.
Blessed are they that mourn, for they shall be comforted.
Blessed are the meek, for they shall inherit the earth.
Blessed are those who hunger and thirst after righteousness, for they shall be filled.
Blessed are the merciful, for they shall obtain mercy.
Blessed are the pure in heart, for they shall see God.
Blessed are the peacemakers, for they shall be called the children of God.
Blessed are those who are persecuted for righteousness' sake, for theirs is the kingdom of heaven."

—Matthew 5:2–11

PRIMARY SOURCE

to baptize: to sprinkle with or dip into water as a sign of purification from sin and of admission into a Christian church

convert: changing religion; one who has changed religion

social outcast: someone who has no power or influence in society; someone a community has rejected

DID YOU KNOW?

The Pentateuch, which is the first five books of the Old Testament of the Christian Bible, comes from the Jewish Torah.

responsible for this was St. Paul, who travelled extensively building Christian communities. His many letters provided guidance for Christians both then and now.

One reason for Christianity's early popularity was that Jesus preached that all people, including the poor, were precious to God. If people were **baptized** and led good lives, they would go to heaven after they died, no matter how poor and powerless they had been in life. This revolutionary message had great appeal in the Roman Empire, where many people were not just poor but kept in backbreaking slavery for their entire lives.

As the new religion spread and the number of **converts** grew, the Romans began to persecute Christians who refused to worship the gods of Rome. For this many were condemned to die in the arena, burned alive as human torches, torn to pieces by wild animals, or slain by gladiators. Rather than destroying Christianity, however, the persecutions made the new religion stronger.

In 313 C.E., the Roman emperor Constantine converted to Christianity and issued the Edict of Milan, which legalized Christianity throughout the empire. Christians quickly moved into positions of power in the army and government. The religion of **social outcasts** soon became the official faith of the Roman Empire.

LINK-UP

What's Right and What's Wrong

You're in a music store and you see someone slip a CD into his jacket and leave. Do you think stealing is wrong? Ever wondered where you got that opinion? In Canada we learn our values from several sources, including our families and friends and the media (for example, television shows). Religious teachings are also a source of social values.

Sometimes we get the same message—for example, that theft is wrong—from several sources. So what's the connection? In all civilizations, religion, entertainment, and personal morality develop together. For example, religion affects community standards, which affect the content of television shows, which affects personal opinion, which affects religion,

and so on. Many Canadians who are not religious hold a set of values similar to those of religious Canadians because we all learn how to behave from our society and our roots. So studying our religious roots makes sense for all of us; we can learn about our history, our ties to one another, and why we now live in peace together.

The Christian Persecutions

Tacitus, a well-respected Roman historian, wrote about Roman civilization during the period in which Christianity began. His comments reveal what the Romans thought of the first Christians. For example, he says that the Christians' "originator, Christ, had been executed in Tiberius' reign by the governor of Judaea, Pontius Pilatus." Normally only criminals are executed. What does the use of the term "executed" tell us about how Romans viewed Christ?

Tacitus goes on to explain how the Roman emperor Nero used the excuse of a fire that burned through Rome to persecute Christians. Read Tacitus's account here, paying special attention to the final sentence. Though Tacitus pities the Christians, he still believes they are "guilty" and deserving of "ruthless punishment." What does this statement tell you about what the Romans thought of Christians?

> First, Nero had self-acknowledged Christians arrested. Then, on their information, large numbers of others were condemned ... Their deaths were made farcical [ridiculous]. Dressed in wild animals' skins, they were torn to pieces by dogs, or crucified, or made into torches to be ignited after dark as substitutes for daylight.... Despite their guilt as Christians, and the ruthless punishment it deserved, the victims were pitied.

Two Early Religious Martyrs

Early Christian **martyrs** Perpetua, twenty-two, and Felicitas, eighteen, proclaimed their Christian faith publicly, even though they knew this action would result in their deaths. These two young women, along with some friends, were arrested and brought to the Roman amphitheatre. This excerpt describes the behaviour of Perpetua after surviving an attack by a wild animal and before she welcomes death from a gladiator. What evidence shows that Perpetua's behaviour affected the young gladiator? How would stories of Perpetua's loyalty to her faith have affected other Christians?

> When she [Perpetua] saw Felicitas crushed, she approached and gave her her hand, and lifted her up. And both of them stood once more.
>
> [Then Perpetua spoke to her comrades:] "Stand fast in the faith, and love one another, all of you, and be not offended at my sufferings." ... The [martyrs], immoveable and in silence, received the sword-thrust.... But Perpetua, that she might taste some pain, being pierced between the ribs, cried out loudly, and she herself placed the wavering right hand of the youthful gladiator to her throat.

Missionaries and the Spread of Christianity

Christian **missionaries** helped spread Christianity and aspects of the Roman culture throughout Europe. The **Roman Catholic Church** and its leader, the pope, believed that spreading the message of Christ was an important duty. The Church encouraged many promising young **priests** to take on the dangerous challenge of converting the peoples of Europe.

The process of bringing Christianity to western Europe took a long time, lasting throughout the early Middle Ages. St. Patrick converted the Irish around the middle of the fifth century, and St. Augustine converted the English in the late sixth century, but most Vikings did not become Christians until the end of the eleventh century. Christianity eventually became the only official religion of every country in western Europe.

martyr: a person tortured or killed because of his or her religious beliefs

missionary: a person sent out by a church to convert people

Roman Catholic Church: the only Christian church in western Europe until the sixteenth century

priest: a person trained and authorized to perform religious ceremonies

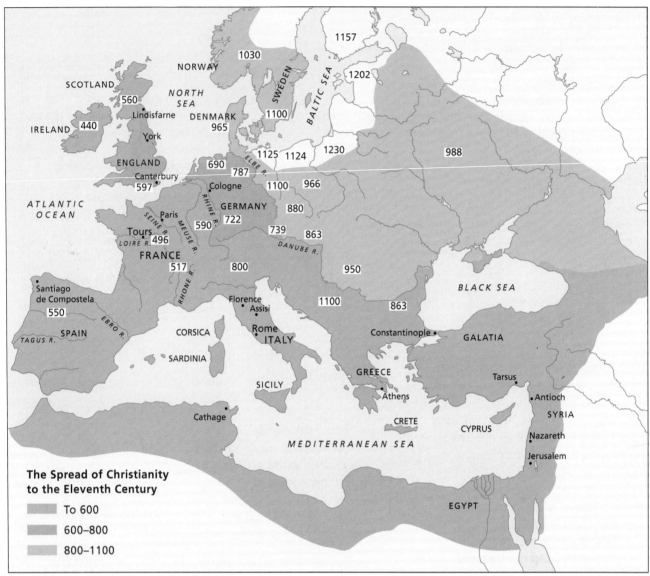

Figure 1–6 This map shows how Christianity spread across Europe during the early Middle Ages. Name two kinds of transportation routes used by the early missionaries. Examine the dates on the map to explain why many of the missionaries who converted the peoples of Germany and France came from the British Isles. Then compare this map to the one on page 120 showing the spread of Islam.

THE BYZANTINES AND ORTHODOX CHRISTIANITY

Constantine the Great (280–337), the first Christian Roman Emperor, decided to make Byzantium his capital. After he refortified the city with protective walls and buildings, the city became known as Constantinople. (Today it is known as Istanbul.) On the Bosporus Sea between the Black Sea and the Mediterranean, Constantinople lay right between Europe and Asia, and eventually became a major centre for trade. After the western Roman Empire collapsed, the Byzantine Empire, with Constantinople as its centre, became the last stronghold of Christianity. With its great walls and a mighty navy, the city withstood the attacks of Muslim invading armies for centuries.

Until the tenth century, Christianity in the Byzantine Empire continued to develop, eventually becoming Orthodox Christianity, which is quite different from the Catholicism of western Europe. For one thing, Orthodox Christians do not recognize the authority of the Catholic pope, except as a respected leader of Christianity. Instead, Orthodox Christians turn to the Patriarch of the Eastern Church for guidance.

Justinian and Theodora

The Byzantine emperors were usually very religious and had important church duties to perform. After Constantine himself, two of the most important Byzantine rulers were Justinian I and Theodora, who ruled together from 527 to 565. Born a commoner, Justinian became one of the most capable leaders in the history of Europe. He had a brilliant mind and was passionately interested not just in politics but also in art, literature, religion, music, and the sciences.

Justinian collected all the written laws of the Roman Empire into a **legal code** now known as the Justinian Code. This code eventually became the basis for the law in every western European country except England. For example, Napoleon used Justinian's work as the basis for the Civil Code for France, which in turn greatly influenced the Civil Code for Quebec.

Theodora, like Justinian, came from humble origins. Her father had been a bear trainer in the Byzantine circus. For this and other reasons, her enemies ridiculed and criticized her. As a ruler, though, Theodora was just as effective and powerful as Justinian. For example, she brought in reforms that gave women the right to keep any

property they inherited. The resolute and resourceful Theodora coped well in emergencies, as well. For example, when an attempt was made to overthrow Justinian, Theodora stopped him from fleeing, and organized the defence of the throne.

Figure 1–7 The Byzantine Empire under Justinian and Theodora, about 550 C.E. How does the outline for this empire differ from that of the Roman Empire in Figure 1–1.

legal code: a collection of written laws

Figure 1–8 The church of Hagia Sophia (Holy Wisdom) was built in Constantinople during Justinian's reign. The building was converted to a mosque (an Islamic place of worship) in the fifteenth century and is now a museum. Suggest two reasons why Justinian would want to build such an impressive church.

Figure 1–9 This **mosaic**, showing the Empress Theodora and her court, is one of the finest works of art to survive from the Byzantine period. Identify two ways that the artist made Theodora and her companions look royal.

mosaic: a picture made with many pieces of stone or glass fixed in place

ACTIVITIES

1. What was the most important difference between Judaism and the religions of the ancient Greeks and Romans?

2. **a)** What was the Diaspora? What effect did it have on the pattern of Jewish settlement in Europe?

   b) Over the centuries many Jews have had to leave their homes because of persecution. Where did this happen in World War Two? Why did this modern migration happen?

3. Compare the Jewish Covenant with the Islamic Covenant on page 116.

4. In pairs, create a comparison chart with the headings Judaism, Christianity, and Islam. On the side of your chart, write the headings Origin, Basic Beliefs, Important People and Leaders, Turning Points, and Other. Fill in the chart with information from this chapter and The Foundations of Islam on pages 116–19. (For help in making a comparison chart, see the feature on page 59.)

5. Explain how and why Christianity emerged as a major European religion.

6. Review the Biblical quotation on page 15.

   a) What level of society do you think would be most drawn to this message? How could this have contributed to the spread of Christianity?

   b) Do you think parts of this passage could hold meaning for Canadians who are not Christian? Explain.

7. Write a comment about a missionary from three different points of view:

   a) the pope

   b) someone who has recently converted to Christianity

   c) someone who does not want to convert

8. Why did Constantinople became the "last stronghold" for Christianity?

9. Explain what made Justinian and Theodora great rulers.

10. Examine the mosaic of the Empress Theodora. What do her clothing and her bearing say about her? Christ preached poverty. How do you think Theodora would justify her extravagant costume?

11. Research Orthodox Christianity, using a CD-ROM and other electronic information sources if possible. What factors make it different from Roman Catholicism? In what regions did it spread? How many people are Orthodox Christians today?

THE FRANKS

As the Roman Legions withdrew from western Europe, various Germanic peoples moved into the territory, fought wars, and established settlements. One of these groups, the Franks, conquered much of the Roman province of Gaul (now France) in the late fourth and early fifth centuries. Although they were farmers, they also loved making war. Most free men went about armed, often with a special kind of throwing axe called a *francisca*. Both men and women were fond of jewellery, and both genders wore their hair long. Their name for themselves—"Frank"—meant free. "Franchise," the English word for the right to vote, comes from this Frankish word.

THE MEROVINGIANS

The Merovingian royal family ruled the Franks for almost three hundred years. The most successful ruler in the family, Clovis I, reigned from 481 to 511 C.E. He founded the country of France and made Paris its capital.

After the death of Clovis, the kingdom was divided among his children, who were not very capable leaders. Before long, this royal family became famous for its treachery and murderous infighting. Kings and queens often committed murders with their own hands, and many were killed by members of their own family. For the next two centuries, the Merovingian royal family was weakened by this constant infighting, and the kingdom fell into chaos.

DID YOU KNOW?

In many parts of Asia, Europeans are still called Franks. For example, the Thai call Europeans "Farang."

VIEWPOINTS IN CONFLICT

Here we have two descriptions of the Franks. In one, Tacitus, a Roman historian of the first century, offers his opinion of the Germanic peoples, which included the Franks. Compare this with the other statement, in which the Franks describe themselves. In what ways do these statements agree? How do they differ? How does each reflect the speaker's point of view?

The materials … come through war and foray. You will not so readily persuade them [the Germanic peoples] to plow the land or await the year's crop as to challenge the foe and earn wounds. Besides it seems [to them] limp and slack to gain with the sweating of your brow what you can win with blood.

—Tacitus

[We are a] glorious people, wise in council, noble in body, radiant in health, excelling in beauty, daring, quick, hardened…. This is the people that shook the cruel yoke of the Romans from its neck.

—Preface to the Frank Legal Code

THE LAWS OF THE FRANKS

As a Germanic people, the Franks had their own legal code, which differed greatly from Roman law. When these laws were written down and collected, they were called the Salic Code, after the Salian Franks, who had settled in France.

The Salic Code placed a monetary value on every piece of property and on every person. If property was stolen or a person injured or killed, a fine called **wergild** had to be paid to the owner of the property or the victim's family. In the case of murder, the family could refuse to accept the fine, and instead could demand the guilty person's death. If a relation of the victim took revenge by killing the murderer, the law did not hold him or her responsible.

wergild: man-money, that is, a person's value in money

arson: intentionally setting fire to property

betrothal: a promise to marry

Figure 1–10 Finely decorated jewellery such as this was often placed in the coffins of Merovingian nobles. Consequently, grave robbing was a common offence. Why do you think the Merovingians placed jewellery in their graves?

Crime and Punishment in the Salic Code

Some of the laws in the Salic Code seem strange to us today, but they made sense to the Franks. For instance, cutting a child's hair was a serious offence because the Franks believed that a person's strength could be measured by the length of his or her hair. Grave robbing was a common problem among the Franks because of the jewellery they placed in the caskets of wealthy people. After analyzing the data carefully, make three conclusions about Frank society. Note that the Franks fined people more for killing a boy than for killing a girl. Why did they do this? Do Canadian laws make similar distinctions? Why or why not?

Note: *Solidi* were gold coins worth $50–$100 in today's money.

Crime	Punishment
Theft of a slave:	120–150 lashes
Arson:	slavery in the mines, banishment, or death
Theft:	fine, torture, or death

Crime	Fines
Breaking a **betrothal**:	65 gold solidi
Touching a woman's hand:	15 gold solidi
Cutting the hair of a free boy or girl:	45 gold solidi
Grave robbing:	200 gold solidi

A Person's Value by Law (Wergild)

Fines for killing a	
free woman of childbearing age:	600 gold solidi
pregnant woman:	700 gold solidi
boy under twelve:	600 gold solidi
girl under twelve:	200 gold solidi

Using Primary Sources

CATALOGUE CARD

What is it? An excerpt from the ten-volume History of the Franks

Who wrote it? Gregory of Tours, a Frankish bishop and historian

When? Late sixth century

Why? To record the history of his people

> Before the great **plague** ravaged Auvergne [a region in France], **prodigies** terrified the people of that region in the same way. On a number of occasions, three or four shining lights appeared round the sun. Once on the first day of October, the sun was in eclipse, so that less than a quarter of it continued to shine.... Then a star, which some call a comet, appeared over the region for a whole year, with a tail like a sword, and the whole sky seemed to burn and many other **portents** were seen.

PRIMARY SOURCE

Much of what we know about the Franks and their rulers, the Merovingians, comes from a book called the *History of the Franks* by Gregory of Tours, a mild-mannered person who was shocked by the bloodthirsty deeds of the Merovingian rulers.

The *History of the Franks* is what historians call a "primary source." In other words, this document provides a first-hand account of historical events by a person who actually participated in them or was able to interview eyewitnesses. An account of Roberta Bondar's flight in space written by Bondar herself during the flight would be a good primary source to have. Documents such as charters, chronicles, historical paintings, and records of births and deaths are also considered primary sources. A "secondary source" is an account put together long after the events it describes. When historians research a particular period, they prefer to work with primary sources.

Even though Gregory's book is a primary source, modern historians have to interpret what Gregory wrote to decide how much of what he wrote actually occurred and how much was the result of superstition or wishful thinking.

WHAT DO YOU THINK?

1. The above extract tells us several things. First, Gregory was superstitious. Second, a disease killed many people in Auvergne. What did Gregory see that would interest an astronomer studying historical astronomical events?

2. Gregory called these astronomical events "portents," or omens. Do you think he was right? Explain.

3. Think of three modern-day beliefs that people a thousand years from now might think were silly or superstitions.

EVERYDAY LIFE AMONG THE FRANKS

By reading Gregory's *History of the Franks*, we also learn about the everyday life of the Frankish people, and we find that some things never change. The Franks had **social classes**: some people were very rich and some were incredibly poor. The majority of people at this time (around 60 percent) were serfs, or peasants, people who worked the land on their lord's manor, or estate. Although they were considered free and not slaves, serfs were not allowed to move away from the manor. Because they were farmers, the serfs were at the mercy of the weather. Storms or drought could cause great hardship. The lords and rulers could steal serfs' crops at any time. Further, as Gregory of Tours complained, merchants often tried to profit from the misfortunes of ordinary people by raising prices when food was scarce.

plague: a contagious disease that is out of control and kills many people

prodigies, portents: omens, occurences that predict future events

social class: the group that one belongs to in a society. Class can be determined by money, role in society, or one's parentage.

Make a Bar Graph

Sometimes we need help in grasping the significance of statistics. Graphs help us by providing a "picture" of the information. For example, a bar graph comparing the life expectancies of Frankish and Canadian women helps us see the extraordinary difference:

Life Expectancy for Frankish and Canadian Women

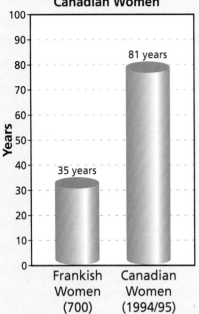

Statistics: The Franks in 700 and Canadians in 1994/95

	The Franks	Canadians
Infant mortality rate	45%	0.6%
Population under twelve years	22%	16%
Population under twenty-five years	60%	34%
Average life expectancy for men	45 years	75 years
Average life expectancy for women	35 years	81 years
Age of marriage (for women)	12 years	30 years
Size of average family	2.9 persons	3.0 persons
Average height for men	165 cm*	180 cm*
Average height for women	150 cm*	165 cm*

* Estimated

PRIMARY SOURCE

Every bar graph has two axes. The horizontal axis shows the categories (for example, year, city, gender), while the vertical axis shows the values (for example, degrees of temperature or distance in kilometres). The bars, always of equal width, show the value for each category by their height.

NOW YOU DO IT

1. a) Following these instructions, make a bar graph comparing the life expectancies of Frankish and Canadian men.

   ◆ Draw and label two axes.

   ◆ Add categories on the horizontal axis and a scale on the verticle axis. To help choose your scale, look at the largest value you will show.

   ◆ Draw and shade one bar for each category, using the statistics in the table above.

   ◆ Give your bar graph a title.

   b) Why do you think life expectancy for men and women in Frankish times was so much lower than life expectancies today? Why do you think Frankish women died so much earlier than men?

2. Now make a similar pair of graphs comparing the heights of Frankish and Canadian women and Frankish and Canadian men. Speculate on why Franks were shorter than Canadians are today.

CHARLEMAGNE

Charlemagne came to power in western Europe in 768 C.E. His father, Pepin the Short, had made himself king by throwing out the last of the Merovingian rulers, who had come to be known as the "do-nothing" kings. The pope agreed to recognize Pepin as king because Pepin's father, Charles Martel, had defeated a Muslim army that had threatened to conquer Europe in 732.

Unlike many of the Germanic rulers who had come before him, Charlemagne, or Charles the Great, was very interested in rebuilding civilization, and he had the intelligence and power to do so. Through his military successes he expanded the old Merovingian Empire in every direction. At the height of his power, on Christmas day in 800, he was crowned Emperor of the Romans by Pope Leo III. The **Carolingian Empire** gave much of western Europe a brief rest from the wars that had torn it apart since the fall of Rome.

Charlemagne governed his empire from his palace at Aachen in what is now Germany. Although he allowed local governments much freedom, he also sent out agents, called *missi dominici* (the lord's messengers), to make sure that people were treated properly. He created a single code of laws for the whole empire. Unlike those who came before him, Charlemagne tried to make things better for the serfs and tradespeople.

We learn from Charlemagne's biographer, Einhard, that Charlemagne could also be hardhearted and merciless. After a long war with the Saxons in northwest Germany, Charlemagne defeated them and insisted that they convert to Christianity. When the Saxon leaders refused, Charlemagne ordered his soldiers to kill about 4000 Saxons in a single day.

Carolingian Empire:
Charlemagne's empire, from about 770 to 814

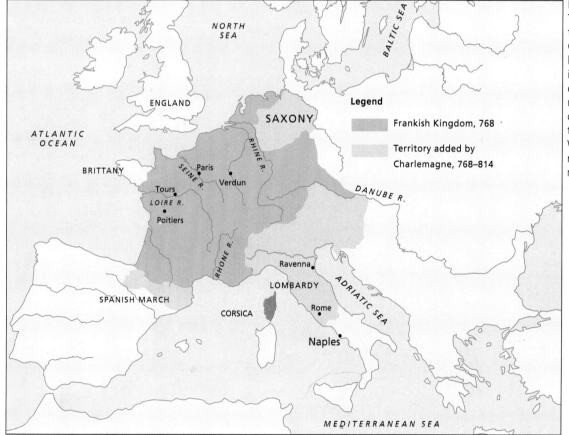

Figure 1–11
This map shows the extent of Charlemagne's kingdom. Check in an atlas to discover what modern countries lie in this region. Which mountain ranges formed natural borders?

Describing Charlemagne

Einhard, Charlemagne's secretary, wrote a biography of Charlemagne, the first biography of a medieval person who was not a saint or otherwise connected with the Roman Catholic Church. Are there any indications of exaggeration in the account at right?

Charles [Charlemagne] was large and strong, and of lofty stature, though not disproportionately tall.... In accordance with the national custom, he took frequent exercise on horseback and in **the chase**, accomplishments in which scarcely any people in the world can equal the Franks. He enjoyed the **exhalations** from natural warm springs, and often practised swimming, in which he was such an adept that none could surpass him; and hence it was that he built his palace at Aachen, and lived there constantly during his later years until his death.

DID YOU KNOW?

Charlemagne learned to read, though he never quite succeeded in teaching himself to write. He kept a writing slate under his pillow and practised his letters before going to sleep but finally gave up, saying he was too old.

Charlemagne's Renaissance

Improving education throughout the empire was a special concern of Charlemagne. He established new schools in monasteries and encouraged the learning of the Latin classics. Charles insisted that his sons and daughters be educated.

Charles was an energetic and thoughtful ruler. He took a keen interest in reviving the practice of architecture and had many stone churches and palaces built in France and Germany. He was interested in science and literature, and he loved talking with interesting people. Because Charlemagne succeeded in bringing about a rebirth of learning and the arts, historians today often refer to his time as the Carolingian **Renaissance**. He died at the age of seventy-two, after ruling for forty-seven years. The peace and security Charles had worked for fell apart because of feuds among his decendants, and their weakness in the face of Viking invasions.

Figure 1–12 A carving from the outside of Charlemagne's coffin, showing Charlemagne dressed in bishop's clothing and seated between two saints. What impression do you think Charlemagne wanted to leave?

the chase: the hunt

exhalations: vapours

renaissance: a rebirth or revival, especially of the arts

1. Who were the Franks? What did they think of themselves? Write a description of Canadians to go in the Canadian Constitution. You may wish to consider ethnic origins, culture, and commonly held principles, ideals, and goals. Compare your description of the Canadian people with the Franks' description of themselves.

2. a) Calculate the worth of the fines listed on page 22. Under Canadian law, murder, arson, and theft would all be punished with a prison term. How did the Franks punish people guilty of these crimes? Why do you think the Franks never punished with prison terms?

   b) What punishments did the Franks use that Canadians do not use? How can you account for these differences?

   c) Under Canadian law, breaking an engagement or touching a person's hand *usually* would not be considered a serious crime. How did the Franks punish these actions? How can you account for these differences?

3. Describe the role played by the serf in Frankish society. Identify three threats to a serf's wellbeing.

4. Look at the statistics on page 24.

   a) At what age did young Frankish women get married? Identify three effects an early marriage might have on a girl's life. Consider her relationship with her parents, the age at which she would begin bearing children, and her relationship with a much older husband.

   b) The infant mortality rate shows that almost half of all Frankish babies died in infancy. What might account for this?

   c) Make up three questions of your own about this chart. With a partner, speculate on answers for each question.

5. In a small group, discuss if Charlemagne deserves the title "the Great." Give evidence to support your view.

6. As one of Charlemagne's advisors, you have been asked to advertise for people to help rebuild civilization at Charles's capital at Aachen. Prepare an advertisement for Charles's approval. Your advertisement should demonstrate your knowledge of the world of the Franks.

THE ANGLO-SAXONS AND THE CELTS

Celtic peoples: (pronounced Keltic), a western European culture. The Scottish, Irish, Welsh, Cornish, and Bretons are all Celts.

While the Franks settled in France after the fall of Rome, Britain was invaded by a different group. When the Roman soldiers left Britain in the fifth century, warriors from the area now known as Germany—the Angles, Saxons, and Jutes—moved in, driving out the native **Celtic peoples**. Soon large numbers of these Germanic invaders began to settle in Britain and pushed the Celts into Wales, Cornwall, and Scotland, and across the sea to Ireland. The Celts had once been a powerful people, inhabiting much of Europe, from Spain all the way to southern Russia. Now, in Britain, the Celtic language and culture disappeared from the seven kingdoms (see page 29) established by the invaders, who became known as the Anglo-Saxons, or English.

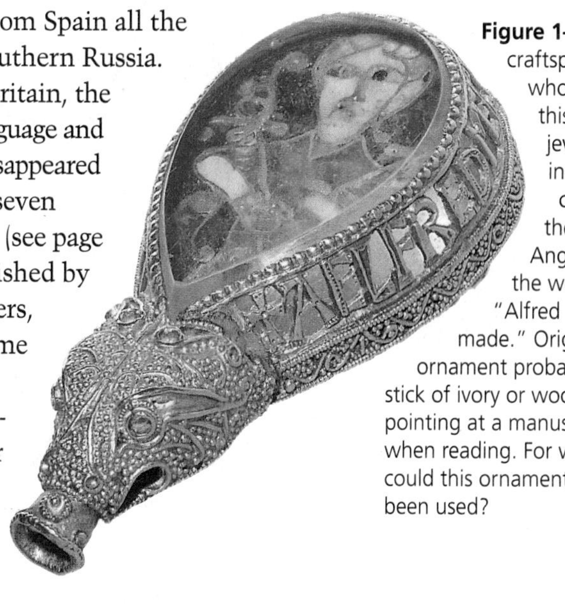

Figure 1–13 The craftsperson who made this piece of jewellery inscribed (or carved) on the work, in Anglo-Saxon, the words, "Alfred had me made." Originally, the ornament probably held a stick of ivory or wood for pointing at a manuscript when reading. For what else could this ornament have been used?

ANGLO-SAXON ENGLAND

Although they thought of themselves as warriors, the Anglo-Saxons, like the Franks, were farmers. They lived in small villages, and men and women shared the hard work of agriculture between them. Some trade and business took place, but even the largest towns, such as London, would seem very small by today's standards. Like other Germanic peoples, the Anglo-Saxons had skilled metal workers. Many examples of their highly elaborate sculpture and jewellery have survived. The Anglo-Saxons were also great storytellers who created wonderful **epics**, such as *Beowulf*.

Beginning in the ninth century, Anglo-Saxon England, like Carolingian France, suffered from devastating Viking raids. Alfred the Great, an early ruler of Anglo-Saxon England, lost many battles with the Vikings before he learned how to beat them. At his death, Alfred left western and southern England united and **prosperous**. England as a whole, however, would suffer from a deadly combination of weak kings and Viking invaders until the time of William the Conqueror.

Beowulf and the Monster Grendel

The Anglo-Saxon, Old English poem *Beowulf* is an ancient epic that would have been told around the fire on long winter evenings. It tells the story of a Swedish hero's battles with three monsters: a troll named Grendel, Grendel's mother, and a fire-breathing dragon guarding a golden treasure. Beowulf slays all three monsters but dies himself after being burned and bitten by the dragon. This story helps us understand the fear in which many people lived in the early Middle Ages: fear of wild animals (which still populated Europe), fear of enemies, and fear of the unknown.

Only one copy of the poem has survived from the Middle Ages. The segment shown at the top right describes the dark night when the monster Grendel and Beowulf engage in battle. The Old English words are given above, along with a translation. Can you pick out the Old English words that resemble modern English?

OLD ENGLISH AND TRANSLATION

Tha com of more under misthleothum
Then came off [the] moor under mist-hills

Grendel gongan, Goddes yrre baer;
Grendel going, God's ire [he] bore;

mynte se manscatha manna cynnes
thought the evildoer of mankind

sumne besyrwan in sele tham hean.
some to entrap in that high hall.

Wod under wolcnum to thaes the he winreced,
Went under clouds until he [the] wine-building,

goldsele gumena, gearwost wisse
gold-hall best, clearly saw

faettum fahne. Ne waes thaet forma sith
with gold plates decorated. Nor was that [the] first time

thaet he Hrothgares ham gesohte.
that he Hrothgar's home had sought.

PRIMARY SOURCE

HOW WE MIGHT TELL THIS STORY

The evil monster Grendel came out of the misty wild lands with evil on his mind. Under stormy skies, the monster saw a beautiful golden palace. The evildoer planned to attack the hall and capture some people. It was not the first time he had attacked Hrothgar's home.

Using a Translation as a Primary Source

CATALOGUE CARD

What is it? *Two translations of one line from the ancient poem Beowulf*

Who translated it? *Two scholars of Old English*

When? *Twentieth century*

Why? *To allow more people to understand the poem*

Then his heart laughed;
evil monster, he thought he would take the life from each body, eat them all before day came.

And his heart laughed, he relished the sight,
Intended to tear the life from those bodies
By morning.

In the feature on page 28, you saw the monster Grendel make his way to Hrothgar's Hall, which he intends to attack. Here are two **translations** of the line describing the thoughts going through Grendel's mind after he breaks into the hall and sees a room full of sleeping warriors.

For each translation, decide if the monster intends to eat the warriors or not. How can two translations of the same line disagree on such an important point?

It is true that translators sometimes make mistakes. More often they disagree about what particular words or phrases mean. Sometimes they are writing for different audiences. Next time you read a primary source document in translation, keep in mind that a translation is never as accurate as the original.

Figure 1–14 England in the time of Alfred the Great. The Anglo-Saxons drove the Celtic peoples into Scotland, Wales, and Cornwall and divided England into seven kingdoms. Pick these out. Why do you think Alfred allowed the Vikings to live in the Danelaw?

THE PIVOTAL ROLE OF THE IRISH

translation: writing changed from one language into another

The Celts, who had settled on the western and northern edge of the British Isles, had practised a form of nature worship called Druidism for many centuries. They fought in bloody battles, kept slaves, and made human sacrifices. All this changed in the fifth century, when St. Patrick, who became the patron saint of Ireland, brought to the Irish both Christianity and a healthy respect for learning. Because Ireland had few cities, large monastic communities sprang up in the countryside and along the coasts. These monasteries became centres for learning not just for Irish monks but also for scholars from the rest of Europe who were fleeing from the Germanic invasions.

Until the time of Charlemagne's renaissance, Ireland was the greatest centre of learning in Europe.

Irish monks played a critical role in training missionaries and in spreading Christianity. They travelled through Scotland, England, and then Europe, spreading knowledge and Christianity. They carried their books hooked to their belts, just as their warrior ancestors had once carried the heads of their fallen enemies.

The Irish monks also played an important role in preserving the cultural legacy of ancient Ireland, Greece, and Rome. Monasteries functioned as something like book factories. In the age before the printing press, every new book had to be carefully copied out by hand on sheets of dried sheepskin called "parchment." The Irish monks did not limit their copying efforts to religious works such as the Bible. They also copied out many of the Latin and Greek classics and ancient Celtic stories that might otherwise have been lost forever.

credit: trust

figment: a made-up story

A Monk's Aside

At the end of a copy of the Book of Leinster, a collection of ancient Irish tales that must have taken months to copy, the copyist added in Latin his own opinion of the material. Because of their respect for literature, Irish monks copied out books of all sorts, even those of which they disapproved.

I who have copied down this story, or more accurately fantasy, do not **credit** the details of the story, or fantasy. Some things in it are devilish lies, and some are poetical **figments**; some seem possible and others not; some are for the enjoyment of idiots.

A C T I V I T I E S

1. Describe the relocations of the Celtic peoples starting from their origins in Europe. What caused these massive migrations?

2. Describe Anglo-Saxon England.

3. **a)** Who was Alfred the Great and what was his greatest accomplishment?

   b) Alfred the Great is supposed to have hidden in the marshes and disguised himself as a minstrel to spy on the Viking leaders. Draw your own cartoon strip of Alfred the Great disguised as a minstrel in the Viking camp. What kind of information could he have gathered?

4. How did Anglo-Saxon storytellers help preserve their culture even though they could not read or write?

5. The Anglo-Saxons were fond of making poetic two-word combinations they called "kennings" to describe people or objects. Sometimes, for instance, they would call soldiers "slaughter-wolves." Beowulf's name, "Bee-wolf," was a kenning for Bear.

   Make up your own kennings to describe these objects and people: the sky, a pencil, a sword, a shoe, a car, a teacher, an actor, and an airplane. Share your kennings in groups.

6. Describe the factors that contributed to Ireland's role in providing a safe haven from Vikings and in preserving ancient knowledge. Consider location, population distribution, and religious influences.

7. **a)** What did the monk who copied out the Book of Leinster think about the material he was copying? Why do you think he completed his task?

   b) A historian documenting a particular event will try to collect and preserve sources that represent all points of view. How are this monk's efforts similar to the historian's efforts?

THE VIKINGS

On Easter Sunday in the year 855, a Viking force attacked and plundered Paris, far from the sea, striking a blow at the very heart of Charlemagne's old empire. France was not the only target. The Vikings were everywhere. Their war parties devastated whole regions in the Low Countries (modern Netherlands and Belgium), Ireland, and England. They roamed into the Mediterranean Sea, they attacked Spain and Italy, and they sailed down the great rivers of Russia all the way to Constantinople.

The Vikings came from the north looking for plunder and glory. They travelled in swift longships that allowed them to strike without warning and disappear quickly before local rulers could raise a force to oppose them. Their raiding forces ranged from the crew of a single ship to large fleets of a hundred ships or more. The peace of mind Europeans had gained under Charlemagne's rule was shattered.

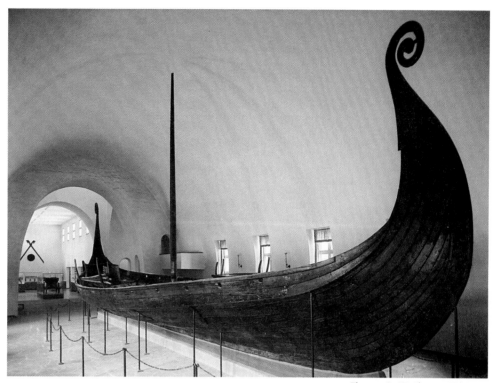

Figure 1–15 Almost 25 metres long, 5 metres wide, and 2 metres deep, this typical ninth-century Viking ship could carry a crew of thirty-two and sail into water just over a metre deep. In 1893, a small crew sailed a replica of a Viking ship across the Atlantic Ocean.

Of Lightning and Dragons

An entry in *The Anglo-Saxon Chronicle* for 793 records the Vikings' destruction of the great monastery at Lindisfarne off the coast of northeastern England. Would this account serve to calm people or to make them more fearful of the Vikings? How do you think reputation assisted the Vikings? Compare this passage with the one from Gregory of Tours's *History of the Franks* on page 23. What is similar about the two excerpts?

In this year terrible portents appeared... exceptional flashes of lightning, and fiery dragons were seen flying in the air. A great famine followed soon upon these signs, and a little after on the Ides of [June] the harrying of the heathen miserably destroyed God's church in Lindisfarne by rapine and slaughter.

PRIMARY SOURCE

THE VIKING REPUTATION

The Vikings were mercilessly destructive. Especially in their early raids, before they began to settle in lands such as England and France, their common practice was to kill or enslave every man, woman, and child they found. The Vikings were so savagely cruel in their attacks that many people thought they had been sent by God to punish the world for its wickedness. To understand the fear people felt, imagine that the coastal communities in British Columbia were regularly invaded by forces that burned everything in sight and killed everyone they found. Would you feel safe living in places such as Mission or Powell River? What might you, with your community, do to protect yourselves in that situation?

Some monarchs and church leaders were so terrified that they paid the Vikings to leave their lands. In England, the Vikings took payments called *Danegeld* from rulers such as Ethelred the Unready. Over the course of a few years, French monarchs paid the Vikings almost 300 kilograms of gold and 15 000 kilograms of silver. All these payments came from taxes collected from the common people. Only a few rulers, such as Charlemagne and Alfred the Great, could fight the Vikings effectively, but even they weren't able to stop the raids completely.

Figure 1–16 By looking at the places the Vikings usually attacked, why do you think it was so difficult to stop these raids? What geographical feature allowed the Vikings to move inland on their raids?

EVERYDAY LIFE AMONG THE VIKINGS

It is important to remember that most of our information on the Vikings comes from the people they attacked and plundered. For this reason, many of us tend to have a somewhat slanted view of their lives. Whatever the Vikings did to the Anglo-Saxons in England was probably not much different from what the Anglo-Saxons had done to the Celts many years earlier.

Viking life was not all wars and raiding parties. Most Vikings were farmers and fishers living in small villages close to the sea. They came from the region we now call Scandinavia—the modern countries of Norway, Sweden, and Denmark. They probably began their raids because the farmland available in Scandinavia could not support the growing

Figure 1–17 The Vikings made their houses of turf, stone, or clay or dung plastered onto woven sticks. The long, low houses frequently sheltered more than one family. Attached to the houses were buildings for slaves and a barn for the animals. Some farms also had saunas. Toilets were outside, often near the well.

population. People lived at the ends of **fjords** and wherever else they could find fertile land. Viking farms tended to be small, only a few hectares in size.

Men and women shared the work in Viking society, although some jobs, such as weaving, were always done by women. Free Viking women had many rights under the law. They could own property, they could divorce their spouses, and they could sue in court. Gunnhild, the "mother of kings," was a legendary leader. Freydis Eriksdottir, the sister of Leif the Lucky, led an expedition to Newfoundland early in the eleventh century.

Life was not good for everyone in Viking society. Viking landowners almost always owned slaves, called *thralls*, who did much of the heavy work on the farms. Most thralls had either been taken captive on Viking raids or been sold into slavery because they could not pay debts or fines. Thralls had no legal rights in Viking society, and could be killed by their masters at any time. The children of

thralls automatically became slaves.

Despite their reputation as ruthless "barbarians," the Vikings had a rich culture. They were highly skilled woodworkers and smiths, and many artworks have survived, especially from the grave sites of wealthy and powerful leaders. Viking art shows gods such as Odin, Thor, and Freya, as well as scenes from everyday life.

The keepers of Viking history and legend were called **skalds.** These poets needed to have excellent memories and be good singers. They carried whole histories in their heads, and could recite, word for word, stories that might take several days to tell. This was an important skill for a society in which most people could not read or write.

Viking Law and Government

The Vikings were great lawmakers, and they designed many laws to

fjord: a long, narrow. saltwater bay with high cliffs along its sides

skald: a Scandinavian poet who recited poems at formal gatherings

DID YOU KNOW?

Like many Canadians, the Vikings ate a varied diet of vegetables, meat, fish, bread, and porridge. Unlike Canadians, they considered beer to be a drink for everyone, even small children.

DID YOU KNOW?

The practice of using juries in the courtroom comes from the Vikings. Also, the next time (or the first time) you take a sauna, remember that you are enjoying one of the more pleasant contributions the Vikings made to later civilizations.

The Value of Writing

Some civilizations have maintained an oral tradition to remember their history, but most have developed some form of writing. Writing has many advantages over oral histories, the main one being that a written document, if cared for properly, can last forever. For example, a case known as the "Franks Casket," shown at right, still survives, though it was made about a thousand years ago. The letters carved into it are **runes**, the letters of the Viking alphabet used mainly by Vikings but also by other Germanic peoples. Many Vikings thought the runes had magical powers. Which runic letters are similar to letters in the Roman alphabet, which we use? What connection can you see between the shapes of the runic letters and the fact that the Vikings did not write with pens and paper but rather carved their letters into stone and wood?

runes: letters based on those in the Roman alphabet

ᚠ	ᚢ	ᚦ	ᚨ	ᚲ	ᚷ	ᚹ	ᚺ	ᚾ	ᛁ	ᛃ
f	u	th	a	r	k	g	w	h	n	i	j

ᛈ	ᛃ	ᛦ	ᛊ	ᛏ	ᛒ	ᛖ	ᛗ	ᛚ	◇	ᛜ	ᛞ
p	E	R	s	t	b	e	m	i	ng	o	d

North America's First European Visitors

The Vikings were an incredibly adventurous people. They sailed their ships far and wide, even across the Atlantic Ocean. Newfoundland's L'Anse aux Meadows National Historic Park is the site of the earliest Viking settlement in North America. In this recent photograph, you can see sod huts reproduced to look like the ones Vikings erected here about a thousand years ago.

Who had already been in North America long before the Vikings came?

WHAT DO YOU THINK?

Evidence proves that Vikings reached North America centuries before other Europeans. Why do you think Christopher Columbus was long considered the first European to reach the Americas?

protect people and their property. Usually these laws were not written down. Instead, people called Law Speakers memorized the law and recited it as needed. The Vikings usually fined criminals, but some dangerous offenders were punished more harshly. The most dreaded penalty was to be declared an outlaw, which meant that the person was to be treated under the law "as if he were dead." Anyone could kill an outlaw on sight and then be entitled to some of his or her property.

THE END OF THE VIKING AGE

The Viking age ended in the eleventh century. Gradually European monarchs grew stronger and learned how to deal with their northern enemies. English monarchs gave half of England, the Danelaw, to Viking lords who then protected their new lands from other Vikings. The king of France gave the Viking Rollo the province of Normandy to rule and protect (Normandy means "land of the Northmen"). Viking settlements in North America and Greenland were destroyed or disappeared. The people of Norway and Denmark became Christian. By the middle of the eleventh century, dragon ships filled with warriors were no longer seen in the rivers and seas of western Europe. The Viking Age was over forever.

Thing: a parliament where free adults could give their opinions on important matters. Viking kings were not crowned; instead, they were lifted up standing on shields, at the Thing.

Figure 1–18 Free Vikings met regularly in a kind of parliament called a **Thing**. Here they made decisions on law, government, and their leaders. The Thing of Iceland is now one of the oldest parliaments in northern Europe.

ACTIVITIES

1. How did the level of population and availability of resources in Scandinavia encourage the Viking strategy of ransacking Europe?

2. Study the pictures of Viking ships on pages 3 and 31. Make four observations about Viking ships. Analyze these ships as a technology. For what purpose were they particularly suited? Why?

3. Who were the skalds? What part did skalds play in maintaining Viking culture? In a small group, brainstorm what or who serves the various purposes of the skalds in Canadian society.

4. Why do you think being declared an outlaw was the most dreaded penalty in Viking society? Consider how this declaration would affect your status in regard to the law, your community, and your identity.

5. Examine the excerpt on page 31 about the destruction of the church at Lindisfarne. Whose view does this represent? What might be the Viking view of this event? Pretend you are one of the Vikings who participated in the raid on Lindisfarne. Write a brief account of the raid in the form of a speech you will give to your friends in Denmark.

SUMMARY

In this chapter, we have begun to explore the concept of civilization. Civilizations have developed all over the world at various times. One of these, western European civilization, began in the region of the Mediterranean Sea. You saw that the climate and geography of the area around the Mediterranean Sea encouraged large communities of people to settle there and build cities. You explored some of the lasting contributions of the Greek and Roman cultures to western European civilization and Canadian society. You saw that the collapse of the Western Roman Empire left western Europe in chaos.

You also considered the role of the Jewish, Christian, and Islamic religions in the early development of western European civilization. During the early Middle Ages, most people in Europe converted to Christianity. Even though many wars would be waged between peoples of different religious beliefs, Christianity emerged as a major unifying force.

You also focused on four of the peoples who settled in western Europe after the fall of Rome: the Anglo-Saxons, the Celts, the Franks, and the Vikings. As the threat of Viking invasions lessened in western Europe, people began to lead more settled lives. Over time, some of the major social structures of western Europe, such as feudalism, began to take recognizable shape.

SUMMARY ACTIVITIES

1. How do you think lawlessness, such as the on-going conflicts between the Vikings and the other western Europeans, affected people's everyday lives during the early Middle Ages?

2. The epic poem *Beowulf* (excerpt on page 28) explored an emotion common during the early Middle Ages: fear of what was beyond the protective walls. Considering that dangerous wild animals were still common in Europe and that enemies or thieves would not hesitate to attack you, do you think this fear was reasonable? Picture yourself on a dark night hiding in a forest in the Rocky Mountains. Draw a picture that shows how you feel in this situation. Then write a one-page story that opens with this scene and touches on the benefits of living in homes and close to other people.

3. a) On a blank map of Europe, locate and label Rome and the lands of the Vikings, Anglo-Saxons, Celts, and Franks.

   b) How would you describe Europe during the early Middle Ages?

4. Justinian, Charlemagne, and Alfred were all considered great leaders. Make up a comparison organizer to find the similarities and differences among the accomplishments of the three leaders. What did they do to benefit their peoples? What makes a good ruler? (For help in making a comparison organizer, refer to the feature on page 59.)

5. After the Vikings converted, Christianity became the major religion of all Europe. How could one common religion help unify the peoples of Europe? Write a paragraph to show how this Christian Europe differed from Europe at the time of the fall of Rome.

ON YOUR OWN

1. English has borrowed words from cultures around the world. Using a good dictionary, find out the original, or root, meanings of the following words, as well as their modern meanings

   Latin: procrastinate, guest, social, curriculum

   Viking or Old Norse: berserk, odd, thing , steak

   Anglo-Saxon: quick, lady, weird, under

2. Write a brief report about Newfoundland's L'Anse aux Meadows National Historic Park, as pictured on page 34. Possible sources of information are the park itself, at 709 623-2608, and the Parks Canada Internet site at **http://parkscanada.pch.gc.ca**.

2 EUROPE'S HIGH MIDDLE AGES

HAROLD

CHAPTER OUTCOMES

In this chapter you will focus on the high Middle Ages (1066–1300), when feudalism formed the basis of the social order in western Europe. By the end of the chapter you will

- explain how and why feudalism developed in Europe
- describe the feudal contract
- compare the rights and responsibilities of various people on the feudal manor
- explain the importance of religion to medieval people
- demonstrate an understanding of early legal systems
- describe the short- and long-term consequences of the Crusades
- make a map

The Story of the Bayeux Tapestry

*By the eleventh century England had been invaded many times. In 1066 England suffered yet another invader: William the Conqueror, from **Normandy**. At the Battle of Hastings he fought for and won the right to call himself King of England.*

*The Bayeux **Tapestry**, a 70-metre-long piece of embroidered fabric, tells the tale of William's victory. This rich primary source reveals how the Normans viewed the whole episode. In a sense the tapestry is like a medieval cartoon strip. Its scenes are arranged in panels, each panel having its own brief caption in Latin. The tapestry panels shown on these pages tell us a great deal about life in eleventh-century England and France. We learn not only about political affairs, warfare, and armour, but also about everyday life. Primarily, though, the tapestry tells us a story.*

A Vassal's Disloyalty

Years before the Battle of Hastings, an English earl, Harold Godwinson, had been shipwrecked on the coast of Normandy (in present-day France) and was taken prisoner.

The Bayeux tapestry tells us that William of Normandy spared Harold's life and befriended him. William took Harold with him on a military campaign, where the English earl distinguished himself by various acts of bravery.

A grateful William honoured Harold with gifts of armour and weapons. According to the tapestry, Harold in turn swore an oath of loyalty to William, thereby becoming William's **vassal**. Harold then returned to England.

William listens to Harold's tale of misfortune.

Some time later, in 1066 the English king, Edward the Confessor, died, leaving no heir to the English throne. William immediately claimed the throne for himself. On his mother's side, the Norman duke was related to Edward. Further, William said that Edward had promised the throne to him. At the same time, the Anglo-Saxon Harold claimed that Edward had offered *him* the throne on his deathbed. This claim, according to William, was a great act of disloyalty. No vassal should ever take something that his **lord** claimed for himself. By taking a throne that William wanted, Harold broke the **feudal contract**. William felt he had every right to declare war on his faithless vassal.

About this time, Halley's comet appeared in the night sky, an event that struck fear in the heart of **Anglo-Saxon** and Norman alike. The Anglo-Saxon Chronicle describes it thus: "Then over all England there was seen a sign in the skies such as had never been seen before." You can see the comet, along with a messenger telling King Harold about it, on the opening page of this chapter. People believed that such a dramatic natural occurrence must predict a coming disaster. Elsewhere on the panel are shown people pointing at the comet. Why do you think this panel was included?

Preparing for War

When Harold was crowned king by the other Anglo-Saxon nobles, William collected an army, built a fleet of ships, and sailed to England. The tapestry records the considerable achievement of building a fleet, collecting stores, and then

William's army got the food for this feast by raiding the surrounding countryside. He did this for three reasons: to supply his large army with food, to strike fear into the hearts of the English people, and to anger Harold. It was an effective tactic.

transporting an army of seven thousand knights—complete with their armour, horses, weapons, servants, and supplies—across the English Channel.

After reaching England, William holds a feast in a celebration that is shown in the panel on the previous page. Here we see the first course of the meal, with rounds of bread, fish, and wine. How do the Normans drink their wine? This contrasts with another scene in which the Anglo-Saxons guzzle ale from horns. Also in this picture you see a servant waiting on table. How does his clothing differ from that of the nobles being served? The caption above the scene reads "And here the Bishop [Odo] blesses the food and drink."

The panel of the Norman feast shows that the Norman army was well fed and rested before going into battle. In contrast, Harold's army, which had just defeated an invading Viking army in the north, was tired and hungry. As Harold's **housecarls** raced south to defend their country, William's soldiers feasted—and waited.

The Tactics and Technology of a Battle

The battle was a savage affair. On the field at Hastings the two armies tore away at each other from about nine o'clock in the morning until four in the afternoon. In most medieval battles, knights were taken prisoner and later exchanged for hefty ransoms. At Hastings, however, the soldiers fought to

the death, and casualties on both sides were unusually high.

The English tactic was to battle on foot using lances, swords, and axes in a formation called the shield-wall, as shown below. The troops stood shoulder to shoulder with their kite-shaped shields overlapping to make a protective wall. This battle formation made it difficult for enemy soldiers to break through the English line without being cut down.

The Normans did not battle on foot like their English foes. Instead, they rode into battle on the horses they had brought with them across the English Channel. These horses gave the Norman **cavalry** two advantages. First, the power of a horse charging across open ground could drive a **lance** right through

Even though the Normans were on horseback, they could not break the Anglo-Saxon shield wall.

In the scene above, a mounted Norman knight cuts down an Anglo-Saxon soldier, possibly Harold. Some historians believe Harold was killed when an arrow smashed into his eye.

a wooden shield and into the soldier's body. Second, the extra height of the mounted knight gave him a longer reach when swinging his sword. Despite these advantages, the repeated charges of the Norman knights on horseback failed to wear down the Anglo-Saxon housecarls. In frustration, William ordered his knights to pretend to retreat. When they did so, some inexperienced soldiers in Harold's army broke ranks to chase their enemies. They were slaughtered, and Harold's **impenetrable** shield-wall was broken.

Without the shield-wall formation to protect them, Harold's foot soldiers were butchered by their mounted foes. This day of battle was a sad day for England. William of Poitier, a chronicler of the time, wrote that "the bloodstained battleground was covered with the flower of the youth and nobility of England."

Medieval Propaganda

The Bayeux Tapestry was created under the direction of Bishop Odo, William's half brother, who fought at William's side in the battle. Because Odo participated in the events, historians treat the tapestry as a primary historical source. William had the tapestry made to convince people that he was the rightful king of England, thereby discouraging others from claiming the throne. In a sense, the tapestry is more than a work of art or a source for historical research; in its time the tapestry served as a very effective piece of **propaganda** for a medieval politician.

Making the Tapestry

After Bishop Odo ordered the tapestry for William, sketches would have been made of the various scenes to be portrayed. At this point, a team of highly skilled needleworkers began the embroidery work. The needleworkers outlined the figures in dark thread and filled in the outlines with threads of various colours. These needleworkers were either English nuns or daughters of the English nobility who had perfected their needleworking skills from an early age. When the tapestry was finished, Bishop Odo hung it from the pillars of Bayeux Cathedral in Normandy. By doing so, he claimed God's blessing for William's kingship.

Normandy: an area, now part of France, that was home to the Normans, who were descended from Vikings

tapestry: a thick, embroidered cloth picture used as a wall hanging

vassal: one who swears loyalty to a lord

lord: a feudal superior

feudal contract: the bargain between a lord and his vassal

Anglo-Saxon: the earliest English, a Germanic people

housecarl: soldier

technology: things humans make to use as tools

cavalry: soldiers on horseback

lance: a long spear

impenetrable: impossible to pass

propaganda: an effort to spread opinions or beliefs, sometimes by distorting the truth

audience: a hearing, an interview

The Bayeux Tapestry was so long that sections of it were produced separately and then sewn together. Englishwomen were so talented with the needle that embroidery work was often referred to as *opus Anglicanum*, or "the work of the English."

ACTIVITIES

1. Summarize the story told by the Bayeux Tapestry.

2. Examine the tapestry panel that shows William giving Harold an **audience**. Who is standing and who is seated? What does this say about the relationship of the two men? Why do you think William wanted to show this scene?

3. In the panel showing the Norman feast, Bishop Odo lifts his arm to bless the meal. Elsewhere in the panel, the Pope's flag is shown flying over William's troops. Why would William want these touches included?

4. Describe the purpose of the Anglo-Saxon shield wall. What military advantage did the Normans have? Describe the tactic that finally allowed the Normans to use this advantage to achieve victory.

5. In a group of four or five students, select one panel from the Bayeux Tapestry to dramatize for the rest of the class. Think about what happened just before and just after the moment captured in your chosen panel. Then create some dialogue for all the characters pictured.

6. Give two reasons why the tapestry is called a primary historical source. What would be a secondary source about the Battle of Hastings?

TIME LINE

1066	WILLIAM OF NORMANDY CONQUERS ENGLAND
1085	THE DOMESDAY BOOK IS MADE
1096	THE FIRST CRUSADE BEGINS
1147	THE SECOND CRUSADE BEGINS
1169	SALADIN BECOMES SULTAN
1170	MURDER OF THOMAS BECKET
1189	THE THIRD CRUSADE BEGINS
1198	INNOCENT III BECOMES POPE
1204	ELEANOR OF AQUITAINE DIES
1215	KING JOHN SIGNS THE MAGNA CARTA
1227	DEATH OF CHINGGIS KHAN

[King Harold] gathered a great army and assembled them at the ancient apple tree. William came upon them unawares, before they had gathered; the king, nevertheless, fought very hard against them with those men who would stay with him, and there were many killed on both sides. There King Harold was killed, earl Leofwine his brother and earl Gyrth his brother, and many good men. The French held the field of the dead as God granted them because of the sins of the people.

—THE ANGLO-SAXON CHRONICLE, 1066

PRIMARY SOURCE

This brief account of the defeat of King Harold's forces at Hastings presents the Anglo-Saxon view of the battle, just as the Bayeux Tapestry presents the Norman view. What do the Anglo-Saxons say caused their defeat? What other reasons are suggested? Do these agree with the reasons presented in the Bayeux Tapestry?

INTRODUCTION

The Battle of Hastings was a historical milestone for two reasons. It marked the point at which the mounted, armoured knight became the deadliest fighter in western Europe, an advantage he would hold until the introduction of the English longbow during the Hundred Years' War. William the Conqueror's victory also opened England to a complete social and political reorganization through the introduction of Norman feudalism, a social system based on land, loyalty, and religious faith. During the centuries that followed—known as the high Middle Ages—feudalism reached its highest point of development in western Europe.

The centre of feudal life was the manor: a self-sufficient community where most people lived out their lives as serfs or free landowners. On the manor, religion and the Church played a major role in people's day-to-day lives. New laws and systems of justice helped people live together in peace. Because life on the manor was all that people knew, the world view of the Middle Ages differs greatly from the one we hold today.

The feudal system was primarily a military arrangement. The manor's main purpose was to support the lord of the manor, a knight. The feudal knights—and many ordinary people—finally looked beyond their isolated world when the Church called people to arms to defend the Christian Holy Land during the Crusades. In the end, this **monumental** military campaign would change Europe forever.

Figure 2–1 This infrared satellite image of the Quebec City area shows the narrow strips of farmland characteristic of the seigneurial system, which the French used when they first settled in Quebec. This system, by which tenants of the land held personal contracts with a seigneur, or lord, comes straight from feudal times.

monumental: very important

WILLIAM THE CONQUEROR AND THE FEUDAL SYSTEM

Soon after William the Conqueror took possession of England, he decided that the feudal system he was familiar with in Normandy would also work well in his new kingdom. Armoured knights need a large land base to support them, so William immediately began taking land away from the defeated English earls and giving it to the Norman knights who had fought with him at Hastings.

Norman feudalism was very different from the old English system in which free people lived in free villages. The English landowners and serfs at first resisted William's changes, but William brutally suppressed all opposition. Within five years, William had established feudalism throughout England.

THE FEUDAL CONTRACT

A feudal system like the one set up by William was based on the "three Fs" of fief (land), fealty (loyalty), and faith (religion). Under feudalism, land was the basis of all wealth; land was given to nobles, who were all knights, in exchange for loyalty. The oath formed the cement in this bond, and religious faith bound every knight to the oath he swore.

The monarch parcelled out all the lands in the kingdom to faithful nobles as fiefs, or estates. In return for these fiefs, the nobles promised the king their loyalty, which meant living up to a number of obligations. First, all the nobles had to serve in the king's army for a certain number of days each year, usually around forty. Second, they had to supply the king with additional knights in time of war. Third, the nobles were expected to serve in the king's court and to give him advice on political matters. Finally, they had to give the king money on certain occasions, such as when his oldest son was knighted or when a daughter got married.

In return for performing these duties, nobles had the right to their monarch's protection and justice. The king defended his nobles from attack and settled disputes that arose between two or more nobles.

This relationship was sealed in a ceremony in which nobles swore an oath of **allegiance**. In this way they

allegiance: loyalty

homage: formal acknowledgment

VIEWPOINTS IN CONFLICT

Oaths of Allegiance

Here are two oaths of loyalty: the medieval vassal's oath of allegiance to his lord and the oath taken by a new Canadian citizen of Canada. In what ways are these oaths similar? How do they differ?

Vassal's Oath of Allegiance
And then they did their **homage** thus. The count asked if he was willing to become completely his man, and the other replied, "I am willing;" and with clasped hands, and surrounded by the hands of the count, they were bound together by a kiss. Secondly, he who had done homage gave his fealty to the representative of the count in these words, "I promise on my faith that I will in future be faithful to Count William, and will observe my homage to him completely against all persons in good faith and without deceit," and thirdly, he took his oath to this upon the relics of the saints.

PRIMARY SOURCE

The Canadian Oath of Citizenship
I Swear (or Affirm) that I will be faithful and bear true allegiance to Her Majesty Queen Elizabeth the Second, Queen of Canada, Her heirs and successors according to law, and that I will faithfully observe the laws of Canada and fulfill my duties as a Canadian citizen.

PRIMARY SOURCE

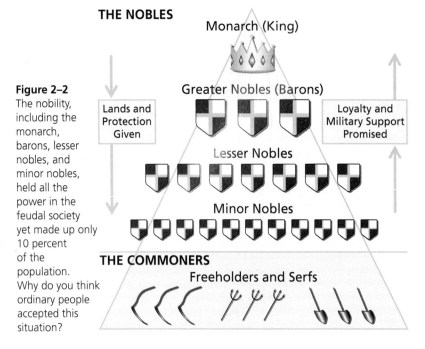

THE NOBLES
Monarch (King)

Greater Nobles (Barons)

Lands and Protection Given

Loyalty and Military Support Promised

Lesser Nobles

Minor Nobles

THE COMMONERS
Freeholders and Serfs

Figure 2–2
The nobility, including the monarch, barons, lesser nobles, and minor nobles, held all the power in the feudal society yet made up only 10 percent of the population. Why do you think ordinary people accepted this situation?

contract: a formal agreement

lord of the manor: the tenant of a noble, who has the inherited right to run a manor and profit from it

freeholder: a person who owns his or her land

became the king's vassals. In similar ceremonies, stronger nobles took lesser nobles as vassals, who in turn took their own vassals. This is the very basis of the feudal system: the deal, or **contract**, between the lord and the vassal. Both parties to the agreement, even when one was the

monarch, were expected to live up to the bargain, which was known as the "feudal contract." And as long as all parties maintained their part of the bargain, peace was maintained.

The vassals of the king, the barons, became the tenants-in-chief of estates. (The word "tenant" comes from the French word meaning "holder.") The vassals of these nobles became tenants, and the vassals of the tenants became sub-tenants. The nobles always kept some land for themselves, so that, in the end, all nobles had some land under their direct control. Each noble would live on his land, called a manor, and, as the **lord of the manor**, had the right to profit from it. The lord of the manor had serfs and **freeholders** to work the land.

The serfs and freeholders— usually forming about ninety percent of the population—were kept outside the circle of power and had few rights. Freeholders actually owned the land they farmed, for which they paid a yearly fee to the lord of the manor.

The Domesday Book

William the Conqueror arrived in England as an outsider. To learn more about his new kingdom, William sent officials all over the land to record how many people lived in each region, what they owned, and how much land was being farmed. He especially wanted to know if people were living on land he had not granted them, and if he could charge higher taxes. At right, the Anglo-Saxon Chronicle describes the enormous task of collecting the information.

shire: county

hide: about 40 hectares; generally enough land to sustain one family

livestock: farm animals

All the information was gathered together into the *Domesday Book*. "Dome," or doom, was the Anglo-Saxon word for judgement. The title of the book refers to the comment

made by many Anglo-Saxons that under William the "day of judgement" had arrived. What is the modern Canadian equivalent of the *Domesday Book*?

[William] then sent out his men over all England into each **shire**, and had it made out how many **hides** of land were in each shire . . . what and how much each man had who was holding land in England, in land, in **livestock**, and how much money it was worth. So closely did he let it be searched out that not a single hide nor rod of land, nor indeed (it is a shame to tell it, but it seemed no shame to him to do) one ox nor one goat nor one pig was left out, that was not set in his document; and all the documents were brought to him afterwards.
—*The Anglo-Saxon Chronicle, 1085*

PRIMARY SOURCE

The serfs, at the very bottom of the feudal pyramid, had virtually no power. They were considered part of the property. Nonetheless, the lords could not take away their right to farm and live on the manor.

to exploit: to make selfish use of

ACTIVITIES

1. Explain how a vassal gained protection as well as land from the feudal contract. What services did the vassal offer his lord?

2. **a)** Feudalism was a social order based on contracts. What is a contract?

   b) Contracts can be written or unwritten. For example, when you give money to a store clerk and then leave the store with a chocolate bar, you take part in an unwritten, unspoken contract. Think of an example of a contract, written or verbal, that you made. In a group, share these examples.

   c) Describe the nature of the feudal contract.

3. **a)** How did feudalism bring an organized political system to Europe? How did feudalism contribute to social order?

   b) How did feudalism suppress individual freedom? Who was **exploited** by whom?

4. **a)** Most medieval people were serfs with no power even over their own lives. What one fundamental right did they enjoy?

   b) Suppose that a school friend jokingly suggests that serfdom be introduced to Canada as a means of reducing unemployment. How do you respond?

5. Considering that neither the printing press nor pen and paper existed when the Domesday Book was made, what technologies do you think were used to collect and organize the statistics? Compare the process and technology involved with that used by a modern data collection organization such as Statistics Canada.

MEDIEVAL LIFE AND CUSTOM

THE MANOR

Throughout medieval Europe, large fiefs were divided into parcels of land called manors. Each manor had farming lands, woodlands, common pasture, and at least one village. Almost completely **self-sufficient**, the manor usually provided enough food for everyone who lived on it. The manor village had a church, a mill, a blacksmith's shop, and a tannery. Each manor also had the skilled people needed to do most jobs, from **thatching** a roof to **fletching** an arrow.

The manor village was almost always located by a river or stream, from which the villagers drew water. The stream also powered the mill to grind grain for bread, and along the river banks were hay fields that provided winter feed for livestock. People gathered firewood in common woodlands. Other forests were set aside for the lord's hunting parties.

The lord of the manor always kept some land on the manor for his own use and personal profit. Called the **demesne**, this land consisted of the gardens and orchards around the manor house and some strips of land in the manor fields. All the rest of the manor fields belonged to freeholders or were for the use of serfs. Some lords took a personal interest in the work of their estates but most had managers, called **bailiffs**, to look after day-to-day affairs and to keep the peace.

self-sufficient: independent

thatching: using special grass to make roofs for buildings

fletching: fitting feathers on arrows

demesne: lands set aside for the lord of a manor

bailiff: the person who collected rents and supervised serfs and freeholders on a manor

DID YOU KNOW?

"Demesne" is pronounced "di-mane," like the English word "domain." Can you see a similarity in meaning also?

Sustainable Farming

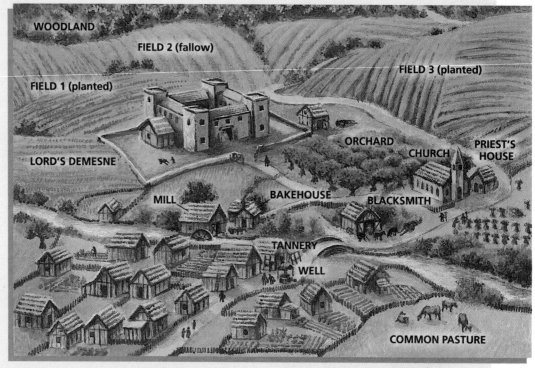

Figure 2–3 A small medieval manor. Can you pick out the three fields, the church, the common pasture, and the lord's manor house?

During medieval times, self-sufficiency was absolutely necessary. Manors had to grow enough food on the manor lands to feed the community all year.

To encourage their lands to produce sufficient quantities of food year after year, medieval farmers fertilized their fields by allowing the farm animals to roam freely on the crop fields after the crops were harvested. Animal manure is an excellent natural fertilizer used by farmers all over the world.

By the eleventh century, manor farmers had developed a three-field system of crop rotation to increase their harvest. For each field, they grew cereal one year and a nitrogen-generating crop the second. (Adding nitrogen to soil ensures healthy, vigorous plant growth.) In the third year, the field was left **fallow**: no crops were planted, and weeds were ploughed under twice. This loosened the soil, controlled plant diseases, and

killed weeds. With three fields, the farmers could always have two fields producing crops while the third lay fallow. They thereby struck a **sustainable** balance between maintaining the productivity of their fields and planting enough crops to feed the local population.

All farming communities face the challenge of growing enough food for everyone. Various communities find different solutions. For example, the Pima, a

Central American Aboriginal people, developed many kinds of maize (corn) suited to various weather conditions and soil types. One type of corn ripened quickly. The Pima would plant this variety if spring came very late. In this way, the Pima could get the most out of every growing season, no matter the weather.

fallow: ploughed and left unseeded

sustainable: can keep going, year after year, without deteriorating

WHAT DO YOU THINK?

1. Why did manor communities have to be completely self-sufficient?

2. Sustainable farming does not ruin the soil. Describe two practices that made medieval farming sustainable. How did this contribute to the manor's ability to be self-sufficient?

3. Within three centuries, the Pima lost seven varieties of maize because lush conditions changed to near desert. Explain why preserving the knowledge and accomplishments of all peoples is important.

HOW TO...

Make a Map

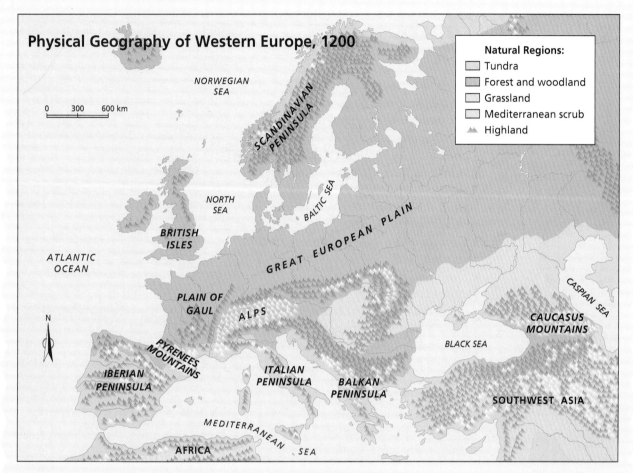

Physical Geography of Western Europe, 1200

0   300   600 km

NORWEGIAN SEA

SCANDINAVIAN PENINSULA

NORTH SEA

BALTIC SEA

GREAT EUROPEAN PLAIN

BRITISH ISLES

ATLANTIC OCEAN

CASPIAN SEA

N

PLAIN OF GAUL

ALPS

CAUCASUS MOUNTAINS

BLACK SEA

PYRENEES MOUNTAINS

IBERIAN PENINSULA

ITALIAN PENINSULA

BALKAN PENINSULA

SOUTHWEST ASIA

MEDITERRANEAN SEA

AFRICA

Natural Regions:
- Tundra
- Forest and woodland
- Grassland
- Mediterranean scrub
- ⛰ Highland

The map above provides several clues about why the feudal system flourished where it did in western Europe. To make a map that will pull together those clues, follow steps 1 to 9, using an outline version of this map provided by your teacher.

1. Label the major water bodies.

2. Draw an arrow to indicate north.

A successful manor needs to support a large group of people. Manors benefited from flat land, fertile soil, and a plentiful supply of water.

3. **Flat land.** On your tracing, mark on the mountain ranges using upside-down *V*s. The plains (areas of relatively flat land) are everywhere there are no mountains or large hills. Label the Plain of Gaul and the Great European Plain.

4. **Fertile soil.** Next, show the fertile land by outlining and shading in light green all the forest and woodland areas. Forests also provide firewood and building materials.

5. **Source of water.** Trace all the rivers with a blue pencil, thereby showing which regions have plentiful access to water.

6. Now use red slanted lines to show all areas that are flat, have fertile soil, *and* have plenty of water nearby. These

are the areas where feudal communities flourished.

7. Add a legend to show what colours or symbols you used to show mountains, fertile land, rivers, and areas with feudal communities.

8. Give your map a title.

9. Write a summary of your map by finishing the following two sentences:

◆ To grow enough crops to support the community, manors needed…

◆ According to my map, the most successful manors were located…

ORDINARY PEOPLE

wattle and daub: woven sticks covered with clay or mud

vermin: lice, fleas, and bedbugs

louse: a small, wingless insect that lives and feeds on mammals, including human beings

The serfs and freeholders on a manor provided all the labour but had the lowest standard of living. The serfs were considered part of the property of the estate and were not free to come and go as they pleased. All serfs had to donate two or three days of work each week to ploughing, planting, weeding, and harvesting the lord's demesne. Although they could not own land, most serfs had the right to farm a particular strip of land within the manor fields. On the satellite image on page 44 you can see how farms were divided into strips so that each serf would have easy access to water on the river. The rights to strips were passed on within families from generation to generation. Serfs turned over a percentage of the produce they grew to the lord of the manor. They were allowed to sell any produce left over after they had fed their families and paid their lord.

Most serfs also had small vegetable and herb gardens. Many owned a few cows, some sheep, a horse or two, a few pigs, and some chickens or ducks. The average male serf consumed about 5000 calories every day, mostly in the form of bread (2 kilograms each day) and beer. They also ate herring, onions, leeks, cheese, fruit, peas, and eggs. Besides beer, they drank the milk of cows, sheep, and goats. Most of the manure from these animals would go on the serf's own strip of land or garden plot.

Freeholders, unlike serfs, actually owned their land. They paid money to the lord but did not have to work on the lord's demesne. These free farmers also had the right to leave the village or the farm whenever they pleased.

Village Homes

The serfs and freeholders, and the few tradespeople such as the blacksmith and candle maker, all lived in the manor village. The villagers built their houses from wood or **wattle and daub**, and roofed them with thatch. The floor of a typical house was packed dirt. There was a place for a fire, with a hole in the roof to let out the smoke, but no chimney. The houses were quite small, just 9 or 10 metres long by 3 or 4 metres wide. The whole family, usually about five or six people, shared one dirty room, often with some of their farm animals and enough **vermin** to make a **louse** comb a common possession.

Plumbing and electricity were non-existent. Most people had only a few pieces of furniture: a stool or two, some wooden boxes, a rough bench, and a homemade table. They slept on low beds heaped with straw. In the Middle Ages, feather mattresses were very rare. Even great lords and ladies slept on straw mattresses.

Work and Cooperation

Men and women worked hard in the Middle Ages, and even young children had to do their share. Babies went to the fields with their mothers, and children quickly learned how to do farm work. The whole family helped with planting and harvesting. Children of serfs and freeholders did not go to school.

For a woman living in a medieval village, a great deal of time was taken up just keeping her family fed and clothed. She wove cloth, made clothes, brewed beer, baked bread, cooked meals, preserved food for winter, and cared for the children. Grandparents were seldom available to help with child care because most people died young. Women also gathered firewood, and hay and cornstalks for the farm animals. They collected nuts, berries, and herbs, which they used both to flavour food and to cure sicknesses. Many women also kept a kitchen garden next to the house.

Most of a medieval man's time was taken up with farm work: ploughing, planting, weeding, and harvesting, all without benefit of modern machinery. If he was a serf, not only did he work on his own piece of land, he also worked on the lord's demesne.

Men and women alike worked from sunrise to sunset. On larger jobs, they usually worked with their neighbours, partly because the laws of the manor required that people work together for ploughing and harvesting.

pullet: young chicken

green cheese: unripe cheese

curds: cottage cheese

collop: slice of meat

dung: manure

drought: a long period without rain

Lammas: August 1, a feast to celebrate the first wheat harvest

Piers the Ploughman: A Peasant's Diet

The medieval English poet William Langland movingly describes the poverty of a ploughman named Piers, who worked as hard as he could but still had difficulty feeding his family. In winter, many poor peasants like Piers went hungry.

Following the example of the *Beowulf* poet, Langland uses alliteration. This means that in each line of poetry two or three words start with the same letter or sound. Which initial letter is repeated in the first line? The third? The others?

> "I have no penny," quoth Piers, "**pullets** for to buy,
> Neither geese nor young pigs, but two **green cheeses**,
> A few **curds** and cream and an oaten cake,
> And two loaves of beans and bran baked for my children.
> And yet I say, by my soul I have no salt bacon,
> Nor any cook, by Christ, **collops** for to make.
> But I have parsley and leeks, and many cabbage plants,
> And also a cow and a calf, and a cart mare too
> To draw afield the **dung** while the **drought** lasts.
> And by these means we must make do until **Lammas** tide."

PRIMARY SOURCE

WHAT DO YOU THINK?

1. Make a list of all the foods and livestock that Piers has and a list of those he does not have. Analyze your list and the poem to decide if Piers lacks variety, quantity, or balance in his diet. Explain.

2. How do you think farming technology, refrigeration technology, and transportation technology—or their absence—influenced Piers' diet?

Figure 2–4 Servants wait on nobles at a wedding feast. How did the lifestyle of the nobles differ from that of their servants?

LORD AND LADY OF THE MANOR

The Manor House

Compared with the typical villager, the lord and lady of the manor lived very well. They occupied the largest, best house on the manor and were attended by a whole team of servants. Most manor houses had several rooms, including a large hall where the lord would look after the affairs of the manor and entertain guests. The walls were draped with elaborate tapestries to keep out the cold, and every room had furniture: a small table, some wooden chests, a few good chairs, maybe even a book or two—all very expensive items. Servants laid fresh rushes on the stone floor several times a year.

By modern standards, these houses were not comfortable. There was no running water, toilets, or central heating, and rooms were drafty and cold. Further, people had very little privacy. Servants slept near the bed of their lord and lady. Medieval people were used to these conditions and didn't complain. They spent much of their time outdoors anyway.

The Privileges

The nobles lived as well as they could, with the help of their many servants. Then, as now, people loved to possess costly, rare things, which they kept as status symbols. Lords liked to own fine hunting **falcons**, beautiful horses, expensive furniture, and big houses. Both men and women hunted for recreation. Singers, called **troubadours**, and other entertainers occasionally visited the manor and performed for the lord and lady.

The Obligations

Although the lord of the manor had a great deal of power over his serfs and freeholders, he was also a tenant himself and had certain **obligations**. In return for the manor, the tenant-in-chief expected a pay-back. If the lord failed to live up to his end of the bargain, perhaps by not sending the required number of knights to fight for the tenant-in-chief, he could lose the manor.

One of the duties of all nobles was to marry and have children. If a lord died childless, then his tenant-in-chief could take back the manor. Parents usually arranged the marriages of their children, finding a partner with as much land as possible. Young men and women were rarely asked who they would like to marry. Noble marriages were much more about land and power than about romance. The good of the family was considered more important than an individual's wants or needs.

A Woman's Rights

As boys and girls grew up, the boys' rights increased dramatically, whereas the rights of girls did not. Before marriage, a girl's father controlled her life; after marriage, her husband did. Women who expected to inherit property were often treated like prizes to be won in the feudal age. Because the tenant-in-chief expected military service in return for land, he might take back the estates of an unmarried heiress, so she would try to marry before that happened. Orphans such as Maid Marion in the Robin Hood story became **wards** of the ruler, who selected a husband for them. Once married, a woman's property came completely under her husband's control.

Medieval women who had never been married had few legal rights. Widows, however, kept their rights, their property, and their freedom. Many rich widows absolutely refused to remarry, even when pressured by the king to do so.

ward: an orphan who is put in another person's care until he or she becomes an adult

◄ LINK-UP ►

Women and the Right to Own Property

Land was the most precious commodity in feudal times. The more land one owned, the more powerful one became. Therefore, a noble would always leave his land to his eldest son. In this way, the family's power was not divided and lessened. In modern England, titles and ancestral homes still go to the eldest son.

Similarly, in other civilizations, such as ancient India and Greece, women could not own land. In some African countries, for example, farmland has been passed on from father to son through many generations. A daughter would never inherit land because her family would not want her to take the land out of the family group when she married and went to live with her husband's family. By tradition, a woman had the right to farm her husband's land and to live in the couple's family home, especially as she did the farming, cooking, and home care. But if her husband were to die, her son would inherit her husband's land, not the woman or her daughter.

Not all civilizations followed the same rules. In ancient Babylonia, nearly 4000 years ago, King Hammurabi wrote a single code of law for everyone in his empire. Under his rule, women could own property, buy and sell land, and even lend and borrow money. In ancient Egypt, women could own, buy, and sell property, run a business, and testify in court.

Figure 2–5 Many women the world over farm land owned by their husbands.

WHAT DO YOU THINK?

1. In societies all over the world, in the past as well as today, men keep control of the land. What are the benefits of this system? What are the drawbacks? To whom?

2. Does modern Canada differentiate between the rights of men and women? Brainstorm various ways that women have been and are still treated unfairly. Do some research to find out when one unfair practice came to an end in Canada. Why does unequal treatment still occur?

1. During the Middle Ages in Europe, most people never travelled more than 10 kilometres from their place of birth. What methods of transportation were available to villagers? How does this help explain why manors were isolated, self-sufficient organizations?

2. People called Miller, Fletcher, Tanner, Thatcher, and Smith all have ancestors who practised certain trades in feudal times. Can you identify what work each ancestor did?

3. Create a large-scale map for a manor that has all the features of a typical manor of the eleventh or twelfth century. Give your manor a name. Be sure to include a manor house, village, fields, a water source, and other features. Label all the important places.

4. All serfs worked long hours. Make a list of women's tasks. Make a list of men's tasks. Comment on the differences. Have things changed? How?

5. At harvest time men, women, and children worked together in the manor fields. Why would this be common? Today children still help in the harvest all over the world. What are the benefits and drawbacks of this practice?

6. a) In a group, make a chart comparing the rights and responsibilities of serfs and lords.

   b) Still in your group, make another chart to compare a serf's rights and responsibilities with those of a Canadian citizen.

7. a) Compare women's rights with men's rights in the Middle Ages.

   b) Feudal society was primarily a military arrangement, whereby nobles protected and maintained their lands and power. What does this say about the power of women?

BELIEF AND DEVOTION

Medieval people lived in a world filled with religious signs and meanings. Christian churches appeared throughout Europe, and most people attended church services frequently. Almost all western Europeans were devoutly Christian. They believed absolutely that every person had to struggle between good and evil throughout their lives, and that each person would be judged after death. They learned as children that good people went to heaven and bad people suffered in hell for eternity. They believed that by taking part in various religious ceremonies their sins—the evil they had done—would be forgiven and they could avoid the agonies of hell.

Medieval people also saw evidence of God's hand in their everyday lives, bringing them success or failure, sickness or health, rain or drought. When things went badly, they believed they were being punished for their sins. We saw one example of this in the quote on page 43, when King Harold's defeat was blamed on "the sins of the people."

In the medieval calendar, every day was dedicated to a different saint. Many Canadians still mark St. Valentine's Day on February 14 or St. Patrick's Day on March 17. Every medieval ceremony had a religious aspect, and no important event could proceed without God's blessing.

Medieval people accepted without question things that many modern people would be **sceptical of**—the miraculous power of a holy **relic**, for example. Medieval people also accepted their position within society

sceptical of: doubting the truth of

relic: an item associated with a saint; thought to have great powers

as part of God's plan. People took their spiritual urges so seriously that it was not at all unusual for men and women to devote their entire lives to God in monasteries or convents. Some even chose to live as hermits, walling themselves up in prison-like cells in hopes that through their solitude they would grow closer to God.

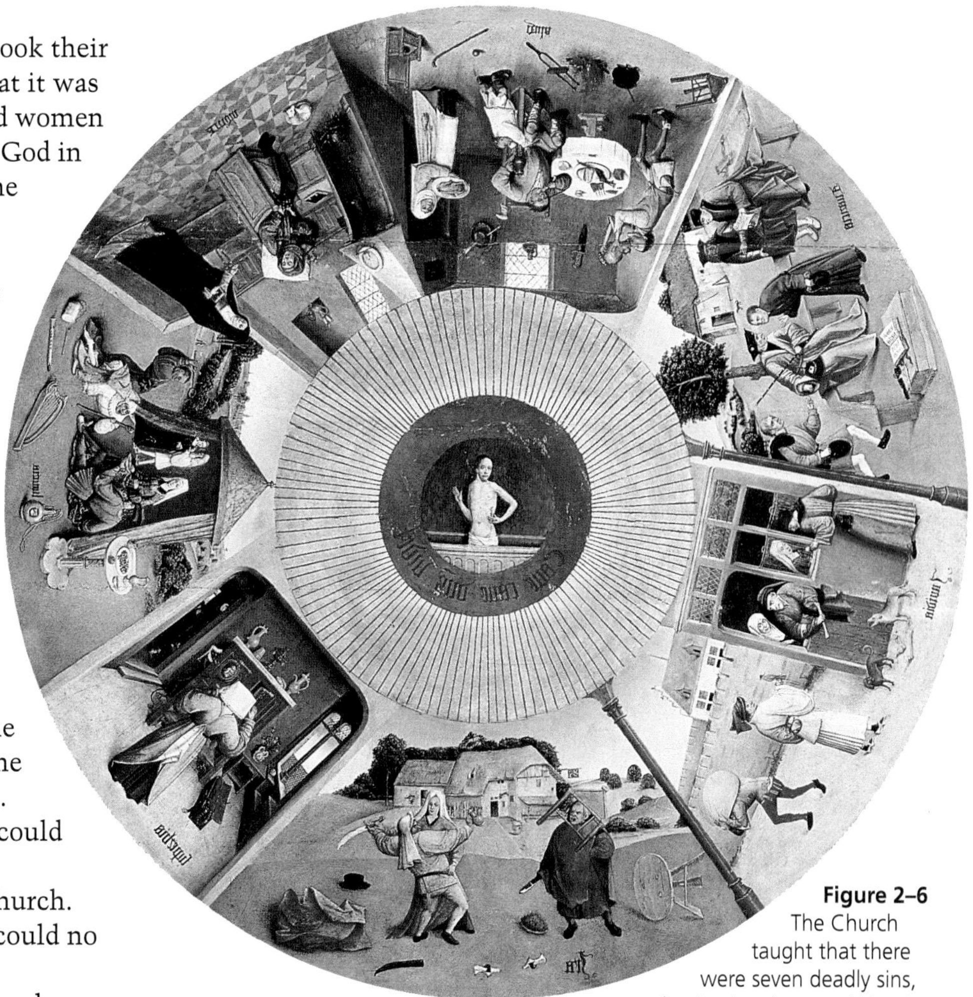

THE CHURCH

In the Middle Ages, the Catholic Church was the only Christian religious institution in Europe. Christians could practise their religion only through the Church, so the Church became very influential and powerful. One of the worst things that could happen to a person was to be **excommunicated** from the Church. An excommunicated person could no longer participate in church ceremonies; for instance, he or she could not be married or be blessed before death. People greatly feared excommunication because they felt certain it meant they would go to hell. The Church thus had great power over the lives of everyone from serfs to monarchs. The Church's considerable power over everyone, including monarchs, brought a balance to medieval life, putting church and state on an equal footing.

Almost every village had at least one church and one priest. The Church provided for all the religious needs of the people. It performed marriages and burials, and witnessed agreements. The Church also assisted people in desperate need.

The Church was supported by a tax on villagers called a **tithe**, worth about one-tenth of their incomes, in either cash or crops. Some churches grew very rich because they had their

Figure 2–6
The Church taught that there were seven deadly sins, that is, sins that would lead to spiritual death. These were pride, anger, envy, greed, lust, gluttony (eating too much), and sloth (laziness). Can you match each sin to the scene that represents it in the picture above?

own lands and were situated in rich towns or villages. Some priests got rich by keeping most of the income from their churches and paying replacements low wages.

For some young people inspired by a love of God, the Church offered a chance to devote their lives to study and prayer. For others an **ecclesiastical** career was an inviting alternative to the drudgery and routine of village life and a chance to improve their social standing.

MONASTIC LIFE

Many men and women became monks and nuns in medieval times. Men entered monasteries; women entered convents, also called "nunneries." These religious

to excommunicate: to cancel a person's membership in the Church

tithe: money or produce given to the Church, worth approximately one-tenth of one's income

ecclesiastical: having to do with the Church

chastity: virtue; modesty; doing without sex

communities provided a life of work and prayer. New members took vows of poverty, **chastity**, and obedience. Monks and nuns woke up several times during the night to pray, and rose very early in the morning. In some religious houses, no one was allowed to speak except to say prayers. Food was simple and comforts few. Nevertheless, there was never a shortage of applicants.

Although their lives were hard, nuns and monks did have some free time each day and some choice about what to do during this time. Some spent the time studying, some praying, and others doing various kinds of work. The copying and illustrating of books was both common and encouraged.

A C T I V I T I E S

1. In what ways did Christians of the Middle Ages express their faith? Why was religion so important to them?

2. **a)** Describe three ways in which the Church was central in people's lives.

   b) In what ways was the Church's influence over people a positive thing? A negative thing?

3. The Church was the only organization offering education. How did this role give it power? What benefits did the Church bring through education?

4. Why did some people choose to live in monasteries or convents? What was monastic life like?

5. Write an imaginary journal entry for either a nun or a monk who lived in the Middle Ages. Describe a typical day and have your monk or nun give their thoughts and feelings about the events of the day. In a group, read one another your journal entries. Discuss the benefits and drawbacks to monastic life.

THE LAW

Many Canadian legal customs have been handed down to us from the Middle Ages. We might not feel completely at home in a medieval courtroom, but we would certainly have a good idea of what was going on. As in our own courts, someone would be **prosecuted** or **sued**, witnesses would swear to tell the truth, a jury would hear the case, and a sentence would be passed by a **judge**.

Some things, however, would definitely surprise modern people. For example, we would not think of putting rats on trial because they ate the village grain supplies. Medieval people did **try** rats, toads, and even, on occasion, insects. Anything that brought evil into a person's life could be brought to justice. "Evil" could include the death of a cow, an accident, or having your food stolen by rats.

TRIAL BY ORDEAL AND TRIAL BY BATTLE

Trial by **ordeal** and trial by battle were common ways of deciding if a person was innocent or guilty in the Middle Ages. People reasoned that God would certainly help an innocent person. So,

to prosecute: to present evidence to prove a person's guilt

to sue: to seek compensation for a personal wrong

judge: one who hears and decides cases in court

to try: to determine guilt or innocence

ordeal: dreadful experience

to test a person's innocence, why not expose a person to danger to see if God would protect him or her from harm?

Trial by ordeal came in several varieties. A person might have to swallow poison, pull an object from boiling oil, walk over nine red-hot ploughs, or carry a red-hot piece of iron a certain distance. If the burn from the ordeal became infected, the judges would rule the person guilty. Trial by ordeal was outlawed later in the Middle Ages.

In trial by battle, two nobles would fight, often until one of them died. The winner was assumed to be innocent, because God protected innocent people. Only noblemen had the right to trial by battle. A noblewoman had the right to select a champion to fight on her behalf.

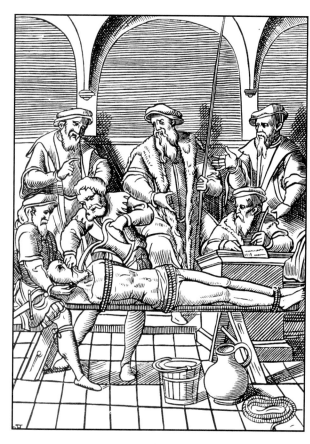

Figure 2–7 In this trial by ordeal, a person's innocence is tested by his ability to withstand poison. Does this form of trial endure in Canadian law? Why or why not?

MANOR COURTS

Various courts—manor courts, royal courts, and Church courts—looked after different legal matters. A person accused of any major crime would be sent to the royal court. Church people (the clergy) were tried by Church courts. The most common kind of court was the manor court, which settled minor disputes and punished petty criminals.

Many of the disputes settled in the manor court had to do with farming and property. Villagers might be in trouble for using too much manure, for not "bringing their oxen to the plough," for ploughing another person's strip of land, or for other civil matters. Even serfs could sue. This court also dealt with charges of **assault,** public drunkenness, petty theft, and other small crimes.

The manor court was like a village meeting, and most of the villagers would attend. Witnesses were very important, and there were heavy fines for lying to the court. The villagers decided who won the case, and a representative of the lord, called the steward, acted as judge, deciding the sentence of the court, which was usually a fine.

ROYAL COURTS

The royal courts dealt with serious crimes such as murder, **treason**, rape, and burglary. Poaching game from the royal forests, cutting trees there, or even taking deadwood to use as fuel were also considered serious crimes. Wardens of the royal forest treated these crimes with as much earnestness as they would a murder.

Royal courts used the common law; this law was called "common" because it was the same for the whole kingdom. Only this court could order the execution of murderers and thieves. In 1300, the theft of anything worth more than a shilling (about a week's wages) was considered a

assault: an attempt to physically harm another person

treason: betraying one's country or ruler

DID YOU KNOW?

Unlike today, very few people were put in prison in the Middle Ages. Instead, the royal court punished serious crimes with death, mutilation (a thumb or an ear might be cut off), banishment from the country, or a hefty fine.

capital crime punishable by death. After executing a criminal, the court would take away all of his or her property.

CHURCH COURTS

God's direct representative on earth was the pope, who had absolute authority over people who held office in the Church or belonged to recognized religious orders. Therefore, only Church courts could judge bishops, deacons, priests, clerks, monks, and nuns. Church courts usually gave out lighter sentences than the royal courts, and they could not sentence a person to death. Because all members of the clergy could read and write, a literacy test was sometimes used to prove that a person worked for the Church, and therefore should be tried in the more lenient Church court. For this reason, some criminals tried to educate themselves.

lenient: mild, merciful

meddlesome: interfering

canonize: to declare that a person is a saint

shrine: a place of worship

Henry II and the Murder of Thomas Becket

The pope had authority over kings and queens in all religious matters. Nonetheless, disputes arose in the Middle Ages whenever the powers of the monarch and the Church seemed to overlap or conflict.

In 1164, King Henry II of England wanted all members of the clergy who were convicted of criminal offences to be handed over to the royal courts for sentencing. He felt the sentences they received in Church courts were too light. Thomas Becket, the archbishop of Canterbury, refused to obey the king's command even though he had been appointed by Henry and had been his good friend. To punish Thomas, Henry took away all his property and forced the archbishop to flee to France.

Six years later, Henry agreed to let Thomas return to England as head of the English Church. Not long after his return, Thomas angered the king once again. Henry is supposed to have said, "Will no one rid me of this **meddlesome** priest?" Four knights who heard the remark took Henry at his word. They rode to Canterbury and on December 29, 1170, they killed Thomas Becket at the foot of the altar in Canterbury Cathedral.

All of Europe was outraged at this murder. Even though King Henry denied that he had meant for Thomas to be killed, Pope Alexander III forced the king to submit to a public flogging at Thomas's shrine and to stop interfering with the Church courts. Two years after his death, Thomas was **canonized** and quickly became the most popular saint in England. Canterbury Cathedral became the country's greatest religious **shrine.**

Figure 2–8
Thomas Becket about to be killed in Canterbury Cathedral. Why do you think so many people were outraged at this murder?

Make a Comparison Organizer

Comparison organizers are charts that help us compare two or more things. To clarify the purpose of your chart, first think of a title. Write your title at the top of the chart.

Next decide exactly what you will compare. These have to be things that can be compared easily. Write your choices across the top, leaving the far-left column blank.

Next decide on your points of comparison. These will depend on the information you have available and the purpose of your comparison. You don't want to compare hair colour if the information isn't useful or easy to find. Your points of comparison will go in the column at the far left.

Now go to your sources and complete the chart. Usually point-form notes are fine. A short version of a comparison organizer comparing serfs and nobles in medieval Europe might look like this:

Title   Things to be compared

SERFS AND NOBLES IN MEDIEVAL EUROPE

	Serfs	Nobles
Portion of Population	• 90% (with freeholders)	• 10%
Level of Power	• lowest	• high, though with obligations

Points of Comparison   Data

NOW YOU DO IT.

1. Make up a comparison organizer to help you understand the differences between the three types of medieval courts. To get you started, here are five points of comparison:
   - What crimes could the court try?
   - Whom could the court try?
   - Who was in charge?
   - How did the court operate?
   - What penalties could the court hand down?

   If you have access to a computer, try making up your chart using a suitable word-processing or spreadsheet program. It takes time to get started, but once you get the hang of it, making tables on computer will become easier than making them by hand.

2. In a paragraph, comment on the similarities and differences among the three types of medieval courts. Organize your thoughts by developing a fourth column in your chart called "Similarities and Differences."

ACTIVITIES

1. What were trials by ordeal and trials by battle? How did medieval people justify using these methods to decide a person's guilt or innocence? Do you think these were sound methods of determining guilt or innocence? Explain.

2. What types of offences did manor courts try? Why do you think manor courts dealt with these offences?

3. What was common law? Why was it called common law?

4. Why did Church courts have the right to try and punish members of the clergy? Do Church courts exist in Canada? Why or why not?

5. a) What issue did Thomas Becket and Henry II disagree about? What did Henry want to do, and why do you think Thomas refused to give in?

   b) Role play this situation in class. One person can play Henry, one can play Thomas. Have a class discussion to work out a compromise.

   c) Why did Henry and Thomas fail to compromise?

WORLD VIEW

MEDIEVAL GEOGRAPHY

The vast majority of medieval Europeans were uneducated. Most serfs had no knowledge at all of the world that existed beyond the boundaries of their lord's manor because they never saw maps and never travelled. Taking journeys was very dangerous. Outlaws were common all over Europe. People seldom went from one town to another unless they could join a group of travellers for safety. Almost all travellers carried weapons to defend themselves and journeyed only by day.

Most nobles learned about the world beyond their manor when they visited relatives and other nobles, and when they went to war. Yet even well-travelled people, such as traders and emperors, had limited knowledge of the world. Maps were rare and full of errors. Map makers created what are now known as T-O maps, which always placed Jerusalem, the holy city of Christianity, at the centre of the known world.

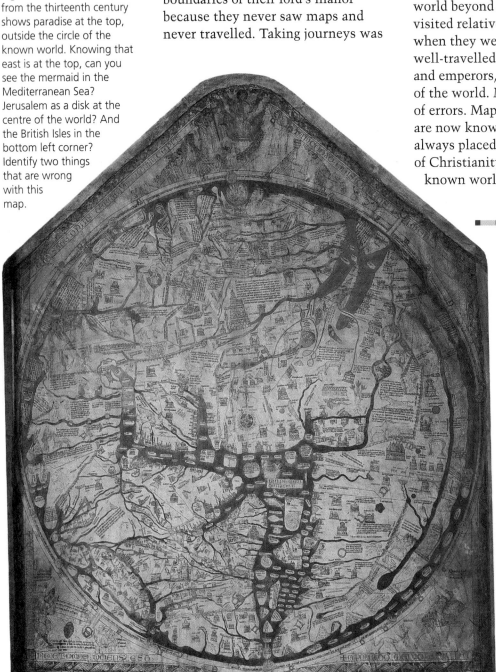

Figure 2–9 This T-O map from the thirteenth century shows paradise at the top, outside the circle of the known world. Knowing that east is at the top, can you see the mermaid in the Mediterranean Sea? Jerusalem as a disk at the centre of the world? And the British Isles in the bottom left corner? Identify two things that are wrong with this map.

CONTACTS WITH ASIA

In spite of their misguided notions about world geography, western Europeans at this time were still affected by events in other parts of the world. In the thirteenth century, Chinggis Khan conquered much of Asia and created a vast Mongol Empire that included China. For the first time, Europeans were permitted to travel along the ancient trade route known as the Silk Road all the way to China.

Using the Early Travelogue as a Primary Source

CATALOGUE CARD

What is it? *Part of a book called Travels*

Who wrote it? *Sir John Mandeville, an English noble*

When? *1360*

Why? *To document his travels, perhaps to make money*

One way that medieval people formed their perceptions of the world beyond their immediate surroundings was by hearing the stories travellers told, or, for those who could read, through travel books. Sir John Mandeville wrote one such book, his very popular *Travels*. Sir John had fled England after murdering a fellow noble, and had then travelled to Constantinople, Cyprus, Jaffa, Jerusalem, and Egypt. He later settled in France, where he wrote about his travels.

Sir John's accounts of the places he visited, or imagined he visited, are not entirely factual. For example, he claims to have drunk from the Fountain of Youth. He also describes Prester John, a legendary Christian ruler who protected his kingdom with a valley filled with thousands of unrotted corpses of people killed by demons. Believable? Now read Sir John's description, at the top right, of a few of the "peoples" of far-off lands.

All the men and women of that isle have hounds' heads ... and they be full reasonable and of good understanding, save that they worship an ox for their God....

In one of these isles be folk of great stature, as giants. And they be hideous to look upon. And they have but one eye, and that is in the middle of the front. And they eat nothing but raw flesh and raw fish....

And in another isle be folk that have horses' feet. And they be strong and mighty, and swift runners; for they take wild beasts with running, and eat them.

On the face of it, this book would seem useless as a source of facts. But let us consider what this document can tell us. For example, what can we learn from it about the people of the Middle Ages? We do know that people loved Sir John's fantastic tales and took them at face value. This shows us that the medieval person was gullible. But is that fair? If a group of astronauts travelled to another galaxy, and then wrote a book about the intelligent life they encountered there, many of us would love to believe them.

WHAT DO YOU THINK?

1. Make a point-form list of all the outrageous claims in the material above. What claims have to do with religion? What claims involve monsters? What does this tell you about the concerns of medieval people?

2. Write a fantastic travel tale of your own. What weird and wonderful things will you write about? How will these things reflect your culture?

In 1255, the Venetian merchants Nicolo and Maffeo Polo completed the long journey to China, something no other European had yet done. In 1271, they journeyed there again, this time accompanied by Nicolo's son Marco. Young Marco impressed Chinggis Khan's successor, Khubilai Khan, who made him an official of the Chinese court. After a stay of seventeen years, Marco returned to Europe. Although some historians question the accuracy of Marco's accounts, the book in which he described his travels had great influence on Europeans and vastly increased their knowledge of the world. A few years after Marco's return to Europe, the Silk Road was once again closed to Europeans.

DID YOU KNOW?

Unlike most people of his time, Sir John Mandeville believed the world was round, not flat. His book later inspired Christopher Columbus.

Khubilai Khan's Capital

At right, Marco Polo describes the capital city of Khubilai Khan. Marco's book about his travels in Asia became a best seller in thirteenth-century Europe. Why do you think Europeans at this time were so anxious to read about the marvels of Asia?

disposed: arranged

> The new-built city received the name of Tai-du. This new city is of form perfectly square, and twenty-four miles in extent. The whole plan of the city was regularly laid out in line, and the streets are consequently straight. In the public streets there are booths and shops of every description. In this manner the whole interior of the city is **disposed** in squares, so as to resemble a chess board, and planned out with a degree of precision and beauty impossible to describe.

PRIMARY SOURCE

ACTIVITIES

1. Imagine you lived in a community with no high technology and no books. Identify one or more ways that you could gain information about the outside world. How could you be sure of what was true? Describe how **tall tales** might become respected sources over time.

2. Give three reasons why nobles had a better understanding of the outside world than serfs.

3. Examine the medieval map on page 60. Is this a primary source or a secondary source? Summarize what this map tells us about the medieval European view of the world.

4. Without consulting a printed map, draw a rough map of North America from memory. Compare this map with the maps drawn by your classmates. Why would a lack of scientifically made maps make it difficult to determine whose map is most accurate?

5. Why might Marco Polo's accounts be important to European traders? Monarchs? Ordinary people?

6. Compare Marco Polo's account of Tai-du (above) with the map of Chang'an on page 96. What does this comparison confirm?

THE CRUSADES

tall tale: an exaggerated, unlikely story

DID YOU KNOW?

The term "crusade" refers to the cross the Christian knights displayed on their jupons, flags, and shields.

The Crusades were wars in which the Christians of Europe fought against Muslims for control of the Holy Land, the area around modern-day Israel where Jesus lived and died. The Holy Land, filled with sacred places and pilgrimage sites, had once been part of the Christian Byzantine Empire. In the eleventh century, however, this area (also known as Palestine) came under the control of the Seljuk Turks, who were Muslims. The deep religious feelings of the medieval Christians, in combination with prejudice against those of another religion and a lust for booty, made many Europeans want to drive the Muslims out of the Holy Land.

But the holy places of the Middle East were also important for Muslims. Jerusalem, for example, is the second most holy city in Islam because Muslims believe that Muhammad rose to heaven from this place.

Medieval knights, like the Muslim warriors, looked on fighting in such a holy war as a way of guaranteeing

Pope Urban II Preaches the First Crusade

The First Crusade began with a speech by Pope Urban II on November 27, 1095, at Clermont, France. The pope described in vivid detail cruelties that the Muslim conquerors of the Holy Land had supposedly committed against Christian pilgrims and settlers. He mentioned the riches that could be won. He especially stressed that Christian knights would have their sins forgiven and would find paradise if they went on a crusade to free the Holy Land. At the end of his speech, the crowd cried out in one voice, "Deus volt!" (God wills it!). This was to become the battle cry of all the crusaders.

> **PRIMARY SOURCE**
>
> It is the **imminent** peril threatening you and all the faithful which has brought us hither. From the confines of Jerusalem and from the city of Constantinople a horrible tale has gone forth. A race utterly **alienated** from God has invaded the lands of those Christians and has depopulated them by the sword, pillage, and fire.... On whom, therefore, is the labor of avenging these wrongs and of recovering this territory **incumbent**, if not upon you? Enter upon the Road to the Holy Sepulchre [Jesus' tomb]; wrest that land from [them], and subject it to yourselves.

WHAT DO YOU THINK?

1. Identify phrases the pope uses to excite the knights. Why do you think he uses such emotional terms?

2. Assume you are a Muslim who has just battled to regain what you consider to be your own Holy Land. Write to the pope to argue against statements he makes in his speech.

themselves a place in heaven. The crusader could also gain an honourable reputation through his warlike deeds. Many of the knights were land-hungry feudal nobles who hoped to win fiefs and even kingdoms from their enemies. Altogether, there were seven crusades between 1096 and 1254.

DISASTERS AND VICTORIES

Even before the first military crusade, ordinary people gathered from all over Europe to do battle. Thousands of men, women, and children walked across Europe in response to the pope's message. Peter the Hermit and Walter the Penniless were the leaders of this People's Crusade. On the way to Constantinople, this ragged band of wanderers was responsible for several massacres of Jews and fellow Christians. In return, they were attacked and driven from place to

place. A Turkish army wiped them out in Asia Minor. In the thirteenth century a disastrous Children's Crusade ended when most of the children were killed or sold to Arab slave traders in North Africa.

The arrival of armed knights was to have more effect. The First Crusade created a Christian kingdom in the Middle East that lasted for about a hundred years. In 1187, a bold new

imminent: immediate

alienated: turned away

incumbent: resting on as a duty

Figure 2–10 Christians and Muslims battle for control of Palestine. List all the tools of war you see in this picture.

Muslim leader, the Sultan Saladin, recaptured Jerusalem. The strength of the united Muslims under Saladin, combined with a lack of direction among the Crusaders, eventually brought an end to the Crusades. The Muslims regained all their lands.

Long-Term Consequences

The Crusades did not result in the long-term military victories for which the pope and Christian kings had hoped. The Crusades did change life for many people, however. Western Europeans learned that the Muslim world was a highly advanced civilization.

At this point in time the Muslim peoples were flourishing in the scholarly pursuits of medicine, astronomy, philosophy, mathematics, and literature. The exchange of knowledge among Muslim, Jewish, and Christian scholars, which the Crusades brought about indirectly, resulted in advances in learning in Europe that would lead eventually to the Renaissance.

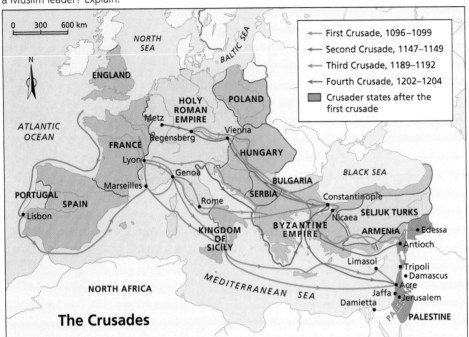

The Crusades

Legend:
- ← First Crusade, 1096–1099
- ← Second Crusade, 1147–1149
- ← Third Crusade, 1189–1192
- ← Fourth Crusade, 1202–1204
- ▊ Crusader states after the first crusade

Atrocities of War

As in any war, very cruel acts were committed on both sides. In the passage below, a Muslim writer tells of a massacre of Muslim prisoners by the army of Richard the Lion-Hearted, of England.

> [Richard] ordered all the Muslim prisoners, whose martyrdom God had decreed for this day, to be brought before him. They numbered more than three thousand and were all bound with ropes. The Christians then flung themselves upon them all at once and massacred them with sword and lance in cold blood. On the morrow morning, our people gathered at the spot and found the Muslims stretched out upon the ground as **martyrs** for the faith. They even recognized some of the dead, and the sight was a great affliction to them. The enemy had only spared the prisoners of note and such as were strong enough to work.

PRIMARY SOURCE

WHAT DO YOU THINK?

1. What is meant by the phrase "prisoners of note" in the quoted passage? What did the Christians do with these prisoners?

2. How would you describe the actions of the Christian army as described in the quotation? Do you see any contradiction in soldiers fighting a war in the name of religion and yet engaging in such actions? Explain. Referring to Pope Urban II's speech, on page 63, suggest how the Christian knights might have explained their participation.

3. Richard was considered a great hero in England. Explain how a person can become a hero in one society and hated in another.

martyr: someone who is killed for their religious beliefs

The Crusades also sparked trade and expanded Europeans' knowledge of the world. The Crusaders brought back many new products from the Muslim world, including silk, silkworms, spices, and new varieties of fruit, such as plums and figs.

Unintentionally, the Crusaders created a desire for foreign goods that would later lead to the European voyages of discovery. The resulting increase in trade would open up the European economy, improving the standard of living for many Europeans.

ACTIVITIES

1. **a)** Examine the map of the Crusades on page 64. Consult an atlas. What modern countries were once at least partly within the Crusader kingdoms?

   b) Give at least three reasons why the Crusaders could not keep control of their conquests.

2. **a)** Compare the Crusaders' reasons for travelling to Jerusalem with John Mandeville's reasons (see page 61).

   b) Why did so many people take part in the Crusades, not only knights and soldiers but also ordinary people and even children?

   c) Write a one-page story about two friends who participate in the Children's Crusade. Exchange stories with another student and edit each other's work. Then revise your own story.

3. Many historians today think that the Crusades were not justified. Why might they think this way? Is it always fair to criticize an event that occurred hundreds of years ago? Explain.

4. **a)** List the positive and negative consequences of the Crusades for Europeans.

   b) How did the Crusades help end the feudal age?

ROYAL POWER AND DEMOCRACY

In Canada we value the right to take part in our government and to elect our leaders. Medieval people had no concept of democracy as we understand it. They believed that monarchy—that is, rule by a king or queen—was part of God's plan.

THE BALANCE OF POWER

By custom and under law, the feudal monarch had the power to make and change laws, to collect some kinds of taxes, to choose advisors, and to give titles and estates. The monarch's power was not unlimited, however. As a player in the feudal system, he had to obey the feudal code. The king was kept in check by a small but powerful group of people: the wealthiest and most powerful nobles, who were called barons.

If a monarch did anything to break the feudal contract, the barons would feel justified in making war on their sovereign. The barons were a considerable threat. These warriors had large armies and strong castles, and could call upon their vassals on short notice to fight for them. The royal army, on the other hand, needed time to collect knights from all over England. Even in good weather a royal messenger might have to travel for

Figure 2–12 A medieval king and queen of France. The artist has taken care to include four symbols of authority in this portrait. Identify these symbols.

ELEANOR OF AQUITAINE

Eleanor of Aquitaine led the sort of life of which legends are made. Over the course of her eighty-two years, she was the queen of both France and England, joined the Second Crusade, gave birth to two kings of England, committed treason by encouraging her sons to rebel against their father (the king of England), and spent sixteen years in prison as a result. She also helped popularize the ideal of "courtly love" by patronizing writers and poets and by holding "courts of love" in which she and her ladies-in-waiting gave judgements on fictional love affairs. Eleanor was so passionate about literature that the figure on her tomb does not show her dead or at prayer but reading a book.

Eleanor came to believe that there should be equality between the sexes—a disturbing idea for many in feudal society. With her first husband, Louis VII of France, Eleanor went on a crusade to Jerusalem. For the journey, Eleanor dressed herself and her ladies in knightly armour, something that shocked all of Europe. Louis, who was impatient for an heir, ended the marriage. Eleanor then married Louis's greatest political rival, Henry II of England.

With Henry, Eleanor had ten children. Because Henry did not want to share power with Eleanor or his sons, Eleanor encouraged her children to rebel against her husband. On discovering the plan, Henry threw Eleanor into prison, where she stayed for many years. After Henry's death, Eleanor helped rule England while her son Richard the Lion-Hearted was fighting in the Crusades. After Richard died, Eleanor helped her other son, King John I, defeat his enemies in England and France. By the time of her death, Eleanor was easily the most famous person in Europe.

weeks to reach some parts of the kingdom. An unexpected rebellion by one or more barons could prove hard to put down.

Because the barons posed a real threat, the monarch made great efforts to fulfill his feudal obligations to them. Further, he had to treat them with the utmost respect. This was a time when people took offence easily; even relatively slight insults were considered a blot on the family's honour if they were not revenged.

Figure 2–13 Eleanor of Aquitaine was one of the first people in medieval Europe to encourage writing by and about women. This picture shows the writer Christine de Pisan presenting a copy of her book *The City of Women* to her patron, Eleanor.

KING JOHN

King John I of England is known to many of us as the villain of the Robin Hood legend. John first lost the support of his people because he quarrelled with Pope Innocent III over who should appoint the archbishop of Canterbury. The pope excommunicated John and placed the whole of England under an **interdict**, which banned all church services in the kingdom. No one could be properly married, baptized, or buried. For medieval people, this was a terrible sentence and they complained bitterly. When the pope encouraged the French king, Philip Augustus, to invade England, John swung completely the other way. He gave England to the pope as a fief and agreed to raise a tax for the pope called "Peter's pence," which every person in the kingdom had to pay.

To make matters worse, John behaved badly, even to his own vassals. He stepped over the bounds of the feudal code many times. So he could hunt better, he tore down hedges that protected people's crops from wild animals. He imprisoned barons without trial and confiscated their property. He took the relatives of barons as hostages and sometimes tortured them. King John raised illegal taxes and even hired foreign soldiers to fight his own people.

The Magna Carta

By 1214, John was so hated that the barons rebelled. Even townspeople and the Church rose up against the king. On June 15, 1215, the barons forced John to go to a meadow near London called Runnymede. There he put his seal to a great charter, called the "Magna Carta," in which he agreed to respect the rights of the English people. He guaranteed that the free people of England would not be preyed upon by their own ruler; that taxes would not be taken without the consent of a parliament; and that no person could be arrested or thrown into prison without a proper trial. These rights are now part of Canada's tradition of law and government. With the signing of the Magna Carta, England took a big step towards democracy.

interdict: an official act of the Catholic Church that keeps a person or group of people from participating in religious ceremonies

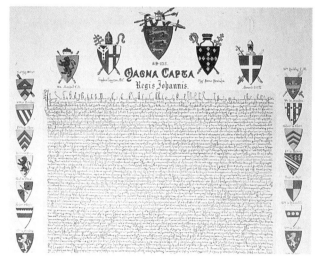

Figure 2–14 The opening lines of the Magna Carta. The large coat-of-arms at the top is King John's. The other coats-of-arms are those of barons and high church officials. Why do you think all parties, including the king, had to add their seals at the bottom of the document?

ACTIVITIES

1. What powers did the monarch have in medieval times? How did strong rulers deal with barons? What qualities made medieval rulers strong? What could the barons do about a bad king?

2. Who was Eleanor of Aquitaine? Give five reasons for considering her a remarkable person.

3. **a)** Compare Queen Eleanor's two sons, King Richard and King John.

   b) What two things did the Church do that demonstrates its great power.

   c) In what ways did King John break the feudal contract?

4. What was the Magna Carta? What rights did the Magna Carta give to free people? Why is the Magna Carta important to Canadians today?

5. Create a modern Magna Carta that enshrines the rights you think should be important in our society. Decorate your charter with coats of arms, ribbons, and round wax seals.

Many changes took place in western Europe during the high Middle Ages. In England, for instance, the Norman invasion introduced a highly organized social structure called feudalism, which became the norm throughout Europe.

You have seen in this chapter that most medieval people were farm people. They lived close to the land and according to the natural rhythms of the seasons. For the most part, they lived the same lives their parents and grandparents had lived before them. Generally they were conservative people, used to their customs and traditions and disliking change.

You have also seen that medieval society was organized by classes into a kind of pyramid, with the king at the top and the serfs at the bottom. Even though medieval rulers were supreme, they were expected to honour the feudal contract they had with their barons and other subjects. And even though serfs were at the bottom of the pyramid, they did enjoy some legal rights. People during this period often used the courts to settle disputes. The manor court involved the active participation of ordinary people.

The Middle Ages was a time of great religious devotion. Christianity, because it was the common religion of most western Europeans, provided a bond between peoples and helped build a common identity for western Europeans.

Living conditions were, to say the least, uncomfortable. But medieval people loved life. They wrote and sang songs, played music, told stories, gossiped, and played games; backgammon and chess were two favourite board games. The high Middle Ages was a robust time: the boisterous childhood of modern Western society.

SUMMARY ACTIVITIES

1. As a class, create a medieval meal to celebrate a wedding of two serfs. Check the chapter to see what foods would be typical. Make a shopping list and menu as a whole class. Then groups of four or five students can each make one dish and bring it to school. For the meal, dress in the style of the times. Consult the pictures in this chapter for ideas.

2. **a)** In feudal society your social position was based on birth, not ability. Why did people never move from one social class to another? How did this social structure benefit the society as a whole?

   b) Does modern Canadian society assign people to social classes? If so, how are people kept in one class? Discuss these questions in a small group.

3. **a)** Thomas Becket, Eleanor of Aquitaine, and Richard the Lion-Hearted were heroes during the Middle Ages. What did they do that made them so popular with people all over Europe? How do these people's character and accomplishments reflect the values of medieval society?

   b) Name one living person who is a hero to you. List three reasons why you consider this person heroic.

4. Although not everyone benefited equally from the feudal system, most gained relative peace and everyone enjoyed certain rights. Explain how the feudal system supported the good of the group more than the good of the individual. Alternatively, explain how the feudal system benefited one individual—at the expense of everyone else. Present your explanation to the class in a brief oral report.

ON YOUR OWN

1. In a group of five, plan a tapestry in five panels, each panel having a brief caption. Use any medium you wish, such as paper, paint, cloth, or cardboard. Your tapestry can tell the story of an important event in school life or of a war or natural disaster such as a hurricane or tornado. Show the effect the event had on ordinary people.

2. Referring to Chapter 6, write a report comparing medieval Europe with medieval Japan.

3. Europeans fought in the Crusades because of religion and land. The Middle East continues to experience turmoil to this day. Research a recent war in the area. Identify any connections to religion, land, and historical conflict. Identify various ways in which people have tried to resolve the conflict. If possible, conduct some of your research on the Internet or using CD-ROM.

3 THE CIVILIZATION OF EARLY CHINA

CHAPTER OUTCOMES

In this chapter, you will learn about the civilization of early China. China is the longest continuous civilization in the world. Its empire began in approximately 1650 B.C.E. and lasted into the twentieth century. By the end of the chapter, you will

- describe the development of Chinese civilization
- use a Landsat image as a source of information
- compare Chinese philosophies and assess their impact on society and culture
- assess the importance of geography as a factor in historical development
- draw historical and social information from poetry
- describe the status of women in Tang Dynasty China
- trace the source of some modern technologies

The Mystery of the Oracle Bones

This is a true story about some ancient bones discovered in China in the nineteenth century. An unfortunate aspect of this story is that the people who found the bones did not know what they were, so they accidentally destroyed many of them.

Artifacts of early civilizations are often lost to the modern world because they cannot survive the passage of time. They are destroyed by the natural environment; they rot or decompose; or humans destroy them through carelessness, superstition, or warfare.

Sometimes, artifacts of the ancient world do survive, but no one can **interpret** them. That's what happened in China. In the rural district of Anyang, in the province of Henan,

farmers began finding unusual bones after heavy rains or when they ploughed their fields. These bones were like no others. They were small, and their edges were highly polished. The surface of the bones contained small notches and cracks. Some of the bones had mysterious markings on them—pictures and designs.

The people of the district decided they knew what the bones meant. "These must be dragon bones," they told their neighbours excitedly. Bones thought to be dragon bones

were used in Chinese medicine. They were found to be effective in curing nervous disorders. The farmers of Anyang knew they could sell their bones to local **apothecaries** for money.

For many years, the apothecaries were happy to buy the "dragon bones." The only problem was that customers did not want to buy old, marked up bones. They wanted smooth, clean bones. So the apothecaries told the farmers to scrape off all the markings. That is how most of the bones were destroyed.

Then in 1899, a learned antique dealer saw some of these bones before the strange markings had been erased. He studied the markings and realized that they must be some form of writing. The dealer was able to determine that the bones were approximately 3000 years old. They came from the time of 1100 B.C.E., the end of the Shang Dynasty. Chinese scholars did not know much about this period of their history until then. All the information they had came from other artifacts, such as pottery, which often says very

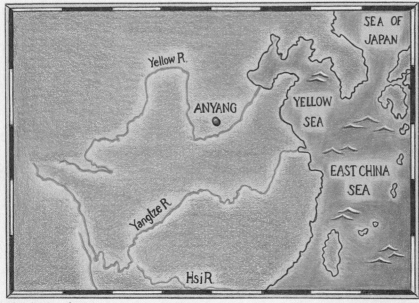

The district of Anyang

"Surely these are dragon bones!"

little about how people thought or felt.

By analyzing the writing, scholars realized that the bones contained questions to the gods. The dragon bones were really **oracle** bones. Before people of the Shang Dynasty would decide to do something—take a trip or go hunting, for example—they would ask the gods for advice. They did not want to undertake any serious activity without direction from the gods. After all, if the gods were displeased, they could send famine or other hardships to plague the people.

The people of the Shang Dynasty used the leg bones of cattle or turtle shells as a writing surface. After the question was etched on the surface of the shell or bone, heat was applied with a hot poker. This caused cracks to appear. The cracks were interpreted by a priest who would decide if the gods had returned a favourable or unfavourable answer to the question.

Not all the questions were serious in the way you might think. Consider these two: "Would an offering of a cow be appropriate?" and "Are you causing the king's toothache?" Other questions concerned issues of basic survival, such as

"Will rain be granted?" or "Who is sending this epidemic?" Before a hunt, one king asked, "We are going to hunt at Ch'iu. Will there be any capture?" It was recorded that the king captured "1 tiger, forty deer, 164 foxes, and 159 hornless deer."

Sometimes, the people did not approach the gods but posed questions to their dead ancestors. In this case, another person would act as an **intermediary** by **impersonating** the dead. He or she would be offered many glasses of wine and the best possible food and entertainment. At the right moment, those attending the

71

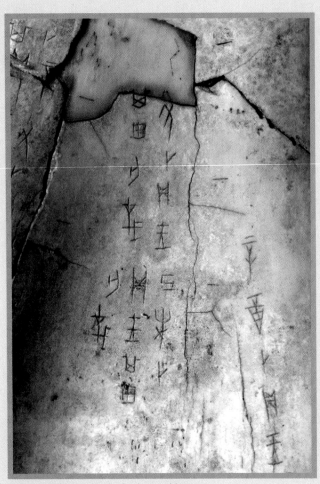

This oracle bone clearly displays writing.

impersonator. It was extremely important to perform these rites correctly because that made the ancestors happy.

By 1903, the story of the oracle bones reached the rest of the world. At that time, a number of the oracle bone writings were published to worldwide interest. The farmers of Anyang were understandably thrilled and began digging to find more bones. Official excavation did not begin until 1928 and, in 1936, many new bones were discovered.

feast would feel themselves in communion with the ancestor through the body of the

But the process of explaining the oracle bones was not quick. It took a very long time before even knowledgeable scholars could read the writing on the bones. They had to work back from the earliest Chinese writing they knew.

And many people declared the bones were a **hoax**. It seemed as difficult to interpret this writing as it had been to interpret the Egyptian hieroglyphs.

By the middle of the twentieth century, the oracle bones were still not ready to give up all their mysteries.

artifact: something made by humans

to interpret: to explain the meaning

apothecary: a pharmacist or druggist

oracle: a prediction

intermediary: a go-between

to impersonate: to act as another person

hoax: a trick or fraud

hieroglyphs: pictures or symbols used instead of alphabet letters

conventional: accepted because it is customary

ACTIVITIES

1. You are a farmer in China in the nineteenth century who has just discovered an oracle bone. Write a diary entry expressing your emotions and wishes. Remember, you are not exactly sure what the bone means.

2. Find out more about the symbol of the dragon in Chinese culture. Does your research help explain the Chinese attitude towards dragon bones as described in the Window on the Past?

3. Select an artifact from your room that you believe people a thousand years from now might have

trouble understanding. Now imagine that you are a visitor from the future. Interpret this artifact as a member of this "future" culture. What are your beliefs and values as a member of that culture? How does your interpretation of this artifact reflect those beliefs and values?

4. The antique dealer who looked more carefully at the oracle bones must have sensed that their true significance had not yet been uncovered. What leads people to doubt **conventional** wisdom? Is this a good thing? Explain.

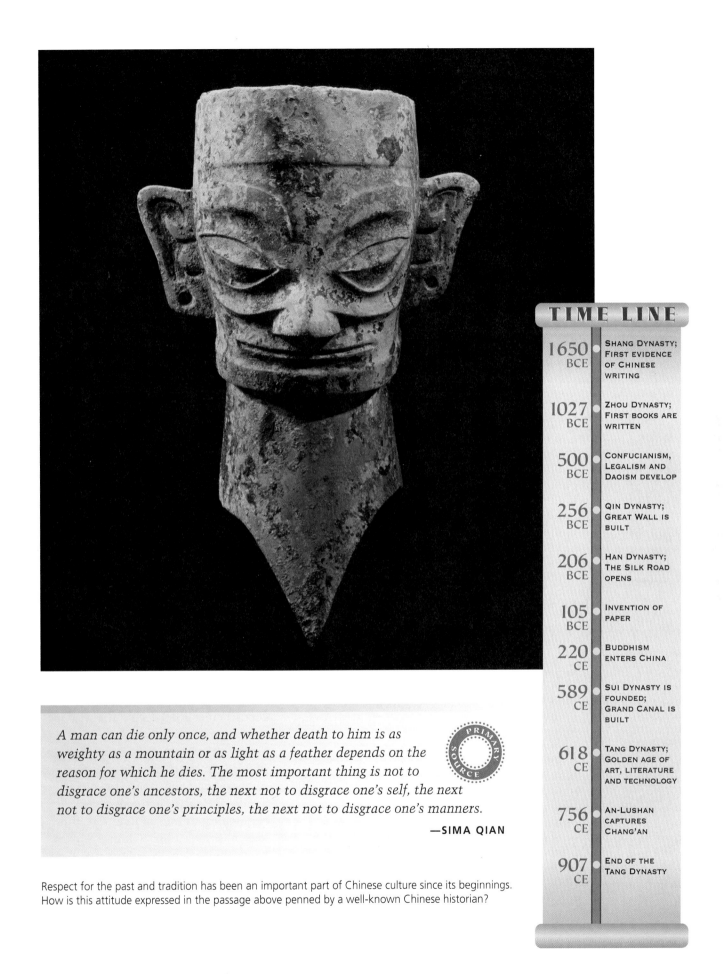

A man can die only once, and whether death to him is as weighty as a mountain or as light as a feather depends on the reason for which he dies. The most important thing is not to disgrace one's ancestors, the next not to disgrace one's self, the next not to disgrace one's principles, the next not to disgrace one's manners.

—SIMA QIAN

PRIMARY SOURCE

Respect for the past and tradition has been an important part of Chinese culture since its beginnings. How is this attitude expressed in the passage above penned by a well-known Chinese historian?

TIME LINE

1650 BCE	SHANG DYNASTY; FIRST EVIDENCE OF CHINESE WRITING
1027 BCE	ZHOU DYNASTY; FIRST BOOKS ARE WRITTEN
500 BCE	CONFUCIANISM, LEGALISM AND DAOISM DEVELOP
256 BCE	QIN DYNASTY; GREAT WALL IS BUILT
206 BCE	HAN DYNASTY; THE SILK ROAD OPENS
105 BCE	INVENTION OF PAPER
220 CE	BUDDHISM ENTERS CHINA
589 CE	SUI DYNASTY IS FOUNDED; GRAND CANAL IS BUILT
618 CE	TANG DYNASTY; GOLDEN AGE OF ART, LITERATURE AND TECHNOLOGY
756 CE	AN-LUSHAN CAPTURES CHANG'AN
907 CE	END OF THE TANG DYNASTY

INTRODUCTION

The ancient civilization of China is different from all other early civilizations because it lasted so long. From its beginnings around 1650 B.C.E., the Chinese people established traditions that have endured to the present day. Over the years, many aspects of that way of life changed, but many other aspects remained the same. Today in China, certain ideas and values that developed thousands of years ago are still respected.

THE ORIGINS OF CHINESE CIVILIZATION

Chinese civilization began to take shape in the Huang He River valley with the Shang and Zhou **Dynasties** over 3500 years ago.

dynasty: a succession of rulers from the same family; the period of time during which they reigned

steppe: a vast, treeless plain

loess: very fine wind-blown silt. In North China, loess is yellow in colour. Loess was deposited by glaciers during the last ice age.

silt: a fine-grained sediment

dike: a barrier built to prevent flooding

DID YOU KNOW?

In atlases, you may find the Huang He listed as the Yellow River, and the Chang Jiang River as the Yangtze River. He means "river" in Chinese.

THE IMPORTANCE OF GEOGRAPHY

China, an enormous country, is isolated from the rest of the world by geography. In the west and southwest, high mountain ranges and wide deserts separate China from the rest of Asia. In the southeast, dense jungles protect China, as does the Pacific Ocean in the east. To the north, however, China has no geographic protection. There, the land consists of **steppes**, or grassy plains, that provide an easy entry into China.

Within China itself geography separates the country into north and south. China's two major rivers, the Huang He, or Yellow, in the north, and the Chang Jiang, or Yangtze, in the south, both flow from east to west. In between these two rivers are the high Qing Ling mountains, which separate the northern part of the country from the southern part.

Climate also divides China. The north has harsh winters and sporadic rainfall in the summer. The south, on the other hand, enjoys a subtropical climate. The temperature is moderate year-round, and rain falls abundantly in the summer.

The fertile, crop-growing parts of China are the river valleys of the Huang He and the Chang Jiang. These rivers are among the longest in the world. Rising in the mountains to the west, the Huang He meanders for 4300 kilometres through deep deposits of fine yellow **loess** on the flat North China Plain on its way to the ocean. The yellow **silt** gives the river its name, and also colours the Yellow Sea into which the river flows.

The Huang He floods often and deposits its silt so deeply that it changes its own course. In some places, the river passes between **dikes** that rise many metres above the surrounding countryside to control flooding. Huang He floods have claimed thousands of lives. For this reason, some call it "China's Sorrow." Nevertheless, the North China Plain, with its deep deposits of rich, yellow loess is very fertile. It was here that Chinese civilization began because people settled in the area to farm.

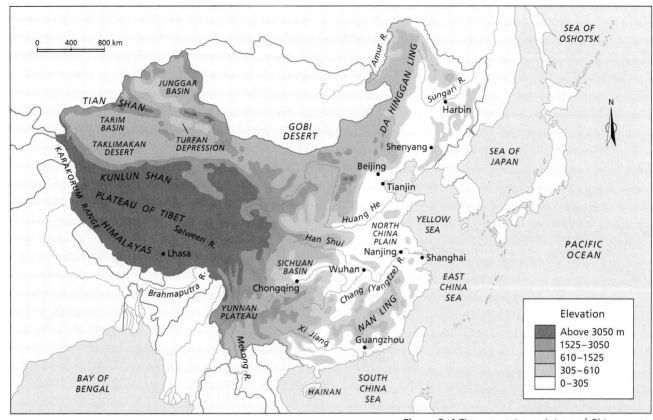

Figure 3–1 The mountains and rivers of China create distinct areas, often quite separate from one another. One of the most important regions is the North China Plain, one of the "cradles of civilization."

The Chang Jiang River is longer than the Huang He, flowing for about 5200 kilometres before reaching the sea. The Chang Jiang is a much easier river to navigate than the Huang He. In later times, this river became an even larger centre of Chinese civilization because boats could travel on it so easily.

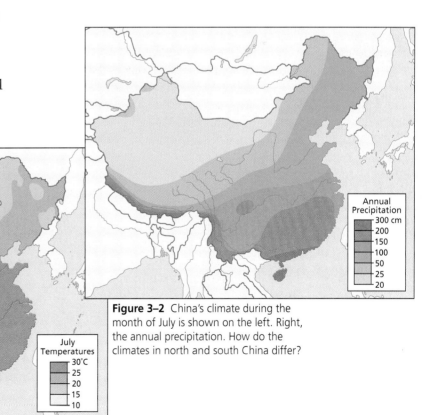

Figure 3–2 China's climate during the month of July is shown on the left. Right, the annual precipitation. How do the climates in north and south China differ?

Read a Landsat Image

We understand a society better when we know about its physical environment. Landsat images have given us a new tool for understanding the physical environments of different societies.

Landsat images are created by satellites equipped with sensors. These satellites, travelling hundreds of kilometres above the Earth's surface, "see" and record huge areas of the planet—areas much larger than those captured by an **aerial** photograph. They also record different information.

A Landsat image is a recorded image created by a computer. These images have a distinctive appearance and are able to display details that photographs miss. For example, Landsat images can show the location of mineral deposits or sources of heat.

Landsat colours do not necessarily compare to those found in nature. For example, the colour red on a Landsat image usually indicates trees and other vegetation. Darker, greyish areas of land usually indicate much sparser vegetation.

aerial: as seen from the air

Figure 3–3 A Landsat image of the North China Plain

NOW YOU DO IT

1. Examine the Landsat image and locate the North China Plain. Look for the following information:
   - the extent of the plain
   - the present course of the Huang River
   - other courses of the Huang River
   - mountain peaks around the plain
   - the sediment dumped into the Yellow Sea by the river (most of the sediment will appear at the mouth of the river)

2. What might be the large, straight-edged areas be? Hint: They are not buildings!

3. What would be the similarities and differences in the kind of information provided by a Landsat image and an aerial photograph?

4. For what reasons might you use a Landsat image? Explain your answer.

5. For what reasons might you use a photograph? Explain your answer.

THE SHANG DYNASTY, 1650–1027 B.C.E.

People had been living on the North China Plain for many hundreds of years. They lived in relatively small agricultural communities, each with its own leaders. By 1650 B.C.E. many of these communities had been merged into a small kingdom in northern China under the leadership of the Shang rulers (see Figure 3-4). It was here that Chinese civilization began to take shape.

The Shang controlled their territory politically from a walled city at Anyang—where the oracle bones were found thousands of years later. The Shang kings were not strong enough to rule the entire area on their own. They divided the territory into small regions, and appointed loyal **nobles** to rule these regions. These nobles were the friends of the king, heads of important clans, or the previous rulers of the area. Their positions became **hereditary**. Clans were groups of families claiming a common ancestor.

The Shang possessed fine bronze weapons and they used horse-drawn chariots in war. They often had to fight off attacks from the nomadic people who lived on the steppes to the north of China.

The upper class—the Shang kings and the nobles—lived in large timber or stone houses. Merchants and artisans collected around the capital at Anyang because only the upper class could afford to buy the products that the **artisans** and merchants made and sold.

Most of the people were farmers, growing **millet** and other crops in the rich loess soil of the Huang He valley. The fertility of the Huang He Valley made it possible for farmers to grow surplus food. As with other earlier

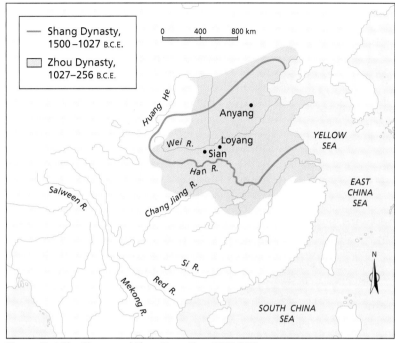

Figure 3–4 The Shang and Zhou Dynasties, 1650-256 B.C.E.

civilizations, the surplus of food meant that it was possible for Shang society to increase its population.

The peasants lived in small farming communities. Their homes were pits dug into the ground and roofed with thatch. These houses were warm in the winter and cool in the summer. The peasants laboured endlessly in their fields to produce food, some of which was owed to the local ruler. The peasants were also expected to work on public projects such as dike building, and to be soldiers in time of war.

Arts and Culture

The Shang had a remarkable culture. They developed an early form of writing. Modern Chinese writing can be traced directly to this writing system. They also made fine pottery. Some of the dish shapes the Shang made are still popular in China today.

The Shang were also skilled metal workers. They used bronze to cast a variety of artifacts, often decorated with elaborate "monster masks" representing gods and spirits. Moulds

hereditary: passed on from generation to generation within a family

nobles: people who received a high rank in society because of the family they were born into

artisan: someone who makes things. A potter is an artisan.

millet: a cereal grass

Figure 3–5 Bronze dishes were used by priests and rulers to make offerings to the gods. Many of them have fierce faces on their sides and bronze animals on their lids known as monster masks. This wine jug includes the monster mask. Can you find it? Look for two sets of square patterns over two bulges — then you can start to see a face. Why might the bronze makers have wished their work to look ferocious?

silk: cloth spun from fibres made by silkworms. People have eagerly purchased this delicate fabric for thousands of years.

working day: one person working for one day

were used, which contained the design for the bronze on its inner surface. The core mould determined the interior shape of the bronze. Molten bronze (a mixture of copper and tin) was poured between the moulds, which were removed once the bronze had hardened.

Bronze was a valuable substance, so it was only used in religious ceremonies or for weapons. The skill of the Shang bronze makers has never been surpassed, and Shang bronzes are so rare and valuable they are often faked. Scientific testing is needed before they can be declared authentic.

The Shang were also skilled in **silk** making. This was a very advanced technology, and it was kept secret from outsiders for many years.

Figure 3-6 Silk making continues in China today. The process begins when a female moth lays an egg. Approximately forty days after hatching, the silkworm will begin spinning its cocoon by sending out one silken strand. Usually the strands of many cocoons are needed to create one silk thread.

Much of our knowledge about the Shang has been gained from their burial practices. When Shang rulers died, they were buried in deep pits, along with artifacts of bone, stone, pottery, jade, and bronze. Servants were sacrificed and buried with the kings as well. One Shang king was buried with his war chariot and horses.

Shang tombs were immense. One tomb was 10 metres deep; archaeologists estimate that it took at least 7000 **working days** to complete this tomb. Shang burials also tell us much about life in Shang times, as well as some of their beliefs. Clearly, the Shang believed in an afterlife, as did many other early civilizations.

Shang Beliefs

The Shang believed in many gods and natural spirits. One of the most important gods was Di, the Lord on High, who was responsible for sending good harvests, help in battle, rain, thunder, wind, or drought. The king's ancestors were also important. The Chinese believed that the family was a union of both the living and the dead members of the family. The dead needed their family to give them offerings in the tomb and also after burial. The living needed their ancestors to protect them, or at least not be angry with them. If the ancestors were angry with their family members, they would not protect the family.

The Shang king acted as a priest in the worship of Di and the royal ancestors. Shang people thought that the high gods would prefer to deal with the ancestors of royalty rather than with the ancestors of ordinary people. The current king was better able to communicate with his royal ancestors than anyone else. The king's role as priest was therefore an important one since it helped make life on earth better for everyone. The ancestors were consulted before any important decision was made, and

Figure 3–7 Many Canadians consult fengshui experts today to ensure the best placement of furniture in the home. The principles of fengshui dictate how people should arrange their surroundings in order to be in harmony with the spirit world.

people made regular offerings of food and drink to them.

The Shang believed that nature was **dual**. This duality was symbolized by *yin* and *yang*. Yin and yang were opposites. Yin was linked to earth, darkness, cold, and feminine forces. Yang was linked to the opposite forces of heaven, light, heat, and masculinity. However, these opposites were not in conflict with each other. They were part of a harmonious whole. The yin-yang symbol, with its black and white halves—each containing a dot of the opposite shade—reflects the idea that everything contains its opposite within itself and is **interdependent**.

The Shang also believed that the earth was made up of five elements. The five elements were wood, metal, fire, water, and earth. Everything on earth was some combination or other of these natural forces. They also believed that there was an essential life force, called *qi*, that governed the universe. They thought of qi (pronounced "chi") as travelling beneath the surface of the earth in currents. It was important not to

disturb this life force when locating a building or a tomb.

The early Chinese called on a *fengshui* expert before deciding where to build anything. (*Feng* means "wind" and *shui* means "water.") The expert used special instruments to check a location for negative influences, and recommended solutions to fengshui problems. Fengshui experts helped plan whole cities.

The Shang kings were constantly at war with

dual: having two parts

interdependent: mutually dependent, each is dependent on the other

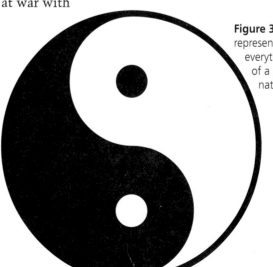

Figure 3–8 The yin-yang symbol represents the idea that everything in existence is part of a pair, and that all parts of nature are interdependent.

other kingdoms surrounding their territory. Eventually, one of these kingdoms defeated the Shang. The victorious kingdom was the Zhou, which was located along the Wei River, a tributary of the Huang He.

THE ZHOU DYNASTY 1027–256 B.C.E.

The Zhou Dynasty replaced the Shang Dynasty around 1027 B.C.E. The Zhou rulers defended their attack on the Shang by saying that the Shang rulers had lost the Mandate of Heaven. The concept of the **Mandate of Heaven** has its origins in myth. China's first ruler was thought to be the son of the sky god and an earthly mother. His children were called the Sons of Heaven. During the Zhou period, this myth became a theory about the right of rulers to rule—a theory used by all the dynasties that followed the Zhou. According to the theory, a ruler obtained the authority to rule from the highest spiritual power in the universe, or "heaven." The ruler kept this authority to rule only by being worthy and by governing properly. If natural disasters such as famine, or human disasters such as war, occurred, the ruler was revealed as unworthy to rule and lost the Mandate of Heaven.

The Zhou set up a feudal state similar to that of the Shang. The kingdom was divided into territories, each ruled by a lord. The lords were responsible for managing the land and the peasants. In return they owed loyalty and tribute to the Zhou king. Over the years, the Zhou extended the boundaries of China by spreading out throughout central China as far south as the Chang Jiang River (see Figure 3–4, page 77).

Mandate of Heaven: the idea that the emperor, the son of Heaven, has the support of the gods as long as he rules correctly

irrigation: supplying water to land through artificial means

nomadic: moving one's home from place to place according to the season

Society during this period was divided into two classes. The upper class was made up of the king and the lords ruling the different territories. The lower class was made up of the peasants who owed food, labour, and military service to their lord, as they had under the Shang. Merchants and artisans were also members of the lower class, as they had been in Shang times.

Like the Shang monarchs, the Zhou king acted as a priest, practising ancestor worship and holding ceremonies to mark the important seasons of the agricultural year.

The Zhou did not have the skills of writing or bronze making at the time they conquered the Shang. However, they eagerly adopted the Shang culture. Because the Zhou ruled for a long time, Chinese culture and technology was able to develop to new heights.

Under the Zhou, China launched an ambitious program of public works. Large-scale **irrigation** projects increased the amount of food that could be grown. Roads and canals made it easier to travel throughout the kingdom. To protect China from the **nomadic** people of the steppes, the Zhou constructed a wall across the north. Bronze making continued, although there were some changes in design. The Zhou introduced the use of iron, used for agricultural tools and military weapons. They also introduced the use of money.

Writing improved considerably during this period. By the end of the Zhou period, Chinese writing had taken on its modern character. The first Chinese books were written during the Zhou period.

The Zhou gradually began to lose control of their kingdom. The lords who were subordinate to the Zhou king began to rebel against the kings. About 770 B.C.E., the king was forced to flee east and establish a new capital at Luoyang. Over time, the

Chinese Writing

The Chinese language is spoken by 20 percent of the world's peoples and has many dialects. Some modern dialects are Mandarin, Cantonese, Shanghainese, Hakka, Hunanese, and Fujianese. These dialects are very different, so people cannot necessarily communicate with one another verbally. But because all Chinese people use the same writing, it is relatively easy for people with different dialects to communicate in writing.

The earliest Chinese writing developed during the Shang Dynasty. Characters were painted on bamboo strips, cast into bronze, and written on oracle bones (see the Window on the Past at the beginning of this chapter).

The earliest Chinese writing used characters based on simplified pictures. These later became more stylized, so that the picture was no longer evident. A character can represent a thing or an idea, or it can have a "meaning" part and a "sound" part. Over the years, the simple pictures evolved into characters of great complexity and beauty.

Chinese is best written with a brush, traditionally in columns from left to right. Through the centuries, people have taken pride in their writing skill—their calligraphy. Many styles of calligraphy are popular, often depending on the purpose of the writer. The examples in the box at centre show how different one stroke style can be from another.

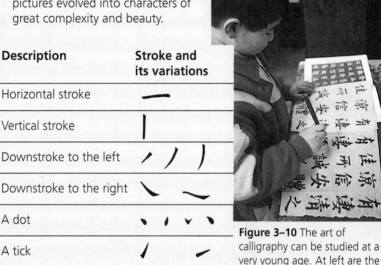

Figure 3–10 The art of calligraphy can be studied at a very young age. At left are the basic brush strokes.

Period	Example
	fly
5000–4000 B.C.E	NO SYMBOL
4000–3000 B.C.E	NO SYMBOL
2690–827 B.C.E	兄
827–221 B.C.E	飛
213–206 B.C.E	飛
206 B.C.E –353 C.E	飛
220–PRESENT	飛

Figure 3–9 The evolution of Chinese characters from before the Shang Dynasty to the present day. Can you detect the evolution from simple characters to more complex ones?

Description	Stroke and its variations
Horizontal stroke	—
Vertical stroke	│
Downstroke to the left	ノ ノ ノ
Downstroke to the right	＼ ＼
A dot	丶 ノ ⌄ ﾍ
A tick	／ ⌐
A hook	⌐ ⌐ ⌐ ⌐

WHAT DO YOU THINK?

1. Why do you think Chinese writing evolved from simple to complex instead of the other way around?

2. What are the advantages of a large population sharing the same written language?

3. Research the origins of the English alphabet. You could begin by looking up the word "alphabet" in an encyclopedia.

Zhou kings lost all their political and military control. They still kept their role as priests, however. The lords spent a great deal of time fighting with one another, trying to increase their territories at the expense of their neighbours.

The political unrest became so severe that the years from 481 to 256 B.C.E. are often called the "Warring States" period. Yet the Zhou managed to keep their dynasty in power, technically at least, until 256 B.C.E. During these tumultuous years, three important schools of thought developed. These schools of thought influenced Chinese culture tremendously.

ACTIVITIES

1. Examine the Landsat image on page 76 and the climate data on page 75. Based on this examination, draw five conclusions about agriculture, warfare, the layout of villages and towns, vegetation, and climate.

2. Is geographic isolation beneficial or harmful to cultural development? Make a list of the positive and negative effects of isolation on cultural development. Discuss this issue with classmates. Prepare a **brief** on the conclusions you reach.

3. Summarize the society of the Shang people in a chart. Use the following headings:
   - religion and belief
   - art
   - government
   - social structure
   - links to Chinese culture

4. What is the basic difference between Chinese and Western writing? How would this difference affect the process of learning to write?

CHINESE PHILOSOPHY

CONFUCIANISM

brief: a paper about an issue. A brief summarizes the information, draws conclusions, and outlines possible actions.

philosopher: one who searches for knowledge and wisdom

turmoil: confusion and chaos

virtue: good quality

conscientious: careful to do things properly

No other **philosopher** had as much influence on China as Kongfuzi (Confucius). He probably lived from 551 to 479 B.C.E. Confucius was influenced by the political **turmoil** of the times he lived in. He thought that the disorder was because the rulers were not governing as they should.

Confucius believed that people were basically good, but that they needed to be trained to behave well. This training would start with the family and then later be assumed by society. Confucius identified five **virtues** and five relationships that were the building blocks of a harmonious society.

To be considered virtuous, people had be honest, upright, **conscientious**, charitable, and loving in all personal relationships. Rulers were expected to display the same five virtues towards their subjects. The ruler had to set a good example of behaviour so that the subjects would also behave well.

Confucius also believed that everyone in society had duties and responsibilities, depending on their station in life. The five relationships that Confucius identified were father and son; ruler and subject; older and younger brothers; husband and wife; and friend and friend. Those who were in a superior station of life, such as the father, the ruler, or the older brother, had to treat their inferiors with love and kindness. Those who were inferior in status, such as sons, subjects, or younger brothers, owed respect and obedience to their superiors. As in many societies, women were regarded as less important than men.

After his death, Confucius was respected and honoured as one of China's great teachers. For over 2000 years, Confucian teachings have been important in China, and in other Asian countries as well. Confucius did not try to create a religion, but he did believe strongly that society should be moral and ethical.

LEGALISM

Another philosophy developed around the same time as Confucianism. It was known as Legalism. Han Feizi was the most prominent writer on Legalism. Legalists believed that government was more important than the people and that it should be strong—not virtuous. According to Legalists, humans by nature were selfish and greedy. This meant that people would not follow the example of a good ruler, as Confucius thought. The only way to have an orderly society was for the government to control the people through strict laws and harsh punishments.

For most of Chinese history, people followed Confucian ideas of government. However, Chinese criminal law seemed to follow Legalist ideas. It was very strict, and major crimes were punished severely. Minor crimes were usually dealt with by families or local government.

Figure 3–11 The philosopher Confucius. No one knows for sure what Confucius looked like. This statue is one of many representations of him.

China's first recorded code of laws was prepared in 400 B.C.E. under the Zhou. It had six sections: laws on theft, violence, detention, and arrest, miscellaneous laws, and general laws. The law code was amended many times by later dynasties, but the law always kept this basic framework.

In addition to assessing the case, judges investigated the crime itself. The accused had to prove his or her innocence in court—the opposite of the situation in Canada today. There were five basic penalties: death by **strangulation** or **decapitation**; **exile** (with the distance depending on the severity of the crime); imprisonment (with various lengths of time); beating with a heavy stick (with five degrees of severity); and beating with a light stick (with five degrees of severity).

Collective punishment was also used by judges. This meant that whole families or villages would be punished for a crime committed by one of its members. Families and communities were expected to control their members and to be responsible for their behaviour. If a person committed

DID YOU KNOW?

The Chinese legal system still hands down harsh sentences. In 1996 it executed at least 4300 people for everything from murder to pig stealing.

to strangulate: to kill by squeezing around the neck to stop the breath

to decapitate: to cut off the head

exile: the forced removal and banishment of a person from his or her country or region

Confucius and Han Feizi

Here are two excerpts from the writings of Confucius and Han Feizi. Both men were interested in the best way to govern society, and their writings explain their thoughts on this subject. Confucius himself did not write about his philosophy. His followers, however, collected his sayings in a book called *The Analects*.

CONFUCIUS

The Master said, "When your father is alive observe his intentions. After he passes away, model yourself on the memory of his behavior. If in three years after his death you have not **deviated** from your father's ways, then you may be considered a **filial child**."

The Master said, "You can be of service to your father and mother by **remonstrating** with them tactfully. If you perceive that they do not wish to follow your advice, then continue to be reverent towards them without offending or disobeying them; work hard and do not murmur against them."

The Master said, "Lead the people by means of government policies and regulate them through punishments, and they will be **evasive** and have no sense of shame. Lead them by means of virtue and regulate them through rituals and they will have a sense of shame and moreover have standards."

HAN FEIZI

If an infant's head is not shaved, his sores will not heal; if his boils are not **lanced**, his illness will worsen. Even when someone holds him and his loving mother does the shaving or lancing, he will howl without stop, for a baby cannot see that a small discomfort will result in a major improvement. Now the ruler wants people to till the land and maintain pastures to increase their production, but they think he is cruel. He imposes heavy penalties to prevent wickedness, but they think he is harsh. He **levies** taxes in cash and grain to fill the storehouses and thus relieve them in time of famine and have funds for the army, but they consider him greedy. He imposes military training on everyone in the land and makes his forces fight hard in order to capture the enemy, but they consider him violent. In all four cases, he uses means that will lead to peace, but the people are not happy.

to deviate: to move away from

filial child: one who has done his or her duty as a son or daughter

to remonstrate: to plead in protest

evasive: hard to catch, showing avoidance

to lance: to break

to levy: to collect or raise

NOW YOU DO IT

1. According to Confucius, what do children owe their parents? What do parents owe their children?

2. What is Han Feizi's attitude towards people? To whom does he compare them?

3. How would Confucius describe a good ruler?

4. How would Han Feizi describe a good ruler?

treason, for example, all his or her male relatives over sixteen might be killed—including grandfathers, uncles, and nephews. All female relatives, and males under sixteen, might be made slaves.

DAOISM

Another new philosophy, Daoism, also began during the years of the Warring States. Daoism was based on the teachings of the philosopher Laozi. The basic goal of Daoists was to live **in harmony** with nature. Following the Dao, or "the way," was the means to achieving that harmony. Daoists believed that by studying nature closely, people would come to understand how it worked. Then they would be able to live in harmony with nature. It was important not to interfere with nature in any way because this could upset the natural order.

A Quotation from *The Laozi* (the book)
Do not honour the worthy,
And the people will not compete.
Do not value rare treasures,
And the people will not steal.
Do not display what others want,
And the people will not
have their hearts
confused.

PRIMARY SOURCE

Daoists thought that the harmony of nature could be copied in human society. They believed that rules and customs forced people to behave in certain ways, instead of allowing them to behave naturally and **spontaneously**. They were opposed to rules and regulations, and to social tools such as money and education. Money, for example, could lead to conflict and disharmony as people

Figure 3–12 Chinese medicine still incorporates the use of herbs. In recent years, many North Americans have become interested in herbal medicine.

tried to become wealthy, perhaps at the expense of others.

From the beginning, Daoists were in conflict with Confucians, who believed in many rules and proper conduct. Confucius and Laozi are supposed to have met and argued about their beliefs—often with Laozi getting the upper hand!

In later times, Daoists began to seek **immortality**. People could achieve immortality by following the Dao and strengthening their life force, called *qi*. This could be done by breathing properly and by taking the proper medicines. While searching for these medicines, many Daoists became **alchemists**, experimenting with various plants and metals that they hoped would produce the **elixir** of life. Daoists tried to achieve immortality by making special pills from **mercury**. Mercury is highly poisonous, and those who took the pills died, including several emperors. The experiments of Daoists in their search for immortality led to many important discoveries in the fields of medicine and **metallurgy**.

in harmony: in peaceful coexistence

immortality: endless life

spontaneously: with freedom, on impulse

alchemist: an early chemist; alchemists were heavily influenced by magic

elixir: medicine

mercury: a silver-white metal that is liquid at ordinary temperatures

metallurgy: the science of the composition of metals

1. Compare Daoism and Confucianism using an organizer. Consider categories such as the goals of each, the values of each, the roles people should play, and the role the government should play.

2. As the emperor of China, you are faced with three new philosophies. Which one would you select to dominate your court: Confucianism, Legalism, or Daoism? Explain your choice.

3. Compare the Chinese view of nature, as shown in yin-yang, fengshui, and Daoism, with that of any modern Canadian environmentalist.

4. Compare the values of a traditional Confucian society with values of modern Canadian society. What are the main similarities and differences? How closely do our values match Confucian ones? Explain your answer, giving reasons for your choice.

UNITY AND CONFORMITY

The political unrest of the later Zhou Dynasty (the Warring States period) eventually led to the dynasty's downfall. A prince of one of the Warring States conquered the last Zhou king in 256 B.C.E. and then went on to conquer all the other warring states. This process was completed in 221 B.C.E. The dynasty the prince founded was called the Qin (pronounce "Cheen") Dynasty. The prince called himself Shi Huangdi, which means "first emperor."

The Qin Dynasty lasted only a short time, but it was an extremely important dynasty. It established a new system of government. The dynasties that followed the Qin kept and refined this new system of government, which lasted until 1911. The word "Qin" is the root of the word "China." Shi Huangdi turned China into one of the world's great empires. He ended the feudal system of government that the Shang and Zhou kings had used. That system gave the nobles too much power, and led to situations such as the Warring States period in which the nobles fought one another and ignored the Zhou kings.

THE QIN DYNASTY, 256–202 B.C.E.

Shi Huangdi decided to set up a strong central government. He created thirty-six districts, each of which was ruled by an official he appointed. The officials were chosen on the basis of their ability and their loyalty to Shi Huangdi. Inspectors toured the districts regularly, making sure that these officials ruled properly.

Shi Huangdi wanted to make sure that no one would have a chance to disobey him, so he forced the nobles—who no longer had territories to rule—to live in the capital. This way, he could keep a close eye on their behaviour. He then divided the land among the peasants, so that the peasants had an adequate amount of land to support their families as well as pay taxes. Peasants were still required to provide labour for public works and the army.

Shi Huangdi fought several wars to expand China's size. In addition, he carried out many measures to improve China's economy and defences. He built more roads and

The Qin Empire, 221–210 B.C.E.

CENTRAL ASIA

TALKA MAKAN DESERT

KUNLUN MTS.

XIZANG (TIBET)

HIMALAYA MTS.

MONGOLIA

GOBI DESERT

MANCHURIA

SEA OF JAPAN

KOREA

Handan

Huang He

YELLOW SEA

C H I N A

Chang'an (Xian)

Chengdu

Chang R.

EAST CHINA SEA

Si R.

VIETNAM

SOUTH CHINA SEA

PACIFIC OCEAN

N

■ Qin Empire
221–210 B.C.E.

□ Area of silk
production during
the Han Dynasty

ⅉ the Great Wall

0   300   600 km

Figure 3–13 Qin territory under Shi Huangdi. The emperor expanded China's borders to include most of south China. Compare this map with a modern map showing both China and Vietnam.

canals. He standardized the system of money, weights, and measures so that trade was easier. He standardized the characters in the writing system, so that people could communicate with one another more easily.

One of Shi Huangdi's greatest accomplishments was the construction of the Great Wall. The Great Wall was built to stop attacks from the nomads who lived on the steppes and who often raided north China. Agriculture was not possible on the steppes because of the climate. As a result, the nomads were greatly attracted by China. Shi Huangdi's wall linked earlier walls together, and was part of a project that lasted for 2000 years. The Great Wall was strengthened and improved many times by the emperors who followed Shi Huangdi.

In spite of his many accomplishments, Shi Huangdi was not a popular emperor. He was a Legalist and believed that the state was more important than the people, so he treated people harshly. The nobles resented losing their power and land. The peasants resented working on the public projects because the conditions of work were inhumane. Thousands of people died

while working on the Great Wall.

As a Legalist, Shi Huangdi disagreed strongly with Confucianism and wanted to make people forget all the traditions of the past that did not conform to Legalism. He thought that these would weaken the new form of government he had set up. Thousands of classic books, including the works

DID YOU KNOW?

It took approximately 500 000 workers to complete the Great Wall. Many died in the effort.

Figure 3–14 The Great Wall of China was strengthened by the Qin emperor and later by the Ming emperors. The wall stretched for 2200 kilometres, was 7.5 metres high and 4.5 metres thick. If the Great Wall stretched across Canada from the Pacific coast, in which province would it end?

of Confucius, were burned because Shi Huangdi did not like the opinions they contained. Many scholars and their families were killed to erase the knowledge of the past.

Shi Huangdi was also a very suspicious man. Because he was so hated, he feared for his life. He moved frequently from palace to palace, often in disguise. It was said that he never slept in the same bed twice. He had his own son executed because he thought the prince planned to **assassinate** him. As he grew older, Shi Huangdi ordered his servants to search for life-preserving potions.

Shi Huangdi died in 210 B.C.E. Legends say that his officials were so afraid of what would happen if the death were reported that they kept it secret, transporting the decaying body in a cart of dead fish. The Qin Emperor was buried in a great tomb filled with thousands of life-sized **terra cotta** figures to guard the body.

Archaeologists have not yet finished excavating the tomb. There are rumours that it is filled with treasures yet to be found. The floor may be a giant map of the empire with rivers of mercury. The ceiling may be a map of the heavens with planets and stars of jade, silver, and gold.

After his death, Shi Huangdi's successor was unable to control the empire. Shi Huangdi had made too many enemies, and the people rose in revolt against the Qin. Rival generals struggled for power. Eventually one of these generals defeated the others and founded a new dynasty, the Han Dynasty.

to assassinate: to kill for political reasons

terra cotta: a brownish-red material used to make pottery

Figure 3–15 Shi Huangdi's tomb. In all, 6000 life-sized terra cotta soldiers guarded this burial site.

THE HAN DYNASTY 206–220 C.E.

The first Han emperor was Gaozu. After establishing his capital at Chang'an, he made the Han Empire strong and prosperous. Gaozu did not restore the feudal system of government. Instead, he kept the centralized system of the Qin, appointing capable and loyal people as government officials. He did, however, ease the harsh Legalist policies of the Qin and build a government based on Confucian principles. Confucian scholars were hired as advisors to the emperor.

The Han believed that officials should win their appointments through **merit**, not birth. Officials had to prove their worth by passing difficult examinations set by the Han. As well as being good scholars, officials also had to show that they appreciated art and literature. One of China's most famous historians, Sima Qian, was a government official. He wrote the first major history of China. Although the Han government was not Legalist, some Legalist ideas were maintained. Opposition to the government was not allowed, and lawlessness was dealt with promptly. Laws remained very strict.

The Han waged many military campaigns to enlarge the empire. During their rule, the empire expanded in the south, and grew to include Manchuria and Korea. By a combination of conquests and alliances, the Han Empire expanded far into central Asia.

With the expansion into central Asia came contact with India, the Middle East, Africa, and Europe. The famous Silk Road across Asia was constructed. This trade route linked China with distant lands— even to Europe. The Silk Road began in the great Chinese cities such as Chang'an and crossed the deserts and

merit: being worthy of reward or honour because of one's efforts and abilities

Figure 3–17
A photograph of the Silk Road taken in 1940. In this photograph, you can see where beams have been used to prop up the side of the road and the overhang near the route. How would you feel if you were travelling along this road?

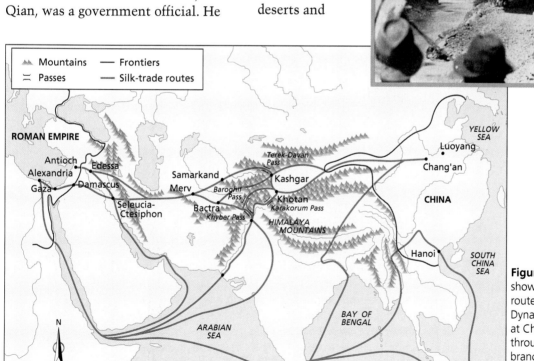

Figure 3–16 This map shows all the silk trade routes during the Han Dynasty. The Silk Road starts at Chang'an, moves west through Kashgar, and then branches out in many directions. What factors would have made this a long and difficult route?

mountains of central Asia to the Middle East and the Mediterranean. Few travellers could cover the whole distance because the journey took years. Camel caravans transported the trade goods from one city to another along the route. Then a new caravan would take over and transport the goods to the next city.

China's economy boomed from the trade along the Silk Road. China exported products—mainly silk—and imported raw materials from within Asia and elsewhere. The Romans bought so much Chinese silk that they almost caused the Roman Empire to go bankrupt! The number of artisans and merchants increased as a result of this trade.

The Han emperors strengthened the economy in other ways as well. They built more roads and canals, as well as more flood-control and irrigation projects. They also established granaries throughout the empire, to help feed people during periods of famine.

During the Han Dynasty, farmers continued to follow the traditional pattern of agriculture. The farmers lived in small villages close to their farming lands. Within a day's walk was a market town, where farmers could buy and sell products. Village life was very important in China, as it is to this day. Farmers still owed taxes to the government, as well as labour on public works and in the army.

The family also played a key role in society. Several generations of a family would live together as a family unit. Usually an elder male, such as a grandfather, would be considered the head of the family and would have a great deal of power. He would choose his children's future marriage partners and even the kind of work they could do. Elders were to be respected without question, especially by the youngest members.

Paper was one of the many important inventions of the Han Empire. According to tradition, an inventor named Cai Lun first showed paper to the emperor in 105 C.E. The Han also invented breast-strap harnesses and **stirrups**, the stern-post **rudder**, and the magnetic compass.

stirrup: a foot support that hangs from a saddle

rudder: a broad, flat piece of wood used for steering a boat

The Life of the Peasant

It is sometimes difficult to find out much about the lives of ordinary people who lived long in the past. Most people were not interested enough in peasants to write about their lives. The author Chao Chu, who lived in 178 B.C.E. and wrote the piece at right, was an exception.

arbitrary: unpredictable

They [the peasants] labour at ploughing in the spring and hoeing in the summer, harvesting in the autumn and storing foodstuffs in winter, cutting wood, performing labour service for the local government, all the while exposed to the dust of the spring, the heat of the summer, the storms of the autumn, and the chill of winter. Through all four seasons they never get a day off. They need funds to cover such obligations as entertaining guests, burying the dead, visiting the sick, caring for orphans, and bringing up the young. No matter how hard they work they can be ruined by floods or droughts, or cruel and **arbitrary** officials who impose taxes at the wrong times or keep changing their orders. When taxes fall due, those with produce have to sell it at half price [to raise the needed cash], and those without [anything to sell] have to borrow [at such high interest rates] they will have to pay back twice what they borrowed. Some as a consequence sell their lands and houses, even their children and grandchildren.

PRIMARY SOURCE

All these inventions helped the people of China be more productive.

The Han also made beautiful dishes and sculptures of bronze, silver, and gold. Chinese people believed that **jade** had the power of preservation. When rulers died, some were clothed in jade suits sewn with gold thread. Other grave goods show that the wealthy enjoyed many luxuries.

Eventually, the Han Dynasty lost the Mandate of Heaven. There were many reasons for this. The later emperors were less capable. Factions at the imperial court undermined the work of the government. There were some natural disasters that ruined the lives of many peasants. Rebellions broke out, and the Han Dynasty was overthrown. It was replaced by a time period sometimes called the "Period of Chaos." This period lasted for a long time (220–589 C.E.). During these years, no one was powerful enough to unite China. It fragmented into a number of small kingdoms that competed with one another in trying to found a new dynasty.

In spite of the political chaos, life for most Chinese people went on much as usual. The kingdoms followed the type of government that had been established by the Qin and the Han. The major difference was that there was no overall empire. Authors continued to produce great works of literature, and artisans became more skilled at pottery and metal working. Farmers continued to farm as they always had.

At this time, a new and influential religion—Buddhism—spread through China. At first, only the wealthy and influential people adopted Buddhism. Later it became popular with everyone. Its philosophy appealed to people living in a time of political uncertainty.

BUDDHISM

"As in the ocean's midmost depths, no wave is born, but all is still, so let the monk be still, be motionless…"

Buddhism is different from many religions because it does not include worship of a god or gods. Instead, it is based on the teachings of an Indian prince, Siddartha, who gave up wealth and family to seek an answer to the misery of the world. After much searching, he received **enlightenment** —the answer—and became the Buddha, or "enlightened one."

Buddha said that suffering occurred only when people were too concerned with themselves and their own desires and needs. In other words, suffering

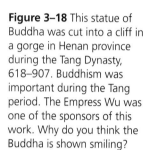

jade: a precious mineral, usually green or white

enlightenment: seeing the light of truth

Figure 3–18 This statue of Buddha was cut into a cliff in a gorge in Henan province during the Tang Dynasty, 618–907. Buddhism was important during the Tang period. The Empress Wu was one of the sponsors of this work. Why do you think the Buddha is shown smiling?

existed when people were too involved in the physical world. People should instead seek to free themselves of worldly concerns through retreat into a **monastery** or through **meditation**. All kinds of aids could be used to help in meditation. Mandalas, for example, are colourful paintings of the spiritual world. They help unfocus the mind so that it can find its way to higher truths. Buddhists also believed in reincarnation—the idea that a soul is reborn until it finds enlightenment, which is true knowledge of self. Ultimately, the soul would find nirvana, or peace and freedom from desire and suffering.

Buddhism became very popular in China and spread quickly. It was sponsored by wealthy and influential people. It was an appealing faith in a time of political unrest. Many Buddhist monasteries were founded, and Buddhism inspired much literature and art. Eventually, many semi-deities associated with Buddhism were created as well as *bodhisattvas*. A bodhisattva was a kind of god, a person who put off nirvana in order to help other people in their search for enlightenment.

THE SUI DYNASTY, 589–618

After the fall of the Han, China had numerous small kingdoms. In 589 an official of one of the many kingdoms managed to reunite China. He formed an army that successfully defeated the other kingdoms. Calling himself "Wendi," this official founded the Sui Dynasty. This was a very short-lived dynasty, but it accomplished a great deal in the short time it was in power.

Most importantly, the Sui Dynasty reunited China into one empire, and undertook many measures to strengthen it. The Sui rebuilt many sections of the Great Wall that had fallen into disrepair. It revived the examination system that was used to select government officials.

One of the most important contributions the Sui made to the economy was the construction of the Grand Canal. The Chang Jiang region had become a very important source of food, but it was very difficult to ship this food north because of the Qing Ling mountains. Wendi decided to link a number of small canals into one large one—the Grand Canal—that would run from the Huang He River to the Chang Jiang River and then to Hangzhou on the coast. A little later, the canal was extended north to Beijing.

The Sui were very successful in the improvements they made. Their capital at Chang'an became the largest city in the world, with a population of over 1 million people. The Sui ruled with great cruelty, however, and tried to do too much too soon. Over 1 million people were required to work on the many public works projects, and many died because of the harsh working conditions. The people rebelled, and a new dynasty, the Tang Dynasty, was founded.

Figure 3–19 The Grand Canal was designed to link the rice-growing areas of the Chang Jiang region with the cities of the North China Plain. The longest artificial waterway in the world, the canal was 40 metres wide and 2000 kilometres long. Scholars estimate that more than 5 million people helped build the canal.

1. Assess the importance of the Qin and Sui emperors. Did the benefits of long-term projects such as the Grand Canal justify their cruelty? Give reasons for your answer.

2. List the inventions of the Han Dynasty identified in this chapter. Prepare a short report on one invention, explaining how the invention was discovered, how it worked, and its benefits.

3. How long was the Silk Road? Assuming that a caravan might cover 10 kilometres in a day, how long would it take to travel from Chang'an to Aleppo? Describe the environments travellers would pass through on such a journey. Use an atlas and other references to obtain the information you need.

4. Develop an organizer to summarize the achievements of the Han Dynasty. What categories of information should you include in your organizer?

5. What is better: a government official who receives office based on birth or one who receives office based on merit? Give reasons for your answer.

6. Would you prefer to be a Chinese official under the Han or a modern politician in Canada? Explain, giving reasons for your answer.

7. The scale of some Chinese projects, particularly that of the Great Wall and the Grand Canal, was almost unbelievable, considering that most of the work was "hand" labour. What does this tell us about the power of the emperors and the efficiency of the government?

THE GOLDEN AGE: THE TANG DYNASTY, 618–907

The Tang Dynasty ruled during China's Golden Age. The dynasty was founded by a government official named Li Huan, who took the name of Gaozong. Gaozong was soon replaced by his son Taizong, one of the most dynamic of the Chinese emperors. Building on the Sui accomplishments, the Tang made China a flourishing and **cosmopolitan** empire that was the envy of the world. It was a remarkable achievement considering the long period of chaos that had gone before.

The Han Empire, which you read about in the previous section, is often compared to the Roman Empire because they existed at approximately the same time. They were both large and powerful empires, although the Han Empire contained more people than the Roman Empire. Both empires were brought down, and their fall led to years of great political unrest. The Roman Empire, however, was never revived. The Tang not only revived the glory days of the old Han Empire, they made it more powerful and prosperous than ever.

The Tang extended the boundaries of the empire, expanding west as far as Afghanistan, and forcing Tibet, Vietnam, and Korea to become **tributary states**. Tributary states were required to send a gift each year to the Tang, in recognition of Tang power and supremacy.

At home, the Tang worked to expand and strengthen all aspects of Chinese life and culture. During the Period of Chaos (see page 91), many peasants had become very poor. They had been forced to sell their land and

cosmopolitan: worldly, sophisticated

tributary state: a country forced to make regular payments to a more powerful country for peace or protection

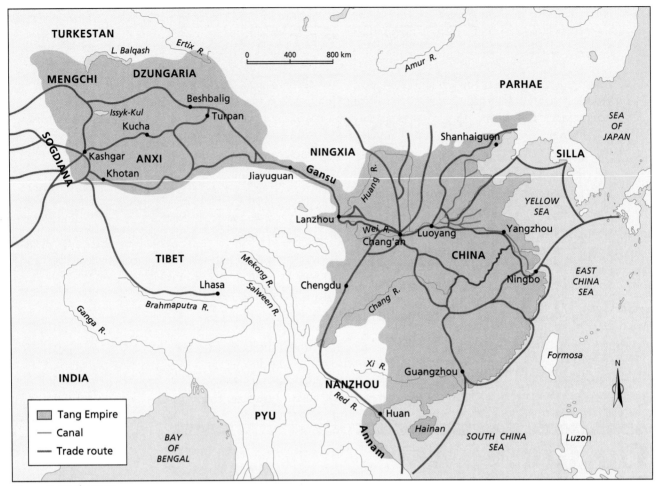

Figure 3–20 The Tang Empire, circa 700. Can you name one reason why Chinese society became open to the world during the Tang empire?

become tenants for wealthy landowners. As a result, the government had lost a great deal of income from taxes. To increase the taxes it could collect, the Tang gave land to ordinary people. The Tang also carried on the tradition of public works, such as the construction of roads and canals, to increase the prosperity of the empire.

One unusual event occurred during the Tang Empire: China had its first and only empress, the Empress Wu. Women were often influential in the Chinese Empire. Some ruled as **regents** for infant sons, for example. But they always ruled in the son's name. The Empress Wu was different. After ruling for her husband and two of her sons for thirty years behind the scenes, she seized power in 690 in her own name—after **deposing** her sons.

regent: a person who rules for a monarch who is too young, sick, or old to do so

to depose: to put out of office

EDUCATION AND THE EXAMINATION SYSTEM

The Tang improvements to the education and examination systems were among their most important achievements. They expanded the examination system used to select government officials. They built schools and standardized the courses so that all students studied the same topics. Until the Tang period, schools were not provided by the government. The wealthy hired private tutors to educate their children. Ordinary citizens might join together to hire a teacher, or the local community might pay for a school, but this was not common.

Preparing a bright child for the examinations was a major family project. It was an expensive undertaking, and not many families were able to provide the opportunity. But government officials had high status in Chinese society, and the family of a successful student would share this status. It was one of the few ways for an ordinary family to improve its social standing in China.

Students studied the Four Books and the Five Classics. These books explained the fundamental concepts of Chinese society and contained China's greatest literature. Students were expected to be obedient and to memorize what they had learned. Calligraphy was also important.

Government examinations were held regularly. Candidates wrote a series of examinations beginning at the local level and finishing with the finals exams in the capital. Students were isolated for days in individual small cells. They were tested on their exact knowledge of the classics, and on government practice. Only 2 or 3 percent of all candidates passed the highest level. However, all students earned a privileged role in society and were treated with respect.

Years later, when visitors from Europe visited China, they were impressed by the examination system as a way of selecting government officials because candidates qualified on the basis of merit, not class. The visitors encouraged their own governments to copy the idea.

COSMOPOLITAN TIMES

Under the Tang, China reached out to the world. China was visited by people from all over Asia. Many of them lived in the capital at Chang'an, a large, bustling, and highly cosmopolitan city.

The imperial palace was at the north end of the city so that the emperor could face south, considered to be the most favourable direction. The city was divided into 108 wards, or areas. Each ward was enclosed by walls, the gates of which could be closed at night. Certain wards were set aside for markets, and some were set aside for the Jews, Muslims, Christians, and other foreigners who lived in China.

The Chinese eagerly bought the goods of many different countries— horses, jewels, musical instruments, and textiles were among

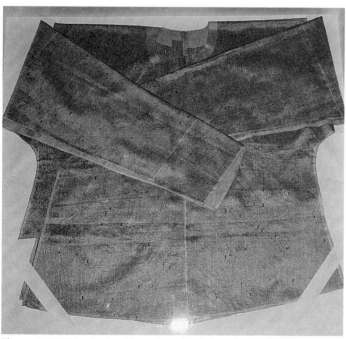

Figure 3–21 This nineteenth-century cheat sheet is actually underwear with portions of the classics written on it! The Chinese civil-service examinations were so difficult—and the rewards for success so wonderful—that historians believe cheating was common even in early times.

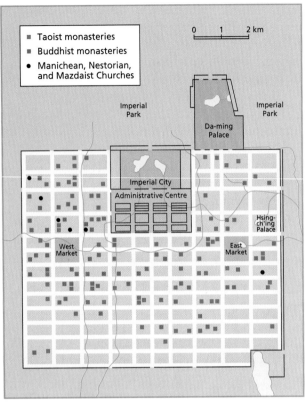

Figure 3–22 The Tang capital at Chang'an. Chinese cities were built on a grid plan. The outer walls of Chang'an extended more than 8 kilometres on one side and almost 10 kilometres on the other. The walls were made of pounded earth 4 metres thick and 11 metres high. Why do you think this grid plan impressed visiting Europeans?

■ Taoist monasteries
■ Buddhist monasteries
● Manichean, Nestorian, and Mazdaist Churches

0   1   2 km

Imperial Park

Imperial Park

Da-ming Palace

Imperial City
Administrative Centre

Hsing-ch'ing Palace

West Market

East Market

polo: a game played by two teams on horseback, who use a mallet to get a ball into the opponent's net

Figure 3–23 This beautiful figurine of a high-born Tang woman shows that she lived a life of comfort and luxury, delighting in the finer things of life.

the favourites. Foreign fashions in clothing and hairstyles were copied, and foreign games such as **polo** became popular activities.

The number of merchants in China increased enormously because the amount of trade was growing. Merchants were not well-respected in society, however. Confucianism did not value their work, because he thought it was not beneficial to society. Farmers produced food, and artisans produced goods, but merchants only produced profits of benefit to themselves. As a sign of the disfavour in which they were held, merchants

were forbidden to ride horses or wear rich clothes. As a result, most merchants tried to enter the upper class by buying land, by marrying into a landowning family, or by having a son pass the examinations and become an official.

Tang women enjoyed more rights and privileges, and more freedom of movement, than women of earlier times. People did not stick to the Confucian ideas about the proper behaviour for women during this cosmopolitan era. The Empress Wu successfully broke tradition by governing in her own name until 705, when she was over eighty and in poor health. More women received an education, and were not forced to stay in their homes as they had been in the past. Upper-class women became writers and artists. Some of them played polo. The wives and daughters of artisans helped run the family business. Other women were midwives, nurses, or entertainers. Women on farms had always worked.

ART AND SCIENCE

The arts flourished during the Tang period. Potters, painters, jade carvers, and other artists created many masterpieces. The style of art became more realistic and dynamic. Although a great deal of art was devoted to Buddhist and Daoist themes, people also began to paint scenes of everyday life. These paintings conveyed a sense of vitality and movement in contrast to the serene and other-worldly feeling of Buddhist and Daoist art. During this period, design elements from other parts of the world became visible in Chinese art as a result of the increased contact with other cultures. One major change at this time was the introduction of chairs and stools to China. Before this time, the Chinese had sat on mats on the floor.

The Inventions of the Tang

Many scientific and technological inventions that we enjoy today were discovered by the Chinese long ago. Later, their inventions were borrowed and carried to other parts of the world. The following are a few examples of inventions developed during the Tang Dynasty—and how they travelled to the twentieth century.

Invention	China	Elsewhere	Today
Gunpowder	Invented in 850. Used in fireworks and later in weapons.	Knowledge carried by Arab traders to Europe in the 1200s.	Gunpowder, with much the same formula, is still used for fireworks and weapons all over the world.
Smallpox **vaccine**	Invented in China in the 900s.	Knowledge spread to Asia in the 1600s. Europe discovered its own vaccine for smallpox in 1796.	Led to the invention of later vaccines and the science of **immunology**.
Block printing	Invented in China in the 700s. By 1040, the Chinese had invented movable type.	Knowledge spread throughout Asia. Printing invented in Europe in the 1400s.	Block printing used mostly for book illustrations and decorative arts. Movable type being replaced by computers.

vaccine: a preparation injected into the body to protect from a disease

immunology: the branch of medicine dealing with resistance to disease

WHAT DO YOU THINK?

1. Why do countries like to claim that they were the first to make important inventions or discoveries?

2. Does it really matter who invented something first, if the invention is of benefit to all people? Explain.

3. Are scientific and technological inventions always a benefit? Explain your answer by outlining the positive or negative effects of a particular invention. You can use the list in this Link-Up or identify other inventions in an encyclopedia.

4. Why did it take so long for Chinese inventions to spread throughout the world?

source: beginning

league: about 5 kilometres

carnage: killing

Huns: a nomadic people from Central Asia

image: picture in the mind

LITERATURE DURING THE TANG DYNASTY

Some of the greatest poets of Chinese history lived and worked during the Tang Dynasty. The first books in China were written during the Zhou Dynasty. During the Han Dynasty, scholars worked feverishly to recreate the books that the Qin had burned. They wanted to regain China's literary heritage, and to write new classics as well. By the time of the Tang, there were literally millions of works of literature available to read and study.

Using Poetry as a Primary Source

CATALOGUE CARD

What is it? *A poem*

Who wrote it? *Li Bai, of the Tang dynasty*

When? *After a battle*

Why? *To express his feelings*

Good poetry is honoured in China. It usually follows strict rules about the number of syllables in each line and the type of rhyme that may be used. Li Bai was one of China's favourite poets. He chose an unconventional style that emphasized strong images and made the reader feel as if he or she were part of the scene.

Fighting South of the Ramparts

Last year we were fighting at the **source** of the Sang-kan [River];
This year we were fighting on the Onion River Road.
We have washed our swords in the surf of Parthian seas;
We have pastured our horses among the snows of the T'ien Shan.
The King's armies have grown old and grey
Fighting ten thousand **leagues** away from home.
The **Huns** have no trade but battle and **carnage**;
They have no fields or ploughlands,
But only wastes where white bones lie among yellow sands.
Where the house of Qin built the Great Wall that was to keep away the Tartars,
There, in its turn, the House of Han lit beacons of war.
The beacons are always alight, fighting and marching never stop.
Men die in the field, slashing sword to sword;
The horses of the conquered neigh piteously to Heaven.
Crows and hawks peck for human guts,
Carry them in their beaks and hang them on the branches of withered trees.
Captains and soldiers are smeared on the bushes and grass;
The general schemed in vain.
Know therefore that the sword is a cursed thing
Which the wise use only if they must.

PRIMARY SOURCE

WHAT DO YOU THINK?

1. What was a Chinese soldier's life like, as described in "Fighting South of the Ramparts"? Where did the fighting take place? How long had it been going on?

2. What was Li Bai's attitude to war? How does he convey this viewpoint?

3. In your opinion, what is the most vivid **image** in this poem?

4. In your own words, describe what you think Li Bai was trying to say in this poem.

5. What can you learn about the social and cultural values of a society from poetry? What did you learn about Chinese society from this poem?

6. What is the best use you can make of this kind of information?

One Tang poetry collection, for example, contained 48 000 poems of a single type—written by 2200 poets. Good poetry, which was honoured in China, followed strict rules about the number of syllables and type of rhyme that could be used, and new styles of poetry were always being developed.

THE DOWNFALL OF THE TANG

One of the most interesting of the Tang emperors was Xuanzong, meaning "Brilliant Emperor." Xuanzong's government was good for a time, but he preferred court life to the cares of government. He was interested in both Buddhism and Daoism, and in poetry. Gradually Xuanzong retreated into his own private world, and various government officials began to compete for power. At the age of sixty, Xuanzong fell in love with a young woman in the imperial court, Yang Guifei. Yang Guifei took sides in the scheming of the court officials. She favoured a man named An Lushan.

An Lushan commanded a large part of China's northern army. In spite of the favours heaped on him by the emperor through his friendship with Yang Guifei, An Lushan was angry at not receiving a post he wanted. In 755, An Lushan rebelled and marched on Chang'an, forcing Xuanzong and Yang Guifei to flee west. The troops that accompanied Xuanzong rebelled and forced him to have Yang Guifei strangled. Xuanzong was so depressed that he gave his empire to his son.

Xuanzong's son fought for eight years before finally putting down An Lushan's rebellion. The Tang Dynasty never fully recovered from this rebellion. The sad tale of Yang Guifei, killed because the emperor's mutinous troops had demanded her death, showed how powerless the Tang rulers had become. The Tang Dynasty continued for a time, although more rebellions took place. Tang armies that had once ranged far into the west and south now fought in defence of a shrinking empire.

The Tang Dynasty ended in 907 to be replaced by a period called the "Five Dynasties," during which China was again fragmented into regional states. The Chinese Empire was not reunified until the Song Dynasty in 960.

DID YOU KNOW?

The story of Yang Guifei and Xuanzong inspired a classic Chinese opera.

ACTIVITIES

1. In what ways did China experience a golden age during the Tang Dynasty? Make an organizer, choosing your own categories, to summarize this information.

2. Write a letter to a general of the army to plead for the life of Yang Guifei. Explain why you feel she should not be killed.

3. How might the role played by the Empress Wu have affected other women in Tang times? How might it have affected the men?

4. Examine the figurine on page 96. Describe, in detail, what you see. What do you "read" in the face of the woman depicted here?

5. What aspect of Chinese government did the foreigners in China praise? Why do you think they recommended this practice to their governments at home?

6. What were the advantages to Tang society of allowing people from many different cultures to live in China?

By the time the Tang period ended, in 907, China had a written history over 2000 years old, and deeply rooted philosophic traditions. China's diverse landscape, with its mountains, rivers, and plains, also had an influence on the development of the empire. By the time of the Tang, Chinese civilization covered an enormous extent of territory and had spread outward to influence the growth and development of other countries. The empire was held together by shared beliefs in Confucianism as the foundation of the family and the state. In many ways, given the wide range of environments in China, its unity was remarkable.

SUMMARY ACTIVITIES

1. Create a large map of China showing the Huang River, Chang Jiang River, mountain ranges, and the major cities of the North China Plain. Indicate the separation of north and south China.

2. In groups, create sections of an illustrated time line from the Shang to the Tang Dynasties. What are the most important accomplishments of each dynasty?

3. Choose one of Buddhism, Confucianism, or Daoism. In a group, research and prepare a report on the religion or philosophy you have chosen. Be sure to include illustrations and other information to help people understand the most important points of the religion or philosophy. Decide on the best method to present your report to the class.

4. The year is 750 C.E. Write a journal describing a trip across the Silk Road from Chang'an to Damascus. Research the landscape and cultures you would pass through and describe them in your journal. Provide a map of your journey.

5. Pretend you are a student writing the government exam to gain an official post during Tang times. Write a letter to your parents, or a friend, describing your experiences and your thoughts. Note: Cheating may have occurred in Tang times, but for you it is not an option!

6. Prepare an in-depth comparison of ninth-century Chinese society and one European society (Viking, Anglo-Saxon, or Frankish) of the same period. Use the following categories in your organizer:
   ◆ political organization
   ◆ basis of the economy
   ◆ social life
   ◆ religion/philosophy

ON YOUR OWN

1. Gather more information about Shang bronzes. Draw a Shang dish or make a model of one out of papier mâché or other materials. What important stylistic elements will you need to include?

2. With your teacher, plan to invite an expert in Chinese calligraphy to visit your class and instruct you in the art of Chinese writing. After the visit, what new impressions do you have about Chinese calligraphy?

4 THE ARAB WORLD

كوش گردان پلم روح نواز
نم سنن هوش ایما می داد
بامین خدای در تر ریس
دین همین خدا و عقل دلیل
نم محمد در جبریل بر بار
کوش را حلقهٔ غلامی داد

CHAPTER OUTCOMES

In this chapter you will focus on the origins of the Islamic world during the seventh century, and the great Arab empire that developed over the next 400 years. By the end of the chapter, you will

- synthesize information from a variety of map types

- identify and describe contributions of Arab civilization to the world

- outline the early history of Islam and the Islamic Empire

- compare the beliefs and traditions of Islam with those of other religions

- trace the history of Muslim traditions

- describe town life in Muslim societies during the eighth and ninth centuries

- use geographic information to analyze settlement patterns

- interpret and make a climagraph

The Arabian Nights, *sometimes called* One Thousand and One Nights, *is probably the most famous collection of Arab folk tales. It includes the stories about Alaedinn and Ali Baba and the Forty Thieves. According to legend, Princess Scheherazade told the stories to her new husband, Sharyar, every night. Scheherazade always included a fascinating* **cliff-hanger** *so that the stories actually took "a thousand nights and one night" to tell.*

No one is sure where or when the stories were composed. A book called The Thousand Tales *was written by Princess Homai of Persia in the tenth century. Another collection of stories was composed in Egypt in the fifteenth century. The story that follows is an adaptation of the story of "Alaedinn" (Aladdin), also called "The Wonderful Lamp."*

Alaedinn (or The Wonderful Lamp)

As usual, Alaedinn was doing very little except talking to his friends.

When it was the five hundred and fourteenth night, Dunyazad spoke to her sister, Scheherazade: "Please sister, if you're not too sleepy, tell us another story." Sheherazade began to tell the story of Alaedinn and his wonderful lamp to her husband, the King of India.

I heard, O Mightiest King in the World, that there was a poor tailor in China who had an only son named Alaedinn. This boy was so lazy and **unmotivated** that his father despaired of teaching him anything. His friends were a bad influence on him and Alaedinn was always in trouble. In short, Alaedinn was a big disappointment. When the tailor died, his wife was forced to make a living spinning. The family was so poor that they often had little to eat.

Scheherazade was surprised by the dawn, and ended the story.

•••••••

When it was the Five Hundred and Fifteenth Night, Dunyazad asked her sister, Scheherazade, to tell the king more of the tale, and Scheherazade agreed.

One day, when Alaedinn was fifteen, his life took a turn. As usual, he was doing very little except talking to his foolish friends in the marketplace. That particular morning he was distracted and did not notice that he had caught the eye of a strangely dressed man. The man came quickly across the square and stood in front of the boy, searching Alaedinn's face as if he knew him. "You aren't, by any chance, the son of Mustapha, the

"You aren't, by chance, the son of the tailor, are you?"

tailor, are you?" he asked.

"Yes, sir, as a matter of fact, I am," Alaedinn replied. "But my father died some time ago."

With that, tears sprang into the man's eyes, and he threw his arms around Alaedinn and hugged him. "Oh, my boy, your father was my brother. I have lived in the distant west for many years, and I came home hoping to see him. To hear that he is dead is almost too much to bear. Blood can't hide from blood. I knew, as soon as I saw you that we were related, although your father wasn't even married when I left this town."

It seemed that Alaedinn's uncle was also a magician, trained in **astrology**. He listened as Alaedinn told about his father's life and death, and about the family's circumstances. To hear that his brother's wife was so poor was most upsetting. He asked where the family lived, and told Alaedinn that he would visit the family home the next day.

"You, my boy," he said, "are now my only blood connection with my dear brother." He took ten gold pieces from his wallet and gave them to Alaedinn. "Take this money to your mother, and tell her, **Inshallah**, I'll visit in the morning to salute her." He embraced Alaeddin once more, and turned away.

Alaedinn wrapped the gold coins into his sash and ran home. His mother was surprised to see him. He told his mother the story of the meeting in the marketplace.

"Mother," he said, "This man is dressed like a lord, and he has told me that he is also a magician and an astrologer. Do you think that our luck has changed at last? This could be the best thing to ever happen to us."

But his mother looked concerned. "My son, I don't know who this man is, but he is not your uncle. You had an uncle, but he is long dead."

Alaedinn's mother was tired of working hard to keep the ungrateful boy.

"But he wept when he saw me and seemed to know me just by my appearance. And he gave us the gold coins!"

Scheherazade was surprised by the dawn, and ended the story.

• • • • • • •

When night came, she continued the story.

I heard, O Great King, that the magician set out the next morning and found Alaedinn. He went with him to his mother's house. Once inside, he asked to see the **memorial** to Alaedinn's father. He wept when he saw it. His tears were so genuine that the wife became convinced that the man really was her brother-in-law. "So long as you have

children," the uncle sighed, "you never completely die."

The magician asked Alaedinn what skills he had acquired, and what job he did. Alaedinn, of course, was a good-for-nothing, and was very embarrassed. His mother told how she was tired of working hard to **keep** the ungrateful boy, and was thinking of forcing him to go live elsewhere. "He treats me very badly," she said, nodding towards Alaedinn. "He shows up when he's hungry, and refuses to help in any way. I have lost all patience with him."

The magician seemed very disappointed. He told Alaedinn that he was shaming his mother with his behaviour. He suggested that if the boy didn't want to be a tailor like his father, then he could look for something else to do. Alaedinn did not seem interested. So the magician offered to set up a stall in the market and fill it with costly goods. Alaedinn could manage the store. Alaeddin thought this was a great idea.

He would be a rich merchant with many fine things.

As he promised, the magician set up the stall in the market, and outfitted Alaedinn with fine clothes. He gave him **sherbets** and fine food to eat. He also showed Alaedinn the **sultan's** palace and introduced him to the merchants in the **caravanserai**.

If Alaedinn's mother had any doubts about the identity of the magician, these were now satisfied. "Surely we owe you a great debt that we cannot repay," she said. "I pray that God will always help and preserve you."

But the magician replied, "You owe me nothing. It is my duty to look after my brother's son as if he were my own. I cannot open the store tomorrow because it is Friday, the day of meeting and prayer, but on Saturday, Inshallah, we will begin."

On Saturday, as promised, the magician came for Alaedinn. He took him through the city, showing him palaces and other wonders. Many times he asked the boy if he liked what he saw. Alaedinn expressed his wonder and joy.

Later in the day, the two arrived in a desolate valley in the hills near town. The magician told Alaedinn to seat himself. To Alaedinn's surprise, the man began to chant and burn special **incense**. Soon the air filled with smoke and the ground burst open revealing a marble slab to which was attached a great metal ring. Terrified, Alaedinn tried to run, but the magician was too fast. He struck Alaedinn down and told him to be still. "Quiet, boy," he said, "there is a great treasure here that has been buried in your name. Stand fast and all will be well."

Scheherazade was surprised by the dawn, and ended the story.

·······

When it was the five hundred and twenty-fourth night, Dunyazad asked her sister, Scheherazade, to tell the king more of the tale, and Scheherazade agreed.

It was told to me, O mighty King, that the magician told Alaedinn that he must lift the slab to get the treasure. When Alaedinn complained that he was not strong enough to lift it himself, the magician replied that the stone could only be lifted by Alaedinn. He instructed him to lift the stone himself while **reciting** the names of his father and mother. The magician reassured the boy, telling him that he thought of him as his own dear son, and that no harm would come to him. Thus was Alaedinn **coaxed** to lift the stone, which rose as if it had no weight at all, revealing a staircase leading down into the earth.

The magician looked down the staircase. "Now, nephew, you must go down into the chambers below. You will see many gold and silver jars, and other things. Do not touch them, or even let your clothing brush against them. Instead go from room to room, and through the underground gardens, where the fruit of trees are pearls and jewels, until you reach a **terrace** wherein a lamp hangs from the ceiling. Take the lamp and bring it back to me." With that, he placed a ring on Alaedinn's finger, saying that it would protect him from harm, and sent him down the stairs.

And Scheherazade was surprised by the dawn, and ended the story for the night.

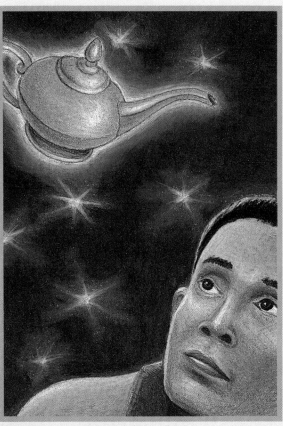

"Take the lamp and bring it back to me."

cliff-hanger: a suspenseful ending to an episode in a long story

unmotivated: lacking an inner drive

astrology: the study of the influence of the planets on human affairs

Inshallah: God willing

memorial: something intended to preserve the memory of someone

to keep: to provide for

sherbet: a frozen dessert

sultan: a ruler in a Muslim country

caravanserai: a hostel with a warehouse and stables for traders

incense: a sustance that provides a fragrant odour when burned

to recite: to repeat

to coax: to encourage

terrace: an open area connecting a main building to the outside

ACTIVITIES

1. Who are the main characters in this tale? Select one character and write two sentences about him or her. Include such information as how that character is related to the other characters, or how he or she helps move the story along.

2. Describe the form, or structure, of Alaedinn in a single word or phrase. Some examples are: "Loose," "And then..." or "Like a soap opera."

3. Give examples of how Scheherazade created suspense at the end of each evening. Which "cliff-hanger" was the most suspenseful? Why?

4. What did Alaedinn's uncle mean when he said: "So long as you have children, you never completely die"? Do you agree or disagree? Explain?

5. Write an ending for the story of Alaedinn.

وشكني ومسكني وحولي وحالي وما بي ومالي ولا تلجي بنفسي ٣٤
سلط على مغيرا واجعل لي من لدنك سلطانا نصيرا اللهم احسني بصرك وغذك

واخصصني باسمك ومنك وتولني اختيارك وخيرك ولا تكلني الى كآءة غيرك
وهب لي عافية غير عافية وارزقني رفاهية غير واهية واكفني مخاني اللاواء

TIME LINE

476	FALL OF THE WESTERN ROMAN EMPIRE
570	BIRTH OF THE PROPHET MUHAMMAD
622	THE YEAR OF THE HIJRAH
633	ABU BAKR IS THE FIRST CALIPH
661	BEGINNING OF THE RULE BY THE UMAYYAD DYNASTY IN DAMASCUS
710	TARIK INVADES SPAIN
749	ABBÂSID DYNASTY OF BAGHDAD TAKES CONTROL OF THE CALIPHATE
809	DEATH OF HARUN AL-RASHID
950	ARAB SPAIN HAS ITS OWN CALIPH
1055	THE SELJUKS TAKE POWER IN BAGHDAD
1071	BATTLE OF MANZIKERT
1097	BEGINNING OF THE FIRST CRUSADE

*And their Lord has accepted of them and answered them:
"Never will I suffer to be lost the work of any of you, be he/she
male or female: you are members of one another..."*

It was in Arabia that the word of Allah was revealed to Muhammad and was later written down in the Qur'ân.

INTRODUCTION

While Arab culture dates back thousands of years B.C.E., historians say that the Arab world was never truly united until the appearance of Islam. Islam—a major world religion—was first revealed in Mecca in the seventh century C.E. Today it provides both spiritual and social guidance for about 1 billion Muslims all over the world.

The Arab world would not have expanded without Islam. It was the Arab Muslims of the sixth and seventh centuries who carried the Arabic language and Arab traditions—along with their Islamic faith—to the far corners of the known world.

However, Islam was to spread so quickly, and over such a large area, that it would eventually lose some of its Arab character. Islam is still the principal religion of the Middle East, North Africa, much of Central Africa, and many countries in Asia. There are millions of Muslims in China and Russia, for example. It is also the second fastest growing religion in North America.

In this chapter, you will focus on the Arab world, which was the birthplace of Islam. You will also learn about the foundations of the Islamic faith and the religious duties of Muslims around the world.

Figure 4–1 The spread of Islam from 632 to 750. Islam spread very quickly before and after the death of its founder, Muhammad.

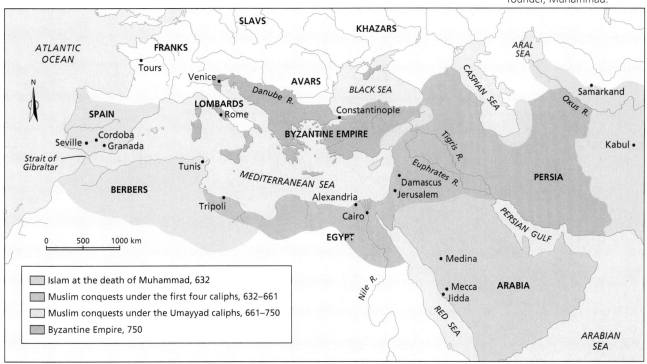

THE MIDDLE EAST

The **Middle East** is a vast territory containing the modern nations of Saudi Arabia, Egypt, Lebanon, Israel, Jordan, Iraq, Iran, Kuwait, Yemen, Oman, United Arab Emirates, Qatar, Bahrain Sudan, and Turkey. The region has always been important. Some of the earliest city-building civilizations in the world—

Middle East: This term is not a geographic designation but a widely used political term for the region.

those of the Sumerians, Babylonians, and Egyptians—developed there.

Christianity and Judaism were born in the Middle East. The cultures of many lands, including Canada, have deep connections to the cultures of the region. English and French literature, for example, contain many references to the Bible, which originated in the Middle East. The modern English alphabet and numbering system originated there. At a personal level, there are many links. Many Canadians who do not have a direct connection with the Middle East have names that originated there. Mary, Rebecca, Ruth, Joshua, Michael, and David are just a few.

Surrounded by Africa, Europe, and Asia, the Middle East is a world crossroad. Ancient and modern trade routes crisscross the region. Countless wars have been fought there, most recently, the Persian Gulf War. This modern war was fought for control of Middle East oil, which is one of the world's most precious **commodities**.

The Middle East and Europe have been in conflict many times. The Romans came and conquered the Middle East. The Crusades were fought there. The Arabs conquered many regions of Europe. European armies fought one another for control of the region in the nineteenth and twentieth centuries. Even now, events in the Middle East (and those involving the Middle East) are featured in newscasts, newspapers, and magazines almost every day.

commodity: an article that is traded

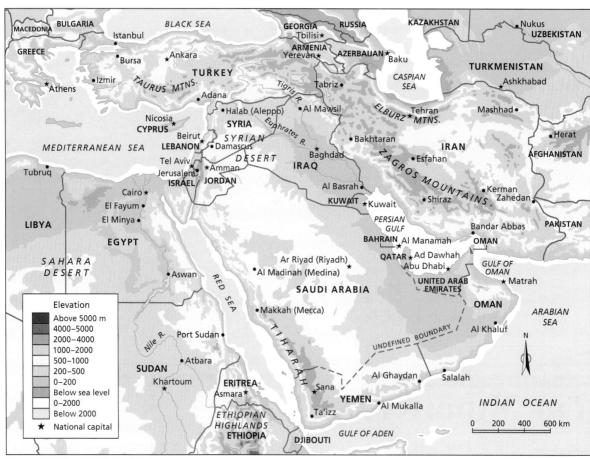

Figure 4–2 The Middle East today

Read a Climagraph

Climagraphs combine temperature and precipitation information in one place. They have three elements. You can identify them by looking at the example shown here of Baghdad, Iraq.

♦ a temperature scale on the left vertical axis

♦ a precipitation scale on the right vertical axis

♦ a horizontal axis at the bottom with twelve letters, each standing for one month of the year

The information in a climagraph is displayed in two ways:

♦ a red line for temperature

♦ blue bars for precipitation

The red temperature line connects a series of dots. Each dot represents the average temperature for one month. Each column in the blue bar graph represents the average precipitation for one month. By viewing the information together, you can easily determine how much the temperature and precipitation fluctuate during the year.

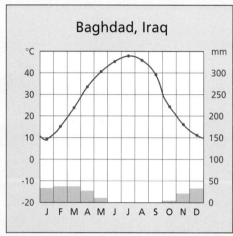

A climagraph for Baghdad, Iraq

NOW YOU DO IT

1. On a sheet of graph paper, draw the left vertical axis. This is your temperature scale. Label the units as shown in the example. Start at –20°C and go up to 40°C in units of 10°C. Hint: You can use two squares of graph paper for one unit to make your graph bigger.

2. Now draw the right vertical axis. This is your precipitation scale. Label the units as shown in the example. Start with 0 mm (millimetres) and go up to 300 mm in units of 50 mm.

3. Draw a horizontal line to connect the two axes at the botton. Divide the line into twelve blocks and label each one, beginning with "J" for January.

4. Use the following information to create a climagraph for Ottawa, Canada. (Your teacher

Temperature data for Ottawa, Canada

month	J	F	M	A	M	J	J	A	S	O	N	D
°C	-11	-10	-3	6	12	18	21	19	15	9	1	-8

Precipitation data for Ottawa, Canada

month	J	F	M	A	M	J	J	A	S	O	N	D
mm	60	57	61	68	70	73	81	82	79	66	78	77

may provide you with a blank climagraph.)

a) On your graph, mark a small dot in the centre of the column for each month to record the average temperature. Connect the dots with a red line.

b) Now use a ruler to draw a line across the column for each month to record the average amount of precipitation. Colour in each bar with blue.

5. Share your climagraph with a partner.

The Middle East Today

You have undoubtedly heard about conflicts in the Middle East on television or in the newspaper. If you have family members living in the region, you may have heard some news first-hand.

Sometimes it is hard for people living far away from a conflict to appreciate why it started—or why it is difficult to resolve.

Conflict in the Middle East partly concerns achieving peace for two groups of people—the Israelis and the Palestinians. Both groups say they want peace, but both groups also say they have a right to occupy the same territory.

Many problems can be traced back to the time when the state of Israel was created in 1948. For over 50 years before that time, many Jews had been fleeing terrible persecution in Europe by moving to Palestine, the Jewish homeland in biblical times. They believed they were entitled to return to territory they had inherited from their ancestors. During World War II, millions of Jews were

murdered by the Nazi followers of Adolf Hitler. After the war, hundreds of thousands of surviving Jews came to Palestine as **refugees**, hoping to create their own state. The Arab majority, who had lived there for generations, did not welcome their arrival, and warfare erupted. Hundreds of thousands of Palestinian Arabs were displaced from their homes and became refugees. As a result, there has been conflict between the two groups ever since. Despite many attempts to reach a lasting peace agreement, tensions in the area remain high.

There are other issues in the Middle East that have a more immediate impact on North America. One of these is oil. Much of the world's oil comes from countries that surround the Persian Gulf: Iraq, Kuwait, Bahrain, Qatar, United Arab Emirates, Oman, Iran, and Saudi Arabia. In 1990, Iraq invaded Kuwait to increase its access to

Figure 4–3 In1947, the United Nations proposed to split Palestine into a Jewish and an Arab state, as shown in this map. By the end of the Arab-Israeli war that broke out in 1948, Israel had taken a larger portion of land. Some of the land was also taken over by Jordan and Egypt.

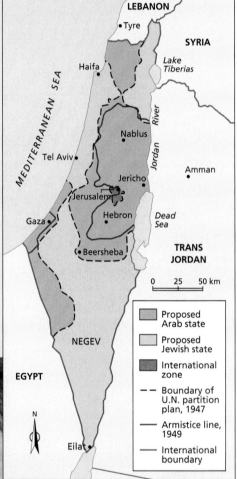

Figure 4–4 Palestinian representative Hanan Ashrawi is one of many politicians and negotiators on both sides of the Israel-Palestine conflict who have been involved in talks aimed at reaching a lasting peace agreement.

the Persian Gulf and to gain control of Kuwait's oil. The United Nations imposed **economic sanctions** against Iraq, in the hope that refusing to buy its oil would force its leader Saddam Hussein to withdraw his forces from Kuwait. When the sanctions failed to have this effect, the Gulf War broke out. A coalition of forces led by the United States, and including Canada, bombed and attacked the Iraqi forces using bases in Saudi Arabia and drove them out of Kuwait. The sanctions remained in effect as a way of keeping pressure on the Iraqi government.

While some people in the countries around the Persian Gulf supported the US-led attack, others did not. For example, some Muslims objected to the American presence in Saudi Arabia, the land of the Islamic holy sites of Mecca and Medina. Long after the end of the Gulf War, they resented what they saw as American interference in their affairs. In 2001, a small group of extremists—most from Saudi Arabia—took dramatic action. They hijacked planes and crashed them into the World Trade Center in New York and the Pentagon (US military headquarters) in Washington. These targets were symbols of US economic and military power. Over 2800 people were killed, in an attack that shocked the world.

The terrorist attacks were planned by an exiled Saudi Arabian, Osama bin Laden, and his organization of Muslim extremists, al-Qaeda. This organization was based in Afghanistan, where the government was controlled by the Taliban, an extremist Islamic group. Declaring a "war on terrorism," the United States led an attack on Afghanistan. The Americans were joined by several other countries, including Britain and Canada, to wipe out many al-Qaeda bases, overthrow the Taliban, and establish a more moderate government in Afghanistan.

refugee: a person who is forced to leave his or her homeland because of war, persecution, or natural disaster

economic sanctions: actions by one nation to force another to comply with international law, e.g., refusing to sell goods to or buy goods from that country

Figure 4–5 Kuwait is much smaller than Iraq but produces 15 percent of the region's oil, the same percentage as Iraq.

Figure 4–6 As Iraqi soldiers retreated from Kuwait during the Gulf War, they set fire to many of the country's oil wells. Some of the oil fires took almost a year to put out. What impact would these fires have on the environment?

WHAT DO YOU THINK?

1. Events in the Middle East are constantly changing. Brainstorm the types of information that would help you keep informed on these events. Where could you find this information? What types would be available in your community? What types would be available through the Internet?

2. There are often opposing viewpoints about issues in the Middle East. Why is it important to seek out several sources of information on issues of this type?

3. Explain why it can sometimes be difficult to determine your own point of view on complex issues such as those in the Middle East.

Write a Letter to the Editor

If you have a strong opinion about a newspaper or magazine article on the Middle East, there is one way that you can respond immediately—by writing a letter to the editor.

Letters-to-the editor sections appear in most daily newspapers and other periodicals. A letter to the editor states an opinion on an issue and is usually written in response to a particular story or event.

A good letter to the editor

♦ **refers to the story in question**
In the first paragraph, state that you are writing about [article title] by [author's name], which appeared in [name and date of publication]. If you have some personal connection with the issue, state this information in the first paragraph as well.

♦ **states a point of view with supporting information, and agrees or disagrees with the story**
In the next paragraph or two, offer facts, examples, and statistics that support your viewpoint. Your evidence should be strong enough to convince readers. State the origin of your information, for example, statistics compiled by the United Nations.

♦ **uses language and tone appropriate for the newspaper or magazine**
While it is important to be informative, if you use a tone that suggests you "know everything," readers may tune you out. Stay calm and reasonable. You can be clever, but do not use **sarcasm**.

♦ **summarizes a position in a conclusion and makes a recommendation**
It is always a good idea to recommend a plan of action after restating your position in a sentence or two.

In this way, your letter cannot be taken as mere criticism. This is the final paragraph of your letter to the editor.

♦ **is printed neatly or produced using a word processor**
Your own address goes in the top right corner of the page followed by the date. The name and address of the newspaper appears below, left.

sarcasm: a sneering attitude

Figure 4–7 It is much easier for the newspaper editor to read your letter if it is neatly printed or produced using a word processor.

NOW YOU DO IT

1. Write a letter to the editor in response to a recent story about the Middle East. Begin by creating the three sections noted above: the introduction, the main section, and the summary.

2. Check your letter for any necessary changes or additions. Review the guidelines during the checking process.

3. Give your letter to a classmate for a "trial read" and offer to read his or her letter. Raise any outstanding issues.

4. Print your final draft and mail or fax your letter. Post the printed and published letters on your class bulletin board.

THE GEOGRAPHY OF THE MIDDLE EAST

The Middle East covers a great deal of territory. Saudi Arabia, for example, with an area of 2 149 690 square kilometres, is over twice the size of British Columbia (948 601 square kilometres). The Red Sea is almost as wide as Vancouver Island is long (approximately 400 kilometres and 450 kilometres respectively). British Columbia's longest river, the Peace, at 1923 kilometres, is less than one third as long as the Nile, at 6671 kilometres.

As you might expect with such a large area, the Middle East has many different landforms. Most of Saudi Arabia is on a large **desert** plateau that tilts from northeast to southwest. Very high mountains are found in Turkey, Iran, and northern Iraq. In fact, many parts of the Middle East are mountainous or rugged.

Much of the Middle East is dry and desert-like. Even the wettest areas, along the Mediterranean coast, receive just 200 millimetres of precipitation a year. The average July temperature is 30°C. The average winter temperature is 16°C. This means that areas with water, such as **oases**, have always been important. Villages and towns were often located near an oasis. People also settled along the Nile, Tigris, Euphrates, and other rivers. Because the soil in many places is very fertile, and the growing season has always been long, agriculture has always been important in areas where water exists.

Many crops can be grown in the Middle East. Oranges originated there (the name comes from the Arabic word *naranj*). Dates, figs, and olives are still important crops. Even in Roman times the Nile valley was the breadbasket of the Mediterranean world. Today, wheat is a major crop in the irrigated areas along the major rivers. Other grains are also grown. Many kinds of vegetables grow in the Middle East and provide much of the daily diet of local people.

The Middle East is

desert: a dry region supporting very little vegetation or none at all

oasis: a green area in a desert region

Figure 4–8 The varied regions of the Middle East are shown here. Top, a typical oasis town. Left, the Atlas Mountains.

Semitic: an ancient people that includes the Jewish people, Arabs, Assyrians, and Phoenicians

herder: one who moves a group of animals kept together for travelling and feeding

nomad: a person who has no fixed home but moves about from place to place with the seasons

domestication: the taming of an animal for human needs, e.g., travel

caravan: a group of travellers who band together for safety while crossing the desert

Figure 4–9 Today, the Bedouin dress much as they have for centuries, while Arab city dwellers observe a variety of traditions and styles. Why do you think that the Bedouin would be less likely to change?

one area of the world where geography has had an important effect on history. Large areas of mountain and desert are very sparsely inhabited. All the major towns and cities of the Middle East are located near water. Historically, this has had an important impact on trade and even the spread of religion. When Islam expanded, it leapt across great distances and established itself in one city and town after another. In this way, many people heard about the new religion in a short space of time.

THE ARABS

Islam was first revealed in Arabia, the homeland of the Arabs. The Arabs are a **Semitic** people who occupy Arabia and other parts of the Middle East. For centuries—as far back as 1000 B.C.E.—many Arabs have lived as **herders** and **nomads**, known as Bedouin, in the vast desert lands. Other Arabs settled

villages and towns around oases and other water sources. The two groups led very different lives, but some people moved their homes from desert to town and back again, depending on the circumstances.

For both groups, trade was important from the earliest days. By 500 C.E., Arabia was situated at the crossroads of two international trade routes—from the Indian Ocean to the Mediterranean Sea, and from Africa, south of the Sahara Desert, to the Mediterranean.

Trade had been made easier with the **domestication** of the camel because it made long-distance journeys possible. **Caravans** of travellers and merchants moved across the desert from one town to another, carrying expensive goods from distant corners of the world. Sometimes caravans were raided by the desert Arabs, who forced the merchants to pay money and establish **treaties** with them. But for

the most part, caravan travellers and the Bedouin respected each other.

From earliest times, Arabs belonged to **clans**. In the desert, where the Bedouin lived, clans were led by chiefs who prided themselves in their generosity, bravery, and fighting ability. Such virtues were much admired. Even in towns, membership in a clan was very important. It gave the person an identity and "connections" to help them through life. When a clan member was attacked, the clan sought revenge by raiding communities of the clan of the attacker. A council of clan chiefs led the local government and met regularly to discuss important issues.

Before the establishment of Islam, many Arabs were **pagans**. They worshipped many different gods and goddesses who were believed to live in various locations. These locations attracted religious pilgrims and worshippers. Some of the most important pagan shrines were in the city of Mecca. There was also a widespread belief in magic, and most people were deeply superstitious. In addition, Arabia was home to many communities of Jews, and some Christians.

treaty: an agreement reached by negotiation between two or more parties

clan: a group of people who are descended from the same distant ancestor

pagan: one who worships many gods and goddesses

Figure 4–10 Islam developed in the oasis towns and cities of Arabia, similar to this one.

ACTIVITIES

1. **a)** On an outline map of the Middle East supplied by your teacher, add the following features and label them:
    - main desert areas
    - main mountain ranges
    - the Mediterranean Sea, the Red Sea, and the Persian Gulf
    - major rivers
    - major cities

    b) How do you think the geography of the Middle East has affected human activities in the region?

2. Which areas in the Middle East seem to be the most heavily populated? Explain why this is so.

3. Create an organizer for the following countries: Egypt, Iraq, Iran, and Saudi Arabia. Find out more information about these modern nations using these headings and any other headings you think are important:
    - style of government
    - important water source(s)
    - industries and occupations
    - major cities
    - major religion(s)
    - climate

4. Using an atlas and tracing paper, trace the area of North Africa and the Middle East above and below the curved line of the thirty-first parallel. (For more information on latitude and longitude, see page 253.)

5. Describe Arab society around 500 C.E. What were the two main groups?

6. Find out more about the contributions of Arab society to Canadian society, for example, in commerce, science, or the arts. Create a list illustrated with pictures cut out from magazines or newspapers and mount it on your class bulletin board.

THE FOUNDATIONS OF ISLAM

When Muhammad, the **apostle** of God, reached the age of forty, God sent him in compassion to humankind, "as an **evangelist** to all men" (Qur'ân XXXIV: 27). Now God made a **covenant** with every prophet whom he had sent before him that he should believe in him, testify to his truth and help him against his adversaries, and he required of them that they should transmit to everyone who believed in them, and they carried out their obligations in that respect. God said to Muhammad: "Do you accept this and take up my burden?"

apostle: a person sent on a special mission

evangelist: a bearer of news, a messenger

convert: one who changes from one religious belief to another

prophet: a person who speaks with divine inspiration

convenant: bargain

revelation: what is revealed

parable: a story that has a moral lesson

Islam was revealed to the **prophet** Muhammad in the seventh century. Muhammad was born in Mecca, a great trading city, around 570 C.E. His relatives were business people and traders, and members of an important clan. He was orphaned by the time he was six, and cared for by his grandfather and uncle. The family was poor. As a young man, Muhammad married the widow Khadijah and joined her in business. He became a skilled trader and manager.

In the year 610, Muhammad retreated to a cave near Mecca where he could meditate and pray. As he meditated, he received a powerful **revelation** from God through the angel Gabriel. Muhammad received many important revelations from God, which give guidance in many areas. These are recorded in the Qur'ân (Koran), the Muslim Holy Book. They describe God's powers and expectations, the Day of Judgment, and other matters.

The new religion revealed to Muhammad was called Islam, meaning "submission to the will of God." The followers of Islam were known as Muslims, meaning "they who submit." Muhammad knew that the idea of one God, Allah, would not be popular in the pagan city of Mecca, where many gods were worshipped. Although he made some **converts**, city leaders and others soon began to persecute Muslims, who fled to the city of Medina. Muslims call this migration the *Hijrah*. It marks the beginning of the Islamic calendar Later, the two cities fought, and the Muslims defeated the forces of Mecca.

THE QUR'ÂN: TRADITION AND LAW

Muslims accept the Qur'ân as the word of God as given to Muhammad by the angel Gabriel. Because it is believed to contain God's actual words, in Arabic, the Qur'ân cannot be changed. Every letter is sacred. The Qur'ân has 114 chapters, 6236 verses, and 77 934 words. In addition to its description of a powerful and merciful God, it includes commandments and **parables**. In many ways, it is similar to the Old and New Testaments of Judaism and Christianity. Moses and Jesus are accepted as prophets by Muslims.

In addition to the Qur'ân, Muslims turn to other sources for spiritual and social guidance. One such guide, the *hadith*, is based on what Muhammad said and did during his lifetime. Since Muhammad lived a model life, his sayings and deeds were recorded as the hadith. The hadith shows believers how a proper servant of God should live and behave (although not all of the hadith is accepted by all Muslims). Islamic law, called the *sharia*, is based on the Qur'ân and the hadith. Muslim scholars taught that religious beliefs, religious duties, and good works were the important elements of Islam.

THE FIVE PILLARS

Islam has Five Pillars of faith. These are the duties that Muslims must follow. The first Pillar requires that a person openly declare his or her faith by repeating the phrase "There is no God but God and he has no partners." Uttering this statement sincerely makes a person a Muslim.

The second Pillar requires that Muslims pray often to Allah, or God. Customarily, this includes five periods of prayer each day, preferably with other Muslims. Those at prayer always face the holy city of Mecca. Prayers take place at dawn, noon, the middle of the afternoon, sunset, and nightfall. Before prayer, Muslims purify themselves—by washing their hands, face, and feet, and by clearing the mind of impure thoughts.

The third Pillar of Islam is charity. Muslims are required to give to the poor. To this day, Muslims consider charity to be good for a person's soul.

The fourth Pillar is **fasting**. Muslims must fast during the daylight hours of the month of

Figure 4–11 This wall painting of the Kaaba indicates that the occupant of the house has made a journey to Mecca. The Kaaba is one of the holiest places in Islam. Muslims believe that Abraham built the Kaaba.

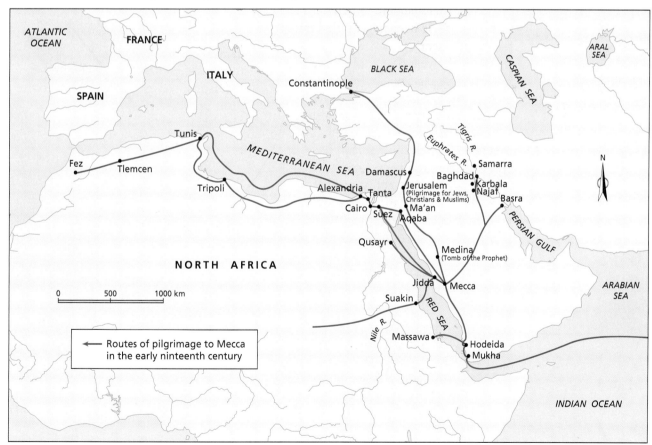

Figure 4–12 Muslim pilgrims, like those of other religions, travelled to important Islamic shrines. The most important pilgrimage was the *hadj* to Mecca, one of the requirements of Islam and the fifth of the Five Pillars. Locate Mecca on this map.

fasting: refusing food for spiritual or religious reasons

pilgrimage: a journey to a sacred place as an act of devotion

ritual: a practice that is performed many times in an established manner

mosque: a Muslim place of worship

to prostrate: to lie face-down

Ramadan (the ninth lunar month)—in other words, from the first light of dawn until nightfall.

Finally, Muslims are expected to undertake a **pilgrimage** to Mecca, known as the *hadj*, at least once in their lifetime. Some Muslims try to make the pilgrimage every year. During the hadj, all Muslims dress alike, eat the same foods, and perform the same **rituals**.

The five Pillars of Islam are considered important for the soul but they also serve other purposes. The public prayer held on Friday at noon brings the Muslim community together, and is an occasion for sermons on religion, society, and politics. The third Pillar, charity, makes Muslims aware of the importance of looking after everyone, no matter what their circumstances. The hadj helps Muslims feel that they belong to a single world religion, and reminds all Muslims that they are equal in the sight of God. Over the centuries, the commitment to practise the five Pillars has made Muslims strong.

Figure 4–13 Daily prayer is important to Muslims, and is the requirement of the second Pillar of Islam. These Canadian Muslims pray in unison, facing Mecca, as tradition requires.

Figure 4–14 The **mosque** is a place for prayer. Because many mosques are built to house large numbers of people, the central prayer hall is spacious and uncluttered. There are no pews or chairs because the faithful bow and **prostrate** themselves in the sight of God. One wall has a mark to show the direction of Mecca. The mosque also has minarets—tall, slender towers. Muslims are called to prayer from these minarets.

1. Describe the main events in the life of Muhammad in **chronological order**. You can make a series of point-form statements, or you can create a paragraph.

2. Compare the lives of Jesus and Muhammad using an organizer with headings of your choice. Some possibilities:
   ◆ early life
   ◆ main message

   Add at least two more headings.

3. Choose one of the five Pillars of Islam and explain in a paragraph how it helps bring the Muslim community together.

4. Find out more information about the holy days of Ramadan, Yom Kippur, and Lent. To which religious faiths do these days belong? Why are these days holy? Compare the rituals observed during these days. How are they similar? How are they different?

THE SPREAD OF ISLAM

Many Arabs were inspired by Muhammad and believed that spreading the new religion was a sacred duty. Arabs who converted and became Muslims were treated well. Those who resisted were destroyed or enslaved. Christians and Jews were allowed to practise their respective religions because they were "peoples of the Book" (the "book" includes the Torah and the New Testament). However, they were not allowed to spread their faith and they paid special taxes.

Muhammad died in 632 and was succeeded by Abu Bakr, one of his first converts. The new **caliph** continued to spread the Islamic faith across Arabia. The campaign was continued by caliphs who came after Abu Bakr. With skilled commanders and devoted troops, Islamic armies swept all opponents before them. By 647, they had conquered Iraq, Palestine, Syria, Egypt, and Iran. Two years later, they reached what is now Pakistan.

The wealth of the empire accumulated with each conquest. When the armies seized Ctesiphon, the capital city of what was then known as Persia, every soldier received 12 000 pieces of silver. In addition, thousands of slaves—residents of the conquered cities—were captured and sold in the marketplace. Slavery was not a Muslim tradition but an Arab one.

DIVISION AND RIVALRY

Because the armies were so successful, and because the Arab Empire grew so quickly, Islamic leaders soon faced the enormous task of administration. There was also the question of leadership. The caliph was considered to be the Head of the Faith, but also commander of the army and the chief lawmaker and judge. Because Muhammad did not have a son to succeed him, many Muslims could not agree on who should have this important position. Many thought that Ali, the husband of Muhammad's daughter Fatimah,

chronological order: arranged from oldest to most recent

caliph: an Arab word meaning "successor"

should be caliph. They thought that the leadership should stay within the family of the prophet. This dispute resulted in warfare between Ali and his supporters on one side, and a group that included the Umayyad family and Muhammad's wife, Aishah, on the other.

Ali resisted his enemies at the Battle of the Camel in the year 656—so named because Aishah commanded her soldiers while mounted on a camel. Ali was **assassinated** in 661, and the Umayyad family of Damascus took control. The problem of the leadership of Islam resulted in a major division in the Islamic world between the Shi'i (Shia), the supporters of Ali, and the Sunni, the supporters of Aishah and the Umayyad family. This political division remains to this day.

to assassinate: to kill for political reasons

siege: a prolonged period of attack

medium: a material or technique used for the expression of art

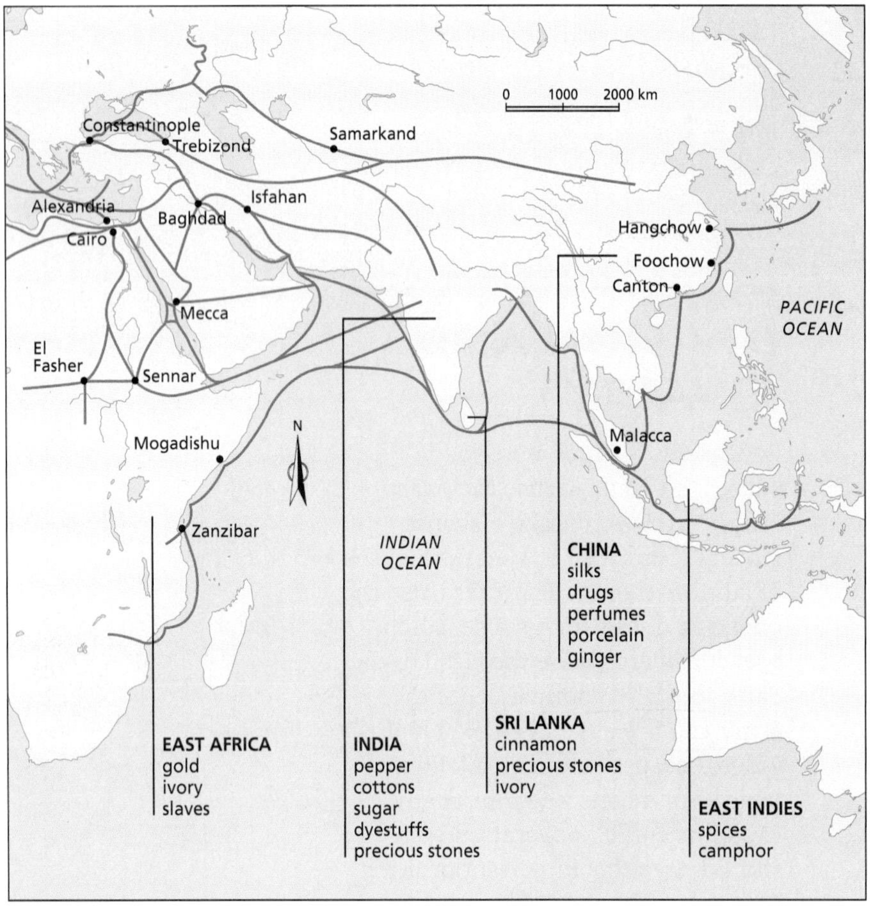

Figure 4–15 The expansion of Islam through Africa, Asia, and the Indian Ocean followed trade routes that had been in existence for more than a thousand years.

THE UMAYYADS AND THE EXTENSION OF EMPIRE

The Umayyads moved the capital of the Islamic Arab Empire to the city of Damascus, in Syria, in 661. There they built a court of great splendour. It rivalled the court at Byzantium, the Eastern Christian Empire, which you read about in Chapter 1.

But war was still going on for control of the Arab Empire. Mecca was often under **siege**, and leaders and challengers were being deposed or assassinated with regularity. Ali's son, Hussein, was ambushed and killed at Kerbala when he tried to challenge the caliphate. Finally, Abd-al-Malik seized the throne and put down all opposition. In the years that followed, the Islamic armies were well organized and determined to spread the faith. They continued to reach out across Asia and North Africa. In 711, they crossed the Strait of Gibraltar and entered Spain. The Arab Empire was growing larger, richer, and more complex every year.

TRADERS AND TRADE ROUTES

The Islamic Arab Empire grew along roads, sea routes, and other trade routes, most of which had been in existence for centuries. As you read on page 114, trade had always been important in the Arab world. The conquest of so much territory encouraged even more trade. It was one reason why the successive Arab empires endured.

Using A Photograph as a Primary Source

At this point in your life you have probably taken many photographs—of your family members, friends, pets, and favourite places. Have you ever wondered what your photographs say to people?

A successful photograph is one that speaks visually to the viewer, much as a painting does, but through a different **medium**. Paintings are created with paint, brushes, and a surface. Photographs are created with light, a camera lens, and a roll of film.

Photographs have certain advantages over paintings for some types of historical research. A photograph is a fairly accurate depiction of what exists. There is a famous saying that "Photographs don't lie."

Figure 4–16 is a photograph of a famous Islamic site in Spain, built after the Arabs arrived there at the beginning of the eighth century. Study the photograph for a few minutes before you proceed to the section below.

WHAT DO YOU THINK?

1. Using this photograph as your only guide, try to answer these questions. You can check your answers against the historical information, which appears upside down.

   ◆ What is depicted?

   ◆ Do you think it took a long time to create? Why or why not?

   ◆ Can you guess at some of the materials used? What are they? What do these materials say about the builders? What do they say about the environment?

   ◆ What features are shown close up? Describe them.

   ◆ What features are shown in the distance? Describe them.

   ◆ Would this photograph be as useful to the historian if it were taken at dusk? Why or why not?

Figure 4–16 What is it?

Answer

Shown is the Alhambra, an Islamic palace in Granada, Spain. Construction began in 1248 and ended in 1354, so it took over one hundred years to build. The walls are made of plaster and painted with intricate designs. The floors are made of marble. In the courtyard, there are trees and flowers (not visible), and fountains. The kings of Granada were wealthy and wanted to display their wealth and might. Shown close up is the famous Court of the Lions. The basin is made of alabaster and the lions are made of marble. Shown at a distance are the outer walls made of sun-dried bricks that contain a type of clay found only in dry, sunny regions. This photograph is most useful because it was taken in daylight, so that all the features can be viewed clearly.

The economies of many locations benefited from the stability and connections provided by Islam. Eventually, the Arab Islamic world became one of the largest economic trade zones in the world. For example, Ibn Battuta, the great traveller and explorer about whom you will read in more detail in Chapter 12, was able to travel safely from Tunis to the Pacific Ocean. He travelled an estimated 120 000 kilometres from his home in Tangier, visiting Zanzibar, India, and Indonesia, among other places. Everywhere he went, he found fellow Muslims.

THE ABBÂSIDS, 750 — 1258

secular: related to the world, not God

token: a symbol of affection

bureaucracy: civil service, government employees

Muslims accept the four caliphs after Muhammad as spiritual heads of their faith. After this time, the title of "caliph" became **secular** and the caliphs did not necessarily rule according to Islamic teachings. This was the case with the Abbâsid caliphs.

Abu'l-Abbas became caliph when the power of the Umayyads declined, after the last family member was killed in battle. In 762, the second Abbâsid caliph moved the Arab capital once again—this time to Baghdad. The power of the caliphs grew ever greater.

The Abbâsid caliphs dressed in the finest clothes, adorned themselves with beautiful jewels, and surrounded themselves with armoured soldiers and learned advisors. Fabulous palaces surrounded by gardens housed the ruler and his wives and attendants. The glory of the Abbâsid court was renowned even in distant parts of Europe and Asia. The European ruler Charlemagne wrote to Harun al-Rashid, the most famous of the Abbâsid caliphs, who sent several elephants as a **token** of friendship. In the excerpt at left, an Arab historian describes one of the ceremonial palace rooms,

There is a tree standing in the midst of a great circular tank filled with clear water. The tree has eighteen branches, each branch having numerous twigs, on which sit all sorts of gold and silver birds, both large and small. Most of the branches of this tree are of silver but some are of gold, and they spread into the air carrying leaves of different colours. The leaves of the tree move as the wind blows, while the birds pipe and sing.

the Room of the Tree, in the year 917. The historian also describes the caliph, as below.

He was arrayed in clothes … embroidered in gold being seated on an ebony throne … To the right of the throne hung nine collars of gems … and to the left were the like, all of famous jewels …. Before the caliph stood five of his sons, three to the right and two to the left.

Such magnificence was designed to impress the people the caliph ruled, and foreign visitors. The money to support the court and its **bureaucracy** came from trade and commerce, and from taxes paid by ordinary people. Christians and Jews paid extra taxes based on their personal wealth. Because the empire was expanding, booty and slaves taken from captured lands were plentiful.

The Abbâsids were always either at war or getting ready for war. Unlike the first caliphs, they used the spread of Islam as an excuse to wage war. They divided the world into two: the land of Islam and the land of War. Their greatest enemy was the Byzantine Empire, and there were many conflicts between the two great powers.

1. Examine Figure 4–1 and review pages 119–22. Give three reasons why Islam spread so quickly. One of your reasons should be geographic, one military, and one religious.

2. What was the cause of the first great split in the forces of Islam? Describe this conflict.

3. In what ways did the spread of Islam help the economies of conquered territories?

4. List the most impressive features of Umayyad and Abbâsid society.

5. Write a letter from Charlemagne to Harun al-Rashid, thanking the caliph for the gift of elephants.

LIFE AND SOCIETY

In the eighth century, the Islamic world soon included people from many cultures, each with their own customs and traditions. So long as these did not conflict with the teachings and customs of Islam, they were allowed to continue.

But Islam did have a powerful influence. Music, art, and architecture were changed by Islamic values. For example, it was considered sinful to show human beings, animals, and other subjects realistically. Often, Islamic artists created works of art using designs and written script. This resulted in beautifully patterned objects, from tiles to carpets. At various times this restriction was overlooked, and people and animals were shown, as they were by the Mughals of India, for example.

The City

Many of the cities in the Arab Empire had been founded centuries before the coming of Muhammad. They occupied key locations on trade routes and in prime agricultural areas near ample supplies of water. The greatest of these cities, Damascus and Baghdad, had large populations that included Jews and Christians.

By the eleventh century, Baghdad had almost a million inhabitants. The Muslim city of Cordoba in far-off Spain had 400 000 inhabitants in the tenth century, with 700 mosques and 300 public baths. Compare this with medieval London, which had 50 000 inhabitants—most of whom had barely heard of bathing, let alone public baths! Mosques, libraries, and universities were built, and became renowned centres of learning. In fact, larger mosques were always focal points in the cities. They always attracted large congregations, and were surrounded by courts and other buildings.

Many cities were surrounded by walls for protection. Poor people were usually forced to live near the walls, or even outside the city. Richer people built palaces and fine houses with gardens. These were located on shaded streets near the central marketplace, or *suq*, or close to the royal palace. Workshops—tanneries, silversmithes, and wood shops—were located near the marketplace but away from the richer residential districts so that noises and smells would not bother the inhabitants. Cities bustled with activity. The government even provided temporary accommodations where traders could stay and display their wares.

In the cities, Arab scholars discussed and studied medicine and science. They also translated the books and essays of the ancient Greeks, whose reasoning skills they admired. Scholars in the Islamic world knew much more about natural science than Europeans did. They

DID YOU KNOW?

Showing people or objects in art is banned by Islam. This law does not come from the Qur'ân, but from the hadith. Muhammad stated that, "The angels will not enter a house in which there is a picture or a dog." Islamic art uses various shapes in decoration. Inscriptions, written in praise of Allah, and verses from the Qur'ân, are also used.

Figure 4-17 The original city plan of Baghdad. The city was founded in 762 and was imagined to be the centre of the Islamic Empire—and the universe. In the outer ring were houses and shops protected by heavy walls. Inside the city were moats and bridges that led to other areas of town. In the heart of the city lay the palace and mosque. Baghdad grew so quickly that it remained in this shape for only a few years. Why do you think the city planners would choose a circle as an ideal shape?

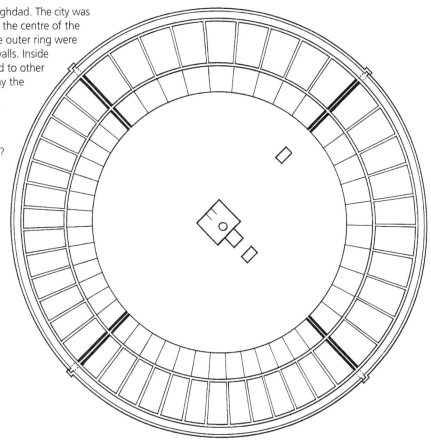

anesthesia: whole or partial loss of feeling of pain or touch

barbaric: uncivilized

DID YOU KNOW?

Two Arab astronomers consulted the heavens to recommend the best time for laying the foundation of Baghdad.

Figure 4–18 Ibn Sina (Avicenna) surrounded by his medical students

preserved and used the ancient learning of the classical world, which was later rediscovered by medieval Europeans in Arabic books.

One of the most famous Arab scholars was Ibn Sina, or Avicenna. He was a physician, philosopher, astronomer, and poet. His most famous work, *Canon of Medicine*, was used as a medical text for 600 years after his death. Today, the Canon is still used in some parts of Asia. Avicenna was one of the first physicians in the world to describe **anesthesia**—a standard practice of modern medicine.

Arab rulers and rich merchants supported the arts. Compared with European society in the eighth century, Arab civilization was refined and wealthy. Later, during the Crusades, rough European knights came into contact with the splendour of the Arab world, and were awed and changed by it. They saw the silks, fine glassware, paper, jewellery, carpets, perfumed soaps, brass, silver, and gold and wanted these treasures. To the refined merchants and princes of the Islamic world, the Europeans seemed utterly uncivilized.

Arab Poetry

Poets were one group of artists who were honoured in Arab society from early times—as early as the fourth century. Even caliphs wrote poetry. The Umayyad Walid I, for example, wrote poetry and music regularly, and supported other poets with rich gifts. Many rulers in the Arab world associated with poets to enhance their own reputations.

Arabic is considered to be a highly poetic language. Some people say this is because it is rich in meaning—it is possible to have many different **interpretations** of one word in Arabic.

One person who did not approve of poetry was Muhammad.

Under his influence, poetry fell into some decline and was replaced by the Qur'ân as the proper object of study. But the love of poetry never completely died out in the Arab world.

This Arabic verse describes the city of Baghdad. What picture do you have in your head after reading these lines? What are the main sounds and colours?

interpretation: personal understanding of meaning

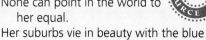

Blessed be the site of Baghdad,
   seat of learning and art,
None can point in the world to
   her equal.
Her suburbs vie in beauty with the blue
   vault of the sky,
Her climate rivals the life-giving breezes of
   heaven,
Her stones in their brightness rival
   diamonds and rubies.

The banks of the Tigris with their lovely
   damsels surpass Kullakh,
The gardens filled with lovely nymphs
   equal Kashmir,
And thousands of gondolas on the water
Dance and sparkle like sunbeams in the air.

The Countryside

Arab cities in the 700s were very **cosmopolitan**. In the countryside, however, life followed ancient patterns. Throughout most of the empire, people lived with their extended family. They had traditional rights to pasture their flocks, grow dates and other crops, and use the wells. In many areas, the right to obtain water from certain wells was held by a clan. Most people lived in flat-roofed houses of plastered mud brick. People spent warm evenings on the roof. Men, not women, owned almost all the property.

Village life was slow-moving and regular. As in the cities, people ate relatively simple foods: bread, dates, goat or sheep meat, fish (where available), onions, garlic, fruit, and vegetables. Most people concerned themselves only with what happened with the neighbours, and didn't think too much about what happened in the rest of the world.

Figure 4–19 Water wheels in Syria. Water wheels were developed in the Arab world, and were used to bring water to irrigation channels. This technology was copied in the West after the Crusades.

THE STATUS OF WOMEN

Women did not have the rights that men had in Abbâsid society, but this was not supported by Islam. Muhammad's wife had been a business woman, and women during

cosmopolitan: worldly, sophisticated

harem: a special place for women in a Muslim home where men were not allowed

the time of Muhammad prayed, taught, worked—and even went to war with men. Abbâsid women, in contrast, had few rights and could not take part in government. Nonetheless they were economically important, particularly if they belonged to the

working class and contibuted through labour. But if a woman was a member of a wealthy family, or married a wealthy man, she lived in a **harem**. This was a special part of the house where males, other than the husband and young boys, were forbidden.

VIEWPOINTS IN CONFLICT

The Status of Women

Ibn al-Hajj and Jâhiz, two Arab writers, were born almost seven centuries apart. In the excerpts that follow they express two different views on the status of women.

In this excerpt (at right), Ibn al-Hajj, who lived in the fourteenth century, seems to agree with the church elders on the subject of women's freedom.

> Some of the **pious** elders (may God be pleased with them) have said that a woman should leave her house on three occasions only: when she is conducted to the house of her bridegroom, on the deaths of her parents, and when she goes to her own grave.
>
> PRIMARY SOURCE

In this excerpt (at right), Jâhiz, born in Persia in 776, writes about the "superiority of women."

pious: religious

emancipate: free

to expostulate: to reason earnestly

> Women are superior to men in certain respects: it is they who are asked in marriage, desired, loved and courted, and they that inspire self-sacrifice and require protection. An indication of the high esteem in which women are held is that if a man is asked to swear by God—there is none greater—and take his solemn oath to go to the House of God, or distribute his possessions as alms, or **emancipate** his slaves, all that comes easily to him…. But let him be asked to swear to put away [to give up] his wife, and he grows pale, is overcome with rage, protests, **expostulates**, gets angry and refuses…. All this is the result of the place God has given wives in their husbands' hearts…. God created a child out of a woman without the help of any man, but he has never created a child out of a man without a woman. Thus it is specially to woman and not to man that He gave this wonderful sign, this signal token, when He created the Messiah in Mary's bosom, without a man.
>
> PRIMARY SOURCE

WHAT DO YOU THINK?

1. According to Ibn al-Hajj, the elders said a woman could leave her home on only three occasions. What are they? Why are these occasions important?

2. Do you think Ibn al-Hajj accepts the opinion of the elders about the place of women in society? Why or why not?

3. In what way do the views of the pious elders and those of Jâhiz seem to contradict each other? In what ways are their views similar?

Women covered themselves to go outdoors, and were always accompanied by a male guardian.

Divorce was easy for a man in Abbâsid society. By stating in front of witnesses that he divorced his wife, the divorce was finalized. For a woman, divorce was more difficult. A **justice** had to agree, and the wife had to have a very good reason—that the husband was suffering from mental illness, for example. A man could have up to four wives (provided he could treat them equally), but a woman could have only one husband. This custom arose because if a woman had more than one husband, it would be difficult to know who had fathered the children. Today, many Muslims are concerned that **polygamy** has been associated with their faith, when it was simply a cultural fact of the Arab world.

■ ■ ■ ■ ■ ■ ■ ■ ■ ■ ■ ■ ■

GOVERNMENT

By the end of the eighth century, the

Figure 4–20 These women have chosen to cover themselves completely, in keeping with a strict interpretation of the *sharia*, the law code of Islam.

supreme leader of the Islamic world was still the caliph. In theory, he had absolute power over everyone. But governing was still difficult. There were many Muslims who did not accept the Umayyad and Abbâsid caliphs. Shi'i Muslims believed that the descendants of Ali should rule because they were the true interpreters of the will of God. Rival families and **factions** also challenged the rule of the caliph. Assassinations and rebellions were not uncommon. Caliphs tended to show little mercy towards their enemies, usually executing captured rivals in the most horrific ways possible as an example to others.

Government was orderly but complex. Every district had a governor, and every city and town had a council. The prime minister, or wazir, was in charge of all the officials of the empire. Like other officials, the wazir was usually a civil servant who had been trained since childhood in the ways of government. Justice was put into force by officials appointed to know and administer the law.

justice: a judge

polygamy: a practice of one person having several marriage partners

faction: political subgroup

The caliph was personally advised by the *ulama*—the learned, pious men who studied and applied the teachings of the Qur'ân. No caliph could rule effectively without the support of the ulama.

The Islamic Arab Empire, which stretched across the Middle East, North Africa, and Spain, eventually became too large for the caliph to control by himself. The distances were simply too great to permit communication. By the ninth century, local rulers across the empire had become sufficiently powerful to defy the caliph. Separate kingdoms were established in Spain, Morocco, and the eastern provinces. These states were sometimes attacked by the forces of the caliph.

Caliphs often used Turkish, African, and European slave soldiers in their armies because they could not depend on the loyalty of their own troops. Converted to Islam, and trained from a young age to serve the ruler, these slaves rose to high positions, eventually seizing control from their masters. In time, the old ruling families were swept aside by the Turkish forces, who set up their own government. It was the Turks who fought the European Crusaders in the religious wars which shook the Middle East beginning in the eleventh century.

Figure 4-21 The Islamic world during the First Crusade

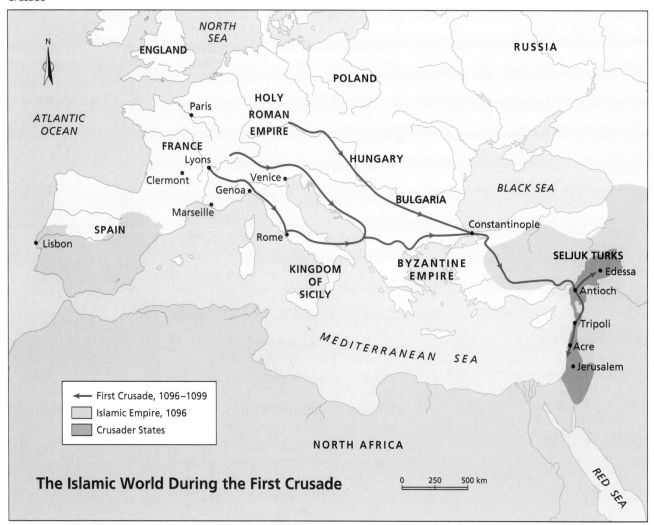

The Islamic World During the First Crusade

1. With a partner create a series of fictional postcards between a resident of a major Islamic city and a villager around 750. Use as many postcards as you need to describe your typical day. You could ask your correspondent about his or her life. Remember that the life of a woman would be quite different from that of a man. On the "picture" side of the card, illustrate with scenes from each location.

2. Find examples of Muslim art by reviewing this chapter. Now examine Figure 1–9, an example of Byzantine art. What is the main difference? What is the reason for this difference?

3. In the encyclopedia, look up some of the world's most famous mosques. Were they all built by Muslims? Find out why or why not.

4. With a partner, create a visual display to illustrate the levels and branches of government in the Abbâsid Empire. Your chart could take the form of a flow chart. You will find an example of a flow chart on page 406.

ISLAM AND THE WEST

The rapid growth of Islam, through conversion, conquest, and trade, brought the new religion to the doors of Europe. The once mighty Eastern Roman Empire, also called the Byzantine Empire, was attacked and lost territory to the Arabs. In the West, the Christian Goths were defeated by the Arabs in Spain. Islamic armies marched far into Europe, finally meeting defeat in France at the Battle of Tours in 732. Afterwards, the forces of the two militant religions were seldom at peace.

THE SELJUKS

The Seljuks were Turkish nomads from central Asia. Renowned warriors, they had been used by the caliphs in Muslim armies, where their skill with powerful **recurved bows** had made them formidable fighters. In the tenth century, they crossed into Anatolia (modern Turkey) and attacked the Byzantines. Next, they sent armed soldiers into Syria and Iraq.

Soon the Seljuks controlled most of the Middle East. The Byzantine army, attacking from the west, was completely destroyed by the Seljuks at the battle of Manzikert in 1071, and the Roman emperor was taken prisoner. By the time the Crusades began, the Turkish ruler, the **sultan**, controlled much of the Muslim world.

THE BYZANTINE EMPIRE

The Western Roman Empire had collapsed in the fifth century, but the Eastern Roman, or Byzantine, Empire lasted until Constantinople fell to the Turks in 1453. Constantinople was a mighty city surrounded by **impregnable** walls. It was strategically situated on the Bosporus, the strait that separates Europe from Asia. Its 1 million inhabitants obtained their food and necessities

recurved bows: a bow that is bent backward

sultan: from al-sultan, Turkish for ruler

impregnable: impenetrable, extremely difficult to attack

from Turkey and Palestine.

The Byzantines were great traders. They filled their markets with the produce of the world: silks from China, **amber** from the Baltic, dates, wheat, and glass from Egypt. To the people of northern Europe, Constantinople was the world's greatest city. Perhaps the Byzantine soldiers were not as aggressive as the Muslim armies, but they were well trained in defence. To the Muslims, Constantinople was a rich prize—not only because of its wealth but because it was the main city of Christendom, and Christians were now considered the **infidels**.

To Christians, the Byzantine emperor was the guardian of the Holy Places of Palestine—the sites of Christ's birth and burial, and Jerusalem, the Holy City. But these sites, particularly Jerusalem, were also important to the warriors of Islam. The Dome of the Rock, for example, had been built by Muslims in Jerusalem in the seventh century. When the Byzantine emperor was defeated by the Turks at the Battle of Manzikert in 1071, western European Christians rallied to fight Muslims over control of the Holy Land. These religious wars, which began in 1097, are known as the Crusades.

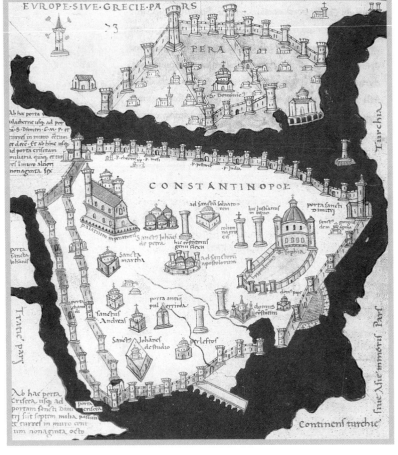

Figure 4–22 This is a sixteenth-century copy of an old map of Constantinople.

ACTIVITIES

1. How did Islam come into conflict with the Byzantine Empire and other parts of Europe?

2. Who were the Seljuks? Name three reasons why they were successful conquerors.

3. Name one natural and one human-made defence system that allowed Constantinople to defend itself so well. Identify these on Figure 4–22.

Islam is one of the world's great religions. It fostered a wonderful civilization within a short space of time. Within a few hundred years, and in spite of civil wars, assassinations, and rebellions, Muslims ruled from Spain to India. Wherever the warriors and traders of Islam travelled, Arabic and Arab values were introduced to local populations who, in turn, added their own customs and ways. Arabs (and others) could travel literally thousands of kilometres within lands controlled by Islam and Islamic law.

During the European Middle Ages, Islamic cities were splendid, both admired and envied by Christian nobles and monarchs. They were great capitals of learning and commerce. The trade of both east and west passed through the Middle East, making all parties richer.

Islam is still a major force in the world today. Millions of people all over the world are practising Muslims—a living legacy of more than 1400 years of history.

SUMMARY ACTIVITIES

1. Did you know that paleontologists believe the camel actually originated in North America and then migrated to Asia? Find out more about the camel, and why it is so well-suited to desert and caravan life.

2. Create a geometric design similar to those found in this chapter and use it to illustrate the cover of a notebook.

3. Interview a member of the Muslim community, and prepare a report on how a Canadian Muslim lives his or her faith.

4. Collect reports of current and recent events involving Muslims from newspapers, magazines and other sources. From these reports, what main issues do you think are of concern to Muslim communities in different parts of the world?

5. In a small group, prepare two posters that describe and compare a mosque, a synagogue, and a cathedral. Highlight any differences and similarities. You could use pictures of actual buildings in your town or city for some of your examples.

ON YOUR OWN

1. Research and prepare a meal based on two or more of these Middle Eastern dishes. You will have to do a little research to discover what you will be eating!
   ◆ hommous
   ◆ falafel
   ◆ tabouli
   ◆ fattoush
   ◆ fried kebbeh
   ◆ baba ghannouj
   ◆ grape leaves
   ◆ yogurt salad (yogurt, cucumber, garlic, and mint)
   ◆ shish kabob
   ◆ katayef
   ◆ baklawa

UNIT 2
MEDIEVAL PERSPECTIVES, 1100–1400

Over time, civilizations evolve. Although civilizations do not evolve in the same way, they all grow, flourish, and decline. Most civilizations go through the cycle of growth and decline at different times.

In Unit 2, we investigate a remarkable exception to this rule. About a thousand years ago, two civilizations, Europe and Japan, went through a similar period at about the same time. Japan and Europe had virtually no contact during this period. Nonetheless, both societies functioned as feudal societies. The land was controlled by the nobles while the vast majority of people toiled as peasants on the land. In both societies, a system of military loyalty, honour, and obligation kept the land—and power—in the hands of the few. The most powerful nobles, barons in Europe and shoguns in Japan, maintained their power by means of castles and warriors. In Europe these warriors were called "knights" while in Japan they were called "samurai." In both societies, a few people enjoyed the finer things in life while everyone else enjoyed few rights and lived short, difficult lives. Unlike modern Canadians, people did not have the opportunity to improve themselves or their social position.

Despite the many similarities between feudal Japan and feudal Europe, the two societies were distinct. Individual societies always find unique solutions to the common problems of life. The similarity in the basic structure of European and Japanese feudal society, however, is quite noticeable. As you read the next two chapters, speculate about why the similarities existed.

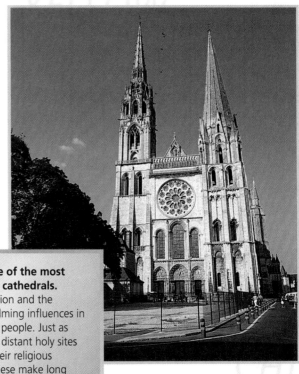

Chartres Cathedral, one of the most beautiful of the Gothic cathedrals.
During feudal times, religion and the Church became overwhelming influences in the daily lives of ordinary people. Just as European pilgrims visited distant holy sites as a way of expressing their religious feelings, so did the Japanese make long journeys to visit Shinto shrines.

SEA

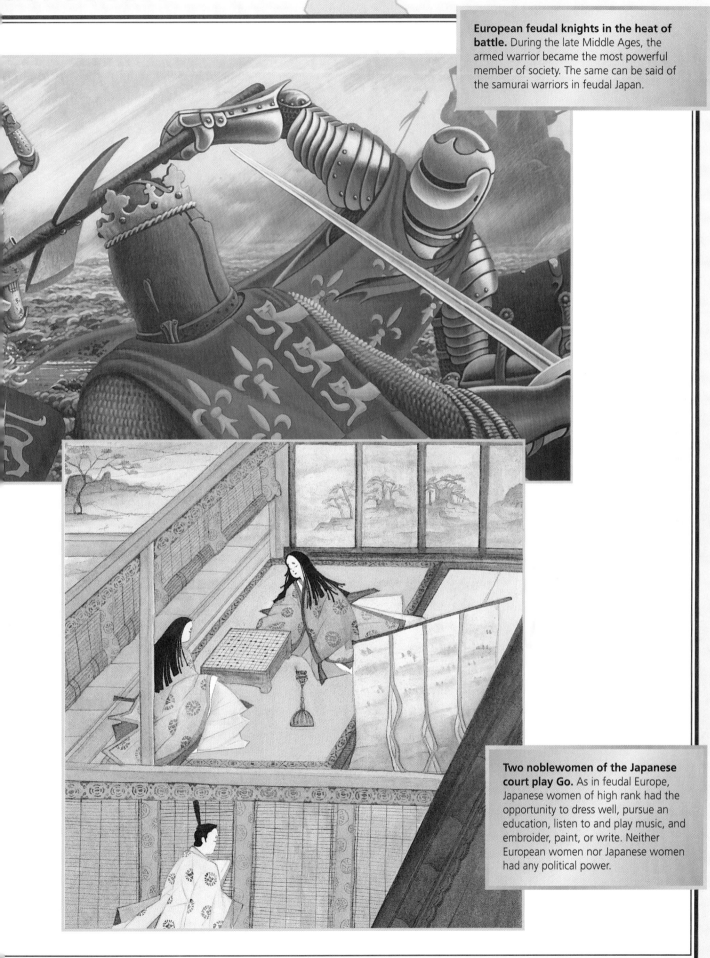

European feudal knights in the heat of battle. During the late Middle Ages, the armed warrior became the most powerful member of society. The same can be said of the samurai warriors in feudal Japan.

Two noblewomen of the Japanese court play Go. As in feudal Europe, Japanese women of high rank had the opportunity to dress well, pursue an education, listen to and play music, and embroider, paint, or write. Neither European women nor Japanese women had any political power.

5 EUROPE'S LATE MIDDLE AGES

CHAPTER OUTCOMES

In this chapter you will learn about the forces that ended feudalism in the mid-fifteenth century and set the scene for the Renaissance in western Europe. By the end of this chapter you will

- explain how the technologies of war changed a society

- identify ways that the growth of trade changed feudal society

- investigate life in a medieval town

- examine the beginnings of craft and merchant guilds in western Europe

- investigate the role of women during this period

- make a graph showing how the Black Death affected the population of Europe

- compare different maps

Sir Percival Pelham and the Battle of Agincourt

Although the story that follows is fictional, it tells the tale of a real battle that happened on October 25, 1415. In a field between the villages of Agincourt and Tramecourt in Normandy (part of France), a knight and his squire are poised to make history in the Battle of Agincourt.

Many accounts of this battle have been written by people who witnessed the events of the day. Through these first-hand, or primary, sources, we know that many young men like Sir Percival and his squire, Ralph, fought in the battle. We also have some idea of what they were thinking about—their hopes and fears.

As you read this story, try to imagine what the people who were there that day experienced.

Sir Percival, a young knight, gazed across the field towards the ranks of French knights who filled the field between the little villages of Agincourt and Tramecourt. He was amazed by the size of the French army: it looked about four times larger than the force commanded by Percival's **liege lord**, King Henry V of England.

The French seemed in good spirits. In their roomy tents they had not suffered much from the rain the night before, and they had eaten well at breakfast. In contrast, most of the English soldiers had slept in the open, and they'd had nothing but a handful of dried wheat to eat. It was all they could find. Percival's stomach growled as he gazed at the French troops.

Just after dawn, the French had noisily assembled into battle formation. Several fights had broken out before the battle order was finally settled; everyone wanted to be in the front where they could capture English nobles for **ransom**.

This confident, terrifying army awed the English knights, **squires**, and **archers** waiting almost a kilometre away. Never before had any of them seen

The English army waits for the French attack.

With an energetic battle cry, King Henry leads his troops into battle.

such a large group of the French **chivalry**. Every knight wore a brightly coloured **jupon** and polished armour; every squire carried a banner with **heraldic symbols** that identified the lineage and accomplishments of his lord. When the armies formed up at dawn, the English had braced themselves for an overwhelming attack by the French **cavalry**. Yet now, after three cold, miserable hours, the French army still showed no signs of moving.

"Percival!" An older man in **full-plate armour** clanked towards the young knight, his breath steaming.

"Yes, my lord Gloucester." Percival nodded his head slightly to acknowledge his uncle's rank.

"The King thinks that the French want to sit back and starve us into surrender. Be ready to move. We may have to draw them into battle."

The English army numbered about six thousand, only a thousand of whom were knights. Most of the rest were archers, ordinary people from the villages of England and Wales. Beside each archer was a sharpened pole driven into the ground with the point set at the height of a horse's chest. The archers had battle-axes and hatchets to protect themselves in the heat of battle, but little armour. Now they all stood silently, waiting for the king's command.

King Henry dismounted and strode to the front to face his army. He was dressed in bright armour with a gold crown on his helmet. The English king's red and blue jupon, which hung across his breast, showed both the **fleur-de-lis** of France, which Henry claimed to rule, and the **leopards of England**. After a brief pause, the king raised his arm and called out to his waiting soldiers. "In the name of Almighty God and **Saint George**, forward banner!"

At the king's command, priests quickly blessed the troops. Every soldier in the army knelt, drew a cross on the ground, and kissed the earth. Some put dirt into their mouths to show that they had just been blessed and could now accept death. With that, the archers rose and cheered. They pulled their sharpened wooden stakes from the ground and began to march forward. The armoured knights, leaving their horses behind, followed noisily. They tried to stay together in defensive formation behind the archers. Their heavy armour dragged them down, forcing them to pause every few hundred metres to catch their breath.

The English army was now only three hundred **paces** from the enemy. Most of the French had dismounted and had cut short their lances.

Percival took his place in the centre **battle** (group of knights) near the king. As he struggled through the mud, he saw the archers preparing for the French attack. Some peeled off their wet shirts. Others adjusted tunics of chain mail or hardened leather. An archer whom Percival knew as the manor blacksmith winked at Percival while he checked his boiled leather cap.

Percival's mouth was dry and he began to sweat. He turned to look at the French line again. The French knights, thousands of them, still hesitated to attack. In frustration, King Henry ordered his archers to shoot into the first battle. With a great shout, five thousand archers drew their bows and **loosed their shafts**. With a tremendous crash, a shower of metre-long arrows smashed into the front ranks of the French army, killing and wounding many. Without waiting, the English archers drew a second time and fired. This time the French knights turned their armoured backs to the arrows.

Angrily, the French commanders ordered their first battle to attack. A small band began to play on flutes and drums. The clash and clatter of the armour of thousands of warriors, the sound of their excited voices, and the low metallic roar of their spectacular approach terrified Percival.

Detachments of French cavalry were the first to reach the English line, trying to ride down the archers on the flanks. The mounted French knights did not see the sharpened stakes driven into the ground until it was too late to stop. Many of the horses rode right into them, piercing themselves and throwing their riders to the ground. Using their axes and hatchets, the nimble archers made quick work of the helpless, armour-clad knights.

The French knights on foot faced a storm of arrows so fierce that many knights lowered their armoured heads to protect their faces. Through the mud they came, bent forward as if fighting a gale. Volley after volley of arrows strummed across the field and smashed into the armoured ranks. The English fire was so accurate that many knights were struck through the visor and killed instantly. Once down in their heavy armour, the wounded struggled in the mud, unable to rise. Many were crushed under the weight of fallen comrades.

The French knights, still in their thousands, huddled together and passed through the arrow storm. Before he knew what was happening, Sir Percival was knocked to the ground by a tall French knight wielding a **mace**. Percival's squire, Ralph, rushed to help his lord, driving a long knife into the unprotected spot under the French knight's arm. He then yanked Percival to his feet. Nearby, King Henry had dismounted and was fighting on foot. With his gold crown and royal banner, the young king was a tempting target for the French. If they could kill or capture him, the victory would be theirs.

The fighting was fierce, but the first French battle was losing. So many French knights were pushing and shoving to get to the front that those already there couldn't swing their weapons or keep their balance. In the confusion, the Duc d'Alençon led the second French battle forward, pushing through the disoriented knights of the first. D'Alençon spied

A shower of arrows rains down on the French knights before they can engage in hand-to-hand combat.

Duc d'Alençon swings his battle-axe at King Henry's head as Percival rushes to help his liege lord.

the king fighting beneath his royal banner. Calling loudly on **Saint Denis**, d'Alençon and his comrades rushed towards Henry, climbing over the heaps of dead knights to reach their prey.

Percival's uncle Gloucester threw himself between d'Alençon and Henry, but the powerful duke pushed him aside and, with a crunching blow from his battle-axe, knocked the old man to the ground. With a shout, Percival and Ralph rushed at the king's attackers.

Percival struck down one attacker with his sword. King Henry was dodging wild swings of d'Alençon's battle-axe. With a mighty effort, d'Alençon threw himself forward, aiming a blow at the king's head. Quickly, Henry dodged to one

side. D'Alençon slipped in the mud and fell heavily to the ground, his axe clipping a piece from Henry's crown. As d'Alençon floundered in the mud, Percival disarmed him and then rushed to the king's side.

"Are you well, your Majesty?" he asked anxiously.

"Aye, well enough. Look, the French have retreated for the moment but there are more waiting to attack. Send messengers to my commanders. I want the prisoners gathered together behind the line."

Percival sent Ralph off with the message and then rejoined the line. The battlefield was a ghastly sight. The English soldiers had taken care to spare the lives of the French nobles who were worth large ransoms, but they had slaughtered the

rest of the French on the spot.

The third French battle waited, horrified by the sight of thousands of dead comrades. The commanders talked among themselves, and arguments broke out. Some French knights drew their swords, threatening their own lords. Suddenly, it was all over. A few of the French returned to their horses, mounted, and rode off. Soon others followed. Within a few minutes, the French third battle had gone, leaving the field to the English. Six thousand had defeated twenty-five thousand. Percival and the others, hardly believing their eyes, stood quietly for a few moments, resting on their swords. Some cheered a little; a few laughed as the tension eased.

Percival heard his name

called. He looked around and saw his uncle Gloucester, head bandaged, motioning him and Ralph to join the king at his standard. When Percival arrived, Henry grasped him by the forearm, and clapped him on the back.

"Lord Percival!" he exclaimed, giving the young knight a new title. "I will require that you **do homage** to me for your new estates in Gloucestershire once we are safely in Calais. You have my thanks. Do you accept your reward?"

Flushed with pride, Percival nodded. "Aye, Sire, I will always serve Your Majesty as a true and Christian knight."

In an exultant voice, King Henry spoke to the army. "Today, we give thanks for a great victory at Agincourt. Tonight, we rest. Tomorrow, on to Calais! God bless you all." With that, the whole army knelt to give thanks.

Sir Percival kneels with his squire and the whole English army to give thanks for the day's victory.

liege lord: the lord to whom a person owes loyalty

ransom: money demanded in exchange for a prisoner

squire: a knight's assistant; a knight in training

archer: a person who shoots a bow. By law, all adult males in English villages had to practise archery.

chivalry: knights and nobles

jupon: a long shirt worn over armour

heraldic symbol: a symbol that represents a family line; a coat of arms

cavalry: soldiers on horseback

full-plate armour: overlapping plates of steel that covered knights from head to toe

fleur de lis: representation of a flower called the iris; the symbol of France

leopards of England: three crouching lions, the heraldic symbol of England

Saint George: the patron saint of England

pace: the length of a stride, about a metre

battle: a military action; a group of knights

to loose a shaft: to shoot an arrow

mace: a war club

Saint Denis: the patron saint of France

to do homage: to swear loyalty

ACTIVITIES

1. During the Middle Ages, people learned news by word of mouth. Many found it easy to remember details of the events of the day by turning them into rhyming poems. When sung, these were known as ballads.

   Choose one of the characters in the story and write a poem about the battle from his point of view. Alternatively, draw a series of pictures to show what happened to that character in the battle. Or imagine you are the mother, father, sister, brother, or wife of one of the slain soldiers and write a poem that describes the events of your loved one's death. Compare your poem or pictures with those of someone who took a different point of view.

2. Pretend you are a French military advisor. What advice would you give your king after the battle? Draw up a list of mistakes the French made and your recommendations to help avoid similar disasters. Remember to be diplomatic. You are speaking to a king who will be furious about the defeat he has just suffered.

3. Draw a series of maps showing the stages in the Battle of Agincourt, or create a scale model of the battlefield. Your maps or model should clearly show the positions of the French and English forces at the time of the battle. Show the location of Henry V, Duc d'Alençon, archers, knights, and their numbers.

TIME LINE

1066	THE BATTLE OF HASTINGS
1097	THE FIRST CRUSADE BEGINS
1327	THE HUNDRED YEARS' WAR BEGINS
1347	THE BLACK DEATH STRIKES EUROPE
1358	THE JACQUERIE IN FRANCE
1381	THE PEASANTS' REVOLT IN ENGLAND
1400	GEOFFREY CHAUCER COMPLETES THE CANTERBURY TALES
1415	THE BATTLE OF AGINCOURT
1429	JOAN OF ARC BEGINS HER CAMPAIGN AGAINST THE ENGLISH
1492	COLUMBUS SAILS ACROSS THE ATLANTIC

The said French were so loaded with armour that they could not support themselves or move forward. In the first place they were armed with long coats of steel, reaching to the knees or lower, and very heavy.... The softness of the wet ground kept them as if **immovable,** *so that they could raise their clubs only with difficulty.... The plain was so narrow that there was no room except for the men-at-arms.*

The said archers were for the most part in their **doublets,** *without armour, their stockings rolled up to their knees, and having hatchets and battle-axes or great swords hanging at their* **girdles***; some were bare-footed and bare-headed, others had caps of boiled leather.*

—JEHAN DE WAVRIN

PRIMARY SOURCE

Jehan de Wavrin, a French knight who fought in the battle of Agincourt, describes the difference in the clothing of the French knights and the English archers. What advantage did the light dress of the archers give them over the heavily armoured French? What was the difference in social class between the two groups? What do you think the triumph of the archers over the knights might mean for the feudal system?

INTRODUCTION

The Middle Ages of Europe seems a romantic period, very different from the world we live in today. We dream of a time when knights and ladies lived in castles and attended colourful tournaments. To some extent, the Middle Ages were as we imagine them. A great many knights lived in castles all over Europe. There were more than 10 000 castles in Germany alone, and many thousands more throughout Europe.

Yet only about 10 percent of the people belonged to the knightly, or noble, class; far more were serfs, many of whom lived in dreadful conditions. Only in the late Middle Ages did some serfs escape the life into which they were born. Their opportunities came with the beginnings of trade.

The late Middle Ages was a time of great change and upheaval, a time when a series of terrible events shook the foundations of Western society. In religion, the unity of the Catholic Church was rocked by the appearance of new **heresies**. In society, the Black Death killed perhaps a third of all the people in Europe, and peasants' revolts spread rapidly, only to be savagely suppressed. In politics, the Hundred Years' War ruined northern France and wasted the energies of England. All these developments were sources of great suffering.

Yet this period was also a time of positive change. Trade developed across the continent, and the nations of modern Europe began to emerge in a recognizable form. Agriculture gradually improved, and so did the wages of the farmers who worked the land. People could now earn money at a trade instead of scraping by as a serf on a farm. Cities grew in importance and size, and beautiful **cathedrals** were built. New ideas grew in the universities and spread to influence rulers and their advisors. All these developments, both bad and good, worked together to bring an end to feudalism and prepare western Europe for the Renaissance and the Protestant Reformation.

immovable: unable to move

doublet: vest

girdle: belt

heresy: a teaching that is contrary to that of the Church

cathedral: the home church of a bishop

KNIGHTHOOD AND CHIVALRY

In the late Middle Ages, knighthood reached its highest state of development before a quick decline. Eventually, two new technologies of war, the longbow and firearms, made heavy plate armour useless. When monarchs could keep their power by using armies of archers, the knight's days were numbered. Before that happened, however, the late Middle Ages was a time when the ideal of the mounted knight, fighting for his

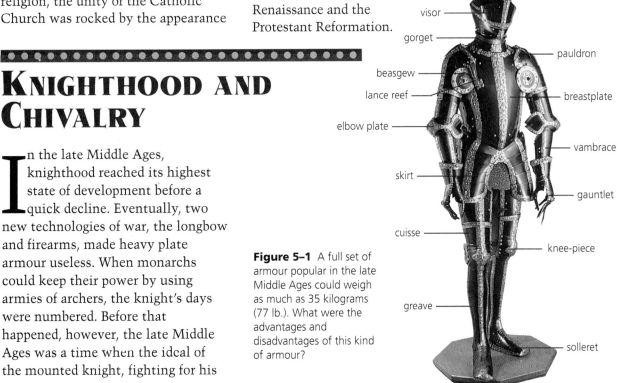

helmet
visor
gorget
pauldron
beasgew
lance reef
breastplate
elbow plate
vambrace
skirt
gauntlet
cuisse
knee-piece
greave
solleret

Figure 5–1 A full set of armour popular in the late Middle Ages could weigh as much as 35 kilograms (77 lb.). What were the advantages and disadvantages of this kind of armour?

DID YOU KNOW?

The word "chivalry" comes from the French word cheval, *meaning horse, and refers to the fact that knights almost always fought on horseback.*

lord and dedicating his life to his lady, was more a reality than it ever would be again.

The code of honour that every knight swore to uphold was known as chivalry. The code of chivalry was based on personal honour. Ideally, all knights were brave, generous, and truthful. They were also supposed to protect women and children and to love and strengthen the Church. In practice, of course, few knights were truly chivalrous. For instance, knights seldom extended their code of chivalry to the serfs who worked on manors to support them. Mistreatment of serfs by knights—including beatings—was so common that laws had to be passed forbidding assaults on peasants.

Virtually all knights admired and practised fighting and war, which they saw as their trade. Even their amusements, **jousting** and hunting, were ways of practising for war. By perfecting their physical abilities, knights increased their value to their lord and so kept their valued **social status** and lands. They also increased

their chances of staying alive on the battlefield.

THE EDUCATION OF A KNIGHT

The education of a young knight took many years. At the age of seven or eight, a noble's son would be sent to live in the household of another knight to get his education. There he would serve as a page, waiting at table, learning to ride and fight, and also learning to play music and sing. The lady of the household and her female attendants usually took a keen interest in the education of the page, teaching him about literature and music and knightly **courtesy**. The warriors of the household taught the page how to hunt and use weapons.

At the age of fourteen or fifteen, the page was usually accepted by an experienced knight as a squire. The young man would serve as the knight's assistant and bodyguard, attending the knight at tournaments

Figure 5–2 Although knighthood was sometimes granted on the battlefield, many knights received "their **spurs**" in a formal ceremony. As part of the ceremony, the lord fixed spurs to the knight's heals. What might this ritual symbolize?

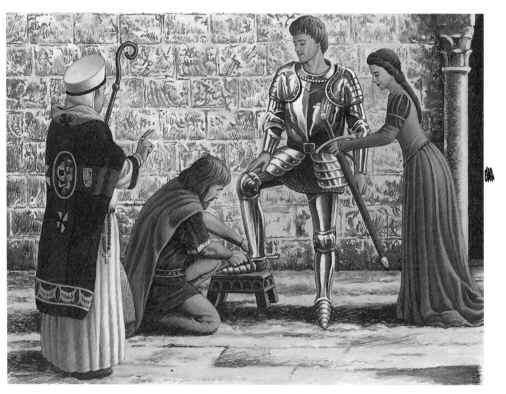

and fighting by his side in battle. The knight shared his knowledge with the squire, instructing him in the use and care of weapons, in heraldry, and in siege warfare. Tournaments, combat training, and hunting with dogs or hawks took up more and more of the squire's time.

Most squires expected to be knighted, but some could not afford the necessary armour and other equipment and so remained squires for life. In modern terms, a suit of good plate armour, like the one used in the fifteenth century when the story of Sir Percival takes place, would cost as much as a modern luxury car.

Those who did advance usually became knights at about the age of twenty-one. Before the formal ceremony, the squire fasted and **kept vigil** over his armour overnight, often in a chapel. In the morning, freshly bathed and purified, the new knight was **dubbed**, robed, and armed by his lord.

to keep vigil: staying awake and praying

to dub: to make a person a knight by touching the shoulder with a sword

-(LINK-UP)-

The Page

The medieval term "page" has not disappeared. Many young Canadians serve brief terms as pages in the House of Commons, the Senate, or a provincial legislative assembly. Pages for the House of Commons must be attending a local university during their term. Their duties are as follows:

◆ to collect and distribute official documents

◆ to link members to their Hill offices

◆ to serve House officials in various ways

◆ to act as messengers for the Speaker, chair occupants, members of Parliament, and table officers

◆ to provide professional, impartial, and efficient service

Does this sound like a good part-time job for your first year of university? Find out more about the page programs by writing to your provincial or federal representatives or the Public Information Office, House of Commons, Ottawa, ON, Canada, K1A 0A9. You could also try your school's career counsellor or a government site on the Internet.

Figure 5–3 Two students, one from Prince Albert, Saskatchewan, and another from Iqualuit, Northwest Territories, serve as pages in the House of Commons in Ottawa.

WHAT DO YOU THINK?

1. Compare the duties of the pages of medieval society and those of the pages who serve in a modern Canadian parliament. Compare the education each gains.

2. What do you think you could gain from a year as a page? Besides the duties, think about whom you would work with and the environment you would work in every day.

3. Conduct some research with the sources listed above to find out what criteria a student must meet to be eligible for the program.

Recognize Our Symbols of Ourselves

Heraldry is the science of representing our family history and accomplishments with symbols. We all use symbols to tell about ourselves. Some symbolism is simple and casual; for example, we wear our team colours on the sports field. Sometimes we protect our symbols fiercely. Companies that use logos to help consumers identify their products would sue anyone who used the same logo.

Many peoples use symbols to represent their family lines. The First Nations of the Northwest Coast display their family heraldry on carved wooden poles, or totems, rich with symbolic meaning. For example, the Haida classify themselves into two ancestral groupings, those descended from the Raven and those descended from the

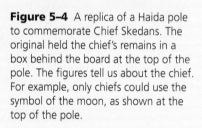

Figure 5–4 A replica of a Haida pole to commemorate Chief Skedans. The original held the chief's remains in a box behind the board at the top of the pole. The figures tell us about the chief. For example, only chiefs could use the symbol of the moon, as shown at the top of the pole.

Eagle. A raven or an eagle usually appears on the top of a Haida totem. Underneath may be animals that remind people of a story significant to the family.

Beginning about 1100, the knights and nobles of Europe began displaying emblems on their shields and banners to identify themselves. These emblems, called coats of arms, helped knights identify one another on the battlefield.

Coats of arms had to be easy to identify. A mistake could be costly. In the War of the Roses, for example, in 1471, the Earl of Warwick attacked a group of his own supporters because he mistook their coat of arms, a white star, for the white rose of his enemies. His supporters fled and Warwick lost the battle.

The symbols and colours used on coats of arms developed into heraldry by which nobles identified their families and ancestry. The symbols often used a pun; for example, the Corbet family used the raven, also known as a corbie, which sounds like Corbet.

The following diagram shows how a family crest would change if a family joined another noble

Figure 5–5 This manuscript illustration shows a medieval English knight being armed for a tournament. Where is the knight's coat of arms displayed?

family through marriage. You can see that the family crest changed only when a woman brought estates into her new husband's family. What does this say about what the society valued? As time went by, complicated coats of arms became a status symbol. Why would this be?

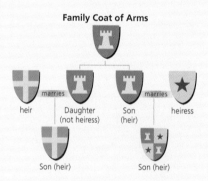

Family Coat of Arms

NOW YOU DO IT

1. Which of the following three coats of arms shows the family with the "most noble" lineage? Why?

2. Find the coat of arms of your own town, city, or province. Research the meaning of the various symbols.

3. Interview an older family member to learn about your family's history. Then create your own coat of arms or totem with symbols representing your family's history, achievements, and values. Explain why you think these symbols are important.

1. **a)** In point form, explain how the code of chivalry guided a knight through life. Give examples.

   b) Given the violent nature of a knight's skills, do you think society would benefit if knights followed a code of behaviour? How?

   c) Write a code of chivalry for young Canadians.

2. Design an organizing chart to show the various stages a young man would go through before becoming a knight. In one column list the stages. In the next column list what occurred at each stage.

3. In Chapter 2 you learned that feudal society is structured into a series of ranks, with the monarch at the top. Draw an expanded diagram of the feudal **hierarchy**, including the king, knights, nobles, as well as squires, children, and pages.

4. **a)** How did a lack of money keep some young men from becoming a knight? Think of a similar situation in Canada today.

   b) How does Canada attempt to help poorer Canadians achieve their goals? Why would this not be available in the fifteenth century?

THE HUNDRED YEARS' WAR

The Hundred Years' War was a struggle between the monarchs and nobles of France and England that lasted from 1338 to 1453. Today it is hard for us to imagine how a war could last so long. Warfare in the fourteenth and fifteenth centuries was not like modern warfare with its terrible weapons of mass destruction. There were frequent long truces, and nobody fought during the winter months, when the roads were impassable. Even during an active military campaign, the armies spent much of their time manoeuvring for position, burning homes, trampling crops, and raiding farmers' food stores.

The war began, like the Norman invasion of England, as a war about who should be king. The French supported a French cousin of the dead ruler. The English king, Edward III, as a nephew of the old French king, believed he had a stronger claim, so he invaded France. Over the course of the war, the English, at various times, controlled vast areas of France but by the end of the war held only the port city of Calais. King Henry V's victory at Agincourt, as told at the beginning of this chapter, was to be one of the last important English successes of the war.

TECHNOLOGY AND TACTICS

The English had one powerful weapon that the French did not have: archers. These archers were ordinary villagers skilled in the use of the longbow. They shot clothyard (metre-long) arrows from bows almost 2 metres in height. It was reported that an arrow from a longbow could penetrate a knight's plate armour and kill him. The thrust from such a bow was so powerful that it could send an arrow through the armoured leg of a mounted knight, the body of his horse, and the knight's leg on the other side.

Although the French knights could fight as well as the English,

hierarchy: the order of ranks in a system

DID YOU KNOW?

Japan, another military society, also had castles. Compare the castle on the opposite page with the one on page 196.

they were defeated many times during the Hundred Years' War. Many of the French refused to fight with anyone of "low birth," so they would not attack the archers. In three important battles, French knights tried to ride past the low-born archers to get at their social equals, the English knights. In each case, the volleys of arrows from the archers were so deadly that the battles turned into disasters for the French, who had to pay large sums to ransom the surviving knights. The lowly English archer made the knight and his armour **obsolete**.

obsolete: useless because it is out of date

siege: the act of surrounding a fortified place in order to capture it

Figure 5–6 At the age of twenty-eight, Henry V of England invaded France. You read about his great victory at Agincourt at the beginning of this chapter. Judging by this peace-time painting, what do you think Henry's character was like?

The Burghers of Calais

Early in the Hundred Years' War, in 1346, Edward III of England besieged the French port city of Calais.

Under the rules of war at the time, the inhabitants of a town or castle under **seige** would be treated mercifully if they surrendered, The rules of chivalry—which were tied to the rules of war—demanded it. The citizens could all be slaughtered, however, if they had not surrendered before the final assault. With this in mind, hold a class debate to decide who was the most chivalrous in the true story at right: the burghers, who volunteered to die to save their fellow-citizens; the Queen of England, who pleaded for the lives of her husband's enemies; or King Edward III, who granted his wife's request.

The story begins when the French king refuses to come to the city's aid, and the citizens finally ask Edward for terms of surrender.

Upon which the king replied: "You will inform the governor of Calais that the only grace he can expect from me is that six of the principal citizens of Calais march out of the town with bare heads and feet, with ropes round their necks, and the keys of the town and castle in their hands. These six persons shall be at my absolute disposal, and the remainder of the inhabitants pardoned."

When Sir Walter Manly had presented these six citizens to the king ... the king eyed them with angry looks ... and ordered that their heads be stricken off.

The queen of England, who at that time was big with child, fell on her knees, and with tears said, "Ah, gentle sir, since I have crossed the sea with great danger to see you, I have never asked you for one favour: now, I most humbly ask for a gift, for the sake of the Son of the blessed Mary, and for your love to me, that you will be merciful to these six men."

The king looked at her for some time in silence, and then said: "Ah, lady, I wish you had been anywhere else but here: you have entreated in such a manner that I cannot refuse you; I therefore give them to you, to do as you please with them." The queen had the six citizens conducted to her apartments, and had the halters taken from round their necks, after which she new clothed them, and served them a plentiful dinner; she then presented each with six nobles, and had them escorted out of the camp in safety.

PRIMARY SOURCE

Figure 5–7 Forces attacking castles used war technology, such as this catapult, as well as battering rams and movable towers. Often they dug mines under walls and lit great fires in the shafts to bring a section of wall down.

Figure 5–8 Knights built castles throughout Europe to protect themselves and their families. A well-defended castle could keep enemies out for months. Often the only way to defeat such a castle was to surround it and wait for the inhabitants to run out of food. Make a list of activities going on in this castle. What factors would allow this castle community to function independently for a long period of time?

JOAN OF ARC RALLIES THE FRENCH

dauphin: eldest son of the French king

hither: here

In 1429, seven years after the death of Henry V, a seventeen-year-old peasant girl named Joan of Arc appeared at the French court claiming that angelic voices had commanded her to drive the English out of France. The **dauphin** was skeptical at first. In the end, however, he gave Joan a plain steel suit of armour, a white banner, and enough troops to battle the English.

Young Joan, brimming with confidence and flying her white banner, was an inspirational leader. After driving the English from Orleans, she escorted the dauphin to the cathedral at Reims where she stood at his side as he was crowned Charles VII, King of France.

Joan of Arc enjoyed other triumphs, but two years after her victory at Orleans, she was captured. King Charles refused to pay her ransom, so she was put on trial for heresy and witchcraft. One piece of evidence considered important at her trial was that she dressed in armour, which was men's clothing. People of the high Middle Ages would have been highly suspicious of a woman who dressed as a man. On May 30, 1431, Joan was burned at the stake. She was just nineteen years old.

Joan's death proved to be as inspirational to the French as her life had been. By helping them rally together behind the French king against the English, she had forced them to start thinking of themselves as one nation rather than as a collection of fiefdoms always at war with each other. In her death, Joan became a heroine of all France. By strengthening the king at the expense of the nobles, she also contributed to the end of feudalism in Europe.

Figure 5–9 Although burned at the stake for heresy and witchcraft, Joan of Arc was eventually made a saint. What view of Joan does this portrait present? Explain.

Joan of Arc Writes to the English Invaders

Joan of Arc could not read or write herself but dictated this letter to be delivered to the English at the beginning of her campaign to drive them from France. After reading this letter, decide what qualities made Joan an inspiration to her troops.

Jesus Maria —

King of England, and you Duke of Bedford, calling yourself regent of France, you William Pole, Count of Suffolk John Talbot, and you Thomas Lord Scales, calling yourselves lieutenants of the said Duke of Bedford, do right in the King of Heaven's sight. Surrender to The Maid sent **hither** by God the King of Heaven the keys of all the good towns you have taken and laid waste in France. She comes in God's name to establish the Blood Royal, ready to make peace if you agree to abandon France and repay what you have taken. And you, archers, comrades in arms, gentles and others, who are before the town of Orleans, retire in God's name to your own country.

If you do not, expect to hear tidings from The Maid who will shortly come upon you to your very great hurt.

PRIMARY SOURCE

1. Why did the Hundred Years' War last so long? Consider both the strategy required for defeating castles (see page 147) and France's failures on the battlefield.

2. What could the long-bow do? How could this capability turn metal armour into a worthless technology?

3. **a)** In the fifteenth century, powerful cannons were developed and widely used in sieges. With this new technology, castles could no longer provide the protection they once had. Why did gunpowder and cannons make both knights and castles out of date?

   b) Think of two modern examples of technology making an institution or practice useless.

4. In war, countries use military might to get their way. Just as in a scuffle on the school ground, the best fighter usually wins. The justness of a cause is irrelevant. Write a brief paper outlining the benefits and drawbacks of war as a way to settle disputes between countries. In a small group, brainstorm other ways to settle disputes and outline the benefits and drawbacks of these.

5. Why do you think Joan of Arc was able to rally the French in the Hundred Years' War? How did she help the French see themselves as a nation?

6. Despite her powerless station as a shepherd's daughter, Joan of Arc beat the odds.

   a) What enabled Joan to succeed? Do some research to find a Canadian who came from humble circumstances to make a mark on history. Describe an imaginary situation in which you achieve a similarly remarkable achievement.

   b) By becoming a military leader, Joan took on a traditionally male role. Do you think this contributed to her fate? How? Describe the difficulty some women face when they take on traditionally male roles in Canadian society.

TRADE AND TOWN

TRADE BEGINS

During the Crusades, western Europeans' eyes were opened to the possibilities of trade with distant lands. Tempted by goods such as silk, spices, tapestries, and sugar, a few brave individuals with the money to pay for the expenses of a trip went into the trading business. Over time, western Europeans began sending ships on trading expeditions to distant lands in search of the goods they desired.

At first, traders sold their goods in regular local markets, or fairs, held in towns and villages and sponsored by the feudal lords. The fairs were fabulous events where people gathered to socialize and browze, not just to buy. Through exposure to the

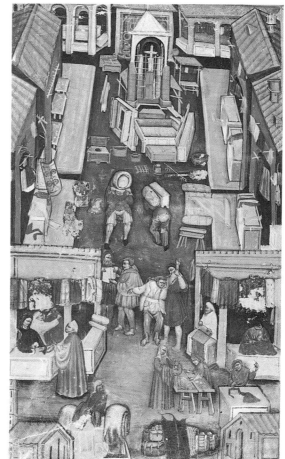

Figure 5–10 Medieval towns were busy places with all kinds of goods for sale. Identify four activities in this street scene.

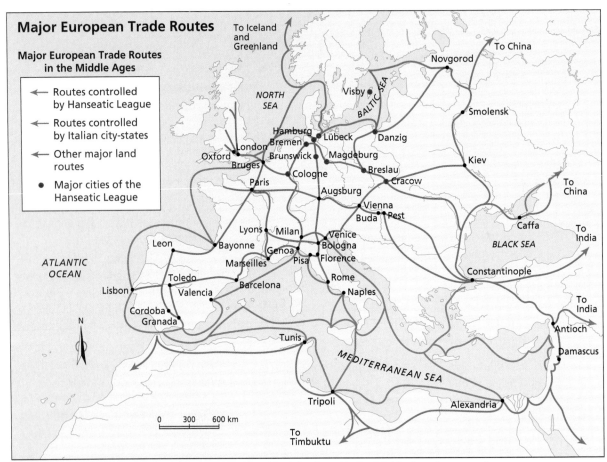

Major European Trade Routes

Major European Trade Routes
in the Middle Ages

← Routes controlled
by Hanseatic League

← Routes controlled
by Italian city-states

← Other major land
routes

• Major cities of the
Hanseatic League

Figure 5–11 Cities such as Oxford, Hamburg, and Frankfurt developed in the Middle Ages because of their location on trade routes. What trade did the Italian city-states of Venice and Genoa control? What trade did the Hanseatic League control?

many goods brought from faraway lands, ordinary people realized that they could make things and sell them in exchange for money. Here was their escape from serfdom. All over Europe, people began learning and perfecting the skills needed to produce the goods that were coming from distant lands. Fairs were soon filled with finely crafted goods—such as copper pots, gloves, and cutlery—made in western Europe as well as in far-off lands.

TRADE LEADS TO TOWNS

After some time, the fair could not satisfy all the needs of traders and consumers. First, they were seasonal, so no one could buy or sell in winter. Second, people would sometimes have to travel great distances to reach the fairs. Travel was dangerous, so many just didn't go. Out of this emerged the need for the stability that could be provided by a town, where permanent shops could be set up and protected by a wall surrounding the town.

TO MARKET, TO MARKET

The appearance of a market in a society marks the beginning of organized **commerce**: the buying, selling, and bartering (trading) of goods and services. In the countryside, the market usually appears on a set day of the week or month. Goods may be sold, as well as various foods. Sometimes a hairdresser or letter writer offers services for sale. In larger towns and cities, the market usually occupies one area, with different squares or streets dedicated to various products. The market has emerged in virtually every civilization. For example, Bernal Diaz del Castillo, a Spaniard who travelled to Mexico with Hernàn Cortéz in 1519, saw the great Tlatelolco marketplace in Tenochtitlàn, capital of the Aztec Empire. He called this market a marvel of organization, with areas for jade, lumber, limestone, salt, and more, as well as streets for herbalists, barbers, and wild animal dealers.

The ancient fair, or market, survives in Canada in amusement parks, trade fairs, and farmers' markets. We even buy and sell bonds and company shares on the "stock market."

Figure 5–12 A young vendor sells her wares in a market in Gujarat, India. Goods and services are sold in markets in virtually every civilization.

WHAT DO YOU THINK?

1. Name a nursery rhyme, song, or story that features a fair or market.

2. a) Identify another form of market (such as the farmers' market) that exists today in Canada.

   b) Why do you think the market in all its forms has become such an important feature of Canadian culture? What does this tell you about Canadian society?

THE CRAFT GUILDS

The emerging towns were populated with people specializing in trades of all sorts. There were bakers, tailors, sword and armour makers, **tanners,** and tavernkeepers, to name a few. Every trade, or craft, was controlled by the experts in that particular trade, who together were called a **guild.**

Guilds were co-operative organizations that set standards for the quality of their products, controlled prices for them, kept out unskilled craftspeople, and eliminated competition. They controlled almost all the merchant and trade activity that took place within and between towns. Guilds also looked after their members in case of death or accident. For example, if a member of the candle-makers guild grew too sick to work, the other candle makers would pitch in to provide food for him and his family. Tradespeople could only operate if they belonged to a guild, and they could only belong to the guild for which they had been trained.

commerce: the buying, selling, and trading of goods and services

tanner: a person who makes hide into leather

guild: a union of persons practising the same craft

Becoming a Master of a Craft

Acceptance into a guild came at the end of a long and difficult apprenticeship. The **apprentice** learned the craft in stages, beginning with the most simple tasks. He or she would receive training, room and board, and a small allowance. Young people were sent to live and work under a particular **master** at a very early age, sometimes eight or nine. Many masters beat their apprentices for making mistakes.

After years of work and learning, apprentices would take a test to become a **journeyman** and would be admitted to a guild. They were called journeymen because they could now be paid by the day (*par journée*). After several more years of study and practice, the journeyman created a "master piece" to be judged by a panel of masters for quality. If the piece was considered acceptable, then the journeyman became a master, an expert in his or her craft.

Using The Written Rule as a Primary Source

CATALOGUE CARD

What is it? A set of rules called an ordinance

Who wrote it? High ranking masters of the **seamstresses'** guild in Memmingen, Germany

When? 1543

Why? To set guidelines about who can be a seamstress and what training is required

Concerning seamstresses: All seamstresses who are not citizens here are to be sent away and forbidden to do work as seamstresses in this city.

For those who are citizens, it is ordered that no one shall serve an apprenticeship of less than one year, and after this a period as a journeyman for at least one year, before she is allowed to become a master. She is also never to do anything which is limited to members of the tailors' or furriers' guild, and is to pay the guild five shillings [when she is taken on as a master]. She is to obey all regulations and ordinances. A woman who wants to become a master is to appear before sworn overseers [guild officers], who will test her on what she knows and explain the ordinances, which she is to follow from that point on.

Guild membership was not limited to men in the Middle Ages. Although barred from most guilds, women were active in others, especially guilds related to the brewing and textile industries. As you can see from the set of rules above, women could become masters of their craft.

Ordinances are rules written by towns, companies, or clubs to help them run their affairs. They do not deal with criminal offences, such as murder or theft. Instead they deal with such things as whether or not you can keep chickens within town limits or empty your **chamber pot** out your window.

Rules are important because they tell us what was important to ordinary people, especially rule makers. When assessing just one set of rules, always keep in mind that the townspeople probably had many other rules about other matters. Also, people in other towns may have had different concerns. In other words, a set of rules gives us a snapshot of the concerns of one group.

WHAT DO YOU THINK?

1. Read the passage again to identify five things that were important to the seamstresses' guild in Memmingen.

2. Here is one clause from a by-law, or rule, for the city of Scarborough, Ontario. "Pinball machines and other electric or manually operated games shall be prohibited in ... commercial zones." What does this clause tell us? Analyze a by-law for your own community.

Figure 5–13 These three young people work in a German automotive plant as apprentice mechanics. After they complete their apprenticeships they will receive their journeyman papers. Identify another trade that uses apprentices.

prohibition: a ban

incentive: something that urges a person on

mandatory: required

LINK-UP

Guilds and Modern Unions

The guilds of the late Middle Ages brought together people working in the same field to achieve common goals. As such, guilds were the forerunners of modern associations of professionals, such as the Editors' Association of Canada. Craftspeople formed guilds for several reasons, one of which was to protect the rights of the guild members. Particularly in this area, guilds bear a striking resemblance to modern unions, such as the Canadian Auto Workers (CAW). The following excerpt from a newspaper article shows what

CAW won after a strike against General Motors of Canada (GM Canada) in the fall of 1996.

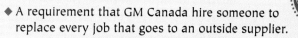
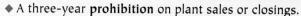

CAW leaders can pat themselves on the back for some short-term victories:

◆ A requirement that GM Canada hire someone to replace every job that goes to an outside supplier.

◆ A three-year **prohibition** on plant sales or closings.

◆ Attractive early retirement **incentives** for workers in Windsor and Oshawa to help compensate them for the sale of those two plants.

◆ A ban on **mandatory** overtime at the Oshawa operations.

WHAT DO YOU THINK?

1. For each of the four "short-term victories" noted above, what was the union trying to achieve? Examine the section "Apprentices and Guilds" to identify three goals of the guilds of the Middle Ages.

   Compare the two sets of goals.

2. With your teacher, look up some modern business unions or associations in the telephone book. You may

even find that some of these organizations still use the word "guild" in their names. As a class, write to one of these groups and ask what the organization does for its members.

LIFE IN THE TOWN

Although medieval towns had many attractions, they were also crowded and smelly and rather small compared with modern cities. London, England, today has a population of more than eight million people, but in the year 1300 only 50 000 people lived there, only one-thirtieth the number living in modern Greater Vancouver.

Figure 5–14 The city of Carcassone, France, is still surrounded by the wall built in the Middle Ages. What effect would such a wall have on the architecture of the houses in the town?

Most towns and cities were the centres for farm communities. They were surrounded by the farms of large manors or they grew around some sort of defensive structure, such as a castle, palace, or large monastery. Citizens usually built an encircling wall of stone to protect against raids from rival cities or feudal lords. The citizens also built gates, which they shut at night. As a village developed into a town and then into a city, ever larger rings of walls were built.

Because of the walls that surrounded medieval towns, space was limited, and houses for the poor and middle-class people were all crowded together. Town houses were often several stories high, with their upper floors overhanging the street. Unlike cities today, medieval towns did not have straight, planned streets.

Instead, streets were narrow and winding, and they usually had open sewers. As there was no plumbing, people routinely emptied chamber pots into the street and dumped their garbage there as well. In some places, swineherds drove pigs through the town at night to eat up the waste.

For all their faults, medieval towns also had their attractions. Compared with small manor villages, there was much more entertainment for people. Guilds and the local church organized many **pageants** and plays, and people could also see **bear baiting** and other blood sports. Life in town was exciting.

SOCIAL CHANGES THAT CAME WITH TRADE

Money had not been very important in the old feudal system, where a person's wealth and power were measured by the amount of land he or she held. With trade, all that changed. Now many people could become independent and even powerful because they could make money. The town was the home of the medieval middle class, most of whom were merchants and skilled tradespeople. These townspeople were called burgesses in England, burgers in Germany, and bourgeois in France. Some merchants grew wealthier than the feudal landowners in the country.

The feudal lords had a hard time adjusting to a system where money, and not position, was most important. Members of the nobility thought trade was beneath them, but they still wanted the finer things available only in the towns. Unknown to the feudal lords, the middle class, with its power, money, and desire for freedom, would spell the end of feudalism.

New Freedoms

The towns drew people longing for freedom. Although the town was walled and cramped, people had the freedom to do as they wished, marry whom they pleased, and make money as they could. According to the law, runaway serfs could gain their freedom by staying in town for a year and a day without being discovered. Because the towns were so small, this was actually quite difficult to do. Nonetheless, some were able to manage it.

Feudal lords could not control the people who lived in towns, nor could manor courts. Most medieval towns were chartered; that is, they paid for or were given the right to exist by the monarch or the local lord. The **charters** of many modern European towns can be traced all the way back to the Middle Ages. A charter gave a town certain privileges, one of which was that the town could govern itself. Wealthy citizens and the guilds usually controlled the town government.

New Powers

The most powerful citizens were those belonging to the merchant guilds. These guilds were for the people who bought and sold goods on a large scale, and who financed ships and overland caravans to trade in distant lands.

Sometimes merchant guilds became very powerful and well organized. By putting together their wealth, for example, the port cities belonging to the Hanseatic League (a merchant guild) were able to support their own army and build a navy. The league became so wealthy and powerful that by threatening to cut off all trade with a country it could force that country's ruler to do what it wanted. In Italy, the port cities of Genoa, Venice, and Naples grew into powerful city-states thanks to their merchant-traders.

charter: a written order authorizing the right to operate as a town

ACTIVITIES

1. Examine the map showing trade routes. How were trade routes affected by major waterways? Referring to a relief map of Europe, explain how the physical features of Europe affected the trade routes.

2. With a partner, skim pages 149–50 to find the answers to the following two questions. When you skim, don't read everything. Instead look for just the information you need.

    a) What factors led to the growth of trade?

    b) How did the growth of trade lead to the need for towns?

3. Compare a medieval fair with a modern Canadian shopping mall. Consider the days and hours of operation, goods sold, type of consumers, and ownership of the shops/booths. What do the differences tell you about the two societies?

4. Explain how medieval guilds worked, why they were needed, and what they did for their members.

5. In a chart, compare the life of a serf and the life of a guild member working in a town. What are the benefits and drawbacks of each person's way of life?

6. Describe what you would see and experience as you entered a medieval town. What conclusions can you draw from the fact that medieval towns always had walls?

7. Define the term "middle class." How did this class fit into medieval society? Why did the middle class grow in size and importance during the Middle Ages? In what way would the growing middle class change feudal society?

8. Why was the Hanseatic League able to become more powerful than some rulers?

WOMEN IN THE LATE MIDDLE AGES

European women of the Middle Ages had fewer advantages in life than men. By referring to passages in the Bible, the Church taught that women's lower social status was justified. Medieval society was male-dominated, so it seemed acceptable to treat all women as inferior to men and to keep them under men's control. Not having any power, most women simply tried to make the best of things.

libel: a false or damaging statement

oratory: a small chapel

redress: set right

Chaucer Defends Women Through the Wife of Bath

In the late Middle Ages, as at other times, many women resented being treated as inferiors. Geoffrey Chaucer must have known one or two of these women because, in his book *Canterbury Tales*, he presents the Wife of Bath. This strong-willed character explains why women got a poor reputation in the first place. Below, Chaucer's original Middle English version of the Wife's words appears on the left. The modernized version appears to the right. What reason does the Wife of Bath give to explain women's poor reputation?

In Middle English

For trusteth wel, it is an impossible
That any clerk wol speke good of wyves,
But if it be of hooly seintes lives,
Ne on noon oother womman never the mo.
Who peynted the leon, tel me who?
By God! if wommen hadde writen stories,
As clerkes han withinne hire oratories,
They wolden han writen of men moore
    wikkednesse
Than al the mark of Adam may redresse.

In Modern English

For take my word for it, there is no **libel**
On women that the clergy will not paint,
Except when writing of a woman-saint,
But never good of other women though.
Who called the lion savage? Do you know?
By God, if women had but written stories
Like those the clergy keep in **oratories**,
More then had been written of man's
    wickedness
Than all the sons of Adam could **redress**.

WOMEN AND SOCIAL LEVEL

All peasants at this time lived hard lives, often in terrible poverty. Women usually had many children, shared the hard work with men in the fields, and died young.

Town women were slightly better off than the women who worked the fields because many earned money. In addition, they maintained their homes, went to market, cooked the meals, spun the wool, wove the cloth, made the clothes, and cared for their children. Many worked as servants. Women who belonged to a guild or who were married to a guild member were better off than most. As towns grew in importance, many merchant families grew rich. The women of these wealthy families had many opportunities. They often received a good education, either through a **parish** school or under a **tutor**.

Figure 5–15 Pieter Breugel's sixteenth-century painting of a peasant. What do you think life was like for medieval peasant women?

parish: church-sponsored

tutor: a private teacher

inventory: a detailed list of items

Margaret Paston Writes to Her Husband

In the fifteenth century, well-off people communicated by letter almost as often as we do today by telephone. The busy head of a household, whether man or woman, would often write six or seven letters a day. In this one, Margaret Paston, a noblewoman, writes to her husband to bring him up to date on estate business. How do you think the day-to-day tasks of Paston's life would compare with those of a medieval peasant woman? What words does Paston use to address her husband? Whose inventory is she beginning? What do these two pieces of information tell you about the relationship of husband and wife?

To my right worshipful master, John Paston, be this delivered in haste.

Right worshipful husband,
I recommend me to you, praying you to know that I have spoken with Newman for his house, and I am through with him therefore....

I have begun your **inventory**, that should have been made ere this time if I had been well at ease; I hope to make an end thereof and of other things by this next week....

I have sent John Norwood this day to Gresham, Besingham, and Matslake, to get as much money as he may. The blessed Trinity have you in his keeping. Written at Norwich, on the feast day of Peter and Paul.

Yours,
Margaret Paston

1. Until recently, many peasant women in various parts of the world did not have a chance to grow old because they died either of a contagious disease or during childbirth. In Canada today, most contagious diseases are under control, and only eighteen Canadian women died in childbirth in 1995. What do you think accounts for these differences?

2. **a)** List three tasks that Margaret Paston describes to her husband.

   b) Examine the painting on page 140 to identify three entertainments enjoyed by privileged medieval women.

3. Write a summary that describes the status and lifestyle of women in the late Middle Ages. Compare the rights and responsibilities of women in different classes.

4. Women played a very responsible role in medieval society. Make a list of the things women did. Medieval women were denied equal treatment and generally accepted this. Are things different in your community? Draw up a chart to compare the life of women of the Middle Ages (most of whom were peasants) with the life of Canadian women (most of whom are middle class).

5. Attempt your own translation of the Middle English version of the comments of the Wife of Bath on page 156. According to the author, how did the "power of the pen" serve men well and women badly?

6. Compare Chaucer's Middle English poetry with the Old English poetry from "Beowulf" on page 28. How has the language changed? Identify one reason why language might change.

THE CHURCH IN THE LATE MIDDLE AGES

PILGRIMAGES

In the late Middle Ages, the Church continued to have great influence over people's lives, both through its position in society and through its spiritual guidance. Pilgrimages were very popular during the Middle Ages, showing that Christians at this time took their religion very seriously. Pilgrims would make a journey to a holy place, especially a place where a Christian saint had been **martyred**. Many pilgrimages were long, dangerous journeys. There were no planes, trains, or cars; people travelled by foot, horse, or sailing ship. The favourite destinations were the shrine of Saint James at Compostela in Spain, the tomb of St. Thomas Becket in England, the holy places in Rome, and the city of Jerusalem. The pilgrimage was a way of making up for sins.

Pilgrims usually tried to bring back souvenirs of their journeys. The symbol of a pilgrimage to Compostela, for example, was a cockle shell; the symbol of a pilgrimage to Jerusalem was a palm leaf. Some Jerusalem pilgrims took the name "Palmer" to celebrate their journey. Pilgrims also brought back pieces of Christ's cross, the nails used in the Crucifixion, and many other holy items. Or so they thought. There were many sly traders on the pilgrim roads who made themselves rich by selling fake **relics** to unsuspecting pilgrims.

martyred: killed for the sake of religion

relic: a sacred object associated with a saint

Figure 5–16 Salisbury Cathedral, at left, and Chartres Cathedral, below, show the architecture typical of Gothic cathedrals.

CHURCH ARCHITECTURE

Churches in the early Middle Ages were relatively small. Engineers had not yet discovered ways of supporting heavy stone walls over a certain height. Then, sometime in the twelfth century, they learned how to build much taller churches with spires and how to replace wall space with huge windows of brilliantly coloured stained glass. To achieve greater height, **architects** pointed the arches that supported the cathedral roofs. By using massive supports called **flying buttresses** to hold up the walls, they made the cathedrals even taller and allowed for the large windows.

Thus began the age of the **Gothic** cathedral. Soon church spires were reaching for the heavens in every town and on every hilltop.

Gothic cathedrals are among the most beautiful buildings ever created. They were constructed with simple tools over long periods, sometimes a hundred years or more. With their intricate carvings, lofty ceilings, and striking patterns in stained glass, these churches struck awe in the hearts of the medieval faithful. Even

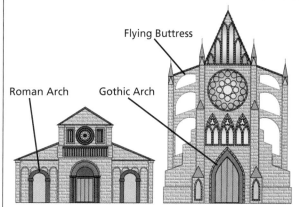

Flying Buttress

Roman Arch   Gothic Arch

Figure 5–17 A cathedral in the Romanesque style is shown on the left; the Gothic cathedral is on the right. What differences can you see between these two buildings?

today, stepping into a Gothic cathedral on a day when the sun streams through the multicoloured glass is like entering another world.

architect: one who designs buildings

flying buttress: an archway built against a wall to help support it

Gothic: a type of architecture featuring steep roofs and pointed arches

RUMBLINGS IN THE FLOCK

During the fourteenth century, the Catholic Church began to lose authority. In England, the teachings of an Oxford professor named John Wycliffe became very popular with commoner and noble alike. Wycliffe believed that priests and bishops, even the pope himself, had no right to tell people what to believe. He thought each person could only gain salvation by following his or her own conscience.

At this time, the Bible existed only in its Latin version. Wycliffe wanted to translate the Bible from Latin into English so that the common people could read it and decide for themselves what was right and wrong. Church leaders were enraged by Wycliffe's teachings. He had powerful friends among the nobility, however, so the Church was unable to prosecute him.

One reason nobles liked John Wycliffe was that he criticized the Church for its wealth. The nobles and the common people alike were tired of paying heavy taxes to the Church on top of what they had to pay to the king.

Wycliffe's teachings were popular not just in England but also in Hungary. There his disciple John Hus had great success in converting people to the new ideas. Hus, however, was condemned by a Church council in 1415 and burned at the stake. The nobles refused to protect him because they were afraid his ideas would lead to a peasants' revolt.

Figure 5–18 John Hus was burned at the stake, the usual means of execution for medieval heretics. Many condemned persons died of smoke inhalation before the flames could reach them, but not all.

ACTIVITIES

1. Describe the medieval pilgrimage and explain its purposes.

2. Tradition holds that the townspeople of Chartres harnessed themselves to carts to haul heavy loads of stone from nearby quarries to build Notre Dame Cathedral. What does this tell you about what religion meant to people of the Middle Ages?

3. Describe what Gothic cathedrals looked like. Considering that church services were given in Latin and that most people could not read, what purpose did sculptures and stained glass windows serve?

4. Describe a place of worship with which you are familiar. Are the architectural style, decoration, and works of art meant to help the worshipper achieve a certain frame of mind? How?

5. Think of a scene that would illustrate one of your own values. Using tissue paper, black construction paper, and glue, design your scene as a stained glass window.

6. What did John Wycliffe believe in? Pretend you have heard some of Wycliffe's sermons. Prepare a journal entry in which you record your thoughts on Wycliffe and the Church. You can do this from the point of view of a noble, a citizen of a town, or a young priest.

7. Compare the fates of John Wycliffe and John Hus. Why was one executed and the other not?

SOCIAL UPHEAVAL

THE BLACK DEATH

In the middle of the fourteenth century, western Europe experienced a disaster so great that many people thought the end of the world had come. Italian trading ships returning from ports on the Black Sea brought back one of the most devastating disease epidemics in history: the Black Death.

The Black Death was a variety of **bubonic plague**. It spread from victim to victim through the fleas on rats, which lived on medieval ships and throughout towns and cities. The diseased person quickly developed buboes (swollen **lymph glands**) and was covered with dark blotches on the skin. Then the patient would be stricken with a high fever and begin vomiting blood and **hallucinating**. Most victims died within one to three days. In some villages and towns, the sick and dying outnumbered the healthy.

Medieval medicine had no cure for the disease. Doctors recommended burning sulphur and smelling garlic as ways of preventing the spread of the plague. Neither was helpful. Probably twenty-five million people — about one-third of all the people of Europe — died from the plague. Thousands of villages became ghost towns, not reappearing until centuries later when their outlines were revealed through **aerial photographs** taken during the Second World War.

The Black Death brought out the best and worst in people. Many priests, nuns, and doctors died because they spent so much time tending the sick. At the other extreme, some parents abandoned their sick children, and thieves robbed corpses or broke into houses where everyone had died. Groups of religious fanatics called "Flagellants" travelled from town to town spreading the idea that the plague was a punishment from God.

bubonic plague: a highly contagious, usually fatal disease; swollen lymph glands were a typical symptom

lymph glands: rounded masses of tissue located under the arms and in the groin

hallucinating: seeing things that do not exist

aerial photograph: a picture of the ground, taken from a great height

Figure 5–19 Victims of the plague were desperate for a cure. Here a doctor attempts to drain a bubo. This treatment would only have helped spread the disease. Why would that be so?

Compare Maps

Early map makers usually attempted to locate towns, rivers, bodies of water, and natural features. Many medieval maps were very fanciful, as we saw with the T-O map on page 60. Nonetheless people wanted maps mainly to show them the rest of the world in relation to themselves. Today we make maps to show us much more, from the routes taken by explorers to the locations of prime fisheries areas. We use maps to help us understand all sorts of information.

By comparing maps of different types but of the same area, we gain even further insight by spotting relationships and patterns. For example, let's look at the following two maps of Canada.

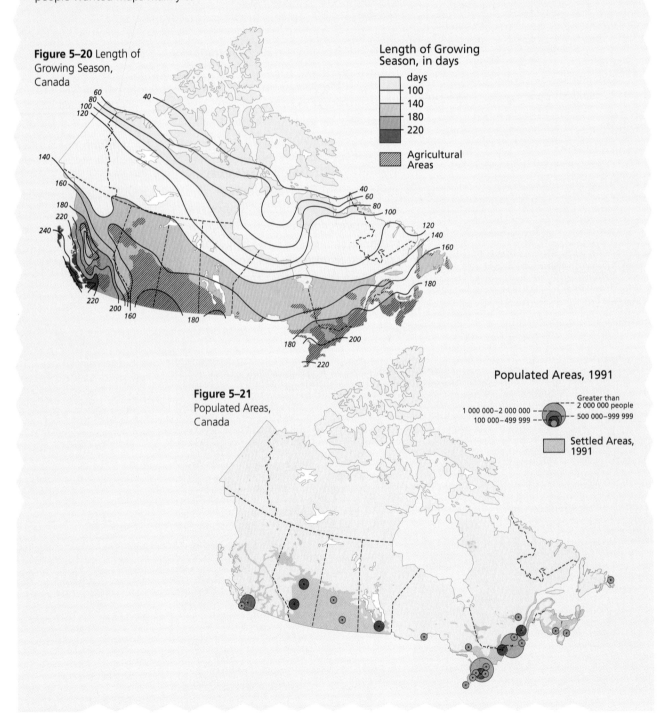

Figure 5–20 Length of Growing Season, Canada

Length of Growing Season, in days

days
100
140
180
220

Agricultural Areas

Figure 5–21 Populated Areas, Canada

Populated Areas, 1991

1 000 000–2 000 000
100 000–499 999
Greater than 2 000 000 people
500 000–999 999

Settled Areas, 1991

Try to find connections between the two maps on page 162. How would you describe where people live in relation to the agricultural areas? Do many live where the growing season is shorter than 100 days? How about where the growing season is more than 180 days? Do you see a major exception in western Canada? Use your knowledge of Canada's natural features or refer to a relief map of Canada to explain this exception to the pattern.

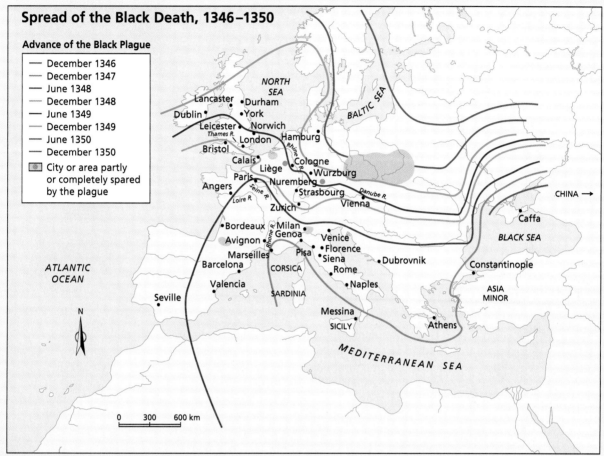

Spread of the Black Death, 1346–1350

Advance of the Black Plague

- —— December 1346
- —— December 1347
- —— June 1348
- —— December 1348
- —— June 1349
- —— December 1349
- —— June 1350
- —— December 1350
- ▦ City or area partly or completely spared by the plague

NORTH SEA
BALTIC SEA
Lancaster • Durham
Dublin • York
Leicester • Norwich
Thames R.
Bristol • London • Hamburg
Calais • Cologne
Paris • Liège • Wurzburg
Angers • Nuremberg
Seine R.
Loire R. • Strasbourg
Zurich • Vienna
Rhine
Danube R.
CHINA →
Bordeaux • Milan
Avignon • Genoa
Rhone R.
Marseilles • Pisa • Venice
Barcelona • Florence
CORSICA • Siena
Rome • Dubrovnik
Valencia
SARDINIA
Caffa
BLACK SEA
Constantinople
ASIA MINOR
ATLANTIC OCEAN
Seville
N
Messina • Naples
SICILY
Athens
MEDITERRANEAN SEA

0   300   600 km

Figure 5–22 Historians think the plague started in China and travelled west along the caravan routes. By 1346 the plague had reached the Black Sea. Here the Italian trading colony of Caffa was besieged by a Mongol army. The Mongol general catapulted the bodies of his dead, plague-stricken soldiers into the city.

NOW YOU DO IT

1. Compare the map above to the map in Figure 5–11, which identifies the main European trade routes in the late Middle Ages. Does your comparison support the historians' hypothesis that the plague spread along the trade routes? How? Describe one route that the plague might have followed in its march across Europe.

Boccaccio's Decameron

Images of the plague haunted artists of the late Middle Ages. The Dance of Death—a popular theme in paintings—shows grinning skeletons leading people from the different classes of society to their graves. The figure of Death became a common character in stories.

The Italian poet Giovanni Boccaccio used the Black Death as background for his collection of stories called *Decameron*, written in 1353. In *Decameron*, ten young people flee the plague-stricken city of Florence to stay in a country estate until the epidemic has ended. To pass the time, they hold a contest to see who can tell the best story. In the opening chapter of his book, Boccaccio tells about the ravages of the Black Death in Florence. Even though this passage comes from a work of fiction, historians consider it primary source material because it was written by an eyewitness to the plague. Explain why those with little money presented a "more pathetic spectacle."

> As for the common people and a large proportion of the bourgeoisie [the middle class], they presented a much more pathetic spectacle, for the majority of them were constrained [forced], either by their poverty or the hope of survival, to remain in their houses. Being confined to their own parts of the city, they fell ill daily in their thousands, and since they had no one to assist them or attend to their needs, they inevitably perished almost without exception. Many dropped dead in the open streets, both by day and by night, whilst a great many others, though dying in their own houses, drew their neighbours' attention to the fact more by the smell of their rotting corpses than by any other means. And what with these, and the others who were dying all over the city, bodies were here, there, and everywhere.

PRIMARY SOURCE

Effects of the Black Death on Economics

The Black Death changed Europe forever, not only by killing so many people but also by damaging the feudal system. Feudalism, as we saw in Chapter 2, was based on farming. The growth of towns and trade had already weakened this system. After the Black Death, labour was in such short supply that workers could travel from estate to estate and ask for higher wages. Because of the labour shortage this brought about and the rise in wages, the Black Death caused many feudal estates to go bankrupt.

Balance Sheet of a Manor

These budgets from a fourteenth-century manor show how the Black Death made the manor lose money. By reducing the labour force, the plague forced lords to pay more to get the labour they needed to run their manors. Furthermore, after the plague the manor had to operate with sixty fewer serfs. What effect would this have on the manor farm and the people left?

BEFORE THE BLACK DEATH:

Two hundred serfs live and work on the manor.

Income
200 serfs x 124 days/serf, valued at 1 penny/day:
200 x 124 x 1 = 24 800 pennies worth of work
Total income for one year: 24 800 pennies worth of work

Expenses
To hire 80 additional workers for 300 days/year at 1 penny/day:
80 x 300 x 1 = 24 000 pennies
Total expenses for one year: 24 000 pennies

Profit from labour for one year before the Black Death:
24 800 - 24 000 = 800 pennies

AFTER THE BLACK DEATH:

Sixty serfs are dead, or have run away to work for higher wages elsewhere. Cost of outside workers is now 3 pennies per day since wages have gone up.

Income
140 serfs x 124 days/serf, valued at 1 penny/day:
140 x 124 x 1 = 17 360 pennies worth of work
Plus
Total income for one year: 17 360 pennies worth of work

Expenses
To hire 80 additional workers for 300 days a year at 3 pennies/day:
80 x 300 x 3 = 72 000 pennies
Total expenses for one year: 72 000 pennies

Loss from labour for one year after the Black Death:
17 360 - 72 000 = -54 640 pennies

Persecution of the Jews

The plague brought out the good in people but also the bad. Some of the worst instances of cruelty during the plague involved prejudice against the Jewish people. This was not unusual.

Jews lived all over Europe in the Middle Ages, particularly in larger villages and towns.

The most skilful and knowledgeable doctors of the Middle Ages were Jewish, though usually they were not allowed to treat Christians. Only a few occupations were open to Jews, so some concentrated on academic studies. Others flourished in business, becoming prosperous jewellers, money traders, and merchants.

Jews were not appreciated for their successes, however. They were usually forced to live in a *ghetto* (a certain section of the town or city), had to wear identifying yellow patches on their clothing, and did not have the freedoms of other

> On Saturday — that was St. Valentine's Day — they burnt the Jews on a wooden platform in their cemetery. There were about two thousand people of them. Those who wanted to baptize themselves were spared. Many small children were taken out of the fire and baptized against the will of their fathers and mothers. And everything that was owed to the Jews was cancelled, and the Jews had to surrender all pledges and notes that they had taken for debts. The council, however, took the cash that the Jews possessed and divided it among the working-men proportionately. The money was indeed the thing that killed the Jews. If they had been poor and if the feudal lords had not been in debt to them, they would not have been burnt.

PRIMARY SOURCE

citizens. Many Christians blamed Jews for the crucifixion of Christ and accused them of secret anti-Christian rituals. At times of trouble, Christians tended to blame Jews for their problems, making them **scapegoats**. Many Jews were massacred during the Crusades and at other times of unrest.

During a time of plague in the French city of Strasbourg, the townspeople accused the Jews of starting the epidemic by putting poison in the city's wells. Despite the objections of city officials, the mob dragged the entire Jewish community to the Jewish cemetery, where they burned them to death in a bonfire. Does this event remind you of a tragedy that occurred during World War Two? Describe links between the two events.

- - - - - - - - - - - - - - - - -

THE PEASANTS' REVOLTS

scapegoat: a person wrongfully blamed, sometimes leading to persecution

Feudalism was further weakened in the fourteenth century when the lowest order of society, the peasants, rose up and demanded better living conditions. In both France and England the revolts at first met with some success but were then savagely suppressed by the nobility.

France

In France, the revolt was called the "Jacquerie," after Jacques Bonhomme, the nickname for the French peasant. The revolt began after the French defeat at the battle of Poitiers in 1356, when the English captured the French king, John II, and held him in London for ransom. While he was gone, a mob attacked the palace of the king's son, the dauphin, in Paris, and drove him from the capital.

In the northern countryside, the serfs broke into open revolt against their lords. Even though the farmlands had been laid waste by years of fighting, manor lords were still demanding high rents from their serfs. Banding together, peasant armies burned manor houses throughout northern France and killed their lords. Reaction was swift and brutal. Ringleaders were rounded up and hanged, and whole villages were burned to the ground.

England

In fourteenth-century England, the ravages of the Black Death caused severe labour shortages in the countryside. Food supplies went down, and prices and wages both rose dramatically. The lords tried to put an end to the trend in 1381. They passed a law returning wages to the pre-plague levels. Then, to help finance the Hundred Years' War, Parliament approved a **poll tax**, which took a fixed amount of money from every person in England, from the lowliest serf to the highest noble.

The serfs had had enough. Two leaders emerged to organize the angry serfs into a fighting force: Wat Tyler, a former soldier; and John Ball, a stirring preacher who believed that since all people were equal in the sight of God there should be no class distinctions.

Before long, a peasant army was marching on London. When the army reached the city, sympathetic guild workers opened the gates of the city. Once inside, the peasants killed any nobles they could find, including the archbishop of Canterbury, and burned

down many great buildings. During negotiations with fourteen-year-old King Richard II, however, Wat Tyler was killed by the lord mayor of London. John Ball was taken prisoner and later beheaded. The revolt collapsed, and the serfs returned to their farms, where vengeful lords hanged many.

Figure 5–23 The Lord Mayor of London strikes down Wat Tyler, while King Richard II and John Ball watch. Write a story about what might have happened if Wat Tyler had dodged the blow and the peasant army had overwhelmed the royal party.

poll tax: a standard tax collected from every person

ACTIVITIES

1. **a)** Rats flourish where there is plenty of garbage and grain to eat. How do you think the conditions in which humans lived in the Middle Ages contributed to the spread of the bubonic plague? Consider systems of waste and garbage disposal, the crowded conditions in town, and the lack of plumbing.

   b) Research other civilizations to find out which ones had plumbing.

2. Make a bar graph showing the population of Europe before and after the Black Death.

3. Imagine you are in the same predicament as the young people of Boccaccio's *Decameron*. Write a story about leaving your family and fleeing your plague-stricken community to join friends at a ski chalet. Be sure to explain how you feel about deserting your family and convey your own worries about becoming infected.

4. Pretend you live on an English manor or in an English town in 1349. Write an account of what happened in your community as a result of the Black Death. Your account, which can appear in diary form, should contain entries for a period of six months or more, and should give details about the social and economic effects of the plague.

5. Examine the chart that shows the balance sheet of a manor before and after the Black Death. Draw a bar graph to compare the profits of the year before the plague, with the losses of the year after the plague. The bar showing profit will rise above the zero line, while the bar showing loss will drop below it.

6. How was the Black Death related to the end of feudalism in Europe? Prepare a detailed response.

7. Identify two causes of the revolt in England.

8. Write a speech, to be read by either John Ball or the leader of the Jacquerie, to inspire the peasants to revolt against the landowners and nobles. Make your speech forceful and dramatic.

By the middle of the fifteenth century, the feudal world of the Middle Ages was disappearing. Monarchs were taking more and more power away from their nobles, and nation states were starting to appear. After the labour shortages caused by the Black Death, serfs were no longer bound to the land. Trade and commerce produced new sources of wealth. This in turn helped cities and towns grow in importance and strengthened the emerging middle class, a class not tied to farming and the land.

The Church, which had tried to create a single Christian empire of the spirit, was still strong at the end of the Middle Ages, but the Church had changed. Because of the rise of new heresies, more and more people began to question its authority. In the sixteenth century, the absolute power of the Roman Catholic Church would be broken by the Protestant Reformation.

The day of the armoured knight ended with the widespread use of gunpowder. One of the last major battles by knights in plate armour was fought during the War of the Roses in England at Bosworth Field in 1485, a year that marks the end of the Middle Ages. All the underpinnings of medieval society—feudal land tenure, the Church, and chivalry—were breaking down, and new social structures were developing to take their places. The European Middle Ages was coming to a close and the Renaissance, a rebirth, was about to begin.

SUMMARY ACTIVITIES

1. **a)** Make a chart to compare the various stages of two medieval young people's education. One wants to become a knight and the other a goldsmith. For both, note the necessary duties and privileges at each stage.

   b) Do some research to find out what education you would need to become a professional soldier in the Canadian Armed Forces. What would be your duties? Your privileges? Compare these with the education, duties, and privileges of a medieval knight.

2. Construct a gothic cathedral or a castle using whatever materials you wish.

3. Write a story featuring at least two of the following: a serf, a feudal lord, a knight, a guild member, an apprentice, and a page. The conflict in your story should stem from the difference in the individuals' social status.

4. The picture on the opening page of this chapter shows a young man drawing his sword to fend off Death. Outline three reasons why people of the late Middle Ages were fascinated by Death.

5. In the late Middle Ages, what was becoming more important: the good of the individual or the good of the group? Give evidence from the text to support your claim.

ON YOUR OWN

1. Research the following words and draw up a chart to show how their meanings have changed from the Middle Ages to today.
   - freelancer
   - jousting
   - gothic
   - masterpiece
   - plague
   - journeyman

2. In 1920, Joan of Arc was declared a saint. To mark this occasion, the Irish writer George Bernard Shaw wrote a play called *St. Joan*. In the preface to his play, Shaw explained why he thought people should know something about Joan. Research one individual mentioned in this chapter and write a short essay explaining why you think people should know about this person.

3. Using the Internet or CD-ROM sources if possible, research a modern epidemic, such as the 1918–20 influenza epidemic, the Ebola virus epidmic, or the AIDS virus epidemic. Write a report to compare this epidemic with the Black Death. How did various aspects of modern civilization allow some people to remain calm? Consider medical knowledge, hospitals, communication, sanitation levels, and knowledge about how the disease is spread.

6 MEDIEVAL JAPAN

CHAPTER OUTCOMES

In this chapter you will focus on the medieval period of Japan, from approximately 700 to 1500. You will also learn about the early years of Japan's civilization. By the end of this chapter you will

- investigate the prehistory and early history of Japan
- use and interpret climate and topographical maps
- compare Japanese and European feudalism
- interpret Japanese literature
- investigate Japanese social structure
- draw conclusions about social structure from evidence
- evaluate the influence of religion on Japanese society
- describe the culture of the samurai

Tale of Genji

The world's first novel, Tale of Genji, was written by Lady Murasaki in Japan before the year 1015 C.E. It is a story about the life and times of a royal prince named Genji, and the period after his death. "Murasaki" is the author's nick-name. No one knows for sure who she really was, except that she was an aristocrat, and that her father was a court official.

Here are five selected passages from Tale of Genji. Because these passages are taken from different parts of the book, try not to look for the actual story line. Instead read to learn about the lives of rich nobles during the Heian Period almost 1000 years ago (794–1185), and about the things that were important to them.

"The Shining Genji is almost too grand a name. Yet he could not escape criticism for numerous little adventures."

Genji Gives a Rehearsal

The royal **excursion** to the Susaka Palace took place towards the middle of the Tenth Month. The emperor's ladies **lamented** that they would not be present at what would certainly be a most remarkable concert. Distressed at the thought that Lady Fujitsobu should be deprived of the pleasure, the emperor ordered a full rehearsal at the main palace.

Genji and To no Chujo danced the "Waves of the Blue Ocean." To no Chujo was a handsome youth, but compared to Genji he was like a **nondescript** mountain shrub beside a blossoming cherry. In the bright evening light the music echoed grandly through the palace and the excitement grew.

Although the dance was a familiar one, Genji scarcely seemed of this world. As he **intoned** the lyrics, his listeners could have believed they were listening to the bird of paradise. The emperor brushed away tears of delight, and there were tears in the eyes of all the princes and high **courtiers** as well. As Genji rearranged his costume at the end of his song and the orchestra took up again, he seemed to shine with an ever-brighter light.

"Surely the gods above are struck dumb with admiration," Lady Kokiden, the mother of the crown prince, was heard to observe. "One is overpowered by such company."

Some of the young women thought her rather horrid.

To Fujitsobu it was all a dream. How she wished that these remarkable experiences had not taken place. Then she might be as happy as the others.

On the day of the excursion the emperor was attended by his whole court, the princes and the rest. The crown prince too was present. Music came from boats rowed out over the lake, and there was an **infinite** variety of Chinese and Korean dancing. Reed and string and drum echoed through the grounds. The most **renowned** players from the high and middle court ranks were chosen for the flutists' circle. The director of the Chinese dances and the director of the Korean dances were both guards officers who held seats on the council of state. The dancers had for weeks been in **monastic** seclusion studying each motion under the direction of the most revered masters of the art.

Genji leaves his hiding place to spy on two ladies of the court playing Go.

Genji Spies on Ladies Playing a Board Game

Hoping to see the ladies at the **Go** board, Genji slipped from his hiding place and made his way through the door and blind. One panel of the screen had been folded back. There was a lamp near the women. One woman seemed to have on a purple singlet with a woven pattern, and over it a cloak of which the colour and material were not easy to determine. She was a small, rather ordinary woman with delicate features. She evidently wanted to conceal her face even from the girl opposite, and she kept her thin little hands tucked in her sleeves.

Her opponent was facing east, and Genji had a full view of her face. Over a singlet of white **gossamer** she had thrown a purplish cloak, and both garments were somewhat carelessly arranged all the way to the band of the red trousers. She was very handsome, tall and plump, and of a fair complexion, and the lines of her forehead and head were strong and pleasing. It was a sunny face, with a **beguiling** cheerfulness about the eyes and mouth. Though not particularly long, the hair was rich and thick, and very beautiful when it fell about the shoulder.

It might help, to be sure, if she were just a little quieter. Yet she did not seem to be merely silly. She brimmed with good spirits as she placed a stone on a dead spot to mark the end of the game.

Ukon is alone with her thoughts.

Ukon Enjoys a Quiet Moment

The evening sky was serenely beautiful. The flowers below the veranda were withered, the songs of the insects were dying, too, and autumn tints were coming over the maples. Looking out upon the scene, which might have been a painting, Ukon thought what a lovely **asylum** she had found for herself. She wanted to **avert** her eyes at the thought of the house of the "evening faces." A pigeon called, somewhat **discordantly**, from a bamboo thicket.

Nakatsukasa Is Infatuated

They were too fond of each other to say good-bye on the spot.

Getting into the carriage, they played on their flutes as they made their way under a pleasantly misted moon to the Sanjo mansion. Having no **outrunners**, they were able to pull up to a secluded gallery without attracting attention. There they sent out for court dress.

Taking up their flutes once again, they proceeded to the main hall as if they had just come from court. The minister, always eager for a concert, joined in with a Korean flute. He was a fine musician, and soon the more accomplished of the ladies within the blinds had joined them on lutes.

There was a most accomplished woman named Nakatsukasa. To no Chojo had designs on her, but she had turned him away. Genji, who rarely came into the house, had quite won her affections. News of the **infatuation** had reached the ears of Princess Omiya, To no Chujo's mother, who strongly disapproved of it. Poor Nakatsukasa was thus left with her own sad thoughts, and

tonight she sat forlornly apart from the others, leaning on an armrest. She had considered seeking a position elsewhere but she was reluctant to take a step that would prevent her from seeing Genji again.

The End of the Tenth Month

It was late in the tenth month. The vines on the shrine fence were red and there were red leaves beneath the pine trees as well, so that the services of the wind were not needed to tell of the **advent** of autumn.

The familiar eastern music seemed more familiar than the more subtle Chinese and Korean music. Against the sea winds and waves, flutes joined the breeze through the high pines of the famous grove with a grandeur that could only belong to Sumiyoshi. The quiet clapping that went with the koto was more moving than the solemn beat of the drums. The bamboo of the flutes had been stained to a deeper green, to blend with the green of the pines. The ingeniously made flowers in peoples' caps seemed to make a single carpet with the flowers of the autumn fields.

The song "The One I Seek" came to an end and the young courtiers of the higher ranks all pulled their robes down over their shoulders as they descended into the courtyard, and suddenly a dark field seemed to burst into a bloom of pink and lavender. The crimson sleeves beneath, moistened very slightly by a passing shower, made it seem for a moment like the pine groves had become a grove of maples and that autumn leaves were showering down. Great reeds that had been bleached to a pure white swayed over the dancing figures, and the waves of white seemed to **linger** on when the brief dance was over and they had returned to their places.

For Genji, the memory of his troubles was so vivid that it seemed like only yesterday.

excursion: a trip

to lament: to grieve for

nondescript: plain, without impressive qualities

to intone: to sing

courtier: a court attendant

infinite: endless

renowned: famous

monastic: characteristic of monks or a monastery

Go: a Japanese game played with black and white stones on a marked board

gossamer: fine fabric

beguiling: appealing

asylum: safe place

to avert: to turn away

discordantly: not in harmony

outrunners: servants who run alongside the cart

infatuation: giddy love or affection

advent: coming

to linger: to stay

Genji and his friend To no Chujo sense that fall has arrived.

ACTIVITIES

1. *Tale of Genji* is not only the first novel in the world—it is also one of the longest, at 1200 pages. Look up the definition of "novel" in a dictionary or encyclopedia. Can you think of any reasons why the novel might have developed in Japan at this moment in history? Once you read more about the Japanese aristocracy and the role of women, you may want to revisit this question.

2. Find five colourful images, or pictures in the mind, created by the author. Select your favourite image and create a sketch or painting that illustrates it.

3. Genji is an officer in the Guards, part of the military. What kind of military leader do you think Genji would make? Explain and give at least one example to support your view.

4. You have already been introduced to several different cultures in *Pathways*. What evidence is there in these excerpts that Japanese culture was influenced by other cultures? Give two examples.

5. List some of the pastimes that were important to Heian aristocrats. Would you enjoy this kind of life? Why or why not?

8000 BCE	JOMON AND AINU CULTURE PRESENT IN JAPAN
250 BCE	YAYOI CULTURE PRESENT IN JAPAN
300	YAMATO PERIOD BEGINS
538	INTRODUCTION OF BUDDHISM INTO JAPAN
710	BEGINNING OF THE NARA PERIOD
1010	WRITING OF THE TALE OF GENJI
1185	MINAMOTO YORITOMO SEIZES CONTROL; START OF THE KAMAKURA PERIOD
1274	FIRST MONGOL INVASION
1318	GO-DAIGO BECOMES EMPEROR
1336	BEGINNING OF THE ASHIKAGA SHOGUNATE
1543	ARRIVAL OF THE PORTUGUESE IN JAPAN
1568	ODA NOBUNAGA CAPTURES KYOTO
1600	BEGINNING OF THE TOKUGAWA SHOGUNATE

In the sound of the bell of the Gion Temple echoes the **impermanence** *of all things.... The proud ones do not last long, but vanish like a spring night's dream. And the mighty ones too will perish in the end, like dust in the wind.*

—**TALE OF HEIKE**

PRIMARY SOURCE

This quotation from *Tale of Heike* captures a melancholy feeling that the Japanese call *aware*. Have you ever felt sad in the presence of something powerful or wonderful?

INTRODUCTION

Japan is a country with a fascinating history. Today Japan is one of the world's most modern nations, and one of its wealthiest. This is a great achievement because Japan cut itself off from the outside world for almost 250 years. During this period of the final **shogunate**, which ended in 1867, foreigners were forbidden to live in or even visit Japan.

After Japan became more open to western influences in the mid-nineteenth century, the Japanese people began to turn their country into a modern nation, partly by borrowing some ideas from the West. They were so successful that by 1900, Japan had fully developed important industries, such as steel making, and had built a powerful army and navy. Today, the Japanese automobile industry is the largest in the world. Do you own a futon? That too is a Japanese invention, born of the necessity to save space.

For much of its history, Japan has seen war. Military ideas and values were important to this culture well into the twentieth century. Most people have heard of Japan's **samurai** warriors. Samurai culture developed during Japan's feudal period, which lasted for hundreds of years. Japanese feudalism is similar to the feudalism of Europe but with some important differences. Of course, Japan was not always feudal. During the Nara and Heian periods, a strong central government ruled a relatively peaceful land.

Through all the years of war, Japan kept and nurtured its strong traditions. Even the samurai loved art and respected the past. In Heian times, Japanese noblewomen made long-lasting contributions to art and literature. In art, as in other things, simplicity and refinement continue to be important. These ideas are supported by two Japanese religions—Shinto and Zen Buddhism (a sect of Buddhism).

Tradition and history—and Japan's status as an island nation—have helped make Japanese culture unique. Its people have always had a strong attachment to their homeland, a value that continues to this day.

shogunate: a military government of Japan led by a shogun, or military ruler

samurai: warriors who worked for the powerful lords who eventually took control of Japan

JAPAN'S GEOGRAPHY

Japan is an island nation made up of four main islands—Hokkaido, Kyushu, Honshu, Shikoku—and many small islands. A group of such islands is called an **archipelago**. From north to south, the Japanese archipelago is over 2000 kilometres long. Japan is close enough to the mainland of Asia to have had important contacts with the cultures of Korea and China. These contacts have been important throughout its history. The southwestern coasts of Kyushu and Shikoku are just over 200 kilometres from Korea.

Japan is both mountainous and volcanic. Only 20 percent of its land is plain and valley, which means that land for agriculture must be used efficiently. Mountain ranges also have an important effect on where people settle and on how they make their living. Most of Japan's population lives on the large coastal plains, such as the

impermanence: mortality changeability

archipelago: a chain of many islands

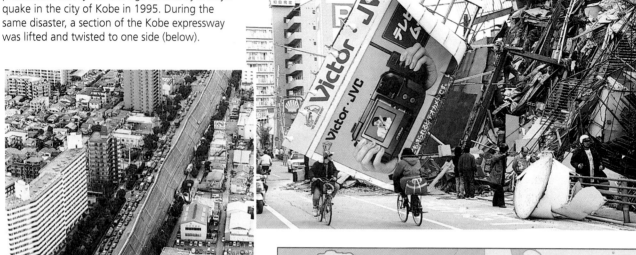

Figure 6–1 Earthquakes are relatively common occurrences in Japan. Right, cyclists and pedestrians survey the damage caused by a major quake in the city of Kobe in 1995. During the same disaster, a section of the Kobe expressway was lifted and twisted to one side (below).

geyser: a boiling hot spring that shoots steam and a column of water into the air at intervals

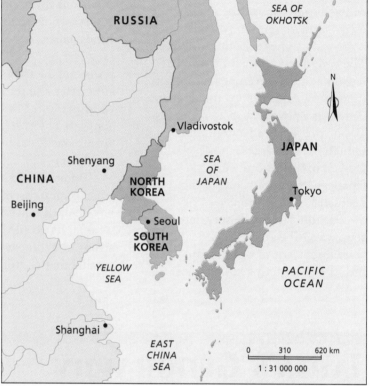

Figure 6–2 Japan and its surroundings

Kantö Plain, which surrounds Japan's largest city, Tokyo. Important boundary lines, which today mark provinces, or prefectures, follow the crests of mountain ranges.

Like British Columbia, Japan is on the Pacific "Rim of Fire." Many volcanoes are active, and there are **geysers** in many places. There are also many earthquakes in Japan. Japan's most famous mountain, Fuji, is a volcano.

Although Japan is in the northern Pacific, its climate is relatively mild because of the warm Kuro Shio ocean current. However, the climate in northern Japan is very different from that of the south. Northern Japan has cold winters, with lots of snow, and cool summers. Southern Japan has a subtropical climate where rice and other warm weather crops grow well. Rice is Japan's most important crop. In the past, rice-growing areas were vigorously defended—probably because land was at such a premium.

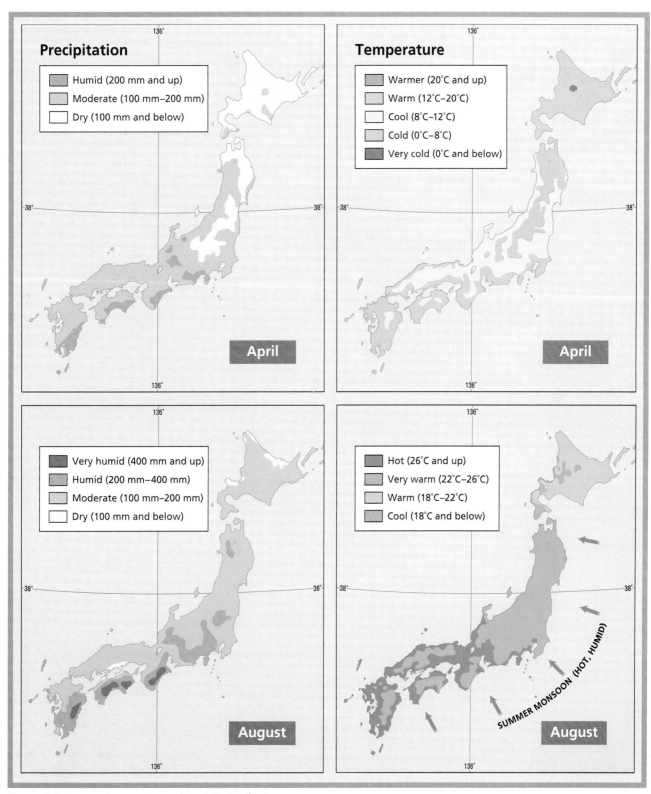

Figure 6–3 Average temperature and precipitation for Japan during the months of April and August

Use Large- and Small-Scale Maps

A large-scale map shows more detail than a small-scale map. Both types of maps are useful but for different purposes.

The map of Japan shown in Figure 6–2 on page 176 is a small-scale map. You can determine the scale by reading the representative ratio in the lower right corner, in this case 1 : 31 000 000, which means that 1 millimetre on the map represents 31 000 000 millimetres of real space. (For more on map scales, see page 212.) A small-scale map is useful for viewing the size and shape of a country in relation to its surroundings.

Figure 6–4 is a large-scale map that shows the area around Fuji-**san**, Japan's most famous mountain. The volcanic cone is clearly visible. Note how the boundary lines of Japan's provinces follow the mountain ridges. Large-scale maps are useful for viewing a country's **topographical** features in more detail. In this map, you can also see

the region's main roadways and buildings

san: a Japanese suffix (word ending) meaning "mountain peak"

topographical: describing the surface characteristics of a region, for example, its lakes, rivers, and mountains

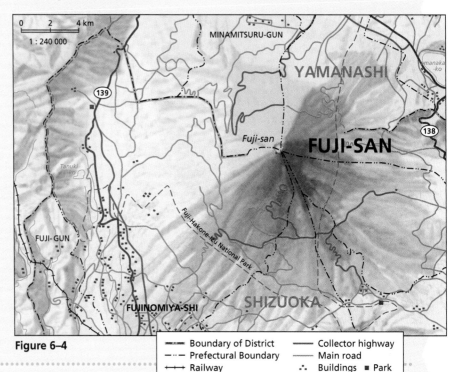

Figure 6–4

- ┄┄┄ Boundary of District
- ─ · ─ · ─ Prefectural Boundary
- ┝┷┷┥ Railway
- ─── Principal highway
- ─── Collector highway
- ─── Main road
- ∴ Buildings ■ Park

NOW YOU DO IT

1. What is the scale of the map shown in Figure 6–4?

2. Would a city map be a large- or small-scale map?

3. Would Figure 6–4 be more useful to a traveller than a small scale map? Explain.

4. Japanese uses many suffixes in words. For example, -gun means "county" and -shi means

"city." Identify the counties and cities on Figure 6–4.

5. Identify the routes of major roads shown in Figure 6–4. Make a general statement about the roads in relation to the topography. Where are the major settlements? Make a general statement about topography in relation to the settlements.

A C T I V I T I E S

1. What three factors helped make Japanese culture unique?

2. With a classmate, brainstorm some brand names that originate in Japan. Do these brand names describe objects that have something in common? What conclusion can you draw about Japan after reviewing your list?

3. Examine the climate maps of Japan on page 177. Can you explain why the pockets of southern Japan are warmer and wetter than the other areas? Hint: Refer to a physical map of Japan in your atlas. What areas of the country get the most snowfall and other precipitation?

THE EARLY DAYS OF THE RISING SUN

The islands of Japan have been occupied for thousands of years. The name "Japan" means "great land of the rising sun." This is fitting, say some historians, because Japan's first peoples may have believed that the sun first rose over their islands.

Japan's first inhabitants were known as the Jomon. The Jomon people originally came from South China, and possibly some islands in the South Pacific, around 9500 B.C.E. They were hunter-gatherers, living by hunting, fishing, and gathering food such as nuts and shellfish.

During this time, another group of people arrived on Hokkaido, Japan's most northern island. Historians believe that these people, known as the Ainu, came from the region around the Amur River, which serves now as part of the China-Russia border. Today the Ainu are known as Japan's Aboriginal peoples. They number only 20 000 and are fighting for **territorial rights** to a group of islands off the coast of Hokkaido.

By 300 B.C.E., a new people called "the Yayoi" had appeared on the scene. They probably came from what is now Korea, and intermingled with the Jomon. The Yayoi developed agriculture in Japan. They knew how to grow rice, which was to become a very important part of the Japanese diet. They also used iron and bronze tools, had mirrors, and raised horses and cattle.

Around 300 C.E., Japan entered what is known as the Yamato period. The Yamato family was a **clan** that claimed to be descended directly from the Sun God. This belief—along with some carefully planned marriages—allowed them to gain power over all the other powerful families living in Japan at the time. This was how the idea of the **imperial sun line** was born, a concept still respected in Japan today.

territorial rights: rights to land

clan: a social grouping made up of related families

imperial sun line: the concept that the Japanese emperor is directedly related to the Sun God, the greatest of all deities

Figure 6–5 This keyhole-shaped tomb near Osaka, Japan, was built for the Yamato emperor Nintoku. Its massive size, and the fact that it has never been looted or opened, are indications that the emperor was highly revered. Why is this tomb in the shape of a keyhole?

How a Written Language Was Born

Around 360 C.E., written language first came to Japan from Korea. Up to this point, the Japanese had lived without writing anything down.

When Koreans began visiting Japan, they wrote down their impressions of the country using Chinese characters. These were the characters you read about in Chapter 3, developed by the Chinese during the Shang Dynasty. The Japanese admired this writing and borrowed the Chinese characters to form the basis of their own written language.

This is why Japanese writing has so many characters that are identical to Chinese characters.

But the Japanese did not rest there. To go with the Chinese characters, they developed new symbols that communicated the grammar of their **oral** language. This new system was known as **kana**. Kana made writing Japanese simpler.

As time went on, it was still considered important for aristocratic males to master classical Chinese. It eventually gained status as the language of "good literature"—as did Latin and classical German in Europe. Noblewomen, on the other hand, were free to write in kana. Many noblewomen of Heian Japan kept lengthy diaries and **pillow books** in kana.

Today, the Japanese language still uses about 1200 Chinese characters in books, newspapers, magazines, and advertising. Every student is expected to memorize them.

oral: spoken

kana: an alphabet developed by the Japanese to write down their oral language

pillow book: a bedside journal in which one records the day's events

WHAT DO YOU THINK?

1. Are there any advantages to a society that has no written language? What are they? What are the drawbacks?

2. Why do you think Japanese noblewomen were encouraged to write in kana while men were still expected to master Chinese? Consider expectations as well as desire to control important documents.

creed: a formal statement of religious beliefs

scriptures: sacred writings

RELIGION IN JAPAN'S EARLY PERIOD

For many years leading up to the mid-sixth century, the Japanese practised a religion called "Shinto." Shinto means "the Way of the Gods" and is still followed in Japan today. Shinto has been influenced by the introduction of Confucianism and Buddhism, which you read about in Chapter 3.

Shinto is based on a series of traditions and customs, most of which involve pilgrimages to famous places and shrines. It has no **creed** or holy **scriptures**. The most important spirits in Shinto are *kami*, which means "above" or "superior." The kami are not gods in the Western sense—they could be mountains, rivers, rocks, streams, or ancestors—any object or person who inspires awe. Shinto gods and spirits sometimes live in temples, where they can be contacted by priests and individuals. The emperor was believed to have the closest connection with the gods, being descended from the Sun God. Among believers, Shinto often brings about a deep love of nature. Shinto shrines have been built on many beautiful natural spots in Japan, even in the water.

Buddhism in Japan

Buddhism came to Japan from China via Korea during the late Yamato period. Although followers of Shinto were initially skeptical of Buddhism, it did offer one attractive belief: people could continue to exist in an afterlife. Shinto had little positive to say about life after death. Instead it emphasized the beauty of the here and now.

Buddhism was formally introduced to Japan in 552 C.E., when a Korean ambassador to Japan brought over a large statue of Buddha. Soon after, a Japanese clan associated with the Sun Line declared that it would follow Buddhism. By the end of the sixth century, Prince Shotoku had declared Buddhism a state religion of Japan. He also determined that other aspects of Chinese culture should take root in his country. He personally organized several missions to China involving hundreds of Japanese monks, painters, musicians, and government officials. These people eventually returned— sometimes after 30 years—with new and wonderful knowledge to pass on to the Japanese.

Figure 6–6 The floating "spirit gate" at Miyajima, a famous Shinto shrine. This gateway has its origins in the Shinto religion. What feeling does this shrine inspire in you?

tradition dictated. Before Prince Ahotoku died in 607, he built at Nara what is now the oldest remaining wooden building in the world—the Horyuji Temple.

For a time, Japan's government seemed rather like Chinese government with many officials ruling from the central capital. Chinese sytems of taxation were introduced, and a code of law, the Taiho Code, was established in 702. This approach was quite different from the feudal system which became so important later on.

Buddhism was very strong during

Figure 6–7 This Buddhist temple was built in the seventh century in Nara. The suffix *ji* means "temple" in Japanese. Traditional Japanese architecture borrowed ideas from China.

THE NARA PERIOD, 700–800

The Nara period lasted fewer than one hundred years, but important events occurred during that time that changed Japanese culture. Many ideas continued to be imported from China, including ways of governing, religious ideas, and taxation systems.

Nara, Japan's first capital city, was a copy of China's capital at Chang'an. It was laid out as a rectangle with the palace at the north end, as Chinese

the Nara period. During this era, Buddhist monks virtually took over the government and angered many people. This was also a period of great hardship for the Japanese because a series of smallpox and measles epidemics claimed many lives. Even the new tax base could not provide enough funds to look after everyone.

However, the rulers managed to build many fine temples and create beautiful art to honour the Buddha. For this reason, the Nara period is an important period for Buddhist art. Buddhists were so influential in Nara that the capital was eventually moved to Heian-kyo (Kyoto) to get away from them.

The Buddha's Sayings

The Buddha was born in India in the sixth century B.C.E. As you learned in Chapter 3, he taught that finding the truth about life was a personal quest. After his death, many Buddhist sects appeared, including Japan's Zen Buddhism.

As one source of guidance in their spiritual quest, Buddhists could turn to the *Dharmapada*, the sayings of the Buddha. There are 423 sayings. Here are three, to give non-Buddhists some sense of what Buddhists value.

- ◆ A speech can be made up of a thousand senseless words. One word of sense is better, which if people hear, they become quiet.
- ◆ If one man conquers a thousand in battle, he is not so great as those who conquer themselves.
- ◆ Canal-makers lead the water; archers bend the bow; carpenters bend a log of wood; good people fashion themselves.

ACTIVITIES

1. In what ways did Yayoi culture differ from Jomon culture? How did these differences advance Japan?

2. Examine the picture of the Yamato tomb on page 179. Make three general statements about the Yamato period based solely on what this tomb tells you about the people who built it.

3. With a partner, create a chart comparing Buddhism with one other religion you have studied. Headings might include

   - ◆ name of God or gods
   - ◆ important beliefs
   - ◆ concept of afterlife
   - ◆ place of origin
   - ◆ role of priests

4. Reread the sayings of Buddha found above. What do they have in common? If you were to identify one attitude these sayings encourage, what would it be?

5. Try to find more information about the Ainu of Japan. How is their situation similar to that of the Native peoples of Canada or Australia?

HEIAN JAPAN, 794–1192

For much of the Heian period, Japan enjoyed relative peace and security. Normally, this would result from strong leadership, but this was not the case. Power was concentrated in the hands of the Fujiwara family, who were second only to the Sun Line, and who used emperors as **puppet rulers**.

The Fujiwara were an important family in the city of Heian, today called Kyoto. When the emperor and the government moved from Nara, the Fujiwara took control. To make themselves even stronger, Fujiwara women and men married members of the imperial family.

During this time, the imperial court and the high nobles occupied themselves by refining their lifestyle. They loved beautiful clothes and textiles. They developed a taste for fine painting and sculpture, much of it religious. They lived in a kind of fantasy world, and were intensely interested in themselves and their own doings. Perhaps you noticed this theme in *Tale of Genji*, of which you read part in the Window on the Past. A weighty discussion could revolve around which of the four seasons was most lovely.

Heian nobles believed that truly civilized people needed to be able to appreciate the beauty of nature and beautiful objects. The term *miyabi* means "refinement," and describes the attitude of these people. They devoted themselves to studying the beauty of flowers, tea bowls, fine paintings, and many other small things.

They also enjoyed thinking about the sadness in life—that it was over quickly, and that all things passed away. This melancholy feeling is called *aware*. It is found in many poems and stories of the period. Some flower arrangements, even today,

Figure 6–8 Heian art was often painted on hand scrolls. This detail from a late Heian painting shows a gathering of literary men.

create the feeling of aware in many Japanese people. The following quote from *Tale of Heike*, the story of the civil war between the Taira and Minamoto clans, conveys the feeling of aware.

> In the sound of the bell of the Gion Temple echoes the impermanence of all things... The proud ones do not last long, but vanish like a spring-night's dream. And the mighty ones too will perish in the end, like dust in the wind.

PRIMARY SOURCE

Outside the court, these aristocratic values were far less important. People went about their business—growing crops, manufacturing pottery and tools, and generally living life—without paying much attention to the imperial court. Gradually, the wealthy landowners who lived in the provinces began to assume more power for themselves. Many peasants resented paying high taxes to the imperial court and decided to relocate closer to the landowners. In return for some protection, they paid the landowners rent. The landowners began to assemble powerful armies of

puppet ruler: an offical ruler who does what another person or group of persons says

fantasy: not real

DID YOU KNOW?

The emperor never appeared in public because it was believed that ordinary people would be overwhelmed by the sight of him. When the emperor appeared before other nobles, he sat behind a screen.

warriors who would defend them. These developments signalled the end of the Heian Empire.

THE RISE OF THE SAMURAI CLASS

The samurai class was born as the Heian capital grew weaker. Samurai were skilled archers and swordsmen employed by the powerful lords who were gaining control over Japan's land. Over the years, while the palace nobles preoccupied themselves with delicacy and refinement, the provincial lords had been developing powerful armies to defend their territories. Now they were ready to take control. Two families, or clans, eventually became very powerful. These were the Taira clan and the Minamoto clan.

The Taira and the Minamoto

The Taira were also called the Heike, while the Minamoto were called the Genji (not the Genji of *Tale of Genji*). As the situation in the capital city became more chaotic, the Taira and Minamoto began their struggle for

absolute power. During this time, small wars were breaking out constantly, emperors were **abdicating** early in their reigns, and nobles were hiring samurai to guard them.

Two major wars resulted in victory for the Taira, who tried to wipe out the surviving Minamoto. Within ten years, however, the Minamoto struck back. In the naval battle of Dannoura, they completely destroyed the power of the Taira clan. To avoid capture, members of the Taira family drowned themselves.

abdicate: to give up a throne

Figure 6–10 This painting shows a famous incident of the civil war between the Taira and the Minamoto. Surrounded by samurai warriors, the emperor is taken away in a covered cart.

ACTIVITIES

1. Explain how the emperors and their officials lost power in Heian Japan.

2. Who were the Fujiwara? What was their role in the government of Japan?

3. Write a letter from a court lady or gentleman to a friend. The letter should express the feelings of aware and miyabi.

4. Draw a picture or write a short story about the Taira and the Minamoto and their wars.

THE FEUDAL AGE

As you read earlier, the civil war between the Taira and Minamoto clans came about because the imperial government of Japan broke down. When this happened, local lords, who could raise and train armies of samurai, became powerful. They supported themselves by collecting taxes from the people who lived on their lands. These lands were known as *shoen*, which is similar to a European fief—a word you may remember from reading about the European feudal system in Chapter 2. After the civil war, Japan became completely feudal.

The victor in the civil war,

Figure 6–11 This portrait of the shogun Yoritomo shows him wearing a sword, a symbol of the real source of his power.

shogun: a military ruler of Japan during the feudal period

shogunate: a period of rule by a shogun

daimyo: a great feudal lord

revere: to admire and honour

Minamoto Yoritomo, ruled Japan from the city of Kamakura. He decided to leave the imperial court in Nara, believing it to be incompetent. For this reason, Japan's first feudal period is often called the Kamakura Period. Yoritomo did not try to become emperor himself, an act that would have been technically impossible because the emperor was descended from the Sun God. Instead, Yoritomo adopted the title of **shogun**, and showed public respect for the emperor. Nevertheless, the shogun had all the real power in Japan. For the next 600 years, Japan would be ruled by three successive **shogunates**.

THE BAKUFU

Yoritomo ruled Japan as a military overlord, and the important officials in his government were soldiers. The government itself was called the *bakufu*, which means "headquarters." The bakufu had three parts. One department ran the military, another ran the day-to-day affairs of the country, and the third dealt with justice.

Yoritomo also appointed military governors and stewards to look after many parts of the land. Later, the governors would become the great feudal lords while the stewards would become the less important ones. Feudal lords were called **daimyos**. The samurai owed allegiance to the daimyo.

In the meantime, many of the government jobs of the old imperial court remained. The emperor became a figure who was **revered**, but who grew less powerful as time went on. Yoritomo also made Japan completely unlike China, where the military was kept from power and was treated with contempt.

Yoritomo died when he fell off his horse in 1199. The title of shogun was taken by members of the Hojo family. Hojo was the family name of Yoritomo's wife. For a time, the Hojo made the bakufu stronger, even defeating an attempt by an emperor to take power. Sometimes the Hojo family gave the title of shogun to others—members of the Fujiwara family, for example. But they kept the real power to themselves, and were able to stay in charge for over a hundred years.

Gradually, though, power began to slip away from Kamakura, and into the hands of the daimyos. The Emperor Go-Daigo took advantage of this weakness and challenged the Hojo family. Another civil war broke out. The Hojo were betrayed by one of their most important supporters, a feudal lord named Ashikaga. In the end, Kamakura was captured and burned.

Although Go-Daigo tried to rule without the bakufu, new struggles broke out. Japan even had two emperors for a time. To control the emperor, Ashikaga brought the bakufu to Kyoto. Unfortunately, the daimyos now had much more power and could not be controlled by Ashikaga's government. In this sense, Japan's feudalism was similar to Europe's feudalism. Powerful lords fought one another and ruled their own **domains**.

FEUDAL SOCIETY

For long periods during the feudal period, Japan did not have much contact with other cultures. This was

domain: land belonging to one person

typhoon: a tropical cyclone or windstorm

sake: rice wine

LINK-UP

The Origins of the Kamikaze

During the Kamakura period, Japan was invaded twice by Mongols from the mainland of Asia, led by Khubilai Khan. You will read more about this period of history in Chapter 13. These invasions, though unsuccessful, had important effects on Japan.

First, the feudal lords led by the shogun showed themselves ready to sacrifice themselves for Japan. This made feudalism stronger. Second, Japan was saved by a great **typhoon** that destroyed the Mongol navy in 1281. To the Japanese, this event seemed to have been sent by the gods to protect their people. Never again, until the Second World War, would Japan be invaded by outsiders. The "Divine Wind," called *kamikaze* in Japanese, helped the Japanese see themselves as a special, protected people.

At the end of World War Two, when Japan was about to be invaded by the Americans, young pilots crashed their planes loaded with explosives into American warships. These planes and their pilots were called "Kamikaze," in honour of their sacrifice and of the winds that had once saved Japan.

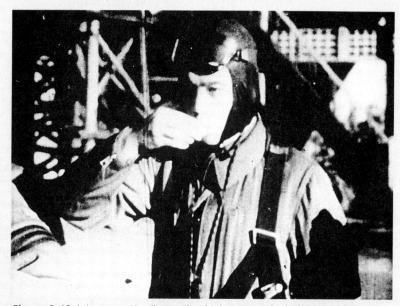

Figure 6–12 A Japanese Kamikaze pilot drinks some **sake** before launching his suicide mission during World War Two, which took place from 1939 to 1945.

WHAT DO YOU THINK?

1. Japan remained free from invasion for hundreds of years. What effect might this have had on its people's view of their own history? Explain.

2. Would you die for your country? Explain why or why not in two or three sentences.

Figure 6–13 This picture of the capital at Kyoto was painted on a screen used to divide rooms in Japanese homes and palaces. Note the architecture, people, costumes, and perspective.

in stark contrast with its early years, when Japan had encouraged the introduction of Chinese culture. Eventually, it became difficult for foreigners to come to Japan. Contact with China was cut off for a time during China's Tang Dynasty.

Later, for over 200 years—until 1853—the nation was completely cut off from the outside world. This isolation put Japan in a unique position. Its traditions and the outlook of its people are very distinctive. In some respects, all Japanese belong to a kind of super-village in which harmony is the most important goal. Japanese society is not, however, one of equals. Almost every person in Japan has higher or lower status compared with another person. Many of these patterns were made more rigid during Japan's long feudal period.

Duty and Obligations

Japanese society is rich with complicated social relationships. This means that people have many duties and responsibilities that they take very seriously, even today. In the past, a person could be killed or be required to kill himself or herself if an important duty was not performed, or performed badly. (For an example, see the story of *The Forty-Seven Ronin* on page 191.)

But it is even more complicated than that. A person becomes obligated to someone else the moment he or she is born. Obligation to others—a kind of debt that must be repaid—is called *on*. Japanese people have an obligation to their parents, teachers, and other important people in their life, such as the emperor. Although it is impossible to repay this debt to some people (parents, ancestors, the emperor), people have a duty to try to do so throughout their lives. Some obligations can be paid back. These obligations are called *giri*.

> Giri is hardest to bear.
> —Japanese Saying
>
> PRIMARY SOURCE

A Person's Rank

In feudal times, every person in Japan knew their **rank** in society. As in Confucian China, a person's rank, as well as their age, gave him or her the right to be treated with respect by less important people. Women were always considered inferior to men, and had to show them respect. Even a young boy could come to rule his mother. Sisters always **deferred** to brothers. Wives were required to obey their husbands.

rank: position in society

to defer: to submit to another's wishes

Respect was offered in the form of bows or, in some cases, **prostration**. High-ranking people received respect and acknowledged it appropriately. When meeting someone new, it was always important to find out who they were and where they fit in society. This still happens today. When Japanese business people exchange business cards, they want to know with whom they are dealing, and how much respect the person should receive. Proper behaviour was, and is, extremely important. The Japanese firmly believe that good manners make society run properly.

Japanese society during the feudal period had eight or nine levels. At the top, the royal family and higher nobles lived apart from the rest of the world. For most of the feudal period, the people who belonged to this class had very little power. They spent their lives performing ceremonies, studying art, and taking part in the complicated politics of the emperor's court.

As you have learned, real power during the feudal period was held by the shogun, and the daimyos, who belonged to the samurai class. They were rather like the knights and barons of feudal Europe. This class had tremendous pride in their family history and in their role in society. They devoted themselves to the military arts, and admired personal bravery and self-control. They had the right to kill any commoner who offended them.

The other members of Japanese society were ranked according to their occupation. This means that a person's job gave him or her high or low status, something that also happens in our own society. But there are important differences.

In feudal Japan, a person was required to do the same job as that performed by his or her parents, a custom that continued for generations. Farmers had higher status than carpenters, potters, and

Figure 6–14 Modern-day Tokyo during rush hour. Do you think good manners can help society run properly? Why or why not??

other craftspeople, who had higher status than merchants. Beggars and actors came next, who in turn had higher status than leather workers. People at the very bottom, who did not fit into any of the categories, were known as the "lowest of the low" and had no rights at all. Unlike present-day Canadian society, there was almost no **social mobility**. You were what you were, and that was that.

prostration: lying on the ground with face downward to indicate humility

social mobility: the movement—up or down—of people's position in society

Figure 6–15 These swordsmiths had fairly high status in feudal Japan because the samurai depended on their handiwork.

THE LIFE OF THE SAMURAI

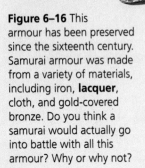

You now know that samurai were trained fighters who served a daimyo, or lord. Their work was to carry out the business of war, much like the knights of feudal Europe. Samurai were not allowed to take part in business, so they paid no taxes or even rent when in the service of a lord. The lord required absolute obedience from samurai, which included committing suicide, if ordered. Like European knights, samurai were proud of their rank in society. They enjoyed special privileges, including cheap travel and many free gifts, which they often **extorted** from the lower classes.

For various reasons, samurai might find themselves without a lord to serve. These men, known as *ronin* (floating men), knew no other life, and often lived as near-outlaws. Samurai women were as fiercely proud as samurai men, willing to fight or to defend castles if necessary.

In the sixteenth century, samurai were given the right to wear two swords, a short *wakizashi* and a long *katana*. Swords were prized weapons. They were carefully made by master swordsmiths, and beautifully assembled. Even the wavy pattern on the edge of the super-sharp blades was admired and discussed. Famous swords were passed on from generation to generation. Armed with two swords, samurai spent their lives ready to fight at a moment's notice. They were also extremely proud and took offence easily. Duels to the death were often started by a single insulting word. Swordless people in the lower classes were very careful to show the samurai proper respect. To do otherwise could be **fatal**.

Figure 6–16 This armour has been preserved since the sixteenth century. Samurai armour was made from a variety of materials, including iron, **lacquer**, cloth, and gold-covered bronze. Do you think a samurai would actually go into battle with all this armour? Why or why not?

lacquer: a coating that creates a durable, glossy surface when dry

extort: to acquire money by means of threats

fatal: causing death

Figure 6–17 This Japanese painting from the sixteenth century shows a samurai on horseback cleaning his sword. What is your first impression of this figure?

THE FORTY-SEVEN RONIN

What sacrifices would you make to keep your honour?

The story of *The Forty-Seven Ronin* is well known in Japan. It describes the lengths to which the samurai would go to keep their honour. It also helps us understand the importance of on and giri. These obligations and duties are still very important in Japan today, but without the extreme Samurai ideas of revenge and death. After you have finished reading the story, supply your own ending.

Figure 6–18 This portion of a remarkable painting shows a samurai dying by his own sword. The painter, Taiso Yoshitoshi, often made sketches on the battlefield and personally witnessed many deaths. Why has the painter made the samurai's lips blue?

A daimyo named Lord Asano was required to perform ceremonies at the shogun's court. These ceremonials were very complicated, and the slightest mistake—or discourtesy— would make the ruling family look bad.

So Lord Asano asked an important official, Lord Kira, to help him prepare. Kira, however, was insulted by the presents Asano had given him on a previous occasion. He decided to insult Asano. This was a direct attack on the honour of Asano. He [Asano] drew his sword and slashed Kira.

Unfortunately, Asano had drawn his sword within the shogun's palace. This was an insult to the shogun. It now meant that Asano had to commit suicide, which he did. His samurai, now without a lord, soon became a ronin.

Asano's samurai were devastated by the death of their lord. Some of them, rejecting mass suicide themselves, planned for revenge. They numbered forty-seven. The forty-seven ronin took great care to make it seem as if Lord Kira's actions were of no concern to them. They tried to live peacefully with their families, and never mentioned the tragedy. Some actually behaved foolishly in public, so that they would seem even less of a threat. Secretly, however, they planned to attack and kill Lord Kira when he was most unguarded.

A year after Lord Asano's death, they raided and fought their way into Kira's house, dragged him from the shed where he was hiding and cut off his head. After placing Kira's head on Asano's grave, they waited to see what the shogun would do. Although many people thought the ronin had behaved correctly, violating the shogun's orders could not be tolerated and the forty-seven were ordered to kill themselves.

The story of the forty-seven ronin quickly spread through Japan. They were sincerely admired for their courage and devotion to the Code of Bushido.

PRIMARY SOURCE

THE CODE OF BUSHIDO

Like European knights, the samurai tried to live by a code, or set of rules. The samurai code is called "Bushido," or "The Way of the Warrior." Unlike the European code of chivalry, Bushido did not require the warrior to protect the weak.

Samurai were expert with weapons and in military tactics. They also worked to develop their sense of beauty. Although it might seem strange that warriors would be interested in tea ceremonies and flower arranging, these pursuits were consistent with **Zen Buddhism**, the samurai religion. The tea ceremony and flower arranging needed perfect concentration and application, as did sword play. To be "perfect" in the tea ceremony showed a high level of mental and artistic development, which the samurai admired greatly.

The most important requirement of Bushido was that the samurai be true to the lord he served, and his comrades. Samurai owed giri both to their lord and to their fellow samurai. This meant that they were willing to give their life if required to "pay back the debt." Samurai also owed giri to themselves, which meant that they would not accept an insult. This attitude is well illustrated in the story of *The Forty-Seven Ronin* on page 191.

Zen Buddhism: a variety of Buddhism

to dispose of: to settle

top knot: a knot of hair at the top of the head

pumice: a light, spongy stone

to buff: to polish

foppish: vain, affected

diligent: careful, steady

Unless a samurai sets his sights on no less than offering up his life for his ruler, dying swiftly and becoming a spirit, unless he is constantly anxious about the welfare of his daimyo and reports to him immediately whenever he has **disposed of** a problem, his concern always to strengthen the foundations of his realm, he cannot be called a true samurai in the service of his lord.

Until fifty or sixty years ago, samurai got ready every morning, shaved their heads, and perfumed their **topknots**. Then they cut their fingernails and toenails, filed them with **pumice**, and finally **buffed** them with kogane herb. They were never lazy about such matters but took great care to be wellgroomed. Then a samurai took a look at his long and short swords to make sure they were not rusting, wiped off the dust, and polished them. Taking such pains over one's appearance may seem **foppish** but the custom did not arise from a taste for elegance or romance. One may be run through at any moment in a vigorous battle; to die having neglected one's personal grooming is to reveal a certain sloppiness of habit, and to be despised and mocked by the enemy... If, always prepared to die, a samurai begins to think of himself as already dead, if he is **diligent** in serving his lord and perfecting the military arts, surely he will never come to shame; but if a samurai spends his days selfishly doing exactly as he pleases, in a crisis he will bring dishonour on himself. Having done so, he will not even be aware of his shame.

ADVICE TO SAMURAI

This advice to samurai (at left) was given by a Zen priest who had been a samurai himself. The priest, Jocho Yamamoto, was concerned that many of the old samurai values were being lost.

ZEN BUDDHISM: THE RELIGION OF THE SAMURAI

Zen Buddhism is a way of looking at the world in which meditation is most important. In fact, the word *zen* means **meditation**. People who practise Zen Buddhism hope to find the truth through discipline and **contemplation**. They try to come to an understanding about the true nature of life.

The samurai class gradually adopted many aristocratic ideas concerning beauty and refinement that had developed at the imperial court. They incorporated these ideas into Bushido, along with Zen. Zen Buddhism became the religion and philosophy of the samurai. It provided them with discipline and **tranquility** for total concentration during battle, and it made many of them seekers of refined beauty.

It may be difficult for you to imagine a samurai at a **tea ceremony**, but this elaborate ritual also became part of their training. A Zen priest created the first tea ceremony and the first teahouse in Japan during the late fifteenth century. It was originally designed to help Zen monks meditate. The four original requirements for the tea service were spiritual: harmony, respect, purity, and tranquility.

meditation: reflecting and concentrating in silence

contemplation: deep thought

tea ceremony: the preparation and drinking of tea in a service that follows strict rules

tranquility: peacefulness

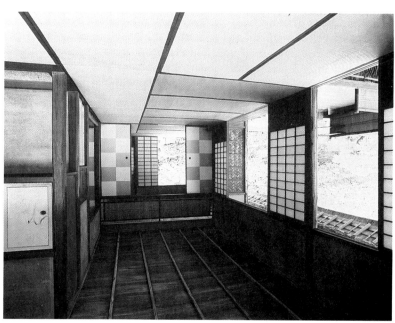

Figure 6–19 Teahouses are very simple in construction. The layout is carefully planned. Even doorways are low to force people to bow on entering. The tea ceremony is highly stylized. At times the only sound is the hissing of the kettle. Both the tea maker and the guests have carefully planned roles.

Figure 6–20 The Zen Garden at Ryoan-ji, Kyoto. Zen is always associated with simplicity, and Zen temples are beautiful but **austere**. This garden, containing nothing but raked gravel and rocks, has no clutter. How would this setting help people reflect and meditate?

austere: severely simple

Using Haiku as a Primary Source

Zen beliefs about discipline and simplicity have influenced more than just the appearance of buildings and gardens. Poetry has also been influenced by these ideals. One of Japan's most famous forms of poetry, *haiku*, is really Zen poetry. With only seventeen syllables per poem, haiku poems are simple yet powerful. Each poem contains an idea on which to meditate.

The first two haiku at right were written by two different Zen monks hundreds of years ago. One haiku is about winter; the other is about a frog. (Or it is about water? Or a pond? You decide.) The third haiku was written by a Grade 8 student living in British Columbia. And by the way, if you notice that the first haiku has only fourteen syllables, remember that it had seventeen syllables in the original Japanese.

Under the winter moon
The river wind
Sharpens the rocks.

This ancient pond here:
A frog jumps into the pond:
Sound of the water.

On a warm afternoon
The hot sun burns the sky
As the cars go by.

WHAT DO YOU THINK?

1. Practise meditating on one of the haiku. One approach would be to repeat the words to yourself with your eyes closed—that way, you will be less distracted. What new insights do you have after about one minute?

2. Does the simplicity of the haiku make its images more or less powerful than you would expect? Explain.

3. Create your own haiku about some event in your life. Remember to keep to seventeen syllables in total.

THE IMPORTANCE OF RICE FARMING

paddy: a rice field

to thresh: to beat the grain out of its husk, or covering

In feudal times, rice was an important crop to Japan, as it is today. Rice was so important that it was Japan's currency; the taxes of the daimyo, and the salaries of samurai, were all translated into measures of rice, or *koku*.

The excerpt at left, from a Shinto harvest prayer, shows how important rice was to the Japanese. It was, and is, Japan's most important food.

The farmer's life was generally hard. Rice farming is time consuming, and there was always something to do. The **paddies** had to be maintained, and crops needed to be planted, cultivated, harvested, **threshed**, and stored. Women and families participated fully in the work. In fact, the complicated process of rice growing was perfected by ordinary people during Japan's feudal period. This is important to remember when it seems as though the entire country was engaged in war.

If the high gods will bestow the harvest in rice ears many a hand's breadth long and abundant, produced by the labour of men from whose arms the sweat drops down and on whose thighs the mud has gathered, I will fulfil their praises by humbly offering a thousand first-fruits of ears, setting up the jars of sake and setting in rows the bellies of the sake jars…

Rice Farming in Japan

Today, rice is still the **staple** food of Japan—along with fish—and rice farmers continue to enjoy a special status. Although Japan has one of the largest rice yields in the world, especially considering its size, the country still needs to import rice to feed everyone. That is how prominent rice is in the Japanese diet.

Rice is also a grain with very special growing requirements. For example, rice must grow in water until it is almost ready to harvest. For this reason, rice farmers enclose their fields, or paddies, with walls so that they make shallow ponds. Later, the ponds are drained and the rice is harvested. Rice also requires very warm temperatures for growing.

The process begins when rice seed are sown in rich mud. When the rice plant is about 5–8 centimetres high, it is removed and planted in the rice paddy. Over the centuries, women have usually done the back-breaking work of replanting the tiny rice plants in the knee-deep water of the paddy.

When rice is ready to be harvested, the rice grain is separated from the plant. At this point, it is covered in a brown **hull**, which must be removed before marketing. Finally, the grains are polished so that they appear pale and glistening.

Rice paddies that are established can be used for other purposes. For example, sometimes fish are raised in the flooded fields. The sides of the paddy can also be used to grow other food plants. Nearby areas can be used to grow a variety of plants and trees, including **persimmons** and mulberry trees. (Mulberry leaves are used to feed silk worms.) After the rice is harvested, other crops can be grown in their space. In some areas of Japan, two rice crops can be grown in a year.

staple: basic, primary

hull: covering

persimmon: an orange-coloured fruit

JAPAN

N

Hokkaido

Honshu

Shikoku

Kyushu

Rice	Forest
Other grains	Urban regions
Horticulture and orchards	Mulberry fields (silk)

Figure 6–21 Land use in Japan. This modern map shows where rice paddies are located, and where other products are raised. These patterns have changed little over time. Notice how rice farming takes place in small pockets throughout the whole country.

Figure 6–22 These rice paddies are located near Matsumoto, Japan.

WHAT DO YOU THINK?

1. What well-known Japanese dish features rice as one of its main ingredients? What are the other ingredients in this dish?

2. North American physicians consider the traditional Japanese diet to be very healthful. Do you know why? Find out more about Japanese cuisine and compare some of the staple foods to those of your diet.

1. Using either the picture of the noblewomen on page 174 or the pictures of the samurai on page 190 as a guide, draw and colour a poster showing an historical Japanese costume.

2. Pretend you are a samurai, or a woman in a samurai family. Write a short guide to a young family member outlining the values of the samurai class.

3. Briefly describe the life of a peasant during the feudal period.

4. Explain why the religions of Zen and Shinto would be important to the samurai, and why these religions had such appeal.

5. What are "on" and "giri"? How did these ideas affect Japanese life and values?

6. Examine Figure 6–21 in more detail. Which category of land use represents the least space? Explain why.

WAR AND UNIFICATION

to reunify: to reunite, to bring together, as one again

ambush: a trap; a secret attack

fortification: an aspect of a structure that gives protection

vassal: one who owes loyalty to a lord

Figure 6–23 A samurai castle built in the fourteenth century. What castle **fortifications** can you see here?

The Ashikaga shoguns you read about on page 187 could never completely control the islands of Japan. There were too many powerful warlords who would not surrender their own rights to a central government. Because the country was filled with castles and armed warriors who were loyal to their daimyo, small wars were frequent.

In 1467, Japan suffered through another devastating civil war, called the "Onin War." This war was fought to gain control of the shogunate and lasted for a hundred years. Daimyos built strong castles and lived in them with their important **vassals**. As in Europe, these castles often became a focus around which towns could grow. Under the protection of a powerful lord, townspeople often became rich and prosperous. Farmers and villagers grew their crops and paid their taxes, hoping to avoid being slaughtered in the wars. Around this time, a daimyo named Oda Nobunaga started the process of **reunifying** Japan.

Nobunaga was from a poor country family. Because of his personal bravery and good leadership skills, he was made a general by the emperor. Instead of becoming shogun, Nobunaga supported a weak member of the Ashikaga family but kept the real power himself. With his generals, Hideyoshi and Tokugawa Ieyasu, he soon took over most of the empire. Nobunaga not only destroyed the power of many daimyos but also that of the private armies of Buddhist temples that had menaced the country. His capital was Yedo, or Edo, which is modern Tokyo.

When Nobunaga was killed in an **ambush**, Hideyoshi took over and continued the process Nobunaga had

begun. Hideyoshi was one of the few commoners to lead armies in Japan. He was a great general and a remarkable individual. He organized an invasion of China, first defeating Korea, through which his armies had to pass. Hideyoshi's invasion failed, partly because of the attacks by the Korean navy.

When Hideyoshi died in 1593, his son and heir was only five years old.

A council was appointed to look after the government until the boy came of age. However, disputes led to a war. In a decisive battle at Sekigahara, Nobunaga's other general, Tokugawa Ieyasu, a member of the Minamoto clan, defeated the other members of the council. Ieyasu took the title of shogun, preventing anyone from contacting the emperor without the permission of his bafuku.

THE TOKUGAWA ERA

Ieyasu moved quickly to consolidate his power. Within two years, he had made his son the shogun, although he kept supreme power until his death. The Tokugawa shoguns ruled Japan until 1867—the year that Canada became a **dominion**.

Ieyasu showed the emperor the same respect as other leaders had done. To ensure the loyalty of the daimyos, the Tokugawa shoguns forced them to spend part of each year in Yedo. When the daimyos went to their fiefs, their wives and families stayed in Yedo. Rich daimyos were taxed heavily, particularly if the Tokugawa shoguns thought they might be disloyal. Daimyos were also watched closely. Loyal lords were given lands next to the fiefs of lords suspected of lacking loyalty. In these ways, as Ieyasu had planned, the Tokugawa shoguns kept power in their own hands, and brought peace to Japan.

English adventurer. Because Europeans were heavily involved in trade, they were welcomed into the country. They also brought guns, which feudal warlords were quick to adopt.

As was usual with the Spanish and Portuguese, Roman Catholic missionaries came with the merchants and began to set up missions and churches. One of the first **missionaries** was Saint Francis Xavier, a Jesuit. Within a few years, thousands of Japanese had converted to Christianity.

But the success of Christianity disturbed Japan's leaders. They saw Christianity as an alien religion. Beginning with Hideyoshi, severe measures were taken to snuff out the new faith. Christians were banned in Japan, and missionaries were killed or driven out. Japanese Christians were put to death. After a rebellion in 1637, almost all contact with the West was cut off. Only a small Dutch trading community on the island of Deshima remained, closely watched and regulated. Japan had closed its door to the world.

dominion: a name for a nation that governs itself and belongs to the Commonwealth of Nations

missionary: a person sent from a church on a religious task, often to convert others

EUROPEAN CONTACT

Europeans arrived in Japan in the sixteenth century, beginning with the Portuguese. The Spanish and Dutch soon followed, as well as the odd

EDO JAPAN

Although Japan was cut off from most

Figure 6–24 Edo painters created highly realistic scenes of life. This screen painting shows two Japanese Jesuit priests. What does the small figure in the centre seem to think of them?

institution: a practice or system

nō: a form of Japanese theatre that often presents a military or courtly story

patriotism: loyalty to one's country

Figure 6–25 This *ukiyo-e* wood-block depicts a fashionable Edo woman looking in her mirror.

contact with the outside world, the country prospered under the Tokugawa shoguns. Edo (Yedo) occupied an excellent geographic position, situated on the Kantō Plain, a prime agricultural area, and on a good harbour. Because the daimyo's family and servants had to spend so

much time in the capital, the city of Edo grew very large. The capital drew craftspeople, workers, and others from many parts of the country. Many of these people came to provide services for the shogun and daimyo.

The arts also prospered during the Tokugawa era. A form of wood-block printing called *ukiyo-e* became popular, and showed scenes from stories and from everyday life. Some of Japan's most renowned screen painters, such as Ogata Korin, worked during this period. **Nō** theatre and kabuki theatre entertained nobles and commoners alike. Craftspeople created and sold beautiful objects to wealthy nobles and rich merchants. Merchants and traders grew wealthy because of the demand for their products and services. As in feudal Europe, these once-despised people were soon lending large sums of money to the cash-strapped nobles.

For almost all of the Tokugawa Shogunate, Japan had little contact with the outside world. Even shipwrecked sailors from other countries were executed. Without foreign influence, the Japanese people turned inwards. They continously refined their traditional ceremonies and artistic **institutions**.

One result of Japan's self-imposed isolation was that the Japanese people began to feel distinct. They continued to develop close social ties, which made for a strong sense of community. In later times, these strong feelings turned into extreme **patriotism**. The Edo period was thus an important phase in the development of modern Japan.

ACTIVITIES

1. In point-form notes, describe the process of unification in Japan from the time of Nobunaga to the time of the Tokugawa shoguns

2. Write a journal entry for a family member of a daimyo that describes life in the capital of Edo during the Kamakura Shogunate.

Japan's isolation ended in 1853 when the American admiral Matthew Perry sailed into Edo Bay. Perry forced the shogun to open Japan to trade, and ended Japan's feudal age. The feudal period lasted for many centuries in Japan, and had long-lasting effects. The feudal warriors—the samurai—and their values helped make Japanese culture what it is today. But Japan's history is about more than feudalism. The Jomon, Yayoi, Yamato, and Nara periods are also part of Japan's rich cultural tradition. The Heian era was, for the upper classes at least, a kind of Golden Age. Japan borrowed many ideas from China, including a whole writing system. Buddhism, which came through China and Korea, also had a major influence on Japanese culture. Nevertheless, Japan is unique. Centuries of isolation, and powerful feudal traditions, have shaped the Japanese nation. Today, Japan is a wealthy and prosperous nation with a deep reverence for the past. Its traditions are very much a part of its national character.

SUMMARY ACTIVITIES

1. Hold a class debate on the following resolution: "Feudalism in Japan developed much as it did in Europe." Ask your teacher for guidance on structuring the debate.

2. Create a poster-sized, illustrated physical map of Japan, labelling the major mountains and volcanoes, bodies of water, important plains, and major cities.

3. Write a story about events in either feudal or Heian Japan. Your story should have two or three main characters, and should teach the reader something about the period. You may, if you wish, illustrate the story or make it into a comic book.

4. Compare the armour of the samurai with that of the European knights shown on page 141. Using the labelling system for Figure 5–1, locate similar elements in the samurai armour, shown on page 190.

ON YOUR OWN

1. With a partner, research Yayoi, Ainu, or Jomon culture, and prepare an illustrated report to present to the class.

2. Find out more about Zen Buddhism or Shinto, and prepare an illustrated report on the topic.

3. The *shoen* of the daimyo was somewhat similar to the manor of a European feudal noble. There was a castle for the daimyo and his samurai (sometimes the samurai lived in town), a village, and lands worked by peasants. Research feudal Japan and construct a model, diorama, or illustrated poster showing the layout of a shoen.

4. Obtain more information about the Pacific Rim of Fire. How did it get its name? Which countries are included in the Rim of Fire?

UNIT 3
EUROPE PROSPERS,
1400–1700

The evolution of civilizations occurs not smoothly but in a series of halting steps. War can slow development, for example, as can disease epidemics. The overwhelming power of one group over another within society can also suppress development.

By about 1400, the people of western Europe had lived in isolated manors under the rule of feudal lords for many centuries. And then the civilization of western Europe made a remarkable leap. With new found confidence and opportunities allowed by trade, Europeans began to stretch the possibilities of their ordinary lives. In Italy, Renaissance thinkers found new faith in the vast potential of humanity. Artists gave expression to these discoveries in works that celebrated the human form. When the printing press was developed, ideas spread like wildfire, people began educating themselves, and northern Europeans made incredible scientific discoveries.

At the same time, Europeans' newfound confidence—as well as their lust for riches—encouraged them to explore the world in search of trading partners. Though they were not the first to explore the world, European

seafarers changed the face of human civilization forever, partly because they forced the peoples of the world to open their doors and partly because the Europeans prospered at the expense of others.

In another extraordinary change, many European Christians rejected the Catholic Church. Wanting to achieve a more personal religion, these reformers developed their own version of Christianity, and thus began the Protestant Reformation. The resulting power struggles contributed greatly to political change in western Europe. Before long, the nobles had lost power to the monarchs and the growing middle class. Europe transformed into a subcontinent of nation-states.

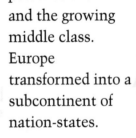

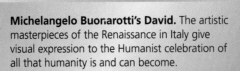

Michelangelo Buonarotti's David. The artistic masterpieces of the Renaissance in Italy give visual expression to the Humanist celebration of all that humanity is and can become.

A replica of Sir Francis Drake's ship, the Golden Hind, in full sail. The advances in ship design and navigation were crucial to the European Age of Exploration. Perhaps even more important was the determination of individuals willing to sail into the unknown to find gold, trading partners, and adventure.

Elizabeth I. Soon after England broke with the Roman Catholic Church, Elizabeth came to the throne of England. Under her accomplished rule, England became one of the most powerful of Europe's new nation-states.

Martin Luther burning a Papal bull. By destroying a written order from the pope, Luther rejected the authority of the Roman Catholic Church. His action encouraged many people dissatisfied with the Church to make a complete break and form a whole new church.

Bona

SICILY

7 EUROPEAN RENAISSANCE

CHAPTER OUTCOMES

In this chapter you will explore a time of spectacular human achievement in the arts and sciences: the period of European history known as the Renaissance, which lasted from about 1450 to 1600. By the end of the chapter you will

- explain how geography and environment can affect trade, settlement, and culture

- analyze the importance of city-states as centres of culture during the Renaissance

- compare family structures of civilizations using statistics

- analyze how and why Renaissance art differed from the art of the Middle Ages

- explain how Humanism opened peoples' minds with revolutionary ideas

- describe the impact of the printing press

- use map scales

The Cartoons

During the Renaissance, European society valued its artists and writers. Most of those who followed these pursuits were men because society decreed that a woman's primary task in life was to serve her family. A few women, however, were fortunate enough to step into the role of artist or writer. Like the character Francesca in this fictional story, these lucky few needed understanding parents, powerful friends, and determination.

Francesca laid aside her heavy lead **maul** and pointed chisel. She wiped the marble grit from around her eyes and tried to clear her nostrils. A cloud of marble dust slowly settled to the floor of the studio. Across the room, Francesca's father, Gentile, cut ridged pathways across the back of a stone **condotierre**, its right arm raised to touch its marble helmet. The statue was almost finished.

Gentile's shop was a small one, with Francesca as the only apprentice. Although Gentile had trained with the great Renaissance sculptor and painter Michelangelo Buonarotti, he had never been able to find a **patron**. Instead, he got work from Michelangelo and other artists, working on parts of a statue or sometimes doing the rough cutting on a marble block.

Feeling his time was almost past, Gentile had decided to enter a competition sponsored

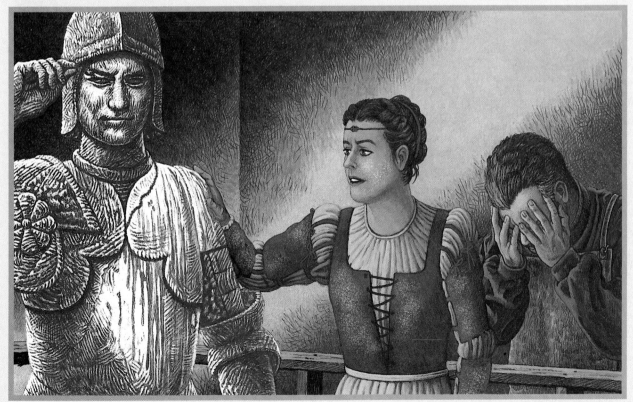

Francesca rushes to see the cause of her father's anguish.

by the Medici family. For the past few months, he had been working on a life-sized statue of the famous Lorenzo de Medici dressed as a condotierre. Gentile had invested all he had in a block of **Carrara marble**. He knew he had to create a winner or his studio would have to close.

Francesca liked working in the studio, but she too longed to create her own works for a patron. She had inherited a strong back and arms from her father's side of the family, stone masons for generations. Her keen eye for detail came from her mother, a cousin of the sculptor Andrea del Verrocchio. In her spare time, Francesca carved small statues with marble her father had rejected. She also liked to paint, especially portraits of friends.

Just like the great masters— Michelangelo, Leonardo, Brunelleschi, and the others— Francesca was talented in many areas of the arts. Francesca's **cartoons**, large drawings in red chalk, covered a wall behind her father's work station.

Suddenly Gentile's hammer stopped ringing.

"Francesca!" the sculptor called out, a note of panic in his voice. "Bring a bucket of water—quickly!"

Francesca ran, filled a leather bucket from the **cistern** near the back door of the studio, and rushed the bucket to her father.

Gentile slowly poured the water over the dusty marble. He closed his eyes and let out a breath. Then, his face pale and drawn, he sank to his knees.

Francesca pulled herself up

onto the scaffold and looked. A long, brown line like a mouldy scribble crossed the wet marble at the base of the neck. Francesca knew the crack went deep and could not be fixed. Her father's beautiful statue would never be completed. The Medici would not think of buying such a work.

• • • • • • •

At sunset, Francesca closed the door of the workshop and walked through the Piazza Santa Croce to Vasari's, a **trattoria** popular among artists and writers. As Francesca entered the restaurant, she was met with the buzz of lively conversation and friendly argument. The long, rough tables and benches were filled. Many of the diners, like Francesca, were covered with marble dust, others with

Seeking dinner and the company of fellow artists, Francesca enters the trattoria.

spatters of paint. Francesca noticed the high-strung writer, Machiavelli, arguing heatedly with Michelangelo and Pico della Mirandola. Her father sat nearby, his head in his hands.

Another man, who did not seem to belong, turned, revealing his face. Francesca shuddered. It was Giuseppe Tassarini, a small-time trader in leather whose proposal of marriage Francesca had rejected just one week before. He sneered and turned away.

Francesca calmed herself and waved to an old friend of her father's, Pico. Like a breath of fresh air, Pico launched into a witty speech about the Medici as soon as Francesca sat down at the end of a bench. But Pico couldn't make her laugh, as he usually could, and when Francesca's meal came she only picked at it halfheartedly. She was depressed about her father's misfortune, and her own, and she really didn't know what to do. Her chances of continuing as an apprentice to her father seemed pretty slim.

Francesca decided to return to the studio for a few more hours of work. Pushing her plate aside, she left some coins on the table, said good bye to Pico, and left. It was now quite dark. The streets of Florence could be dangerous at times, but Francesca wasn't worried. She walked along the River Arno, not even seeing the lights of the Ponte Vecchio, she was so lost in thought. As she turned a corner, a shadow detached itself from the deeper shadows of the nearby buildings.

Tassarini crept across the street until he was right behind Francesca. Turning at the sound

Tassarini learns that Francesca knows how to protect herself.

of a footstep, Francesca found herself looking straight into Tassarini's bloodshot eyes. She gasped and tried to back away, but Tassarini lunged forward, grabbing her by the wrist.

"I'll show you that no one refuses Tassarini," he said. "I didn't even demand a **dowry**. You and your failure of a father will pay for the insult you have done my family."

He spat at Francesca, struck her across the face, and started to drag her towards the shadows. Reaching into her apron pocket, Francesca pulled out the long iron chisel she always carried when walking at

night, and hit her attacker across the bridge of his nose. Tassarini stumbled back, blood streaming from his nose. Then he pulled a sword from his belt.

"I don't think so, my friend." It was a rough voice that Francesca knew: Michelangelo's. Tassarini turned to face the disapproving glare of the great artist and the folded arms of Pico della Mirandola. As Tassarini raised his sword, Michelangelo ducked and threw his arms around the drunken man. Pico took hold of Tassarini's wrist and bent it back until the sword clattered onto the pavement.

Father and daughter come to a decision.

"You'll pay for this," Tassarini sputtered. "All of you. Even you, Maestro."

Without a word, Michelangelo lifted the man into the air. Assisted by Pico, he carried Tassarini across to the bank of the River Arno. "You wouldn't dare," shrieked Tassarini.

"Oh yes we would," laughed Pico. The two men then handily tossed Francesca's attacker into the river. Below them, in the dark, Tassarini yelled and splashed as he swam towards the embankment.

Pico turned to Francesca. "We watched that scoundrel leave Vasari's right after you and knew something must be up. The Maestro suggested we tag along to make sure you got home all right."

Michelangelo looked at his goddaughter with concern.

"Are you all right, Francesca?" he asked.

"I'm fine, Maestro. I wasn't afraid of him. But I am worried about my father."

"Poor Gentile. My own David had a flaw—luckily, on the hand—and it almost broke my heart." Michelangelo stooped, picked up Tassarini's sword, and tossed it into the river. "Let's go back to the studio. Things may not be as bad as Gentile thinks. I've repaired marble before, perhaps we can fix it."

. . . .

Through the open door of the studio, Pico, Michelangelo, and Francesca could hear the crunch of metal on stone. Inside they found Gentile

hammering furiously at his condotierre, spraying large chips of marble into the air. Tears streamed down his dusty face as he pounded the statue. The head was now a shapeless mass.

"Old friend!" Michelangelo called out to Gentile. "Restrain yourself." He and Pico ran forward and dragged the sculptor from the scaffold. Gentile threw down his tools and lashed out at his two friends. It took Francesca and the two men several minutes to restrain him.

Francesca sat down beside her father. "Papa, why have you done this? The Maestro might have known how to repair the flaw."

Recovering himself, Gentile patted his daughter's shoulder. "I'm all right now," he said. "The fever has passed." He looked sheepishly at Pico and Michelangelo. "I apologize for my outburst. The flaw runs the length of the statue. There was no possibility of repair."

Pico tried to comfort Gentile, but only Michelangelo knew exactly what was going through Gentile's mind, as only a fellow sculptor could. He looked searchingly at his old friend. "Gentile, I understand. Forget your condotierre. This is God's will. Accept it."

Michelangelo then looked around the studio until his eye fell on Francesca's cartoons. "Gentile, did you draw these?" he asked. "Hmm. Good form. Very nice."

Francesca's mouth was suddenly so dry that she had to swallow before she could speak. "Maestro," she stammered.

"Excuse me, but these poor drawings are mine."

Michelangelo looked at her with amazement. "Well, well, little daughter. As a sculptor, you are, I might say, nothing special. But with chalk, you draw an excellent line, a little tentative, perhaps, but with real promise. And your understanding of perspective is good. Let me think." He stood for several minutes with his chin in his large, calloused hand.

"Gentile." He addressed the father first. "Listen to me. His Holiness, the pope, and I have made up. Now I can return to Rome and finish the tomb for Julius. Gentile, with so much work, I require assistance. I need your skill. You are someone I can rely on. Will you come?"

Gentile brightened, "Yes, yes, my friend, I will come. I'll make arrangements for Francesca. Her mother's family can take her in. God knows, maybe I'll be able to get a decent dowry together yet."

But Michelangelo wasn't finished. "I must ask that Francesca come also. I'm afraid there may be another task for me—more frescos for the Sistine Chapel. I tell them I'm not a painter, but do they listen? I'll need people skilled with chalk and paint. Francesca has a gift from God. It is only right that she use this gift in the service of the Church. She'll be paid well."

Gentile mulled over Michelangelo's request. Francesca was already sixteen. Soon, she would be almost too old to marry. He looked at his daughter.

"I don't know, Francesca. This is a big move, far from family and friends. I think you should stay in Florence, and I'll send money home."

Francesca flushed. She tried to hold her tongue but could not. "Papa, you don't even have a dowry. Ever since mother died we've worked together; I don't want you to leave me now.

Besides, some women wait to marry. Please reconsider."

Gentile looked around. Pico and Michelangelo were studying Francesca's chalk cartoons on the back wall. Neither wanted to interfere in a family matter of such importance.

Gentile muttered under his breath and sighed. "You are exactly like your mother, Francesca. All right, we'll go together."

maul: heavy hammer

condotierre: a leader of mercenary soldiers in Renaissance Italy (plural: condotierri)

cartoon: a chalk drawing that provides the outline for a painting. Made by drawing the design on paper, outlining the design with small holes, and then dusting the holes with chalk to leave the design on a wall.

patron: someone who buys art and supports artists

Carrara marble: the finest white Italian marble, used for sculpture

cistern: a tank for storing water

trattoria: a simple restaurant

dowry: money paid to the family of a groom by the bride's family

ACTIVITIES

1. What does the story tell you about the relationship between artists and patrons during the Renaissance?

2. Young Renaissance artists learned their profession by working as apprentices to artists who had patrons. Outline the benefits to all three.

3. What are the cartoons Francesca creates? Why would Michelangelo need a skilled cartoonist to help with his paintings in the Sistine Chapel (shown on page 202)?

4. What difficulties would a young woman encounter if she wanted to be an artist during the Renaissance? Do young Canadian women encounter these same difficulties today? How do expectations affect the route one takes in life?

5. How did Michelangelo and Pico punish Tassarini? Would that action be legal in Canada today? What other routes of justice would be available? In which instance is justice better served? Why?

6. The real Pico wrote the quotation on page 208. Read it and then decide why Pico would have admired Francesca. Retell the story from Pico's point of view.

1304   PETRARCH IS BORN

1347   THE BLACK DEATH DEVASTATES ITALY

1434   THE MEDICI BEGIN TO RULE FLORENCE

1445   GUTENBERG INVENTS MOVABLE TYPE

1453   CONSTANTINOPLE FALLS

1492   COLUMBUS SAILS TO AMERICA; LORENZO DE MEDICI DIES

1503   LEONARDO PAINTS THE MONA LISA

1508   MICHELANGELO BEGINS PAINTING THE SISTINE CHAPEL

1513   MACHIAVELLI WRITES *THE PRINCE*

1604   CERVANTES'S *DON QUIXOTE* IS PUBLISHED

1605   SHAKESPEARE WRITES *KING LEAR*

1610   GALILEO BEGINS TO STUDY THE HEAVENS

*You who are confined by no limits, shall determine for yourself your own nature, in **accordance** with your own free will, in whose hand I have placed you. I have set you at the centre of the world, so that from there you may more easily survey whatever is in the world.... You may fashion yourself in whatever form you shall prefer.*

— PICO DELLA MIRANDOLA, 1486

PRIMARY SOURCE

Pico della Mirandola's words display the optimism about humanity typical of the Humanist writers of the Italian Renaissance. He reflects their faith that people, through their own efforts, can shape their own lives. How does this world view differ from the one that was popular during the medieval period? How does this world view compare with your own?

INTRODUCTION

The Renaissance, which began in Italy in the fourteenth century, witnessed the emergence of a new faith in human effort and achievement. This age was a period of intense creativity in both the arts and the sciences. Many of the greatest artists in history, including Michelangelo Buonarotti and Leonardo da Vinci, lived and worked during this time. Renaissance scientists greatly expanded knowledge about the natural world, and Renaissance thinkers changed the way people saw themselves and the world around them.

Renaissance society was quite different from the feudal society of the Middle Ages. The medieval world had been built around the closed system of the manor and the castle. By the time of the Renaissance, towns in southern Europe had grown tremendously in both size and influence. The wealthy people who lived there had more leisure time and money than people during the Middle Ages. This meant they could spend more time studying new ideas and had money to patronize the arts.

The medieval view of the world had been largely pessimistic: people thought of life as short and full of suffering. Most medieval art had had a religious theme. The Church had hired artists to create paintings to teach people about their faith and to encourage them to lead good lives so they could go to heaven.

Renaissance people were tired of the art and world view of the Middle Ages. To them, the feudal period had been a dark age of **stagnation**. Instead, Renaissance people admired the classical age of the great artists and thinkers of ancient Greece and Rome.

Ancient Greek and Roman artists had tried to communicate a sense of beauty. Much ancient art, especially sculpture, had been created to celebrate the beauty of the human form. Greek thinkers had developed systems of philosophy that showed people how they could improve themselves and their society through their own efforts. On the whole, the classical view was optimistic, something Renaissance people embraced wholeheartedly. Renaissance artists and thinkers worked hard to bring the classical culture back to life, and to forge ahead.

As towns and cities prospered in northern Europe, new ideas spread there also, often through the help of the newly invented printing press. The Renaissance of the North was different in many ways from the one in Italy, but at the core of both was a deep-seated faith in human effort.

accordance: agreement

stagnation: sluggish, inactive, not progressing

DID YOU KNOW?

"Renaissance" is a French word meaning "rebirth." Because of its origin, we usually pronounce "renaissance" with the stress on the first and final syllable rather than on the second.

DID YOU KNOW?

This intense period of European history was not called the "Renaissance" until the nineteenth century.

ITALY: THE RIGHT CONDITIONS

It is the responsibility of historians, geographers, and other social scientists to ask questions about people and their activities. In answering these questions, they hope to understand why things happen the way they do. When they study the Renaissance, they ask the following questions: "Why did the Renaissance happen first in Italy and later in places such as England and Germany? Did Italy have special features that made such major changes possible?"

Italy was different from northern Europe in many ways. First, it was the heartland of the old Roman Empire. Most of Italy still used Roman law; therefore, the problems of combining the medieval law with the Roman legal code didn't exist in Italy. Italy's clear legal code made business and trade between different regions much easier.

Also in Italy were many Roman ruins, sculptures, mosaics, and wall paintings. Some ancient works of art were brought to Italy with the fall of Constantinople. These ruins and works of art inspired many Italian artists and architects, partly because it was their ancestors who had created many of them.

Finally, one must consider geography.

Figure 7–1 The ruins of the Roman Forum, the centre of the ancient city of Rome. If you go to Italy today, you can still see some of the ruins of Roman civilization that inspired Renaissance artists to return to their classical roots.

THE IMPORTANCE OF GEOGRAPHY

During the Middle Ages, Italy had developed as a collection of independent city-states. As trade increased, cities situated near or on one of Italy's few good harbours almost automatically became large and powerful because they served as centres for trade. The two largest Italian port cities were Venice on the east coast and Genoa on the west. Venice became a major centre for both trade and ideas.

Italy is a mountainous peninsula, a fact that greatly affected Italy's development. Mountains make communication and travel difficult. Mountainous countries usually have only a few well-established trade routes, but those few tend to be very busy. Cities like Siena and Assisi, located on the old Roman roads that threaded the mountains of Italy, grew rich on the proceeds of trade. Florence, on a plain drained by the Arno River, was located at the hub of a major trade route that ran through mountains to Rome and Naples in the south and through more mountains to Genoa and Venice in the north. Partly because of its fortunate location, Florence became for a time the peninsula's most powerful city.

The climate of Italy was milder than that of the countries north of the Alps. This meant that the winter weather did not disrupt travel, trade, and commerce as it did in Germany and northern France. The milder climate also meant that food was plentiful all year long. People probably had more free time to devote to science and the arts in a place like Italy because they could spend less time earning a living.

Italy had closer ties than the rest of Europe to the Muslim world to the south and east. Muslims had ruled Sicily for a time in the early Middle Ages. During this time Italy was introduced to science, medicine, and astronomy as well as products such as oranges, lemons, coffee, and sugar. Because Italy was near the rich port cities of northern Africa and the Middle East, trade with these lands was easier and cheaper for Italy than for any other country in Europe. With trade came wealth, which in turn allowed the arts to flourish.

Geography in Painting

topography: surface features of a region

Renaissance painters paid far more attention than medieval painters had to the landscapes in their pictures. In the painting of Mary and Jesus on the opening page of this chapter (page 208), Giovanni Bellini used the geography of Italy as the background for his subjects. The distant blue mountains show that Bellini understood atmospheric perspective. To put it simply, things in the distance look cooler and bluer than things close up. The rich brown earth shown in the painting is found in an area in Italy called "Umbria." Artists still paint with a pigment called umber made from the soil of this region.

Figure 7–2 Considering that all travel during the Renaissance was on foot, on horseback, by cart, or by ship, what effect did Italy's **topography** have on communications and trade? In such a mountainous region, which cities would have had the best chance of becoming wealthy?

Italy, about 1500

- • Cities
- ■ Italian City-States
- ▲ Mountains

Use Map Scales

Maps can provide us with a wealth of information about our world, but without several key tools a map would be useless. Most maps provide the following four tools to help us understand what we see. Locate each on the map in Figure 7–2.

◆ **A title:** to indicate the overall purpose of the map (e.g., Roman Trade Routes)

◆ **A direction indicator:** to provide a sense of direction (an arrow or compass rose shows due north and sometimes other points)

◆ **A legend:** to tell what kind of information the map provides through symbols and colouring

◆ **A scale:** to tell what distances are represented on the map

The scale lets you know if you're looking at an area the size of your neighbourhood or the size of a sub-continent—a rather important distinction. The scale also helps you determine the distance between points on a map, for example, the distance between cities, which can be crucial in planning a trip.

Scales help you figure out what distance on earth is represented by a distance you measure on a map. Most maps have at least one of the three basic

types of map scales: **statement scale, linear scale,** or **representative ratio**.

A statement scale tells you the distance in words. For example 1 cm = 100 m indicates that 1 centimetre on the map represents 100 metres. Therefore, if you measure 10 centimetres between two points on a map with this scale, the points are actually 1 kilometre apart (10 cm x 100 m/1 cm = 1000 m = 1 km). Simple!

A linear, or line, scale shows distance represented on a line. By measuring the distance between two points on a map, and then laying your ruler along the numbered line, you can estimate real distance. On the scale below, place a ruler along the line to see what 1 centimetre represents in kilometres.

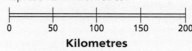
Kilometres

Even more useful is the representative ratio. The ratio indicates what one unit on the map represents in the *same* unit on the earth. If the ratio is 1:3 000 000, then 1 millimetre on the map

Renaissance Trade Routes

← Main overland trade routes
• Cities that traded with Italy

Linear Scale:
0   400   800 km

Representative Ratio:
1 : 40 000 000

Statement Scale:
1 cm = 400 km

ATLANTIC OCEAN

MEDITERRANEAN SEA

represents 3 000 000 millimetres on earth. It also means that 1 centimetre represents 3 000 000 centimetres. Knowing that a town is 3 000 000 centimetres away doesn't mean much, however. Fortunately, the representative ratio offers an easy way to convert metric distances to units we can readily visualize. To convert centimetres to kilometres, always follow this strategy: Begin at the right side of the ratio. Count five digits to the left and place a decimal point between the fifth and sixth digit. You've done it! 3 000 000 centimetres becomes 30.000 00 kilometres, or 30 kilometres! Another example:

1:11 000 000

1 cm : 11 000 000 cm

1 cm : 110.000 00 km

1 cm : 110 km

....

NOW YOU DO IT

1. For each of the following three representative ratios, figure out how many kilometres are represented by a centimetre:

    1:13 000 000   1:700 000   1:5000

2. Using the map Renaissance Trade Routes, above, determine what one centimetre represents in kilometres. What is the actual distance between the cities of Florence and Bruges? Milan and

Cologne? Venice and Marseilles? Calculate these distances in two ways: as the crow flies (along a straight line) and the route distance (the length of the route one would have to travel).

3. Determine the route distances in kilometres between Florence and Hamburg, Venice and Rome, and Genoa and Bruge.

ITALIAN CITY-STATES

The Renaissance did not occur because the Italian people had created a great empire. In fact, the opposite is true. Italy wasn't even a united country until the nineteenth century. The Renaissance flourished in city-states, some of them relatively small. A city-state consists of a city and the rural area immediately surrounding it. The surrounding area, called the **hinterland**, provides food and other necessities. Singapore is an example of a modern city-state that flourishes even without a hinterland. City-states have their own government and their own armed forces. The Italian city-states were democratic for at least part of their history.

Because some parts of Italy were occupied by the Holy Roman Empire, some by Spain, and some by the pope, politics was very complicated. Further, war often broke out between city-states. From the time of the Middle Ages, these city-states hired companies of **mercenary soldiers** led by condotierri, some from as far away as England, to fight for them. Condotierri fought for the pay and had little interest in the reasons for war. Often they were careful not to have casualties, with the result that some battles were more ceremonial than real. Some of the condotierri became the rulers of city-states.

hinterland: area surrounding a city

mercenary soldiers: soldiers for hire

Figure 7–3 Andrea Verrocchio's statue of the Venetian condotierre Bartolomeo Colleoni. What aspects of Colleoni's character did the artist emphasize in this portrait?

Governing the City of Mantua

Like many Renaissance rulers, the Duke of Mantua was often away on military campaigns. During his absence, his wife, Isabella D'Este, governed the city. The portrait of Isabella, drawn by Leonardo da Vinci in 1500, shows Isabella when she was twenty-six. Isabella excelled in governing, in leading Italian society, and in supporting the arts. Governing the state was sometimes complicated by rumour and gossip, so Isabella often wrote to her husband to assure him that all was well. Here is an excerpt from one such letter. After reading it, describe Isabella's method of governing. What problems do you think a woman might face in the absence of her husband?

councillor: advisor

The inventors of these evil tales who have not been afraid to disturb your peace of mind when you are occupied with the defence of Italy, showed little regard for my honour, or for those of my **councillors**. Let Your Highness, I beg of you, have a peaceful mind... for I intend to govern the State... in such a manner that you will suffer no wrong, and all that is possible will be done for the good of your subjects... I not only listen to officials but allow all your subjects to speak to me whenever they choose [so] no disturbance can happen without my knowledge....

From her who loves and longs to see Your Highness,
  Isabella,
  with her own hand.
  Mantua, June 30, 1495

PRIMARY SOURCE

Florence

oligarchy: government by a few powerful people

florin, ducat: gold coins weighing about 3.5 grams

Florence and Venice were the two most important Renaissance cities. Both became rich through the skill of their business people, and both were large enough to dominate their neighbours. Florence made its fortune in the cloth trade and controlled the kingdom of Naples. Today this city is famous for the Renaissance art that fills its galleries and other public buildings. Michelangelo and Leonardo da Vinci lived in this city as did many other painters, sculptors, and architects. The city is located in Tuscany in northwest Italy, on the banks of the Arno River. By 1330, Florence was already one of the largest cities in Europe, with a population of about 100 000.

Early Florence was ruled by a kind of democracy made up of representatives from the city's guilds. Later, the city was ruled by an **oligarchy** that was controlled by the wealthiest and most powerful families. Beginning in 1434, the extremely powerful Medici family ruled Florence.

In 1378, the cloth workers had revolted to protest poor living conditions. After this, the rulers of Florence tried hard to keep their citizens relatively happy. For this reason, and because they were proud of their city, Florence's rulers financed many beautiful public buildings and works of art. The Medicis were great patrons of the arts who sponsored both Leonardo da Vinci and Michelangelo Buonarotti.

The Business of Banking

Florence relied on the wool trade and banking for its prosperity. Florentine merchants would buy the best-quality wool from England and Spain and turn the wool into high-grade cloth that fetched high prices all over Europe. Florentine bankers began as moneychangers visiting European fairs, where they helped foreign merchants change their money to the local currency. At this time in Europe, more than 500 currencies were in use. These early moneychangers worked behind a *banc*, or bench, and so acquired the name "bankers." The Florentine gold **florin**, like the Venetian **ducat**, soon became a standard unit of currency that was accepted throughout Europe.

After becoming the pope's bankers and receiving authorization to collect taxes for him, the Florentine bankers established the wealthiest financial houses in Europe. They also introduced a

Figure 7–4 This woodcut shows the inside of a fifteenth-century Florentine bank. On the left, a banker examines a letter of credit (like a money order) that a foreign merchant has handed him. What do you think is being exchanged on the right? How would the bank make money from these transactions?

number of new banking practices. To make the flow of money easier and to keep detailed records of their transactions, they invented cheques and modern accounting methods.

Banking was often a risky business because merchants who borrowed money to buy or rent ships, purchase cargo, and hire crews, continuously faced the threats of shipwreck, piracy, robbery, and war. Also, rulers sometimes failed to repay their loans. For instance, when Edward III of England refused to repay his loans, two of the most powerful banking families in Florence, the Perazzi and the Bardi, went out of business.

Using Art as a Primary Source

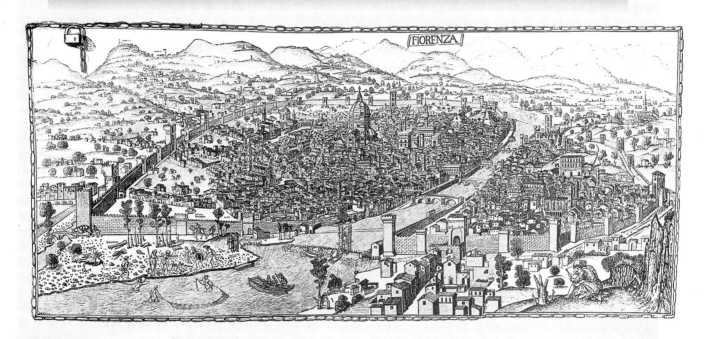

FIORENZA

CATALOGUE CARD

What is it? A print of Florence taken from a wood engraving

Who painted it? Vincenzo Catena, an Italian Renaissance artist

When? About 1480, when Florence was at the height of its power

Many sources other than the written word are valuable tools for understanding the past. Much can be learned about a particular era, event, or person through works of art. For example, this print by Catena provides the viewer with a wealth of information about Florence at the height of its power. Work through the following questions to analyze the print yourself.

NOW YOU DO IT

1. What evidence is there that Florence is a prosperous and growing city?

2. What buildings dominate the skyline? What does this tell you about the power of the institutions that constructed the buildings?

3. Identify and explain what natural features make this an ideal site for a city. What natural feature would benefit enemies attacking Florence?

4. Is the print made to scale? Explain.

5. Find Catena working in the hills. Why would Catena place himself in the picture?

6. Estimate the population of the city. How did you reach your estimate?

7. What are the men doing in the bottom, left-hand corner? What does this tell you about the Arno River?

8. Give two reasons why walls were built along the banks of the Arno River.

Remember, no matter what the historical primary source, one must always consider who is creating the work. This helps determine biases. For example, consider how the painting might have differed had the artist been any of the four individuals listed below. For each hypothetical painter, list possible biases.

◆ a proud Florentine citizen

◆ a foreigner being paid by a proud Florentine citizen

◆ a foreigner being paid by an enemy city

◆ an artist who loves nature, perspective, and the science of art

Which of the four descriptions do you think best matches Catena?

Figure 7–5 Map of Venice in the fifteenth century. With this map in mind, consider why Venice would be such a difficult city for an army to conquer. What kind of natural disaster would pose a real danger to Venice?

pile: a heavy beam driven upright into the earth to support a structure

republic: a state in which the citizens elect representatives to form a government

Venice

Venetians have always referred to their city as "the Most Serene Republic." Venice is a one-of-a-kind city built entirely on **piles** sunk into marshy islands at the head of the Adriatic Sea. The city has hundreds of canals, which function as roads and highways.

With its hinterland, called the *veneto*, Venice was able to grow into one of the foremost cities of the Italian Renaissance. The city had a population of more than 150 000 people. It was

successful because its leaders created a powerful navy through which Venice was able to gain control of the trade routes on the Mediterranean Sea. The Venetians maintained hundreds of merchant ships and warships and thousands of sailors. The city's navy and its watery surroundings made the city very difficult to attack successfully. Venice kept its independence from the Middle Ages until the end of the eighteenth century, when the city was conquered by Napoleon.

Although Venetians referred to their city as a **republic**, which is a form of democracy, the people of Venice in fact had little political freedom. The supreme ruler was the Doge (pronounced "dōj"), who was elected for life. The city also had a senate and a Great Council that passed laws. The Doge and the members of the government all came from wealthy families, however, so Venice in effect was an oligarchy, not a republic. All citizens were at the mercy of the most powerful arm of the government: the secret Council of Ten. This council had the power to imprison, torture, and execute any citizen of Venice—all in secret.

Figure 7–6 This photograph shows modern citizens of Venice costumed for one of the city's festivals. This celebration has its roots in the Renaissance, when wealthy citizens wore masks to attend lavish parties and mingle with the masses. Why do you think they wore disguises?

Venice, like Florence, had many famous artists who were **patronized** by the wealthy merchants of the city. Architects built beautiful palaces and official buildings throughout the city. Titian was the most famous of the Venetian artists. He worked all his life, dying when he was ninety-nine. Many of Titian's works were massive paintings commissioned by the Republic of Venice itself to record its glory. Titian also had a gift for painting people and was able to show emotion and personality better than many other artists. He often painted women with light red hair, a colour still known today as "Titian Red." Thanks to Titian and many other artists, Venice remains one of the most beautiful cities in the world.

to patronize: to support

ACTIVITIES

1. What does the term "renaissance" mean? What factors caused the Italian Renaissance in the fourteenth and fifteenth centuries?

2. Imagine you are a prosperous Florentine wool trader writing to your cousin in Germany in 1420. Try to persuade him to abandon his woodworking business and move to Florence, where the business opportunities are better. In your letter, discuss the following:

   ◆ the local climate
   ◆ the advantageous location of Florence
   ◆ the location of Italy in relation to other trading nations
   ◆ the growing market for all types of goods

   Include a sketch map in your letter showing the location of Florence on the Arno River and its position relative to two trading centres in Italy.

3. What is a city-state? How did city-states manage to avoid becoming part of larger kingdoms or empires?

4. Why is a hinterland important to a wealthy city?

5. Construct a chart to compare Venice and Florence in regard to location, geographical advantages and disadvantages, population, source of wealth, political system, and important artists. What made these two city-states wealthy and powerful? Did they both grow rich for the same reasons?

6. a) Review the feature on early banking (see page 214). Make a list of functions performed by early banks. Then do the same for Canadian banks and credit unions.

   b) In a small group, script and present the following drama. A pair of time travellers has been sent from the Bank of Canada to explain the wonders of machine banking to a group of Italian bankers in the mid-fifteenth century. The time travellers should describe the advantages of the instant teller and the bank card, while the bankers should ask questions. Will the standard bank machine have to be modified to make it useful for Renaissance bankers? In what ways?

   Construct a mock bank machine for your drama.

THE FAMILY

THE ITALIAN FAMILY

The family was very important in Renaissance Italy. Even though the rate of infant deaths was higher than today, and people died earlier, families were usually large. Mothers, fathers, and their children shared a house with their aunts, uncles, grandparents, and cousins. Children generally learned the trade of their parents and worked in the family business.

Getting Married

Middle-class and poorer people gave their children considerable freedom when it came to choosing a marriage partner, but wealthy people arranged the marriages of their children very carefully because the right marriage would promote the family's interest. The new family connections might bring better employment for a family member, valuable business contacts, and acceptance into favoured social circles.

The daughter of a wealthy family was almost always much younger than the man she married, and her father would pay a large dowry to her husband's family. A young woman may not have wished to marry so young or to a man she did not know, but her wishes were not considered important.

Weddings were flashy occasions when wealthy people displayed their finery, spending vast sums on clothing and entertainment. A wedding gown of this period might have been decorated with articles such as peacock feathers, gold leaf, pearls, and flowers. Such a gown would cost as much as hiring a skilled labourer for 500 days. At a rate of $25 an hour, in today's dollars, how much would the gown be worth?

Figure 7–7 This detail of *The Wedding at Cana* by Paolo Veronese shows the clothing of wealthy people in sixteenth-century Italy. African servants were rare and sought after. Why do you think the artist included the young boy shown at the front of the picture? What does this say about Renaissance society?

The Sumptuary Laws

Imagine you are preparing dinner for some special friends. How would you feel if the law insisted that you provide a certain number of food courses depending on the social status of your friends?

Renaissance Italy had many such laws. If you invited a high Church official, a cardinal, to dinner, you had to serve nine courses. If you invited a bishop, archbishop, count, or duke, you served seven. Ordinary government officials would have to be content with six.

By 1460, wedding and social banquets in Venice had become so excessive that the government decided to ban most of them, along with certain foods, such as partridge, pheasant, and peacock.

All these laws were called "sumptuary laws" because they controlled con**sump**tion, or how people spent their money. Sumptuary laws also governed clothing and household goods. They were often directed at the growing middle class. Why would that be so?

Florence in 1427

H ere are some statistics about families in Florence in the fifteenth century. Why do you think women tended to marry at a much earlier age than men?

Average age of head of household:	45 years
Average family size (merchant):	6.16 persons
Average family size (poor):	4.57 persons
Average age difference between bride and groom:	13.6 years
Average age for first marriage (women):	17.9 years
Average age for first marriage (men):	29.9 years
Earliest age for first marriage for wealthy men:	31.2 years
Average age for fatherhood:	39.8 years
Average age for motherhood:	26.5 years
Men who did not marry:	10 percent
Women who did not marry:	unknown but very few

In the countryside around Florence:

Average age difference between bride and groom:	7.3 years
Average age for first marriage (women):	18.3 years
Average age for first marriage (men):	25.6 years

A Betrothal and a Dowry

I sabella D'Este was betrothed (promised in marriage) at the age of six to Giovanni Gonzaga, aged fourteen. The boy's family sent a representative to inspect Isabella. Part of the report appears here.

Madonna Isabella was then led in to see me [the Gonzagas' representative], and I questioned her on many subjects, to all of which she replied with rare good sense and quickness. Her answers seemed truly miraculous in a child of six. I sent the portrait of Madonna Isabella, so that your highness … may see her face, but I can assure you that her marvelous knowledge and intelligence are far more worthy of admiration.

At this time, a marriage involving two wealthy families had little to do with romantic love and quite a lot to do with finances. Here are the particulars of Isabella's dowry, the money paid to her husband's family upon the marriage. This was considered a relatively small dowry. In the end, the marriage took place when Isabella was sixteen, four years later than originally planned.

Jewellery	8000 ducats (about $80 000)
A silver service	2000 ducats
A ruby	7000 ducats
Isabella's own money	3000 ducats
Other money (payable in 18 months)	25 000 ducats
Property and other gifts	10 000 ducats
Total:	55 000 ducats ($550 000)

THE MEDICI FAMILY: POWERFUL PATRONS

The Medici family was the most famous, influential, and powerful family in Italy during the Renaissance. The Medici were an important part of the city's cultural and political life for more than three centuries.

It was almost impossible to have power in Renaissance Italy unless you had great wealth—and vice versa. The Medici family made themselves a fortune as wool and silk merchants and as bankers. They built alliances with other wealthy families, acquired important positions in the Church, and married into the royal families of Europe. By 1434, Cosimo de Medici, a banker and merchant, was wealthy and powerful enough to take complete control of Florence.

Because Florence was a republic, Cosimo could not openly declare himself a dictator. Instead, he used his wealth to buy support and to have his enemies exiled from the city. Under his leadership, Florence attacked certain neighbouring city-states, such as Siena, and made alliances with others, such as Milan. Although Cosimo could be quite ruthless in political matters, he also had a real interest in the arts. He began the Medici tradition of finding and patronizing promising artists.

Like many leading families, the Medici made many enemies. In 1494, important family members were exiled from Florence and not allowed to return for years. Later, as dukes of Tuscany, the Medici once again regained control of the city, which they ruled until the eighteenth century.

assassin: a murderer of a politically important person

to send into exile: to banish

Lorenzo the Magnificent

The most famous Medici was Cosimo's grandson, Lorenzo the Magnificent. Lorenzo was very fond of his brother Giuliano, and the two young men had a grand time in the Renaissance fashion, giving and attending lavish parties. Rivals of the Medici family attacked the brothers when they were at church one Easter Sunday. The attackers stabbed Giuliano to death and wounded Lorenzo. The people of Florence were outraged by this attack and took terrible revenge on the **assassins**. Lorenzo later became absolute ruler of Florence and held power from 1469 until his death in 1492.

Like Cosimo before him, Lorenzo was a patron of art and literature. He sponsored Michelangelo, Botticelli, Leonardo da Vinci, Pico della Mirandola, and other great artists and thinkers. The most famous thinkers of the day were frequent guests in Lorenzo's home. Lorenzo founded a university at Pisa and an academy in Florence. He could talk about art, politics, religion, and culture with his friends in the art world as an equal, not simply as a rich patron. Further, Lorenzo wrote excellent poetry and composed music.

Lorenzo maintained his power in Florence in the same way his grandfather Cosimo had done. He used his wealth to increase his popularity by creating a beautiful and well-run city and by making sure powerful citizens were either on his side or **sent into exile**. Lorenzo made his son Giovanni a cardinal in the Catholic Church when Giovanni was only fourteen years old. Later, Giovanni became Pope Leo X.

Figure 7–8 Lorenzo the Magnificent, ruler and poet. Which aspect of Lorenzo's character—the strong-willed ruler or the sensitive poet—did the painter Giorgio Vasari emphasize in this portrait?

Death in the Medici Family, 1464–1587

As you can see in the account below, Renaissance politics took a high toll on the Medici family. Why do you think so many of the Medici died violent deaths? The account of the Grand Duke Francesco's death, as well as that of his wife, Bianca, may not be true. Some historians believe they died of malaria. As a historian yourself, how would you find out which version is true?

Cosimo the Elder (1389–1464): exiled

Giuliano (1453–1478): stabbed to death

Lorenzo the Magnificent (1449–1492): wounded in an attack on his brother, Giuliano

Piero the Unfortunate (1472–1503): drowned in a shipwreck

Giovanni delle Barde Nere (1498–1526): shot and killed attacking Mantua

Ippolito (1511–1535): poisoned by order of his cousin Alessandro

Alessandro (1511–1537): assassinated by his cousin Lorenzino

Lorenzino (1515–1547): assassinated by order of his cousin Cosimo I

Isabella, daughter of Cosimo I (1542–1576): strangled in bed by her own husband

Grand Duke Francesco (1541–1587): died after eating a tart poisoned by his wife, Bianca. She had been trying to kill Francesco's brother, but her husband ate the tart instead. Bianca then killed herself by eating a slice of the same poisoned tart.

ACTIVITIES

1. How important was the family in Italian society? Give examples from the text to support your view.

2. Why did many young Renaissance women need dowries? What difficulties might arise within an arranged marriage? Compare Renaissance marriage practices with those in Canada.

3. Examine the table titled "Florence in 1427" on page 219.

   a) Compare the average family size with the average family size of the Franks in the similar table in Chapter 1 (page 24). Why do you think that most Florentines had larger families than the Franks?

   b) How do you account for differences between men and women expressed in the table for Florence? Why do you think the age difference between husband and wife is so much higher in the city than in the country?

   c) What do you think was the source of these statistics? Would these sources be reliable? Explain.

4. a) What is a sumptuary law?

   b) Brainstorm a list of possible sumptuary laws for modern Canadian students in Grade 8. With another classmate, write three sumptuary laws around one topic, for example, food or clothing. If you decide to limit the consumption of something, or to ban its use altogether, give a reason why.

   c) Are there any sumptuary laws in effect in Canada today? Why or why not? What right do you enjoy as a Canadian citizen that Florentine citizens did not enjoy?

5. What did the Medici do to advance the arts in Florence?

6. Reread the feature box above on the bloody deaths of members of the Medici family. In a small group, select one of the incidents and create a tableau that captures the drama of the moment. (In a tableau, you pose in a group to create a striking dramatic scene.) Consult some of the paintings in this chapter to get an idea of the appropriate clothing.

RENAISSANCE THOUGHT

THE HUMANISTS

reason: the ability to think and draw conclusions

Old Town: a term used to describe the original city centre of a European city

Unlike the medieval artists, Renaissance artists were Humanists; this means they were more concerned with the goals of human beings than

Figure 7–9 A young Canadian strolls through Warsaw's **Old Town**. Many young Canadians travel the world; some even work overseas for a year or two taking part in programs such as Canadian University Students Overseas (CUSO) or teaching English as a second language. What do you think Petrarch would have said about such adventures?

with spiritual matters. Humanists believe in using the power of **reason** to find truth instead of relying on the Bible or other religious teachings. They believed in each person's ability to choose and create his or her own destiny.

The Italian writer and poet Francesco Petrarch was one of the first Humanists. Petrarch often said that he admired the culture of ancient Rome much more than the culture of his own time, the late Middle Ages. For this reason, he spent much time and money collecting and correcting ancient manuscripts. He wanted to make sure that these writings would continue to delight and inspire future generations, what he called "posterity." Through Petrarch's efforts, many classical works survived that might otherwise have been lost forever.

Petrarch recommended that artists and writers study the ancient masterpieces to move art in a new direction, one that would emphasize beauty. He modelled his writing style on the works of the great Roman

Petrarch's Letter to You

Petrarch wrote his *Letter to Posterity* to all the people who would come after him. In this letter he set down some of the thoughts that had guided his life and were important to him. After reading the excerpt, list three ideas important to Petrarch. What kind of a person do you think he was, based on this excerpt?

antiquity: early ages of history

I have always possessed extreme contempt for wealth; not that riches are not desirable in themselves, but because I hate the anxiety and care which are associated with them. I have, on the contrary, led a happier existence with plain living and ordinary fare.

The pleasure of dining with one's friends is so great that nothing has ever given me more delight than their unexpected arrival.

I possess a well-balanced rather than a keen intellect. Among the many subjects that interested me, I dwelt especially upon **antiquity**, for my own age has always repelled me, so that, had it not been for the love of those dear to me, I should have preferred to have been born in any other period than our own.

PRIMARY SOURCE

speaker Cicero. For Petrarch, the truly cultured person made an effort to read good books, see great works of art, and travel widely.

Many Renaissance artists took Petrarch as their model of the well-rounded person who knew about and was skilled in many different areas—the true "**Renaissance man**." Not only would his ideas inspire the great artists, they were to bring about a transformation in the way people thought of their world and the potential of their lives.

MACHIAVELLI AND THE PRINCE

The shifting alliances, family politics, and constant warfare of fifteenth-century Italy disturbed many people of the time. They yearned for stability and peace. Some hoped that a strong leader would bring an end to all the political chaos.

This view was best expressed by the Florentine writer Nicolo Machiavelli, born in 1469. A victim of politics himself, he worked for a time as a civil servant and diplomat for the Republic of Florence. When the republic was overthrown, Nicolo's enemies first took him prisoner and then sent him into exile.

In his best-known book, *The Prince*, which is still studied today, Machiavelli disagreed with the popular Humanist view that people were capable of improving themselves through their own efforts. People, for Machiavelli, were "wretched creatures" who had to be forced by a strong ruler to do what is right. The wise ruler—who Machiavelli called "the Prince"—would be absolutely ruthless. Only thus could he maintain the power he needed to force his citizens to behave properly. Some people accepted Machiavelli's ideas as wise insights into human nature and politics, but others condemned them as evil.

DID YOU KNOW?
Humanism does not mean rejecting religion. The Humanist Pico della Mirandola believed that humans possess great dignity because we were made in the "image of God."

Renaissance man: a term traditionally used to describe a person skilled in many areas

The Qualities of a Ruler: Better to Be Feared?

Machiavelli describes some of the moral qualities of his ideal ruler. Do you think Machiavelli is right when he says a good ruler must be a good liar? Does this advice apply in politics today? Do you think modern politicians seek to be loved or feared? Explain.

From this arises the following question: whether it is better to be loved than feared, or the reverse. The answer is that one would like to be both one and the other; but because it is difficult to combine them, it is far better to be feared than loved if you cannot be both. One can make this generalization about men; they are ungrateful, fickle, liars, and deceivers, they shun danger and are greedy for profit.... Men worry less about doing an injury to one who makes himself loved than to one who makes himself feared. The bond of love is one which men, wretched creatures that they are, break when it is to their advantage to do so; but fear is strengthened by a dread of punishment, which is always effective.

—*The Prince, Chapter 17*

So it follows that a prudent ruler cannot, and should not, honour his word when it places him at a disadvantage.... If all men were good, this precept [rule] would not be good; but because men are wretched creatures who would not keep their word to you, you need not keep your word to them.... One must know how to be a great liar and deceiver.

—*The Prince, Chapter 18*

SAVONAROLA THE REFORMER

During the Renaissance, the Catholic Church was controlled by powerful families in Italy. High church officials, even the pope, often involved themselves in the political turmoil of the time. The strong interest that people had in advancing their families made this problem worse because they would use the Church as a way of increasing their influence and power. At this time, working for the Church did not mean a life of poverty. Church life was often filled with luxury and excess.

Savonarola was a spellbinding preacher of the **Dominican** order who dedicated his life to reforming the corruption in the Church and in society. After coming to Florence in 1490, he persuaded Michelangelo and other artists and writers to join his cause. Soon the fiery priest was attacking the luxuries with which many Florentines surrounded themselves, and which Savonarola thought were sinful. Under his direction, the citizens of Florence built huge "bonfires of the **vanities**" in their town squares, and threw into them wigs, make-up, fancy costumes, and obscene art and books.

When Savonarola preached against Pope Alexander VI, the preacher's enemies set out to destroy him, although they first tried to bribe him. The crowds who had once thought Savonarola a prophet turned against him. A mob dragged him from his prayers and threw him into prison. After repeated tortures, Savonarola was convicted by a religious court of several crimes. Finally, he and his two closest associates were hanged and then burned. Their ashes were thrown into the Arno River. Each year, people still place flowers on the site of his execution.

Dominican: a Catholic religious order

vanity: a worthless pleasure

Arguing for Social Equality

Figure 7–10 Compare Savonarola's portrait with that of Lorenzo on page 220. What does the comparison tell you about the two men?

Figure 7–11 Savonarola is led to his execution. After reading about Savonarola's opinions, at right, what do you think he would have thought about his conviction?

> This country of ours is like a piece of cloth long enough to make coats for everyone; but it is so unequally divided that one has enough to wrap around him three times and trail upon the ground, another has too little to make even a beggar's cloak.... Equality demands that no citizen should be able to oppress another....
>
> Nowhere in the Gospel have I found a text recommending golden crosses and precious stones; rather have I found: I was thirsty and you gave me something to drink; I was hungry and you gave me something to eat.... I, for my part, will give everything away, beginning with my own coat.
>
> —*Sermon of Savonarola*

The Renaissance: Cultivating Disagreement

During the Renaissance, human thought developed in many directions, and the political and academic climate allowed for and even encouraged differences of opinion. Consider and compare the viewpoints of four Renaissance personalities whose words are quoted in this chapter: Machiavelli (page 223), Savonarola (page 224), D'Este (page 213), and Petrarch (page 222).

1. Do you agree with Machiavelli that a leader is better feared than loved? Explain why Savonarola would likely not agree with such an idea.

2. What advice would Machiavelli give to D'Este on how to deal with those who spread evil tales about her? Considering the ways that Isabella proposes to deal with the problem herself, do you think she would agree? Why or why not?

3. What in the Savonarola primary source hints that Savonarola would agree with sumptuary laws?

4. What opinions do Savonarola and Petrarch share concerning the need for possessions?

ACTIVITIES

1. **a)** Read again the opening quotation for this chapter on page 208, as well the section on the Humanists. What ideas were most important to the Humanists?

   b) In what ways did the attitudes of the Humanists differ from the attitudes of medieval thinkers?

2. Read the selections from Machiavelli's *The Prince*. Are these examples of primary or secondary sources? In your own words, summarize Machiavelli's advice to a ruler.

3. Why did Savonarola criticize the Church and the rulers of Florence? What happened to him?

4. **a)** What were the bonfires of the vanities? Make a list of items from modern culture that you think people would want to throw onto a modern-day bonfire of the vanities. Explain how each item represents an abuse. Would you participate in such an event? Why or why not?

   b) Write a brief sermon in Savonarola's style that preaches against some contemporary abuses.

THE GREAT ARTISTS

The key to the realism achieved by the great painters of the Renaissance lay in two remarkable innovations: **proportion** and **perspective**. The Florentine artist Giotto di Bondone (1226–1337) developed the rule of proportion in painting. Proportion means that everything in the painting is "in scale"; in other words, the people are the right size in relation to the buildings and other objects in the painting. Filippo Brunelleschi, another Florentine, discovered the laws of perspective, which allow artists to add depth to their pictures by showing how distance makes things look smaller. Perspective makes paintings look three-dimensional, unlike medieval artists' paintings, which look flat.

proportion: a correct relation among parts

perspective: giving the appearance of distance on a flat surface

LEONARDO DA VINCI

Leonardo da Vinci (1452–1519) never received the classical education that was so valued in his time. Instead, at the age of fifteen, he was apprenticed to the Florentine painter and sculptor Andrea del Verrocchio (see Figure 7–3). The master was so amazed by his young pupil's talent that he gave up painting for the rest of his life and concentrated on sculpture.

Leonardo's apprenticeship as a painter trained him to be unusually observant of the natural world. He was one of the first great Renaissance minds to try to learn about the truth of the natural world through direct observation and experiment. His experiments led him in many directions. He was not just a great painter but an inventor, engineer, and scientist of genius. He was the first to design a helicopter, a tank, a parachute, and a flying machine. Many regard Leonardo da Vinci as the ideal "renaissance man," meaning that he was highly skilled in many areas.

Leonardo had such a restless mind that he often started a new project before finishing the one he was working on. For much of his life, he planned to write a textbook on **human anatomy,** one of the many projects he never finished. His notebooks do survive, however, and they are filled with detailed anatomical drawings of humans, and sketches of inventions. His notes show that he was something of an **eccentric**; they were all written backwards so that they could only be read by holding them in front of a mirror. Leonardo's most famous work is the *Mona Lisa*, whose entrancing smile leaves one feeling fascinated and perplexed.

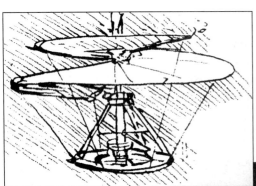

Figure 7–12 This drawing from one of Leonardo's notebooks shows the first design for a helicopter. Why do you think helicopters were not made for another 450 years?

Figure 7–13 Leonardo's *Portrait of Ginevra de' Benci.* Leonardo painted many other portraits of aristocratic women. This woman's first name, Ginevra (meaning "juniper"), is symbolically represented by the juniper tree that frames her head.

blasphemous: showing contempt for sacred things

human anatomy: the science of the structure of the human body

eccentric: odd, peculiar person

Read this passage and then summarize in your own words what Leonardo thought was the painter's most important task.

A good painter has two chief objects to paint, man and the intention of his soul; the former is easy, the latter is hard, because he has to represent it by the attitudes and movements of the limbs. The most important consideration in painting is that the movement of each figure expresses its mental state, such as desire, scorn, anger, pity, and the like. That figure is most worthy of praise which by its action best expresses the passion which animates it.

PRIMARY SOURCE

MICHELANGELO

Perhaps the greatest artist of the high Renaissance, Michelangelo (1475–1564), thought of himself first and foremost as a sculptor. Today, though, he is more famous for the **fresco** paintings he created on the ceiling of the Sistine Chapel in Rome (see page 202). Like many other Renaissance artists, he was apprenticed to a master at an early age, in Michelangelo's case at thirteen. By the time he was twenty-five, Michelangelo had already won fame as the best sculptor in Italy, creating masterpieces of great power and beauty, such as the *Pieta*, his statue of Mary holding the lifeless body of Jesus. In 1501, he began to carve his statue of *David* from a single block of marble more than 5 metres high, a task that took three years to complete. This work and others made Michelangelo what we would call a superstar: he was wealthy and famous.

Though protesting that he was not a painter, Michelangelo agreed to paint the ceiling of the Sistine Chapel in Rome at the insistence of Pope Julius II. Michelangelo painted from a scaffold 23 metres above the chapel floor. He applied his water colours to plaster that was still wet; as the plaster dried, the painting became a permanent part of the ceiling. Not all of the figures on this ceiling are from the Bible. Why do you think the artist would include pagan prophets in a religious painting?

Michelangelo had a fiery temper. Once, in a fight with another sculptor, he got his nose broken. When Pope Julius II thought Michelangelo was taking too long to paint the Sistine Chapel in Rome, the pope remarked that he might as well throw the artist from the towering scaffold. Michelangelo looked the warrior pope in the eye and replied, with some personal risk, "I think not, My Lord." Michelangelo died much later, still carving marble, at the age of eighty-nine.

fresco: painted with water colour on fresh wet plaster

Figure 7–14
Michelangelo carved his David from a single, oddly shaped block of marble that had been abandoned in frustration by another sculptor.

ARTEMISIA GENTILESCHI

Artemisia Gentileschi, born in Naples in 1593, was the daughter of a famous painter, Orazio Gentileschi. In an age when women's options in life were severely limited, Artemisia achieved fame and independence through art. An accomplished portrait painter, she travelled as far as England, where she painted people at the English court. Artemisia's masterpiece, *Judith Slaying Holofernes*, was especially noted for its intensity and the way the light illuminates the faces of the three subjects.

Figure 7–15 Like many of her fellow artists in Renaissance Italy, Gentileschi spent much of her time painting scenes from the Bible for wealthy patrons. Her painting *Judith Slaying Holofernes* shows an Old Testament heroine just after she has cut off the head of the general of an Assyrian army that invaded Israel in the sixth century B.C.E.

ACTIVITIES

1. Review the paintings shown in this chapter. What makes Renaissance art different from medieval art?

2. What is perspective? What is proportion? Why were both these ideas important to Renaissance artists?

3. **a)** How does the detail from *The Wedding at Cana*, on page 218, demonstrate the Renaissance principle of perspective? In a chart, compare the features of this work with those of the banquet scene from the Bayeaux Tapestry on page 39.

   b) In another chart compare the *David* by Michelangelo with the statue of Charlemagne on page 26. What do you think were the goals of the artist in each case?

4. What difficulties do you think Michelangelo may have faced while working on the ceiling of the Sistine Chapel (see page 202), which is over 23 metres high and curved rather than flat?

5. Describe the accomplishments of Gentileschi.

6. Using a CD ROM from the art department or your school library, search a data base of artwork for examples of Renaissance art and medieval art. List three examples of each, describe each work, and make four general comments that describe the differences between the two groups.

7. **a)** Leonardo da Vinci states that the supreme goal of the artist is to convey the passion that animates a person. Choose one Renaissance work of art that you think best accomplishes this task, and explain your choice.

   b) How does Leonardo's description of the Humanist artist relate to the beliefs of the Humanists?

8. The Song Dynasty in China has often been compared to the Renaissance in Europe. For a research project, read up on the Song Dynasty in Chapter 13 and then create an organizer to compare the two periods.

THE NORTHERN RENAISSANCE

Renaissance ideas spread quickly from Italy throughout the rest of Europe. The cities of northern Europe, such as Antwerp, Amsterdam, and London, had many wealthy merchants who responded by patronizing painters, writers, and scientists. writers. The new ideas also attracted the attention of rulers and philosophers, and gave them a fresh view of the world around them. One of the most important contributions of the North to the Renaissance was the invention of the printing press, which revolutionized the spread of knowledge.

PRINTING TECHNOLOGY

To appreciate just how important the invention of printing was, you have to use your imagination. Picture a world in which all information is communicated either by word of mouth or through handwriting. In the Middle Ages, there was no television or radio, no movies or printed books, no computers. When an author wrote a new book, it had to be copied out by hand from the author's manuscript, often by a team of scribes who worked at the same time on different parts of the book. Even with this sort of teamwork, months were needed to produce a single copy of a new book. Authors were lucky if even fifty copies were made.

About the middle of the fifteenth century, Johann Gutenberg, a German, invented the printing press with movable type. Using this new piece of technology, printers could produce thousands of copies of a book in the time it had once taken to make a single copy. These books were cheaper, too. They were printed on paper, which was much less expensive than the parchment (dried sheepskin) used in medieval times.

Unlike writers before them, Renaissance authors could reach thousands of people in the growing middle class, not just a few hundred wealthy individuals. Artists took advantage of the new technology, too, using it to mass-produce wood-block prints. The German artist Albrecht Dürer used the printing press for both purposes, producing wood-block art prints for wide distribution and art manuals that helped popularize the ideas of the Italian Renaissance.

DID YOU KNOW?

Although Europeans did not know it, the Chinese had already invented movable type by 1040.

DID YOU KNOW?

Oil paint, which allows leisurely painting and brilliant colours, was a Flemish development brought to Italy late in the fifteenth century.

Figure 7–16 Interior of an early print shop. Each person pictured here has a separate task to perform. See if you can pick out the people who are doing the following tasks: setting the type, operating the printing press, drying the freshly printed sheets, and binding the dried sheets.

Figure 7–17 Albrecht Dürer's *Hare*. The medieval artist would not have made a picture of a hare, partly because nobody would have paid for such a picture, and partly because the very idea would have seemed odd.

NORTHERN ART

The ideals of Humanism attracted northern European artists, but these artists retained a great fondness for the Gothic art of the Middle Ages, as well as a strong interest in religious themes. One painter, Peiter Breugel, was a major exception because he preferred to paint ordinary people in scenes of everyday life. You can see his painting of a peasant on page 157.

Renaissance art from the North looks very different from Italian art of the same time. It is darker, and because of its serious tone and its focus on religious topics, northern art seems more medieval than the works of the Italian painters. Northern artists such as the master **etcher** and **woodcutter** Albrecht Dürer from Germany sometimes travelled to Italy to study the works and technique of artists there. When he returned from Italy, Dürer wrote a textbook on perspective and proportion. Through this book, he hoped to explain to other northern artists the rules and techniques that

---

LINK-UP

The Renaissance in Many Cultures

When we hear the words "the Renaissance," we usually think of the European Renaissance we're studying in this chapter. But "renaissance" means the "rebirth" of culture, which many civilizations have experienced. For example, China experienced a phenomenal resurgence of its culture during the Song Dynasty. The Chinese of this period rediscovered ancient Chinese arts and sciences, both of which they advanced significantly.

For an example of a current renaissance, though somewhat smaller, we can look at the French-speaking Acadians in Atlantic Canada. The Acadians have been experiencing a renaissance of their culture, which had suffered a dreadful setback when the English expelled them from their lands over 200 years ago. Now Acadians are rediscovering their history, and celebrating their culture.

Figure 7–18 *Viola Léger in Emmanuel à Joseph à Davit*, a play by Acadian playwright Antoinine Maillet at Le Cercle Molière (a Manitoba French-language theatre). How is this play, which celebrates lost Acadian culture and values, similar to the Renaissance works of art?

the Italian masters used to create more natural-looking works of art.

If the Italian painters can be said to have developed the laws of perspective and proportion, the northern painters can be said to have developed the secrets of light and shadow. The way light or shadow falls upon a subject can create many different moods, from cheery to melancholy. Using light and shadow gives the artist another way of achieving realism and conveying more about the subject than just the physical appearance. The Flemish (Belgian) artist Jan van Eyck began this trend in the fourteenth century. Three centuries later, the great Dutch master, Rembrandt van Rijn, would take the exploration of light and shadow to its peak, stressing non-religious themes.

THE SCIENTIFIC REVOLUTION

In the fourteenth and fifteenth centuries, science began to separate from religion. Scientists became convinced that they could learn more about the way things work by studying these things rather than reading about them in the Bible or works of philosophers such as Aristotle and Thomas Aquinas. Their attempts often resulted in discoveries and theories that went against the teachings of the Catholic Church. It was still dangerous at this time for a scientist to challenge the teachings of the Church, as Galileo, the greatest of all Renaissance scientists, was to discover.

Copernicus

Nicholas Copernicus of Poland was the first scientist to state, in 1543, the revolutionary theory that the Earth is not the centre of the universe. A lawyer, doctor, mathematician, and church administrator, Copernicus studied astronomy only in his spare time.

Copernicus did not have a telescope to help him formulate his hypothesis. Instead, he used mathematics to calculate the orbits of

etcher: an artist who engraves a picture onto a metal plate, and uses this plate as a stamp

woodcutter: an artist who carves a picture onto a wood block, and uses this block as a stamp

empirical reasoning: drawing conclusions from physical evidence

Use the Scientific Method

Renaissance scientists developed the scientific method for their research into the natural world and the structure of the solar system. The scientific method still guides scientists today.

1. Identify the problem or question.

2. Experiment and observe the results.

3. Use your reason to analyze the results.

4. Formulate a **hypothesis** based on the results of your experiments.

4. Test your hypothesis by gathering additional information and conducting further experiments.

5. Use your reason to analyze the new results.

6. If your hypothesis is supported by the new experiments, restate it as a **theory**. If not, then formulate a new hypothesis and continue to experiment.

NOW YOU DO IT

1. Working with a partner, solve a straighforward scientific question using the scientific method. For example, "Which falls faster: heavy objects or light objects?"

hypothesis: a proposed explanation

theory: an explanation supported by the observation of evidence

the planets around the sun. He became convinced that the old Ptolemaic system, which placed the Earth at the centre of the universe, was wrong. Copernicus theorized correctly that the Earth moves in two ways: first, by revolving daily on its axis; and second, by orbiting annually around the sun. He also theorized that the sun was just one of many stars, each of which could also have its own system of planets. Copernicus

died shortly after receiving the first printed copy of his book *On the Revolutions of Heavenly Bodies*. In 1616 the Church condemned the book, but by then so many copies had been printed that the ideas of Copernicus had come to the attention of daring thinkers such as Galileo.

Galileo Galilei

Galileo Galilei, was born in the town of Pisa, Italy, in 1564, the same year that Michelangelo died. He studied to be a medical doctor but soon became interested in the astronomy and physics that so fascinated the northern Europeans, who were leading the scientific renaissance. In 1609 Galileo learned about a recent Dutch invention called a *kijkglas*, or "looking glass," made by an eyeglass maker named Hans Lippershey. This looking glass made small objects seem large. Galileo decided to build one to watch the stars. After several attempts, each one better than the one before, Galileo finally made a telescope that made things appear a thousand times larger and thirty times nearer than they

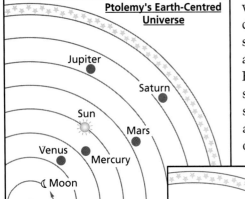

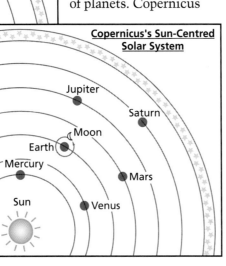

Figure 7–19 For many hundreds of years, people had believed that their world, the Earth, had been placed by God at the centre of the universe, as described by the Greek astronomer Ptolemy and supported by the Bible. Why do you think Renaissance people were shaken by Copernicus's vision of the universe?

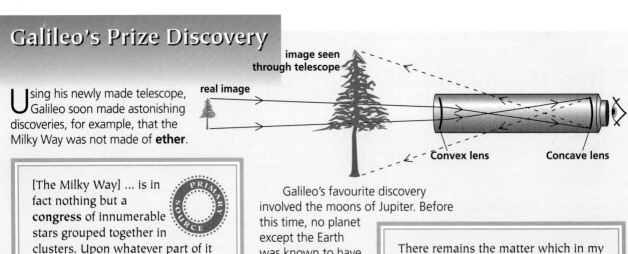

Galileo's Prize Discovery

Using his newly made telescope, Galileo soon made astonishing discoveries, for example, that the Milky Way was not made of **ether**.

[The Milky Way] ... is in fact nothing but a **congress** of innumerable stars grouped together in clusters. Upon whatever part of it the spyglass is directed, a vast crowd of stars is immediately presented to view. Many of them are rather large and quite bright, while the number of smaller ones is quite beyond calculation.

Galileo's favourite discovery involved the moons of Jupiter. Before this time, no planet except the Earth was known to have moons. After reading the following excerpt, how do you think Galileo felt about his discovery?

There remains the matter which in my opinion deserves to be considered the most important of all—the disclosure of four PLANETS [orbiting moons] never seen from the creation of the world up to our own time.

were. This piece of technology allowed him to see things that no one else had seen before. He saw, for example, that the moon was solid and its surface was pitted and scarred. Until then people had believed that the moon and other planets were not solid, but made of a light substance they called "ether." Through his careful observations of the movements of the planets, Galileo came to the disturbing conclusion that Copernicus had been correct: the Earth revolves around the sun.

Galileo's discoveries had an explosive effect on thinkers of the time. Because several of his discoveries went against the teachings of the Church and what was written in the Bible, Galileo was summoned before a Church court called the **Inquisition**. The court ordered Galileo to accept the Church's view that the Earth was the centre of the universe and did not move. Galileo believed that one could believe in both the Bible and the discoveries of science. After the court threatened him with torture, however, Galileo said he would accept the Church's view, and he was sentenced to indefinite house arrest. Legend holds that when Galileo heard the sentence, he whispered "E pur si muove" ("Nevertheless, it does move").

ether: an extremely pure, refined substance once thought to occupy the upper regions of space

congress: collection

Inquisition: a Church court that tried heretics, people who disagreed with Church teachings

DID YOU KNOW?

The word "telescope" comes from the Greek words tele, *for "far away," and* skopeo, *for "look."*

◄ LINK-UP ►

Stargazing

The stargazing begun by Tycho Brahe continues. The very first observatory in North America is believed to have been built in Falmouth, Nova Scotia, in the 1700s. Today's cities, however, with their bright electric lights, make viewing the sky very difficult. For this reason, Canada builds its largest observatories (buildings that house telescopes) far from cities, often in distant countries.

Two of the biggest are the Las Campanas Observatory in Chile and the Mauna Kea Observatory in Hawaii. Now we even have telescopes in space, such as the Hubble.

Research modern telescopes and summarize how they have changed since Galileo's time.

Figure 7–20 Now Canada has several telescopes, such as the J.S. Plaskett Telescope at the Dominion Astrophysical Observatory near Victoria, British Columbia. With a 1.8 metre-wide opening, this telescope was the largest in the world when it was built in 1918.

A C T I V I T I E S

1. Who invented the printing press? Why did this invention have such a great effect on the spread of knowledge in Europe during the Renaissance? Has the Internet had a similar effect? Explain.

2. Compare the developments in art in northern Europe with those in Italy during the Renaissance. Consider the major artists, subjects of painting, techniques used, influences, and time periods.

3. Compare a painting of a northern European artist with one by a southern European artist. In what ways are these paintings similar? In what ways are they different? Which do you like better? Why?

4. Explain how science changed during the Renaissance.

5. Galileo made many discoveries. List the ones mentioned in this chapter. Do some research to find out about another of his discoveries.

6. Why was Galileo tried before the Inquisition? Would such a thing happen in Canada today? Explain.

SUMMARY

During the Renaissance, western European civilization took a great leap forward, greater than any taken before or since. The Renaissance literally changed the way people looked at the world around them. In art, the newly discovered laws of perspective and proportion finally allowed painters and sculptors to create works that looked natural, mirroring the way things appear in reality. In science, inventions such as the telescope meant people could see things that had always been invisible. These new discoveries completely destroyed the old view of the universe and of humanity's place within it. Many people began to rely less on the teachings of the Catholic Church to find meaning in their lives.

Instead they turned to their own powers of observation and reason.

As the Humanists would have liked, the Renaissance opened people's eyes to new possibilities of human achievement. Pico della Mirandola summed up this new attitude when he stated that human beings are "confined by no limits." We will see in Chapter 8 how the seafarers of Portugal, Spain, and England translated this optimism into the great ocean voyages that showed Europeans the world. In Chapter 9, we'll look at explorers of a different kind—those on a quest for spiritual reform. All these explorations took their inspiration from the Renaissance, a time when humanity's creative powers seemed limitless.

SUMMARY ACTIVITIES

1. Write seven entries in the imaginary diary of Isabella D'Este. Include references to things you think would be important to a powerful Renaissance woman who was a leader in Italian society and a major patron of the arts. Keep in mind that she was noted for her brilliant mind as well as her personal grace and charm.

2. Organize an imaginary Renaissance holiday tour for your classmates that will take them to see city-states and important art from the Renaissance. Prepare a schedule, tour map, brochures, and pictures of sights to show potential "customers."

3. Reread the Early Banking feature on page 214. Write a paragraph comparing the economy of medieval Europe with that of Renaissance Europe.

Then analyze how these differences changed European society and culture.

4. a) Read again the opening quotation for this chapter on page 208. In this brief declaration lies the essence of Humanist thought and the spirit of the Renaissance. Summarize Mirandola's ideas in your own words.

   b) Pretend you have a chance to write a one-paragraph letter to everyone in the world. What would you say? Decide what is the most important message you want to get across, and write the letter.

5. What was the greatest achievement of the Renaissance? Explain your choice.

ON YOUR OWN

1. Research and list some discoveries that have come as a result of telescopes such as the one at Mauna Kea (Canada's telescope in Hawaii) and the Hubble telescope. Despite the great power of these modern instruments, have they made any discoveries that were more exciting than those Galileo made with his primitive instrument?

2. Write a research report on one Renaissance artist and one Renaissance scientist. Be sure to explain

how this person changed the way people viewed their world or themselves.

3. The Sistine Chapel is one of the greatest masterpieces of the Italian Renaissance. Prepare a report comparing this work with a tremendous masterpiece of the Muslim world, the mosque built by Abd-al-Rahman in Cordoba, Spain. You can see its picture on page 315.

8 NAVIGATORS AND SEA DOGS

CHAPTER OUTCOMES

In this chapter, you will focus on the Age of Exploration, the period from about 1400 to 1600, when European explorers set out to see the world. By the end of the chapter, you will

- describe the impact of new technologies in ship building and navigation

- analyze the effect of trade on exploration

- relate knowledge of physical geography to patterns of exploration

- demonstrate understanding of the use of grids (latitude and longitude)

- locate and describe the accomplishments of the European explorers, using maps

- compare different historical accounts of Spanish conquests in the Americas

- examine how the conquistadors' conquests affected Aboriginal peoples

An Inca Remembers

Cayalla	*To this tune*
Pununqui	*You will sleep*
Chaupituta	*At midnight*
Samusac	*I shall come*

This ancient Incan love song appears in The Incas, *a book written by Garcilaso de la Vega in the sixteenth century to document the history and culture of the Incan civilization. De la Vega was the son of an Inca princess and a Spanish* **conquistador**. *He was born a few years after Spain conquered Peru.*

The Inca Empire, called "Tawantinsuyu," was ruled from the city of Cuzco in present-day Peru. The empire stretched 3500 kilometres to include most of present-day Peru, Chile, and Equador. The supreme ruler of the empire was The Inca, a ruler said to be the direct descendant of the Sun God. The members of the extended royal family, which included de la Vega's mother, were known as the Incas.

The following selections from de la Vega's book show his view of the Incas and their empire. Historians have criticized de la Vega for downplaying some of the practices of the Inca, which included human sacrifice, and for downplaying the cruelties of the Spanish invaders. Considering his parentage and his audience, can you think why he might be unwilling to criticize? European explorers and conquerers believed they were bringing civilization to uncivilized peoples. As you read, consider whether or not you believe this to be true.

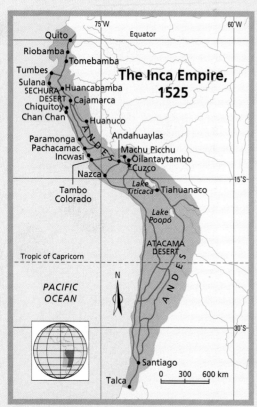

The Inca Empire and its roads. The fine system of roadways meant the conquistator Francisco Pizarro and his troops could travel speedily during their conquest of the Inca Empire in Peru.

D e la Vega begins his story by telling of the discussions he heard as a child when his mother's Incan relations came to visit.

On these occasions, the conversation turned almost invariably to the origins of our kings and to their majesty. It also concerned the grandeur of their empire, their conquests and noble deeds, their government in war and peace, and the very wise laws that they had **promulgated** *for the welfare of their subjects and vassals. In short, nothing of what these great lords had done for our country was forgotten. Then, leaving grandeur behind, my relatives would return to the present, and here they wept over their dead kings and their lost empire. Indeed, I do not believe that there was a single one of these conversations that did not end in tears and wailing, while all those present kept repeating: "Once we were kings, now we are vassals!"*

The Origins of Incan Civilization

After de la Vega asks about the origins of his family, the Inca, his uncle responds, as below.

"My nephew," said he, "I shall answer you with the greatest pleasure, because it is important for you to have heard these things and you should preserve them in your heart. Know then that, at one time, all the land you see about you was

nothing but mountains and desolate cliffs. The people lived like wild beasts, ... [feeding] upon grass and roots, wild fruits, and even human flesh....

"Seeing the condition they were in, our father the Sun was ashamed for them, and he decided to send one of his sons and one of his daughters from heaven to earth, in order that they might teach men to adore him and acknowledge him as their god; to obey his laws ... as every reasonable creature must do; to build houses and assemble together in villages; to till the soil, sow the seed, raise cattle, and enjoy the fruits of their labours like human beings."

The Incan Rulers

The direct descendants of the first two Incas were considered to be both monarchs and gods. They were treated as such, as can be seen by de la Vega's description of the litter bearers for the Inca ruler.

The men who carried the gold litters on which the Inca moved about were chosen from two neighbouring provinces.... If one of these porters fell, he was put to death, and some twenty-five substitutes always followed the royal litter, should it be necessary to replace a porter on duty. This office, like the above-mentioned, was greatly prized because it

allowed those who filled it to approach the Inca's sacred person.

As supreme rulers, the Inca received **tribute** from all citizens except nobles.

The Inca's vassals [citizens] furnished him with four types of ... labour: they tilled his land, spun and wove his wool and cotton, and manufactured shoes and weapons for his troops.

We shall add to these the special tribute that, every year, the poor and disinherited paid to the governors of the territory they lived in; which consisted of a tube filled with **lice**. The Incas said that this token tribute was intended to show

Procession outside the Temple of the Sun in Cuzco

237

that everyone, no matter what his station, owed something to the State, in exchange for the benefits he received from it.

Ordinary People

Married women were generally dedicated to the care of their homes; they knew how to spin and weave wool or cotton, according to whether they lived in cold or hot regions. They did little sewing however, for there was hardly any needed, Indian garments, both masculine and feminine, being generally woven in one piece in the proper length and width ....

Although the care of clothing was **incumbent** upon women, that of shoes was left to the men.

All the men and all the women worked together in the fields. In a few distant provinces that were not as submissive as others to all the details of the Inca laws, the women worked in the fields while the men stayed at home to do the spinning and weaving. But that sort of thing was both barbarous and unusual, so that we can pass it over.

Social Status, Laws, and Schools

The study of science was the exclusive right of the sons of noblemen, and the children of the common people had to be content with learning the same trade as their father. Robbery, adultery, homicide, and willful **arson** were punishable with death by hanging. Male children were bound to work for their fathers until they were twenty-five years old, after which they entered the service of the State ....

Inca Roca was the first Peruvian king to open state schools in the city of Cuzco, for the education of young nobles. The subjects taught them by the amautas [teachers] included the rites, **precepts**, and ceremonies of their false religion, the foundations of their laws, their numbers and the art of equitably interpreting them, the military arts and those of government, how to keep account of the years and of history by means of quipus, oratory, child education, the precepts of domestic life, poetry, music, philosophy, and astronomy.

Astronomy and the Inca Calendar

Besides having an excellent knowledge of geometry, which they used to survey land, the Inca had a developed knowledge of astronomy, which helped them keep an accurate

Farmers working on the terraces required for farming in mountainous regions

A monumental stone Incan calendar at Cuzco, Peru

calendar and determine when to sow crops. They were quite superstitious, however, just like Europeans, as we saw in the excerpt from *The History of the Franks*, page 23.

Despite their primitiveness, the Incas understood the annual movement of the Sun ....

Since they counted the months by Moons, and since, too, the solar year was longer by twelve days than the lunar year, it was thanks to ... observation of the solstices that they restored order to their calendar. They were also familiar with the equinoxes, which were the occasion for important ceremonies ....

They knew, too, about the different eclipses of the Moon and the Sun, without, however, suspecting their causes. For them, when the Sun was in an eclipse, some misdemeanour committed in the kingdom had irritated it, since, at that

moment, its countenance [expression] had the disturbed look of a man in anger, and they predicted, as astrologists do, the imminence of some severe [punishment] ....

On Sacrifices

De la Vega describes the sacrifice of a lamb:

Three or four men held the animal, with its head turned toward the east, without its having to be tied. They then slit it open on its left flank ... and the priest, thrusting his hand into its body, took out the heart, lungs and all the interior organs, taking care that they should be whole and all in one piece, without being torn.

*If the lungs [stirred] ... in broad daylight, there could be no better **omen**, and they looked no further.*

Recording Techniques

The Inca had a remarkable system for recording information.

The word "quipu" means both "knot" or "to knot"; it was also used for accounts, because they were kept by means of the knots tied in a number of cords of different thicknesses and colours, each one of which had a special significance. Thus, gold was represented by a gold cord, silver by a white one, and fighting men by a red cord ....

According to their position,

The mummy of an Incan girl, a sacrificial victim uncovered in an archaeological dig at a Temple of the Sun in Peru

The quipu numbers reminded the Inca accountants of historical events, and so served as a way to record history.

the knots signified units, tens, hundreds, thousands, ten thousands and, exceptionally, hundred thousands ... Indeed, those men, called quipucamuyaus, who were in charge of the quipus, were exactly that, imperial accountants.

Cuzco and the Great Sun Temple

The Incas possessed great quantities of gold, silver, and precious stones. As Tawantinsuyu had no monetary system, these metals were used solely to glorify the palaces of the Inca ruler and the Temples of the Sun. Cuzco received much of the glorification.

*In the whole of old Peru, there was undoubtedly no place that was as deeply **revered** as the imperial city of Cuzco, which is where all the Inca kings held court and established the seat of government. When two Indians met on a road leading to this city, the one who was going there immediately greeted the one coming from there as his superior, and in all the kingdom there was neither vegetable, grain, nor other produce, of however superior quality, to compare with those from Cuzco. All the Incas enriched this city and, among its countless monuments, the Temple of the Sun remained the principal object of their attention. They vied with one another in ornamenting it with incredible wealth, each Inca [ruler] seeking to surpass his predecessor ....*

The four walls were hung with plaques of gold, from top to bottom, and a likeness of the Sun topped the high altar. This likeness was made of a gold plaque twice as thick as those that paneled the walls ... The whole thing was so immense that it occupied the entire back of the temple, from one wall to the other .... There was no other idol in this temple, nor in any other, for the Sun was the only god of the Incas, whatever people may say on this subject.

When the Spaniards entered Cuzco, this likeness of the Sun, as the result of a division of property, fell into the hands of one of the early conquistadors .... He was a great gambler and he had no sooner acquired this treasure than he gambled and lost it in one night.

The End of an Empire

A relatively small group of Spanish conquistadors led by Francisco Pizarro invaded the Incan Empire in 1531. By means of brutal determination and ruthlessness, and because the empire had been weakened by a civil war, the Spanish quickly brought the empire to its knees. The last of the Inca leaders, Huascar and his brother Atahualpa, were both executed, despite a ransom paid of three rooms full of gold and silver. The Spaniards then ransacked Tawantinsuyu for gold. Below, de la Vega relates one incident.

The Spaniards destroyed [the Sun temple in Cacha], despite the fact that it was unique of its kind, in the same way that they destroyed all of Peru's most beautiful monuments ....

They preferred to raze everything, out of cupidity [greed], because they could not believe that the Indians had built such monuments as these, unless it was for the purpose of hiding important treasures. In the case in question, they began by pulling down Viracocha's statue [a *former Inca ruler], in the idea that it contained piles of gold. Then they destroyed and excavated the entire **edifice** to its very foundations, without finding anything. A few years ago, this disfigured statue was still lying in the grass, near the ruins of the temple. Then, one fine day, they broke it in pieces, to be used for* **cobblestones**.

conquistador: Spanish for "conqueror"

to promulgate: to proclaim

tribute: expected gifts made to a ruler

lice: tiny parasitical insects that live on mammals, including humans

incumbent: resting as a duty on

arson: setting property on fire

precept: general rule of behaviour

omen: sign of what is to happen

to revere: to honour and respect

edifice: building

cobblestone: a stone used for paving streets

bias: unintentional distortion of the truth

What do you think the artist is trying to say in this painting? Do both warriors appear brave? Compare the protective armour and weapons of each.

ACTIVITIES

1. What was the weirdest thing you read about in Garcilaso's account? Why did you find it strange? What impressed you most? What did you find shocking? Or sad? What made you laugh?

2. Who did the Inca say brought civilization to the Tawantinsuyu people? Identify four conditions crucial to civilization according to the Inca.

3. Create an organizer on the culture of the Incas. Your chart should include these categories: social structure, government, sciences, arts, religion, calendar, recording techniques, and schools.

4. Look for words and phrases in Garcilaso's account that show his **bias**. (Bias is discussed on page 262.) List these clues. Can Garcilaso's views be completely trusted? Explain.

5. a) After reading about what happened to the likeness of the Sun in the Sun Temple in Cuzco, and the destruction of Viracocha's statue in the Sun Temple in Casha, and all the Incan temples, what can you say about how the Spanish regarded the Incan culture?

   b) Is Canadian society more tolerant? Are all cultures equally tolerant or intolerant? What leads to tolerance and intolerance? Share your observations with a partner.

6. The photograph on page 242 shows Machu Piccu, an ancient Incan city built on a mountaintop deep in the Andes Mountains. Hiram Bingham found it in 1912 on an archaeological expedition. Think of three reasons why archaeologists considered this site to be such a spectacular find. Consider the size of the find, its intriguing location, and its rare, relatively untouched condition.

TIME LINE

1420 Henry the Navigator sends out his first ship

1488 Dias sails around Cape of Good Hope

1492 Columbus sails to the "New World"

1494 Treaty of Tordesillas

1497 Giovanni Caboto sails to Canada

1498 Da Gama reaches India

1517 Martin Luther writes his Ninety-Five Theses

1521 Cortéz sails to Mexico

1522 Magellan's expedition returns to Spain

1533 Murder of Atahualpa

1534 Jacques Cartier's first voyage

1580 Queen Elizabeth knights Francis Drake

1600 End of Spain's Golden Age

> *"Brothers and comrades, let us follow the sign of the Holy Cross in true faith, for under this sign we shall conquer."* And *[Cortéz] ordered a proclamation to be made to the sound of trumpets and drums ... that anyone who wished to accompany him to the newly discovered lands, to conquer and settle, would receive a share of the gold, silver, and riches to be gained.*

— **BERNAL DIAZ**

PRIMARY SOURCE

Bernal Diaz, a soldier and historian who accompanied Hernàn Cortéz to Central America, tells how Cortéz inspired his troops, partly through religious zeal and partly by appealing to their lust for riches. What contradiction, if any, do you see in this message?

INTRODUCTION

By the end of the Middle Ages, Western Europe had changed utterly from what it had been after the fall of Rome. In many places, feudalism had almost disappeared and merchants and traders were responsible for great economic growth.

Medieval Europeans had looked inward. They knew little about world geography and had a superstitious dread of the unknown. Renaissance people were different. Not only did they have a great appetite for knowledge; they also hungered for riches and were eager to explore the world to find them. It was during the Renaissance that the first great voyages of European exploration occurred, from Spain, Portugal, England, France, and Holland. Almost every early expedition was sponsored by a monarch desiring access to the wealth of Asia. In their search for a sea route to Asia, Europe's bold explorers found whole continents and proved that the world was round.

THE RICHES OF ASIA

To western Europeans, China, Japan, and India were places of great wealth and mystery. Europeans knew something about these countries, but only a handful of people had ever travelled to these distant lands. The products of Asia, however—silk, sandalwood, teak, oils, gold, and jewels—had been available to Europeans in limited quantities for centuries. Even the Romans had worn Chinese silk.

After the Crusades, more and more goods from Asia poured into Europe. Over time, so-called luxuries came to seem like necessities. Pepper had once been so exotic that wealthy people ate it for dessert. By the early fifteenth century most Europeans used pepper regularly to flavour meat that had been stored over the long, cold winter months.

By the end of the thirteenth century, Marco Polo had written a book about his seventeen-year stay in China. Europeans were so impressed by what Polo reported that trade with China and Japan became Europe's chief economic goal for several centuries. Some people might say the same thing has happened today, with North America's expanded trade with countries on the **Pacific Rim**.

Asia could be reached, however, only by means of overland trade

Pacific Rim: all the countries bordering the Pacific ocean

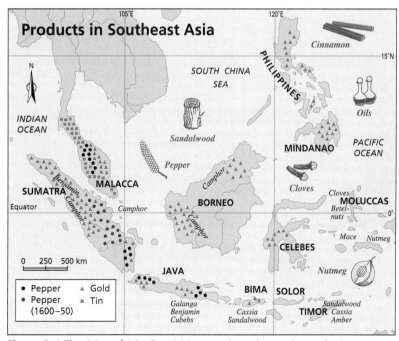

Figure 8–1 The riches of "the East." Many products that we buy today in a supermarket were as rare and valuable as gold in fifteenth-century Europe.

Figure 8–2 In 1453, the Ottoman Turks destroyed the Byzantine army and captured the strategically important city of Constantinople. Thus Islam became the main religion in that area, and Europe was cut off from the overland trade routes to Asia.

routes controlled by rulers such as Chingghis Khan and Tamerlane. Throughout the Middle Ages, Venice and Genoa, two Italian port cities, had become wealthy by carrying Asian goods from Constantinople into the rest of Europe. Others in Europe resented the great profits that these Italian cities made on the spice trade, and they dreamed of finding another way to reach the riches of Asia.

THE DOOR SLAMS SHUT

In 1453, the rich trade with Asia came to a sudden halt when the city of Constantinople fell to a Turkish army, marking the end of the Eastern Roman Empire. For European Christians, the door to eastern Asia slammed shut.

Although the fall of Constantinople was a disaster for Venice and Genoa, people living in Spain, Portugal, France, Holland, and England held a different view. These countries had paid high prices for the luxury goods they bought from the Italian merchant families. If they could find new routes to Asia, the spices of the Orient, the silks and porcelains of China, and even the gold and slaves of Africa would be theirs for the taking. So they began to consider sea routes, an option that offered many rewards—just one ship filled with spice could make a merchant extremely wealthy.

EUROPEANS OPEN THEIR EYES

The old medieval map makers always drew the world as a flat disk with Jerusalem at its centre (see Figure 2–9). The rediscovery of the works of the ancient Greeks and Arabs showed Renaissance people a very different world view. The Greek philosopher Ptolemy had proven with mathematics that the world must be a globe. Ptolemy's conclusions made so much sense that by the late fifteenth century, most scholars believed that the old disk idea was incorrect. They also understood that if the world were round, many things were possible, including reaching Asia by sailing westward.

Had Europeans known the true nature of the world, they might have been less eager to explore it. They were quite ignorant of anything outside Europe. They knew nothing, for instance, of North or South America, which together blocked the way to Asia. Nor did they know anything about the more than 500 nations and

LINK-UP

East and West, Up and Down

For years, North Americans have referred to Asia as the "Far East" simply because that is how Europeans viewed Asia. But people living in Asia have rightly pointed out that they don't consider themselves far from anything! They are home, just as you are home in your own city, province, and country.

In the twentieth century, people have begun to realize that the language used to describe other places sometimes betrays a certain self-centredness, or bias. For example, have you ever caught yourself saying "Up North" when talking about Northern Canada? If the earth is a sphere, where is "the East," really? Or "the West"? Or up or down?

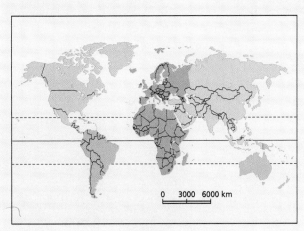
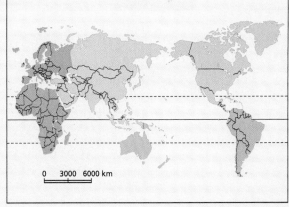

0   3000   6000 km

WHAT DO YOU THINK?

1. In each of these two maps, which countries seem most important? In each, which regions would you call "the East" and "the West."

2. Do you feel more comfortable or familiar with one of the maps? Which one? Explain what might cause this feeling.

3. Use the term "relative" to help you describe the problem of locating places in relation to one another.

junk: a Chinese sailing vessel, sometimes very large. Zheng He had junks that were many times the size of European ships.

pilot: Someone who knows local waters and can guide ships

cultures on these continents. The Europeans thought of Asia as a place of legendary splendour and potential opportunity. They soon confirmed their impressions when they learned about the mighty Ming emperor who ruled China, the richest and most powerful nation on earth.

Before the Europeans arrived and began trading by sea, explorers from China and the Arab lands had already created their own trade routes via the Indian Ocean. Ibn Batutta, a famous explorer from North Africa, had already travelled overland through Africa, Asia, and even into Siberia. Ibn Batutta's journeys lasted for twenty-four years, but even he was following trade routes that had been established by Arab and Indian traders before him. In the fifteenth century, a Chinese admiral named Zheng He led a fleet of enormous ships called **junks** as far as Africa. (See map page 420.) The Chinese abandoned further explorations partly because they felt they had no need of anything outsiders produced.

In every new land they visited, European explorers and merchants would find trade routes, **pilots**, and guides able to help them. By making use of these knowledgeable people and well-established routes on land and sea, the Europeans, with determination, courage, ambition, and luck—often mixed with appalling brutality and treachery!—learned of different lands and other civilizations. Some succeeded in enriching themselves beyond their wildest dreams.

Figure 8–3 After about 1420, Europeans began to learn of peoples all over the world, including the Algonquins in the village of Secota, shown here as a European artist portrayed it just after first-contact with Europeans. What do the orderly farm areas, buildings, and ritual dancers tell you about the artist's impression of these original North Americans?

The Monsoons: A Gift of Predictability

Chinese, Arab, and Indian traders sailed with the monsoons, the seasonal winds of southern Asia. Every summer the monsoons blow from the southwest; in winter they blow from the northeast. These regular winds made trade and travel between mainland Asia and the rich Spice Islands of Southeast Asia predictable. Asian mariners travelled according to the season, with winds that propelled their sailing ships to and from China. European explorers eventually used the monsoon winds to cross the Indian Ocean, from Africa to India and back.

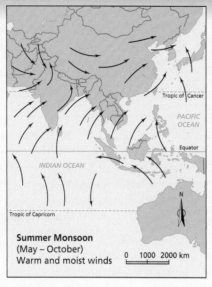

Summer Monsoon
(May – October)
Warm and moist winds

0 1000 2000 km

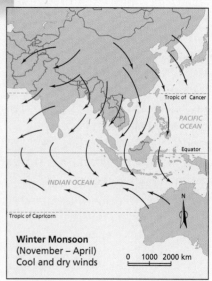

Winter Monsoon
(November – April)
Cool and dry winds

0 1000 2000 km

1. Examine the T-O map on page 60 and a modern map of the world in your atlas. Make a list of six facts about the world that Europeans did not know before the voyages of European explorers.

2. With a partner, or in a small group, prepare a large outline map of the world without showing modern countries. Label the continents and oceans. Lightly shade all the areas of the world about which Europeans knew little or nothing before 1492. Locate and label at least five civilizations in these regions.

3. Describe the accomplishments of Ibn Batutta and Zheng He. What was the Silk Road? (See page 89.) Why weren't Islamic and Asian nations as interested as European nations in sending out explorers?

4. Describe the pattern of European trade with the Middle East and Asia before 1453. What happened in 1453 that changed this pattern? Explain why new trade routes had to be found. Write a paragraph explaining why the Europeans wanted to explore the world.

5. Examine the map on page 246.

   a) Explain how the monsoons helped traders on the Indian Ocean. In which direction would ships sail during the winter monsoon? During the summer monsoon?

   b) On another map, find Malacca. Explain why this port's location made it an important trading city.

6. a) In a small group, compile a list of products that you, as sixteenth-century European merchants, would want the captain of a sailing ship to bring back to you from Asia. Individually, put your order in a letter to the captain. Your letter should also explain why you can no longer get Asian products overland.

   b) In your group, brainstorm a list of products that you, as modern Canadian importers, would like to order for sale in Canada. Compare your list with the one you compiled for part (a). What does the difference tell you about the two societies?

SHIPS AND NAVIGATION

In the fifteenth century, European long-distance voyages and exploration were made possible by technological improvements in two areas. The first of these was in ship design, especially in the development of a new and more **manoeuvrable** ship called the "caravel." The second was in the science of **navigation**, which was improved by the development of more accurate instruments. With the increase in knowledge that these new technologies made possible, European seafarers became masters of the seas.

THE NEW SHIPS

By using **lateen sails** that allowed for greater manoeuvrability, and rounded holds to carry plenty of supplies and cargo, European shipbuilders gradually learned to build useful craft that could withstand the long distances and rough seas that the great explorers would encounter.

The winds of the world flow like rivers of air. In the northern hemisphere, the **prevailing** winds are from the west. Sailing west from Europe to America meant that a ship had to sail partly into the wind, which was slow until the development of the caravel. After a ship sailed south of the Tropic of Cancer, its voyage was made easier by winds from the northeast.

manoeuvrable: easy to handle

navigation: the science of guiding a ship

lateen sails: triangular sail on a short mast

prevailing: strongest, major

DID YOU KNOW?

Columbus's largest ship, the Santa Maria, was a carrack (merchant ship) of 100 tonnes with a crew of 52; the smallest, the Nina, was a caravel of 40 tonnes with a crew of 18. These ships were about the same size as modern fishing trawlers. They could cover about 160 kilometres in a day.

THE DEVELOPMENT OF SHIPPING TECHNOLOGY

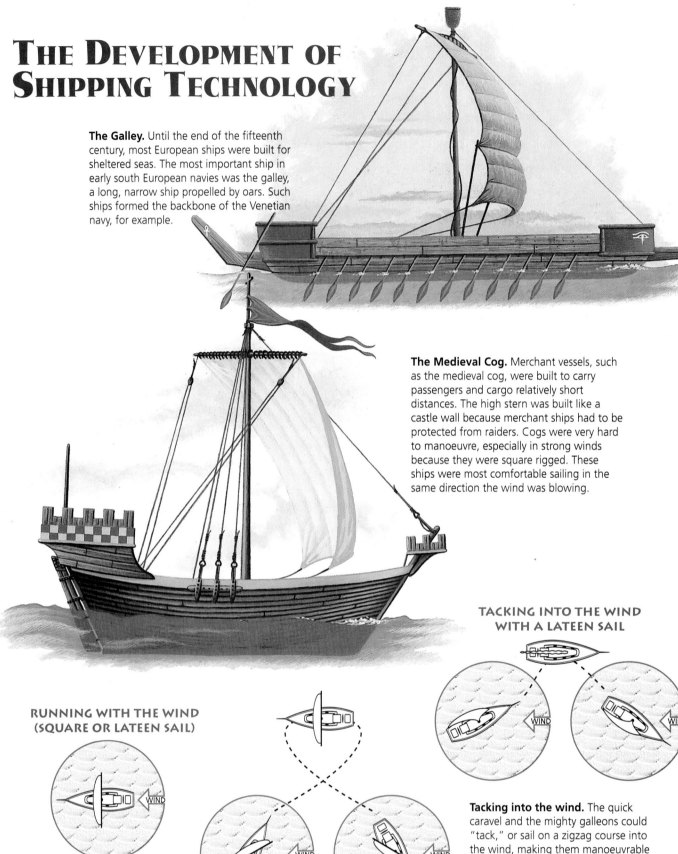

The Galley. Until the end of the fifteenth century, most European ships were built for sheltered seas. The most important ship in early south European navies was the galley, a long, narrow ship propelled by oars. Such ships formed the backbone of the Venetian navy, for example.

The Medieval Cog. Merchant vessels, such as the medieval cog, were built to carry passengers and cargo relatively short distances. The high stern was built like a castle wall because merchant ships had to be protected from raiders. Cogs were very hard to manoeuvre, especially in strong winds because they were square rigged. These ships were most comfortable sailing in the same direction the wind was blowing.

TACKING INTO THE WIND
WITH A LATEEN SAIL

RUNNING WITH THE WIND
(SQUARE OR LATEEN SAIL)

Tacking into the wind. The quick caravel and the mighty galleons could "tack," or sail on a zigzag course into the wind, making them manoeuvrable and safe for long sea voyages. With the lateen sail, sailors did not have to depend so much on having the wind at their back.

CHANGING DIRECTION
WITH A SQUARE SAIL

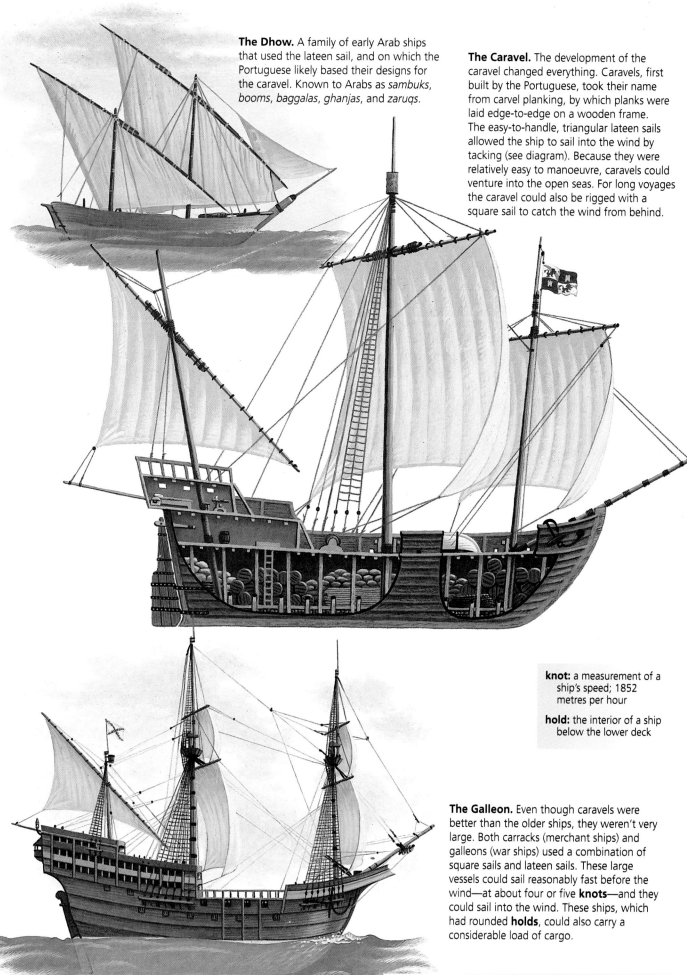

The Dhow. A family of early Arab ships that used the lateen sail, and on which the Portuguese likely based their designs for the caravel. Known to Arabs as *sambuks*, *booms*, *baggalas*, *ghanjas*, and *zaruqs*.

The Caravel. The development of the caravel changed everything. Caravels, first built by the Portuguese, took their name from carvel planking, by which planks were laid edge-to-edge on a wooden frame. The easy-to-handle, triangular lateen sails allowed the ship to sail into the wind by tacking (see diagram). Because they were relatively easy to manoeuvre, caravels could venture into the open seas. For long voyages the caravel could also be rigged with a square sail to catch the wind from behind.

knot: a measurement of a ship's speed; 1852 metres per hour

hold: the interior of a ship below the lower deck

The Galleon. Even though caravels were better than the older ships, they weren't very large. Both carracks (merchant ships) and galleons (war ships) used a combination of square sails and lateen sails. These large vessels could sail reasonably fast before the wind—at about four or five **knots**—and they could sail into the wind. These ships, which had rounded **holds**, could also carry a considerable load of cargo.

NAVIGATION

Fifteenth-century captains liked to "hug the coast," that is, they sailed within sight of land from one familiar landmark to the next. Venturing into the open ocean was far too risky—and frightening. Captains had very few navigational instruments to help them find their way on a long journey by sea. They depended almost entirely on their own knowledge of particular waters, which they acquired through experience and from other captains.

Sea captains did have the compass (what they called the **lodestone**), invented by the Chinese about 1000. Early Europeans rarely used compasses, however, because many superstitious sailors thought that such a mysterious device must be a tool of the devil. Fortunately for navigation, by the fifteenth century Prince Henry of Portugal understood the importance of the compass well enough to make his captains use it openly.

Gradually the superstitions against the compass and other navigational instruments died away and new navigational instruments developed. Soon a sea captain could fix the location of his ship on a map and find the shortest and safest route to his destination. The new tools are illustrated in the diagrams below. Even with these improved instruments, however, the up-and-down motion of a ship could still cause an error of several hundred kilometres.

lodestone: A naturally magnetic stone, also known as magnetite, used as a compass

watch: shift

Figure 8–4 Common navigational instruments during the Age of Exploration. All these devices helped mariners plot their course once they were out of sight of land.

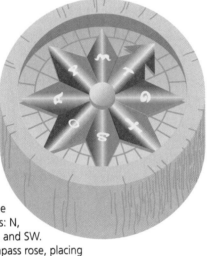

Compass. In early compasses the whole compass rose turned, with the arrow pointing north. The eight symbols stand for the eight main directions: N, E, S, W, NE, NW, SE, and SW. Draw your own compass rose, placing the directions on the appropriate points.

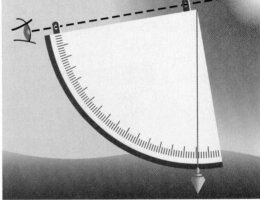

Quadrant. The quadrant and later the astrolabe (which you can see on the back cover of this book) both measured the height of the sun or a star above the horizon. This helped a ship's captain determine how far north or south the ship had sailed.

Log line. This measured the ship's speed. A triangular piece of wood was thrown into the water, and an attached line with evenly spaced knots was drawn out behind the ship. After a set period of time, the line was pulled in and the knots counted. A ship's speed is still measured in knots. A ship travelling at one knot will cover 1852 metres in an hour.

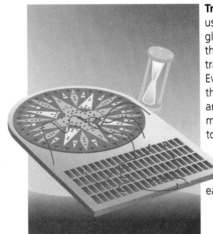

Traverse board. This was used along with an hour glass and a compass to help the ship's helmsman keep track of the ship's course. Every half hour (measured by the glass) a bell would ring and the helmsman would move the pegs in the board to the new location. The helmsman worked a four-hour **watch**. How many "bells" were in each watch?

Usually only the captain had the instruments and knowledge to determine a ship's route, so the sailors had to have unshakable faith in their commander. Living conditions were very bad on board. Food was horrible. Sailors often ate wormy cheese and bread, and drank scummy barrel water. On long voyages, they suffered from **scurvy** caused by a lack of vitamin C. Magellan's crew was reduced to eating ox hides, sawdust, and rats. On long voyages, the chances of survival for the average sailor were no better than fifty-fifty. Most of the European captains of the fifteenth and sixteenth centuries had to deal with **mutinies**; both Francis Drake and Ferdinand Magellan executed mutinous crew members.

scurvy: a potentially fatal lack of vitamin C. Sufferers become weak, their skin gets splotchy, their gums swell and bleed, and their teeth loosen and fall out.

mutiny: an open rebellion of sailors against their officers

ACTIVITIES

1. Identify the characteristics of the caravel that helped make ocean sailing possible. Draw your own sketch of a caravel showing top and side views. Label the sketches.

2. Make a comparison organizer to compare uses, advantages, and disadvantages of the five types of ships featured on pages 248–49.

3. In a group, create an illustrated time line for the history of the ship from the galley to the twentieth century. Make the time line large enough to post on a bulletin board. Place the ships mentioned in this chapter on your time line along with three more recent ships. Some examples:

   ◆ the steamship   ◆ the luxury liner
   ◆ the clipper   ◆ the submarine

   Include one important fact about each ship beside its illustration, along with the approximate dates it was in use.

4. Explain what is meant by the term "navigation." What tools for navigation were used by fifteenth-century captains? Write a two- or three-page instruction manual on navigation for a fifteenth-century mariner explaining the available instruments and the main purpose of each one. Illustrate your manual with sketches.

THE PORTUGUESE

Portugal was a young country in the sixteenth century, but its leaders recognized a great opportunity. The Portuguese were already fishing the Atlantic and maintaining contact with countries in Africa in the late fifteenth century. To gain an advantage in trade, Portuguese monarchs sponsored expeditions that sent caravels down the west coast of Africa, each one travelling farther south. By 1550, before any other European nation, Portugal had established trading posts and colonies in Africa, India, Brazil, and Southeast Asia.

Figure 8–5 Lisbon in the sixteenth century. The city is located on a natural harbour on the Atlantic Ocean. Identify the lateen sail on the caravel leaving the harbour.

PRINCE HENRY THE NAVIGATOR

Portugal's crown prince Henry was so fascinated by ships and navigation that he soon became known as Henry the Navigator. He sponsored voyages of exploration, the gathering of information on new trading routes, and the development of new navigational equipment. He also built an institute at Sagres that was devoted to the study of navigation. Henry himself left court life to live and study at Sagres for forty years.

Prince Henry sent out many expeditions to Africa. He encouraged his captains to sail past the equator, even though crews at the time believed that a ship sailing too far south was doomed to destruction. His ships found new sources of minerals and spices. Unfortunately, Henry's expeditions also had a deplorable outcome: On one voyage, a Portuguese ship met Arab slave traders and brought back a human cargo to resell for a large profit in Portugal. This encounter began a slave trade that would stain the history of Europe and the Americas for hundreds of years to come.

DID YOU KNOW?

The southern route around Africa was a Portuguese state secret. A Portuguese captain who guided any but an authorized Portuguese expedition would have faced execution.

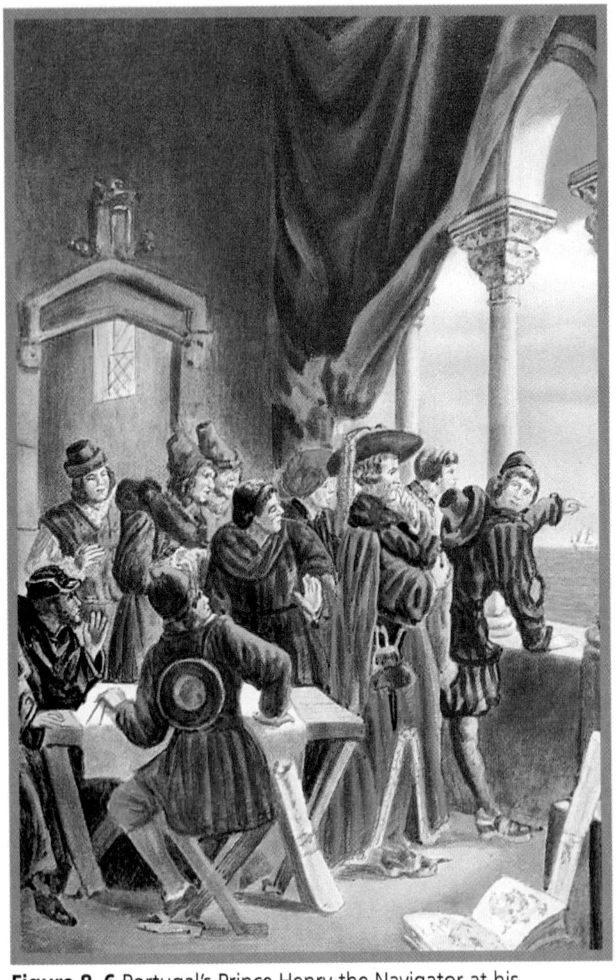

Figure 8–6 Portugal's Prince Henry the Navigator at his navigational school in Sagres. What is going on in the painting?

Bartholomeu Dias

Henry the Navigator died in 1460, but his influence—and Portuguese exploration—continued. Every year, ships travelled farther and farther south along the African coast. One such expedition, commanded by Bartholomeu Dias, set out to find a way around Africa. In 1488 and with two caravels, Dias accomplished what had been considered an impossible feat: he sailed around the Cape of Good Hope.

Although Dias had wanted to travel into the Indian Ocean, his crew was afraid. They rebelled and would not go on. The next Portuguese expedition around Africa did not take place until 1497, five years after Christopher Columbus had landed in the Americas. The expedition to India would be led by a captain who was destined to become as famous for his acts of barbaric cruelty as for his remarkable feats of exploration.

Vasco da Gama

In 1497, King Manuel of Portugal sent Vasco da Gama to find a sea-route around Africa. Da Gama was a tough and ruthless soldier and a brilliant navigator. Unlike Dias, he was capable of overriding the wishes of his crew, a determination that proved necessary for the type of expedition King Manuel planned.

The king gave da Gama four ships. Instead of hugging the African

HOW TO...

Use Latitude and Longitude

Thanks to Ptolemy, a geographer who lived in the second century—and to map makers of the fifteenth century who rediscovered his work—you can determine the location of any place in the world as the meeting of two imaginary lines.

One type of line is latitude. Lines, or parallels, of latitude are rings that encircle the earth and lie parallel to the equator. One such line, the equator, lies on the **circumference** of the earth exactly halfway between the North and South Poles. Latitude measures a location's distance either north or south from the equator.

The other type of line is longitude. Lines, or meridians, of longitude run north-south from pole to pole. One such line, the prime meridian, passes through Greenwich, a suburb of London, England. Longitude measures a location's distance either east or west of the prime meridian.

Latitude and longitude are expressed in degrees. The equator is at zero degrees (0°) latitude. There are 90 degrees of latitude north of the equator and 90 degrees to the south. About 69 miles, or 110 kilometres, separate each degree of latitude.

Longitude is measured in degrees from the Prime Meridian, which lies at zero degrees longitude. There are 180 degrees of longitude east of Greenwich and 180 degrees to the west.

What are the practical purposes of latitude and longitude? For one thing, parallels and meridians form a grid over the map of the world that helps us pinpoint the location of any city or other place. For instance, geographers have identified the coordinates, or position, of Victoria, British Columbia, as latitude 48°N and

longitude 123°W.

Perhaps longitude's most useful purpose is how it allows us to have a common system of time. When it is noon at 0°, it is midnight at 180°, with twenty-four time zones, one for each hour in the day.

Some lines of latitude and longitude serve to fix the boundary line between two countries. What boundary line runs along the forty-ninth parallel north? In the past, latitude and longitude have helped colonizers—people who have just moved into a region—estimate what the weather will be like and what crops they will be able to grow. Can you think of another purpose that latitude and longitude serve today?

circumference: the boundary line of a circle; a line that encircles a sphere

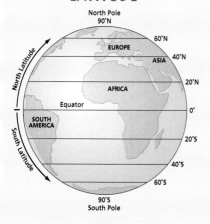

PARALLELS OF LATITUDE

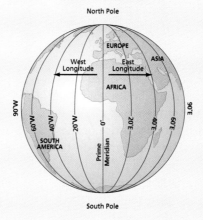

MERIDIANS OF LONGITUDE

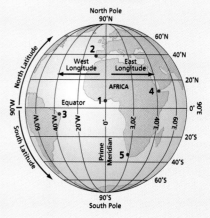

GRID OF LATITUDE AND LONGITUDE

. . . .

NOW YOU DO IT

1. Using an atlas, identify the latitude and longitude of your home town or city.

2. a) Estimate the coordinates of the five locations numbered on the grid, above.

b) Use your atlas to identify the modern-day communities at those locations.

c) Using the gazetteer at the back of your atlas, check to see if your estimate of the locations' coordinates were close.

Figure 8–7 Looking north at the Cape of Good Hope. Imagine what it must have been like to round the southernmost tip of Africa for the first time and see the African coast stretching far to the northeast.

coast on his journey south, da Gama first sailed to the Cape Verde Islands, several hundred kilometres off the west coast of Africa. From there he sailed southeast in a great arc that allowed him to take full advantage of the prevailing winds and swoop around to land near the southern tip of Africa.

Da Gama rounded the Cape of Good Hope after ninety-three days at sea and sailed into the Indian Ocean. Following the guidance of Arab pilots familiar with the sea routes of the Indian Ocean, he then sailed on to India and dropped anchor in the port of Calicut (now Kozhikode). By the time da Gama returned home with a cargo of precious spices in 1499, disease and disaster had claimed more than two-thirds of his crew.

In 1502, Vasco da Gama again sailed for India, this time leading a fleet of heavily armed ships. He and his crew captured other ships they came across, murdering all passengers and crew members, and attacked the city of Calicut. When the ruler of the city tried to arrange for peace, da Gama ordered his men to round up and hang some local fishers. He then sent the bodies in pieces to the ruler, who immediately agreed to da Gama's terms. Da Gama returned to Portugal with ships loaded with treasures, leaving behind five warships to control the Indian Ocean for Portugal.

THE TREATY OF TORDESILLAS

When Christopher Columbus, who sailed for the Spanish, discovered what he thought was a sea route to Asia, Portugal wanted to keep some of the Asian trade for itself. The rulers of Spain and Portugal could not agree on how to share the world, however, so they asked the pope to settle the matter. The pope proposed a secret treaty, such that all lands to the west of an imaginary line running north-south through the Atlantic Ocean would belong to Spain; and everything to the east would go to Portugal. The final line, at 46°W, allowed Portugal to keep its lands in Brazil. Even today, Brazilians speak Portuguese while Spanish is the official language in the rest of South America.

Of course, the rest of the world knew nothing of the Treaty of Tordesillas. We can only imagine the reactions of the Emperor of China, the Great Mughal of India, the Emperor of the Aztecs, and the other rulers and peoples of the world had they heard of this amazing treaty's terms.

European Explorers, 1488–1580

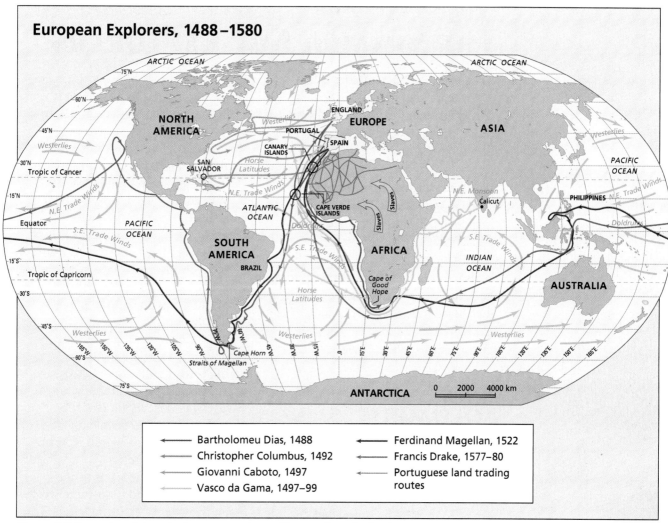

Figure 8–8 The routes of six major European explorers. These explorers had to learn to use the winds and sea currents they encountered on their voyages. Examine the directions of the prevailing winds to see why the explorers took the routes they did.

ACTIVITIES

1. Describe the accomplishments of Prince Henry. This monarch was fascinated with navigation and exploration, yet he never travelled on any voyages. What do you think stopped him? Consider the responsibilities he may have had as well as the personal traits required of an explorer.

2. Examine the routes of Dias and Da Gama, which explorer was most daring—or foolhardy? Explain.

3. Look at the map above. How many kilometres did Dias travel to the tip of Africa and da Gama travel to Calicut, India? How many degrees of latitude did Dias travel through? And da Gama? How many degrees of longitude lie between Lisbon and Calicut?

4. Review the feature on Machiavelli on page 223 of Chapter 7. Note that Machiavelli wrote *The Prince* in the early sixteenth century, at about the same time that da Gama conducted his voyages. What similarities can you see between Machiavelli's advice and da Gama's methods? How do these two reflect the principles of their civilization? Debate the following statement: "Vasco da Gama was a good leader because he was ruthless."

5. Research Portugal and the colonies it once controlled. On an outline map of the world, show Portugal's former colonies in Africa, South America, and Asia.

THE SPANISH SEA EXPLORERS

By 1492, Spanish forces had captured Granada, the last stronghold of the Muslims in Spain. Queen Isabella and King Ferdinand had secured their power and were eager to participate in the rich spice trade with Asia. Fortunately for Spain, a Genoese navigator named Christopher Columbus had a plan to reach Asia by sailing west. Columbus's voyages resulted in the creation of a vast Spanish empire in the Americas and the Pacific Ocean. They also changed Spain from a relatively small and very young country into a world power.

COLUMBUS

Christopher Columbus was born in Genoa, Italy, in 1451. He came from a seafaring family and had wide experience in sailing. According to his own accounts, he had travelled beyond the normal trade routes as far as Iceland.

An avid reader, Columbus had read the stories of Sir John de Mandeville and the tales of Marco Polo. He had studied Ptolemy's *Geography* and became convinced that the world was a globe. Like many knowledgeable people of his day, Columbus accepted an estimate, based on Ptolemy's calculations, that the world was approximately 30 000 kilometres in circumference (about 8500 kilometres too small). Based on this assumption, Columbus reckoned that Southeast Asia was about 8000 kilometres due west of Spain. No one in Europe had any idea that the American continents existed.

Columbus planned to take a ship across the Atlantic and establish a new trade route to Asia. To finance this very expensive voyage, he needed royal support. Although he spent years trying to convince the king of Portugal to sponsor him, the success of Bartholomeu Dias in establishing a route around Africa caused the king to lose interest in Columbus's venture.

Columbus was nothing if not persistent. After being rebuffed by Portugal, he checked to see if Henry VII of England was interested. Finally he turned to Isabella of Castile, the queen of Spain. At first she was reluctant to assist Columbus, but finally decided to give him a chance. In 1492, Isabella and her husband, Ferdinand, gave Columbus permission to undertake the voyage with three ships. The money for the voyage was raised after Isabella offered to pawn her jewels to back the loan. Columbus would receive 10 percent of all profits.

Columbus sailed first to the Canary Islands, and from there west along the twenty-eighth parallel. The voyage took over a month. On several occasions Columbus had to plead with his crew and the captains of the *Nina* and *Pinta* to continue. Finally he promised that if no land was sighted within three days, the expedition would turn back. On the third day, a lookout sighted land: the island of San Salvador.

The inhabitants of San Salvador were astonished to see the strangers. They made them welcome and accepted gifts from the visitors. Columbus did not find the golden treasures he was looking for, however, so he continued his voyage westward. Columbus wrecked the *Santa Maria* on a reef, but he and his crew were rescued by local people. The inhabitants of all the places Columbus visited welcomed the strangers and treated them well. Leaving a

DID YOU KNOW?

Though widely acknowledged as the first European in recorded history to reach the American continents, Columbus never knew it. He always believed he had reached Asia.

settlement behind on Santo Domingo, Columbus returned to Spain in January 1493. He kidnapped twelve San Salvadorans to bring back with him. All twelve died on the voyage.

Columbus made several more trips to the Americas and began the European colonization of these lands. He was, however, unable to produce the gold and treasure he had promised his royal sponsors. Instead, he became a slave trader, sending out expeditions to hunt down and capture the people who had welcomed him so courteously. Many of these people were sent back to Europe as slaves, all of whom died within a few years. As a colonial ruler, Columbus was incompetent and brutal; he ruthlessly executed anyone who opposed him. Finally he was arrested and returned in chains to Spain. He died bitter and poor after his fourth voyage in 1506.

Figure 8–9 Queen Isabella welcomes Christopher Columbus and his Aboriginal captives. Many of the explorers thought of themselves as glorious adventurers. What do you think the captives thought of them? Where does the light fall in this painting? Who is idealized in this painting? What does this tell you about the painter?

HOW TO...

Read an Editorial Cartoon

Editorial cartoons usually appear in newspapers and always present a strong point of view. The cartoonist makes a bold, usually one-sided statement in a visual, humorous way, often by distorting facts or exaggerating physical characteristics. Editorial cartoons are often the subject of angry letters to the editor from people who disagree with the cartoonist.

Ask yourself these questions when reading an editorial cartoon:

1. Who are the people in the cartoon? What are they doing? What are they saying?

2. Is the cartoon about a real incident or issue? If so, identify it.

3. What makes the cartoon funny?

4. Does exaggeration play a role in conveying the message? How?

5. What do you think is the perspective of the cartoonist?

6. Create a cartoon to show your perspective of a topic.

NOW YOU DO IT

Bring to class an editorial cartoon that makes you laugh. Analyze it by asking Questions 1–5. Present the cartoon and your analysis to your class.

The Spaniards in the Caribbean

The following two historical accounts describe the relations between the Spanish explorers and the Aboriginal peoples of the Caribbean. The first is an excerpt from a letter written by Christopher Columbus in which he describes his first voyage to the Caribbean (which he believes are the "West Indies"). In his letter, written in 1493, Columbus takes pains to emphasize that the relations between the Spaniards and the Aboriginal peoples are peaceful and harmonious. Was this true?

> **PRIMARY SOURCE**
>
> Sir:
>
> As I now know that you will have pleasure of the great victory which our Lord has given me in my voyage, I write you this, by which you shall know that, in twenty days I passed over to the Indies with the fleet which the most illustrious King and Queen, our lords, gave me: where I found very many islands peopled with inhabitants beyond number. And, of them all, I have taken possession for their Highnesses. The people of this island, and of all others that I have found and seen or not seen, all go naked. It is true that since becoming more assured, and losing their terror, they are generous with all that they have, to such a degree as no one would believe it but he who had seen it. Of anything they have, if it be asked for, they never say no, but rather do invite the person to accept it, and show such lovingness as though they would give their hearts. They all believe that power and goodness are in the sky, and they believe very firmly that I, with these ships and crew, came from the sky....
>
> At your command,
> The Admiral

The second excerpt was written by a Dominican missionary named Bartolomé de las Casas, who was one of the first Europeans to reveal the atrocities committed against the Aboriginal peoples in the Caribbean and South America. Here de las Casas writes about an incident that took place on the island of Cuba in 1513, just twenty years after Columbus's first voyage.

league: about 5 kilometres

> **PRIMARY SOURCE**
>
> One time the Indians came to meet us and to greet us with food and good cheer and entertainment about ten **leagues** outside of a great city. And coming to the place, they presented us with a great quantity of fish and bread and other food, together with everything else they could think to do for us. But the Devil entered into the Spaniards, and they put them all to the sword in my presence, without any cause whatsoever. More than three thousand souls were laid out before us, men, women, and children. I saw there such great cruelties that no man alive either has or shall see the like.

WHAT DO YOU THINK?

1. Compare these two accounts of the relations between the Spanish and the Aboriginal peoples of the Caribbean. Although these accounts describe different times, what do both confirm?

2. How do they differ? Does Columbus say anything about how the Spanish treated the Aboriginal peoples? Do you think Columbus was telling the whole truth about his dealings with the Aboriginals? Why or why not?

MAGELLAN

Ferdinand Magellan was a Portuguese navigator working for the Spanish monarchs. An experienced sailor, he had travelled with the Portuguese as far as the Philipines by way of the Indian Ocean. The Spanish king, because of the Treaty of Tordesillas, could not use that route, so he ordered Magellan to sail west to find a way around the continent of South America that would give Spain access to the "Spice Islands" in Southeast Asia. These islands, today part of Indonesia, were the only source in the world for the highly valued spice called "cloves."

With five old ships, Magellan sailed down the coast of South America and found a passage between Tierra del Fuego and Patagonia. This passage would later be named the Straits of Magellan. Though pounded by storms, three of his ships cleared the **straits** and sailed northward into the Pacific Ocean. After four months without fresh supplies, Magellan finally anchored in the Philippines, where he was killed while taking part in a local war. His last ship, the *Victoria*, commanded by Juan Sebastian del Caño, returned to Spain loaded with spices. Del Caño and his sailors thus became the first people to **circumnavigate the world**. The two-year voyage had established another sea road for Spain and provided solid proof that the world was round.

strait: a passageway between two land masses

circumnavigate the world: travel around the whole world

Figure 8–10 Ferdinand Magellan falls in a skirmish on an island in the Philippines. He wasn't the only one to die on the voyage. Of the more than 250 Portuguese, French, English, and Greeks that sailed with Magellan, only eighteen made it back to Europe.

Starvation Stalks Magellan's Crew

This diary excerpt by one of Magellan's crew members, Antonio Pigafetta, details some of the hardships suffered by the sailors who made the first complete journey around the world. Why do you think these people were willing to undergo such suffering?

Wednesday, November 28, 1520

We were three months and twenty days without getting any kind of fresh food. We ate biscuit, which was no longer biscuit, but powder of biscuits swarming with worms, for they had eaten the good. It stank strongly of the urine of rats. We drank yellow water that had been putrid for many days. We also ate some ox hides which had become exceedingly hard because of the sun, rain, and wind. We left them in the sea for four or five days, and then placed them for a few moments on top of the embers, and so ate them; and often we ate sawdust from the boards. Rats were sold for one-half ducato [gold coin] apiece, and even then we could not get them. The gums of both the lower and upper teeth of some of our men swelled, so that they could not eat under any circumstances and therefore died.

PRIMARY SOURCE

to chart: to make a map of

itinerary: a scheduled
route plan

VESPUCCI

Amerigo Vespucci was a merchant from Florence who made four voyages across the Atlantic for Spain. Vespucci, according to his accounts, visited the mainland of South America in 1497. He also later sailed down the coast of Brazil and kept a record of his journey. Because Vespucci wrote about and **charted** some of these "new" lands, Dutch and German map makers used his first name when labelling the continents of North and South America. The name stuck.

ACTIVITIES

1. Write a dialogue between Queen Isabella and King Ferdinand about the accomplishments and character of Christopher Columbus.

2. How did Columbus and the other Spanish explorers treat the Aboriginal peoples they encountered? Give evidence to support your view.

3. The 500th anniversary celebrations of Columbus's arrival in the Caribbean in 1492 were held in 1992. In the library or on the Internet, find two documents with different views about this arrival. Summarize and comment on each view.

4. Create a journal from the point of view of a crew member on Magellan's voyage around the world. Your journal should have at least six entries covering the most important events of the voyage.

5. Refer to Figure 8–8. Assume that ships sail about 160 kilometres per day. Plot a course to sail all the way around the world from a port close to your home. How many weeks would you be at sea? Draw your map, indicating where you would need to tack and where you could sail with the wind behind you. Take into account your need to stop for supplies. Finally, write up an **itinerary** for your trip.

THE CONQUISTADORS

Spanish exploits at sea had created new ocean roads and given Spain control of vast new lands. The Spanish conquistadors, or soldiers of fortune, were determined to expand the Spanish Empire into the heart of their "New World," which included North and Central America, and much of South America. These conquistadors —often the younger sons of minor nobles with no fortunes—set their minds to gaining wealth in the new lands.

Their second purpose was to "civilize" peoples that they viewed as primitive. The conquistadors believed they were serving the Church and saving Aboriginal peoples from eternal damnation by destroying the Aboriginal religions and replacing them with Catholicism. As Catholics, the conquistadors felt they had a mission and duty to bring Christianity to the non-Christian peoples of the world.

The Spanish conquistadors were courageous and tough; they were also brutal. Many of them died, as they lived, by the sword. Within a few years of Columbus's voyages, Vasco Núñez de Balboa had crossed the swampy **Isthmus** of Panama and become the first European to see the Pacific Ocean. Coronado led an expedition into the great desert of the

isthmus: a narrow strip of land with water on either side, joining two larger areas of land

American Southwest, and Hernàn de Soto explored the Mississippi. In South America, other Spanish adventurers travelled up the mighty Amazon and Orinoco Rivers, searching for the fabled El Dorado ("the Golden One") and the fabulous treasures they were sure they would find just beyond the next hill or valley.

HERNÀN CORTÉZ

Hernàn Cortéz was a young noble determined to make his fortune in the New World. Hearing of the empires of Mexico, he organized an expedition in 1519. As soon as he reached Mexico, Cortéz burned all his ships to prevent his soldiers from returning home. The soldiers had no choice but to follow him into the Valley of Mexico, which was controlled at that time by the mighty Aztec Empire. Cortéz made an alliance with the nation of Tlascalan, the traditional enemies of the Aztec.

Fierce and warlike, the Aztecs practised human sacrifice on a grand scale, feeding their gods the blood of thousands of victims. A highly developed people, the Aztecs had large cities, larger and more beautiful than any cities the Spanish had ever seen. Even though Cortéz had the help of the Tlascalan and other allies, his plan now seems arrogant. About 25 million people lived in the Valley of Mexico when the Spanish arrived, and the land the Aztecs controlled was extensive. Their capital of Tenochtitlàn (later Mexico City) alone boasted a population of hundreds of thousands. This was the empire Cortéz hoped to humble with a few thousand soldiers.

Cortéz was fortunate. He stepped into Aztec history at a time when the empire was ruled by the very superstitious ruler Montezuma.

Cortéz's appearance and time of arrival coincided with the expected reappearance of the white-skinned god Quetzacoatl and the end of a cycle of Aztec history. To the disgust of many Aztecs, Montezuma welcomed Cortéz to his capital city of Tenochtitlàn with lavish gifts. He was promptly taken prisoner by the Spaniards.

Montezuma gave a great golden treasure to his captors to buy his freedom, but was then stoned to death by his own people, who regarded him as a traitor. After Montezuma's death, the Spanish conquistadors and their Aboriginal allies fought several bloody battles before they finally defeated the Aztecs. They were greatly assisted in this by **smallpox**, a fatal disease that the Spanish unintentionally introduced to Mexico and against which the Aboriginal peoples had no immunity. Within a year of Cortéz's landing, 3.5 million Aztecs had died of the disease. From Mexico, the Spanish expanded their control to the south and destroyed the Maya. The Spanish then began to demolish the religion and culture of the conquered peoples step by step, even burning their holy books.

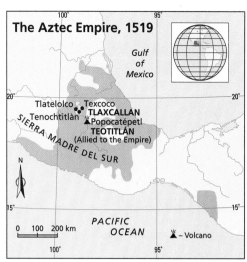

Figure 8–11 The Aztec Empire at about the time of the Spanish arrival

smallpox: a fatal disease, highly contagious among Aboriginal people at the time of first contact with Europeans. Symptoms include fever and blisterlike eruptions on the skin that leave pocklike scars.

immunity: natural resistance

Figure 8–12 Montezuma meets Hernàn Cortéz and his Aboriginal wife, Malinche. Malinche could speak the Mayan and Aztec languages, and quickly learned Spanish. She advised and interpreted for Cortéz during his campaigns in Mexico.

Using A Chronicle as a Primary Source

CATALOGUE CARD

What is it? Part of a historical **chronicle** called The Conquest of New Spain

Who wrote it? Bernal Diaz, a conquistador who travelled with the explorer Hernàn Cortéz

When? After the Spanish invasion of the Aztec Empire, around 1520

Why? Diaz wanted to describe everything that happened during the expedition. In this excerpt, he describes an encounter between Cortéz and the Aztec leader, Montezuma.

> Our captain [Cortéz] said to Montezuma, "Lord Montezuma, I cannot imagine how a prince as great and wise as your majesty can have failed to realize that these idols of yours are not gods but evil things, the proper names of which are devils. But so that I may prove this to you, and make it clear to all your priests, grant me one favour. Allow us to erect a cross here on top of this tower, and let us divide off a place where we can put an image of Our Lady. Then you will see how grievously they have deceived you."
>
> Montezuma, however, replied in some temper (and the two priests beside him showed real anger); "Lord Malinche, if I had known you were going to utter these insults I should not have shown you my gods. We hold them to be very good. They give us health and rain and crops and weather, and all the victories we desire. So we are bound to worship them, and sacrifice to them, and I beg you to say nothing more against them."
>
> On hearing this and seeing Montezuma's fury, our Captain said no more on the subject but observed cheerfully, "It is time for your majesty and ourselves to depart."

Shortly after this meeting, the Spanish took Montezuma hostage.

A chronicle is a continual account of historical events. This written account is like a diary but is much less personal—the writer's purpose is to record valuable information about a historical period.

Historians value chronicles such as the one written by Diaz because they provide **eyewitness** accounts of important events. Sometimes, though, chronicles and other first-hand accounts are not completely accurate. Writers may alter the truth to make themselves look better or to flatter the people they are writing about. For example, Diaz presents Cortéz as polite and "cheerful." An Aztec observer may have seen things differently. Even the best chroniclers can only present their own interpretations of events, often leaving out the other side of the story. Chronicles usually reflect the writer's culture and beliefs.

Unintentional distortion of the truth is called "bias." For example, if you were to write an article about your best friend for the school newspaper, you might fail to note his or her faults. Historians usually try to approach chronicles with a critical eye and do not accept everything the writer says as literal truth. But bias does not destroy a document's usefulness. Recognizing bias gives us more information about the writer.

Ask yourself the following questions when using a historical chronicle as a primary resource:

1. What event is the author describing?

2. Who is involved?

3. Did the author have first-hand knowledge of the event? Do you think it matters?

4. Do you think the author has a bias? Explain.

5. What information might the author have left out? Explain.

6. Do you think this is a reliable primary source? Why or why not?

NOW YOU DO IT

1. With a partner, go to an event such as a concert or baseball game, listen to a report on radio or television, or attend a meeting such as a student council meeting. Independently, each of you can write a one-page description of what you observed. Then compare the two versions. What are the differences? How can you account for these differences?

THE EFFECTS OF THE CONQUEST

On Aboriginal Peoples

The effect of the Spanish conquest on Aboriginal culture was enormous. The Spanish killed or enslaved most of the Aboriginal peoples they met. In the process of promoting Christianity, the Church actively destroyed Aboriginal faiths. The Spanish justified their assault on whole empires by pointing out Aboriginal customs such as human sacrifice. The conquerors' response, however, included the slaughter of thousands.

The conquerors destroyed written records wherever they were found. Both the Maya and the Aztec used a form of **hieroglyphics** and had rich written histories. Archeologists are still painstakingly trying to reconstruct these histories. The Spanish also razed ceremonial buildings to the ground and built churches and cathedrals on the foundations. Many Aboriginal traditions survived, however, sometimes mixed with Christianity.

The conquerors were cruel taskmasters. Everywhere, Aboriginal people laboured under the whip, working in dangerous conditions in mines and on plantations. Any attempt at rebellion was cruelly put down. Many Aboriginal people committed suicide rather than endure the horrible conditions in the Spanish gold and silver mines. Eventually, the Aboriginal populations in the Caribbean dwindled to such a point that the Spanish began importing African slaves to work on their plantations.

The Aboriginal population of the Valley of Mexico is estimated to have dropped from 25 million to just over 5 million in eighty years. One hundred and twenty years later, the population

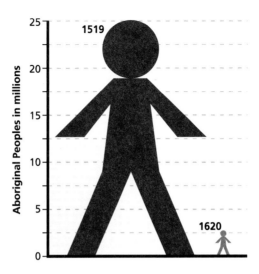

Figure 8–13 How would you describe Mexico's population decline from 1519 to 1620?

was down to 1 million. War, slavery, famine, and, most particularly, disease all contributed to this **decimation**.

On Europeans

The conquest of Central and South America affected Europe quite differently. It gave Spain the riches of Peru, including silver from the fabulous mines of the Silver Mountain at Potosi, and the gold and silver of Mexico. For a time these riches made Spain a great power, but they also had some bad effects on the country. Because all the riches went to the nobles, this class was able to keep its power. The middle class that formed was weak. In the long run, this imbalance hurt Spain's economy. Also, the riches of America increased prices across Europe, almost ruining several European economies.

chronicle: a continuous account of historical events

eyewitness: first-hand

hieroglyphics: writing in which pictures represent words

decimation: literally, one in ten, but usually refers to the destruction of many

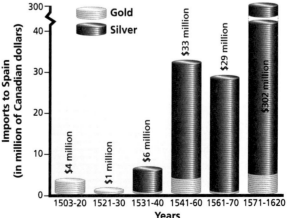

Figure 8–14 This bar graph shows the great increase in gold and silver imports to Spain during the Age of Exploration. At first the shipments were stolen gold treasure. When this ran out, the Spanish maintained their income by forcing Aboriginals to slave in silver mines.

Complaining About the "Price Revolution"

Jean Bodin, a French economist, wrote in 1568 that the vast treasures of gold and silver from America were having a devastating effect on the economies of many European countries because prices were going up everywhere. Further, because Spain failed to develop its own industries, its economy grew completely dependent on the gold and silver it mined in its colonies. Why would this be bad for Spain's economy in the long run?

I find the high prices we see today are due to some four or five causes. The principal and almost the only one is ... the abundance of gold and silver which causes the depreciation of these and the dearness of the things priced.... When the Spaniard made himself master of the new world, hatchets and knives were sold for much more than pearls and precious stones; for there were only knives of wood and stone, and many pearls.

PRIMARY SOURCE

ACTIVITIES

1. How did the Spanish conquistadors make their country both rich and powerful?

2. How was Cortéz able to defeat the Aztec? Read the primary source document on page 262. What two things motivated Cortéz? Are the writings of Bernal Diaz enough to give us a complete picture of Aztec civilization? Explain why or why not.

3. Using this chapter as well as resources from your school library, write a report comparing the civilization of the Inca with that of the Aztec.

4. From the perspective of the Incas or Aztec, what was the effect of the Spanish conquests?

5. What was the economic effect of so much gold and silver from the Americas on the economies of Europe? Write a letter to the ruler of Spain from the ruler of France complaining about the effect the gold and silver is having on the economy of France and suggesting ways of improving the situation.

THE BRITISH, DUTCH, AND FRENCH

Although the Spanish and Portuguese had an early lead in deep-sea navigation and travel, the northern Europeans quickly followed. In 1497, Henry VII of England gave John Cabot and his three sons **letters patent** to sail to the west and north in search of new territories. The Cabots, who were from Venice, travelled to what is now eastern Canada, probably near either Cape Breton or Labrador and recorded what they saw there. Later, England sent William Baffin, John Davis, and Martin Frobisher to the northern waters of Canada to search for the Northwest Passage to Asia. In 1583, Humphrey Gilbert tried and failed to set up an English colony in Newfoundland.

letters patent: an official document giving a person authority to do something

Letters Patent

Henry VII of England authorizes John Cabot to seek out new colonies for England. By what right did Henry authorize Cabot to take lands from the First Nations?

Be it known that we have given and granted to our well-beloved John Cabot, citizen of Venice, full and free authority, leave, and power to sail to all parts, countries, and seas of the East, of the West, and of the North, and to seek out, discover, and find whatever isles, countries, regions, or provinces of the heathen and infidels whatsoever they may be, and in what part of the world soever they be, which before this time have been unknown to Christians...

   And the aforesaid John may subdue, occupy, and possess all such towns, cities, castles and isles of them found as our vassals and lieutenants, getting unto us the rule, title, and jurisdiction of the same villages, towns, castles, and firm land so found.... In witness whereof we have caused to be made these our letters patents.

PRIMARY SOURCE

Figure 8–15 John Cabot says good-bye to King Henry VII just before his voyage to North America. Who are the people in the painting? What emotions are visible on their faces? To see a duplicate of Cabot's ship, the *Mathew*, see page 288.

DRAKE AND THE SEA DOGS

The conquest of the Aztec and Inca Empires by the Spanish in the early sixteenth century resulted in great wealth for Spain. As we have seen, mines in Peru and other places in the Spanish Empire shipped thousands of tonnes of gold and silver and countless glittering emeralds across the Atlantic and the Pacific to Spain, making it by far the richest country in Europe. Elizabethan seafarers looked with envy on the Spanish treasure ships and made plans to capture them.

   Fortunately for the English, their shipyards were making vessels that could travel long distances quickly and outfight any opponents. Fast, low in the water, relatively small, and highly manoeuvrable, the new ships were little more than floating gun platforms that could turn on a dime. This made them ideal for attacks on the lumbering Spanish treasure ships. Soon English captains were raiding ships on the **Spanish Main** regularly. These illegal acts were secretly supported by the English queen, Elizabeth I, who saw them as a way to take a cut of the Spanish profits.

   These English pirates, nicknamed the Sea Dogs, included Captains John Hawkins, Martin Frobisher, and Francis Drake. Some of these seafarers

Spanish Main: coastal waters of northern South America where Spanish merchant ships regularly travelled

Figure 8–16 This Dutch engraving shows the *Golden Hind* (right), under the command of Francis Drake, capturing a Spanish treasure ship on its way from Peru to Panama. What difference, if any, can you see between Drake's actions and those of a pirate?

became famous explorers. Some became slave traders. John Hawkins was one of the first to engage in the trade in human beings between Africa and North America.

After 1567, the Sea Dogs regularly captured Spanish ships and raided towns both in Spain and in the New World. In one especially bold raid, Drake attacked and burned a number of ships in the harbour of Cadiz, Spain. On another raid, he sailed his ship, the *Golden Hind*, through the Straits of Magellan and into the Pacific Ocean. After seizing several galleons and sacking unsuspecting towns along the western coast of South America, Drake sailed to California (and perhaps to British Columbia) before heading across the Pacific. In 1580, after three years at sea, he and his crew arrived back in England, the first English sailors to circumnavigate the globe. Queen Elizabeth knighted Drake on the deck of the *Golden Hind* and took a large part of the loot into her treasury.

THE FRENCH AND THE DUTCH

Beginning in 1534, Jacques Cartier made three voyages across the Atlantic to Canada and sailed up the Saint Lawrence River, claiming the land for France.

Dutch merchants also hoped to establish colonies and take part in the trade. The first Dutch ships to complete a circumnavigation of the globe, led by Olivier van Noort, left Holland in 1598. For a small country, Holland quickly became powerful. The Dutch East India Company, founded in 1602, took over the rich spice trade with Southeast Asia. It established a colony in Indonesia that lasted until after the Second World War.

ACTIVITIES

1. On a large, poster-sized map of the world, mark the equator, the Tropics of Cancer and Capricorn, and the Arctic and Antarctic Circles. Show and label the explorations of the English, Dutch, and French in the sixteenth century.

2. Read the Letters Patent to Cabot on page 265. Make a point-form summary of the details of this agreement. What does this document show about the world-view of the Europeans of the fifteenth century?

3. The photograph on the opening page of this chapter shows a reconstruction of Francis Drake's *Golden Hind*. The English ships were smaller and more manoeuvrable than the enormous Spanish galleons. How could this be an advantage in battle?

What other advantages did the English and French have in their attacks?

4. Examine the map on page 267 and look again at the early T-O map (Figure 2–9) on page 60. Create an organizer to compare the two maps. With a partner, brainstorm the categories to include on the organizer. Some suggestions:

   ◆ date the map was drawn
   ◆ general accuracy (rank from 0 = completely inaccurate to 5 = completely accurate)
   ◆ what is placed at the centre
   ◆ land masses shown
   ◆ bodies of water shown

New World, Old World, One World

To Europeans, the continents previously unknown to them—particularly North and South America—became commonly known as the "New World." The lands and countries they had known for centuries became known as the "Old World." Even today some people use these terms.

The impact of contact among the peoples of the world was great. As we have seen, many Aboriginal peoples suffered greatly under European rule. Many died through war, disease, or slavery; others lost their land, culture, and independence. Some Aboriginal nations were completely wiped out.

Europeans benefited through colonialism, some making their fortunes by bringing products from the Americas to Europe, such as gold, fur, spices, and food products. These new foods, spices,

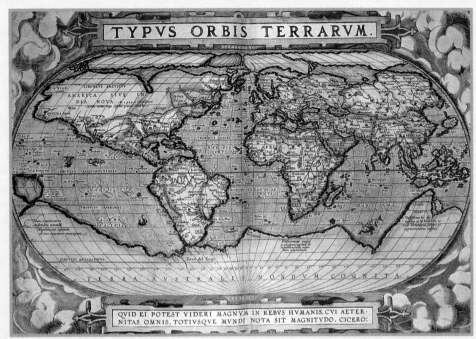

Figure 8–17 Despite some inaccuracies, this map, first printed in 1570, shows that Europeans had gained a much better idea of what the world looked like.

and herbs meant that menus could be expanded to include a variety of dishes. Europeans soon began to depend on foods developed by the Aboriginal peoples of the Americas, including corn (maize), potatoes, pumpkins, sweet potatoes, squash, chilies, and cacao (chocolate), among others. Many of these plants had been carefully developed over centuries from wild plants. The first corn, for example, had begun as a tiny wild plant. Countries such as Ireland soon came to depend on the potato as a basic food. When a disease destroyed most of the Irish potato crop in the 1840s, millions of Irish died or were forced to emigrate. Many came to Canada. The European adventurers also brought to Europe other plants, such as tobacco and medicinal herbs, which have since spread to other societies, including Canada.

WHAT DO YOU THINK?

1. How do you think the Aboriginal peoples felt about their lands being called the "New World"? Explain.

2. In what ways have you benefited or suffered from the exchange of ideas and products that resulted from the Age of Exploration?

3. Do you think the Age of Exploration made the world "one world"? Explain.

SUMMARY

The Age of European Exploration was one of the most significant developments in the history of the world. The European explorers changed the history of countless peoples forever, not always for the better. In places, they succeeded in completely wiping out local cultures and languages, even whole civilizations. They destroyed temples, palaces, fortresses, towns, and villages, or they recreated them in new and different forms. They took the wealth of the nations they colonized to fill their own treasuries and fuel their tremendous economic growth and prosperity. They also expanded the trade in Africans.

The Europeans who set out on the wide ocean to find riches and fame had a religious motive as well. Many sincerely believed in "saving the souls" of the peoples they encountered on their voyages. Cortéz, for example, overturned the blood-soaked images of the war god in Tenochtitlàn and tried to convert Montezuma to Christianity. Often, though, religion was used as an excuse for killing people to get their treasures.

Through their voyages, the Europeans introduced their beliefs, customs, and cultures around the world. We can still see this happening today through the influence of Western media and technology. Europeans also learned from the peoples they met, however, and spread their newfound knowledge and products throughout the world.

It cannot be denied that the conquistadors and other European explorers were courageous. They endured hardships and dangers that seem astounding today. By circumnavigating the world and travelling all over the globe, and by making peoples all over the world aware of one another, these adventurers made the world larger, but also, somehow, smaller. The European explorers can indeed be said to have changed the face of the world forever.

SUMMARY ACTIVITIES

1. Write a modern letters patent for the crew of a starship journeying to a distant galaxy.

2. In a small group, create a poster-sized map of the world in 1500. Indicate the civilizations that existed at that time. Show the major European exploration routes. Indicate products that were taken and shipped to Europe.

3. Look at the various paintings of explorers in this chapter. European explorers saw themselves, as well-dressed, well-mannered conquerors of the "New World" who would bring all the benefits of civilization to the Aboriginal peoples. Choose one picture and explain how it might differ if the scene had been painted by an Aboriginal artist.

4. The Age of Exploration was a time of bold and courageous action as well as brutality. Summarize what you admire about the European explorers, what you deplore about them. Analyze how they affected the future character of the modern nations in the Americas.

ON YOUR OWN

1. Research a civilization that flourished before contact with Europeans. Find out as much as you can about its early religion, technologies, art, and mythology. Then find out the effect of contact with Europeans. Prepare a five-part report.

2. Find and compare ancient maps from India, China, Arabia, and Europe.

3. The Age of Exploration saw the results of unchecked greed, prejudice, and intolerance. In your own words, explain how one of these characteristics affected history during this period. Then explain how this characteristic affects life in your community, country, and world today.

9 EMERGENCE OF THE NATION-STATE

CHAPTER OUTCOMES

In this chapter you will see how the Reformation led to the emergence of the European nation-state. You will also examine one of the most powerful nation-states: England. By the end of the chapter, you will

- explain what factors led to the Reformation
- describe the roles of the key players in the Reformation
- analyze the social and political effects of the Reformation
- identify reasons for the emergence of the nation-state in Europe
- explain how England became a powerful nation-state
- analyze the impact of enclosure on labour and settlement patterns
- show major events on a map

Occurrence at Fotheringhay Castle

In the following fictional story, Zack tags along with his English cousin, Phoebe, on a trip to Cambridge University. Zack ends up assisting Phoebe in her research of Mary, Queen of Scots, the ill-fated monarch who inspired steadfast loyalty in some and hatred in others. Zack learns how this queen lost her throne in two nations, thirsted for the throne of another, and finally died by the executioner's sword.

Zack tossed his Walkman and backpack into the back seat of the **Mini** and ducked into the passenger seat. His cousin Phoebe examined her forehead in the car mirror. Satisfied that no new blemishes had popped up during the night, she started the car, inched out of the narrow parking spot in front of the house, and then sped into the busy city streets. Before long they were headed down the highway.

Zack was still sleepy from the effects of jet lag after the trip from Prince George. After two days here, he still had a hard time believing he was in England. The whole thing seemed a little unreal. It turns out his grandmother had been

Zack and his English cousin, Phoebe, head out for a day's adventure.

squirrelling away money for years so she could send him to England. "It's important for everyone to get in touch with their roots," she had said. "Don't worry, I'll look after Jake for the few weeks you'll be gone. I need the exercise." So Zack's little pug dog was with Nana, and here he was staying with Aunt Marie, Uncle Bill, and Phoebe in busy Kettering, a small city just north of London.

"So what exactly are we doing today, Phoebe?" Zack asked, checking his seat belt. He was still a little nervous in English traffic, with everyone driving, as he saw it, on the wrong side of the road.

"Well, as I said, I've got a project to do on the Tudors—you know, Henry VIII, Good Queen Bess, Bloody Mary—that lot. It's a make-or-break kind of thing, since it makes up most of my term mark."

Phoebe glanced into her rearview mirror and then changed lanes. "We have to demonstrate how well we can use our research skills and that we can pull a whole lot of information together to answer some original questions. Cambridge has one of the best libraries in the world and it's just an hour from home. I've decided to do my research on Mary Stuart, Queen of Scots, and her years in prison. She had her head chopped at a castle not too far from here, as a matter of fact." Phoebe gave Zack a quick look to gauge his reaction.

He laughed and turned to face her. "You're kidding me, right?"

"No, I'm serious, dearie. Lots of famous things happened around here. You have heard of the Queen of Scots over there in Canada, haven't you?"

Zack began turning the radio dial, looking for a good station. "Sure I've heard of Bloody Mary," he said absently. "What about her?"

"Not Bloody Mary, cuz, Mary, Queen of Scots. They're two completely different people. My Mary had her head chopped off by her cousin, Queen Elizabeth."

Zack turned to Phoebe, hesitating. "Her cousin?"

"That's right."

Zack didn't blink.

Phoebe parked the car in a lot near Cambridge University. They found a Beani Burger and had their lunch. Zack was ravenous. As they ate, Phoebe explained her project.

"Mary was held prisoner in several castles, including Fotheringhay Castle, not too far from where I live. It seemed odd that Mary would be kept in prison way up here rather than in the Bloody Tower in London. So that was my first question: Why keep Mary so far from London—or Scotland, for that matter?"

Zack—his mouth full of Beani Burger—nodded as Phoebe continued.

"So I started to read a little and found out that Mary was kept prisoner for twenty years. This didn't make sense to me either, so my second question was 'Why the delay?' In the end, I had a list of half a dozen questions. Here," Phoebe said, pushing over a piece of paper. "Look them over."

Zack peered at the list as he went to work on Phoebe's

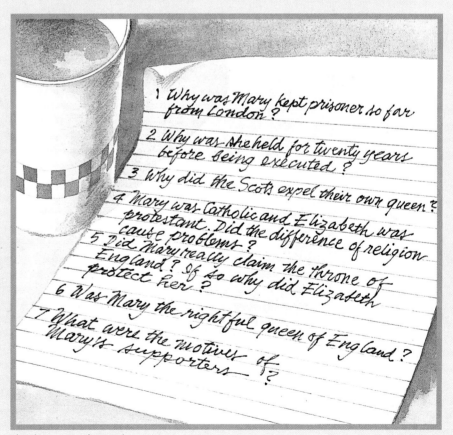

Phoebe's research questions

1 Why was Mary kept prisoner so far from London?

2 Why was she held for twenty years before being executed?

3 Why did the Scots expel their own queen?

4 Mary was Catholic and Elizabeth was protestant. Did the difference of religion cause problems?

5 Did Mary really claim the throne of England? If so why did Elizabeth protect her?

6 Was Mary the rightful queen of England?

7 What were the motives of Mary's supporters?

untouched fries. "So why come all the way to Cambridge? Isn't she mentioned in an encyclopedia?"

Phoebe stared at her cousin for a few moments before continuing. "I started with encyclopedias. Then I checked out some books at the local library. A few questions posted to a newsgroup on the Internet got some useful replies. But my questions aren't answered yet."

"Well," said Zack, stifling a burp. "When do we go to the castle?"

"Later. First we go to the university. Cambridge has letters and other original documents. Fabulous, huh?"

"Uh. Yeah, sure, Phoeb."

Phoebe convinced Zack to help her sort through the documents. They spent three hours poring over the material before the library closed. It turned out that Zack had a pretty good knack for making out scrawled, sixteenth-century handwriting. Afterwards, Phoebe thanked him for his help by treating him to fish and chips from a local shop. As they sat by the River Cam watching the rowers practise, Zack couldn't help boasting.

"You know, Canada has the best rowers around," Zack bragged, "especially in B.C."

"B.C.?"

"Yeah,… British Columbia." Phoebe looked puzzled. "You know," Zack continued, "the

province on the west coast— where I live!"

"Oh, right, in Canada."

Zack sighed and changed the subject. "So, Phoeb. I'm not sure how you're going to use some of those quotations you've got."

"What do you mean?"

"Well, some of them contradict each other. Remember those two quotes from Mary and Elizabeth about whether or not Mary had been treated fairly? Mary thought she'd been pretty badly treated, seeing as she'd been arrested by Elizabeth. Elizabeth, on the other hand, seems to think she's treated her cousin just fine, thank you very much."

"You're right. But remember, Elizabeth didn't

Zack and Phoebe take a break on the bank of the River Cam.

Conflicting Opinions

I am myself a Queen, the daughter of a King, a stranger, and the true **kinswoman** of the Queen of England. I came to England on my cousin's promise of assistance against my enemies and rebel subjects and was at once imprisoned.
—*Mary at her trial, October 1586*

You have planned in **diverse** ways and manners to take my life and to ruin my kingdom.... I never proceeded so harshly against you; on the contrary, I have maintained you and preserved your life with the same care which I use for myself.
—*Elizabeth in a letter to Mary, October 1586*

have much choice but to arrest her cousin. For one thing, Mary had fled Scotland, her own country, because she was accused of plotting the murder of her husband. Elizabeth couldn't just welcome her with open arms without checking up if she was a murderer. Second, Mary had always claimed that she was the true queen of England, not just of Scotland, because Elizabeth's father, Henry VIII (who was also Mary's great uncle), had once said that Elizabeth wasn't really his child. You and I found proof that Mary made this claim because we saw that picture of her dinnerware **impressed** with the **arms** of England, which only the true monarch of England has the right to use."

"You know," said Zack, "for a queen, I think that was a pretty stupid move—I mean, cheesing off her own cousin by claiming her kingdom wasn't such a hot idea."

"I suppose she made some wrong moves," mused Phoebe. "But she was no slouch. She gave speeches in Latin when she was just a kid. Did you?

And what a life. She was married to the king of France, you know, but he died when they were both pretty young. Then she went to Scotland where she was queen in her own right, being the only surviving child of James V. Mary was a Catholic, though, and Scotland was in the middle of the Reformation, so there was all kinds of trouble. The story is that Elizabeth set her up to marry a no-account nobleman named Henry, Lord Darnley. He only made matters worse. He murdered Mary's best friend, David Rizzio, almost in front of her eyes. Then Mary took up with Lord Bothwell. Lord Darnley was murdered, blown to pieces by a bomb, probably on Bothwell's orders. Mary married Bothwell, right away, which was stupid. Everyone thought she was involved in the plot to murder her own husband so she could marry Bothwell. I wonder if I can get to the bottom of that mystery."

"I still can't get over it, though," said Zack. "Why would Elizabeth cut off her

own cousin's head? You remember the description of Elizabeth's reaction to news of Mary's execution, don't you? She cried buckets!"

"Well," replied Phoebe somewhat wryly, "you know they never even met."

"Never met? Even though Elizabeth kept her in England so long?"

"Quite. Partly to keep her distance I think. She didn't want to be associated with the scandal. Even so, now I think she also wanted to protect Mary. Remember that letter Elizabeth wrote in response to Parliament's demands for Mary's head? What a diplomat. Seems to me she did a pretty good job putting off the execution."

"They sure wrote a lot of

Elizabeth's Response to Parliaments' Request for a Death **Warrant**

If I should say unto you that I mean not to grant your **petition**, by my faith I should say unto you more than perhaps I mean. And if I should say unto you I mean to grant your petition, I should then tell you more than is fit for you to know. And thus I must deliver you an answer answerless.

letters in those days," said Zack as he stuffed the last piece of fish in his mouth.

"I'll say. Let's see. We saw Mary's letters complaining about the conditions, others protesting her innocence, and others pleading with Elizabeth," said Phoebe, recalling the letters they'd looked at that afternoon.

"The best was the letter she wrote to the king of Spain, asking him to invade England to free her. Can you believe it?"

Phoebe sighed, squinting at the stream of light reflecting off the surface of the river. "Seeing that letter, I guess I finally gave up wishing that Mary was, well, wronged."

"Come on—she wasn't so evil," said Zack. "She probably never wanted to kill her cousin, just get her throne. That's what she swore to just before her execution, anyway. Besides, even if she did, it sounds like everyone was pretty brutal in those days, according to those letters I read, anyway. I think she had guts."

> ### Mary's Declaration Before her Execution
>
> As for the death of the Queen your sovereign [Elizabeth], I call God to witness that I never imagined it, never sought it, nor ever consented to it.
>
> PRIMARY SOURCE

"It was letters that got Mary in the end," said Phoebe. "Spies seized letters revealing that she and others were planning a rebellion to free Mary and make her queen of England. With the letters as evidence, Mary was done for."

. . . .

It was getting late when Zack and Phoebe finally pulled into the gravel parking lot of Fotheringhay Castle. In the gathering dusk, they left the parking lot and walked down the path in the direction of the ruins of the great hall, passing low, grass-covered mounds that had once been the walls of a mighty castle. As the light disappeared, a heavy dew began to fall. The air was cold after the warmth of the day. Shadows deepened around trees and bushes. Phoebe finished her story.

"Mary died very bravely, apparently. She had a little dog. People around here say it hid in

Contemplating the fate of a queen at Fotheringhay Castle

her skirts after her death and wouldn't leave her."

"No way!" Zack swallowed hard, trying not to think of his own dog. Jake would have stayed with him, too, Zack was sure. "This dog. She must have been good to it."

"I suppose. And come to think of it, remember those letters she wrote? She was always rewarding loyal servants and looking out for them—that shows she couldn't have been all bad."

The two cousins peered into the gloom. It was hard to imagine what the castle might have looked like; it was all broken down and covered with moss and grass. Phoebe seemed to be in a world of her own as they wandered through the grounds. "Not much of a castle anymore, Phoebe," Zack called after her. But she had disappeared around a pile of rubble.

Zack stamped his feet in the sudden quiet, gazing up at the night sky. Had this queen really deserved to die? he mused. After all, she'd already been in prison for twenty years.

Zack peered at the ruins through the gloom, wondering if Mary's little dog had found a good home. Out of the corner of his eye he saw a quick movement. He turned, heart suddenly racing. Could it be...?

"Well, bird-brain. Shall we go?" Zack let out his breath. It was Phoebe.

"Yikes, don't jump out like that."

"Scared ya, huh," laughed Phoebe. "Oh, I don't blame you. I've been here lots of times, Zack, and it always makes me feel rather sad. It was once such an exciting place; things happened here. And now..." She turned towards the castle and smiled wistfully.

"Maybe, you shouldn't visit castle ruins at twilight, Phoeb," said Zack. "It's just ... dark."

Phoebe looked down the long, grassy lawn in front of them.

"You're right, Zack, but I've got a good imagination. If I concentrate, I can almost see Mary walking and talking with her ladies-in-waiting. She was a famous beauty, you know, and very accomplished."

"Were they on their way to a banquet?"

Catching the hint, Phoebe smiled. "Are you ever not hungry, cuz? C'mon, let's go. No time like the present!"

Mini: a small British car popular with students

kinswoman: a female relation

diverse: various

to impress: to stamp

arms: heraldic coat of arms

warrant: a written order giving legal authority

petition: request

ACTIVITIES

1. In point form, list the events of the life of Mary, Queen of Scots, according to this story.

2. a) Sometimes it's hard to figure out what happened hundreds of years ago. What research strategies did Phoebe and Zack use to accomplish this?

   b) List the conclusions Zack and Phoebe came to and what piece of evidence they used in each case.

3. Examine the four primary sources given on pages 273–74. Decide what these documents tell you about
   - Mary
   - Elizabeth

   - the education of Tudor monarchs
   - Elizabeth's diplomatic skills

4. Describe Zack's reaction when Phoebe mentioned Mary's little dog. How did the dog make a historical figure seem more like a real person?

5. a) Why do you think Zack's grandmother felt so strongly about sending Zack on a trip to England? What do you think Zack will get out of the trip?

   b) Would you like to go on a trip like Zack's some day? Prepare a brief oral presentation to explain to others in your class where you would go and what you would like to find out about. You may get some useful help from an older member of your family.

1485	KING HENRY VII CROWNED
1492	COLUMBUS SAILS TO AMERICA
1497	JOHN CABOT SAILS TO AMERICA
1508 −12	MICHELANGELO PAINTS THE SISTINE CHAPEL
1509	HENRY VIII COMES TO THE THRONE
1511	ERASMUS WRITES "IN PRAISE OF FOLLY"
1517	MARTIN LUTHER PUBLISHES HIS NINETY-FIVE THESES
1534	ENGLAND BECOMES PROTESTANT UNDER HENRY VIII
1545	THE COUNCIL OF TRENT BEGINS
1553	MARY I COMES TO THE THRONE
1555	THE PEACE OF AUGSBURG
1558	ELIZABETH I COMES TO THE THRONE
1603	QUEEN ELIZABETH I DIES
1616	DEATH OF WILLIAM SHAKESPEARE

If thou wilt be perfect, go and sell that thou hast, and give to the poor, and thou shalt have treasure in heaven.

—MATTHEW 19:21

Before the Protestant Reformation, the Church maintained its great wealth through the taxes it forced people to pay. Many people of the time felt that the Church was ignoring Jesus's message that a spiritually perfect life could be gained only by those who gave their money away and not by those who craved money.

INTRODUCTION

At the beginning of the sixteenth century, the Catholic Church was one of the largest organizations in the world. Almost everyone in western Europe was Catholic. Because every village of any size had a church, there were tens of thousands of churches in Europe as well as many great cathedrals, monasteries, schools, and universities. All these belonged to the Catholic Church.

Because the Church was very rich and because it taxed everyone—even the poor—to increase its wealth, Christians started to criticize this ancient institution. Important Church teachers and priests, many of whom were influenced by the

Humanist theories that developed during the Renaissance, had serious doubts about the Catholic Church and its teachings. In the sixteenth century, these doubts would grow so strong that they destroyed the unity of the Catholic Church and split the Christian population into two groups: Catholic and Protestant. The political power of the Church was greatly diminished.

At the same time, the political power of the barons was disappearing. With the support of the growing middle class, which had mushroomed with the increase of trade, the kings and emperors gradually gained power at the expense of individual barons. This power, along with a lessening of

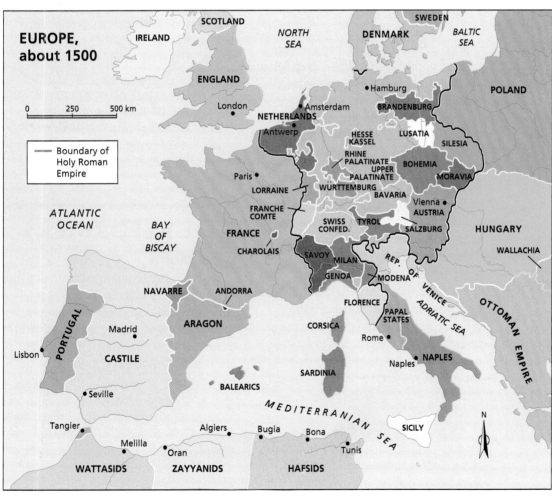

Figure 9–1 This map of Europe shows the states of Europe around 1500. What modern countries can you identify? What modern European countries are missing? Note that the Muslim Ottoman Empire controlled most of southeastern Europe.

the power of the Catholic Church, meant that individual leaders became supreme within their nations.

The modern world is divided into a few hundred nation-states, which we call countries. Each country has its own government, flag, anthem, and traditions. The idea of the nation-state was new in sixteenth-century Europe. For most of the thousands of years of human history, if people had had any idea of their nation, it was very vague. Most Europeans had identified partly with their immediate ruler—the lord of their manor—or with a united, Catholic Europe. Once the Reformation began, all this would change.

THE PROTESTANT REFORMATION

THE NEED FOR CHANGE

The Church had numerous ways of raising money. It could tax people directly, sell Church jobs and positions to the highest bidder, and charge for the services it offered. Church leaders had little interest in the ability of people to pay. They continued to collect taxes even when people were suffering during hard times, even when the Church's demands were driving people into poverty.

Church leaders seemed to be part of the problem. Bishops and cardinals paid great sums for their titles, and then they used the money they received from taxes and fees to build themselves fine palaces and collect works of art. In the sixteenth century, people could buy a position in the Church, and collect the salary that went with it, even if they did not actually perform the religious services that went with the position. This practice, called **simony,** created much resentment. Some officials practised **nepotism;** that is, they gave jobs to their relatives even when these family members were unqualified or undeserving.

Besides spending their time increasing their wealth and political power, some Renaissance popes led scandalous private lives. Members of the clergy, which included the pope, were not supposed to marry. This did not keep a number of popes from having children and then appointing them to powerful positions in the Church. Pope Alexander VI, a member of the Borgia family, was guilty of this practice. He was also famous for the wild parties he threw in the papal palace. Catholics were **scandalized**.

Many parish priests were poorly educated and knew little about the Bible. Although some priests worked hard to provide comfort and spiritual guidance to their parishioners, others drank and did no work. More and more people became disillusioned with the Catholic Church and angry about the way it was run.

THE REFORMERS

Most Christians, even those dissatisfied with the operations of the Church, had no desire to see the Church break up. These reformers hoped that people of good will could reform, or fix, the Catholic Church and that a universal Christian community would last forever.

Reformers who avoided criticizing the fundamental teachings of the Church were left in peace. People who did openly criticize the Church's teachings were considered sinful and were labelled as heretics.

DID YOU KNOW?

"Catholic" means universal.

simony: the buying and selling of church positions

nepotism: giving jobs to undeserving relatives

to scandalize: to offend by doing something thought to be wrong

Selling Indulgences

To raise money, many Catholic monks and priests sold **indulgences**, which were rather like insurance policies for the soul. The Catholic Church taught that, after death, the soul had to stay in **purgatory** until it was purified of all the sins the person had committed during his or her lifetime. Only then would the soul be allowed to go to heaven. To shorten the time spent in purgatory, people were advised to purchase indulgences. The more indulgences one bought, the more of one's sins would be forgiven and the quicker one's soul would go to heaven. The selling of indulgences angered many Catholics who hated the idea that God's justice could be bought and sold for money. Below, Johann Tetzel, a monk, explains how to sell indulgences.

Figure 9–2 In this wood-block print, the pope is shown hurriedly writing out indulgences for which ordinary people pay out their hard-earned coins. What is the artist saying about the pope?

> Tell your priests that for every **mortal sin** a man commits he must, after making good confession, suffer seven years in purgatory, unless he has done seven years' penance. Bid them think how many mortal sins a day are committed, how many each week, each month, each year. All but infinite, then, are the pains they must suffer in the flames of purgatory. This indulgence will mean for them full **remission** of all punishment due to them up to the time they gain the indulgence.
>
> —*Johann Tetzel*

They could be arrested and seriously punished. As we saw earlier in this book, reformers Hus and Savonarola both paid for their activities with their lives. To avoid this fate, those who wanted to fix the Church had to be very careful.

Erasmus

Desiderius Erasmus was born in the Netherlands in 1466. As a young man, he tried to live as a monk but found he was not suited to life in a monastery. Instead, after being ordained a priest, he went to the University of Paris, where, like other Humanists, he studied the Greek and Latin classics. Erasmus soon became famous for his learning and travelled to England where he met King Henry VIII. Often short of money, Erasmus wrote humorous books and taught school to

Figure 9–3 Erasmus of Rotterdam, a famous Humanist, recommended trying to fix the Church from within.

indulgence: a cancellation of punishment for sins

purgatory: the place in which a person's soul was thought to suffer until all sins were punished

mortal sin: the worst kind of sin, e.g., murder

remission: cancellation

dogma: official teachings

add to his income. In his books, Erasmus was very critical of the Church, attacking priests, bishops, cardinals, and even the pope. Some of Erasmus's writings seemed so outrageous that Charles V, emperor of the Holy Roman Empire, made reading them a capital offence. Erasmus, however, was not attacking the fundamental teachings of the Church and so was never considered a heretic.

St. Peter vs. Julius II

Erasmus, the most famous writer of his day, wrote this scathing **satire** about the very **corrupt** Pope Julius II. He presented the satire as a skit in which Julius tries to get past Saint Peter at the gate of Heaven. The pope boasts that he improved the Church by making it richer. How does St. Peter respond? What point was Erasmus trying to make through this dialogue?

satire: a story, poem, or play that criticizes something or someone by using irony

corrupt: dishonest, depraved

Pontifex Maximus: head of the college of priests in Rome

invincible: unconquerable

diligent: putting careful effort

prince: a monarch, not necessarily male—Queen Elizabeth was called a prince

heathen: without religion

Julius: I am Julius ... P.M....

Peter: P.M. What is that? Pestis maxima [big pest]?

Julius: **Pontifex Maximus**, you rascal ...

Peter: You must show your merits first.... Have you been **diligent** in your prayers?

Julius: The **invincible** Julius ought not to answer a beggarly fisherman. However,... I have done more for the Church and Christ than any pope before me.

Peter: What did you do?

Julius: I raised the revenue. I invented new offices and sold them ... I recoined the currency and made a great sum that way ... I set all the **princes** of Europe by their ears. I tore up treaties, and kept great armies in the field.

Peter: The Church had nothing of this when it was founded by Christ....

Julius: You're thinking of the old affair when you starved as pope, with a handful of poor, hunted bishops about you. Time has changed all that.... Look now at our gorgeous churches ... bishops like kings ... cardinals gloriously attired ... Beyond all, myself, Supreme Pontiff, borne on soldiers' shoulders in a golden chair, and waving my hand majestically to adoring crowds.... Look at all this, and tell me, is it not magnificent?...

Peter: Insolent wretch! Fraud, usury, and cunning made you pope.... I brought the heathen Rome to acknowledge Christ; you have made it **heathen** again.

PRIMARY SOURCE

ACTIVITIES

1. What made the Church such an important institution in Europe in the early sixteenth century?

2. Identify three criticisms people had of the Church. What was the difference between criticizing a Church leader and criticizing Church teachings? Which was more seriously punished? Why?

3. **a)** After reading Erasmus's skit, describe the character of Pope Julius II, as portrayed by Erasmus. Did the Renaissance popes seem very religious? Give evidence to support your view.

   b) Working with two or three other students, write a job description for the pope.

THE PROTESTANTS

Unfortunately, many of the Church's problems could not be solved as easily as Erasmus wished. Ordinary people all across Europe reacted bitterly to the continued corruption in the Church, and the high Church taxes they had to pay every year. Rulers began to resent Rome's political power. Many people decided to seek **salvation** within the framework of a whole new Christian church.

Martin Luther

If we wanted to point to a single day and say, "This is the day when the Reformation began," then we might choose October 31, 1517. On this day, a monk named Martin Luther drew up a list of arguments against Church practices and nailed them to the door of the church in the German city of Wittenberg. At the time, this was a common way of inviting debate on an issue. The list, which became known as Luther's *Ninety-Five Theses*, was copied, printed, and then distributed throughout Germany, where it was welcomed by the many people who were dissatisfied with the current state of the Church.

Luther's Beliefs

One day, Luther had been reading St. Paul's Letter to the Romans (part of the New Testament) when he came upon a passage in which Paul said that if a person had faith, then that in itself was enough to be saved, that is, go to heaven. If Paul said this, Luther reasoned, then people were saved by believing in God and because God was merciful, not because they obeyed

Figure 9–4 Does this painting indicate that Martin Luther was the kind of person to spark a religious revolution? Why or why not?

salvation: rescue from the consequences of sin

Angry Questions

When Luther visited Rome, the headquarters of the Church, he was shocked by the corruption and dishonesty he saw. He remarked on one occasion that "the nearer one gets to Rome, the farther one gets from God." In the excerpt at right, from one of the *Ninety-Five Theses*, Luther questions the actions of the pope.

Why does not the pope, whose riches are at this day more ample than those of the wealthiest of the wealthy, build the one Basilica of St. Peter's with his own money, rather than with that of poor believers?

Figure 9–5 St. Peter's Basilica became a symbol of the Church's extravagance because it was built with money gained by selling indulgences. An inside view of this building can be seen on page 276. Using the word "extravagance," think of a statement that a sixteenth-century European might make on first seeing this building.

priests and gave money to the pope.

Luther did not believe that people could choose to save themselves, however. Instead, he thought that God had known, from the beginning of time, all the souls that would be saved. This idea is called **predestination**.

Catholic priests did not marry. This was another idea that Luther attacked. Although he was a priest, he and a former nun got married. They had six children of their own and adopted eleven more.

Luther held conservative, medieval views about many things including heaven and hell, the devil, angels, and witches. He thought society had a duty to burn witches at the stake.

The Catholic Church Responds

Luther's views about the afterlife were not heretical, but his attack on the necessity of the clergy was, as was his view on predestination. Pope Leo X, Lorenzo de Medici's son, published a **bull** disapproving of many of Luther's teachings and threatening the monk with excommunication, or

removal from the Church. Luther responded by burning a copy of the bull at a public assembly in Wittenberg, Germany. The pope then officially excommunicated Luther and put him on trial in the city of Worms. Luther escaped execution only by the skin of his teeth.

TECHNOLOGY, LITERACY, AND THE SPREAD OF THE REFORMATION

Because Luther believed that the Bible, rather than the Church, should be a Christian's true spiritual guide, he wanted to make the Bible available in the **vernacular**, a language in everyday use. He began by translating the Bible from Latin into German. Translations into other languages soon followed.

Figure 9–6 Luther burned a copy of the Pope's bull with his own hands in front of a large crowd at Wittenberg. In Canada today, do ideas about religion stir up this kind of excitement? Why or why not? What topics might inspire Canadians to protest in such a manner?

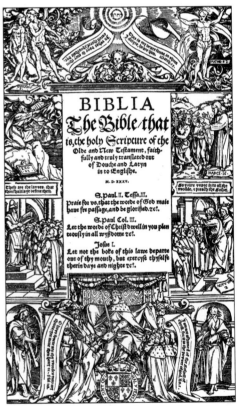

Figure 9–7 The title page, from the first printed English Bible, published in 1535

The newly invented printing press produced multiple copies of vernacular Bibles very quickly and cheaply.

At the same time, respect for education had been increasing because of the influence of Humanism. With the new religious ideas, reading became necessary for salvation. For the first time, literacy—the ability to read and write—became a goal for rich and poor alike.

The combination of increased literacy and the availability of bibles made all the difference to the Protestants. Their ideas spread across Europe like wildfire.

Luther's religious revolution, called the "Reformation," affected many groups in different ways. Unlike Catholics, Protestants had no official dogma, and no established traditions. Religious beliefs changed rapidly as groups of people interpreted and reinterpreted the Bible in their own ways. The Lutheran Church was strong in Germany; elsewhere in northern Europe other churches were popular, and many of them were based on ideas that were very different from those held by Luther and his followers. It soon became obvious that Protestants had as many differences of opinion among themselves as they did with the Catholic Church.

Figure 9–8 This painting by Rembrandt shows a Dutch Protestant couple studying the Bible at home. What statement do you think the artist is trying to make? How would art like this help spread the Reformation?

Calvin's Blue Laws

John Calvin, a French lawyer, set up a Christian state in the city of Geneva in Switzerland. (A state ruled by religious authorities is called a **theocracy**.) Calvin's government was very strict. People in Geneva, Switzerland, had to get used to Calvin's "blue laws," which outlawed all sorts of amusements, from dancing to card playing. Because of Calvinism's emphasis on seriousness and hard work, this new religion appealed especially to people in business. Calvinism spread to many parts of Europe, but was especially strong in Switzerland, the Netherlands, Scotland, and parts of France, where Calvin's followers were known as Huguenots. Here are four of Calvin's Blue Laws for Inns.

theocracy: a system of government in which God's laws are considered the laws of the state

dissoluteness: wickedness

- ◆ The host shall be obliged to keep in a public place a French Bible, in which any one who wishes may read.
- ◆ [The host] shall not allow any **dissoluteness** like dancing, dice, or cards.
- ◆ [The host] shall not allow indecent songs.
- ◆ Nobody shall be allowed to sit up after nine o'clock at night except informers.

Show Major Events on Maps

Visualizing where and when things happen sometimes helps us follow the course of history. For example, Figure 1–6 on page 18 illustrates how Christianity spread gradually northeastward through Europe during the Middle Ages.

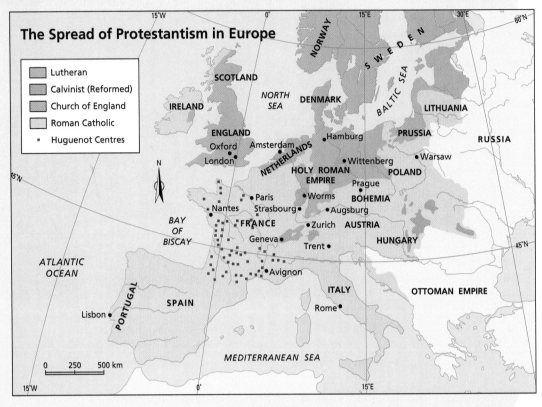

The Spread of Protestantism in Europe

Legend:
- Lutheran
- Calvinist (Reformed)
- Church of England
- Roman Catholic
- Huguenot Centres

NOW YOU DO IT

The map above, The Spread of Protestantism in Europe, shows the areas in which people broke away from the Roman Catholic Church to embrace Protestantism. You can improve this map to show the major events of the Reformation.

1. Begin by acquiring a black-and-white copy of this map from your teacher. Shade the areas for each Christian group in a different colour.

2. Add the labels for the following events at the cities indicated:

   ◆ At Oxford: Wycliffe calls for reforms, 1300s

   ◆ At Amsterdam: Erasmus born, 1466

   ◆ At Rome: Pope Alexander VI elected, 1492

   ◆ At Wittenberg: Tetzel sells indulgences, 1517

   ◆ At Wittenberg: Luther posts *Ninety-Five Theses*, 1517

   ◆ At Worms: Luther's trial, 1521

   ◆ At London: England declared Protestant, 1534

   ◆ At Geneva: Calvin sets up Protestant Theocracy, 1541

   ◆ At Trent: Council of Trent, 1545–63

   ◆ At Augsburg: Peace of Augsburg, 1555

   ◆ At Paris: Saint Bartholomew's Day Massacre, 1572

   ◆ At Nantes: Edict of Nantes, 1598

3. Add arrows to indicate the route of Calvinism:

   ◆ Geneva to Paris

   ◆ Geneva towards central France

   ◆ Geneva to Avignon

   ◆ Geneva to Scotland

   ◆ Scotland to England

4. Comment on the patterns you discovered while making your map.

Protectors of Protestants

At the beginning of the Reformation, Protestants depended on the protection of powerful rulers, without whom they would have been arrested by the Church. A few of these protectors were educated women deeply interested in spirituality. One such woman was Marguerite of Navarre, the sister of the king of France. Marguerite spoke or read six languages and was one of the best poets in Europe.

Marguerite was attracted to the ideas of the Protestants, probably because she was a **freethinker** herself in matters of religion. She criticized the Roman Catholic Church and even suggested that God may not have inspired the Bible. Because she bravely protected Protestants, important writers, such as Rabelais, dedicated their work to her. A Protestant French historian's remembrance of Marguerite appears below.

freethinker: a person who forms a religious opinion without consulting organized religion

pyre: pile of wood, on which one would be executed by burning or strangulation

Figure 9–9 The first Protestants would not have survived had not powerful people such as Marguerite of Navarre offered their protection. How would this protection have encouraged the spread of Protestantism?

Let us always remember this tender queen of France, in whose arms our people [Protestants], fleeing from prison or the **pyre**, found safety, honour, and friendship. Our gratitude to you, lovable mother of our Renaissance! Your hearth was that of our saints, your heart was the nest of our freedom.

PRIMARY SOURCE

ACTIVITIES

1. **a)** Draw an eight-frame comic strip to describe important events in the life of Martin Luther.

   b) Who was Martin Luther? What did he protest against? How did he protest? What was the result? Were his views heretical? Explain.

2. Compare sixteenth-century Catholic and Protestant beliefs on three religious matters.

3. Calvinist and Lutheran churches tended to be very plain. The walls had no pictures or statues. How does this simplicity compare with St. Peter's, shown on page 276?

4. Describe Geneva as governed by Calvin. Why do you think many people embraced Calvin's rules of conduct? Why would some reject them?

5. According to the Protestant work ethic, which affects Canadian society even today, one gains virtue by working hard. Why would business people agree with this idea?

6. Two centuries before the Reformation, John Wycliffe had also attempted to make the Bible available to ordinary people. Wycliffe's ideas spread slowly, however, and were easy to stamp out. Identify five factors that explain the huge success of the sixteenth-century Reformation.

DID YOU KNOW?

Jesuit priests accompanied the early French explorers to Canada and set up **missions** *among the First Nations. Several Jesuits were put to death by the Iroquois Confederacy. A reconstruction of their mission stands at Saint-Marie-Among-the-Hurons in Ontario.*

mission: headquarters for Jesuit efforts to convert others to Catholicism

to commission: to hire for a specific purpose

baroque: an elaborate artistic style typical of 1550–1750

THE CATHOLIC COUNTER-REFORMATION

The Catholic Church did not accept the Protestant Reformation without a fight. The Church struck back with reform, propaganda, and—most frightening—the Inquisition.

Reform

In response to the Reformation, the Church called the Council of Trent, which met from 1545 to 1563, to fix the Catholic Church and get rid of the corruption. Those who attended did not believe it would be easy to end the Reformation. In the end, the council confirmed the Church's approval of everything the Protestants had objected to, including indulgences. The council also restated that only the Church—not the individual—could properly understand the Bible. This was completely opposite to Protestant ideas. The council did end much corruption, however, particularly in monasteries.

Propaganda

Ignatius Loyola, a Spanish soldier, had a religious reawakening while recovering from battle wounds. To stem Protestantism, he organized the Society of Jesus—the Jesuits—to protect the Church and spread the Catholic message. The Jesuits reconverted many people in Poland, Germany, Hungary, and what is now the Czech Republic.

As part of its attempt to stem Protestantism, the Catholic Church banned books that might lead Catholics to question dogma. Works by Luther and Galileo were both forbidden. The Church also **commissioned** artists and set strict rules for artists to follow. The **baroque** art that resulted emphasized the glory and good deeds of the Church and its saints.

The Inquisition

For several hundred years, the Church had used the Inquisition to stop heresy; this organization was now given more power to question, torture, and kill the "enemies" of the Church. The Spanish Inquisition, in particular, was most enthusiastic in pursuing heretics. This court had absolute powers and could arrest and imprison anyone on the slightest suspicion. Officers of the Inquisition regularly tortured people to get confessions. The court always confiscated the property of heretics, so Inquisition officers had good financial reasons for finding a person guilty.

Art For a Purpose

The Council of Trent directed Catholic artists to create paintings that would inspire people "to adore and love God and to cultivate piety." Look at Caravaggio's *The Calling of St. Matthew*, on page 269. How would you describe the figures' poses? The painting shows Jesus approaching Matthew, the tax collector. As Jesus reaches out his hand towards Matthew, a beam of light shines upon the small group. What could the light represent? Does the painting make you curious about what is about to happen? Do you think Caravaggio's painting would have succeeded in inspiring religious feelings in Catholics? Explain.

Figure 9–10 The Inquisition could sentence someone to a variety of punishments, of which the most horrible was to be burned alive in an elaborate ceremony called the *auto-da-fé*. Describe the costume of the condemned prisoners in this sketch of an auto-da-fé in Seville, Spain.

WARRING FAITHS

Once the Reformation started, Catholics and Protestants were soon at war with each other. The Reformation was not an age of tolerance—quite the contrary. States fought wars over differences of opinion, and people committed horrible **atrocities** in the name of God.

Only the Peace of Augsburg of 1555 provided temporary peace in the German States. The warring parties agreed to let the ruler of each German state set the state religion. Protestants had won a great victory with the peace treaty. The Catholic Church in the Northern States was forced to accept that Protestantism was a fact and that history could not be reversed.

The Saint Bartholomew's Day Massacre

In the sixteenth century, many French business families became Calvinists, even though France was officially Catholic and Protestantism was against the law. The Calvinists, called Huguenots, were hard-working, industrious people who helped make the French economy strong.

Nevertheless, they had many enemies, including the French queen, Catherine de Medici.

On the occasion of a royal wedding on Saint Bartholomew's Day in 1572, Catherine urged the murder of all the Protestant guests. Within hours, Protestants were being hunted down and killed in towns and cities throughout France. The resulting religious war lasted until 1598, when Henry IV issued the Edict of Nantes. This royal announcement allowed Protestants to practise their own religion in France.

atrocity: an extremely wicked deed

Figure 9–11 During the Saint Bartholomew's Day Massacre, the streets of Paris were said to have "run red with blood." Do you think people sometimes use a difference of religion as an excuse for violence? Explain.

ACTIVITIES

1. **a)** How did the Catholic Church show that it recognized the need for change and was willing to take action?

   b) Outline the three ways the Catholic Church responded to the Protestant Reformation. Which method was honourable, in your opinion? Which was effective? Explain.

2. **a)** What part did Ignatius Loyola and the Jesuits play in the Church's efforts to rebuild itself?

   b) Many peoples in the world are Christian now as a result of the Jesuits' efforts. How do you think the Catholic Church views this feat?

3. What happened to a heretic found guilty by the Spanish Inquisition? What made the Inquisition so powerful?

4. Why was the Peace of Augsburg a victory for Protestants? How could this treaty strengthen the nation-state?

5. **a)** What was the Saint Bartholomew's Day Massacre?

   b) In small groups identify and research conflict that has arisen as a result of religious differences in recent history. Use the Internet as an information source, but beware of bias.

progressive: puts new ideas into practice

cottage industry: a business in which hired workers produce goods in their own homes

victor: conqueror

merchant adventurer: an independent merchant who bands with others to finance business ventures

to sponsor: to pay expenses in return for part of the profits

jousting: knightly combat, usually two people try to knock each other off horses with lances

THE ENGLISH REFORMATION AND THE TUDORS

The Reformation in England was a squabble over political power as much as a struggle about religion and corruption in the Church. Henry VIII was largely responsible, but his father, Henry VII, unknowingly laid the groundwork by strengthening the English nation-state.

During the fifteenth century, England had experienced a long series of civil wars, called the Wars of the Roses, that caused great hardship and suffering. These wars finally ended in 1485, at the Battle of Bosworth Field. The **victor**, young Henry Tudor, came to the throne as Henry VII. Because Henry's claim to the throne was relatively weak, he built support wherever he could, particularly with the merchants of the new middle class. This would be the key to the success of his monarchy, and the strengthening of the English nation-state.

Figure 9–12 In 1997, modern ocean adventurers duplicated Cabot's voyage to North America in the *Mathew*. Henry VII encouraged **merchant adventurers** to **sponsor** voyages such as Cabot's. How would this system benefit Henry? And England? See Cabot's letters patent on page 265.

HENRY VII AND THE BUSINESS OF MONARCHY

Young Henry VII was determined to restore law and order to his new country. His first task was to destroy the power of the feudal barons. He accomplished this by supporting the middle class, by forbidding the barons' private armies, and by using the Court of Star Chamber to persecute individual barons in secret. The barons' power was quashed.

Henry also began to modernize the economy. The medieval guilds were controlling prices, restricting manufacturing to small groups, and deciding who could buy and sell. Henry took away the guilds' power and instead supported **cottage industries**, by which merchants paid people to make products in their homes. The king helped English woollen merchants by undermining the Italian and Hanseatic leagues.

Henry VII was a modern ruler in the sense that he ran the country rather like a business, with the help of trained civil servants. By the time he died, England was a prosperous, peaceful country, and one of the most **progressive** in Europe.

HENRY VIII

Henry VIII was the second son of Henry VII. As a young king, Henry seemed the ideal Renaissance

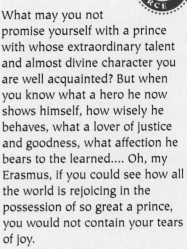

Praise for a Young King

What may you not promise yourself with a prince with whose extraordinary talent and almost divine character you are well acquainted? But when you know what a hero he now shows himself, how wisely he behaves, what a lover of justice and goodness, what affection he bears to the learned.... Oh, my Erasmus, if you could see how all the world is rejoicing in the possession of so great a prince, you would not contain your tears of joy.

—*William Blount, Baron Mountjoy, in a letter to Erasmus*

monarch. He was handsome with golden red hair and a good build, and he impressed everyone he met with his vitality, intelligence, and sense of humour. He loved learning and read a great deal, inviting famous teachers such as Thomas More and Erasmus to talk with him.

In practical matters, Henry made himself an expert in government affairs, shipbuilding, war, and engineering. Thomas More said that Henry was the most knowledgeable ruler in English history. Later, Henry would prove that he also possessed all the negative qualities of a Renaissance ruler as described by Machiavelli—especially the quality of absolute ruthlessness.

The Divorce Controversy

For political reasons, Henry married Catherine of Aragon, the widow of his older brother Arthur, who had died of a fever. Although this was an **arranged marriage**, and Catherine was several years older, the two seemed to become very fond of each other. Unfortunately, the marriage produced only one child, a daughter named Mary. Because there had never been a reigning queen of England, Henry felt he needed a son to succeed him as ruler. At the same time, he fell in love with young Anne Boleyn, one of his wife's ladies-in-waiting. When Anne insisted the king marry her before she would return his affections, Henry sought a divorce from Catherine.

Unfortunately, a divorce was almost impossible to obtain at this time for anyone, even a ruler. The most one could hope for was to have the Church end a marriage on technical grounds. In Henry's case, he claimed the marriage should end because Catherine had been his sister-in-law. The pope turned him down.

Henry was not a person to take no for an answer. Further, he had his eye on the Church's extensive lands in England. Henry called a meeting of

Figure 9–13 Henry VII, the first of the Tudor monarchs, stands behind his more famous son, Henry VIII. Judging from this picture, how would you compare the two men's characters?

the English Parliament and took the first steps to separate the English Church from the Catholic Church. This process took several years, but by 1533, the head of the new English Church had finalized Henry's divorce from Catherine, and the king married Anne Boleyn.

In 1534, Parliament made Henry the supreme head of the Church of England, which, though Protestant, kept many Catholic ceremonies and **rituals**. Henry then closed all the monasteries in England, and persecuted anyone who refused to accept his new church. He also took all the monasteries' lands and wealth, which he needed because he had spent the money collected by his father. Henry liked to live the high life, spending the money he had taken

arranged marriage: one in which the parents choose the marriage partners

ritual: ceremony

DID YOU KNOW?

Henry VIII composed musical pieces, played musical instruments well, and was an accomplished dancer. He was also an all-around athlete, who excelled in jousting, wrestling, and archery.

Using MUSIC as a Primary Source

Today we know that King Henry VIII was an accomplished composer of songs. Some historians claim that Henry composed the **ballad** "Greensleeves," five verses of which appear at right. Although today we sing the haunting melody at a slow tempo, "Greensleeves" was originally written as a vigorous dance tune. Music can tell us a great deal about the composer, through the **lyrics** and the melody. Keep this in mind as you read the verses at right or listen to the song.

ballad: a poem that tells a story in verses, usually sung

lyrics: the words for a song

gelding: a calm horse

Alas, my Love! ye do me wrong
To cast me off discourteously;
And I have lovéd you so long,
Delighting in your company.

Chorus:
Greensleeves was all my joy,
Greensleeves was my delight;
Greensleeves was my heart of gold,
And who but my Lady Greensleeves?

I have been ready at your hand,
To grant whatever you would crave;
I have both wagéd life and land,
Your love and goodwill for to have.

I bought thee petticoats of the best,
The cloth so fine as fine might be;
I gave thee jewels for thy chest,
And all this cost I spent on thee.

My sweetest **gelding** I thee gave,
To ride wherever likéd thee;
No lady ever was so brave,
And yet thou wouldst not love me.

Greensleeves, now farewell! adieu!
God I pray to prosper thee;
For I am still thy lover true.
Come once again and love me.

Figure 9–14 Jane Seymour, Henry VIII's third queen

WHAT DO YOU THINK?

1. What do the lyrics of this song tell you about sixteenth-century English society? What objects are valued? What characteristics are valued?

2. If possible, listen to a recording of the song "Greensleeves." Loreena McKennitt sings one version. Then write out the lyrics for "Greensleeves" in your own words. What feelings does the composer of this song express in the melody and lyrics?

3. Does the knowledge that King Henry wrote dance tunes, perhaps even "Greensleeves," agree with what else you know about Henry? Why or why not?

Henry's Persecution of the Clergy

Henry VIII ordered the persecution of Catholic monks and rebels in 1536. Many of those who rebelled against Henry were left hanging in chains for months on the scaffold or were drawn and quartered. What do you think was the purpose of such extreme punishments? What do you think "drawn and quartered" means? Do some research to see if your guess is correct.

Our pleasure is that before you close up our banner again you shall cause such dreadful execution to be done upon a good number of the inhabitants of every town, village, and hamlet that have offended, as they shall be a fearful spectacle to others hereafter. You shall, without pity, cause all to be tied up without delay.

from the Church on entertainments, spectacles at court, and foreign wars.

A King Becomes a Tyrant

Henry Tudor married six times in all. Anne Boleyn and Henry had a daughter, Elizabeth, but no sons. Anne was beheaded after being convicted of high treason in 1536. Henry's next wife, Jane Seymour—perhaps the woman he loved best—died after giving birth to a son who would become Edward VI. Some historians claim that she died because the attending doctors were too eager to save a royal son at the expense of his mother. On the advice of his advisors, Henry then married Anne of Cleves, a Protestant from the Low Countries, but Henry disapproved of her and had the marriage ended. His fifth wife, Catherine Howard, was much younger than Henry, and she soon lost interest in the king. Like Anne Boleyn, she was beheaded after being convicted of high treason. Catherine Parr, Henry's sixth wife, was lucky enough to outlive him.

Henry executed many people close to him, including his close advisors, Cardinal Wolsey and Thomas Cromwell. In his later years, the handsome, generous young prince had changed into a bloated, unpleasant, and suspicious **tyrant**. He had grown so large that, when he was in armour, a crane was needed to get him on his horse. By the end of his life, open sores on his legs so plagued him that he could not even walk.

tyrant: a person who rules without regard for others

Figure 9–15 Canadian actress Genevieve Bujold portrays Anne Boleyn in the classic film *Anne of a Thousand Days*. Why do we continue to be fascinated by the lives of the "royals"?

ACTIVITIES

1. **a)** How did Henry VII become king? As king, from whom did he take power and how did he do it?

   b) Compare the strategies that Henry VII and William the Conqueror used to secure their power (see Chapter 2).

2. Who benefited in Henry VII's reign? How? What economic changes took place in this period? In a small group discuss ways in which England became more of a modern nation.

3. **a)** Develop a list of the important events of Henry VIII's life.

   b) Assume you are one of Henry VIII's wives. Develop a journal that describes three of the events you listed above.

4. Why was Henry VIII so desperate to have a son? Explain the divorce controversy that took place during the reign of Henry VIII. What effect did this power struggle have on a) politics and b) religion?

HENRY VIII'S SUCCESSORS

Edward VI

Henry's son Edward was a nine-year-old orphan when he became king. Because he was so young, he was placed under the control of a group of Protestant **regents**. As a result, Edward developed strong Protestant sympathies and persecuted Catholics. He became ill with **tuberculosis** when he was still very young and died when he was only sixteen. Because he had no heirs of his own, and to keep his

Catholic half-sister Mary from the throne, Edward named his Protestant cousin, Lady Jane Grey, to succeed him. The throne was not really Edward's to give away, however, and many powerful people in England thought Mary had a much better claim to rule than Jane.

Mary I

The army that supported Lady Jane Grey was easily defeated by the Catholic forces led by Henry VIII's eldest daughter, Mary. After Mary became Queen of England in 1553, she launched a campaign to make England a Catholic country once again. Her courts burned nearly three hundred people, and imprisoned many more. Nevertheless, she seems to have been a much nicer person than her nickname, "Bloody Mary," might suggest. Unlike many monarchs, Mary visited the poor in disguise, and in other ways showed a sincere interest in the welfare of her people.

As a young princess, Mary was often unhappy, shunned, and friendless. She was twelve when Henry VIII divorced her mother, Catherine of Aragon. Later, Henry forced Mary to state publicly that she was not a princess, and made her a servant to her sister Elizabeth. Mary was forbidden under any circumstances to see her mother, even when Catherine was on her deathbed. We can easily forget that important historical figures are people, too. Mary's unhappy childhood no doubt affected her view of the world.

Mary's attempts to bring all of England back into the Catholic Church nearly succeeded. However, by 1553 many English had grown strongly anti-Catholic, and more proudly English. By allowing popular Protestants to be burned as heretics, Mary lost whatever good feelings her people felt for her. When Mary died in 1558, few of her subjects mourned. After Mary's death, Henry's second

regent: a person appointed to rule in place of a monarch who is too young, ill, or old to rule

tuberculosis: a disease of the lungs, common and always fatal until recently. Also called "consumption."

Figure 9–16 Edward VI was a sickly, frail boy. In this portrait Edward is dressed and posed to look like his athletic, imposing father (see Figure 9–13). What do you think was the purpose of this strategy?

Figure 9–17 Some considered Lady Jane Grey the "marvel of the age" because of her learning and beauty. After being made queen against her wishes, Jane was beheaded at the age of sixteen. Few people, it is said, did not weep when they heard news of the death of the "Nine Days' Queen."

daughter, Elizabeth, made England once again Protestant.

Elizabeth I: A Renaissance Queen

Elizabeth was Henry VIII's daughter by his second wife, Anne Boleyn. Like Jane and Mary, Elizabeth had an unhappy childhood. After the execution of Elizabeth's mother, Henry would refuse to see Elizabeth for long periods of time. During Mary's reign, Elizabeth was in great danger, both as a Protestant and as a potential rival for the throne. She spent these years on a country estate, trying not to attract attention. When Mary died in 1558, Elizabeth became queen.

Like her father, Elizabeth was very well educated and skilled in many areas. She spoke and read both Latin

Figure 9–18 This portrait of Mary I is very revealing. What does her clothing and jewellery tell you? On first glance, she appears cross, but look closer. Mary was a woman who endured great sadness, and who was capable of great compassion and devotion. What do you see in her eyes?

Build a Bibliography

Nightmare scenario: 11:30 p.m. You've finished your report on Anne Boleyn. It looks great, but you never kept track of sources. The report is due tomorrow.

Going back to find bibliographic information is no fun. To avoid this nightmare, plan ahead. Keep a separate sheet with a running tally of every reference you use for ideas as well as for quotations. Your bibliography shows your readers that you've done your research. It also gives other authors credit for their ideas. And if anyone gets inspired by your great paper, he or she can track down more information on the topic by using your bibliography. You can set up your tally sheet as above. (Add page numbers for quotations.)

Author	Title	City	Publisher	Date
Michael Cranny	Pathways: Civilizations Through Time	Scarborough	Prentice Hall Ginn Canada	1998

Don't forget to record non-book sources too. When you've finished your research, just assemble your sources in alphabetical order, using appropriate bibliographic style:

Cranny, Michael. *Pathways: Civilizations Through Time.* Scarborough: Prentice Hall Ginn Canada, 1998.

NOW YOU DO IT

1. For practice, make up a bibliography including any five resources with information on the Tudors.

and Greek, the classical languages so admired by the Humanists. She was also fluent in the modern languages of French and Italian. Elizabeth was a great patron of the arts, which flourished under her rule. The playwrights William Shakespeare, Ben Jonson, and Christopher Marlowe all lived in **Elizabethan** England, creating some of the finest works in the English language. Unlike her father, however, Elizabeth was notoriously stingy, and never spent a penny if she could avoid it.

Elizabeth never married even though she was under considerable pressure to do so. Philip II of Spain, who had been married to Elizabeth's sister, Mary, was particularly anxious to marry Elizabeth. The young queen, however, did not wish to share her power with anyone. She had several famous love affairs but never allowed sentiment to stand in the way of her policies.

As queen, Elizabeth worked hard to maintain a good relationship with Parliament, and did everything she could to make England peaceful and strong. She treated Catholics with some fairness and did her best to soften religious tensions.

Elizabeth I was remarkable for the way she changed herself from a shy, bookish young girl into a powerful monarch. She was loved by most of her subjects, who referred to her affectionately as "Good Queen Bess" and "Gloriana." By careful statesmanship, good money management, and **diplomacy**, Elizabeth transformed England from an isolated nation into a world power.

Figure 9–19 Around 1600, most people thought that a country should be ruled by a man. To fight this impression, Elizabeth commissioned paintings showing herself as a powerful monarch: Gloriana. Why do you think a ship was painted into the background?

ACTIVITIES

1. Why was Mary I given the name "Bloody Mary"? Were her attempts to control Protestantism successful? Why or why not?

2. Elizabeth was just the second woman to become queen of England in her own right. What did she do to protect her position? Explain why Elizabeth was such an effective, beloved monarch.

3. Make a list of the Tudor monarchs and their periods of reign. Then, using information from this chapter, draw a family tree showing the Tudor family from Henry VII to the time of Elizabeth I.

4. During Tudor times, the monarch became an extremely important individual, serving both as head of the nation-state and as head of the Church of England. Compare the role of the Tudor monarchs with that of the early caliphs of Islam (see page 119 in Chapter 4), who were considered the successors of Muhammad.

MAKING A NATION-STATE WORK

A WISE MONARCH

Under Elizabeth I's rule, the English experienced a renaissance. Because their culture was developing so quickly, the English people began to develop nationalistic and patriotic feelings, which gave them pride in their language, traditions, and institutions. The Elizabethans had tremendous confidence and optimism; they considered themselves renaissance people in charge of their own destinies, with a renaissance queen at the helm.

This climate of opportunity was largely a creation of Elizabeth herself. Through diplomacy, she kept England from falling under the control of more powerful countries such as Spain. She also saved England from much of the religious troubles that were beginning to tear Europe apart in the sixteenth and seventeenth centuries. Elizabeth brought peace to her realm but, even more important, a sense of confidence.

ENGLAND'S NAVAL MIGHT

Besides diplomatic manoeuvring, Elizabeth's primary tool for achieving and maintaining England's power was the British navy. Her sea captains, Francis Drake, John Hawkins, and the other English **Sea Dogs**, challenged the power of mighty Spain by raiding Spanish ships and settlements. When King Philip II of Spain protested to Queen Elizabeth, she listened patiently to the complaints of the Spanish ambassador and agreed that something "ought to be done." Meanwhile, she knighted Drake and the others and

kept part of the treasure taken from the Spanish galleons and towns for herself.

Finally Philip decided he had had enough: he would crush England and occupy it with troops. To do this, Philip assembled a great fleet, called an **armada**. The Spanish Armada entered the English Channel in July 1588. The English attacked the huge Spanish galleons using new strategies, **gunnery**, and fire ships. These fire ships, unmanned old ships loaded with pitch and gunpowder, were sent to collide with the Spanish ships, at which point both exploded. The Spanish would have done much better if the English had come close enough to allow the Spanish soldiers to jump onto the English ships to do battle, but the English ships—manned with sailors, not soldiers—wisely kept their distance. The English tactics succeeded in breaking the formation of the Armada, and the stormy seas destroyed the Spanish ships. The defeat of the Spanish Armada made England a **maritime** power to be reckoned with.

Populations in Europe, 1500	
Region	**Population (estimated)**
England	2 million
France	16 million
Spain	8 million
Holy Roman Empire	20 million
Europe	**60 million**

Figure 9–21 Although always pictured in a crescent-shaped formation, the Spanish Armada likely travelled in a compact bird-shaped formation. The English harassed the Spanish ships in the rear, causing them to crowd forward. What effect do you think this tactic had?

Sea Dogs: English sea captains authorized to raid Spanish ships and towns

armada: a fleet of war ships

gunnery: the art of firing cannons quickly and accurately—difficult on a rolling ship

maritime: having to do with the sea

Figure 9–20 How does England's population compare with Spain's? With Europe's? Nevertheless, by 1600 Spain had lost control of the high seas. On the open sea, England's relatively small population was not a factor in the balance of power. Why would that be?

OVERSEAS BUSINESS

In the late sixteenth century, English ships seemed to be everywhere. They sailed into the Pacific Ocean, into the Indian Ocean, and across the Atlantic. Elizabethan sea captains were supremely confident. They had the skills and daring to go wherever they wanted—and they wanted to go anywhere they could make money. New trading companies backed by merchant investors sponsored many expeditions to new lands. Queen Elizabeth also supported the captains in their endeavours, always, of course, for a cut of the profits.

Realizing that the Americas blocked the way to Asia, the Elizabethans turned their eyes to North America, some to trade and some to set up colonies. One such colony was established in Newfoundland in 1583 by Sir Humphrey Gilbert. He arrived in his ship, the *Squirrel*, with a small fleet, and found fishing boats from all over Europe already anchored in St. John's harbour. Gilbert took possession of the country for England anyway, and warned that anyone who said anything against the English queen would have his ears cut off. Gilbert was lost at sea shortly afterwards, and the Newfoundland colony failed.

Gilbert's half-brother, Sir Walter Raleigh, then tried to set up a colony farther south. Raleigh named the colony Virginia after Elizabeth, the queen who never married. Raleigh found little that would make the quick profits investors demanded—except tobacco, a plant smoked by the Aboriginal peoples of North America. Raleigh introduced tobacco into England. Although people were shocked at the new habit, it took hold. The colony at Roanoke failed, but the trade in tobacco would persist.

courtier: an attendant at a royal court

Figure 9–22 Sir Walter Raleigh—pirate, **courtier**, business person, poet and writer, scientist, and explorer—was a favourite at court. His ruffed collar, pointed beard, and curled hair marked him as a fashionable dresser.

SLAVE TRADE MONEY

The Elizabethan economy was booming, partly because of new money from piracy and overseas trade. Besides trading in goods, England began trading in human beings. Numerous English merchant traders prospered directly from their participation in this ancient practice. Their prosperity in turn contributed to England's economic well-being, a fact that stains the history of Elizabethan England.

Slavery was very profitable. West Africans were captured by Arab and African slavers in the African interior and brought to the coast. There these unfortunate people were traded to Europeans for European goods, and packed on board slave ships. A human being cost about 5 pounds [$10] in Africa and could be sold for 17 pounds [$34] in the West Indies [Caribbean islands]. The cost of the voyage was about 5 pounds per slave. Usually, one slave in four died from disease or despair on the transatlantic crossing.

—*James Lawrence, Historian*

The Memoirs of Olaudah Equiano

England's participation in the practice of slavery began during Elizabethan times. First-person accounts of the experience of slavery are rare because slaves were not permitted to learn to read or write. One of the few accounts was written by Olaudah Equiano, an **Ibo** from the country in Africa that is now called Nigeria. Equiano was captured at the age of eleven and sold to English slave merchants who in turn sold him in Barbados. Equiano educated himself and eventually purchased his freedom—rights not allowed most slaves. He travelled widely and joined the anti-slavery movement in England.

A truly remarkable person, Equiano later recorded and published the story of his life. Although Equiano lived more than a hundred years after the Elizabethan period, his account helps us learn about the horrors of the slave trade, which changed little over the century. In this excerpt

Equiano describes the conditions aboard the English slave ship.

Ibo: a member of the Ibo people in Africa

to flog: to beat with a strap, stick, or whip

brute: an animal

We were all put under the deck... The closeness of the place, and the heat of the climate, added to the number in the ship, which was so crowded that each had scarcely room to turn himself, almost suffocated us ... and brought on a sickness among the slaves, of which many died... This wretched situation was again aggravated by the galling of the chains now become insupportable; and filth of the necessary tubs [for toilets], into which the children often fell, and were almost suffocated. The shrieks of the women, and the groans of the dying, rendered the whole scene a horror almost [impossible to imagine].

The crew used to watch us very closely who were not chained down to the decks, lest we should leap into the water: and I have seen some of these poor African prisoners most severely cut for attempting to do so, and hourly whipped for not eating. This indeed was often the case with myself....

Still I feared I would be put to death, the White people looked and acted, as I thought, in so savage a manner; for I had never seen among any people such instances of brutal cruelty; and this not only shown towards us Blacks, but also to some of the Whites themselves. One White man in particular I saw, when we were permitted to be on deck, **flogged** so unmercifully with a large rope near the foremast, that he died in consequence of it; and they tossed him over the side as they would have done a **brute**.

WHAT DO YOU THINK?

1. In point form, list the conditions on board the slave ship Equiano describes.

2. Speculate on what Equiano lost.

3. Equiano describes a situation in which one group of human beings has complete power over another group. Explain why you think this situation is acceptable or not. Speculate on why Elizabethan society's views of the slave trade were so different from those of Canadian society.

4. Equiano was "purchased" with certain coins. Assume that those coins paid the wages of the sea captain, who in turn used them to purchase a fine hat in London. How do you think the shopkeeper would react to the charge that the coins were tainted? Would you agree with this opinion? Explain.

1. Explain what qualities made Elizabeth I a remarkable ruler. What did she do for England?

2. **a)** What was the Spanish Armada? How was it defeated? What effect did the defeat of the Armada have on the English view of themselves?

   b) Draw a picture of the sea battle to demonstrate one of England's tactics.

   c) Why was naval power so important to England?

3. Convert the chart Populations in Europe, 1500 into a bar graph. Describe what your bar graph demonstrates.

4. Where did the Elizabethans try to establish settlements? Did they succeed or fail? Why?

5. In a group, decide why the slave trade took place. Debate who was responsible: individual slave traders or European society. How could slavery be prevented in future?

6. Research the events in the life of either Sir Francis Drake or Sir Walter Raleigh. Then make a map to illustrate the major events of this knight's adventures.

THE ELIZABETHAN WORK FORCE

Enclosure

The building of a modern nation in Tudor times created good times for some but disrupted the lives of thousands of others. In the Middle Ages, the manor system had provided most people with a livelihood. The Tudor monarchs allowed the nobles to **enclose** their estates, throwing serfs off land their families had farmed for generations. The nobles put fences all around the manor lands to make enormous pastures for sheep. Soon wool became England's major staple product. Contrasting with the enormous numbers of people required to raise crops, very few people were needed to tend sheep. Many farm labourers were driven out of their villages and farms, or were forced out by high rents. All over England, deserted villages fell into ruin.

to enclose: to fence off

cottage: a house, usually small

Consequences for Ordinary People

Enclosure made farming more efficient, but had disastrous consequences for farm workers. Because there was no social welfare, the unemployed had no means of supporting themselves. Many tried to find work in the towns and cities. Failing that, many of them turned to lives of crime. It is no wonder that vagrancy and petty crime were serious problems in Elizabeth's time. Parliament did pass a Poor Law in 1601, which was designed to provide some help to the poor. This law was perhaps the first piece of legislation in Europe to recognize that society had an obligation to find work for poor people.

Cottage Industries

Towns grew enormously, their populations swollen by thousands of farm labourers looking for work. This large pool of potential workers fuelled the economy because people would accept low wages, they were so eager for work. Investors discovered that they could make a profit by hiring independent labourers to make goods for them cheaply. Usually raw materials were sent to a worker in his or her home, or **cottage**. When the goods were finished, the investor

Sturdy Vagabonds and Rogues

The Tudor governments were very concerned about lawlessness and rebellion. The thousands of desperately poor people who roamed the country found themselves suspected of criminal activity (often with good reason!) everywhere they went. In the literature of the time, these people were referred to as "sturdy **vagabonds and rogues**." Parliament passed a law to deal with them. Travelling without a purpose anywhere in England became illegal.

vagabonds and rogues: idle wanderers and rascals

enjoined: ordered

forthwith: immediately

An Act to Control Vagabonds—1531

Be it further enacted ... that if any man or woman being whole and mighty in body and able to labour having no land, master, nor any lawful merchandise, craft, or mystery, whereby he might get his living ... be vagrant ... then it shall be lawful ... to arrest said vagabonds and idle persons and to bring them to any Justices of the Peace ... [who] shall cause every such idle person ... to [be taken to] the next market town ... and there to be tied to the end of a cart ... and be beaten with whips throughout the same market town ... until his body be bloody; and after such punishment ... shall be **enjoined** on his oath to return **forthwith** without delay ... to the place where he was born, or where he last dwelled.

PRIMARY SOURCE

WHAT DO YOU THINK?

1. What does this law reveal about how Elizabethans thought about people without work? Who do you think was responsible for the situation. Why?

would pick them up and sell them for a profit. Because of the number of people wanting work, wages were low, the work hard, and the hours long. Labour laws did not exist, and families had to struggle to support themselves, so many children worked alongside their parents. All these unreasonable work conditions were bad for most people and families, but they did encourage an enormous growth in manufacturing, which in turn helped make the Elizabethan nation-state strong.

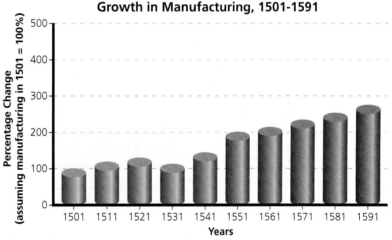

Growth in Manufacturing, 1501-1591

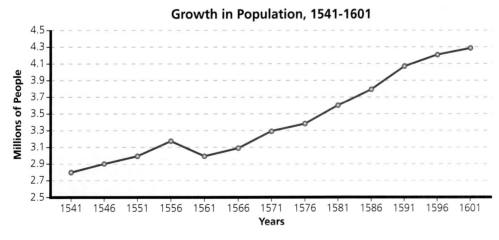

Growth in Population, 1541-1601

Figure 9–23 As in most of the countries of Europe, the population of England grew quickly during the sixteenth century. At the same time, manufacturing grew in importance. Did manufacturing encourage people to have more children because they had jobs, or did growing populations create a bigger market for goods? Historians still argue about it.

Child Labour Then and Now

Figure 9–24 This child works probably eight to twelve hours a day on this silk-making loom in Uttar Pradesh, India.

In a consumer society, the bottom line is usually money. To make a profit, producers try to manufacture a product at a low price and sell it at a high price. To keep costs down, some producers hire children: children will work for lower wages than adult workers; the nimble hands of the young can do unskilled labour very quickly; and children can be controlled.

In Elizabethan England, children were an important part of the labour force, working in small cottage industries alongside their parents. Child labour increased greatly during the Industrial Revolution, when large numbers of children were hired to work in factories and mines. Canada also has a history of child labour. Canada's 80 000 "Home" children were orphans shipped from the British Isles to work as cheap farm help. The fictional character Anne of Green Gables was brought to Green Gables for the same purpose.

Although Canada now has virtually eliminated child labour within the nation's boundaries, it still profits from the work of children. Some Canadian companies hire other companies in **less developed countries** to produce their goods cheaply, perhaps not realizing that children may be employed by these companies. With the increase in trade among nations, probably all Canadians use products made by children.

less developed country: a country with a poorly developed economy

WHAT DO YOU THINK?

1. Assume you are employed full-time as a sweeper in a textile factory. How would your position affect the following?
   ◆ your unemployed parents
   ◆ your younger brother, who is in school
   ◆ your education
   ◆ your future

2. a) In a group, brainstorm ways that governments and international organizations could help put an end to child labour. Then brainstorm ways that you as individuals could take action.

   b) As a class, consider the suggestions for action you developed in part (a). Choose one that your class can achieve and implement it.

ACTIVITIES

1. How did settlement patterns change in England after enclosure?

2. Compare life in feudal England with life in England after enclosure. Whose rights were ignored with enclosure? Who benefited? Explain.

3. Explain why beggars and "sturdy rogues" were a problem in Elizabethan times. Where did they come from? How did Elizabethans deal with the problem?

4. Hold a class debate to argue for and against the following statement: "The changes in Elizabethan England benefited the group more than the individual."

SUMMARY

The Protestant Reformation, which began with Martin Luther's protest in Wittenberg in 1517, broke the domination of the Catholic Church over religious life in Europe. New churches sprang up all over the continent. More than that, the Reformation created a different set of beliefs, one that made each person responsible for his or her own soul. This changed everything because individual responsibility meant that each person was important. This in turn caused changes in business and politics.

The Reformation began as a religious revolt but ended as a political one. Religious conflict caused nations to fight with nations. Political leaders enjoyed their new powers, which they gained at the expense of Rome and the feudal barons. Without the need to be tied to Rome, the people of Europe began to identify more with their own nations. The European nation-state was born.

Elizabethan England is an excellent example of a nation-state that emerged from the Reformation. By the time Elizabeth I died in 1603, England was a great world power. It had gained a professional government, and the medieval way of life with its manors, guilds, and civil wars was gone forever. The Catholic Church had been replaced by an English national church. During this robust, colourful period, England produced, among other things, some of the best literature in the English language.

Larger-than-life monarchs, such as Elizabeth I and Henry VIII, held centre stage in the sixteenth century, but even they had to adapt. The new middle class was coming into its own. For a time, this class would be content to help the monarchs rule, but soon these people would demand true power. Eventually, these demands would lead to elected governments, but that would not occur for many years.

SUMMARY ACTIVITIES

1. Compare Rembrandt's painting on page 283 with Caravaggio's painting on page 269. Consider dress, subject, style, use of light, setting, and activity. How do these paintings reflect the religious struggles of the Reformation and the Counter Reformation, respectively? How do these paintings compare with Renaissance paintings (see Chapter 7)?

2. a) Explain how the Reformation helped lead to the formation of the European nation-state, and indirectly to democracy.

   b) Identify four other factors that led to the nation-state.

3. Write a letter from Elizabeth to her late grandfather Henry VII that describes the changes that have taken place in England since Henry's death, and that also describes Elizabeth's accomplishments.

4. In a small group, prepare a chart comparing the Elizabethan nation-state with the Italian city-states you learned about in Chapter 7. Decide why one system survived and the other did not.

ON YOUR OWN

1. Research one Protestant Canadian church. In class, present a report that describes the group's major beliefs, history, and current membership.

2. A theocracy is a government in which the laws of a religion become the laws of the state. Research and prepare a report on a modern theocracy. Possibilities include Iran and Tibet before 1959. A Lutheran minister once praised Geneva, a theocracy, as a "perfect republic." Analyze what people may gain or lose by living in a theocracy.

3. In this chapter, we saw how life changed drastically for ordinary people during the Elizabethan Age. Newly landless serfs flocked to the towns and cities, taking work if they could get it, often working at low rates of pay. Yet this era is also considered a time of extraordinary economic development, during which trade and manufacturing boomed. Research Canada's jobless recovery of the 1990s, using search engines on the Internet if possible. Prepare a brief report comparing the two eras.

UNIT 4
KINGDOMS AND DYNASTIES, 900–1600

In this unit you will investigate the civilizations of Spain and Portugal, eastern Europe, Africa, and China during its later dynasties. You will discover that each area of the world developed its own distinct traditions in language, religion, art, architecture, law, government, communication, technology, foods, science, economics, and ways of living together.

Some civilizations had extensive contact with other civilizations. The Arab world benefited by expanding its power and influence far and wide. As Islam spread, so did Arab power. The Ottoman Empire expanded from modern-day Turkey across eastern Europe all the way to the Byzantine Empire. From northern Africa, the Arabs conquered Spain and Portugal, where they reigned over a Muslim kingdom for 300 years.

India is an excellent example of a civilization that flourished because of rather than in spite of contact, even in the form of foreign conquest. Every time India was invaded—whether by the Aryans, the Mughals, or the British—the Indian people absorbed the conquerers into their society and culture. In turn, India has strongly influenced other world civilizations, especially in the area of religion.

In Africa, the birthplace of humanity, civilization developed in isolated, closely knit village communities because the continent was so vast and physical barriers kept people apart. The natural resources of Africa made it a rich centre of trade by 1000 C.E. The wealthy kingdoms of West Africa became legendary.

In China, the mightiest empire on earth for many centuries, physical barriers kept foreigners away. At the same time, good environmental conditions within China allowed many peoples to flourish and join together in one huge civilization. The Chinese civilization has remained intact—though under different dynasties—for thousands of years.

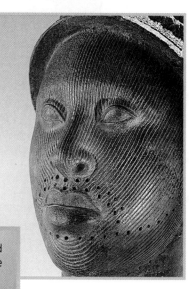

Portrait of an Ife king. A sculptor used the difficult "lost-wax" process to create this work of art. This portrait shows a king who ruled about a thousand years ago in western Africa.

Mehmed II surveys the walls of Constantinople. The walls of this ancient city had kept the Byzantine Empire safe for centuries. The city fell, finally, to the Muslim conqueror Mehmed II after a brilliant assault. Thus began the heady reign of the Ottoman Empire, which soon spread Islam far and wide.

Hindus celebrate the Khumba-mela. Once every three years, millions of Hindus descend upon the Ganges in an unparalleled religious celebration. The Indian people's eternal spiritual quest has brought about many world religions.

Ordinary life in the Ming Dynasty. History often records the doings of rich people, and the lives of ordinary people are forgotten. This painted porcelain vase shows ordinary people at work during the Ming Dynasty around 1400.

10 ISLAMIC SPAIN AND THE OTTOMAN EMPIRE

CHAPTER OUTCOMES

In this chapter, you will examine the effects of Islamic expansion into Spain and Eastern Europe. In both areas, distinctive cultures arose that profoundly affected surrounding and following cultures. By the end of this chapter, you will

- investigate the cultural development and contributions of Islamic Spain

- describe the effects and results of the Reconquista

- demonstrate understanding of the origins and development of the Ottoman Empire

- describe the events of Ottoman expansion into southeast Europe

- identify and analyze the social contributions of the Ottomans

- examine the reasons for the slow decline of the Ottoman Empire

- complete a PMI

The Fall of Constantinople

By the spring of 1453, the once vast and powerful Byzantine Empire had been reduced to one city, Constantinople. For a thousand years, the Byzantines had survived in the Middle East. Gradually, the empire had been losing power and prestige. Frequently attacked, nearly overrun but never defeated, the Byzantines represented a last living link with the glories of the Roman Empire.

That was all to change on a fateful spring day.

While the fortunes of Byzantium were falling, those of the Ottoman Empire were rising. The Ottomans had attacked Constantinople in 1422, but had been unable to capture it, owing to the city's massive fortifications. Now, in the spring of 1453, the new sultan, Mehmed II, prepared to take Constantinople and make it the new capital of his empire. The Ottomans' leader was young—twenty-two years old—intelligent, ruthless, and patient. Their army numbered over 100 000 soldiers, and was supported by a strong fleet of ships blocking the way from the sea to Constantinople.

The Byzantine emperor, Constantine XI Dragases, was also young and resourceful. His city lay behind walls of triple thickness, but he only had 7000 troops, and the walls stretched some 21 kilometres around the city.

The following diary account was written by a fictitious person but is based on actual eyewitness accounts of the fall of Constantinople.

My name is Bartolemo Paggliacci, and I am a native of the town of Genoa, Italy. In the spring of 1453, I was a soldier under the command of Giovanni Giustiniani and, with the rest of our force, was charged with the task of preventing the loss of Constantiniple, Queen of Cities, to the Turks. I was able to write an account of our brave defence, and by God's mercy I escaped the destruction of the city, bringing with me a tale of great sadness and cruelty. I invite you now to go back to the beginning in 1453.

March 20, 1453 — An Ottoman fleet has appeared in the Sea of Mamara, and it blocks the way to Constantinople. We fear it is now impossible for any assistance to reach the city from Europe. Our position is very grave, and we pray daily to the Lord for deliverance.

March 26 — We hear that an Ottoman army of 100 000 marches from Adrianpole towards Constantinople. We are told it consists of 20 000 *bashi-bazouks*, semi-trained irregular troops of great **ferocity**, and 12 000 elite Janissary infantry who attack without mercy. The remainder of the army is made up of the **cavalry**, and it includes a **corps** of artillery— massive cannons that will be used to batter the walls of Constantinople into rubble. The largest of these has an 8-metre-long barrel and fires a 500-kilogram stone cannon ball. We do not know how we can withstand them.

April 5 — The Ottoman army has reached Constantinople. It is under the personal command of the Sultan Mehmed II. I stand on the **battlements** of the city's walls and watch him surveying our defences. We know that he is determining the best place to try to **breach** these walls. And such walls! They were built centuries ago, at the height of the Byzantines' strength and glory. It is said that no invader could ever destroy them.

They consist of a triple wall system. First is a massive ditch, some 20 metres wide and 3 metres deep. Parts of this ditch can be flooded to form a

Sultan Mehmed II surveys the walls of Constantinople with his Ottoman army.

partial moat. The city side of this ditch is a stone **rampart** 6 metres high. Beyond this is an open space, directly before the Outer Wall of the city. The Outer Wall is 8 metres high, and has a series of towers placed 50–100 metres apart. Any attackers able to **scale** this wall would find themselves in another open space between the Outer Wall and the Great Wall.

The Great Wall is truly massive; some 13 metres high, with a **parapet**, it too has stone towers placed along its length. From its heights, we could drop missiles, stones, and boiling oil on any attacking force stuck between it and the Outer Wall. Strong as these defences are, there are two points of weakness. At the northern end of the wall system, near the **Golden Horn**, there are a royal palace and other buildings built between the walls and the harbour. Here, the walls are only of single depth. Also, along the wall system is the valley of the River Lycus, and here, where the river comes close, the walls are of less height.

From where I stand, I can see Mehmed gesturing to his officers—I can tell that he has decided that this is the best place to begin a **bombardment**.

The Emperor Constantine too has been surveying the situation. The size of the Ottoman army fills him with dismay, as his troops are far too few to defend the entire Outer Wall. He has decided to make a show of force along the walls. We spend the day marching visibly along the parapets of the

"We spent the day marching visibly along the parapets of the walls."

walls in an effort to appear more numerous than we are. All the towers have flags flying above them, indicating they are fully manned, even though they are not.

April 12 — The Ottoman bombardment has begun. The great **artillery** pieces are placed so they can batter the walls along the valley of the Lycus. The great 8-metre-long cannon can only fire seven times a day, but it soon blasts great holes in **fortifications** that were built before the invention of gunpowder. The boom of the cannons and the crash of explosions can be heard throughout the city.

April 17 — After five days of bombardment, two towers and the walls in the valley of the

Lycus have been reduced to **rubble**. Constantine and Giustiniani direct us to build temporary **stockades** in an effort to replace them, but the situation is grim. We know that the walls could not long withstand assaults by the Turkish troops.

April 18 — The Ottomans launched an assault today on the broken walls. Wave upon wave of bashi-bazouks attacked, but with God's help we **repulsed** them. I fear that we cannot do so again.

I have heard also today bad news from the harbour. In order to attack us from the sea, Mehmed must have his fleet enter the harbour of Constantinople—the famed Golden Horn. But our wise emperor, Constantine, foreseeing this, has erected a massive iron chain across the harbour. No Turkish ships can pass over this defence. We hear that Mehmed has decided on another approach. He has gathered some eighty ships on the far side of the harbour. These vessels are fully manned. A **slipway** some 1300 metres is being built up the steep sides of the outer harbour, across the peninsula of Galata, and down the other side to the shores of the Golden Horn.

April 23 — I stand on the seaward walls of Constantinople with some of my fellow soldiers. We watch, thunderstruck, as hundreds of troops and oxen drag and push the eighty ships up the slipway. The crews of the ships pull at their oars, giving the impression that they are sailing up the side of the harbour. It is a fantastic sight, and we are powerless to stop the progress of these vessels. By nightfall, the Turks have a fleet in the Golden Horn.

May 2 — For the past week, there has been a **stalemate**. The Ottomans cannot break through the city's defences, yet we are too weak to drive the attackers away. The Turkish fleet attacked the Christian vessels (mainly our Genoese galleys) in the Golden Horn, but our brave sailors drove them off.

May 12 — Mehmed has moved his cannon north to the other weak spot in our defences. After a bombardment that breaches the walls at the northern end, some 50 000 Ottoman troops attack the gap. We fear, with full justification, that this is the end, and we desperately move to repel the attack. Miraculously, we succeed, and Ottoman dead fill the breach. Constantinople is still unconquered! We all fall to our knees and give thanks to the Lord for his divine aid.

May 18 — There has been little action in the past week. We and our opponents are both resting. I know not what the Turks are planning, but we are all praying for **salvation** from this terrible fate.

"We watch, thunderstruck, as hundreds of troops and oxen drag and push the eighty ships up the slipway."

May 28 — The Turks have again bombarded the walls that have been breached, and they are making ladders with which to climb over the walls and the temporary stockades. It seems to us that Mehmed has decided to launch an all-out assault on the defences. Departing from his previous strategy, he will now try an attack at all points of the walls. As it is now late in the day, the attack will begin at night. We fear the worst. We have placed ourselves along the Outer Wall, and the gates of the city are closed and locked behind us. We prepare for the final assault.

May 29 — Shortly after midnight, we hear the Turkish order to attack. The bombardment begins again, and the walls and the stockades crumble before the fire of the massed cannons. There is a massive amount of noise from the Ottoman troops—drums, cymbals, and the cries of "Allah, Allah" from thousands of men. The bashi-bazouks pour forward against the weak points, and we desperately attempt to repel them. Hundreds of Turkish dead litter the breaches. After about two hours, Mehmed gives another order, and the Janissaries rush forward.

Disaster! A small gate near the northern end of the walls, from which some of us had made raids against the Ottomans during the siege, has been left open. Janissaries fight their way inside the walls. They are defeated and killed, but not before some manage to pull down Christian banners and replace them with Turkish flags. I am further along the walls and see this, and hear a cry that the Ottomans have breached the defences.

Now more terrible news! Near the breach at the River Lycus, Giustiniani is severely wounded. He decides to quit the walls, and some of us carry him back into the city. We take him to one of our galleys in the harbour. On our ship I later learn the rest of what happened in Constantinople from one of our men who managed to escape to the ship later in the day.

Our troops waver, not certain of the fate of our commander. Mehmed notices the resulting confusion. He orders the Janissaries forward again. The defenders are forced back against the great wall and are massacred. More and more Ottoman troops pour into the breach. Flinging scaling ladders against the Great Wall, they reach the top and gain the city. They open the Military Gate of St. Romanus, and the rest of the Ottoman army streams into the city. I hear that the noble Constantine has fallen defending his city, and with that final **calamity**, the battle has ended. The agony of Constantinople has begun.

Mehmed had offered us the option of surrender when he approached the city in April. Once we refused, we knew that when the city fell, his troops were entitled to three days' **pillage**. This pillage has now begun, and the Ottoman troops now turn the streets into a **charnel house**. Defenders and civilians alike are being brutally massacred in the streets. Churches are attacked, and anything movable and of value is carried away. Holy **relics** and **icons** have been smashed or taken away.

Constantinople, the Queen of Cities, which had stood as a symbol of Roman power and continuity with ancient times, is no more. At nightfall, our ship managed—I know not how— to escape the harbour, and sail away down the Bosporus. Almost all of our brave **compatriots** were slaughtered in the city, and we survivors feel unworthy to have survived.

ferocity: extreme fierceness

cavalry: soldiers trained to fight on horseback

corps: a formation made up of divisions

battlements: a low wall for defence at the top of a tower or wall

breach: break through; a break in a wall

rampart: a bank of earth used for defence

to scale: to climb

parapet: a low wall to protect soldiers

Golden Horn: the portion of the Bosporus Strait that was close to the double wall of Constantinople built by Theodosius II (408–450), and the Gate of the Christians—a strategic location

bombardment: attack, assault

artillery: mounted guns, cannons

fortifications: protective walls, defences

rubble: broken fragments of rock

stockade: a barrier of stakes, often logs, driven into the ground side by side to make a wall

to repulse: to force away

slipway: a platform that slopes into the water, often serving as a landing place

stalemate: a complete standstill

salvation: divine rescue

calamity: a terrible event

pillage: plunder, robbery, and violence

charnel house: a building full of bodies

relic: an object that has survived from the past and has a religious association

icon: an image of Jesus, Mary, or the saints used in the Orthodox and Eastern-rite Catholic Churches

compatriot: someone who also is a citizen of your country

ACTIVITIES

1. Why did the Ottomans want to capture Constantinople?

2. Do you feel the defenders of Constantinople should have surrendered without a fight? With a partner, discuss the possible outcomes had the Byzantines done so. Share your findings with the rest of the class.

3. Describe three strategies of assault and three defensive strategies presented in Paggliacci's diary.

4. What factors allowed the Ottomans to capture the city?

5. Based on the information given here, draw a diagram that shows the triple-fortified walls of Constantinople.

6. Imagine you are a soldier in the Ottoman army or a citizen of Constantinople. In a poster, poem, or letter, describe your feelings and perceptions during the siege.

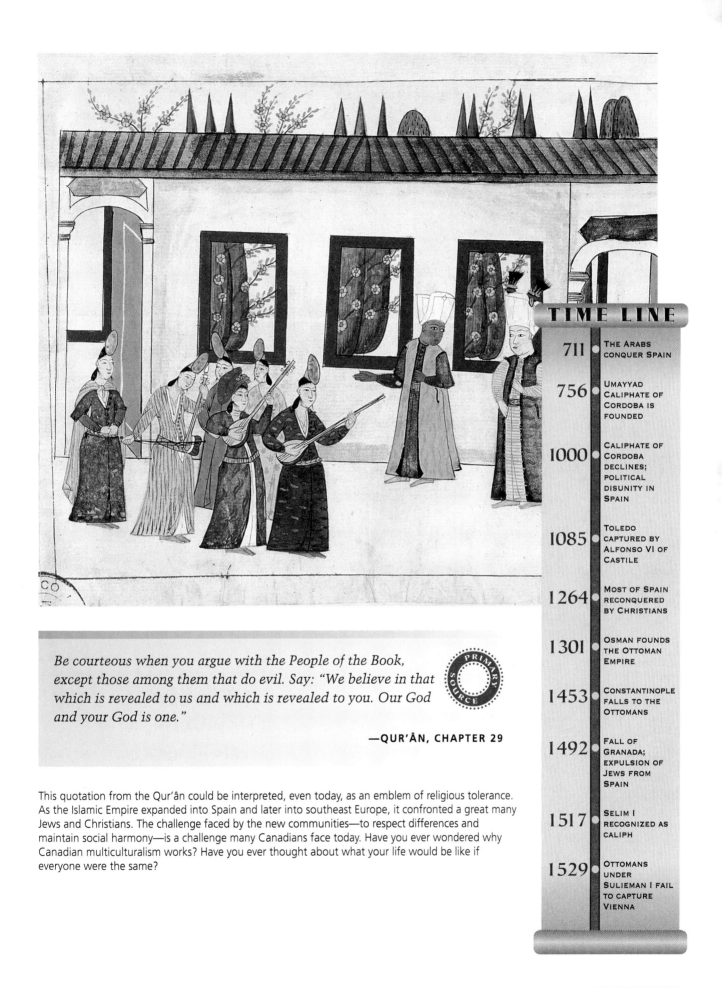

711 THE ARABS CONQUER SPAIN

756 UMAYYAD CALIPHATE OF CORDOBA IS FOUNDED

1000 CALIPHATE OF CORDOBA DECLINES; POLITICAL DISUNITY IN SPAIN

1085 TOLEDO CAPTURED BY ALFONSO VI OF CASTILE

1264 MOST OF SPAIN RECONQUERED BY CHRISTIANS

1301 OSMAN FOUNDS THE OTTOMAN EMPIRE

1453 CONSTANTINOPLE FALLS TO THE OTTOMANS

1492 FALL OF GRANADA; EXPULSION OF JEWS FROM SPAIN

1517 SELIM I RECOGNIZED AS CALIPH

1529 OTTOMANS UNDER SULIEMAN I FAIL TO CAPTURE VIENNA

Be courteous when you argue with the People of the Book, except those among them that do evil. Say: "We believe in that which is revealed to us and which is revealed to you. Our God and your God is one."

PRIMARY SOURCE

—QUR'ÂN, CHAPTER 29

This quotation from the Qur'ân could be interpreted, even today, as an emblem of religious tolerance. As the Islamic Empire expanded into Spain and later into southeast Europe, it confronted a great many Jews and Christians. The challenge faced by the new communities—to respect differences and maintain social harmony—is a challenge many Canadians face today. Have you ever wondered why Canadian multiculturalism works? Have you ever thought about what your life would be like if everyone were the same?

INTRODUCTION

In Chapter 4, you read about the beginnings of Islam in the seventh century and how Arab culture spread across Europe, Asia, and Africa. In this chapter, you will read how one western European country, Spain, became a flourishing Islamic civilization. Spain did not keep its Arab character. Nonetheless, this area was once a centre for an Islamic civilization that lasted 700 years, until 1492.

In Chapter 10, you will also follow the expansion of Islam under the Ottoman Empire from modern-day Turkey, across eastern Europe, and into the very heart of the Byzantine Empire. Islamic civilization under the Ottomans was quite different from the civilization that developed in Spain, but it was also highly successful. The Ottoman sultans ruled a complex military state that provided a good life for its people. The Ottomans had strong views on how to wage war, and how to manage affairs. Ironically, loyalty to some of these ideas during the dawn of the seventeenth century would also speed their decline.

ISLAMIC SPAIN

As you learned in Chapter 4, the Arabs first came to Spain in 711. Within forty years, Spain was home to an independent Islamic kingdom, a civilization that would last for more than 700 years.

to intermarry: in a historical sense, to marry someone from a different group, for example, a different nationality or religion

Only about 40 000 Arabs actually came to Spain during this period, and there were few later immigrants. But over the years, many people **intermarried**, creating a varied and rich culture. Islamic Spain was a sophisticated, tolerant, and technically advanced society. Its influence on European culture can be felt to this day.

THE GEOGRAPHY OF SPAIN AND PORTUGAL

Spain and Portugal are the two modern countries that occupy the Iberian Peninsula. Together they form the westernmost and southernmost European countries. The peninsula is surrounded on three sides by water and on the fourth side by the Pyrenees Mountains. The mountains form a natural barrier to the rest of Europe. The Strait of Gibraltar divides the peninsula from the north shore of Africa.

Figure 10–1 The topography of modern-day Spain and Portugal

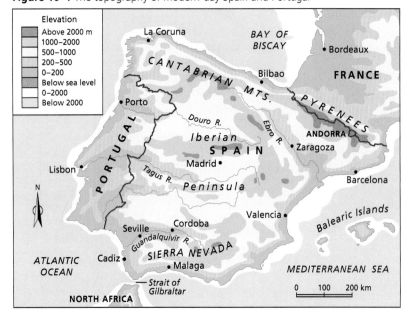

The Iberian Peninsula consists primarily of an elevated plateau that has moderate to high temperatures, and low rainfall. Along the northern coast and the southern coast, there are high mountains. The Mediterranean range, the Sierra Nevada, features some of the highest peaks in Europe.

The peninsula has three major rivers—the Tagus, the Ebro, and the Guandalquivir. These rivers are the source of much-needed water for **irrigation**. With the exception of the river valleys and the northern coast, the climate of Spain is so dry that the country must rely on dry-land farming or extensive irrigation.

The location of the Iberian Peninsula has also influenced its history. Before the Arabs arrived in Spain in the eighth century, the area was occupied by a Germanic tribe known as the "Visigoths." They had been living there for approximately 300 years and had made Spain their kingdom. However, the government of the Visigoths was troubled by violence and scheming. Historians believe that it was only able to survive for two-and-a-half centuries because geography shielded it from outside threats. The only neighbours, the Franks, were safely located on the other side of the barrier of the Pyrenees mountains.

irrigation: supplying the land with water using artificial means

HOW TO...

Do a PMI (Plus, Minus, Interesting)

A PMI lets you see several paragraphs of information in a chart form. It also allows you to classify information. Once you view information in this form, it is easier to gain new insights into a topic.

To set up a PMI, draw a horizontal line across the top of a page and section it into four columns. You will be writing in the first column, so make it sufficiently wide. In this column, summarize your paragraphs in point form. An example of a blank PMI appears at right.

After you have summarized the information in point-form notes, you are ready to classify it. Rate the information **Plus** if it reveals something positive. For example,

there is a benefit to people or to the environment. Rate it **Minus** if the statement reveals something negative. For example, there is hardship, danger, loss of life, or damage to the physical

environment. Rate the information **Interesting** if it makes you wonder why, or makes you want to know more. If the information is neither plus, minus, nor interesting, do not rate it at all.

Statements (point form)	Plus	Minus	Interesting

NOW YOU DO IT

1. In groups of four to six students, do a PMI on the geography of Spain and Portugal using the four paragraphs on pages 312–313 as your information base. Share your findings with other groups in the class.

2. In a class discussion, what conclusions can you make about the impact of Spain's geography on human activities?

THE VISIGOTH KINGDOM OF SPAIN AND THE ARAB CONQUEST

As you read in Chapter 4, during the seventh century, the Arabs expanded across North Africa. By 700, they controlled all of it. In their search for new lands to bring under the control of Islam, they decided to cross Spain.

In the early 700s, the Visigoths were experiencing another period of unrest. The new king, Roderick, was trying to establish control of Spain but he was having little success. In the spring of 711, the Arabs landed near Gibraltar with some 7000 troops. They defeated Roderick and killed him in battle. This marked the end of the Visigoth kingdom.

As they had done on many occasions, the Arabs—or **Moors**, as they came to be known in Spain—did

Using a Treaty as a Primary Source

CATALOGUE CARD

What is it? A treaty of peace

Who wrote it? Abd-al-Aziz to the Visigothic nobleman, Theodimir, ruler of the province of Murcia

When? After the Arab conquest of the Visigoths, in 713

Why? To record the treatment of the Visigoths under Arab rule

A **treaty** is a contract — usually in writing—between governments. Not all treaties are the same, however. Some treaties deal with everyday issues such as trade; others deal with matters of power. In some instances, the leader of a conquered people may have no choice but to sign a treaty that favours the conquerors. History is full of such examples.

On the surface, this particular treaty seems reasonable, and the Moors appear to have shown courtesy to the defeated Visigoths. When you are examining a treaty as a primary source document, examine the tone of the agreement as well as its content. Are there restrictions placed on some persons? Does the language of the agreement seem harsh or fair? Who benefits the most from the agreement?

In the name of Allah, the Clement, the Merciful! A letter addressed by Abd-al-Aziz to Tudmir-ibn-Abdush:

This last obtains peace and receives an engagement, guaranteed by Allah and his Prophet, that nothing will be changed in the position of him [the Visigoth noble Theodimir] and his; that his right of sovereignty will not be contested; that his subjects will not be killed, nor reduced to captivity, nor separated from their children and wives; that they will not be burned, nor **despoiled** of their holy objects; and that this will hold good as long as they satisfy the charges we impose ... he will not give **asylum** to any person who has fled from us or is our enemy, nor injure anyone who enjoys our **amnesty**, nor keep secret information about the enemy from falling into his hands.

WHAT DO YOU THINK?

1. Why might the Moors have chosen not to persecute non-Muslim inhabitants of Spain?

2. In pairs, examine the treaty of peace between the Moors and the Visigoths. Are the conditions reasonable? What sort of attitude on the part of the treaty writers do the conditions reflect? Would you make any changes to the document? Why? Share your findings with the rest of the class.

not forcibly **convert** the inhabitants of Spain to Islam. At this time, Spain was a primarily Christian country, with a large minority of Jews. Under the Arabs, the non-believers were allowed to worship as they chose.

The Arabs soon conquered the whole Iberian Peninsula. They made the city of Cordoba the capital and they governed in the name of their caliph in Bagdad.

SPAIN UNDER THE UMAYYAD CALIPHATE

In 756, Abd-al-Rahman of the Umayyad Caliphate in Damascus crossed North Africa and landed in Spain. He defeated the local Arab governor and established himself as the leader of the Spanish territory. He and his descendants would rule Spain for the next three centuries.

Like the earlier Arab conquerors, the Umayyad rulers were careful to encourage, but not to enforce, conversion to Islam. In time, many Christians did convert to Islam, but some did not.

AN EXPANDING SOCIETY

The new rulers were also interested in creating a sense of **national identity**. For this reason, they began construction of a large mosque at Cordoba, located on the Guandalquivir River. As you have learned, a mosque is more than a place of worship—it is also a centre of learning. Eventually the area surrounding the Mosque of Cordoba became the centre of the city, surrounded by many schools and a marketplace. By the tenth century, Cordoba was the largest city in Europe, with a population of some 400 000 people. One library contained several hundred thousand volumes. Many prominent citizens, following

their ruler's example, also built personal libraries.

For many years, Arabic had been the language of **scholars** in Spain, and people were encouraged to learn it for that reason. However, it did not become the everyday language of the people. They continued to speak Romance, the local form of Latin that had been used before the arrival of the Arabs. This language was understood by Christians, Muslims, and Jews in Spain.

There were also developments in ways of governing. The Moors created two new offices in Spain. The *hajib* acted as a chief bureaucrat on behalf of the caliph. He supervised less important officials who had responsibility for the army, finances, taxation, and the management of the royal household. Justice was provided by another official, who was expected to be both fair and impartial. This official provided

Figure 10–2 The mosque at Cordoba (below). Inside there are 106 pillars supporting the archways. You can also see the expansive area used for prayer.

civil: having to do with citizens

mercury: a silver-white metal that is liquid at room temperature

rulings based on both Islamic law and local laws governing **civil** matters, and was also responsible for the police force.

When Abd-al-Rahman III came to power in 912, he accepted and encouraged non-Muslims, and gave Christians and Jews positions of power and influence in his government.

Abd-al-Rahman III also built a magnificent palace outside Cordoba—Madinat al-Zahra. It was constructed by some 10 000 workers. The centrepiece was a reception hall that was dominated by a pool of **mercury**, which gave off a shimmering light that brightened the hall.

LINK-UP

The "Modern" City of Cordoba

By the end of the ninth century, everyday life in Cordoba was characterized by two themes—prosperity and enlightenment.

Around 825, an inventor and thinker known as "Ziryab" came to Cordoba from Baghdad. Ziryab was the "Miss Manners" of his time. He recommended that the formal sequence of a meal should consist of soup, followed by **entrées** of meat, and then dessert—a sequence still followed by many people today. He thought that drinks should be served in glasses rather than metal goblets for reasons of cleanliness. He even introduced toothpaste to the Cordobans.

Ziryab was also keenly aware of fashion. Have you or your family members ever shopped for a "fall" or "spring" wardrobe? Ziryab was one of the first to suggest that people wear different wardrobes according to the seasons of the year.

During this time, most people of Cordoba lived in houses on paved streets. Their homes were austere but beautiful, and were constructed according to an inward-facing plan. The outer walls of the house had no windows or other openings, except the main entrance. Inside, however, there was an open courtyard that contained plants and fountains—a mini-oasis around which the family could relax and engage in contemplation. While private homes did not have indoor plumbing, there were several hundred public baths in the city. These baths were also used for **ritual** bathing by all devout Muslims.

Tradition dictated that the woman ran the household, but many women also worked outside the home. Some went to university while others worked as **copyists** of Greek and Arabic manuscripts, which were in great demand at local libraries. Men also spent a great deal of time away from the home. They worked in Cordoba's 100 000 shops, went to the mosque to pray, and chatted with other men. Whether the subject was science, philosophy, or literature, it seemed as though there was no shortage of ideas—or of lively discussion.

Cordoba was truly one of the great cities of all time.

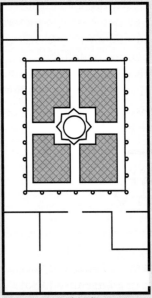

Figure 10–3 This diagram shows the floor plan of a typical Moorish house in Spain. Locate the doorway. Why would the courtyard be situated as shown?

NOW YOU DO IT

1. Make a list of the innovations in manners introduced in Cordoba in the ninth century. What impact do you think these guidelines have had on your day-to-day life?

2. Find out the size of Cordoba's population today. How does it compare with its population in the tenth century? After you finish this chapter, make a list of factors that might have contributed to this change.

3. Describe a modern equivalent to the explosion of Cordoban interest in books.

entrée: the main course of a meal

ritual: solemn, ceremonial

copyist: one who makes written copies

IMPROVEMENTS TO FARMING

When the Moors arrived in Spain, they were impressed by its rich agricultural resources. They compared it to Paradise as described in the Qur'ân. Over the centuries, they made a number of improvements to farming practices.

The Romans had been in Spain since 150 B.C.E. and had built **aqueducts** to deliver water for irrigation. The Muslims repaired and extended the Roman system of water delivery. This was especially necessary in the semi-dry areas of central Spain, where crops needed to be watered regularly. The Moors also used water wheels to scoop water from streams and irrigation canals onto the fields. Many new plants were introduced to Spain from the Arab world at this time. These would not have survived without improvements to irrigation. Some of the new crops were pomegranates, sugar cane, bananas, coconut palms, maize (corn), and rice.

Where the land was steep—along parts of the coastline and in the Sierra Nevada—the Moors introduced terraced farming. Terracing of land involves packing the soil into stepped levels, or terraces. The levels are held together by rocks and gravel. Together,

Figure 10–4
These soldiers' quarters from Madinat al-Zahra still remain.

aqueduct: a structure for moving large quantities of water

the terraces resemble a staircase. Terracing increases crop yields by increasing the amount of flat land. It also allows the farmer to control irrigation because each layer of terracing can be watered individually.

DID YOU KNOW?

Spanish names for certain foods are very similar to the Arabic word. For example, the Spanish word for rice is "arroz"; the Arabic word is "al-ruz."

Figure 10–5
Because much of Spain is quite steep and rocky, the Moors built extensive terraced fields in order to produce a bigger yield from the land. This photograph shows the village of Trevelez in southern Spain surrounded by its terraced fields.

ACTIVITIES

1. Give two examples of how the Umayyad rulers attempted to create a sense of national unity among the different peoples they ruled.

2. Create a sketch of the "downtown core" of Cordoba as you imagine it. Place the Mosque of Cordoba at the centre. Use the information on pages 315–16 to create your sketch. Label the mosque, library, schools, marketplace, and include at least one street with private homes.

3. It could take several years to make one copy of a manuscript in tenth-century Spain. What effect would this have on people's attitude to books and learning?

4. How did terracing and irrigation increase the effeciency of agricultural production in Spain? Draw a diagram of a terraced field and label it, using the information and photograph found above.

SOUTHERN SPAIN AND THE RECONQUISTA

Figure 10–6 This map shows how Spain was divided up in the middle of the eleventh century. How many kingdoms can you spot? What could result from having so many rulers in such a small area?

By the early 1000s, the **caliphate** in Spain had begun a period of decline. A series of ineffective rulers had led to a period of civil unrest and the sectioning of the countries into a number of independent **principalities**. The loss of a unified Muslim state led to much quarrelling among local leaders. It also led to the beginning of an event that would gather force over the next 200 years.

When the Moors had come to Spain, they had reduced the Christian-controlled areas to a narrow strip along the northern coast. Now these areas began to expand southward. The Christians called this expansion

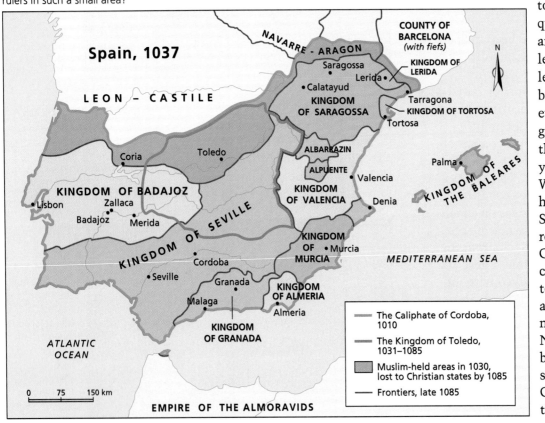

The Poetry of Seville

Seville was one of the most culturally advanced Spanish principalities. By the middle of the eleventh century, Seville controlled much of southern Spain, including Cordoba. It was governed by a series of well-educated rulers who did much to encourage the development of the arts and sciences.

The poets of this region have been credited with the refinement of rhyming poetry. The common form in Seville (and in other cities) was the **rhyming couplet**, with the rhyme scheme of AA, BB, CC, DD, and so forth. Many poems were team efforts. One writer would create the first

half of a couplet and another writer would complete it.

Here is a couplet by Emir al-Mu'tadid:

> The wind scuffs the river and makes it chain mail

PRIMARY SOURCE

… completed by his wife, Rumaykiyya:

> Chain mail for fighting could water avail.

the **Reconquista** because they were bringing Muslim areas under Christian rule once more. The Reconquista would eventually become a religious war. In the beginning, however, it was a way for the Christian kingdoms to expand their power and influence.

Castile was the most powerful of the Christian kingdoms in northern Spain. The Castilian kings wanted to control other principalities directly or, at the very least, obtain tribute funds from them. In 1085, after the principality of Toledo failed to pay tribute money, Alfonso VI of Castile decided to conquer the city. Other local leaders, fearing the Castilians would attack their territories, looked

Figure 10–7 Why would Toledo have been built at the top of this hill? What fortifications can you identify?

for a military power to assist them.

The Almoravids were conservative Muslims from West Africa. They wanted a return to religious purity and

The Legend of El Cid

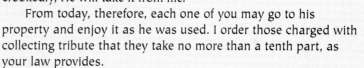

One of the most interesting characters of medieval Spain was Rodrigo Diaz de Viva (1042–1099). Popularly known as El Cid, he became known as a fine example of Christian **chivalry**—on a par with King Arthur and Charlemagne's great knight, Roland.

In fact, El Cid was a complex individual who has baffled historians. He was not just a crusading knight, but a Spanish **nationalist** who fought both with and against Muslims in Spain. His main enemies were the Almoravids. During the 1090s, he gained the reputation as the only soldier—Christian or Muslim—who could defeat the Almoravids.

In 1094, after a twenty-month siege, El Cid captured Valencia, the capital city of an important principality. The terms of surrender imposed on the inhabitants were not at all what one would expect from a crusading Christian knight, as you can see in the accompanying excerpt.

El Cid died in 1099. He was never defeated in any conflict, and the Spanish accorded him the title of *Campeador*, which means "winner of battles."

I am a man who never possessed a kingdom … but from the day I first came to this city, I set my heart on it…. Now, if I order its affairs justly and deal fairly, God will leave it in my hands; but if I deal ill, proudly or crookedly, He will take it from me.

From today, therefore, each one of you may go to his property and enjoy it as he was used. I order those charged with collecting tribute that they take no more than a tenth part, as your law provides.

I have further established that I shall judge your **suits** twice a week … but if any of your complaints are urgent, come to me on any day which you wish and I will hear you…. I wish to be for you both qadi who judges and vizier who governs; and when you quarrel, I will always see that justice is done.

Figure 10–8 This woodcut of El Cid shows him as a typical European knight. Is this the image you have of El Cid after reading about him?

chivalry: the qualities of an ideal European knight in the Middle Ages

nationalist: a person who believes in and identifies with his or her nation

suit: case

did not approve of religious tolerance. They began to expand their territories in the middle of the eleventh century. In the summer of 1086, the Almoravid army landed in Spain and defeated the forces of Alfonso of Castile near Badajoz.

Between 1090 and 1108, the Almoravids conquered all of southern Spain and Portugal, although they were unable to recapture Toledo. As the new rulers, they made several changes to the way that country was governed. Not all of these changes were popular. Christians, Jews, and **intellectuals** were **persecuted**, as a long tradition of religious tolerance came to an end. Works of art and literature that the Almoravids considered **decadent** were publicly

burned. Many Christians and Jews fled to the Christian north.

By 1172, the Almoravids in Spain had been replaced by a second wave of people from North Africa, known as the "Almohads." In July 1212, Alfonso VIII of Castile attacked the Almohad army at Las Navas de Tolosa. This battle marked the end of Moorish supremacy in Spain. The Almohad army was defeated and a new period of rule by independent principalities began again.

Between 1228 and 1264, the Reconquista gathered strength. The stronger Christian kingdoms conquered the independent principalities one by one. By 1264, only Granada remained in Muslim hands.

ACTIVITIES

1. How was classical learning preserved in Moorish Spain?

2. **a)** In a group, read the rhyming couplet from Seville aloud. Discuss it and try to reach a consensus as to its meaning. Share your findings with the rest of the class.

   b) With a partner, try the "make a poem" game. Write a couplet with a particular idea, but do not complete the thought. Your partner's task is to

provide the next two lines so that they finish the thought. Begin again, swithching roles. Post your four-line poems on the classroom bulletin board.

3. In an organizer compare the terms of surrender written by El Cid with the treaty between the Moors and the Visigoths (page 314). What are the broad similarities and differences?

4. Why do you suppose later Christian writers represented El Cid as a great Christian hero?

scholarship: learning

intellectual: one who is interested in knowing and understanding

to persecute: to harass to the point of injury

decadent: having or showing declining morals

SPAIN AFTER 1264

By 1264, most of Spain was in Christian hands. Landowners and the rulers of the principalities were the first to suffer losses. Large Muslim estates were given to high-ranking Christian soldiers as a reward for military service. Ordinary people such as farmers were allowed to work as before, but Jews and Muslims were

now subject to a special tax. Under Muslim rule, Christians and Jews had also paid a special tax.

During this period, many Muslims were agricultural workers or highly skilled artisans. These artisans had developed a way of making intricate tiles to decorate walls of Moorish buildings, both public and private. Spanish authorities continued

Figure 10–9 The technique for creating these decorative tiles was developed during the thirteenth and fourteenth centuries. Muslim artists also produced a new variety of ceramics that featured a **metallic glaze**.

to use these tiles as building materials during the thirteenth and fourteenth centuries.

Many Moors, especially those for whom Islam was important, eventually made their way to Granada. This principality became a **haven** for Muslim refugees. Outside of Granada, it became more difficult for Muslims to participate fully in society. In the late thirteenth century, more than 100 000 Muslim refugees from southern Spain flooded to Granada.

Granada survived mainly because of the **diplomatic** skills of its rulers. The first of these, Ibn-al-Ahmar, made an alliance with Ferdinand III of Castile. He became Ferdinand's vassal, and paid an annual tribute to him.

But Granada remained an Islamic land, isolated from the rest of Spain. Arabic, not Spanish, was its language. The **emir** of Granada, as the ruler came to be known, created and maintained a standing army, which operated under a strict code of conduct. One rule stated that the army was forbidden "to murder children, old people, invalids and the sick, and Christian **hermits** and **friars** not actually caught in armed aid to the enemy."

Granada survived for over 200 years. It eventually was attacked and overrun by its Christian neighbours at the end of the fifteenth century. This was the final episode of the Reconquista, which was now a religious war.

THE SPANISH INQUISITION

After the capture of so much Spanish territory by Christians in the thirteenth century, Muslims and Jews began to feel the sting of **discrimination**. Both groups were hard working and law abiding. They tended to keep to themselves and did not mingle much with their Christian neighbours. By the fourteenth century, they were required to wear distinctive clothing, perform certain jobs, and live in certain areas of cities. As the century progressed, many non-Christians were forced to convert to Christianity.

Figure 10–10 This engraving depicts the expulsion of the Jewish people from Spain. Can you determine how the artist viewed this event? What elements of the engraving guided your answer?

metallic glaze: a hard, glossy finish that contains and looks like metal

haven: place of safety

diplomatic: tactful and skilfull in dealing with people

emir: title of Muslim ruler

hermit: a person who lives alone in a secluded spot, sometimes for religious reasons

friar: a member of a religious order of brothers

discrimination: different treatment based on prejudice. Sexism and racism are examples of discrimination.

In 1474, the two major Spanish kingdoms, Aragon and Castile, were united with the marriage of Ferdinand of Aragon and Isabella of Castile. They decided that the new Spain should have a unifying religion—Catholicism. By 1485, the Spanish Inquisition had begun. Anyone could be investigated to determine the sincerity of their Catholic beliefs. Those who did not believe or who failed the investigation were burned at the stake. The Christian rulers also decided that no Christian should have any Moorish or Jewish ancestors.

to banish: to send away permanently

to expel: to force out

financier: one active in matters involving large sums of money

The Expulsion of the Jewish People

In 1491, Ferdinand and Isabella gave the Jews four months to accept baptism or be **banished** from Spain. Many Jews fled to Portugal, hoping for refuge, but they were quickly **expelled** from that country as well. (Portugal had gained independence from Spain in 1139.) More than 50 000 Jews accepted forced baptism. Another 160 000 left Spain forever to live in the Ottoman Empire (see page 323). Of these, more than 20 000 died on their journey east.

Jews in Spain had formed a large part of the educated middle class. Many were scholars, **financiers**, and business people. The loss of their skills made it difficult for Spain to maintain economic growth at the end of the fifteenth century.

The Expulsion of the Moors

Ferdinand and Isabella completed the Reconquista by conquering Granada in 1492. The Moors now had the choice previously offered to the Jews: convert or be exiled.

By 1526, there were—officially—no Muslims in Spain because the Moors were technically Christian. However, they continued to speak Arabic, primarily in Granada, and they continued to practise their religion in secret, as did many Jewish converts. Both groups lived in constant fear that they would be exposed to the Inquisition and burned.

By 1566, speaking Arabic or possessing Arab documents in Spain was forbidden. Between 1589 and 1614, all Moors were expelled from Spain, even those who had become Christian. It is estimated that some 300 000 were exiled. Southern Spain was hit especially hard. For many years after the explusion, once-rich farmland was abandoned because there were no knowledgeable farmers to work the land.

ACTIVITIES

1. Why did no great changes in the society of southern Spain occur in the years immediately after 1264?

2. The rulers of Granada maintained diplomatic relations with Ferdinand III, but did they have complete trust in their Christian neighbours? What is the evidence for your conclusion?

3. Imagine you are a Spanish Jew or Moor living in Spain in 1491. Although your life has been dominated by discrimination, you still have your family and your life savings. Your children do not want to move. What would you do under the circumstances? Provide reasons for your choice.

4. What was the social and economic impact of the expulsion of the Jews and the Moors on Spain? Give several concrete examples.

5. In a group, discuss possible options that Ferdinand and Isabella might have followed instead of the course they chose. Share your findings with the rest of the class.

THE OTTOMAN EMPIRE

THE OTTOMANS TO 1402

In this section, you will move eastward from Spain to Anatolia—what is now the modern nation of Turkey—and revisit the last days of the Byzantine Empire.

As you learned in Chapter 4, the Mongols under Chinggis Khan came to this region in the 1220s. As a result, two events occurred. First, the Seljuk Turks who lived there under their sultan became a **vassal state** of the Mongols. Second, many Turks decided they did not want to live under Mongol rule and moved into **frontier** area between the Byzantine Empire and Mongol territory. This area was mountainous and difficult to travel in, but it represented a haven for those groups seeking refuge from Mongol rule.

By this time, the Byzantine Empire was no longer as strong as it had been. It had been weakened by conflicts with the Seljuk Turks in the twelfth century, and had been severely damaged by the Crusades of 1202–1204. It could no longer recapture the territory it had lost to the Crusaders or to the Mongols, or even maintain its borders.

In order to gain territory from the Byzantines, the Turkish nomads declared war against the Byzantine Empire. There were many raids on Byzantine territory, and new Turkish principalities were formed between 1260 and 1320. In 1301, a Turk known as "Osman Gazi" defeated the Byzantine army at Baphaeon. He established the most important Turkish principality, which would eventually bear his name—the Ottoman Empire.

From the beginning, the Ottoman state permitted everyone to practise their religion freely and to follow their own customs. The only condition was that Christians and Jews must obey their Ottoman rulers and pay a special **poll tax** imposed by the state on all non-Muslims. The poll tax created much revenue and was collected primarily from the peasants and the townspeople.

vassal state: a state that is loyal to another state in return for protection

frontier: the margin of a settled country or region

poll tax: a fixed tax collected from each person

Figure 10–11 The Ottoman Empire in 1355

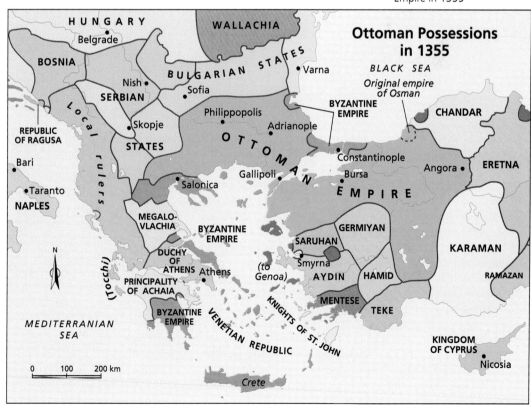

ISLAMIC SPAIN & THE OTTOMAN EMPIRE   **323**

In 1345, the Ottomans enlarged their state as far west as the Dardenelles, a strait between Asian and European Turkey. Sixteen years later, they captured Andrianpole, the second most important Byzantine city after Constantinople. Throughout their campaigns, the Ottomans maintained one attitude towards those they conquered. Communities that did not resist were allowed to remain as before. Communities that refused to submit were captured and the inhabitants expelled, leaving the Turks in charge.

The Byzantine Empire was by now a kingdom in name only. It lacked unity and consisted of a number of small, struggling principalities. The Ottomans, by contrast, were united and mindful of a common goal. They possessed the military and diplomatic skills needed to conquer the Byzantine Empire.

Between 1365 and 1395, the Ottomans took control of almost all of the Balkans as far north as the Danube River. They achieved a total military victory over some principalities. However, some local lords were permitted to keep their territories. In return, they were required to accept Ottoman overlordship, pay a small **tribute**, and provide military assistance as required. Sometimes the Ottomans

tribute: money paid regularly by one ruler or nation to another

elite: special, the best

rations: a specified amount of food supplies

to mutiny: to rebel

barracks: soldiers' living quarters

The Janissary Corps

Figure 10–12 Why would the Janissaries choose the cooking pot as a symbol of prosperity and power? Would a military corps be likely to choose this symbol today?

The Janissaries were an **elite** military unit used by the Ottomans to conquer the Balkans. They were the personal servants of the sultan. Their role was to protect him and his possessions—to the death, if necessary.

Only the most intelligent and physically fit were selected for the Janissary Corps. The corps quickly gained a reputation as an extraordinary fighting machine. In return for their service, the Janissaries were well paid (at a rate double that

of ordinary troops), and were provided for in their old age. In the beginning, they were not allowed to marry or possess property. In this way, they were similar to the Christian religious fighting orders.

Because they enjoyed a comfortable standard of living—much higher than that of other troops—their crest displayed a cooking pot and spoon. Their titles also reflected a preoccupation with cooking. Some official ranks were

"First Maker of Soup," "First Cook," and "First Carrier of Water." The most prized possession of each Janissary regiment was its enormous copper cooking pot. It was used routinely for the preparation of **rations**, and all soldiers in the regiment ate from it. However, if the Janissaries were displeased with the sultan's orders, or if they were not given sufficient military duties, they could **mutiny**. The signal for a mutiny was a ceremonial overturning of the cooking pot, indicating they no longer accepted the sultan's rations or his orders.

Originally a small force of about one thousand, the Janissaries grew rapidly in size. By 1600, they numbered some 50 000 men. As time went on, the corps included more Muslim volunteers because so many people had converted to Islam.

The Janissaries eventually established a permanent **barracks** in Constantinople, and were allowed to marry and possess both property and a craft, which they practised in times of peace.

would hold a vassal's son hostage and insist the vassal swear an annual oath of **allegiance**.

A New Civil Service

During a period of rapid expansion in the fourteenth century, the Ottoman Empire created a new **civil service**. Only Christian males who had been carefully selected on the basis of their intelligence and obedience were accepted. Known as **pages**, they moved to the sultan's palace, converted to Islam, and trained to perform specific tasks in government. The most physically fit were recruited into the Janissary Corps, which you read about in the Window on the Past and in the feature on page 324. Others trained to become **bureaucrats**, **administrators**, and religious officials.

Until the seventeenth century, most of the officials of the Ottoman Empire were converted Christians. As servants of the sultan, they enjoyed both prestige and power. Only Christians were permitted to join the civil service because their religious conversion forced them to cut off ties with their relatives. In this way, they could not pass on any special privileges to their families. "If Christian children accept Islam, they become **zealous** in their faith and enemies of their relatives," said one observer.

Improvements to the Empire

Before the Ottomans conquered the Balkans, the area had been divided into a number of small kingdoms that operated under a feudal system. Peasants were tied to the land, and provided several days of labour every week for their feudal lord. The Ottomans reformed this system by creating a centralized administration. Land was distributed to soldiers in the sultan's army. However, this land was still technically under the sultan's control. Peasants were now required to provide three days labour every year to the *sipahi*, soldiers granted land by the sultan. The peasants were protected from unfair treatment by law, which was enforced by a judge who was appointed by the central government. As a result, conditions for most of the general population under the Ottomans improved considerably.

As the empire expanded, the Ottomans repaired and extended the system of old Roman roads in both Anatolia and the Balkans. These roads were needed to move the Ottoman army and to transport goods. By the sixteenth century, the usual travel time between Belgrade and Constantinople was a mere four weeks. A similar distance in western Europe during the same period took at least two months to cover. The Ottomans improved communications by building stone bridges across the many rivers in the Balkans. An especially fine example was the bridge at Mostar in Bosnia, which was virtually destroyed in the recent war in the Balkans (1991–95).

The sultans also created an extensive system of **hostels** to ensure travellers' safety and comfort. These were actually charitable institutions. The sultan would often grant estates to his officials on the condition that they build hostels on the land. These estates were exempt from taxation and they often became the focal point of new Turkish villages. Travellers were entitled by law to three free nights of lodging— after that, they were expected to be on their way.

allegiance: loyalty

civil service: body of government workers

page: young men who train while serving the sultan

bureaucrat: an official in a government department

administrator: one who oversees day-to-day affairs

zealous: enthusiastic, earnest

hostel: a reasonably priced or free accommodation for travellers

Figure 10–13 The bridge at Mostar, built by the Ottomans in the fourteenth century. How do you think the local inhabitants felt when the bridge was destroyed during wartime in the 1990s?

1. Examine Figure 10–11 on page 323. Locate the original Ottoman Empire founded by Osman. Why did the location of their territory give the Ottomans an advantage over the other Turkish principalities?

2. What steps did the Ottomans take to make their control of newly conquered territory more secure?

3. Imagine you are a farmer living in the Balkans in the fourteenth century. Would you welcome the Ottomans as your new rulers? Why or why not? In a poem, poster, or letter, express your feelings to other people not yet under Ottoman control.

4. How did the Ottomans improve land transportation and communication in their empire? Why were these measures necessary?

5. Why was it essential for the sultan to have loyal civil servants? Why did the sultans not select Muslims for positions of trust? What is your opinion of this practice?

6. How did the Janissary Corps change as time went on?

THE OTTOMAN EMPIRE, 1402–1566

In the Window on the Past, you read about the young ruler Mehmed II. He was responsible for the expansion of the Ottoman Empire during the mid-fifteenth century. His army captured Constantinople in 1453, thereby ending the Byzantine Empire.

Mehmed was determined to make this city his new capital because it was the most important and centrally located city in the region. After he captured it, he renamed it Istanbul.

Mehmed kept the Ottoman Empire in a state of continual war. He fought and defeated the other Turkish principalities. In the Balkans, he established the Ottoman frontier along the Danube. Because of his success in gaining territory, he earned the title "The Conqueror."

Figure 10–14 Areas that the Ottomans controlled in 1481

Ottoman Possessions in 1481

Unfortunately, Mehmed's conquests resulted in political and economic chaos within the Ottoman Empire. By the time of his death, the Janissaries were close to mutiny because they were required to fight more or less all the time. In order to pay for his campaigns, Mehmed increased taxes. He also seized freehold land in Anatolia, which angered the people who owned it.

THE EMPIRE EXPANDS

Mehmed's successor was Bayezid II (1481–1512). He was concerned with tightening central control and restoring security within the empire. His son, Selim I, was more interested in expansion. Selim attacked the Mamluks in Egypt. Next, he conquered Syria, Palestine, Egypt, and, most importantly, Arabia. Arabia was close to Selim's heart because it was home to the Muslim holy cities of Mecca and Medina. The Islamic officials in Mecca recognized Selim as caliph—the protector of the entire Islamic world. At the end of Selim's reign, in 1520, the Ottoman Empire was one of the most powerful empires the world has ever known.

Selim's son, Sulieman I, ruled from 1520 to 1566. Sulieman began his reign by attacking Hungary—his most powerful adversary. In August 1526, the Ottoman and the Hungarian armies met on a plain between a range of low hills on one side, and the marshes of the Danube River on the other. The battle was a decisive victory for the Ottomans. They massacred the Hungarian infantry, and took no prisoners.

Three years later, Sulieman decided to attack Vienna and conquer Austria. Despite losing many large cannons in the swamps along the Danube, the Ottoman army eventually reached Vienna and attacked it. However, the loss of cannons (combined with several unsuccessful attempts to blow up the city walls) forced the Ottomans to retreat. This marked the end of Sulieman's efforts to conquer Austria.

European Alliances

After 1530, the Ottomans were ready to enter into **alliances** with other European nations to secure their power. The most powerful European states at this time were France, Spain (under the rule of the Hapsburg family), and Austria (under the rule of another branch of the Hapsburgs). Eventually, the Ottomans and the French became allies against Austria.

Through their alliance, the French and the Ottomans were able to maintain their relative positions against the Hapsburgs. The Ottomans strengthened their hold on Hungary and their other territories in the Balkans, and the French received special trading rights within Ottoman territory. By the time the "great sultan" Sulieman I died in 1566, the empire was still one of the world's great powers.

alliance: a group of people or nations who co-operate for mutual benefit

Figure 10–15 The Ottomans were the first to use artillery as an effective means of destroying city walls and fortresses. In this painting, gunpowder smoke is clearly visible around the walls of Vienna. However, as the Ottomans moved through the holes created by the blasts, the Viennese placed all their available cannons and muskets on the other side of the gap.

YENI SARAY: THE HEART OF THE EMPIRE

When Mehmed II captured Constantinople, he set aside one area of the city as the site of his new palace. The palace, known as "Yeni Saray" (new palace), was built between 1459 and 1466. It would remain the centre of Ottoman power for the next 400 years.

Yeni Saray, sometimes called "Topkapi," is an example of the complexity of the Ottoman system of governing. Refer to the plan of the palace below and the accompanying photographs, and take a tour of the heart of the empire. (The palace complex is so large that only the area beyond the Middle Gate is shown in the plan.) Remember that the sultan was technically an absolute ruler, with the power of life and death over his subjects. The purpose of the palace was to enhance his greatness and majesty.

The palace complex was bounded by a stone wall some 12 metres high. Its **battlements** were patrolled day and night by Janissaries. The point of entry from the rest of the city was the heavily guarded Imperial Gate, which led to the enormous First Court, an open space about the size of fifteen football fields. Any person was entitled to enter the First Court. On great occasions, many thousands gathered there.

The First Court included stables, barracks, and craft shops. One thousand gardeners laboured to keep the vast gardens in perfect order. Visitors to the First Court were always struck by its silence despite its size and the large number of people within it.

At the far side of the First Court was another high wall. In it was the Gate of Salutation, which led to the Second Court. The Second Court was designed to be an earthly paradise of beautiful and rare plants. Fountains dotted its expanse, and neatly trimmed paths led to the various parts of the inner palace. Few people from outside the palace were ever permitted to enter the Second Court—it was reserved for the sultan and his high officials.

On one side of the Second Court was the Hall of the **Divan**, with its polished and pointed roof. Here the sultan consulted with his officials, who would move—in a dignified procession from the First Court—several times each week. The sultan did not always make himself visible. He could choose to remain behind a screened window in the Hall in order to make himself seem more powerful.

battlement: a low wall or fortification with open spaces for shooting

divan: a royal room or court

bliss: a state of pure happiness

to depose: to remove from the throne

Figure 10–16 Part of the plan of Yeni Saray showing the area of the palace beyond the Middle Gate

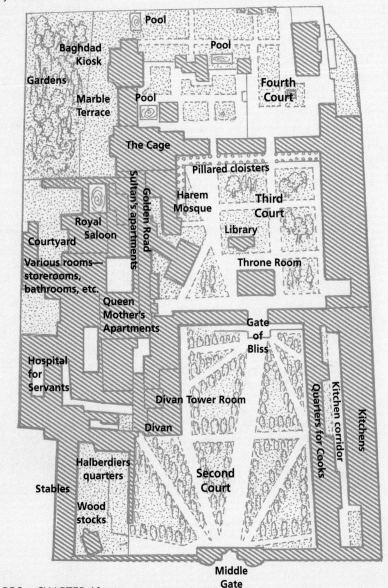

Pool
Pool
Baghdad Kiosk
Gardens
Fourth Court
Marble Terrace
Pool
Pool
The Cage
Pillared cloisters
Sultan's apartments
Harem Mosque
Third Court
Golden Road
Library
Royal Saloon
Courtyard
Throne Room
Various rooms—storerooms, bathrooms, etc.
Queen Mother's Apartments
Gate of Bliss
Hospital for Servants
Divan Tower Room
Divan
Kitchen corridor
Quarters for Cooks
Kitchens
Halberdiers quarters
Stables
Second Court
Wood stocks
Middle Gate

At the far side of the Second Court was the Gate of **Bliss**. This led to the inner world of the sultan. Three thousand people had personal contact with the sultan, including the pages being trained for government positions and their teachers, the sultan's bodyguards and personal servants, and the sultan's family members and their servants.

The mother of the sultan had a great deal of power and was entitled to her own secretary. She would often have great influence over the sultan and the princes. During the seventeenth century, there were instances of sultans being **deposed** by the sultan's mother in favour of one of her grandsons.

The inner world of the sultan was seldom entered by outsiders—it was known as forbidden territory. The sultan's family members, including the royal princes, were confined to a relatively small space—probably not much larger than a medieval monk's cell. But the sultan enjoyed extensive and luxurious quarters. He had his own mosque, a personal library, and his own parklike gardens, which extended to the shores of the Bosporus.

Figure 10–17
The sultan's library was located safely behind the Gate of Bliss.

Figure 10–18
A fountain near the sultan's library

ACTIVITIES

1. Imagine you are a citizen in the Ottoman Empire at the time Bayezid II became sultan. You could be a sipahi, a Christian farmer, a Jewish merchant, or an official of the sultan. In a letter, tell Bayezid what steps you feel he should take to improve life in the Ottoman Empire.

2. Why did Selim I's conquest of Arabia add greatly to the prestige of the Ottoman Empire?

3. In a group, do a PMI on the military campaigns of Sulieman I. Think about what the Ottomans wanted when you label information Plus or Minus. Would your PMI look different if you considered the situation from the standpoint of the Hungarians or the Viennese? Why or why not?

4. You are a citizen of Vienna in 1529. In a poem, poster, or letter, describe what you witness during the Ottoman siege of your city. You will need to examine the text on page 327 and Figure 10–15 for details.

5. How did the sultans use the layout of their palace to emphasize their power? Examine Figure 10–16 and identify the rooms near the palace exterior and those in the interior. How are these locations related to the prestige of the occupants?

6. As the sultan's mother, draw up some guidelines—including some do's and don't's—for the sultan-to-be. Think about the ideal characteristics and duties of a sultan as you are creating your guidelines.

THE OTTOMAN EMPIRE IN DECLINE

Under Selim II, the Ottomans began their decline as a major power. The first major indication of this decline came with the great naval battle of Lepanto, which took place off the Greek coast in 1571. It was the last battle in which the galley ship took part. Two hundred and eight Venetian and Spanish vessels under the command of Don Juan of Austria defeated 230 Ottoman galleys. The Ottomans lost thousands of men and all but 30 of their ships because the European navies had developed a new kind of warship—the Ship of the Line—for which the galley was no match.

manoeuvrable: easy to handle skilfully

musketeer: a soldier armed with a gun

cavalry: soldiers trained to fight on horses

corruption: dishonesty, wrongdoing

inflation: an increase in the amount of money being circulated resulting in a decrease in its value

mercantilism: the theory that the economic interests of a nation as a whole are important

market: the people who would want to buy a product

AN ECONOMY IN TROUBLE

By now the Ottomans also had government and financial problems at home. The major wars of conquest were now over and the army needed to be downsized. The Janissary Corps, along with many salaried **musketeers**, replaced most of the non-salaried **cavalry**. The cavalry was put to work building and maintaining fortifications and roads.

The empire was faced with the problem of paying for an army dominated by Janissaries—all of whom expected salaries. It tried to solve this problem by seizing property held by landowners and renting it to tenant farmers. There was much **corruption** in this system, and in many cases the revenue from such lands never reached the treasury. In addition, positions within the civil service were now available to Muslims, who regarded this work as employment and were entitled to draw a salary.

There was one more financial worry—**inflation**. In the middle of the sixteenth century, there was a great influx of gold and silver into Europe. This wealth had been brought to Europe by the Spaniards, who had conquered the Americas and were raiding the treasures of the Aztec and Incan Empires. Inflation was a major problem. This effect was greatest in the Ottoman Empire. While gold prices in the empire stayed relatively stable, the value of silver, the principal currency, fell.

During the 1580s, prices for items paid for in silver doubled, and then doubled again. People on fixed incomes had their savings wiped out. By 1591, the value of the taxes the government collected was half what it had been in 1534 because all taxes were paid in silver. Between 1576 and 1600, taxes had been raised more than five-fold. The effect of all this taxation was rising unrest within the empire, especially among Christian subjects, who traditionally paid higher taxes than others.

The Ottoman attitude towards trade was also out of step with the trends of the European world. By the late sixteenth century, the European nations had turned to **mercantilism**, an economic system that encouraged exports and controlled imports to protect home industries. The Ottomans did the opposite. They continued to import goods but discouraged exports so as not to deprive their home **markets**. By 1600, the Ottomans had lost control over much of their external trade, and European merchants controlled the buying and selling of most commodities. The Ottoman Empire would last in name only until the twentieth century, but it was never to recover its glory days of the fifteenth century.

Inflation: A Problem in Every Age

Inflation was not only a problem in the ancient world. Cycles of inflation have existed ever since the invention of currency. The late 1980s, for example, was a period of great inflation. Inflation also occurred in North America during the 1920s.

But what is inflation? In one sense, inflation is merely the tendency of prices to rise over time. Ask an older relative what he or she paid for a candy bar back in Grade 8, and you will get the point.

More specifically, inflation means there is more money around than goods to buy. Consumers naturally compete with one another to buy things, so the prices go up—that's inflation.

Inflation often occurs during wartime because the industries that usually make consumer items are busy making weapons. There is then more money available to spend on a smaller pool of goods.

"Runaway" inflation occurs when the increase in available money is so great that there is a financial crisis. This is what occurred in the Ottoman Empire when there was a great increase in silver. In the twentieth century, runaway inflation occurred in Germany after World War One. The government could not finance its own spending by collecting taxes, so it printed so much extra money that people needed a suitcase of bills to pay for one loaf of bread. Now that's inflation!

Figure 10–19 Have you experienced inflation recently?

WHAT DO YOU THINK?

1. What are your own experiences with inflation since the time of your early childhood until today?

2. a) Ask an older member of your family what a chocolate bar cost forty years ago. Has the price of chocolate bars been affected by inflation? Explain.

   b) Track the price of a CD from today back to the time when CDs were first introduced to the marketplace. Has the price of CDs been affected by inflation? Why or why not?

ACTIVITIES

1. Why do you suppose the Ottomans continued to use the galley ship in the seventeenth century?

2. With a partner, investigate how technological changes affect the nature of warfare. You may wish to consider both changes in the period covered by this book and changes in warfare in this century. Create a poster to summarize your findings.

3. How did the activities of the Spanish in the Americas affect the economy of the Ottoman Empire?

4. With a partner, create suggestions on how the Ottomans could have lessened the effects of inflation on taxes. Share your findings with the rest of the class.

SUMMARY

Islamic culture in Spain from the eighth century to the fifteenth century had a significant impact on all of western Europe. The Moors in Spain created a tolerant and sophisticated society that, at its height, had all the flavour of a twentieth-century community.

The Moors modernized agriculture in the region by using irrigation and terracing. They made southern Spain one of the most productive agricultural regions in Europe. They also practised religious and intellectual toleration, encouraging men and women to engage in the pursuits that interested them. Indeed, respect for science and philosophy allowed Moorish scholars to translate and preserve much ancient learning that had been lost to Western Europe. When the Christians conquered Islamic Spain in the eleventh century, this knowledge was carried to Europe and eventually contributed to the European Renaissance.

At the other end of the Mediterranean Sea, the Ottoman Turks rapidly expanded into territories ruled by older kingdoms, creating their own powerful empire by 1400. They were skilled at exploiting the weaknesses of other kingdoms, and used a central government to make their lands secure. They transformed feudalism into a system that favoured the ordinary person. They recruited Christians into their ranks as public servants, making some of them the finest soldiers in Europe.

Unfortunately, their system was not very adaptable to the rapid changes occurring in Europe and other parts of the world in the later sixteenth century. By not keeping pace with technological advances and new ideas about nations' economies, the Ottomans gradually declined in power. Their empire came to an end in the twentieth century.

SUMMARY ACTIVITIES

1. Compare and contrast the architecture of Islamic Spain with that of the Ottoman Empire. What other culture had a great effect on the style of Ottoman architecture?

2. The rulers of Islamic Spain and the Ottoman Empire exhibited tolerance towards other cultures in their realms. Discuss how this practice helped strengthen both empires.

ON YOUR OWN

1. Find out more about the development of music and dance in southern Spain. You could begin by looking up the word "Flamenco."

2. What Moorish sites still exist in southern Spain? Create a travel brochure that encourages Canadians to visit one or more sites.

11 INDIA: SURVIVAL OF THE SPIRIT

CHAPTER OUTCOMES

In this chapter, you will study the ancient civilization of India from the time of its origin in the Indus River valley around 2500 B.C.E. You will also learn about the long lasting impact of the Muslim conquest of India beginning in the tenth century. By the end of the chapter, you will

- describe the geographical conditions that affected India's history
- describe important periods in India's history
- demonstrate an understanding of India's major religions
- analyze information in charts
- summarize an episode from a classic of Indian literature
- identify important differences between northern and southern India
- make a pie graph

The Battle Between Rama and Ravana

PRIMARY SOURCE

This selection comes from a modern version of the Ramayana *by R.K. Narayan, one of India's most famous modern writers. The original Ramayana was composed as an epic poem over 2000 years ago in Sanskrit, the ancient language of India. It has 24 000 verses, and tells the story of Rama, who is the* **reincarnation** *of the god* **Vishnu***.*

The Ramayana is one of the most important stories in Asia. Its episodes are well known by people from India to Indonesia, and are featured in the art, drama, song, and dance of many lands. In this excerpt, Rama fights Ravana, the monster-like ruler of Lanka, who has kidnapped Rama's wife, Sita. Rama is aided by the monkey army of the wise monkey god, Hanuman.

Sita is kidnapped by Ravana, the enormous ruler of Lanka.

Every moment, news came to Ravana of fresh disasters in his camp. One by one, most of his commanders were lost. No one who went forth with battle cries was heard of again. Cries and shouts and the wailing of widows of warriors came over the chants and songs of triumph that his **courtiers** arranged to keep up at a loud pitch in his assembly hall.

Ravana became restless. He left the hall and climbed a tower from which he could obtain a full view of the city. He surveyed the scene below but could not stand it. One who had spent a lifetime in destruction now found the **gory** spectacle intolerable. Groans and wails reached his ears. He noticed how the monkey army seemed to revel in their handiwork. This was too much for him. He felt a terrific rage rising within him, mixed with some admiration for Rama's **valour**. He told himself, "The time has come for me to act by myself."

He hurried down the steps of the tower, returned to his chamber, and prepared himself for the battle. He had a ritual bath and performed special prayers to gain the **benediction** of **Shiva**. Then he donned his battle dress—armour, armlets, and crowns. He had on a protective armour for every part of his body. He **girt** his sword belt and attached to his body **accoutrements** for protection and decoration.

When he emerged from his chamber, his appearance was breathtaking. He summoned his chariot, which was drawn by horses or could move on its own if the horses were hurt or killed. People stood aside when he came out of his palace and entered his **chariot**. "This is my resolve," he said to himself. "Either Sita or my wife, Mandodari, will soon have cause to cry and roll in the dust in grief. Surely before this day is done, one of them will be a widow."

. . . .

Meanwhile, Rama fastened his sword, slung two **quivers** full of rare arrows over his shoulders, and climbed into the chariot.

The beat of the war drums, the cries of soldiers, the trumpets, and the rolling chariots created a deafening noise. While Ravana instructed his charioteer to speed ahead, Rama very gently ordered his chariot driver, Matali: "Ravana is in a rage. Let him perform all the antics he desires and exhaust himself. Until then, be calm. You must strictly follow my instructions. I will tell you when to drive faster."

Rama's army cleared and made way for Ravana's chariot, unable to stand the force of his approach. Ravana blew his **conch**, and its shrill challenge **reverberated** through space. Then Matali picked up another conch, which was **Indra**'s, and blew it. This was the start of the actual battle.

Next, Ravana sent a shower of arrows on Rama. Rama's followers, unable to bear the sight of his body being studded with arrows, **averted** their

Rama's friend and ally, Hanuman

335

Ravana prepares for battle.

heads. The chariot horses of Ravana and Rama glared at each other in hostility. The flags topping the chariots, which displayed the crests of Ravana and Rama, clashed. Ravana continued to send a shower of arrows at Rama but they were neutralized by the arrows from Rama's bow, which met arrow for arrow. In the end, Ravana used ten bows with his twenty arms, multiplying his attack tenfold. But Rama stood unhurt. Ravana suddenly realized that he should change his tactics. He ordered his charioteer to fly the chariot up in the skies. From there he attacked and destroyed a great many of the monkey army supporting Rama. Rama ordered Matali: "Go up in the air. Our young soldiers are being attacked from the sky. Follow Ravana, and don't **slacken**."

There followed an **aerial** pursuit at dizzying speed across the dome of the sky and the rim of the earth. Ravana's arrows came down like rain— he was bent on destroying everything in the world. But Rama's arrows diverted, broke, or neutralized Ravana's. Terror-stricken, the gods watched this pursuit.

Presently Ravana's arrows struck Rama's horses and pierced the heart of Matali. The charioteer fell. Rama paused for a moment in grief, undecided as to his next step. Then he recovered and renewed his offensive. At that moment the divine eagle Garuda was seen perched on Rama's flagpost, and the gods who were watching felt that this could be an **auspicious** sign.

After circling the globe several times, the duelling chariots returned, and the fight continued over Lanka. It was impossible to be very clear about the location of the battleground as the fight occurred here, there, and everywhere. Rama's arrows pierced Ravana's armour and made him wince. Ravana was so insensible to pain that this wince was a good sign. The gods hoped that this was a turn for the better.

But at that moment Ravana suddenly changed his tactics. Instead of merely shooting his arrows, which were powerful in themselves, he also invoked several **supernatural** forces to create strange effects. He was an **adept** at using various **asthras**, which were activated with special **incantations**. At this point, the fight became one of supernatural powers. Among the asthras sent by Ravana was *danda*, a special gift from Shiva, capable of pursuing and **pulverizing** its target. When it came flaming along, the gods were struck with fear. But Rama's arrow neutralized it.

Now Ravana said to himself, "These are all petty weapons. I should really get down to proper business." And he **invoked** the one called *maya*—a weapon that created illusions and confused the enemy.

With proper incantations and worship, he sent this

weapon. It created the **illusion** of reviving all the dead soldiers and returning them to the battlefield. This was very confusing and Rama asked Matali, also now revived, "What is happening now? How are all these coming back? They were all dead."

Matali explained: "In your original identity you are the creator of illusions in this universe. Please know that Ravana has created **phantoms** to confuse you. If you make up your mind, you can **dispel** them immediately." Matali's

explanation was a great help. Rama at once invoked a weapon called *gnana*, which means "wisdom" or "perception." This was a very rare weapon, and he sent it forth. All the terrifying armies suddenly evaporated into thin air.

Ravana now sent his deadliest weapon—a **trident** endowed with extraordinary destructive power. It came flaming on towards Rama, its speed or course unaffected by the arrows he flung at it.

When Rama noticed his arrows were ineffective against

the trident, he lost heart for a moment. When it was near, he uttered a **mantra** from the depth of his being. While he was breathing out that incantation—a syllable in perfect timing—the trident collapsed.

Ravana was now weakening in spirit. He realized that he was at the end of his resources. All his learning and equipment in weaponry were of no **avail**, and he had nearly come to the end of his special gifts of destruction.

Rama's spirit was soaring. The combatants were now near enough to grapple with each other. Rama realized that this was the best time to cut off Ravana's heads. He sent a crescent shaped arrow, which sliced off one of Ravana's heads, and flung it into the sea. But every time a head was cut off, Ravana grew another head in its place.

Now Rama had to consider how to bring this campaign to an end. After much thought, he decided to use Bramasthra, a weapon designed by the Creator Brahma. The Bramasthra was a gift to be used when all else failed. Now Rama invoked its fullest power and sent it in Ravana's direction, aiming at his heart rather than his head, because Ravana was vulnerable at heart. While Ravana had prayed for indestructibility of his heads and arms, he had forgotten to strengthen his heart. The Bramasthra entered and ended his career.

Rama watched him fall headlong from his chariot face down upon the earth. That was the end of the great campaign.

Ravana dies and is transformed.

Then he noticed that Ravana's face was aglow. The arrows had burned off the layers of anger, deceit, cruelty, lust, and egotism that had encrusted his real self. His true personality seemed to come through—of one who is devout and capable of tremendous achievements. His constant meditation on Rama, although as an **adversary**, now bore fruit. His face shone with serenity and peace. Rama noticed it from his chariot above and commanded Matali: "Set me down on the ground." When the chariot descended and came to rest on its wheels, Rama got down and commanded Matali: "I am grateful for your services to me. You may now take the chariot back to Indra."

reincarnation: rebirh of a human soul in a new body

Vishnu: the Hindu god known as "the preserver." Vishnu is thought to have many forms.

courtier: one who is in attendance at court

gory: bloody

valour: personal bravery

benediction: a blessing

Shiva: the Hindu god of fertility and destruction

to girt: to encircle with a belt to

accoutrements: equipment, trappings

chariot: a two-wheeled horse-drawn battle car

quiver: a case for holding arrows

conch: a spiral-shaped shell that can be used as a trumpet

to reverberate: to echo, to resound

Indra: the Hindu god who presides over the air

to avert: to turn away

ensign: a flag or banner representing a country, group, or organization

to neutralize: to make useless

to slacken: to slow down

aerial: in the air

auspicious: favourable

supernatural: above or beyond the natural

adept: expert

asthra: a supernatural weapon

incantations: the chanting of words that have spiritual power

to pulverize: to destroy, demolish

to invoke: to call forth by magic

illusion: a false idea

phantom: something that appears but has no physical being

to dispel: to scatter, drive away

trident: a three-pronged weapon

mantra: a word chanted as an aid to meditation

avail: use

adversary: opponent, enermy

ACTIVITIES

1. Why is Rama at war with Ravana?

2. Name the five spiritual weapons used by Rama and Ravana during the course of battle. Choose one weapon and illustrate its impact in a scene from the story.

3. What remarkable thing happens to Ravana at his death? What lesson about humanity is being communicated in this episode of the *Ramayana*?

4. Create a character sketch for Rama or Ravana. Use point-form notes to describe their physical and personal qualities, for example:
   – restless
   – angry but still admires Rama

TIME LINE

2500 BCE	BEGINNINGS OF THE INDUS CIVILIZATION
1500 BCE	START OF THE ARYAN INVASIONS
327 BCE	ALEXANDER THE GREAT INVADES INDIA
269 BCE	THE REIGN OF ASHOKA BEGINS
200 BCE	RAMAYANA AND MAHABHARATA EXIST
320 CE	GUPTA EMPIRE FOUNDED
405	FA-HSIEN ARRIVES IN INDIA
490	HINDU ASTRONOMERS KNOW THE EARTH IS ROUND
500	GUPTA EMPIRE DESTROYED
950	THE CHOLA DYNASTY CONTROLS SOUTH INDIA
1206	THE DELHI SULTANATE IS FOUNDED
1605	DEATH OF AKBAR
1627	RETIREMENT OF EMPRESS NUR JAHAN
1632	FOUNDATION LAID FOR THE TAJ MAHAL

I looked at the crescent moon
hidden behind the tamarisk tree outside my window.
As if the dear departed one is smiling
and playing hide-and-seek with me.

–RABINDRANATH TAGORE

These lines, from a poem entitled "Ungrateful Sorrow," were penned by India's most famous modern poet. What kind of mood has the author created with his image of the moon playing hide-and-seek? What line tells you that spirituality is an important part of Indian culture?

INTRODUCTION

India is one of the world's oldest civilizations. Its traditions and cultures have sustained its people through many invasions and foreign occupations. These traditions have also inspired many non-Indians. Indian religious beliefs, for example, have been adopted by people all over the world.

The study of India's past—its culture, traditions, and beliefs—is not easy. Hinduism, the principal religion, is ancient and complex. Further, India has been invaded many times, and each conqueror has left a mark. At the same time, a strong thread of Indian culture has lasted thousands of years, virtually unchanged by foreign influence. India is a land of **paradox**. Another of the

paradox: contradictions

world's great religions—Buddhism—was founded in India, and was once a powerful force there. Then it almost disappeared completely.

In this chapter, you will be introduced to India's long history, beginning with ancient civilization around the Indus River and ending with the Mughal age of the sixteenth and seventeenth centuries. No history of India would be complete without a look at India's Golden Age, when the Gupta family ruled in the north. It was during this period that many cultural traditions took firm root. You will also learn how India's geography influenced its past, and how India's religious traditions are still influential today.

THE INDIAN LANDSCAPE

The modern nation of India occupies most of a peninsula called the Indian **subcontinent**—also referred to as South Asia. Other countries of the subcontinent are Pakistan, Bangladesh, Nepal, and Bhutan. Off the southern tip of India lies the island nation of Sri Lanka.

subcontinent: a large land mass separated from a continent by geography

In the north, some of the highest mountain ranges in the world—including the Himalayas—divide the subcontinent from the rest of Asia. India has many other mountains, hills, and plateaus. The high, dry Deccan Plateau lies at its heart, protected by mountains called the Eastern and Western Ghats. North of the Deccan Plateau, the Vindhya Range cuts across India from west to east, and divides the North from the

South. This physical division has been an important factor in India's history.

Mountain barriers have made invasion difficult though not impossible. Moreover, the Indian coast has few good natural harbours. Consquently, until the arrival of the Europeans, beginning in the late fifteenth century, India was rarely threatened by invaders from the sea. Instead, conquerors, including Alexander the Great, from ancient Greece, came through the mountain passes and deserts of the northwest frontier. Although parts of India have been conquered—some many times—the entire subcontinent was never controlled by any one empire. The British, for example, controlled most of India by the nineteenth century but

Figure 11–1 The physical geography of India. Locate the Eastern and Western Ghats, and the Vindhya Range, on this map. Which parts of India would be protected from invasion by these mountain ranges?

monsoons: a seasonal wind

often governed through local rulers.

The Indian subcontinent is vast. The modern nation of India has an area of 3 287 590 square kilometres and is over 3000 kilometres long, from north to south. There are three major rivers—the Indus, the Ganges, and the Brahmaputra—and many smaller ones. The Indus and the Ganges form the Indo-Gangetic Plain, the subcontinent's richest agricultural area—and its most heavily populated. The coastal plains, on each side of the Eastern and Western Ghats, also provide fertile agricultural areas. India's rivers are very important for agriculture, but they often flood because of heavy seasonal rains caused by **monsoons.**

Figure 11–2 Floods bring devastation to India. Flood water not only destroys homes and lives, but also creates hazards for survivors. After a flood, drinking water is often unsafe. Do you know why?

THE CLIMATE OF INDIA

tropical: the hot climate typical near the equator, from the Tropic of Cancer to the Tropic of Capricorn

suptropical: The climate of the region that borders the tropical area

The climate of the subcontinent of India is **tropical** or **subtropical**. Most of India does not have winter and summer as Canada does. Seasons change as a result of monsoons, winds that bring in either moist or dry air.

The monsoons are very regular. They arrive at almost exactly the same time every year. Monsoons result from large differences in temperature among land, sea, and air. This variation occurs because land heats up and cools much faster than water.

In the summer, warm, moist air blows from the Indian Ocean towards Asia, bringing heavy rains. In the winter, cool winds flow from central Asia towards the ocean. Winter monsoons are not only cool but dry.

Throughout history sailing ships depended on the regularity of the monsoons. Farmers, of course, wait anxiously each year for the life-giving rains.

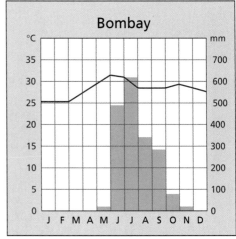

Figure 11–3 Examine the temperature and precipitation information given in this climagraph for the city of Bombay. By how many degrees does the temperature vary in one year? Why would it be easier to identify the seasons of Bombay by checking its precipitation rather than its temperature?

The Asian Monsoons

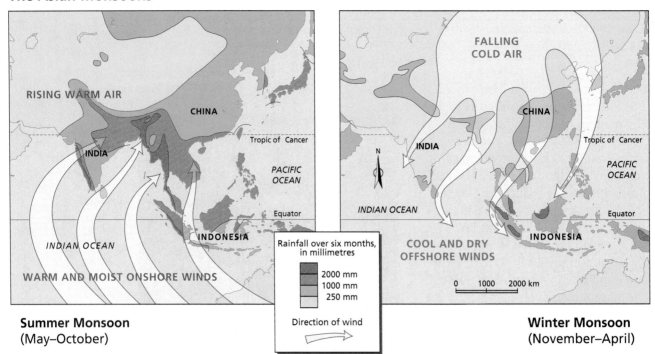

Summer Monsoon
(May–October)

Winter Monsoon
(November–April)

Figure 11–4 The monsoons are winds that blow regularly across the Indian subcontinent, and are the single most important influence on the climate. The summer monsoons bring rain; the winter monsoons bring dry air.

1. Calculate the length of the Ganges River.

2. Examine the physical map of India on page 341 and identify the most prominent physical features. Explain why the Deccan Plateau would be very dry.

3. Solve this puzzle. Hint: Think about the monsoons.

    a) First create a climagraph for the city of Madras, India, based on the following data. To review how to make a climagraph, see Chapter 4, page 109.

    Temperature data for Madras, India

month	J	F	M	A	M	J	J	A	S	O	N	D
C°	25	26	28	31	33	33	32	31	31	29	27	26

Precipitation data for Madras, India

month	J	F	M	A	M	J	J	A	S	O	N	D
mm	40	20	20	30	35	50	90	100	125	300	350	140

b) Now locate Madras, India, on the map shown in Figure 11–1. Keep your thumb on that page so you can refer back to it.

c) Compare the climagraph for Madras with the climagraph for Bombay shown in Figure 11–3. How are the two climagraphs different? Go back to Figure 11–1 and try to account for this difference by noting the respective locations of Madras and Bombay.

EARLY DEVELOPMENTS

India's history has deep roots. The earliest cities on the subcontinent were built in the Indus River valley, and were part of the Indus civilization (2500 B.C.E. to 1500 B.C.E.). The most famous of these cities are Harappa and Mohenjo-Daro (Mound of the Dead). Their **ruins** were discovered in 1921.

Archaeologists say that these ancient cities, built of brick, were home to large populations. This is not surprising. Like other ancient river valleys, the region had many advantages, including fertile soil, and water for irrigation and trade. The Indus people built streets, private homes, public baths, and shops. They also learned how to grow cotton and developed the first cotton textiles. They were probably in contact with the peoples of Mesopotamia, and the cities of Sumer and Ur. Very likely, there were important trade and cultural links between the two civilizations. Harappa and Mohenjo-Daro were abandoned more than 3000 years ago, and were forgotten until archaeologists rediscovered them.

THE ARYAN INVADERS

Archaeologists think that the great Indus civilization had begun to decline gradually but that the real blow occurred about 1500 B.C.E. At this time, a warlike people from west-central Asia—the Aryans—began arriving. This was one of a remarkable series of invasions that also sent Aryan tribes into Europe. In Europe, Aryans almost completely replaced the original inhabitants.

The descendants of the Indus Valley civilization fought with the Aryans but eventually retreated to the south. Known as Dravidians, they were able to establish southern kingdoms that would last, in various forms, for approximately 1800 years. The people who stayed in the North were assimilated by the Aryans.

The Aryans were fair-skinned and tall, living primarily as herders. They were originally **nomadic**, and devoted much of their energy to wars with other peoples and with other Aryan

ruins: what remains after decay or destruction

archaeologist: one who studies historic or prehistoric peoples and their cultures

nomadic: characteristic of peoples who travel from place to place according to the seasons

DID YOU KNOW?

Dravidian is still spoken today and is divided into four major languages, each with its own literature.

groups. They used chariots in battle, and were skilled archers. They had many gods, such as Agni, the god of fire, whom they worshiped and to whom they **made offerings**.

The Aryans developed **castes** for organizing the different functions of society—for example, warfare and agriculture—and for keeping the people they conquered under control. Castes at this point were not inherited. Under later empires, the caste system of India would become complex and **restrictive**.

The four original castes were: the *Brahman* (priest), *Kshatriya* (warrior), *Vaishya* (commoner), and *Sudra* (slave or non-Aryan). Some of the earliest traditions of the Aryans are recorded in books of hymns called the *Vedas* (knowledge). The excerpt (top left) from the ancient *Rig-Veda* illustrates how the Aryans viewed caste.

The second excerpt, also from the *Rig-Veda*, is part of a funeral hymn. It shows that war was important to the Aryans.

to make an offering: to give a gift as an act of worship

caste: a social group limited to persons of the same rank

restrictive: limiting, meant to control people's position in society

primal: first

to wield: to use, control

> When they split up the **Primal** Man, into how many parts was He divided? What represented his mouth, arms, thighs, and feet? The Brahmin was his mouth, the Kshatriya his arms, the Vaishya his thighs, and the Sudra were born from his feet.
>
>

> From the dead hand I take the bow he **wielded**,
> To gain us dominion, might, and glory.
>
>

The Aryan Language

The Aryan language, which is the ancestor of both the European and Indian languages, belongs to a language group known as Indo-European (see feature below). Aryans who occupied northern India used a language called "Sanskrit," which developed into modern languages such as Hindi and Punjabi. Although it is difficult for many of us to see the similarities between Punjabi (an Indian language) and English (a European language), a language specialist could spot many similarities. Both Punjabi and English belong to the same Indo-European language family—a family that includes more speakers than any other language family.

Figure 11–5 In a multicultural society, Urdu (left), English, and Punjabi (right) live side by side, as shown by this Canadian store sign.

Say What? The Indo-European Language Family

Sanskrit and most European languages belong to the same family. This means that they came from the same language "parent." As in all families, the closer the relationship, the more similarities you can see between the family members. See if you can find some family resemblances in this chart. You may find it helps to sound out the numbers.

Sanskrit	English	French	Latin	Punjabi
ek	one	un	unus	ikk
dwee	two	deux	duo	do
tree	three	trois	tres	trai
chatoor	four	quatre	quattuor	car
panch	five	cinq	quinque	panj

Make a Pie Graph

As you learned in Chapter 1, there are many ways of displaying statistics, or numerical facts. For example, you could create a table with columns for the numbers. Let's take the languages of modern India as an example:

Table 1
Modern Languages in India

Language	Number of Speakers (percentage)
Hindi	37.9%
Other	9.9%
Telugu	7.8%
Bengali	7.4%
Marathi	7.1%
Tamil	6.4%
Urdu	5.1%
Gujarati	4.8%
Kannada	3.9%
Malayalan	3.7%
Oriya	3.3%
Punjabi	2.7%

The only problem with a numerical table is that you must read all the numbers carefully before you have a sense of what is going on. There is a much quicker way of displaying information. You could create a bar graph, as you did in Chapter 1—or you could create a pie graph.

In a pie graph, each slice of the "pie" represents one item. Each slice is identified by a different shade of colour. The size of the pie slice tells the number story. For example, imagine that the whole pie represents 100 slices. The number of people who speak Punjabi would be represented by 2.7 slices.

The diagram at right shows how it would look.

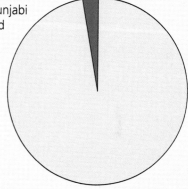

NOW YOU DO IT

1. Assign a shade of colour to each of the Indian language groups noted in Table 1.

2. Draw a circle. This represents your pie. In very light pencil, section your pie into quarters. Each quarter is worth 25 out of 100 slices. This will make it easier for you to draw the smaller pie pieces.

3. Colour the pie slice for the Hindi language first. It represents 37 out of 100. Compare your slice with that of a classmate. Are you on the right track? Now fill in the other slices.

4. Convert your pie graph into a bar graph, following the steps outlined on page 24. Which of the three ways—table, bar graph, or pie graph—do you prefer for displaying these numbers? Why?

5. What conclusions can you make about the modern languages in India?

NORTH AND SOUTH: EARLY EMPIRES

For centuries after the Aryans came to India, the country was made up of many rival kingdoms. Each kingdom had a different language and religion, though each was rooted in both Aryan and Dravidian traditions. These kingdoms were often at war with one another. Geography for the most part protected the south from invasion by outside conquerors. The Vindhya Range and the high, rocky Deccan Plateau made invasion of the south difficult. In addition, the Deccan Plateau is flanked on either side by the Eastern and Western Ghats, and it has many hard-to-reach places.

The northern region was more **vulnerable**. In 330 B.C.E., Alexander the Great was able to invade northern India. He claimed what is now Pakistan, and part of the Indus River valley. But this empire did not last long after. Alexander died in 323 B.C.E.

A new ruler, Chandragupta Maurya (325–184 B.C.E.), rose quickly to power. He was able to overthrow the ruler of Magadha, a northern **Hindu** kingdom. Once in power, Chandragupta attacked and **subdued** the whole of northern India. The Maurya Dynasty, which he founded, led one of the most powerful and important empires in the ancient world. Chandragupta established the capital at Pataliputra, one of the largest and most prosperous cities at that time.

Chandragupta ruled from a luxurious wooden palace. His week was carefully divided into sessions of ninety minutes each, during which he took care of state and personal business. According to legend, he gave up his throne for religious reasons, and eventually starved himself to death.

Ashoka

Ashoka (273–232 B.C.E.) was Chandragupta's grandson and the greatest of the Maurya rulers. He was also one of India's most interesting leaders. Under Ashoka, nearly all of India was brought together as one large empire. In one military campaign, against the kingdom of Kalinga, thousands and thousands of people were killed or wounded. This slaughter had a transforming effect on Ashoka. He converted to Buddhism, a religion you read about in Chapters 3 and 6, and which began in India several hundred years before Ashoka's birth. He came to believe that killing was deeply wrong. From that time on, Ashoka worked to make life better for the subjects of his empire.

Ashoka's officials improved villages and towns by ordering wells dug and trees planted. Free medical aid was also available. Ashoka was a merciful ruler who required that his officials also be kind. He even asked that people be kind to one another, in keeping with Buddhist ideals. Ashoka insisted on religious **tolerance**, and he supported the spread of Buddhism throughout India and beyond. Eventually he became a monk. After Ashoka's death in 185 B.C.E., the Maurya Empire began to wither. Centuries of war and disunity followed.

vulnerable: open to attack

Hindu: having to do with Hinduism. Hinduism was brought to India with the Aryans and developed through contact with the Dravidians.

to subdued: to suppress, conquer, control

tolerance: allowing beliefs and actions with which one does not agree

frugal: avoiding waste or unnecessary spending

go to law: sue people in court

A Greek ambassador described life during the Maurya dynasty as simple but prosperous.

They the people live happily enough being simple in their manners, and **frugal**. They never drink wine except at sacrifice.... The simplicity of their laws and their contracts is proved by the fact that they never **go to law**.... Truth and virtue they hold alike in esteem.... The greater part of the soil is under irrigation, and consequently bears two crops in the course of the year.... It is accordingly affirmed that famine has never visited India, and that there has never been a general scarcity in the supply of nourishing food.

PRIMARY SOURCE

Ashoka devoted himself and his government to the principle of *dharma*, a word that means "duty" in Buddhism. For Ashoka, dharma required him to prevent the killing of animals and the eating of meat, to practise and encourage religious tolerance, and to be like a kind and loving parent to his people. The ruler ordered the creation of **inscribed** pillars all over his empire. They recorded Buddhist texts, laws, and Ashoka's own ideas about life and justice. This excerpt is one **edict** on Ashoka's First Pillar of Law. Many of Ashoka's pillars still exist today.

For this is my principle;
To protect through Dharma
To administer affairs according to Dharma
To please the people with Dharma
To guard the Empire with Dharma

PRIMARY SOURCE

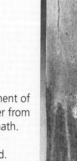

Figure 11–6 This fragment of an inscription is left over from an ancient pillar in Sarnath. Ashoka ordered many inscriptions to be carved.

INDIA'S GOLDEN AGE: THE GUPTA EMPIRE, 320–550

inscribed: with carved writing

edict: a decree, a public order

Tamil: a descendant of the Dravidians

After many centuries of upheaval, the Gupta Empire was founded by another ruler named Chandragupta. He dreamed of recreating the glory and stability of the Maurya Empire. By a series of manoeuvres, Chandragupta managed to have himself crowned Maharaja (king of kings) in the ancient capital of Pataliputra. Thus began a century-and-a-half of Gupta rule, during which great strides were made in Indian art, science, music, and literature. It is often called India's "Golden Age." The Guptas ruled the north but could never subdue the kingdoms of the Deccan Plateau or the Dravidian and **Tamil** kingdoms of the south. But the influence of Gupta art and science spread far beyond the borders of the empire.

THE GUPTA ECONOMY

India's economy in Gupta times was based on agriculture. Farmers lived in villages, as Indian farmers still do. Villages have always been very important in India. Villages are the home of extended families, and are

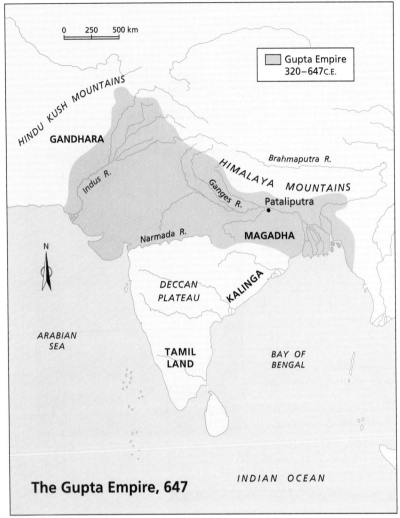

The Gupta Empire, 647

Figure 11–7 This map shows the extent of the Gupta Empire in the north of India in 647.

Artisans were well organized in Gupta India. Many belonged to specialized guilds known as *shreni* and produced cloth, pottery, and metalware. There were even guilds whose members were occupied solely with making special oils from palms and other plants. Members of each guild pooled their resources and shared in the profits, with more experienced members receiving a larger share. Because membership in a shreni was usually hereditary, people followed their parents into an occupation. Under a system similar to the European guild tradition you read about in Chapter 5, a worker started as an apprentice, then became an advanced student, then an expert, and finally a teacher. Teachers received four times as much of the profits as apprentices.

The Guptas were also traders and explorers. They carried on regular trade with China and even, indirectly, with the Romans. Indian art from this period has been found in Roman ruins, such as Pompeii. Indian ships under the Guptas sailed as far as China and Arabia.

micro-: very small

artisan: craftsperson

really **micro**-societies, each with its own place of worship and ways of doing things.

Farmers were taxed for part of their income, and the money went to the royal treasury. Most farmers paid the value of one fiftieth of their cattle and one sixth of their produce to the tax collectors. They also paid special water taxes if their lands were irrigated. **Artisans** were also taxed. But most of the wealth of the Indian states came from taxes paid by landowners and the people who worked the land. India's temples and priests were supported by offerings and fees, mostly from farmers, and by the produce of lands owned by individual temples.

Figure 11–8 This lovely terra cotta figurine depicting a musician was created by an artisan during the Gupta period.

Only the Right Hand...

Fa-Hsien was a Chinese monk who travelled widely through India about 400. Although his goals were to learn about Buddhism and make a pilgrimage, he also left a record of his impressions of Gupta India. In this excerpt, Fa-Hsien describes an orderly and relatively peaceful society. He also refers to the "untouchables."

The climate of this country is warm and **equable**, without frost or snow. The people are well off, without poll tax or official restrictions. Only those who **till** the royal lands return a portion of the profit of the land. If they desire to go, they go; if they like to stop, they stop. The kings govern without **corporal** punishment; criminals are fined, according to the circumstances, lightly or heavily. Even in cases of repeated rebellion they only cut off the right hand. The king's personal attendants, who guard him on the right and left, have fixed salaries. Throughout the country the people kill no living thing nor drink wine, nor do they eat garlic or onions, with the exception of the Chandalas [outcasts] only.

SOCIAL LIFE

As you have read, the Aryans brought the beginnings of the caste system to India. In the intervening years, more than 3000 castes developed, based on heredity and occupation. People were forbidden to marry outside their caste and their occupations in life depended solely on their caste. During the Maurya and Gupta Empires, the caste system gradually became even more restrictive. Now people of different castes were forbidden to socialize with one another, for example, to talk to one another, or to share a meal together. The "untouchables"—those with no caste (literally "outcast")—were completely isolated.

While earlier Aryan society provided some degree of freedom for women, female equality declined during the Gupta Empire. Women were sill permitted to own property, but they had fewer rights and opportunities than before. Higher caste Hindu women were increasingly **confined** to home. When they went outdoors, they were expected to be completely covered. Widows were **shunned** and many threw themselves on their husband's funeral fires rather than face a life of isolation. Sons were valued more than daughters because, by tradition, they looked after their parents when they were old. Only sons were permitted to perform sacred rituals.

INTELLECTUAL LIFE

Under the Guptas, intellectual life flowered in India. Large monasteries offered education not only in religion and philosophy but also in mathematics, physics, and languages. Gupta mathematicians invented the Arabic numbering system that we still use today. Some people say they invented the concept of zero. They were definitely the inventors of the decimal system. Both zero and the decimal system made the calculation of large numbers possible for the first time.

Gupta art, famous throughout the world, is mostly about religion. It shows Hindu and Buddhist **deities**, and important episodes in religious history. Some scenes are carved into the sandstone of cliffs and caves. These large works of art are dramatic and beautiful.

equable: uniform

till: cultivate

corporal: physical

confined: restricted

to shun: to avoid, to treat as a social outcast

deity: god or goddess

DID YOU KNOW?

In many instances, widows were expected to kill themselves by throwing themselves on the funeral fire so that they would not be a financial burden to the husband's family. Occasionally, the widow was thrown onto the fire.

DID YOU KNOW?

Today, there are so many museums in India that no one has been able to count them.

1. Create an illustrated time line for the early history of India beginning with the Indus Valley civilization. Review the previous section for key dates.

2. Name two aspects of culture that the Aryan invaders brought to India.

3. What great **revelation** did Ashoka have after the war against the kingdom of Kalinga? How did this revelation affect his government?

4. You are a Gupta tax official who has been transported forward in time to meet with officials at Revenue Canada. They want to hear about your tax system. Prepare some point form notes that will allow you to give a brief oral presentation. What aspects of your tax system will the modern Canadian officials find surprising?

5. In an organizer, compare the Gupta guild system with the European guild system described in Chapter 5 on pages 151–52.

6. Why was the discovery of zero so important?

revelation: something revealed

relevant: having meaning, significance

reborn: born again

meditation: silent prayer filled with concentration

yogi: one who practises yoga, a series of exercises that aid meditation

rigid: stiff, unchangeable

Figure 11–9 The greatest Hindu event—the Khumba-mela—is held once every three years at one of four sacred sites. Millions of worshippers move into the river to bathe and be blessed. The Khumba-mela celebrates the dropping of heavenly nectar to the earth.

THOUGHT AND BELIEF

India is the birthplace of Hinduism and Buddhism, and several other religions, including that of the Jains and the Sikhs. It also has communities of Christians, Jews, and Zoroastrians, known as "Parsees." Many people are drawn to India because it has such deep religious traditions. Great religious festivals, such as the Khumba-mela, attract millions of people today, as they have done for centuries.

Religion guides the lives of most of India's peoples. Every day millions perform *pujas* in homes and temples. A puja is a ceremony to honour a god or goddess with an offering. These ceremonies keep religion alive and **relevant** to everyday life.

HINDUISM

> Know that all of nature is but a magic theatre; that the great Mother is the master magician, and that this whole world is peopled by her many parts.
> —*Shvetashvatara Upanishad*

PRIMARY SOURCE

Hinduism is the major religion of India. Unlike other world religions such as Islam and Christianity, Hinduism has no known founder. It arrived in India with the Aryans, and was changed by contact with the Dravidian peoples.

Hindus call their beliefs "dharma," which, as you learned, means "duty"

or "way of life." The oldest holy books in Hinduism are the *Vedas* and the *Upanishads*. They describe the actions of the Hindu gods and goddesses, and have answers for many of the important questions about life, suffering, and death.

Hinduism has many gods and goddesses, all of which are forms of the one God. There are three "great" gods: Brahma the creator, Vishnu the preserver, and Shiva the destroyer. Some followers devote their whole lives to one god or goddess. For example, the followers of Shiva are known as "Shivites." They are identified by three stripes on their foreheads—symbols of Shiva's trident.

Rebirth of the Soul

Hindus believe that the soul, called *atman*, does not die with the body. Instead it is **reborn** many times into different bodies. *Karma* governs this cycle of death and rebirth. According to the law of karma, every human action has an effect. Hindus believe that actions in your previous lifetime affected your birth, and that actions in this lifetime will affect your next birth. Because the soul lives in a physical body, it can be "caught up" in the desires and disappointments of the physical world. It forgets that it is part of the universal soul, called *brahman*, and must relearn its true identity before it can escape the cycle of rebirth.

Hindus hope to free themselves from the illusions of the world, and achieve *moksha*, which means "freedom of the soul." The ideal Hindu life is one of selfless service and action. The more a person is caught up in selfish desires, the less able is he or she to gain moksha. Those closest to moksha are able to escape the physical world by living a life of discipline and **meditation**. They become **yogis**, pilgrims, and saintly women and men—in the world but detached from it.

Caste

Hindus recognize thousands of castes. You have already read that the caste system developed over a period of a thousand years from the time of the Aryan invasion of India to the time of the Gupta Empire. Today in India, castes are rigid social groupings, and the boundaries between them are difficult to cross. For Hindus, caste is also determined by the law of karma. Depending on one's actions in this life, one can reach a higher caste in the next life.

Some members of society have no caste. These people are called the "untouchables." They do jobs that other Hindus cannot do because they are considered unclean (for example, working in the leather industry).

The caste system has five principles.

◆ **Ritual pollution.** It is believed that an upper caste person can be "polluted" by a lower caste person by being near them, touching them, eating the same food, or drinking from the same well. Some Brahmins even consider the shadow of a person with no caste to be polluting.

Figure 11–10 The much-loved Elephant-Headed God, Ganesha, is shown holding one of his tusks—with which he writes—and a conch shell.

Figure 11–11 A Hindu Brahmin gives sweets to an "untouchable." Why is he holding the package of sweets so carefully above the man's hand?

◆ **Commensality.** Members of the same caste eat together. When different castes occupy the same place, they eat in separate groups.

◆ **Marriage within the caste.** Men and women of the same caste marry each other. Members of different castes do not marry each other.

◆ **Hereditary occupation.** Traditionally, people have learned the same occupation as their parents. This is less true now than in the past.

◆ **Economic links.** In traditional village life, each caste member had a job to do. Brahmins acted as priests and teachers to the lower castes. Lower castes in turn provided services for upper castes.

LINK-UP

Nominated for President: An "Untouchable"

In June 1997, something unusual happened in India. An "untouchable" was named president. Kocheril Raman Narayanan, age seventy-five, was nominated by India's coalition government. The nomination was supported by the Congress Party, which has traditionally been led by Brahmins alone, India's highest caste.

The nomination means that the caste system in India is gradually breaking down. In the twentieth century, the great leader Mahatma Gandhi encouraged ending the "untouchable" caste. **Discrimination** based on caste was officially abolished in India in 1950. During the 1950s and 1960s, the government set official **quotas** for enrollment in schools that would benefit the lowest castes. However, intermarriage between castes is still rare, as are opportunities for people of lower castes.

Following the nomination of Narayanan, a resident of Pakistan wrote a letter to the editor of a North American magazine, saying that: "It is certainly a great step forward toward the end of discrimination by caste and creed. God made us all equal. No one, rich or poor, should be treated differently. Intermarriage should be encouraged for a better and healthier society. All other countries that have class and sect discrimination can take the example of India and go forward toward the twenty-first century…"

Figure 11–12 Kocheril Raman Narayanan, India's first "untouchable" president. Bottom, Mahatma Gandhi shown with his daughters. Gandhi was assassinated in 1948.

WHAT DO YOU THINK?

1. Why is it so difficult for India to stop discrimination against people with no caste?

2. Why does discrimination against certain groups of people continue even after the government has declared it illegal? What should be the penalty for discrimination?

3. Name groups of people in North America who have suffered discrimination. How long have they suffered? What steps, if any, have been taken to stop this discrimination?

4. People with no caste are often converts to other religions such as Christianity and Islam. Can you explain why?

Holy Days and Pilgrimages

Hindus celebrate many holy days and festivals. In addition, many places in India are considered holy—often because of their association with great events. Religious pilgrims travel to **shrines** at such locations to worship and meditate.

Water is very important in Hinduism, and the waters of the rivers are considered to have special properties. This is particularly true of the Ganges, India's largest river, which is said to have the power to purify the faithful.

Some cities, such as Varanasi, on the Ganges, are also considered holy. Varanasi is so holy that pilgrims travel there to die, or have their corpses taken there to be **cremated** on the cremation *ghats* (steps). The ashes are then scattered in the river. Because India is considered by Hindus to be a sacred land, a pilgrim who travels to the important holy sites in the north, south, east, and west, has gone all around the sacred world.

Important holy days, feasts, and festivals take place throughout the year in India, but more occur during the rainy season than at any other time. Festivals held in the gloomiest part of the year are intended to cheer people up and give them hope. *Divali* is held around October and celebrates Lakshmi, the goddess of **prosperity.**

Divali is the Festival of Lights. People light lamps, wear new clothes, and have fireworks. They also give gifts to friends and family.

Holi is another important festival, which takes place in March. Holi is an occasion for partying and mischief. People feast, eat sweets, and throw brightly coloured powder and water at one another. Holi and Divali are the great spring and fall festivals of the Hindu calendar.

Figure 11–13 These remarkable rock carvings were made to honour the Ganges River and important Hindu deities. They are in the Tamil lands of southern India, and were carved in the seventh century.

shrine: a holy place

cremated: burned

prosperity: good fortune, success

Figure 11–14 This body was covered in flowers before it was placed on the cremation ghats. Its ashes will be scattered in the river.

Figure 11–15 During the Hindu festival of Holi, people throw coloured powder at one another. Others use squirt guns. Many restrictions on behaviour are forgotten during Holi. Even these baby goats could not avoid being doused with festive colours!

Hindus revere cows and bulls and will not kill or harm them. Today, cows and bulls wander freely even through India's major cities. The custom of treating these animals as sacred is very ancient, going back to the Aryan invasions. The Aryans measured their wealth in cows and bulls. In addition, the milk and butter of cows provided a source of wealth. Cattle continue to be protected.

Many devout Hindus will touch the forehead of a cow as part of a request for good fortune. The hoof prints of cows are often painted on doorsteps to bless anyone who enters the house.

Figure 11–16 These bulls are taking a rest on the streetcar tracks of Calcutta. Could this scene take place in your town or city? Explain why or why not.

sanctity: sacredness

traumatic: shocking

reincarnation: the Hindu idea of rebirth

vegetarianism: the practice of not eating meat or, sometimes, dairy products

ethical: according to right belief or practice

THE JAINS

The Jains believe their religion to be one of the world's oldest—older than Hinduism. It came into existence around the sixth century B.C.E. in northeastern India. Jains teach that their faith has been handed down by twenty-four successive saints.

Like Buddhists, Jains believe in the **sanctity** of life. However, Jains respect life to such an extent that they will go to great lengths to avoid killing or harming any living thing. Some Jains wear face masks to avoid breathing in micro-organisms, and gently sweep a path when they walk to avoid stepping on insects.

Jains also believe that the soul can be reborn in the body of some other living thing. A person's actions in life determine the form of their rebirth, a path that ultimately leads to nirvana—the "nothingness" to which the soul returns when it has finally learned its lessons.

Jains worship the Hindu gods, but do not have castes. Because they have always been forbidden to harm living creatures, Jains have gone into occupations such as trade and banking. They also run hospitals for sick and injured animals.

BUDDHISM

Buddhism was founded in India over 2500 years ago and became one of the world's great religions. Buddhism is no longer a major Indian religion but its influence on Indian art and history has been enormous.

Its founder, Prince Siddartha, was a member of a warrior caste who led a protected existence. It is said that Siddartha had the marks of greatness at birth. It was prophesied that he would be an important leader and teacher. To prevent him from seeing

Jains Gather to Celebrate Non-Violence

by Maddhavi Acharya

When Paulomi Gudka was four years old, she accidentally ate a piece of meat.

"I regretted it so much. I remember my mom was trying to calm me down and tell me it was a mistake. It was really a **traumatic** event," she says with a laugh.

Gudka, now twenty-one, is a practising Jain. The religion, which originated in India about 500 B.C.E., is based on the principle of achieving enlightenment through non-violence and non-injury to all living beings. **Reincarnation** and **vegetarianism** are the cornerstones of the Jain philosophy.

Gudka recently had the chance to meet other Jains from around the world, thought to number about four million.

The Ninth Biennial Jain Associations in North America (JAINA) Convention was held in Toronto during the summer of 1997. About 8000 people attended the three-day event.

Among the sixty-five guest speakers was Ingrid Newkirk, founder of People for the **Ethical** Treatment of Animals (PETA).

For younger members, like Gudka, it was an opportunity to learn more about Jainism.

"It's a platform for youth to meet each other and talk about Jain principles. It's important to have, especially in Canada with all the other cultures," says conference organizer Shan Jain.

In Sanskrit, Jain means "one who has conquered his or her inner enemies" of anger, greed, ego, and deceit.

Gudka is a vegetarian. "It does limit your choices sometimes," she says, "but you find ways around those products. You have to walk a few more steps to look for them."

Non-violence does not end with vegetarianism. Gudka says her family will usher insects out of their Scarborough home rather than swatting them.

But it is also important to be non-violent in words and thought,

a difficult task for even the most disciplined. Gudka says she doesn't swear and tries not to think negative thoughts about others.

"I get annoyed at a few people along the way. You have to consciously say, these are the facts; what should I be doing instead of getting annoyed and angry."

But it does get easier. "I think when you start doing all this, you kind of quickly step away from a lot of negative emotions and negative ideas," Gudka adds.

Figure 11–17 Jainism is an important part of Paulomi Gudka's life. Gudka, who studies computer science and economics at the University of Toronto, recently attended a North American convention of Jains that attracted 8000 people.

WHAT DO YOU THINK?

1. Why were representatives from People for the Ethical Treatment of Animals at the Jain convention?

2. Have you ever tried to tell yourself not to get angry, as Paulomi Gudka describes? What happened?

3. The largest Canadian cities have only a few hundred Jains. Why would it be important for young Jains to meet and talk with others about the principles of their faith?

Figure 11–18 This stone carving of Siddartha shows him surrounded by young people.

Buddha, understood the true nature of the world, and of reincarnation. These understandings he developed into the Four Noble Truths—the essential teachings of Buddhism.

The Four Noble Truths

1. There is suffering. Nothing is permanent. Everything changes, include the self. The self is an illusion.

2. Suffering is caused by desire.

3. Suffering can be eliminated when desire and selfishness are eliminated.

4. The Eightfold Path—right understanding, right speech, right determination, right conduct, right living, right effort, right meditation, right peace of mind—can eliminate desire and selfishness.

The Buddha had many followers during his lifetime. After his death, Buddhist ideas quickly spread through India, and to other parts of Asia. Rulers such as Ashoka were important to the success of Buddhism because they set up temples and schools, and sent out **missionaries**. Later, monks from other countries—China, for example—travelled to India and what is now Sri Lanka to learn more about the religion. As it grew it changed, far beyond what the Buddha's disciples could have imagined.

what life was really like, Siddartha's parents kept the young prince in his palace. His servants were always young, and he was never allowed to see sickness, old age, or death.

After marrying Princess Yashodhara, he longed to see beyond his small world. Leaving the palace on a number of occasions, he saw for the first time an aged person, a sick person, and a corpse. These sights disturbed him so deeply that he determined to find a solution to human misery. Leaving his beautiful wife and new son, he mounted his horse and rode away forever.

Buddhists believe that Siddartha was helped by the gods as he rode far from the palace. On the banks of a river, he said good-bye to his charioteer and his horse, cut off his long hair, and began a life of **deprivation**. For years, he lived close to starvation, meditating and hoping to find the answer to his questions. Finally, while meditating under a bodhi tree, he "saw" the truth and became enlightened. Siddartha, now

deprivation: doing without

missionary: a person sent on a religious mission

guru: a religious advisor or teacher

THE SIKHS

The Sikh faith began in the sixteenth century, and was founded on the teachings of **Guru** Nanak. Sikhs rejected many of the beliefs of Hinduism and Islam, the dominant religions of India at that time. Sikhs oppose the Hindu caste system and believe there is only one god.

Persecuted by the Mughals (Muslim rulers you will read about in the next section), Sikhs were organized into an effective fighting force by Govind Singh, the tenth and last guru. Govind Singh wanted to raise all Sikhs to the warrior caste. Sikh men began to wear the outward signs of both their religious beliefs and their community—uncut hair, a sword, and a steel bracelet.

The Sikhs conquered most of the Punjab by the eighteenth century. Sikh soldiers formed a large part of the British armies in India after World War Two, and many Sikh families eventually emigrated from India to Canada.

Figure 11–19 This Canadian Sikh family has arrived for a celebration of Khalsa Day.

make obeisance: show deep respect

The Faith of Guru Arjun

Guru Arjun was the fifth Sikh guru. Here he writes about his faith, and teaches about some of the differences between Sikhism and other religions. Why do you think Guru Arjun spends so much time telling us about what Sikhism is not?

I practise not fasting, nor observe the month of Ramazan.
I serve Him who will preserve me at the last hour.
The one Lord of the earth is my God,
Who judgeth both Hindus and Muslims.
I do not make a pilgrimage to Mecca, nor worship at the Hindu places of Pilgrimage.
I serve the one God and no other.
I take the Formless God into my heart, and there **make obeisance** unto Him.
I am neither a Hindu nor a Muslim.
The soul and the body belong to God whether He be called Allah or Ram.
Kabir hath delivered this lecture.
When I meet a true guru or pir, I recognize my own master.

PRIMARY SOURCE

ACTIVITIES

1. Explain how Hinduism came to India. Why has it continued to have such an important influence on Indian society?

2. Illustrate the Hindu law of karma in a diagram. Review the section on karma and the soul on page 351.

3. Research one of the Hindu gods or goddesses. Write a short paragraph on your choice, including information about his or her main identity and symbols. For example, Ganesha is important because he removes obstacles. His symbols are his tusk, the conch, and the mouse.

4. How are Jain and Buddhist beliefs similar to those of Hindus? How are they different? Create an organizer to illustrate the comparisons.

5. Find out how Canadian Sikhs who joined the Royal Canadian Mounted Police (RCMP) fought for the right to wear their turbans. Why was this issue so important to Sikh RCMP officers?

THE MUSLIM CONQUEST

As you remember from Chapter 4, Islam was founded in 622 C.E. and spread rapidly out of Arabia during the next centuries. In a little over a hundred years, Islam was the dominant faith from Spain to the Indian Ocean. In the seventh century, Muslim armies attacked the northwestern regions of India. In the tenth century, the Muslim conquest of India began in earnest.

What was India like at this time? The Gupta Empire was no more—it had collapsed during the invasion of the Huns, which had begun about 450 C.E. (The Huns were a nomadic people from Central Asia.) In the wake of these invasions, India returned to a period of instability. Rival Hindu princes fought for land in the north. To the south, the Tamils—the descendants of the Dravidians—maintained a prosperous kingdom but had little in common with their northern neighbours. There was no one ruler or government to unify the people. For this reason, India found it difficult to withstand the invasion of the Muslim armies.

sultanate: rule by a sultan, a Muslim ruler

Some of the most effective invasions were led by Mahmud of Ghanzi, known as the "Sword of Islam." He conquered the Punjab about 1025. For the next two centuries, Hindu rulers fought to keep the Muslim invaders out. The Rajputs, rulers of the Deccan Plateau, were never completely defeated. However, in 1206, the Muslims founded the city of Delhi in northern India, which led to the founding of the Delhi **Sultanate**. This Muslim empire would last over 300 years under leaders known as "sultans."

THE DELHI SULTANATE AND THE SOUTHERN KINGDOMS

The rulers of the Delhi Sultanate, Turkish Mamluks, used a combination of diplomacy and warfare to maintain their power. Hindu rulers were usually left alone provided they paid tribute to the

The Sultan Was a Woman

Sultana Raziyya ruled the Delhi Sultanate for three years after her father, the sultan, died. Raziyya stepped into power in spite of serious opposition from those who thought that a woman had no right to govern.

Raziyya was, by all accounts, an intelligent and effective monarch. To make herself look as the sultan ought to look, she wore men's clothing in public. She even led her troops in person. Raziyya was eventually murdered by rivals who had the support of the army. She died in 1240.

Figure 11–20 Sultana Raziyya wore this kind of clothing in public. Why do you think she did so?

sultan. The sultans often used murder and **intrigue** to fend off **rivals**. One sultan, Balban, poisoned at least thirty-nine rivals, including some former friends, after he seized the throne. For many years, the Turkish rulers kept power to themselves. Eventually, however, Indian-born Muslims rose to positions of power in the army and government.

The Delhi Sultanate could never defeat the Tamil kingdoms in the south. There, the Chola Dynasty had been in power for centuries. The mighty Chola navy defeated Muslim fleets in several naval battles.

The Rajput dynasties, which controlled states in the desert regions of the Deccan Plateau, were similarly fortunate. Protected in their castles and **sanctuaries**, Rajput warriors resisted the Muslim invaders from the North. Rajput means "sons of kings," and the Rajputs believed they were descended from fire, the sun, and the moon. Like the knights of Europe, these Rajput nobles had high ideals of personal bravery and **prowess** in war. For them, war was a way of life. They even fought one another.

The clash of North and South was essentially a clash of belief systems—the Muslims in the North and the Hindus of the South. This conflict has endured in India until the present day and is reflected in the creation of Muslim Pakistan in 1947.

■■■■■■■■■■■■■■■■■■■■■■

THE MUGHALS

The Delhi Sultanate was ended in 1526 by another group of Muslim invaders led by Babur, a Mongol prince from Afghanistan. Babur said he was descended from Chinggis Khan and Tamerlane (a conqueror who also claimed to be related to Chinggis).

The Mughals, as they were known, came from central Asia and

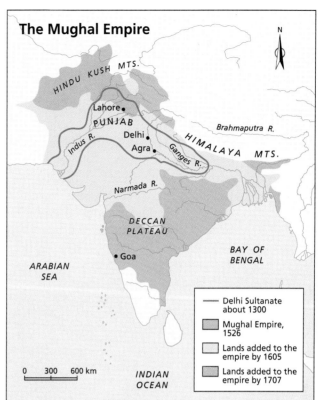

The Mughal Empire

HINDU KUSH MTS.
Lahore
PUNJAB
Indus R.
Delhi
Agra
Ganges R.
HIMALAYA MTS.
Brahmaputra R.
Narmada R.
DECCAN PLATEAU
ARABIAN SEA
• Goa
BAY OF BENGAL
0   300   600 km
INDIAN OCEAN

— Delhi Sultanate about 1300
▨ Mughal Empire, 1526
☐ Lands added to the empire by 1605
▨ Lands added to the empire by 1707

Figure 11–21
Over a period of 300 years, the Mughals conquered most of India. According to this map, which part of the country was not conquered by the Mughals?

were fierce warriors. (The word "Mughal" is Persian for "Mongol" and is sometimes written as "Mogul.") They understood the weaknesses of the Delhi Sultanate and **capitalized** on them. They defeated the sultan's armies easily. Even the mighty Rajputs suffered defeats.

Once in power, the Mughals contributed much to India. They built great and beautiful monuments, such as the Taj Mahal, and developed a rich culture. One Mughal leader, Aurangzeb, managed to conquer almost the whole of India.

Babur

Babur first invaded India in 1505. Over the next twenty years, he continued to raid the northern regions of the subcontinent. When his soldiers seized the city of Lahore, in Punjab, Babur made plans to move his government to India. Thus began a dynasty that would rule in India until the eighteenth century. Babur died in 1530.

intrigue: scheming, plotting

rival: one who competes for power

sanctuary: a safe place

prowess: skill

capitalize: to make the most of

Akbar

Babur's grandson, Akbar, came to power in 1556. He was an effective ruler who reformed the empire and made it strong. Akbar was a truly **enlightened** monarch. A Muslim and a leader of Muslims, he believed in religious tolerance, and tried to make it easier for Hindus and those of other faiths to follow their own beliefs without penalty. He appointed well-qualified Hindus of many different castes to work in his government, and he married a Hindu princess. Later in his life, Akbar tried to create his own religion based on parts of Islam, Christianity, and other faiths that appealed to him. Akbar's new religion was not accepted very widely, and it disappeared when he died.

Akbar was a progressive ruler in other respects. The old government had used advisors and officials who were supported by land grants—somewhat like the feudal system of medieval Europe. Akbar reformed his government and paid his new officials fixed salaries instead of granting them land. In this way, he ensured that they were loyal to him and were not becoming rich at the country's expense. He made taxes for landowners more fair by basing them on actual crop yields, and he established a new and better **currency**. Even weights and measures were reformed so that they were the same throughout the empire. Protected and secure transportation routes encouraged trade. All of these measures made the economy of the Mughal Empire stronger.

enlightened: forward looking and thinking

currency: money in actual use

Figure 11–22 In this painting, Akbar is ordering the slaughter of an animal to be stopped. Why would Akbar give such an order?

THE MUGHAL ZENITH

Following the reign of Akbar, three Mughal rulers went on to extend the empire to its largest size: Jahangir (Akbar's son), Shah Jahan (Jahangir's son), and Aurangzeb (Jahan's son). These monarchs could be both sentimental and warlike. Shah Jahan, for example, built the beautiful Taj Mahal as a tomb for his wife in 1630 (it was completed in 1648). But he also made war on his son Aurangzeb. Aurangzeb in turn deposed his father and imprisoned him for the rest of his life. He did, however, give his father prison rooms that had a view of the Taj Mahal.

Figure 11–23 Shah Jahan built the Taj Mahal as a memorial for his beloved wife, Mumtaz Mahal. Many people think the building is the most beautiful and perfect structure in the world. This is a view you don't often see. These Indian villagers are fetching water from a well behind the Taj Mahal. Most Indian villages lack drinking-water facilities and depend on public wells such as this one. What does this photograph encourage you to think about?

Of the three monarchs, Jahangir, who lived from 1569–1627, was the most devoted to art. He brought Persian artists to India, and made the appreciation of literature an important part of court life in his palace at Fatehpur Sikri, near Agra. Many beautiful miniature paintings were made during Jahangir's reign.

Jahangir was a popular ruler in some respects. Every day he personally heard petitions from his subjects. A devout Muslim, he also set aside times for prayer every day. But Jahangir had some family troubles. He was married to Nur Jahan, a Persian whose accomplishments were well known. Not only was she a patron of the arts and architecture, but she also hunted and travelled. Fiercely ambitious, she ensured that her father and other members of her family received powerful government jobs. She also ruled together with her husband and signed official orders. Jahangir once complained that he "had given her the kingdom for a goblet of wine." Jahangir spent the last few years of his life dealing with the rebellion of his son, Shah Jahan,

who succeeded him in 1627. Shah Jahan then forced his mother to retire.

Shah Jahan was often involved with war. He appears to have had little real interest in the welfare of his people. Instead he spent fortunes on gardens, such as that at Shalimar, in Kashmir, and on architecture and decoration. During **famines**, his officials did very little to relieve the misery of the population. He taxed his people heavily and spent most of the money on beautiful

famine: a lack of food resulting in widespread starvation

Figure 11–24 The Red Fort (*Lal Qila*) at Agra was established in 1639, at the height of Mughal power. It was built by Shah Jahan and contains gardens, private and public halls, offices, a harem, and a mosque. The Mughals kept their power through force, and the seat of their government had to be protected with armed soldiers and strong walls.

objects. His Golden Peacock throne was studded with the finest and largest gems he could acquire. Cruel and corrupt, Jahan had few friends when his son Aurangzeb forced him to give up the throne.

While the early Mughals had tried to accommodate the non-Muslims in their empire, Aurangzeb was not so tolerant. He ordered Hindu shrines destroyed and persecuted those who would not follow Islam. Thirsty for power, he executed two of his brothers and sent the head of one in a box to their father. Aurangzeb caused many rebellions because of his **suppression** of Hinduism, but this did not concern him. He once sent **rampaging** elephants into a crowd of protestors. His enemies included the Sikhs, Hindus, Sunni Muslims, and many others. Yet Aurangzeb survived. Moreover, his armies conquered most of the Indian subcontinent. He died, lonely and in doubt and fear, in 1707, telling his son that he had "sinned terribly, and I do not know what punishment awaits me."

THE EUROPEANS INVADE INDIA

Figure 11–25 This painting depicts a British East India Company representative surrounded by his employees. The British East India Company began exporting Indian tea to Britain in the seventeenth century. What does the posture and body language of the British man in the centre reveal?

After the brief reign of Alexander the Great (see page 346), the first Europeans to make an impact on Indian history were the Portuguese. Led by Vasco da Gama, they arrived in India after sailing around the Cape of Good Hope in 1498. Next, a larger fleet of Portuguese ships arrived in the Indian Ocean in 1502.

The Portuguese used violence and terror to secure an advantage in India. They established a "factory" in Goa, a Portuguese colony that lasted until the middle of this century. Like many of the European trader-explorers of the sixteenth century, the Portuguese were deeply religious, and anxious to spread their faith. Many Indians were converted to Catholicism, some forcibly.

The Portuguese were followed by the French, who established a colony at Madras, and then by the British. Of all the Europeans, the British had the most impact on India. After a slow start, they gradually extended their power over the whole subcontinent. India was part of the British Empire until 1948. Even today, India's government, court system, and sporting life display the British influence.

Using Clothing as a Primary Source

Clothing keeps us warm but also allow us to express ourselves. What information is given by the clothing worn here?

Figure 11–26 Everyone shown in these photographs lives in India today.

WHAT DO YOU THINK?

1. As you are making your decision, consider the following:

   ◆ Who is wearing the clothing? What is the occasion?

   ◆ How much of the body is covered? What could this indicate?

   ◆ Does the clothing seem Western? What could this indicate?

   ◆ Are there any symbols you recognize after reading this chapter?

2. Are social groupings in your school identified by clothing or jewellery? Explain.

3. Is it wrong to make a judgement—positive or negative—about someone because of his or her appearance?

ACTIVITIES

1. Why was it possible for Islamic invaders to capture much of northern India but not the southern region? Which dynasties resisted the Muslim invasion?

2. No pictures of the Sultana Raziyya have been handed down to us. Draw a picture of the sultana as you imagine her.

3. Who were the Rajputs? Find out more about the Rajputs in an encyclopedia. Create a comparison organizer for the Rajputs, the samurai, and the European knights. Brainstorm your headings with a classmate. Some possibilities include "clothing" and "mission."

4. Role play a chance encounter between Akbar and Aurangzeb in which each leader expresses his views on the purpose of government and religious tolerance.

5. Examine the Mughal artwork on pages 358 and 360. Make four or five generalizations about this art, considering colour, realism, the elements that are included, and any other factor you think is important.

SUMMARY

India became a fully independent state in 1948 and ceased to be a British possession. But the dream of some political leaders—such as Mahatma Gandhi—that the entire subcontinent would be united under one government was not to be. History and religion are powerful forces. Hindus, Muslims, and Sikhs remained in conflict. Eventually, one group of Muslims led by Mohammed Ali Jinna created the Islamic state of Pakistan. In 1972, East Pakistan became a separate nation, Bangladesh. Pakistan has since been at war with the Hindu state of India, suggesting how difficult it can be for a country to escape its history.

Perhaps no historical force has as much impact on societies as do strong religious beliefs. Certainly, religion has always played an important role on the Indian subcontinent. It is reflected again and again in the literature, art, and traditions of its people. The Golden Age of the Guptas was a religious age, as was the age of the great Mughals. Some of the world's great religions have emerged from India, and their influence is still very strong. Even today, spirituality is a core feature of Indian society. The *Ramayana* and the *Mahabharata*, for example, are still the most popular stories in India even though they are thousands of years old.

SUMMARY ACTIVITIES

1. Research and prepare an illustrated comparison of the architecture of the Taj Mahal, shown on page 361, and the Gothic cathedral, shown on page 159 of Chapter 5. Consider such features as size and dimensions, purpose, construction methods, and other factors.

2. Prepare a large map of India showing the various empires and kingdoms in the year 1500, or another year of your choosing. Your map should be large, colourful, and informative.

3. Write five or six journal entries, either from the point of view of a European visiting India, or of an Indian visiting Europe, during the time period of the late Middle Ages. If you wish, your journal writer can be Chinese or Japanese. You must demonstrate your knowledge of your home culture during the time period, and the differences between it and the culture you are visiting.

ON YOUR OWN

1. Contact a Hindu or Sikh temple, or the representatives of any other religion native to India. With a partner, prepare and present an informative talk on Indian religion—preferably with the help of a guest speaker.

2. Present a brief oral report on Mahatma Gandhi and his legacy of non-violence.

3. Research one of India's current industries, such as publishing, television and film production, textile manufacturing, or hydro-electricity production. Write and illustrate your report or present it as a videotaped newscast.

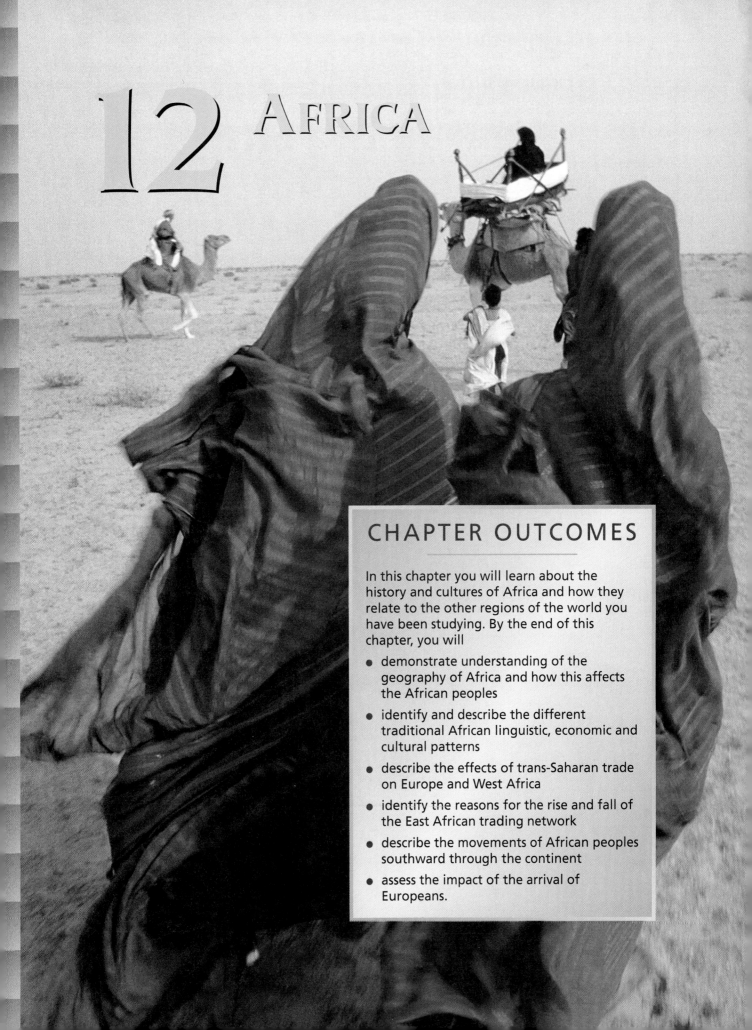

12 AFRICA

CHAPTER OUTCOMES

In this chapter you will learn about the history and cultures of Africa and how they relate to the other regions of the world you have been studying. By the end of this chapter, you will

- demonstrate understanding of the geography of Africa and how this affects the African peoples

- identify and describe the different traditional African linguistic, economic and cultural patterns

- describe the effects of trans-Saharan trade on Europe and West Africa

- identify the reasons for the rise and fall of the East African trading network

- describe the movements of African peoples southward through the continent

- assess the impact of the arrival of Europeans.

A Year in the Life of Ibn Battuta

Ibn Battuta was a world traveller—one of the greatest of all time. He was born in Tangier, Morocco, in 1304. Battuta left his native city for the first time at age twenty-one. A devout Muslim, he visited Mecca and Arabia several times. He also travelled to East and West Africa, central Asia, India, the East Indies and China. It is said that between 1325 and 1354, he covered over 120 000 kilometres.

His last journey was perhaps his most dangerous. As you will see, crossing the Sahara desert with a camel caravan was difficult. Traders who crossed the desert did so because of the great profits to be made in the kingdoms of the Sudan. On the other side of the desert, Ibn Battuta found a way of life very different from his own part of the world.

The following excerpts are adapted from the journal kept by Ibn Battuta during a journey to West Africa that lasted a year and a half.

In Taghaza, the houses are constructed of salt, with camel-skin roofs. There are no trees—the soil is just sand.

I left from Fez in my travelling clothes for the land of **Sudan** on February 18, 1352, in the company of a group of merchants of Sijilmasa. We arrived after twenty-five days at Taghaza. It is a village with no good in it. Amongst curiosities is the fact that the construction of its houses and its mosques is of rock salt with camel skin roofing and there are no trees in it—the soil is just sand.

There is a salt mine there. Salt is dug out of the ground and is found there in huge slabs, one on top of another as if it had been carved. A camel can carry two slabs of salt. Nobody lives in it except slaves of the **Massufa** who dig for the salt. People come here and carry away the salt. The people exchange the salt as one would exchange gold or silver. They cut it up and trade with it in pieces.

We stayed in the village for ten days in miserable condition, because its water is bitter and it is most full of flies. This desert is a travelling distance of ten days and there is no water in it except rarely. However, we found water in pools left behind by the rains. There are so many **lice** in the desert that people put strings around their necks in which there is mercury, which kills the lice.

After ten days we arrived at Tasarahla, where the caravans stay for three days repairing their water bags and filling them with water. From there the *takshif* is sent. The takshif is the name given to every man of the Massufa who is hired by the people of the caravan to go ahead to Walata to rent houses for them and to come out to meet them with water, a distance of four days. That desert has many devils, and if the takshif be alone, they play with him and **lure** him on until he loses his way and **perishes** since there is no way which is clear there and no tracks. There is only sand blown by the wind. You see mountains of sand in a place, then you see they have moved to another.

We used to set out after the later afternoon prayer and travel all night, dismounting in the morning because of the intense heat of this desert. We arrived at Walata after a journey of two whole months from Sijilmasa.

My stay in Walata was about fifty days. Its people were generous to me and entertained me. The town of Walata is very hot and and there are a few date palms in whose shade they plant melons. The clothes of its people are of fine Egyptian material. Most of the inhabitants belong to the Massufa. As for their women, they are extremely beautiful and are more important than the men.

One day I came upon Abu Muhammad Yandakan, a man of the Massufa, one in whose company we had arrived. I found him sitting on a mat and in the middle of his house was a bed with a **canopy**. On it was a woman and with her a man was sitting, and the two were talking. I said to him, "Who is this woman?"

He said, "She is my wife."

I said, "What is the

Abu Muhammad Yandakan sat on a mat in his home, while his wife and another man sat on the bed.

Ibn Battuta's journey to West Africa

relationship of the man with her to her?"

He said, "He is her companion."

I said, "Do you accept this when you have lived in our country and have known the matters of the **shar**?"

He said to me, "Women's companionship with men in our country is honourable and takes place in a good way: there is no suspicion about it. They are not like the women in your country." I was astonished at his thoughtless answer, and I went away from him and did not go to him after this.

I then decided to make the journey to Mali, which is twenty-four days of travel from Walata. Between these two places is a forest with many different kinds of trees, the fruits of which the inhabitants use for food. One such fruit is *gharti*, which is like a plum—very sweet and harmful to

white men when they eat it. The hard part inside is crushed, and an oil is **extracted** from it. They cook with it, fuel the lamps, use it as an ointment, and they mix it with a kind of earth to plaster their homes. After ten days' travel from Walata, we arrived at the village of Zaghari, and then proceeded to the great river, the Nile. We followed the course of the Nile to Timbuktu, to Gao, then to the town of Muli, and finally to Nupe. During this journey I saw a crocodile on the Nile near the shore like a small canoe. I went down to the river to answer a need and a man came and stood between me and the river. I was astonished at his bad manners and the paucity of his shame. I mentioned this to someone. He answered, "He only did that for fear on your behalf of danger from the crocodile. He made a barrier between you and it."

I spent a total of two months at Nupe, engaged in making and receiving formal visits with the Sultan of Mali, Mansa Sulieman, and his officials. I was also able to observe the way in which the people behave towards their

ruler. The sultan has his audiences in a great courtyard that faces his house. He gives his audiences in a raised **cupola**, which he enters from this house. The cupola has an audience chamber attached to it. The chamber has six arches of wood that are covered in beaten silver.

When the sultan is ready to give audience, a **grille** in one of the arches is raised and a silken cord is displayed. A great noise of bugles and drums comes forth, and people assemble. Three hundred slaves carrying spears and shields emerge from the palace and take up their positions. Two mares and two rams are brought forward as protection from the **evil eye**. The interpreter Dugha stands at the entrance to the cupola. He is dressed in magnificent robes and a turban with fringes (the people of Mali have a superb way of tying a turban). He is **girt** with a sword with a golden **scabbard**, and is booted and spurred. Only Dugha wears boots during an audience.

Those who wish to speak to the sultan approach Dugha and speak to him. He speaks to the sultan's deputy, Qanja Musa, and he speaks to the sultan. The people are humble before their king and most extreme in their **self-abasement** to him. They come before the sultan wearing patched clothes. When they come before Dugha, they **prostrate** themselves, hitting the ground hard on their elbows. When they receive an answer from the sultan, they take off their clothes and throw dust on their head and back, in the manner of a person bathing with water. I used to wonder how they did not blind their eyes.

While in Mali, I observed many strange beasts with enormous bodies, both in the river and along its banks. I was told that these were hippopotami, or "horses of the river." I was astonished by them. The boatmen of the river fear these beasts, and make for shore when they are about, lest they be drowned. They hunt these horses by spearing them with weapons with ropes attached. The animals are dragged from the river, killed, and eaten. I saw great heaps of their bones on the river bank.

While on my way back from Mali, at Takadda, I received a message from my ruler that I was commanded to his presence. I speedily complied with this order, and travelled back to my own country.

Ibn Battuta sees a hippopotamus for the first time.

Sudan: a term that once applied to all of Africa south of the Sahara, not just the modern nation of that name

Massufa: desert tribe living on the southern edge of the Sahara

louse: small insect that feeds on people and animals (plural: lice)

mercury: a silver-white metal that is liquid at ordinary temperatures

to lure: to tempt

to perish: to die

canopy: drapery, often over a bed

shar: *sharia*, the law code of Islam

to extract: to draw out, often by pressing

paucity: small amount

cupola: a small structure built on a roof

grille: an open screen of metal or wood

evil eye: a stare that can bewitch

to gird: to encircle with a belt

scabbard: sheath for a sword

self-abasement: self-humiliation

to prostrate: to lie face-down on the ground

counterpart: an equivalent

ACTIVITIES

1. Why are Ibn Battuta's accounts still so important to people living today?

2. How does Ibn Battuta measure the distances in the desert? Why would he express distance in this way?

3. Ibn Buttata says that he arrived at the Nile. Did he? Consult the map on page 368 to find out.

4. Why would Ibn Battuta be so surprised at what he saw at the home of Abu Muhammad Yandakan?

5. Do you think Ibn Battuta has any modern-day **counterparts**? Why or why not? Remember that what Ibn Battuta did in his day was extraordinary—most people never travelled anywhere.

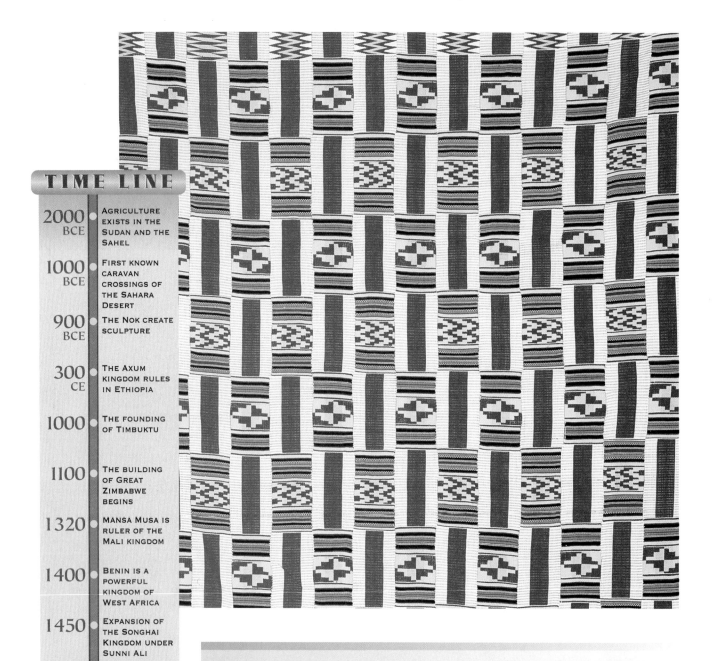

TIME LINE

2000 BCE	AGRICULTURE EXISTS IN THE SUDAN AND THE SAHEL
1000 BCE	FIRST KNOWN CARAVAN CROSSINGS OF THE SAHARA DESERT
900 BCE	THE NOK CREATE SCULPTURE
300 CE	THE AXUM KINGDOM RULES IN ETHIOPIA
1000	THE FOUNDING OF TIMBUKTU
1100	THE BUILDING OF GREAT ZIMBABWE BEGINS
1320	MANSA MUSA IS RULER OF THE MALI KINGDOM
1400	BENIN IS A POWERFUL KINGDOM OF WEST AFRICA
1450	EXPANSION OF THE SONGHAI KINGDOM UNDER SUNNI ALI
1509	THE PORTUGUESE CONTROL THE EAST AFRICA COAST
1590	THE MOROCCAN ARMY DEFEATS THE SONGHAI—THE END OF THE DESERT KINGDOMS
1600	THE EUROPEAN SLAVE TRADE GROWS IN WEST AFRICA
1830	THE SLAVE TRADE ENDS

A child is the beginning and the end of happiness
One must not rejoice too soon over a child.
Only the one who is buried by his child.
Is the one who has truly born a child.
On the day of our death, our hand
    cannot hold a single **cowrie**.
We need a child to inherit our belongings.

—YORUBA POEM

According to the philosophy of the Yoruba people of West Africa, having a child carries much significance. Dead ancestors may be reborn into the same family, and the great cycle of life and death depends upon the child laying the parents to rest. This poem was translated by Ulli Beir, a distinguished scholar who specializes in Yoruba literature. What does this poem teach you about Yoruba culture?

INTRODUCTION

Paleontologists believe that Africa is the homeland of the world's peoples. Human life probably developed in Africa many millions of years ago, and then spread to the rest of the world. Africa is where humans first learned to use fire, make tools, and create art. It is truly the cradle of civilization.

Africa is a vast continent, much of it covered with desert and forest—Africa has more desert and dry regions than any other continent. Farmland is scarce, and there are few **navigable** rivers.

Africa is a land of lost kingdoms and cities. The Empire of the Nile flourished in Egypt from 3500 B.C.E. until approximately 400 B.C.E. The Kingdom of Ethiopia—the second oldest African country—has been traced to approximately 300 B.C.E. The ancient cities of Timbuktu, Tangier, and Zimbabwe thrived between 800 and 1500 C.E. At their peak, these centres of commerce and culture rivalled those of Europe.

In this chapter, you will become acquainted with the continent of Africa and its peoples. You will learn about the development of the kingdoms of West Africa and the importance of trade in gold and salt. You will read about the kingdoms of the Guinea Coast and the origins of the European slave trade, which did much to disrupt both the African economy and its political stability. Finally, you will examine the peoples of Central and Southern Africa—home to Great Zimbabwe.

> **DID YOU KNOW?**
> *Africa is three times the size of Europe.*

> **cowrie:** a type of sea shell, used as money in some cultures
>
> **paleontologist:** a scientist who studies fossils
>
> **navigable:** able to be travelled by ships

THE GEOGRAPHY OF AFRICA

Africa's geography and climate have had a great impact on the continent's historical development. Africa lies primarily between 30°N and 30°S latitude. Temperatures are warm to hot, without the variations that occur in the more temperate parts of the planet. However, Africa's rainfall is highly variable, and has had a great effect on where and how people live.

While West Africa is relatively low-lying, the southern and eastern parts of the continent are uplands or highland plateaus. Almost all the major rivers of Africa are navigable inland, but as they flow towards the coast, they spill over the edges of these plateaus as rapids or waterfalls. As a result, it is very difficult to

Figure 12–1
Topographic map of Africa

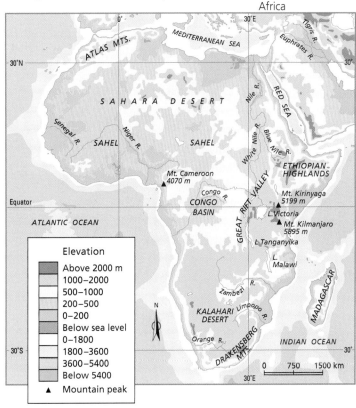

Figure 12–2 The African **savanna**.

savanna: a plain that has coarse grass and scattered trees

The Sahel: transition zone between the desert and the savanna

dunes: sand hill formed by the wind

oasis: an area in the desert made fertile by water

travel inland from the coast in most of Africa.

CLIMATE, VEGETATION AND SOILS

Along the equator—in the Zaire River basin and along the coast of West Africa—lies the tropical rain forest. It makes up about 8 percent of Africa. The rain forest with its giant trees, is hot, wet, and deeply shaded. Rain falls every day.

Different wind patterns and higher land result in a much drier, equatorial climate in East Africa. Farther from the equator, to the north and south, the Trade Winds create an area of dry to extremely dry conditions. In the south, the Kalahari and Namib Deserts are also dry. To the north, the continent is dominated by the world's largest desert—the Sahara.

The Sahara Desert lies between the Mediterranean coast of North Africa and the rest of Africa. It covers nearly a quarter of the total area of the continent. Until about 8000 years ago, the Sahara was an area of streams and grassland. But gradually its climate changed. Rainfall decreased and the temperature began to rise. The Sahara became a region of sand **dunes**, barren mountains, and isolated **oases**. The average rainfall in the Sahara is less than 100 millimetres per year. Many regions have recorded no rainfall at all over periods lasting many years.

The grasslands of Africa are called savanna and are similar to the Canadian prairies. They extend across the continent, south of the Sahara. They are also found in eastern Africa and parts of southern Africa. The savanna is mostly made up of grasses and scrub trees, but larger trees and wetter areas may be found along the banks of rivers. Rainfall in the savanna is light (100–500 millimetres per year). The savanna has a short, wet season and a long, dry season. Periods of lower-than-usual rainfall lead to an expansion of desert regions, especially the Sahara.

The narrow, semi-dry belt immediately south of the Sahara is called the **Sahel**. The Sahel expands and contracts depending on the general level of moisture. It grows smaller in drier periods and expands when the climate is moist. The word "Sahel" is Arabic and means "shore" because the Arabs thought of the Sahara as an ocean of sand.

The most important event in the Sahel and in the East African savanna is the yearly rainfall. In some years,

Figure 12–3 Villages such as this one in the **Sahel** must struggle to survive in the expanding desert.

the rains arrive on time and last long enough for crops to be grown and harvested. But the rains can also be late. In these years, crop yields will not be large enough to feed everyone, causing considerable hardship. Sometimes there is no rainfall, resulting in famine and widespread death and disease.

African farmers often farm land that is generally not suited to agriculture. Most farmland has been cleared from forest, and therefore lacks humus, a dark, organic material produced by decaying vegetation. Humus holds water in the soil near the surface, where plants can reach it. Because the soil is poor, African farmers use one patch of soil for only a limited period. Then they move on to another patch. Most farming is also of a **subsistence** nature. Crop yields are low, and **surpluses** are rare. The danger of famine is always present.

humus: the organic part of the soil formed by rotting vegetation

subsistence farming: farming that provides only for the needs of the family or community

surplus: extra

ACTIVITIES

1. Why is long-distance travel so difficult in Africa? What impact would this have on the ability of people around the continent to trade and communicate with one another?

2. Why are rainfall and rainfall patterns so important to the peoples of Africa?

3. Create an organizer to describe the differences between the savanna and the Canadian prairies. Think of five categories, including location and rainfall. You could subdivide your rainfall category into two categories: quantity and pattern.

4. What effect have poor soils had on African agriculture?

THE PEOPLES OF AFRICA

The peoples of Africa have intermarried over thousands of years, especially in the region immediately south of the Sahara Desert. But language has always distinguished groups of Africans from one another.

THE IMPORTANCE OF LANGUAGE

When humans occupy an area for hundreds of years, they develop a distinctive way of speaking—a native language. In Europe, for example, the French language developed in France over a period of 1500 years. Groups of people who live close to one another develop similar languages over time.

These groups of people are said to belong to **linguistic groups**, a concept you read about in Chapter 11. For example, in Europe, the different peoples whose languages developed from Latin belong to the Romance linguistic group. These include French, Italian, Spanish, Portuguese, and Romanian. In Africa, there are four major linguistic groups.

In North Africa, the regions of the Sahara, Nubia, and Ethiopia are home to the Afro-Asiatic speakers, such as the Berber, Tuareg, Galla, and Somali peoples. They have occupied this area for several thousand years. Since the seventh century, many people in North Africa have also spoken Arabic.

The southern tip of Africa has been the homeland of Khoisan speakers, such as the !Kung San. They

linguistic group: the family of languages to which several languages belong

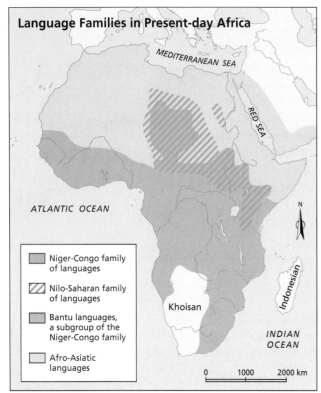

Figure 12–4 Identify one way that geography influenced the spread of languages in Africa.

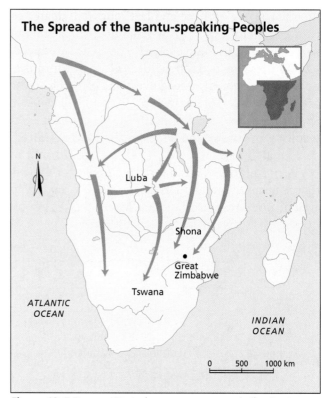

Figure 12–5 Because Bantu languages are very similar, Bantu speakers must have migrated across Africa within the last 2000 years.

migration: a movement of a large number of people or animals over a long distance

clan: a group of related families that all have one common ancestor

speak a distinctive language that probably developed there in the distant past.

Scattered across the Sahel and the southern Sudan are Nilo-Saharan speakers. While they have occupied this area for thousands of years, there have been considerable movements of peoples in this region. As a result, Nilo-Saharan languages are found in isolated pockets.

By far the largest linguistic group in Africa is Bantu, which is spoken today from the West African coast to central Africa, and in southern Africa. While there are many regional differences between languages in the Afro-Asiatic and Nilo-Saharan groups, Bantu languages are very similar. This has caused linguistic historians and archaeologists to conclude that there was a great **migration** of Bantu speakers across Africa in recent years. From their core area in West Africa, these peoples probably travelled across central and southern Africa in

the period between 0 C.E. and about 1500 C.E.

LIVING OFF THE LAND

For thousands of years, many Africans —even city dwellers—have lived off the land. In Africa, south of the Sahara Desert, it is estimated that farming is the single occupation of 80 percent of all people, including those who live in towns.

In the past, villages in rural Africa were made up of members of an extended family or **clan** group. The village was surrounded by the fields where crops were grown. Many of the villages were not permanent because farmers could use their fields for only a short period. As you just read, most soils became exhausted of nutrients after a few years. Therefore, the buildings in these communities were

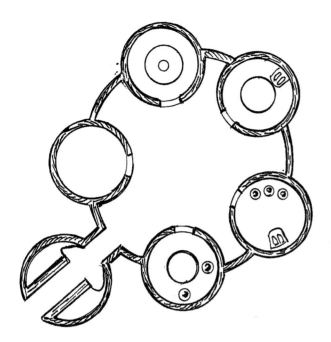

Figure 12–6 This type of family compound is still used by some rural Africans.

Figure 12–7 An African healer. In Africa, there is a strong tradition that links a person's health with his or her spiritual state. Do you think most North American physicians accept this link between mind and body?

not designed to last a long time. They were usually made of **mud-wattle** walls and thatched roofs.

Most villages did not use a money economy. Instead, goods and services were exchanged through **barter**. Markets—except in areas where trade was important—were not common. Most farmers were primarily engaged in growing enough food to feed their families. Some of these traditions continue in Africa today.

RELIGION AND BELIEF

Both Islam and Christianity have taken root in Africa. Today, there are more than 125 million Muslims in Africa, and more than a quarter of the population is Christian. The earliest known Christian convert was an Ethiopian king who lived in the fourth century.

However, indigenous African beliefs about God and the created world existed long before both Islam and Christianity. The ancient Egyptians, for example, worshipped many gods and goddesses. They believed that some animals were sacred, and they developed complex ideas about **immortality**.

Animism is an ancient belief system still practised by some Africans—sometimes in combination with Islam or Christianity. According to animism, all natural things have some form of spirit, which the creator has placed in them. Understanding how these spirits operate is necessary in order to live in harmony with them. There are spirits in the air, in the rivers and lakes, in the soil, and in plants and animals. Animism has influenced Japanese Shinto as well as some forms of Buddhism, religions you read about in Chapter 6.

In rural African societies, clans often had mythical heroes. People believed that the spirits of the clan's ancestors stayed close to the village.

Great respect was given to persons who were skilled in dealing with the spirits of

A Creation Myth From the Fang People of Gabon

All human societies have myths and legends that explain how the universe, the earth, and living things came to be. The following is an adaptation of an African creation myth.

Figure 12–8 This Saharan rock painting depicts the beginning of the world.

At the beginning of things, when there was nothing, neither man, nor animals, nor plants, nor heaven, nor earth—nothing, nothing. God was and he was called Nzame. The three who are Nzame, we call them Nzame, Mebere, and Nkwa. At the beginning, Nzame made the heaven and the earth, and he reserved the heaven for himself. Then he blew onto the earth, and earth and water were created, each on its side.

Nzame made everything: heaven, earth, sun, moon, stars, animals, plants—everything.

When he had finished everything that we see today, he called Mebere and Nkwa and showed them his work.

"This is my work. Is it good?"

They replied, "Yes, you have done well."

"Does anything remain to be done?"

Mebere and Nkwa answered him, "We see many animals, but we do not see their chief; we see many plants, but we do not see their master."

As masters for all these things, they appointed the elephant because he had wisdom; the leopard because he had power and cunning; and the monkey because he had **malice** and suppleness.

Nzame, Mebere, and Nkwa wished to do even better, so they created a creature almost like themselves, giving him power, force, and beauty. This was the first man, whom they called Fam, which means power—and they said to him: "Take the earth. You are **henceforth** the master of all that exists. Like us you have life, all things belong to you, you are the master."

But the first man grew wicked and arrogant, because of his power, and did not worship Nzame again, and he scorned him. Nzame heard this, and he grew angry. He called on Nzalan, the thunder, and the thunder and lightning fell from heaven, and the earth and all that was on it was consumed by fire and destroyed, even Fam. Yet Fam could not die, for Nzame had told him at his creation that he would not, and what Nzame gives, he does not take away.

So Fam was burnt, but he lives. Yet where?

When Nzame saw the burnt earth, he was ashamed. So he took **counsel** with Mebere and Nkwa and they covered the black earth with a new layer of earth, and on this they planted a tree. From the seeds of this tree came all the plants of the earth, and from its leaves, all the animals. And they decided to create a new chief to command the animals. "We shall make a man like Fam," said Nzame, "the same legs and arms, but we shall turn his head and he shall know death."

This was the second man and the father of all. Nzame called him Sekume, and as he did not want to leave the man alone, said "Make yourself a woman from a tree." So Sekume made a woman, and called her Mbongwe, and she was the mother of all. Nzame made the man and woman into two parts—an outer part called Gnoul, the body, and another which lives in the body, called Nsissin. It is Nsissin which makes the body live. Nsissin goes away when a person dies, but Nsissin does not die. Do you know where Nsissin lives? He lives in the eye—the little shining point you see in the middle—that is Nsissin.

Sekume and Mbongwe lived happily on earth and had many children. But Fam escaped from the prison in which Nzame had placed him. He is furious that the second man took his place. He hides in the forest to kill them, and under the water to **capsize** their boats.

Remain silent,
Fam is listening,
To bring misfortune;
Remain silent.

NOW YOU DO IT

1. In groups of two or three, consult your school library to investigate the creation story of another culture. Each group should investigate a different culture's myth. Possibilities include the *Book of Genesis* in the Bible, stories of the First Nations peoples, and stories of the indigenous peoples of Australia.

2. What are the similarities and differences between the African creation story and the story you selected? Present your findings to the class. Have a class discussion about the elements these stories have in common.

the world, including the spirits of ancestors. Most clan and village leaders were chosen for their abilities as spiritual guides. Magic and witchcraft were highly regarded—a powerful magician who controlled the spirits could be the leader of a group. If the group experienced misfortune, the magician would be expected to make things better through **intercession** with the local spirits. The magician who failed repeatedly could be stripped of power—especially if the disaster were a major one.

Disease was often interpreted to mean that the sick person was possessed by evil spirits. In this case, an **exorcism** was performed by a witch-doctor. This was a way to stop the illness and restore the person to standing in the group.

Clans had stories other than the creation story. These stories explained the rules of good behaviour and the importance of certain social customs. They explained the origins of the group, significant events in the group's history, and the nature of death.

African story tellers had a great deal of training, and their stories were a part of a long oral tradition. The stories were often so complex that the oral histories of many groups could cover several hundred years of history.

malice: spite, a wish to hurt others

henceforth: from this time on

counsel: wise advise

to capsize: to overturn

intercession: a spiritual request on behalf of others

exorcism: a ceremony to drive out a spirit

Why Some Animals Behave the Way They Do

Many cultures create folk tales to explain why things are the way they are. As technology develops, it too becomes part of new folk tales. Here is a modern folk tale from Swaziland that does just that.

One hot and sunny day, a dog, a goat, and a donkey were walking through the bush. They came to the edge of a dusty road just as a car was passing by. The driver stopped and offered a ride. As you can imagine, the hot and weary animals all sighed with relief and climbed aboard. They went a long way before the driver stopped and demanded five *emalangeni* [Swazi currency] apiece. The donkey paid his fare, climbed out of the car and continued walking along the road. The dog handed the driver ten emalangeni and asked for change. Meanwhile, the goat (who did not have any money) jumped from the car and ran off into the bush.

Seeing this, the driver turned to the dog and said in a gruff voice, "If your friend will not pay for his ride, you will!" And with that, the mean and angry driver quickly started up the car and left the dog standing in the road, cheated out of his money. The dog started to run.

"Wait!" yelled the dog. "What about my change? Give me back my money!" But the driver kept on driving—so the dog kept on running.

That is why, to this day, if you happen to see a donkey on the road, he will stay where he is. If you happen to see a goat, he will run away. And if you happen to see a dog, he will be chasing after a car.

PRIMARY SOURCE

NOW YOU DO IT

1. Think of a common situation, such as the one described in this folk tale, and create an amusing explanation for it. Share your tale with the rest of the class.

2. Make a display of all the modern folk tales your class created. Alternatively, you could publish your stories as a class book with illustrations.

MUSIC AND DANCE

While sculpture and weaving have flourished in Africa since 900 B.C.E., perhaps the most important form of artistic expression has been dance. In the past, nearly all important activities were accompanied by a special dance—for example, birth, puberty, marriage, and death. Dance was also a way to bring the community together because most dances involved all members of the village—men, women, and children. In some cases, dances were **spontaneous**. People danced because they enjoyed being with other members of the community. If the

spontaneous: not prearranged

ceremony were important, dancers would dress in a symbolic costume. The style and nature of the costumes helped tell the story of the dance.

Dancing was always accompanied by drum music. Most African cultures have used the drum as their major musical instrument. Other important instruments were the lute and the xylophone.

Patterns in African music are complex. European music is sometimes characterized as being **polyphonic**. Many different instruments, including voices—each with its own distinctive sound—are combined to produce a musical display. African music, by contrast, is **polyrhythmic**. A lead musician—usually the drummer—begins a piece by playing a distinctive rythmic theme, which is then taken up by the other musicians. These musicians play a **variation** of the main theme. The production becomes even more complex as dancers move different

Figure 12–9 In Africa, dancing remains a way to bring the community together. What role does dancing play in your society?

parts of their bodies in time with different instruments.

polyphonic: consisting of many voices or sounds

polyrhythmic: consisting of an interplay of different rhythms

variation: something that is slightly different from another of the same kind

LINK-UP

Drumming the Long-Distance Feeling

Drums have also served a unique function in African societies—long distance communication.

"Talking drums" have been used by many groups. By varying the **pitch**, strength, and frequency of the tapping on the drum, a drummer can **mimic** human speech.

Among the Yoruba people of West Africa, talking drums are still used to transmit messages across great distances. Their drums are shaped like an hourglass, with two **membranes** at each end. The membranes are connected by leather strips. By pressing the strips while tapping on the surface, the drummer alters the pitch of the drum.

Relays of drummers create, hear, and pass on messages so that communication can travel a great distance. It is said that a message can be sent over a distance of 200 kilometres in the space of two hours.

pitch: the highness or lowness of a sound

mimic: copy

membrane: a soft, thin covering, often animal tissue

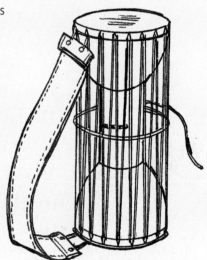

Figure 12–10 A Yoruba "talking drum"

1. Why would language be used to distinguish African cultures?

2. Examine Figure 12–5. Which linguistic group undertook a migration within the last 2000 years? Suggest reasons why they did so.

3. How important are spirits in African religions? Why would magicians be needed?

4. Compare the treatment of disease in traditional African culture with the treatment that was popular in medieval Europe. (See Figure 5–19 on page 161.)

5. In what ways are dance and music so important in African cultures? What practical purposes did drums serve?

THE HISTORICAL DEVELOPMENT OF AFRICA

TRANS-SAHARAN TRADE AND LIFE IN THE SUDAN

Eight thousand years ago, when the Sahara was an area of streams, lakes, and rich grasslands, the peoples who lived there fished and farmed for a living. They left many rock paintings that tell much about their ways of living.

As the African climate slowly changed and the Sahara dried out, the area became a vast waste of scrub vegetation, rock, and sand. Surface water disappeared, to be replaced by a "sea" of sand. Most of the peoples of the Sahara migrated to the margins of the desert by 4000 B.C.E. Only a few managed to survive in the tiny oases that dot the desert.

An Agricultural Economy

Traditionally, the economy of the Sahel and the Sudan was dominated by agriculture. In the Sahel, some people farmed crops by about 2000 B.C.E., but most were herders of animals, especially cattle. Farther south, in those areas where rainfall was slightly more plentiful, farming was the main occupation. However, only a limited variety of crops could be grown, mainly sorghum and millet. These two grains produced a nutritious flour, high in protein and vitamins. The basic diet item was porridge, sometimes enlivened with

Sudan: a term that once applied to all of Africa south of the Sahara, not just the modern nation of that name

Figure 12–11 This rock painting from the Sahara is thousands of years old.

Figure 12–12 Two views of an oasis. In the photograph on the right, it is easy to see how fragile an oasis really is.

green vegetables and herbs. Meat was not a significant part of the diet.

Fields were cleared by fire, and the ash that was left over was used as a **fertilizer**. In general, the men cleared the fields and prepared the land for planting. Women weeded and cared for the developing crops. Harvesting was performed together by all members of the community. Grain was stored in raised container, to guard against **termites**, monkeys, and other pests. The women were also responsible for **winnowing** grain and preparing meals.

While agricultural work was performed collectively, working teams were flexible. Sometimes teams were organized by age, not sex, or sometimes certain families negotiated contracts to perform specific tasks.

THE IMPORTANCE OF TRADE

While agriculture was essential for providing people's basic needs, trade was the driving force behind the organization and development of West African civilization. Both the Sahel and the Sudan produced trade items much in demand in both North Africa and Europe—gold, salt, and eventually slaves.

The greatest obstacle to the development of trade was the Sahara Desert. The first known trans-Saharan crossings occurred about 1000 B.C.E., and involved horse-drawn chariots. But the horse was not a suitable animal for crossing the desert, and trade across the Sahara remained **intermittent** until the camel was introduced from Asia in the fourth century. For the next thousand years and more, the trans-Saharan trade was of great economic importance to the peoples on either side of the Sahara.

Desert caravans travelled along two major routes between the Maghrib (North Africa) and the Sahel.

The first route began in Sijilmasa, in Morocco, and ran across the western Sahara to Awdaghost, in the far west of the Sahel, or to Timbuktu and Gao in the western Sahel. Both of

fertilizer: a substance placed on soil to increase its ability to grow plants

termite: a small white ant

to winnow: to separate the husks from the grains

intermittent: occurring from time to time

All About the Camel

Did you know that the camel is not especially suited to working with humans? It is bad-tempered and difficult to train. When angered, it responds by spitting. Those in the know say the spit of a camel is extremely unpleasant. There's lots of it and it smells terrible!

However, camels can store large quantities of fluid in their bodies for a long time. They can carry a heavy load for a great distance—travelling faster than either a horse or a donkey. The camel is also a source of milk, which can be made into butter or cheese. It even has built-in

sunglasses—thick eyebrows that shield its eyes from the sun. With careful handling, the camel is the perfect transport animal in the desert.

Two types of camel were used in early African desert crossings. The smaller white camel was used for the high-speed transport of small loads. The larger brown camel was slower and better suited for transporting heavy, bulky loads.

It was considered extremely important to use experienced camel drivers. A wounded camel—or one with a badly packed load—could delay a caravan for days. In the desert, such a delay could mean death for the entire caravan group.

Figure 12–13 Can you identify the camel's eyebrow? The eyelid of the camel is also adapted to the desert. Even when it is closed, the camel can still see. Why would this be an advantage?

WHAT DO YOU THINK?

1. If camels are such difficult animals, why would they be used in the desert?

2. How does the camel store all that water? Find out more about the camel's stomach in an encyclopedia.

these routes went through Taghaza, a desert town in the middle of the Sahara. As you learned by reading the Window on the Past, Taghaza was a source of salt, an important product for trade.

The second route began in Tunis and Tripoli and ran across the desert through the Fezzan, terminating at Kano and Gazargamu. A third route, less frequently used, connected the Sahel to Egypt in the east.

By 600 C.E., four types of caravans were regularly crossing the Sahara. The first was the military caravan. Its purpose was to acquire wealth and trade goods by raiding villages. The second type of caravan was the religious caravan, which was usually made up of Muslims on their way to Mecca or to the tomb of a respected holy person.

Commercial caravans were of two varieties. The small commercial variety consisted of five to one hundred camels—these usually moved much faster than larger caravans. Small caravans could average 32 to 36 kilometres per day. The large commercial caravan could include 500 to 2000 camels. It was often made up of smaller caravans that banded together for protection. A large caravan would average 26 kilometres per day.

Generally, groups of travellers left the Maghrib in September and October. The return journey was made from the Sahel at the beginning of the rainy season in April or May. Most caravans made the journey in approximately 80 days.

A Dangerous Journey

The Sahara Desert is an **inhospitable** place. Daytime maximum temperatures can easily reach 45°C; at night it can be as low as -5°C. Sandstorms could materialize within minutes and **obliterate** an entire caravan. Thirst, however, was the greatest enemy. Each person in the caravan would need four litres of water per day. Water was carried in goat-skin bags, which were refilled at desert springs and oases. These locations were well-marked and usually guarded and maintained by caravan traders.

The nomads of the desert, the Tuareg people, were either a help or hindrance to the caravans. They would often guide and protect caravans, for a price. Merchants were careful to employ local desert peoples as their special protectors.

Horses, slaves, gold, and salt were traded most frequently. The Arabs of the Mediterranean and Europeans were always eager for slaves, who were supplied by the peoples of the Sudan. It is not clear exactly how much this traffic was worth, nor how many people were sent north, but travellers' accounts indicate that a large caravan

Figure 12–14 This Tuareg nomad lives a lifestyle that is similar to that of his ancestors.

might carry as many as 500 men and women destined for slavery.

In return, the Arabs of the Mediterranean offered a large number of horses. Arabian horses did not breed well in the Sahel but the rulers of the Sudanic kingdoms were eager to use horses in their wars with one another.

Gold and Salt

The two most important **commodities** were salt and gold. The operators of the caravans purchased salt on their way south once they entered the desert. Salt was the only preservative for food, especially meat and fish. The biggest salt mine of all was the town of Taghaza, which you read about in the Window on the Past.

Farther south, in the Sudan, salt was scarce and "worth its weight in gold."

Gold was always in demand in both the Mediterranean and in Europe, where it formed a major source of new wealth in the economy.

inhospitable: not welcoming

to obliterate: to destroy totally

commodity: a good that has trade value

The exact sources of African gold remained a mystery until the nineteenth century because the miners were careful to guard the secret locations of their mines. The gold was actually dug from the river banks of West African rivers. Afterward, the mud and gravel was **panned** and the gold—usually in the form of fine grains—was stored in hollow feather **quills**.

Gold and salt miners exchanged their commodities in "silent trade," which helped the gold miners maintain their secrecy. The salt merchant would place a portion of salt on the ground. The miner would respond by placing an appropriate amount of gold by its side. Once the amount of salt was satisfactory, the miner would take it, leaving the gold. No word was ever spoken. The miners would often appear and disappear under cover of darkness— never to be seen by the salt trader.

The total amount of gold mined in a year amounted to between 2 and 9 tonnes. Two thirds of this amount was usually exported. The kings of the Sudan took the rest and many grew extremely rich from this trade. Great displays of gold were a characteristic of all the kingdoms of the Sudan, and the wealth of these kings was legendary in the kingdoms of medieval Europe.

By the eleventh century, the majority of the people in the Sudan lived as they had always done, as herders of animals and growers of food. Most kept the customs of their ancestors, although some converted to Islam.

In the great trading cities in the Sudan, Timbuktu and Gao, the populations were often a mix of local people and the Muslim newcomers from the Maghrib. To assist in their trading activities, the northern merchants set up branch offices in

to pan: to search for gold by washing sand and separating the gold from the other particles

quill: the hard, partly hollow stem of a bird's feather

Timbuktu

The most famous city of the kingdom of Sudan was Timbuktu. It is located just north of the Niger River, and was founded about 1100. By the middle of the fourteenth century, it was the largest of the trading cities, with a population of about 25 000.

Timbuktu was surrounded by large farms, which provided food for the population. These farms were well irrigated and produced a wide variety of crops.

Within the city was the great Sankore Mosque, which also served as a university. Many Islamic scholars travelled to Timbuktu to take advantage of the intellectual life there. There were libraries and public baths, and many shops and merchants' offices. A wide range of

Figure 12–15 The remains of Timbuktu as they look today.

goods was available: fabrics, gold, ostrich feathers, and exotic foods— just to name a few. The inhabitants were friendly and welcoming, and the city was noted for a thriving night life, with much public singing and dancing.

Timbuktu remained an important centre as long as the Sudanic kingdoms remained strong. As these declined in the sixteenth century, so did Timbuktu. It slowly became a small outpost on the edge of the desert.

these cities. They also brought with them their religion and culture.

GHANA, MALI, AND SONGHAI

The earliest known kingdom of the Sudan in West Africa is Ghana. By the time Arab traders first arrived in the Sudan in the eighth century, Ghana was a thriving kingdom. Its wealth and power was based on the gold deposits of the region. Ghana was most powerful in the ninth and tenth centuries. It controlled an area from the Senegal River to the Niger River. After conquering the Sanhaja Berbers of the western Sahara, Ghana gained control of the important trading town of Awdaghost. The kings of Ghana became known for their grand court and lavish style, including the wearing of gold ornaments.

In the eleventh century, one Mulsim group decided to conquer Ghana. Known as the Almoravids, they overran both Ghana and Morocco. As a result, Ghana began to lose in its power and prestige.

Meanwhile, the Mandinka peoples, who lived farther south along the Niger, were gaining more power. In the early thirteenth century, they pressed northward into the Sahel and conquered the remnants of Ghana. This was the beginning of the kingdom of Mali. While originally an agricultural kingdom, Mali quickly took control of the caravan trade routes. It extended its rule as far north as Taghaza, and allowed Timbuktu to become the foremost trading centre of the region.

The most important Mali ruler was Mansa Musa, who lived from 1312 to 1337. He undertook a pilgrimage to Mecca in 1318–19. He arrived in Cairo on his way to the holy city with 500 slaves and 300 camels. Each slave and each camel

Figure 12–16
Panning for gold continues in Africa today. Here, a man pours the contents of a pan into a **sluice** that is fitted with special grooves for catching the gold.

carried 150 kilograms of gold. While in Cairo, he and his followers spent so much gold in the markets that there was a serious drop in the worth of gold. Upon his return to Mali, Mansa also attracted many Muslim scholars to his cities, creating a sophisticated urban culture.

Mali was an important kingdom for another century. Difficulties over the rules for **succession** led to war, and the kingdom was seriously weakened. The way was left open for the rise of the kingdom of the Songhai.

Songhai developed along the Niger River in the fourteenth century. By the end of that century, it had gained control of the trading centre of Gao. Songhai expansion took place under Sunni Ali, who lived from 1464 to 1492. In almost thirty years of continual warfare, he conquered and held much of the former lands of both Mali and Ghana. His conquests were **consolidated** by his successor, Askid Muhammad, who created a professional slave army. Askid Muhammad also made a pilgrimage to Mecca, like that of Mansa Musa two centuries before. This action strengthened relations with the

sluice: a structure having a gate to control the outflow of water

succession: the right to come next to the throne

to consolidate: to join together into a whole

Maghrib states and also renewed stories of the wealth of the kings of the Sudan.

As with the kingdom of Mali, there was no rule for succession in Songhai. After Muhammad lost the throne in 1528, a number of civil wars were fought to gain control of the kingdom. By the end of the sixteenth century, Songhai was seriously weakened by these wars. In 1591, a small Moroccan army crossed the Sahara and defeated the much larger Songhai army. The Moroccan troops had one important advantage—they were armed with **muskets**.

musket: a firearm

Because of the vastness of the desert, the Moroccans were unable to maintain control of the region. Around this time, there was a famine that devastated the Sudan and put an end to the desert kingdoms. It was also during this period that European merchants became active along the Guinea Coast, a region you will read about in the next section. As a result, the once profitable trade of gold and slaves that had formerly gone north across the desert now turned south to the coast.

Figure 12–17 The kingdoms of the Sudan

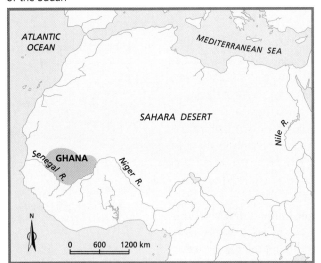

Ghana (700–1200 c.e.) was the first great Sudanese empire.

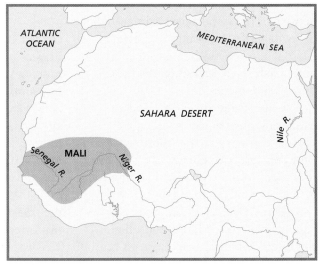

Mali (1200–1500) absorbed Ghana and extended it westward.

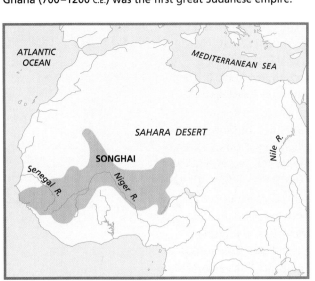

Songhai (1350–1600) slowly took over the territory of Mali.

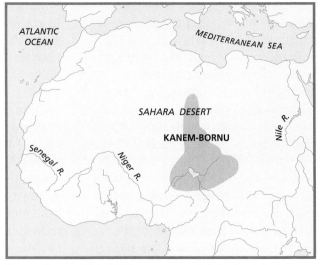

Kanem-Bornu (800–1800) grew separately in the interior.

ACTIVITIES

1. How did the physical environment affect the development and history of the kingdoms of the Sudan? What were the three major kingdoms of the Sudan? In what ways were they similar? How were the Sudanese kings renowned for their wealth and power?

2. What commodities were traded across the Sahara? Why were gold and salt the most important trade items?

3. How was agriculture performed in the Sudan? What difficulties did farmers there face? Why would there be a division of labour between men and women?

4. Do you know of any modern Canadian towns that have suffered a decline in population and prestige? What factors led to their decline?

WEST AFRICA AND THE GUINEA COAST

West Africa includes a coastal region that stretches from the mouth of the Senegal River to the modern nation of Cameroun. It has been called the "Guinea coast" for many centuries. The natural environment is varied, with a rain-forest belt along the coast, and a savanna-dominated hinterland, which gradually gives way to the Sahel.

VILLAGE LIFE

For thousands of years, life centred around small agricultural villages within the forest. Village fields were cleared during the dry season using a technique called "slash and burn." Trees were cut down, and the debris was burned. The resulting ash provided soil nutrients. As in other regions, because the cleared land had relatively few soil nutrients, fields could only be cultivated for a few years. Once fields were no longer productive, new areas were cleared and former farms were allowed to return to forest. Farms were generally small—less than 5 hectares per family.

The primary crop was yams. Yams provided a large number of calories—more calories than the grains cultivated in the savanna farther north. When harvested, yams were soaked, and then pounded into a paste that was mixed with water and boiled. The resulting porridge/dough would be combined with vegetables and meat (if available) and served in a sort of stew. Meals in the villages were **communal** affairs, with family members gathering around the cooking pot, each dipping handfuls of yam dough (known as *fufu*) into the stew.

The forest farmers produced two other crops, both of which had trade value. The first was the palm, which produced an oil-rich nut. Palm oil was extremely attractive. It had an olive-oil taste, the aroma of violets, and a rich yellow colour. It was heavily traded with the peoples of the Sudan, and was very versatile. It was used in cooking, as a fuel, and as a cosmetic.

communal: public

Palm trees were considered to be the private property of individual families, even if they grew on another's farm plot. The more palm trees a family owned, the higher their social status.

The second important crop was the kola nut. Kola nuts contained an ingredient that acted as a stimulant. Because other stimulants were unknown, kola nuts were valued by people as far north as the Maghrib. Growers of kola trees were also granted high social status. Kola nuts were given to travellers and guests to show hospitality.

While the peoples of the forest were not as wealthy as the peoples of the Sudan, they still engaged in trade. Palm oil and kola nuts, as well as salt produced along the sea coast, were exchanged for leather, iron, and gold produced farther inland.

Although most of the forest peoples lived in small villages, larger societies developed there. These were formed mostly in the eastern part of the region, in what is now Nigeria and Cameroun. The rulers of these states of the Guinea Coast seem to have immigrated into the area around the seventh century. An early ancestor of the Yoruba culture, for example, was a Mulsim named Oduduwa. Tradition states that he arrived from Mecca and established several kingdoms, including Oyo, Ife, and Benin. During the tenth century, many peoples from the Sudan moved into this region.

■ ■ ■ ■ ■ ■ ■ ■ ■ ■ ■ ■

THE KINGDOMS OF THE GUINEA COAST

The kingdoms of the Guinea Coast remained quite small—in physical size and power—until the fourteenth century. Most of these kingdoms were city-states scattered throughout the region. The most important of these was Ife. This city has always been considered one of the most sacred of the Yoruba peoples. By about 1200, the people of Ife had grown wealthy enough for sculptors to produce the beautiful bronzes for which Ife has remained famous. Still, Ife remained physically small, although it was the most influential centre in the region.

By 1400, Benin had become a powerful kingdom—the first of the Guinea Coast to grow beyond the status of city-state. The most important Benin ruler was Ewuare the Great (1440–1473). He was, according to oral tradition, a wise man, a warrior, and a great magician. He ruled 201 towns and villages. By controlling trade, the kings of Benin were able to maintain their power, which was further enhanced with the arrival of the Portuguese in 1471.

Contact With the Portuguese

On the West Coast of Africa, the Portuguese had been busy trying to conquer territory since 1474. After some time, they became allies and trading partners of the kingdoms and city-states there. One of their most important allies was Benin. The Benin king even sent **ambassadors** to Lisbon to act as his representatives there. The sons of the king were taught Portuguese so they could deal easily with the newcomers.

The Portuguese were impressed with the business-like Benin. African traders were shrewd bargainers, and negotiations about the price and quantity of goods could go on for days or weeks. Moreover, the Africans insisted on fairness and honesty—if they encountered dishonesty, they would refuse to engage in trade.

Using Sculpture as a Primary Source

It has been said that no art form provides a clearer record of a culture's development than sculpture. The tradition of sculpture goes back 20 000 years to the Paleolithic Period, sometimes called the Old Stone Age.

Sculpture has one advantage over other art forms. It physically represents a culture's ideals. The Romans and the Europeans of the Renaissance, for example, idealized the human body in their sculptures.

In one area of West Africa, artists created a tradition of sculpture that lasted more than 3000 years. The earliest sculptures were created by the Nok, who worked in both terra cotta and bronze. The Nok made their art between about 900 B.C.E. and 200 C.E. Figures were often life-sized. Artists paid much attention to the head because the Nok believed that the head was the origin of a person's life force.

The Ife people began to create their works around 1000 C.E. Ife sculpture is extremely lifelike. The sculptures were used to enhance the power and prestige of Ife rulers.

The sculptural tradition of the Nok and Ife reached its greatest development among the Benin people, beginning in the fourteenth century. This tradition lasted into the nineteenth century. Like the Ife, the Benin had a well-developed urban life, with rulers who became very wealthy and powerful through trade.

The purpose of Benin sculpture was two-fold. The Benin sculpted for religious and spiritual reasons. Sculptures were also used to decorate the royal palace of the Benin kings. These sculptures depicted the great events of the ruler's life and his or her actions.

The Ife and Benin peoples created bronze art, which was difficult to **execute**. The copper for the bronzes came from the Air region of the Sahara, and was acquired through trade with the peoples of the Sudan.

The sculptures themselves were created using the lost-wax process. The lost-wax method involves making a mould of wax of the figure and then pouring the molten bronze into the mould. As the wax melts, the bronze takes its place, leaving a finished piece of art.

The Benin created both figures and **bas-relief** plaques. The plaques, eventually numbering about a thousand, adorned the king's palace and provided a unique historical record of the Benin royal family.

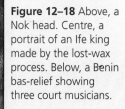

Figure 12–18 Above, a Nok head. Centre, a portrait of an Ife king made by the lost-wax process. Below, a Benin bas-relief showing three court musicians.

to execute: to carry out

bas-relief: a sculpture in which the figures are carved on a flat surface and are raised only slightly

NOW YOU DO IT

1. On your own, examine the art of the Nok, Ife, and Benin peoples. Which do you prefer? Why?

2. In a group of three, compare your findings. Try to reach some sort of agreement as to what you see in the art. What do you like about the art? Why? What do you dislike? Why? Share your group's findings with the rest of the class.

3. Nok, Ife, and Benin art was created for many reasons. Identify three. Can you tell which reason the artist had in mind by examining the finished product? Which details of the sculptures guided your answer?

THE SLAVE TRADE IN WEST AFRICA

Slavery in Africa had always been a part of traditional life, but the African concept of slavery had more in common with the Roman tradition than it did with later European slavery.

Until the arrival of the Portuguese, African slaves were usually prisoners of war or criminals.

They were considered to be unpaid labourers who could be bought and sold. However, they were not considered to be the property of their purchasers. In fact, a slave became a low-status member of the purchaser's tribe or clan group. Slaves were able to buy their freedom, often from proceeds from their own garden. These plots were actually provided by the slaves' owners. A slave could marry into his or her new clan, which also resulted in freedom. It was not

A Slave's Journey

The voyage from Africa across the Atlantic was called "The Middle Passage." The journey represented one of the truly horrific chapters in human history. The following account is adapted from a work by the British historian Edmund d'Auvergne. He based it on testimony from slave-ship captains and crew members given to British parliamentary committees in the early 1800s.

musty: stale, smelling like mould

unfettered: not chained or shackled

intolerable: unbearable

slaughterhouse: the place where animals are killed for food

Figure 12–19 This diagram illustrates the terrible physical confinement forced on men and women during the journey from Africa.

A common type of slaving vessel was the snow, about 30 metres in length, 8 metres in beam [width], with 1.5 metres space between decks. Legally, such a vessel could carry 450 persons, but one such vessel departed Africa with a crew of 45 and 609 slaves (351 men, 127 women, 90 boys, 41 girls) aboard. The passage from Guinea to Antigua in the West Indies was reckoned at five or six weeks. In extreme cases, the passage could take as much as three months. During this time, the slaves were fed a diet of **musty** corn mush, given little water, and only rarely were they allowed on the upper deck while their prison was cleaned.

Between decks, where a tall man could not stand upright, the human cargo was stowed, males and females in separate compartments. The women were left **unfettered**. The men were chained in pairs, wrist to wrist, ankle to ankle. "They were about as comfortable," said one witness, "as a man might be in his coffin." In many cases, a slave might be healthy one evening and dead the next morning—the dead and living were often found chained together.

A ship's surgeon says: "Some wet and blowing weather having occasioned the port-holes to be shut and the grating to be covered, and diarrhea and fevers resulted. While they were in this situation, my profession requiring it, I frequently went down among them, till at length their deck became so extremely hot as to be sufferable for a very short time. The deck, that is the floor of their rooms, was so covered with blood and mucus that it resembled a **slaughterhouse**. Numbers of the slaves had fainted, they were carried on deck, where several of them died…

To these horrors must be added the agonies of sea-sickness. One researcher noted that of 7904 slaves purchased on the Guinea Coast, 2053 died on the Middle Passage.

unusual for a slave to rise to a position of power and wealth.

European attitudes were different. Slaves were considered to be possessions, to be bought and sold. Most slaves were not able to buy their freedom; nor were they allowed to marry the relatives of their purchasers. African slaves purchased by Europeans were shipped from their homelands to work as agricultural labourers in the Americas. Almost none ever returned.

After 1600, the Europeans wanted many more slaves than could be provided by the Africans. This demand led to a breakdown of the traditional relationships among African states and groups. Raids and wars to capture slaves resulted in continual conflict from the sixteenth century to the early nineteenth century. When the West African slave trade finally ended in the 1830s, all the states of West Africa had been devastated by it.

Benin itself was a victim of this aggression. It became a **vassal state** of the rising Oyo kingdom in the seventeenth century.

The Oyo came to power in the seventeenth and eighteenth centuries.

Like the kingdoms of the Sudan, the Oyo had seized power through military conquest and through income from trade. The military strength of the Oyo lay in their cavalry. To get the horses, the Oyo first traded slaves for European goods in the coastal areas they dominated. The Oyo then brought these foods, along with more slaves, to the Sudan, where they traded for the horses.

Oyo power endured only as long as there was a slave trade. Slavery declined at the end of the eighteenth century for a number of reasons, including the ending of slavery by the British in the early nineteenth century. The Oyo rulers were forced to raise taxes to make up for lost revenues. This led to civil unrest, which caused the collapse of the Oyo kingdom in the mid-nineteenth century.

vassal state: a state whose people owe loyalty to another state, often in exchange for protection

Figure 12–20 What does this sculpture convey about the artist's attitude to the Portuguese?

ACTIVITIES

1. What was the main food crop of West Africa? How were fields cleared for agriculture? How did the West Africans deal with the effects of poor forest soils? What two non-food crops were important? Why would they be valuable as trade items?

2. Why did Benin become a powerful and wealthy kingdom? How did European contact enhance this power at first? What eventually led to the downfall of Benin?

3. Why do you suppose sculpture was so important to the peoples of Ife and Benin?

4. Compare the African slave trade with the European slave trade using an organizer or through a creative representation such as a poem. If you choose to use an organizer, keep your account factual. If you choose to use a poem, introduce your feelings and personal images.

5. Imagine you are a slave captured from your village, and placed aboard one of these vessels. In a poem, or letter, describe your feelings about the ship you are on, and what your fate might be. (For a real slave's account, see page 297.)

6. How do you feel the peoples of the Guinea Coast felt about the European slave trade? What longstanding effects do you think it had on them?

EAST AFRICA AND ETHIOPIA

The coastal region of East Africa, which stretches from the Red Sea south to the southern borders of modern Tanzania, has a long history. This area formed part of an extensive ocean trading network for several thousand years, going back at least as far as 1000 B.C.E.

The Romans who participated in this network seem to have had no knowledge of the interior of Africa along its east coast. One reason is the nature of the rivers of the region, which, while broad enough to be **navigable**, descend to the coast in a series of rapids and waterfalls that make penetration inland impossible by water.

With the collapse of the Roman Empire in the fourth and fifth centuries, the East African maritime trade was taken over by the Arabs and

Trade in East Africa

In this excerpt, a first-century Roman official describes East African trade. He provides evidence that long-distance trade in the ancient world was both common and extensive.

Ships depart from the Red Sea port of Berenice in Egypt loaded with cloth goods, metals such as copper, brass, and iron, cooking utensils, tools, olive oil, and wine. They make their first stop at Adulis, the seaport of Axum. Here, some of the cargo is exchanged for ivory, tortoise shell, and rhinoceros horn. The ships then sail down the Red Sea, stopping at both sides of the sea, picking up **incense** from Yemen, and slaves and cinnamon. Once out of the Red Sea, the ships turn south along the coast of Africa. This coast is uninhabited, being both extremely hot and dry, and the ships do no further trading until they reach the mouth of the Juba River.

Further south along the coast there are many trading ports populated by local peoples who are ruled by merchants from Yemen. Here, more ivory, horn and tortoise shell is obtained, in exchange for the original cargo loaded in Egypt. The port farthest south is called "Rhapta" [near present-day Zanzibar]. Beyond this, the coastline continues westward, stretching out from the south and mingling with the western sea. Here, the ships turn eastward across the Indian Ocean, to make landfalls in Malaysia and India, where their African cargo is exchanged for sugar, grain, oils, and spices, which are sold when the ships return to their home port.

PRIMARY SOURCE

Figure 12–21 Victoria Falls is an example of a barrier to the interior of Africa.

Persians. They greatly extended the sea-borne trade of the region.

By the tenth century, most of the inhabitants of the region were Bantu. They had arrived in the region over the previous 500 years. The coastal trading towns also had a population of Arab traders. These traders mingled with the **indigenous** peoples to produce a distinct coastal culture. The people spoke a dialect known as "Swahili," still the primary language of East Africa. Swahili is a Bantu language, but it also has a strong Arabic character, and it reflects the mix of cultures that existed along the coast.

TRADE IN EAST AFRICA

To the trade items described in the feature box on page 392, the Arab traders added gold. They also extended the region of trade as far south as Sofala in present-day Mozambique.

Outside the trading towns, the local people grew African grains such as sorghum and millet. They also produced rice, cucumber, coconuts, and bananas. They practised traditional African religions and were concerned with the spirit nature of the world. They were ruled by kings who were thought to be skilled in magic.

In Madagascar, a different group had arrived in the early part of the Christian era. These people had travelled across the Indian Ocean from Malaysia, and established themselves on that island's east coast. They introduced many Asian foods to Africa at that time, including the banana.

A series of trading centres developed along the East African coast by the tenth century. These towns grew fairly large, to about 10 000 people. The town farthest north was Mogadishu, on the Somali coast. Farther south were the ports of Mombasa, Gadi, Pemba, Zanzibar,

Mafia, Kilwa, and Sofala. By the thirteenth century, all these towns contained a mosque, a palace for the Arab rulers, and other permanent buildings that reflected the prosperity of these centres. The architectural styles of the mosques and palaces were distinctly Islamic.

By the end of the fifteenth century, East Africa was one part of an extensive and prosperous maritime trading network that included Arabia, Persia, India, China, and Indonesia. Kilwa dominated the coastal trade, controlling it from Pemba Island in the north to Sofala in the south. Sofala served as the outlet for gold from the inland plateau—an average of nearly 6000 kilograms was exported annually. This trade also led to the development of Zimbabwe. Kilwa's palace was especially grand, extending over almost a hectare on a cliff overlooking the ocean.

Many and varied items were exported from the East African ports, including gold, ivory, pearls, amber, coral, copper, citrus fruits, sugar,

indigenous: aboriginal, native to the areas

Figure 12–22 The ruins of the palace at Kilwa

timber, and pitch. With the exception of gold, these goods were locally produced or harvested, and there was little contact with the peoples inland. At the end of the fifteenth century, however, an external event took place that very nearly destroyed the entire East African trading network.

Portugal, as you have learned, had been exploring south along Africa's west coast since the middle of the fifteenth century. Following Vasco da Gama's voyage along the East African coast to India in 1497–98, the Portuguese began to participate in the African trade. They decided that in addition to controlling the East Indies, they should also control the trade of East Africa.

In 1502, the Portuguese captured Kilwa. In 1503, they seized Zanzibar. By 1505, they controlled Sofala. And in 1509, the Portuguese defeated a combined Persian, Egyptian, and Arab fleet. In just ten years, Portugal completely controlled the East African coast. However, this violent takeover did not benefit the Portuguese.

Trading restrictions imposed by the Portuguese strangled what had been a free trade network. Further, the local inhabitants did not like taking orders from the Portuguese newcomers. They reacted by adopting a policy of **passive resistance**. By 1512, Kilwa was largely abandoned. Its trade was destroyed and its population had dispersed to other towns.

What happened at Kilwa was repeated at Sofala. As the sixteenth century progressed, Portuguese attempts to dominate the coastline north of Zanzibar also failed. The Portuguese attacks left ruined cities that had to be rebuilt, and surviving merchants tried to avoid the Portuguese. By the end of the sixteenth century, the Portuguese had political control of this region of Africa, but the once thriving trade was a shadow of its former self.

ETHIOPIA

While the coast of East Africa was directly connected to the rest of the known world, the opposite was true for the Ethiopians. Ethiopia is situated in a naturally isolated highland area. Before the coming of Islam, the area had been dominated by the kingdom of Axum. This kingdom had extensive contacts with Roman Egypt and the peoples of the Arabian peninsula, with whom they traded. The Axumites also adopted a form of Christianity in the fourth century. The expansion of Islam had the effect of cutting off the Christian Axumites from their old Mediterranean connections, leaving them culturally and physically isolated.

In the ninth and tenth centuries, the Axumites gradually moved south into the mountainous centre of the Ethiopian highlands. Here they came into conflict with the local people, the Agau, who were primarily **pagans**. The Agau rebelled frequently, nearly destroying Axumite Christianity. However, by the eleventh century, a new society had developed. This society was a mixture of Axumite and Agau characteristics—this was the new kingdom of Ethiopia.

Figure 12–23 This Ethiopian stone church has been carved from solid volcanic rock. There are eleven of these structures in all, built during the reign of King Lalibela (1181–1221). Many are cross-shaped, and use all the traditional elements of Christian churches of the medieval period, including arches, vaults, naves, and chapels.

The Ethiopians tried to prevent their culture from being overwhelmed by their largely Islamic neighbours. From 1200 to 1500, they were generally successful. The most powerful king of this era, Zara Yakob (1434–68) was even able to establish relations with the Roman Catholic Church.

During the sixteenth century, the Ethiopians faced a Muslim invasion from the south under Ahmad ibn Ghazi, who nearly conquered them. In 1541, the Ethiopian king appealed to the Portuguese (who had been in contact with the Ethiopians) for assistance. The arrival of some 400 **musketeers** was the response. In a decisive battle near Lake Tana, the Muslims were defeated and Ibn Ghazi was killed.

From the mid-sixteenth century on, the Ethiopians faced another crisis. This was not a military attack, but a slow and continuous **infiltration** of the country by Galla herdsmen from Somalia. The Galla did not want to **assimilate**, and by the eighteenth century, Ethiopia had become a fragmented land. The Ethiopians and the Galla lived side by side, yet apart, and were always suspicious of each other.

musketeer: soldier armed with a musket (an old firearm)

infiltration: the gradual movement into an area

to assimilate: to become like other people by being absorbed into their society

isolation: the state of being apart from others

ACTIVITIES

1. Why was there little contact between the peoples of the coast of East Africa and the peoples farther inland? What commodity was traded between them?

2. How did the Arabs contribute to the distinctive culture of East Africa? Why was trade so successful for so long in this part of Africa?

3. How did the Portuguese destroy the East African trading network? Why were they unable to work cooperatively with the peoples of East Africa?

4. What were the effects of **isolation** on the development of Ethiopian culture? What group were the Ethiopians able to resist successfully? Why? What group were they less able to deal with? Why?

5. How are the church buildings of Ethiopia and Medieval Europe different? How are they similar? How do you account for these differences?

THE BANTU PEOPLES OF CENTRAL AND SOUTHERN AFRICA

The drying of the Sahara not only influenced the subsequent history of the Sahel and Sudan—it also had a great effect on the settlement of **sub-equatorial** Africa.

As the Sahara became unsuitable for agriculture, its peoples slowly moved south. Reaching the forest margin, probably about 6000 years ago, they began farming. In the savanna and forests of West Africa, settlement was permanent. No more long-range migrations took place.

Farther east, the population movements continued. Some peoples spread eastward along the edge of the forest, as far as the upper reaches of the Nile River. A second group moved south and southeast, into the forest. These people spoke a Niger-Congo language known as Benue-Congo. It gave rise to the nearly 300 Bantu languages spoken today in central and southern Africa.

The southward movement of the Bantu began about 1000 B.C.E., with a relatively slow progress through Gabon

sub-equatorial: south of the equator

into the watershed of the Zaire River. At about the time of Christ, this movement gained speed. Bantu speakers reached the region of Lake Victoria by 300 B.C.E. and Lake Kisale about 400 C.E. By the fifteenth century, the Bantu had occupied nearly all of southern Africa, with the exception of the Namib and Kalahari deserts. These areas were still occupied by their original Khoisan peoples.

Figure 12–24 This is an aerial view of a village in central East Africa. It belongs to a group of people who graze cattle for a living. How does the plan of this village suit the occupation of the inhabitants?

Bantu culture evolved as two distinct groups. On the savanna of eastern and southern Africa, they became primarily cattle herders because the dry climate made farming impractical. As a result, communities moved about seasonally, and were never large. Because of these factors, political organization was firmly based on the village, and larger states did not develop.

In the forests of Zaire and in the wetter parts of southern Africa, the Bantu were able to maintain their original lifestyle as farmers. They cultivated local yams along with Asian imports such as taro root and the banana. If the soil was poor, social groupings remained small, as with the savanna herders. In areas where soil was of higher quality, or where fishing or mining provided additional wealth,

Bantu groups adopted more complex social systems.

GREAT ZIMBABWE

The most notable of these groups lived in what is now the modern nation of Zimbabwe. One of these states, the Zimbabwe Kingdom, created one of Africa's most famous ruins—Great Zimbabwe, part of an enormous complex of stone ruins.

The word *zimbabwe* comes from the Shona language and probably means "stone houses." During the development of the Zimbabwe Kingdom, large stone buildings and fortifications were built to maintain control of the area. These were usually erected on the tops of hills. Terracing of agricultural land led to the first structures in the eleventh century. By the fourteenth century, the buildings had expanded to include hilltop defences and the royal enclosure of Great Zimbabwe itself. The stone structures reflected religious as well as political power. Because the kings usually lived apart from their subjects, these stone buildings added to their status.

The largest of these structures was the Elliptical Building, which encompassed a series of smaller structures. Its walls were up to 10 metres high, built of granite blocks without the use of mortar. The largest structure within the Elliptical Building was the Great Tower, also 10 metres high.

The creators of this remarkable complex were the ancestors of today's Shona people, who still live in the area. A combination of cattle herding, farming, and trade with coastal East African ports generated enough wealth to enable the Shona to develop a kingdom.

Shona kings, who were considered to be divine, lived in a grand manner, yet were **secluded** from their subjects. Public audiences were held, but the king would remain hidden. Persons who were granted access to the king did so while performing ritual acts of proper homage and submission. When a king died, several of his wives and officials would be executed as well, so they could accompany the king on his journey to the spirit world. All fires in the kingdom were put out—new fires could only be started from the fire of the new king.

Despite all this authority, Shona tradition had its limitations. Because the king was divine, he was expected to be perfect. Any hint of disease or deformity would require a king to commit suicide. Further, as the king was kept apart from ordinary people, he was also subject to control by his officials and courtiers.

The Shona kings of Zimbabwe grew wealthy from trade with East African ports, especially Sofala. Gold was shipped to the coast, and cloth and other goods were imported in return. By the thirteenth century, the state was powerful enough to create the imposing palace at Great Zimbabwe.

No one really knows why the kings of Zimbabwe abandoned their city around 1450. Some historians say that the land around the complex could no longer support all the people who lived there. It is also possible that a great **drought** forced everyone to leave. Nevertheless, the economic reasons for the success of Zimbabwe

Figure 12–25 The ruins of Great Zimbabwe.

secluded: kept apart from others

drought: an extended period of no rain

still existed, and it was eventually replaced by a series of new states in the region.

To the north of Zimbabwe the kingdom of Mutapa grew to prominence about 1450. Mutapa maintained its power until the seventeenth century. The economy was based on cattle and, like Zimbabwe, it controlled the production of gold and its export to the coastal ports. When the Portuguese arrived on the coast in the sixteenth century, they established a series of inland trading posts in Mutapa country, and slowly developed a degree of control of this part of the interior plateau. By 1629, they gained direct control of Mutapa, making its king a vassal of Portugal.

ACTIVITIES

1. Locate Zimbabwe on a modern map of Africa. Why would good rail and road systems be so important to this country?

2. Describe the movements of the Bantu peoples. Why did two different types of local cultures develop in southern Africa?

3. How was Zimbabwe able to develop? What were the advantages of the kind of rule its kings practised? What were the disadvantages? What factors might have led to its downfall?

In this chapter, you have examined the development of Africa over a long period of time. The natural environment of the continent has made it difficult for the people of Africa to create large political units. Instead, the movements and interactions of many different peoples across the continent has created many varied cultures.

By 600, the kingdoms of West Africa were thriving. In addition to their obvious wealth and power—which so impressed the visiting Arabs—the Ife and the Benin peoples created longstanding artistic traditions that still influence the arts today.

In both the Sudan and along the East Africa coast, long-distance trade brought wealth and fame to Africa during the time of the European Middle Ages. Europeans always desired African trading goods, particularly its gold and salt.

However, the eventual expansion of Europeans into Africa would have a terrible effect on the continent. In East Africa, the greed of the Portuguese explorers and traders, who arrived in the fifteenth century, nearly destroyed a trading network that had lasted for more than 1000 years. The European slave trade also damaged a network of cultures in West Africa that had existed in harmony for an even longer period.

Today Africa is independent once again. Its future is entirely, and rightfully, in its own hands.

SUMMARY ACTIVITIES

1. Make an organizer that describes the forms of agriculture in the Sudan, West Africa, and southern Africa. Areas you should include could be types of crops and their origins, methods of land clearing and cultivation, use of animals, and the effects of the environment.

2. Imagine you are a trader in a caravan travelling across the Sahara. In a poem or letter, or using visuals such as a poster, discuss your feelings about the dangers of the journey, the trade items you will be buying and selling, and how you might spend your time when you arrive at your destination.

3. In West Africa, the Sudan, and southern Africa, kings held great power. In what ways did they maintain their control over their subjects? The word "protocol" means "how one behaves in certain formal situations." Why was protocol so important in the dealings of subjects with their kings?

4. What were the effects of the arrival of Europeans in various parts of Africa? How did Europeans disrupt traditional ways of doing things? What were the motivations of Europeans in coming to Africa? How did these differ from traditional African motivations?

5. How did African religions differ from those of Europeans in the medieval period? How do you suppose Europeans misinterpreted traditional African beliefs?

ON YOUR OWN

1. Part One of the television mini-series *Roots* contains a dramatization of the slave trade and the voyage on the Middle Passage. You can get it from most video outlets. Screen it in class and hold a class discussion afterwards.

2. Construct a model of the ruins of the Great Zimbabwe. There are many diagrams of the complex in books about South Africa, including those that imagine what the entire complex would have looked like. Label your model.

13 CHINA: THE WORLD POWER

CHAPTER OUTCOMES

In this chapter you will study the civilization of China from about 1000 to 1650. China was one of the greatest civilizations of the world, with an advanced culture and technology. By the end of the chapter, you will

- explain how the collapse of the Song Dynasty led to the period of Mongol rule
- describe the technological developments during the Song era
- identify the basic elements of Song architecture
- describe the Golden Age of the Ming Dynasty
- demonstrate an understanding of the concept of economic recovery
- identify social norms as presented in Chinese literature
- use guidelines to analyze Chinese art
- identify patterns in statistics

The Dream of the Red Chamber

PRIMARY SOURCE

One of China's most popular novels, The Dream of the Red Chamber, *was written during one of the later dynasties.* The Dream of the Red Chamber *is still known today—sometimes through movies and television shows based on its story.*

The Dream of the Red Chamber *offers us a glimpse into daily life in China hundreds of years ago. In this excerpt, a young woman known as Lin Dai-yu has been sent to live with her grandmother after her mother's death. She has just arrived at the Rong mansion in the capital. We also meet Granny Jia and Dai-yu's cousin, the vivacious Lady Wang Xi-feng.*

Lin-Dai-yu at the Rong mansion

On the day of her arrival in the capital, Dai-yu stepped ashore to find **covered chairs** from the Rong mansion waiting for her and her servants. A cart for the luggage also stood waiting for her by the **quay**.

Dai-yu got into her chair and was soon carried through the city walls. Peeping through the gauze panel, which served as a window, she could see streets and buildings more rich and elegant and throngs of people more lively and numerous than she had ever seen in her whole life. After being carried for what seemed a very great length of time, she saw, on the north side of the street through which they were passing, two great stone lions crouched on each side of a triple gateway whose doors were decorated with animal heads. In front of the gateway, ten or so splendidly dressed **flunkeys** sat in a row.

Parts of the Rong mansion probably looked something like this modern artist's rendition.

Ignoring the central gate, her bearers went in by the western entrance. After **traversing** the distance of a **bow-shot** they turned a corner and set the chair down. The places of Dai-yu's bearers were taken by four handsome, fresh-faced pages of seventeen or eighteen. They shouldered her chair and, with the old women now following on foot, carried it as far as the ornamental gate. There they set it down again and then retired in respectful silence. The old women came forward to the front of the chair, held up the curtain, and helped Dai-yu get out.

Each hand resting on the outstretched hand of an elderly attendant, Dai-yu passed through the ornamental gate into a courtyard, which had **balustraded loggias** running along its sides and a covered passage through the centre. The foreground of the courtyard beyond was partly hidden by a screen of polished marble set in an elaborate red **sandalwood** frame.

Passing round the screen and through a small reception area beyond it, they entered the large courtyard of the mansion's principal apartments. These were housed in an imposing five-frame building **resplendent** with carved and painted beams and rafters that faced them across the courtyard. Running along either side of the courtyard were galleries hung with cages containing a variety of different-coloured parrots, cockatoos, white-eyes, and other birds. Some gaily dressed maids were sitting on the steps of the main building opposite. At the appearance of the visitors they rose to their feet and came forward with smiling

Peppercorn Feng seemed to gleam like some fairy princess.

seated once more, a maid served tea, and a conversation began on the subject of her mother: how the illness had started, what doctors had been called in, what medicines prescribed, what arrangements had been made for the funeral, and how mourning had been observed. This conversation had the **foreseeable** effect of upsetting the old lady all over again. She had scarcely finished speaking when somebody could be heard talking and laughing in a very loud voice in the inner courtyard behind them.

"Oh dear! I'm late," said the voice. "I've missed the arrival of our guest."

"Everyone else around here seems to go about with **bated** breath," thought Dai-yu. "Who can this new arrival be who is so brash and unmannerly?"

Even as she wondered, a beautiful young woman entered from the room behind the one they were sitting in, surrounded by a **bevy** of serving women and maids. She was dressed quite differently from the others present, gleaming like some fairy princess with sparkling jewels and lovely embroideries.

Her **chignon** was enclosed in a circlet of gold **filigree** and clustered pearls. It was fastened with a pin embellished with flying **phoenixes**, from whose beaks pearls were suspended on tiny chains.

Her necklet was of red gold in the form of a coiling dragon.

Her dress had a fitted bodice and was made of dark red silk damask with a pattern of flowers and butterflies in raised gold thread.

faces to welcome them.

"You've come at just the right time!" they cried. "Lady Jia was only this moment asking about you."

As Dai-yu entered the room she saw a silver-haired old lady advancing to meet her, supported on either side by a servant. She knew that this must be her grandmother Jia. Dai-Yu would have fallen on her hands and knees and made her **kowtow**, but before she could do so her grandmother had caught her in her arms. She

pressed her to her bosom with cries of "My pet!" and "My poor lamb!" and burst into loud sobs while all those present wept in sympathy, and Dai-yu felt herself crying as though she would never stop. It was some time before those present succeeded in calming them both down and Dai-yu was at last able to make her kowtow.

Grandma Jia now introduced those present.

Dai-yu rose to meet them and exchanged curtsies and introductions. When she was

Her jacket was lined with **ermine**. It was of slate-blue stuff with woven insets in coloured silks.

Her under-skirt was of a turquoise-coloured silk crepe embroidered with flowers.

She had, moreover:

eyes like a painted phoenix
eyebrows like willow
    leaves,
a slender form,
seductive grace;
the ever-smiling summer
    face
of hidden thunders showed
    no trace;
the ever-bubbling laughter
    started
almost before the lips were
    parted.

"Don't you know her?" said Grandmother Jia merrily. "She's a holy terror, this one— what we used to call in Nanking a 'peppercorn.' You just call her 'Peppercorn Feng.' She'll know who you mean!"

Dai-yu was at a loss to know how to address this Peppercorn Feng until one of the cousins whispered that it was "Cousin Lian's wife." She remembered having heard her mother say that her elder uncle, Uncle She, had a son called Jia Lian who was married to the niece of her Uncle Zheng's wife, Lady Wang. Peppercorn had been brought up from earliest childhood just like a boy, and had acquired in the schoolroom the somewhat boyish-sounding name of Wang Xi-feng. Dai-yu accordingly smiled and curtsied, greeting her by her correct name as she did so.

Xi-feng took Dai-yu by the hand and for a few moments examined her carefully from top to toe before leading her back to her seat beside Grandmother Jia.

covered chair: a covered "box" used to transport important people, supported on poles and carried by bearers

quay: the dockside, pronounced "key"

flunkey: a person who waits on others

to traverse: to walk across

bow-shot: about 250 metres

balustraded loggia: a covered walk or gallery, with pillars

sandalwood: a fragrant wood

resplendent: splendid

bated: held in

kowtow: a formal bow that involves touching the forehead to the ground to show respect

foreseeable: predictable

bevy: a group

chignon: a knot of hair at the back of the neck

ermine: fur from an animal in the weasel family

filigree: a delicate work of intertwined metal

phoenix: a mythical bird

ACTIVITIES

1. This excerpt from *The Dream of the Red Chamber* is filled with details to help us imagine what people and things in the novel look like. Using details from the story, make a coloured sketch of a scene or person described in the excerpt.

2. Find three examples from the story that show how formality and respect were important in China.

3. Compare the personalities of Lin Dai-yu and Wang Xi-feng. How many servants did Lin Dai-yu encounter during the few hours covered in this excerpt from *The Dream of the Red Chamber*? Having a lot of servants tells us that a family is wealthy. What else does it tell us about the society of China during this period?

4. Why do you think the author suddenly broke into poetry when describing the physical attributes of Wang Xi-feng? Is this passage entirely serious? Why or why not?

907	SONG DYNASTY BEGINS
1000	INVENTION OF THE MAGNETIC COMPASS
1012	CHANGSA RICE INTRODUCED FROM VIETNAM
1040	INVENTION OF MOVABLE-TYPE PRINTING
1044	INVENTION OF GUNPOWDER
1126	NORTHERN SONG EMPEROR, HUIZONG, IS CAPTURED
1271	KHUBILAI KHAN CAPTURES NORTHERN CHINA; YÜAN DYNASTY BEGINS
1275	MARCO POLO ARRIVES IN BEIJING
1279	KHUBILAI KHAN CAPTURES SOUTHERN CHINA
1368	MING DYNASTY BEGINS
1404 to 1433	ZHENG HE VOYAGES TO SOUTH AND SOUTHEAST ASIA AND AFRICA
1644	QING DYNASTY BEGINS

Do you know the old man who
Sells flowers by the South Gate?
He lives in flowers like a bee.
In the morning he sells mallows,
In the evening he has poppies.
His shanty root lets in the
Blue sky. His rice bin is
Always empty...

...What does
He care if new laws are
*   posted*
At the Emperor's palace?
What does it matter to him
If the government is built
On sand? If you try to talk
To him, he won't answer but
Only to give you a
Smile from under his hair.

—LU YU, CIRCA 1100 C.E.

PRIMARY SOURCE

This poem from the Song Dynasty captures many of the contrasts of Song society. While the period favoured artists and academics, the government was weak and many emperors were corrupt. The Song Dynasty eventually fell to the Mongols in 1271. Why is this poet concerned about his society? Why are poets sometimes social critics?

Introduction

Do you remember the changes that took place in western Europe during the Middle Ages?

During these years, China was one of the greatest civilizations in the world. Its art, technology, and ways of governing were highly developed. By comparison, Europe was backward and warlike. Europeans knew little or nothing about China. Nevertheless, they benefited from Chinese technologies. Gunpowder, paper, the horse collar, the clock, and the wheelbarrow all came to Europe from China, mostly by way of the Islamic world, which traded with China.

As you have learned, China's history is usually studied by referring to its dynasties. Dynasties are ruling families who give their name to the time period during which they ruled. In this chapter, you will learn about China during the Song, Yüan, and Ming Dynasties.

During the Song Dynasty, China experienced a great cultural flowering. Before this period there had been about fifty years of political, social, and economic upheaval. The Song set about restoring peace and order and the traditional Chinese system. As a result, Chinese art, technology, government, economics and culture flourished.

In a military sense, the Song were less strong than earlier dynasties. The empire was sometimes under attack from Mongol groups to the north and northwest. Eventually, the Song lost northern China to the Jurchen Mongols in 1126. The Song moved south and continued their rule for another 150 years.

In 1279, the Mongols from central Asia led by Khubilai Khan captured all of China. Khubilai established the Yüan Dynasty. Khubilai controlled the government, but he allowed Chinese artists, writers, and scholars to work in the old ways. The Chinese were able to keep many of their traditions intact during these years of foreign rule.

China was not ruled by Chinese again until the founding of the Ming, or "brilliant," Dynasty in 1368. The Ming Dynasty restored the traditional Chinese government and brought back strict Confucian values. Under the Ming, Chinese life continued its traditional path. Chinese arts, technology, and civilization prospered and reached even greater heights.

The Chinese were the envy of the world.

The Song Dynasty: Renaissance in China, 907–1276

Historians often refer to the **continuity** of Chinese history and culture. They are really saying that core values and ways of doing things did not seem to change much over time. While this is true, it is also true that some changes did occur. There were many exciting periods of change and development in Chinese history. One of these took place between the tenth and thirteenth centuries under the Song Dynasty. Many historians call this period the Chinese Renaissance—a comparison to the later Renaissance in Europe.

In the fifty years following the failure of the Tang Dynasty, many

continuity: the state of being continuous, having no breaks small kingdoms had grown up. It was a period of chaos, when no one was strong enough to establish orderly government. Finally, an ordinary soldier, Taizu, became emperor following a mutiny by the palace guards in one of these small kingdoms. Taizu was just thirty-two years old when he became emperor.

The first thing Taizu did was to defeat the rulers of the other small kingdoms that had appeared. This reunited China. His next task was to make the country safe from attack by the Mongols who lived to the north and northwest of China. Taizu used many strategies to do this. Sometimes he went to war and defeated China's enemies. Sometimes Taizu used diplomacy to achieve his goals. He entered into **alliances** with some groups of Mongols. He fostered rivalry among other groups, so that they would not unite against China. Taizu and his successors kept China strong and well governed for many years.

alliance: a close association for a common purpose

bureaucrats: workers in various departments of government

However, the northern enemies remained a constant threat to China.

GOVERNMENT

After ensuring that China's borders were safe, Taizu began to rebuild China's government. The emperor was the supreme ruler of China. In theory he had absolute power—the power of life and death over all his subjects and the power to make whatever laws he wished. In reality, an emperor had to be very strong to have his wishes carried out. This was because wealthy landowners were often very powerful, and could influence the emperor. The trained **bureaucrats** who actually ran the government could ignore or dawdle over any new laws they did not like. The bureaucrats were conservative and slow to accept change. Within the royal court, women often had considerable power. The Empress Wu and Yang Guifei are some examples you read about in Chapter 3. However, most women worked behind the scenes.

The Song government was very centralized. China was divided into provinces, each ruled by a governor in the emperor's name. Laws were strictly enforced by magistrates, who were also chosen by the emperor. The government wanted power to be kept in the capital so that the provincial governments could not become too strong.

Figure 13–1 Levels of the Song government

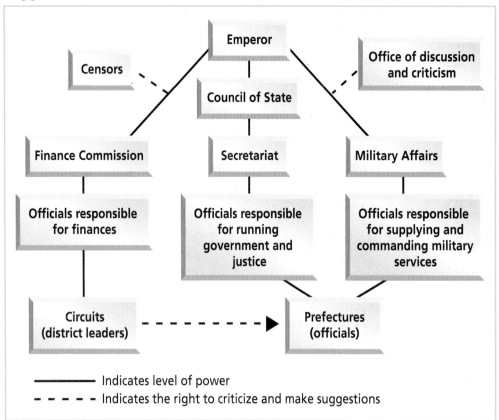

Emperor

Censors

Council of State

Office of discussion and criticism

Finance Commission

Secretariat

Military Affairs

Officials responsible for finances

Officials responsible for running government and justice

Officials responsible for supplying and commanding military services

Circuits (district leaders)

Prefectures (officials)

——— Indicates level of power

- - - - Indicates the right to criticize and make suggestions

The government was divided into three main parts: economy and finance; military affairs; and administration and justice. The most powerful body was the Council of State with nine members. The emperor sat in on all meetings and cast the deciding vote if necessary. The council freely discussed matters of government and listened to advice from all over the empire (even from representatives of from the lower classes). By law, council members could not be arrested by the emperor even if he did not like what they said.

During the Song Dynasty, as at other times, government officials were selected by examination. Candidates were tested on their ability to remember and understand literature and history, and on their skill in poetry. Those who did well on the examinations were eligible for government jobs. Song mandarins—another name for Chinese officials—were very powerful. Those who passed the examinations but did not get a government job were still part of the highest social class and enjoyed a great deal of influence.

THE SOUTHERN SONG

By the twelfth century, the Song Dynasty was in decline. Many government officials were corrupt, and the emperors were not interested in ruling the country. There were

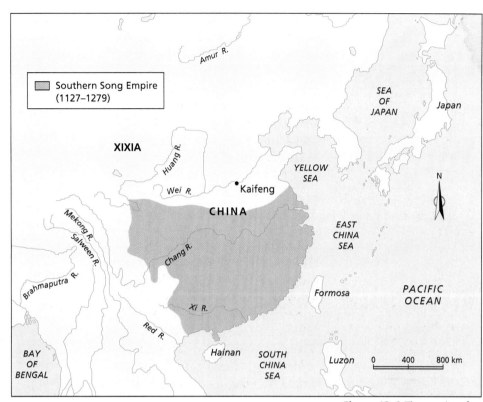

Figure 13–2 The empire of the Southern Song

ransom: money that is demanded to release someone who has been kidnapped or something that has been stolen

famines in the countryside, and peasant rebellions broke out. Then, in 1126, the Song capital at Kaifeng was attacked by Jurchen Mongols. The Jurchen demanded an enormous **ransom** of 5 million ounces of gold, 50 million ounces of silver, and 1 million rolls of silk. Eventually, the Jurchen captured Kaifeng and took the emperor Huizong north to spend the rest of his life in captivity.

The Song Dynasty did not end with the capture of Huizong. His younger son, Gaozong, escaped to the south and continued the empire. Known as the Southern Song, its capital was at Hangzhou. Hangzhou was located in the fertile lands near the Chang Jiang River. The Southern Song Dynasty prospered for another 150 years. The great culture of the Song continued, and many great works of art were produced.

Analyze and Compare Statistical Tables

You have encountered a variety of statistics throughout your reading of *Pathways*. Statistics are numbers with a difference. They are organized, or classified, in a way that tells you something meaningful about people, places, or events. When you have the opportunity to compare two or more statistical tables about the same thing, it becomes easier to **hypothesize** why events happened as they did.

Here is an interesting statistical table. Examine it for a few minutes and try to determine what is unusual about it.

Year	Population of China
2 C.E.	50 000 000
742 C.E.	50 000 000
1100 C.E.	100 000 000

Did you notice anything unusual?

For many years, China's total population remained stable, but then it suddenly started to grow. This is the kind of pattern that researchers look for when they are analyzing statistics. The shift in pattern suggests that something happened between 742 C.E. and 1100 C.E.—during the Song Dynasty—that did not occur earlier. When you see this kind of "blip" in the numbers, you know something's up.

Here is another statistical table.

Year	Population density in the Chang (Yangtze) River valley
2 C.E.	low
742 C.E.	low
1100 C.E.	high

And here is one more.

Crop	Area of land	Calories produced
Wheat	1 hectare	1 500 000
Rice	1 hectare	7 350 000

Are you beginning to get the picture? Interpreting statistics is a little like solving a mystery—the questions you ask are as important as the conclusions you draw.

hypothesize: develop a theory to explain something

NOW YOU DO IT

1. What does each table say? Summarize the information from each table in one sentence and write them down.

2. Now look for patterns of information. Patterns can occur when two or more statistical tables describe related topics and use similar categories. Look again at the first two tables. Which categories are identical?

3. What might be the relationship between the third table and the other two tables? Think about the relationship between people and their location. Brainstorm some possibilities with a partner. Eliminate those possibilities you think are not reasonable.

For the answer, turn the book upside down.

Answer

If you hypothesized that rice might have something to do with the population growth and change in population distribution in China during the Song Dynasty, you are absolutely correct. Rice growing began in China during the Song Dynasty around the Chang (Yangtze) River valley. The climate of this region was perfect for rice production. By 1012, a new variety of rice had been introduced into China from Vietnam. Champa rice ripened much more quickly, and farmers could grow two or even three crops a year. Overall, rice had a tremendous impact on where people lived in China and how many children they could sustain because it provided more calories than wheat.

The Origins of Paper Money

The Chinese government was the first government in the world to issue paper money.

During the Shang Dynasty (1700–1027 B.C.E.), the Chinese used cowrie shells as money. The Zhou Dynasty (1027–256 B.C.E.) introduced the use of bronze coins. Bronze coins were very heavy to carry around in large amounts. During the Han Dynasty (202 B.C.E.–220 C.E.), bolts of silk were used as currency for larger amounts. This cumbersome practice was abandoned by the Tang Dynasty (618–906). Silver, measured by weight, was also used. By the time of the Song, iron or bronze coins and silver were the only legal forms of money.

But by then, trade had expanded so much with the growth in the population that the government could not keep up with the demand for coins. In 997 it issued 800 million coins. By 1085 it needed to issue 6 billion coins. As well, it became impossible for merchants to carry the number of coins they needed for their transactions.

Merchants started to deposit money or goods with trusted shop keepers. The merchants then used the receipts to prove they had deposited the money. These receipts were a form of currency. By the early twelfth century, the government took over, issuing the world's first government-issued paper money.

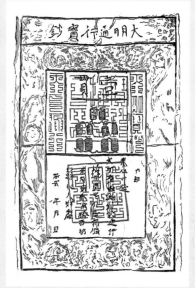

Figure 13–3 This example of Chinese paper currency dates from approximately 1400.

WHAT DO YOU THINK?

1. Why was paper money such an improvement over other forms of currency?

2. In our society, paper money is becoming outdated. What new ways of payment are being used today?

3. Why do many people today prefer not to use money?

Nevertheless, the Song Empire was weak. High taxes weakened the economy, and the army lacked good generals. For years, the Song armies fought battles with their neighbours to the north, but neither side could win decisive victories. The Southern Song also lacked good government in its final years. Eventually the Southern Song fell to the Mongol armies of Khubilai Khan in 1279. Khubilai Khan had established the Yüan Dynasty in north China in 1271, and south China now also became part of his empire.

THE ARTS OF THE SONG

Like the Italian Renaissance, the Song Dynasty was a time when the arts flourished. **Artisans** produced beautiful **porcelain**, **jade** carvings, and other luxury items. Painters and calligraphers made famous masterpieces that are still admired today. Even emperors were often skilled painters. The emperor Huizong was one of the best painters of his day.

artisan: a craftsperson

porcelain: a type of ceramic

jade: a semi-precious stone

karst: a landscape of limestone cliffs, worn away by water, leaving large caverns and strange, rounded mountains where the caverns have collapsed

Figure 13–4 This painting by Ma Yuan, a painter of the Southern Song Dynasty, shows the dreamy, airy effect popularized by Song artists. Notice that most of the painting is on the right-hand side. How does the painting still manage to appear balanced?

Painting and Calligraphy

Because Chinese characters were written with a brush, people could use writing as a form of art. In fact, painters and calligraphers used the same brush strokes. Usually painters and calligraphers were experts in both areas. Brushes were made of animal hair set in bamboo, and cut to a point. Different-sized brushes gave the artist or calligrapher the ability to make large, powerful strokes, or to create fine detail. The ink was made of charcoal, which gave a good effect. With these simple writing tools, Chinese artists created priceless works of art.

There were many themes in Song art. Some artists chose to paint realistic scenes of everyday life or famous people. Nature was another favourite subject. Artists especially liked to show the misty, spectacular **karst** mountains of southern China. Painters were often poets as well. They were interested in expressing the emotions they felt at a particular time and place.

Figure 13–5 This famous painting is called *Spring Festival Along the River*. This picture, by the twelfth-century artist Zhang Zeduan, shows everyday life in amazing detail. How many activities can you identify in this scene? Based on this picture, what do you think Song society was like?

Analyze a Chinese Painting

Paintings give us a very valuable glimpse into the past. They show us scenes of daily life, portraits of famous people, and the landscape of the area where they were painted. Paintings can also tell us about a culture—about its customs and values, about what was considered important to the people who lived in that culture.

Over time, the Chinese developed six rules that painters should follow.

◆ **Brush Strokes.** In Europe, artists were more interested in light and shadow than in line. To the Chinese, however, lines were everything, in both calligraphy and painting. Brushwork was used to give life to paintings. The brushstrokes should resemble a dance—full of movement, energy, and life

◆ **Accurate likenesses.** The artist's goal was to portray the spirit through the form. An accurate copy of whatever was being drawn was not sufficient. The artist also had to make it alive and show its inner spirit.

◆ **Versatile colours.** In earlier dynasties and in Buddhist art, colour was supposed to be varied and bright. By the Song Dynasty,

Figure 13–6 Traditional Chinese painting techniques are still used today. This painting, created by Wang Yani when she was only ten years old, shows how the tradition of Chinese painting has been passed on.

landscape painting became more popular. In this kind of painting, colour was used to reflect the shades of nature. In paintings of everyday life, colour was supposed to be realistic.

◆ **Well-planned space.** Chinese painters paid great attention to the balance of objects in the painting, so that they could create a harmonious whole. They were also very concerned with creating a sense of three dimensions. Western artists used **perspective**, but many Chinese artists did not. They painted on scrolls, which were slowly

unrolled, revealing the painting gradually.

◆ **Tradition.** Copying the work of earlier artists was an honourable thing to do. Chinese artists did not always attempt to be innovative or creative. Copying showed reverence for the traditions of the past.

◆ **Lifelike spirit.** The ability to impart life to a painting was the highest goal. It was considered a gift from heaven. Artists were expected to be so in harmony with the world so that they could recreate the spirit of their subjects.

NOW YOU DO IT

1. Look at the various paintings included in this chapter. Have they followed the six rules?

2. Which painting is your favourite? Why?

3. What can you **infer** about Chinese values from these paintings?

4. Can you identify some of the six rules for good paintings in Wang Yani's work? Which ones? How did you identify them?

5. Can you identify some aspects of her painting that do not seem to follow the rules exactly? What are they?

6. What is the value of maintaining ancient traditions? What are some possible drawbacks?

perspective: the appearance of distance on a flat surface

to infer: to conclude or decide about something

Chinese Drama

Plays and skits have been popular in China for thousands of years. Like the drama of ancient Greece, early plays probably had religious significance. During the Song Dynasty, large towns attracted storytellers, actors, and entertainers of all kinds. In time, actors and other show people became part of a class of entertainers, often passing both trade and skills from generation to generation. Actors had very low social status in early times.

Traditional theatre in China involved music, singing, reciting, dancing, and acting. An orchestra took part, and actors sang their lines. Plays often told stories about love or about historical events. One popular subject was Yang Guifei (see Chapter 3). Stock plays, sometimes called operas, were very familiar to most theatregoers. Most had characters that everybody knew. Actors used masks, make-up, and elaborate costumes, and often played the same character for most of their lives. As in Shakespeare's day, female parts were played by men. Theatre in China today still carries on many of these traditions.

eaves: edges of a roof projecting beyond the walls of the building

SONG BUILDINGS

The Chinese developed a style of **architecture** that has not changed much over time. Most of the buildings of China's earlier ages have not survived to the present. The Chinese used wood, tile, plaster, brick, and stone to construct buildings, but the basic material was wood, which rarely survives for centuries.

The basic structure of a building was a timber frame with wooden pillars to support the roof. The homes of the wealthy were roofed with tiles made from glazed ceramic. The roofs had projecting, curved **eaves** to protect the walls from rain. The brackets supporting the eaves were elaborately decorated, as were the ends of the roof tiles. The roofs of peasant homes were made from thatch as they were in Europe. The walls of the building were made from brick, stamped earth, or mud plastered on woven branches, depending on the wealth of the family.

Chinese houses were built around courtyards. The main house was located on the north side. Housing for married children was on the east and west sides. In keeping with the rules of *fengshui* (see Chapter 3), buildings were arranged along a north-south line.

Figure 13–7 An actor dressed in an elaborate costume for a twentieth-century Chinese opera

Important buildings always faced south, as did the imperial palace in the Forbidden City in Beijing. The homes of the wealthy might contain many courtyards. Most people wanted at least two courtyards, one for entertaining, and one for family use. Those with less money also built their houses around a courtyard whenever possible.

Kitchens were usually located away from the main building, to lessen the danger of fire. In the north, where the climate was cold, houses usually had a heated, raised platform called a *kang*. The kang was made of ceramic, and a fire could be lit under it. People used the kang as a couch or a bed. The heating inside kept them warm in the cold winters.

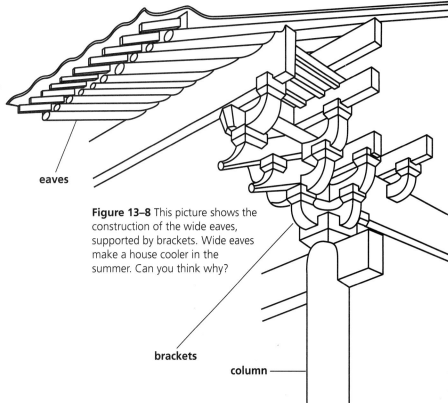

Figure 13–8 This picture shows the construction of the wide eaves, supported by brackets. Wide eaves make a house cooler in the summer. Can you think why?

eaves

brackets

column

Figure 13–9 Most houses in this Chinese village are built around courtyards. Where would the head of the household live? Where would the married children live?

1. Compare the performances of Taizu and Huizong as emperor. What did Taizu accomplish? What were Huizong's interests? How important was it for China to have a strong and dedicated emperor?

2. Examine Figure 13–2. How did location help the Southern Song continue for 150 years?

3. Compare the Chinese Renaissance with the Italian Renaissance. Find two ways in which they were similar, and two ways in which they were different. Display your answer in an organizer.

4. The painter Su Shih expressed a Song Dynasty view of art in the following passage:

   When one savours Wang Wei's poems, there are paintings in them,

   When one looks at Wang Wei's pictures, there are poems.

   Could this quotation be applied to Italian Renaissance art? Explain your answer.

5. You are a scholar-official at the emperor Huizong's court. He has called you in to admire one of his paintings. You have just received word that the Jurchen are invading China. What do you say to him?

6. Would you like to have been an actor in Song China? Why or why not?

7. What are the benefits of a large population for a country? What can be the drawbacks? Was China in a good position in the 1100s in terms of the size of its population? Why or why not?

8. Consult an atlas, encyclopedia, or both to determine the size of China's population today.

   a) How much has it increased since 1100?

   b) What is China's population distribution today? Is it the same as or different from that of the Song era?

   c) What is Canada's population today? Where do most Canadians live? Why?

CHINA UNDER THE MONGOLS: THE YÜAN DYNASTY, 1271–1368

THE MONGOLS

The rulers of the Yüan Dynasty were Mongols, not Chinese. In 1206 the conqueror Chinggis Khan had made himself the overlord, or great khan, of many Mongol peoples, who were herders on the **steppes** of central Asia. He then formed a large army, and created one of the largest empires the world has ever seen.

The Mongol soldiers were fierce, disciplined warriors who could travel for days at high speed. Using waves of mounted archers, they were very difficult to defeat. Chinggis was ruthless, and any city that refused to join him was **obliterated**. Before his death in 1227, Chinggis ruled an area from the Caspian Sea on the west to the Pacific Ocean on the east.

to obliterate: to destroy totally

steppes: a plain of southeast Europe or Asia having few trees

KHUBILAI KHAN GOVERNS CHINA

Chinggis's grandson Khubilai established the Yüan Dynasty and made Beijing his capital in 1271. From there, he went to war against the Southern Song, defeating them in 1279.

To ensure victory, Khubilai built a river fleet instead of relying on **cavalry** as the Mongols had always done. Cavalry forces could not be used effectively because of all the canals and rivers in south China. The Mongols also used the **catapult** to help them storm city walls. Chinese experts taught the Mongols how to use catapults. The Southern Song lacked strong leadership, but the decisive factor in their defeat was likely the Mongol threat to destroy everyone and everything that opposed them.

cavalry: soldiers trained to fight on horseback

catapult: an ancient weapon for hurling stones

nomadic: characteristic of a group that moves from place to place with the seasons

to remove: to go to

to hawk: to hunt using a hawk

Figure 13–10 In this European painting, Khubilai Khan is shown sending his messengers to the provinces to deliver—or possibly obtain—information. How does this painting convey Khubilai's personality?

The Mongols

As you remember from Chapter 2, during the thirteenth century, the Venetian explorer Marco Polo travelled to China and remained there for seventeen years. This is his eyewitness account of the **nomadic** life of the Mongols.

Now that I have been speaking of the Tartars [Mongols], I will tell you more about them. The Tartars never remain fixed but, as winter approaches, **remove** to the plains of a warmer region. During two or three months they ascend higher ground and seek fresh pasture, the grass being not adequate in any one place to feed the multitudes of which their herds and flocks consist. Their huts or tents are formed of rods covered with felt, and being exactly round, and nicely put together, they can gather them into one bundle, and make them up as packages, which they carry with them on their migrations. The women it is who attend to their trading concerns, who buy and sell, and provide everything necessary for their husbands and families; the time of the men being entirely devoted to hunting and **hawking**, and matters that relate to the military life.

PRIMARY SOURCE

compulsory: mandatory, required

In the past, many conquerors of China had adopted Chinese culture, favouring it over their own. Khubilai did not want this to happen to the Mongols. He tried to keep the different cultures in his empire separate. He divided the population into three "races": the Mongols, the Various Races (not Chinese), and the Chinese (which included anyone with a Chinese-like culture). It was illegal for people of one group to marry someone of another group. The Chinese population was punished much more severely than the Mongols for any wrongdoing. In addition, Khubilai appointed only Mongols to the highest offices of government and administration. The Chinese were reduced to the lowliest offices in the capital, although local administration was left in their hands.

Khubilai collected heavy taxes, and called on the population for a great deal of compulsory labour. He needed both the money and the labour for the many public projects he undertook. A new highway was built from Beijing to Hangzhou, as well as many smaller roads. The Grand Canal was extended to Beijing. Hospitals were also built.

Apart from these measures, the daily life of most Chinese people carried on much as before. With the political stability imposed by the Mongols, the economy prospered and the arts continued to flourish.

The Earliest Foreign Exchanges

During Mongol rule, travellers were free to come and go in Asia. Who took advantage of the ability to travel from Europe to China—or from China to Europe—during the era of Mongol rule? History gives us a few names. Most people were explorers, members of religious orders, or merchants. In some cases, the dates are approximate. Perhaps because Ibn Battuta was so well travelled, we know what route he took.

Known Foreign Travellers to China During the Yüan Dynasty

Date	Name	Remarks
1275	Marco Polo	Arrives in Beijing
1307	Monte Corvino	Appointed Archbishop of Beijing
1320	Odoric of Pordenone	Italian Franciscan
1335	Ibn Battuta	North Africa explorer and envoy
1340	Caterina and Antonio de'Vilioni	Probably merchants from Genoa; their tombstone in Yangzhou is dated 1342

Known Chinese Travellers to the West During the Yüan Dynasty

Date	Name	Remarks
1222	Chang Chun	Daoist monk; arrives at Chinggis Khan's camp in Afghanistan
1260	Chang Di	Journeys to Iran
1287–90	Rabban Bar Sauma	Nestorian monk; visits Constantinople and Rome; meets with the kings of France and England in France

CHINA AND THE WORLD

During the Yüan Dynasty, many foreigners such as Marco Polo visited China. The Mongols made it safe for traders to cross Asia along the old Silk Road. Muslim traders, in particular, were made welcome by Khubilai. These foreign visitors spread word of the wealth of China, which westerners began to call "Cathay." During the same period, Chinese travellers, often monks, travelled to the West. Some went as far as France.

To western eyes, the court of Khubilai was fabulous, in other words, like a fable or story . In the eighteenth century, the English poet Samuel Taylor Coleridge wrote of Khubilai's summer palace at Shangdu (Xanadu) in a poem that reflects European's fascination with Asia. Have you ever heard "Xanadu" described in other poems, songs, novels or movies?

> In Xanadu did Kublai Khan
> A stately pleasure dome
> decree: Where Alph,
> the sacred river,
> ran Down to a
> sunless sea...

PRIMARY SOURCE

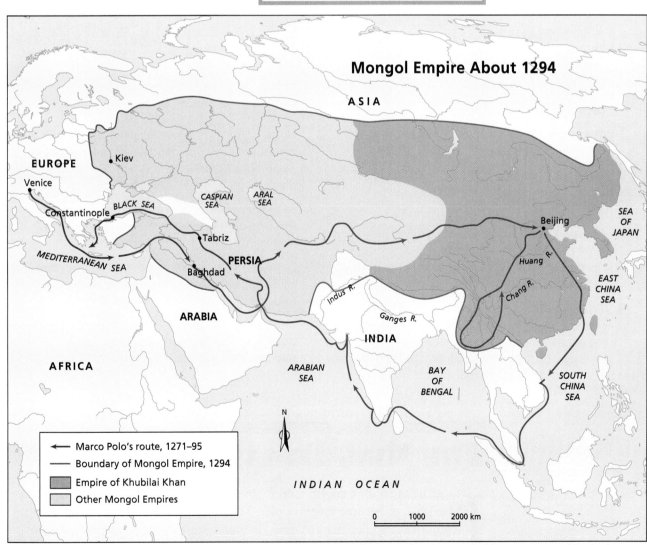

Figure 13–11 The empire of the Mongols. This map also shows the route of Marco Polo, who travelled from Venice to China in the thirteenth century.

Figure 13–12 This photograph shows the typical tent like home found on the grasslands of Mongolia today. What are the advantages of such a home? What else can you see in the picture?

gradually joined together, making them strong enough to fight the hated conquerors. In addition, when a Mongol ruler died, all those who claimed his throne had to travel to Mongolia for a vote on the successor. As a result, there were long periods of time when no one was really in charge at Beijing. The Mongol rulers who followed Khubilai were less able than he had been. In 1368 a new dynasty, the Ming, was founded by Taisu, a commoner who had gained control of the rebellious groups.

The Mongols' high taxes and harsh treatment of the Chinese people eventually caused many rebellions. Different rebellious groups

ACTIVITIES

1. Why were the Mongols able to conquer China? How did the Mongols keep control of their empire?

2. In what ways was Mongol society different from Chinese society? Were some of Khubilai's ideas racist? Explain.

3. Why could the Mongols not use cavalry effectively against the southern Song? Why do you think that Chinese people would help the Mongols defeat their own friends and neighbours?

4. Marco Polo begins the book he wrote as follows: "In this book, it is our design to treat of all the great and admirable achievements of the great khan now reigning, who is styled Kublai-kaan; the latter word implying in our language lord of lords…" How does

Marco Polo describe Khubilai? Read about Khubilai in another book—your teacher can make some suggestions. What differences do you find? How do you account for these differences?

5. Write a secret letter from Marco Polo to Italy in which he describes life for the Chinese under Mongol rule.

6. Compare the size of the Mongol Empire with that of the Shang and Tang Empires by examining the maps on pages 77, 94, and 417.

7. Is it important for people of one culture to get to know the people of another culture? Explain the reasons for your answer.

THE MING DYNASTY, 1368–1644

I t was unusual for a commoner like Taisu to become emperor of China. Taisu called his dynasty "Ming," which means "brilliant," and established his capital at Nanjing.

He ruled for thirty-two years. Taisu was a ruthless and cruel man, but he reunited China and restored the Chinese government, economy, and social system, which had been weakened under the Mongols. To do this, Taisu destroyed thousands of his opponents.

Taisu's successor, Chengzu, moved the capital to Beijing. The Ming emperors realized that China's most dangerous enemies were the nomadic peoples from the northern area, such as the Mongols. They moved the capital to Beijing to be closer to the source of trouble, even though most Chinese now lived in the south. To prevent attacks, the Ming strengthened the Great Wall (see Chapter 3).

For many years China had demanded and received **tribute** from other countries. These countries were expected to send gifts, known as tribute, to China. They were not allowed to trade with China unless they recognized China's superior wealth and power by sending this tribute. Chengzu wanted to continue this system. To do so, he sent out ships proclaiming his rule. Admiral Zheng He led several expeditions to many parts of south and southeast Asia, and to Africa. Zheng He commanded a great fleet of junks. The ships' captains found their way using magnetic compasses, an invention of the Chinese. Chinese junks were large enough to hold a thousand sailors, and had watertight compartments. These technologies were unknown in Europe at this time, and the world had never seen such feats of seamanship.

China sponsored seven great maritime expeditions between 1405 and 1433. They suddenly ceased in 1433. No one is quite sure why. The imperial court may have felt that the

Figure 13–13 This picture shows an idealized version of Taisu. Apparently he was an ugly man, with a pockmarked face and jutting lower jaw. Few portraits show him as he really was. Why would court painters portray him as a handsome man?

tribute: money paid by one nation to another for peace or protection

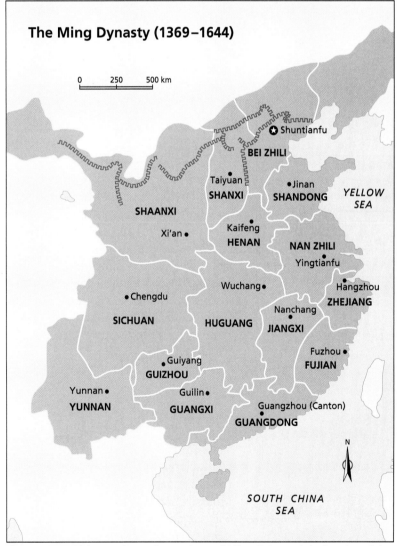

Figure 13–14 This map shows the provinces of Ming China and the location of the Great Wall, which was strengthened by the emperors. How much of the modern People's Republic of China was included in Ming China?

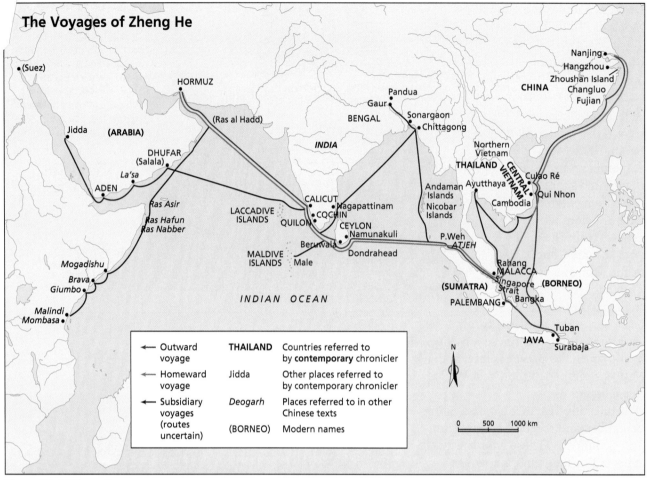

The Voyages of Zheng He

← Outward voyage	**THAILAND**	Countries referred to by **contemporary** chronicler
← Homeward voyage	Jidda	Other places referred to by contemporary chronicler
← Subsidiary voyages (routes uncertain)	*Deogarh*	Places referred to in other Chinese texts
	(BORNEO)	Modern names

0   500   1000 km

Figure 13–15 Zheng He was sent on voyages to impress southern states with the power of China and to maintain the tribute system. Thirty-seven thousand people went on his first expedition. What was Zheng He's furthest destination?

voyages were too costly, or that the trips benefited merchants too much. (In Confucian society, merchants had a low social position.) Whatever the reason, the Ming turned away from sea power, and concentrated on China itself instead. This was to have a lasting impact on the Chinese. The Chinese decided to abandon their sea power just when western societies were increasing theirs.

contemporary: living in the same period of time

hierarchic: having a clear order based on rank and importance

benevolence: wisdom paired with kindness

eunuch: a man with some sex organs removed

GOVERNMENT

The Ming Dynasty restored the Confucian basis of government and the examination system that the Mongols had ended. The government was extremely **hierarchic** and had many levels of power. Each level was more important than the one below it. One had to know exactly how to speak to a person in the level above, so as not to give offence. Within the government, officials had special symbols of their rank. Only they could wear certain clothes or use certain ornaments. It was illegal for anyone else to do so. The importance of such a person also made the family important.

Although the Ming restored Confucianism, the emperors seemed to ignore the fact that, according to Confucius, they were supposed to rule with **benevolence**. The Ming court became noted for its quarrelling. The emperor's friends competed with the bureaucrats for influence and power. The court **eunuchs** gained much more power than they had previously enjoyed. They almost took over the government during the Ming Dynasty. They were able to gain power because Taisu was enormously suspicious and always thought that government officials were plotting against him. He turned the palace guard, largely controlled by the eunuchs, into a secret police force to spy on officials. Over time, Taisu had a total of about 100 000 government officials executed, even though, by law, government officials were exempt from such punishment. The eunuchs eventually controlled the army, the diplomatic corps, taxation, and imperial workshops as well as the palace guard.

Figure 13–16 A Ming official sits in a formal chair for this portrait. He is richly dressed and holds a jade sceptre, a symbol of rank. He would undoubtedly have the power of life and death over much of the population.

REBUILDING THE ECONOMY

The Ming emperors worked hard to restore the economy of China. The rebellions and wars at the end of the Yüan Dynasty had damaged China's business and agriculture. The whole country was in chaos. Some regions had almost zero population at the start of Taisu's reign.

Beginning in 1370, the imperial government began to rebuild the empire's shattered economy. It offered food, animals, and seeds to peasants to help rebuild the country's agricultural base. Peasants who moved to empty areas of land received special supplies and freedom from taxes for three years. A million hectares of land were put back into production this way. Canals and **reservoirs** were rebuilt and **dredged**. Even the forests were replanted. Every family in Anhwei province had to plant 600 trees. Historians estimate that 100 million trees were planted during the reign of Taisu. Although thousands of people suffered terribly from forced labour during the years of rebuilding, the result was a strong and united empire.

The economy under the Ming was strong and healthy. The canal system was enlarged, stimulating the growth in trade between southern and northern China. The volume of trade grew, and so did the production of handicraft and industrial goods. Many of these goods were traded to the rest of the world.

MING CULTURE AND SOCIETY

Building on the great technological advances of the Song era, Ming artisans continued to produce the world's most valuable manufactured goods. Ming porcelain was sought by people in Eastern Africa, Asia, and Europe. Silk, **lacquer** work, and other

reservoir: a place where water is stored

to dredge: to clean out, often with a net

lacquer: a coating that creates a durable, glossy surface when dry

Porcelain: A Booming Industry

Figure 13–17 The two bowls at the top were made centuries and half a world apart. The one on the left is the handpainted Chinese original. The one on the right is a British version made around 1800. The modern covered jug shows that the Chinese influence is still visible in European china patterns. Is there anything unusual about the scene on this jug?

Have you ever wondered why we call our tableware "china"?

For hundreds of years, the Chinese were much more advanced than the rest of the world in the technology of ceramics. By the time of the Ming, the Chinese had perfected the art of making porcelain. Ming porcelain, especially the blue-and-white variety, was in demand all over the world. It was so prized that many European ceramic companies rushed to produce their own blue-and-white tableware in imitation.

Porcelain is different from other ceramics. It is whiter and smoother and **translucent**. If you hold a piece of porcelain up to the light, you can see your hand through it. In spite of its apparent fragility, porcelain is actually very strong. It requires special clays and an extremely hot **firing temperature** of 1280–1400°C.

The special clays needed for porcelain were found near Jingdezhen in Jiangxi province. Jingdezhen was surrounded by the forests needed to stoke the **kilns**, and it was located on a good river for transportation.

The imperial court was one of the biggest customers for porcelain. Eventually, workshops devoted solely to producing porcelain for the imperial court were established. Quality control was exacting—only the highest standards were acceptable. There were enormous piles of smashed porcelain around the imperial workshops, because nothing with imperial markings could be sold to anyone else, so slightly imperfect pieces were destroyed. Private workshops produced the non-imperial porcelain.

Mass-production techniques were used in the production of porcelain. Potters worked on only one part of the production process. As many as seventy potters might be involved in the production of a single piece of porcelain.

WHAT DO YOU THINK?

1. What advantages did Jindezhen have to enable porcelain to be produced there?

2. Why do you think porcelain bearing imperial markings would not be sold to anyone but members of the imperial court?

3. Does your family, or anyone you know, have pieces of blue-and-white ceramics? Where were they produced? How did you find out?

products commanded high prices everywhere. Artists produced beautiful works of calligraphy and paintings.

The upper classes of the Ming Dynasty enjoyed their wealth and power, and the many luxurious clothes, furniture, and works of art that they were able to buy. These goods were far too expensive for ordinary people to afford. Then, as now, most of China's people were farmers living in villages. They travelled very little and knew almost nothing of the world beyond their own countries. Other people worked in factories and workshops, producing the goods that provided much of China's wealth. They lived in cramped housing in the poorer sections of towns and cities.

In theory, Ming society was strictly organized and controlled. There was very little social mobility.

This meant that it was extremely difficult to become a member of a higher social class. In reality, some peasants and workers became richer and more influential than others, as eventually happened with the serfs in Europe during the Middle Ages.

The tax system, for example, tended to make some people more important than others. For taxation purposes, people were organized into groups of ten families. These groups collected their own taxes and decided who would do the labour on public works that all peasants were required to perform. Within these groups, natural leaders often took over, making a profit out of the labour and taxes of others. For this reason, some peasants lived better than others.

The examination system also provided some social mobility. If a family was able to raise the necessary

translucent: letting some light pass through

firing temperature: the temperature required to harden pottery

kiln: the oven for firing pottery

Using a Letter of Instruction as a Primary Source

CATALOGUE CARD

What is it? *A letter from a woman to her daughters*

Who wrote it? *Ban Zhao, a highly regarded scholar*

When? *During the Han Dynasty*

Why? *To instruct her daughters in behaviour suitable for women in a Confucian society*

Throughout the history of the world, people have used letters to teach as well as to communicate socially. The word "epistle," for example, means "letter," but Christians understand it to mean the writings of Christ's apostles. In some societies, parents write letters to their children offering them sound advice. Sometimes these letters are intended to be opened after the parent dies. In societies in which a great deal of emphasis is placed on the authority of parents, children would have no choice but to consider this advice carefully.

In this letter, Ban Zhao passes on valuable information to her daughters. Ben Zhao was a scholar who lived during the Han Dynasty but her writings were still considered important during the Ming period. There is one glaring contradiction in this document. Can you spot it?

I, the unworthy writer, am unsophisticated, unenlightened, and by nature unintelligent, but I am fortunate both to have received not a little favour from my scholarly Father, and to have a cultured mother and instructresses upon whom to rely for a literary education as well as training in good manners. More than forty years have passed since at the age of fourteen I took up the dustpan and broom at the Cao household [her husband's]. During this time with trembling heart I feared constantly that I might disgrace my parents, and that I might multiply difficulties for both the men and women of my husband's family …. Being careless, and by nature, stupid, I taught and trained my children without system … But I do grieve that you, my daughters, just now at the age for marriage, have not at this time had gradual training and advice; that you have still not learned the proper customs for married women. I fear that by failure in good manners in other families you will humiliate both your ancestors and your clan … From this time on every one of you must strive to practise these lessons.

Humility

Let a woman **modestly** yield to others; let her respect others; let her put others first, herself last. Should she do something good, let her not mention it; should she do something bad let her not deny it. Let her bear disgrace; let her endure even when others speak or do evil to her. Always let her seem to tremble and to fear. When a woman follows such **maxims** as these then she may be said to humble herself before others.

Womanly Qualifications

A woman ought to have four qualifications: 1. womanly virtue; 2. womanly words; 3. womanly bearing; and 4. womanly work. Now what is called womanly virtue need not be brilliant ability … Womanly words need be neither clever in debate nor keen in conversation. Womanly appearance requires neither a pretty nor a perfect face and form. Womanly work need not be done more skilfully than that of others.

Implicit Obedience

Whenever the mother-in-law says, "Do not do that," and if what she says is right, unquestionably the daughter-in-law obeys. Whenever the mother-in-law says, "Do that," even if what she says is wrong, still the daughter-in-law submits unfailingly to the command. Let not a woman act contrary to the wishes and opinions of parents-in-law about right and wrong.

WHAT DO YOU THINK?

1. What are Ban Zhao's qualifications for giving this advice? What is her objective?

2. Do you believe that she is really "careless, and by nature stupid"? What reason would she have for describing herself in this way? How does her self-description reflect Chinese society at the time?

3. Do you think Ban Zhao's daughters will ignore this advice? Why or why not? What passages in the letter support your viewpoint?

4. To what extent can you accept this letter as reliable evidence of Chinese thought?

money for one of its sons to study and pass the examinations, the entire family would move up the social ladder because of the son's success in gaining government office.

Merchants could also move up the social ladder. They could use their wealth to buy land, marry into an upper class family that needed money, or send their sons through the examination system.

THE ROLE OF WOMEN

At all levels of Ming society, women were considered inferior to men, according to the teachings of Confucius. During the Ming Dynasty, Confucius's teachings were revived. After the cultural disruptions of the Yüan Dynasty, many Chinese people were anxious to "purify" society, which they felt had been damaged by the Mongols. Philosophers wanted to turn society back to its ancient roots and make Confucianism something like an official religion for the empire.

This movement was particularly hard on women, who lost the freedom they had gained under the Song and Yüan Dynasties. Under the Song, many women had run inns, been **midwives** and nurses, written poetry, or run their husband's artisan business. Many had gained control over their **dowries**.

One cultural practice, called footbinding, symbolized the control that was being placed on women. In Chinese society, women with tiny feet came to be considered more beautiful than women with average-size feet. Without footbinding, a woman had little chance of marrying well. Some parents bound the feet of their daughters starting at the age of five or six, so the feet could not grow normally. Over the years, the four small toes were bent under the arch of the foot in a very painful process that limited the size of the foot to just over 7 centimetres. Such feet were known as "golden lilies" and were a sign of social status. Women with bound feet could only hobble for short distances—they could not walk freely. This communicated to society that the women of the family did not have to work. It also forced women to stay at home, as Confucius thought they should. The practice of footbinding began during the Song Dynasty, continued during the Ming Dynasty, and did not end until the nineteenth century.

THE FALL OF THE MING

Eventually, the Ming rulers began to lose touch with the people. After the great ocean expeditions of the early years of the dynasty, China cut itself off more and more from the world. Outside contact was discouraged. Pirates, some from Japan, **infested** the seas around China and made commerce difficult. China was invaded by the Japanese in the mid-1500s, and by Mongols from the north. At home, powerful officials stole from the government, and emperors lost interest in providing good government. At last, forced into action by droughts and bad harvests, peasants rebelled against the corrupt Ming government. Attacked by rebel armies, the last Ming emperor hanged himself on a little hill outside the palace. So ended the so-called Brilliant Dynasty established by Taisu.

modestly: with humility, having no vanity

maxim: rule of conduct

midwife: a person who helps a woman give birth

dowry: the property that a woman brings to her marriage

to infest: to overrun

European Ideas about Chinese Society

In the late days of the Ming Dynasty, a number of Jesuit priests travelled to China, hoping to convert people to Christianity. They soon discovered that the only way they would be accepted by the Chinese was to conform to Chinese culture. One of these priests, Matteo Ricci, was eventually allowed to live in Beijing in 1601. Ricci was a careful observer, but he was looking at Chinese culture through the eyes of his own world. Keep this in mind as you read the excerpt below.

Figure 13–19 Matteo Ricci as an artist imagined him in China during the sixteenth century.

The extent of their kingdom is so vast, its borders so distant, and their utter lack of knowledge of a **transmaritime** world is so complete that the Chinese imagine the whole world as included in their kingdom. Even now, as from time beyond reckoning, they call their Emperor, Thiencu, the Son of Heaven, and because they worship Heaven as the Supreme Being, the Son of Heaven and the Son of God are one and the same.

Another remarkable fact and quite worthy of note as a marked difference from the West is that the entire kingdom is administered by the Order of the Learned, commonly known as the Philosophers [educated people]. The responsibility for the orderly management of the entire realm is wholly and completely committed to their charge and care … Policies of war are [made] and military questions are decided by the philosophers alone, and their advice and counsel has more weight with the king than that of the military leaders. In fact very few of these and only on rare occasions, are admitted to war consultations. Hence it follows that those who aspire to be cultured frown upon war … realizing that the Philosophers far exceed military leaders in the good will and respect of the people and in opportunities of acquiring wealth.

There are no ancient laws in China under which the republic is governed [forever], such as our laws of the twelve tables and the Code of Caesar. Whoever succeeds in getting possession of the throne, regardless of his ancestry, makes new laws according to his own way of thinking. His successors on the throne are obliged to enforce the laws which he [set] at the beginning of the dynasty, and these laws cannot be changed without good reason....

Their method of making printed books is quite **ingenious**. The text is written in ink, with a brush made of very fine hair, on a sheet of paper which is **inverted** and placed on a wooden tablet. When the paper has become thoroughly dry, its surface is scraped off quickly and with great skill, until nothing but a fine tissue bearing the characters remains on the wooden tablet. Then, with a steel graver, the workman cuts away the surface following the outlines of the characters until these alone stand out in low relief. From such a block a skilled printer can make copies with incredible speed, turning out as many as fifteen hundred copies in a single day.... This scheme of engraving wooden blocks is well adapted for the large and complex nature of Chinese characters, but I do not think it would lend itself very aptly to our European type, which can hardly be engraved on wood because of its small dimensions.

PRIMARY SOURCE

transmaritime: the world across the sea, in this case, Europe

ingenious: imaginative, clever

inverted: turned over

1. What were Taisu's positive achievements? What aspects of his rule were negative? Would you have liked to live in China under Taisu's rule if you were a government official? A peasant? Why or why not?

2. Consult the map showing the routes of Zheng He's expeditions on page 420. Imagine you are a passenger on one of the ships. Make up a journal that recounts your experiences on one of his journeys. Your journal should have at least six entries, and should be illustrated with sketch maps and pictures.

3. Suppose that one of Zheng He's expeditions had reached North America. How might the history of North America be different? Write a story in which western North America has been colonized by the Ming.

4. Compare Zheng He's routes with those taken by Vasco da Gama (Chapter 8).

5. Was the cancellation of the large-scale overseas voyages harmful or beneficial to the Ming in the long run? Support your answer with evidence.

6. Using Figure 13–5, select several of the groups of people illustrated, and write a story about what they are doing during the Spring Festival.

7. You are a scholar-official at the Ming court. You got your job because you know a lot about the history and literature of China. Your subordinates report to you that there is famine in the countryside. What actions do you take?

8. In response to Ban Zhao's letters to her daughters advising them on proper behaviour, write your own letter explaining the differences in the roles of women in today's society.

9. Write a letter from Matteo Ricci to the Jesuit superior in Rome explaining why it is necessary for Jesuits to learn Chinese ways to be successful in spreading Christianity in China.

10. How accurate are Ricci's observations about Chinese ways? Did Ricci like or dislike the Chinese? How would a Chinese person of the time have responded to his observations? Explain why Ricci interpreted Chinese culture in the way he did.

SUMMARY

Throughout the 600 years covered by this chapter, Chinese traditions in government, art, literature, architecture, drama, and ways of thinking about life and the world survived great rebellions and foreign invasions.

The Song Renaissance helped revive Chinese culture and withstood the Mongol invasion. Even under Mongol rule, cultured people regarded long-dead writers and painters as old friends and continually quoted them, thus keeping Chinese ways alive. Confucius's teachings were so much a part of everyday life that they glued the parts of Chinese civilization together in an unbreakable pattern. In the countryside, village life went on in time-honoured ways as people lived and died in their small agricultural villages, often unaffected by catastrophic events in other parts of the vast empire.

China never really lost its status as a world power, even when it was part of the empire of the Mongols. During the Ming Dynasty, China's strength and power grew even more. The voyages of Zheng He impressed the peoples of southeast Asia, and the rest of the world, with the glory and strength of the Ming Dynasty. Zheng He was actually worshipped in some areas as a god. Nevertheless, it was during the Ming Dynasty that China grew more conservative and less interested in the world outside. This was the China that the growing powers of Europe encountered—strong, confident, and arrogant. Only by adopting Chinese ways could people like Matteo Ricci hope to prosper in China. China was the most powerful nation on earth until the eighteenth century—it was the envy of the world.

SUMMARY ACTIVITIES

1. With a partner, make a Time-Link chart comparing China with a European country in the year 1200. Use the following headings:

   ◆ geography
   ◆ religion
   ◆ art
   ◆ government
   ◆ dress
   ◆ technology
   ◆ role of women
   ◆ view of the world
   ◆ city and town life
   ◆ major developments

   Illustrate your chart or re-enact a scene depicting one of these categories as a tableau.

2. Pretend you are a government representative from Europe or any other continent to China in the year 1600. Prepare a speech to the emperor explaining that your nation would like to have good relations with China, and outlining the benefits that each would receive.

3. Prepare an illustrated time line for China between the years 960 and 1600.

4. Make a model or large wall map of China. Show the major physical features and bodies of water, the locations of the various capital cities, the Grand Canal, and the Great Wall.

ON YOUR OWN

1. Try to create a painting in the traditional Chinese style. Review the rules for Chinese paintings, look at the examples provided in this chapter, and then draw your own. When your painting is completed, explain how and why your painting turned out as it did.

2. Research Chinese architecture. Design a palace like the one mentioned in *The Dream of the Red Chamber*. Your plan should include housing for the head of the household and their families: gardens; servants' quarters; kitchens; studies; entertainment areas; and any other features you think important. Give your palace and its main buildings names.

PHONETIC GLOSSARY

Use this glossary to help you pronouce some of the more difficult words in *Pathways*. When you are sounding out the word, place the stress, or emphasis, on the syllable that is written in capital letters.

A

Abd – **ahb**
Ainu – **EYE-noo**
amautas – **a-MAW-tas**
Aryan – **AIR-ee-an**
archipelago – **ar-ki-PEL-a-go**
atrocity – **a-TRAW-si-tee**
auto-da-fé – **AW-tow-da-FAY**

B

bakufu – **ba-KOO-foo**
bailiff – **BAY-liff**
Bayeux – **BY-yoo**
beatitude – **bee-A-ti-tood**
betroth – **bee-TROWTH**
Boccaccio – **bow-KA-chee-oh**
bubonic – **bew-BAWN-ik**
Buddhism - **BOO-dis-um**
bushido – **boo-SHEE-do**
Byzantine – **BI-zan-teen**

C

caliph – **ka-LEEF**
calligraphy – **ka-LI-gra-phee**
carrack – **ka-RAK**
Celtic – **KEL-tik**
Chang Jiang – **TUNH-gee-UN**
chronicle – **KRAW-ni-kal**
cistern – **SIS-turn**
condotierre – **kon-do-tee-AIR**
Confucianism – **kon-FEW-shun-ism**
conquistador – **kon-KWEES-ta-dor**

D

daimyo – **DY-mee-oh**

dauphin – **dau-FEEN**
democracy – **deh-MAW-kra-see**
demesne – **deh-MAYN**
dharma – **DAR-ma**
dhow – **DOW**
Diaspora – **dee-AS-por-uh**
doge – **DOJ**
ducat – **DUH-kut**
dynasty – **DIE-nas-tee**

E

ether – **EE-ther**

F

fealty – **FEE-al-tee**
fengshui – **feng-SHWAY**
feudal – **FEW-dull**
fjord – **fee-ORD**

G

geyser – **GUY-ser**

H

hadith – **ha-DEETH**
hadj – **HAWGE**
haiku – **HY-koo**
hieroglyphic – **hire-oh-GLIF-ik**
hijrah – **HIJ-rah**
Huang He – **Hwong-HAY**
hypothesis – **Hy-PAW-the-sis**

I

Inca – **INK-ah**
Inquisition – **in-kwi-SI-shun**
isthmus – **IS-mus**

J

Jomon – **JOE-mun**

K

kamikaze – **Ka-mih-KAH-zee**
kana – **KAY-nah**
kijkglas – **KYK-las**

L

L' Anse aux Meadows – **LAWNCE-oh-MEH-doze**

M

Merovingian – **mer-oh-VIN-yan**
missi dominici – **MEE-see daw-mi-NEE-chee**
mosque – **MAWSK**

N

navigation – **na-vi-GAY-shun**

O

oasis – **oh-AY-sis**
oligarchy – **aw-li-GAR-kee**
oracle – **OAR-uh-kul**

P

Pax Romana – **PAKS row-MA-nah**
philosophy – **fil-AW-saw-fee**
Ptolemaic – **tawl-eh-MAY-ik**

Q

Qin – **CHEEN**
quipu – **KWEE-poo**
quipucamuyus – **KWEE-poo-kah-MOO-yoos**
Qur'ân – **kor-AN**

R

reconquista – **ray-kon-KEES-ta**
reincarnation – **ree-in-kar-NAY-shun**
Renaissance – **REH-nay-SAWNCE**
Ricci– **REACH-ee**
ronin – **ROW-nin**
rune – **ROON**

S

samurai – **SAM-ur-eye**
Sikh – **SEEK**
simony – **SI-muh-nee**
skald – **SKAWLD**
solidi – **so-LEE-dee**
Sui – **SWEE**
sumptuary – **SUMP-tew-air-ee**

T

Taj Mahal – **TAZH ma-HALL**
Tenochtitlàn – **tay-nawch-tee-TLAN**
theocracy – **thee-AW-kra-cee**
topographic – **top-oh-GRA-fik**
Torah – **TOR-uh**
troubador – **TROO-ba-door**

U

Umayyad – **OO-may-ad**

V

vernacular – **ver-NA-kew-lur**

W

wergild – **WEAR-gild**

X

Xuanzong – **shew-AN-jong**

Z

Zhou – **JOW**
Zimbabwe – **Zim-BAHB-way**

INDEX

CREDITS

Images

Introduction (bottom left) Bridgeman/Art Resource, NY, (top right) Nik Wheeler/Corbis, (bottom right) Corbis-Bettmann; p. 2 Werner Forman/Art Resource, NY; p. 8 Scala/Art Resource; p. 10 (bottom left) Michael Cranny, (bottom right) Al Harvey/The Slide Farm; p. 13 Erich Lessing/Art Resource, NY; p. 14 Dick Hemingway; p. 15 Scala/Art Resource, NY; p. 16 Dick Hemingway; p. 19 Jan Becker; p. 20 Scala/Art Resource, NY; p. 22 Erich Lessing/Art Resource, NY; p. 26 Scala/Art Resource, NY; p. 27 Ashmolean Museum, Oxford; p. 28 Cotton vitellius AXV Folio 148 by permission of The British Library; p. 31 The Granger Collection, New York; p. 34 (top) The Franks Casket, transparency #PS235451 The Trustees of the British Museum, (bottom) Greg Locke; p. 37 Gianni Dagli Orti/Corbis; p. 38 Gianni Dagli Orti/Corbis; p. 39 Nik Wheeler/Corbis; p. 41 Giraudon/Art Resource, NY; p. 43 Giraudon/Art Resource, NY; p. 44 Geomatics Canada, Canada Centre for Remote Sensing, Natural Resources Canada; p. 51 Bridgeman/Art Resource, NY; p. 52 Giraudon/Art Resource, NY; p. 53 Victor Last/Geographical Visual Aids; p. 55 Scala/Art Resource, NY; p. 57 Corbis-Bettmann; p. 58 Archive Photos; p. 60 The Granger Collection, New York; p.85 Jan Becker; p. 66 (top) The Pierpont Morgan Library/Art Resource, NY [detail]; p. 66 Bridgeman/Art Resource, NY; p. 67 Corbis-Bettmann; p. 69 Pierre Colombel/Corbis; p. 72 Lowell Georgia/Corbis; p. 73 Asian Art & Archaeology, Inc./Corbis; p. 76 EOSAT; p. 78 (top) Giraudon/Art Resource, NY, (bottom) Jeff Greenberg/Archive Photos; p. 79 Nikki Abraham; p. 81 Al Harvey/The Slide Farm; p. 83 Jeff Greenberg/Archive Photos; p. 85 Jan Becker; p. 87 Al Harvey/The Slide Farm; p. 88 Russell Thompson/Archive Photos; p. 89 Corbis-Bettmann; p. 91 Al Harvey/The Slide Farm; p. 92 Al Harvey/The Slide Farm; p. 95 Crib Garment, Gest Library, Princeton University; p. 96 Werner Forman/Art Resource, NY; p. 101 Or. 2265, Folio 194r by permission of The British Library; p. 106 Superstock; p. 110 Greg Marinovich/AP/Canapress; p. 111 Corbis-Bettmann; p. 112 Dick Hemingway; p. 113 Nik Wheeler/ Corbis; p. 114 Greg Marinovich/AP/Canapress; p. 115 Kurt Scholz/Superstock; p. 117 Jan Becker; p. 118 Dick Hemingway; p. 118 Roger Wood/© Corbis; p. 121 Adam Woolfitt/Corbis; p. 124 Corbis-Bettmann; p. 110 Eyal Warshavsky/AP/Canapress; p. 124 Corbis-Bettmann; p. 125 Michael Nicholson/Corbis; p. 127 Burhan Ozbilici/AP/Canapress; p. 130 Giraudon/Art Resource, NY; p. 132 Michael Cranny; p. 134 Scala/Art Resource, NY [detail]; p. 140 Bridgeman/Art Resource, NY; p. 141 Corbis-Bettmann; p. 143 Jim Young/Canapress; p. 144 (left) Karen Taylor, (right) Additional Manuscript 42130 Folio 202V (miniature only) by permission of The British Library; p. 146 By courtesy of the National Portrait Gallery, London; p. 147 (top right) Michael Cranny; p. 148 Giraudon/Art Resource, NY; p. 149 Scala/Art Resource, NY; p. 151 Jan Becker; p. 153 Michael S. Yamashita/Corbis; p. 154 Al Harvey/The Slide Farm; p. 156 Bridgeman/Art Resource, NY; p. 157 Scala/Art Resource, NY; p. 159 (both) Michael Cranny; p. 160 Corbis-Bettmann; p. 161 The Granger Collection, New York; p. 167 Bridgeman/Art Resource, NY [detail]; p. 169 The Granger Collection, New York; p. 174 Courtesan with Attendant, Utagawa Toyokuni, Hanging scroll; ink and colors on silk, Japan, early 19th century. Gift of Dr. Nathan V. Hammer, Long Island, New York (HAA 6158.1) Honolulu Academy of Arts; p. 176 (top left) Archive Photos/ Reuters/John Pryke; p. 176 (top right) Reuters/Corbis-Bettmann, (top left) Reuters/Corbis-Bettmann; p. 179 Courtesy of Osaka Prefectural Government; p. 181 (both) Al Harvey/The Slide Farm; p. 183 Scala/Art Resource, NY; p. 184 Albert Rose/Archive Photos; p. 185 Werner Forman/Art Resource, NY; p. 186 Corbis-Bettmann; p. 187 Corbis-Bettmann; p. 188 *Gion Festival Procession: In and Around Kyoto* 1615-1867, Six fold screen, painted in ink, color and gold. Each panel: 62 x 24". Overall: H: 62", W: 144", Brooklyn Museum of Art #54.144 A and B. Gift of W.W. Hoffman, Brooklyn Museum of Art; p. 189 (top) Adrian Bradshaw/Archive Photos, (bottom) Werner Forman/Art Resource, NY; p. 190 (top) Werner Forman/Art Resource, NY, (bottom) The Granger Collection, New York; p. 191 Asian Art & Archaeology, Inc./Corbis; p. 193 (top) Werner Forman/Art Resource, NY, (bottom) Corbis-Bettmann; p. 195 Al Harvey/The Slide Farm; p. 196 Courtesy of the Embassy of Japan; p. 198 (top) Werner Forman/Art Resource, NY, (bottom) Scala/Art Resource, NY; p. 200 Todd Gipstein/ Corbis [detail]; p. 201(top left) Joel Rogers/Art Resource, NY, (middle right) The Granger Collection, New York, (bottom left) Corbis-Bettmann; p. 202 Corbis-Bettmann; p. 208 *The Madonna of the Meadow* by Giovanni Bellini/The National Gallery, London/Corbis; p. 210 Michael Cranny; p. 213 (top) Corbis-Bettmann, (bottom) Scala/Art Resource, NY; p. 214 Corbis-Bettmann; p. 215 Corbis-Bettmann; p. 216 (top) Alinari /Art Resource, NY, (bottom) Reuters/Michele Gregolin/Archive Photos; p. 218 Erich Lessing/Art Resource, NY [detail]; p. 220 Scala/Art Resource, NY; p. 222 Jessica Pegis; p. 224 (both) The Granger Collection, New York; p. 226 (top) Archive Photos, (bottom) Corbis-Bettmann; p. 227 Todd Gipstein/Corbis [detail]; p. 228 Francis G. Mayer/Corbis; p. 229 Giraudon/Art Resource, NY; p. 230 (top) Erich Lessing/Art Resource, NY, (bottom) Courtesy of Hubert Pantel and Le Cercle Molière, Saint-Boniface, Manitoba; p. 233 Courtesy of the Dominion Astrophysical Observatory, Victoria, BC; p. 235 Joel Rogers/Corbis; p. 239 (top) Barnabas Bosshart/Corbis, (bottom) Hulton Deutsch Collection/Corbis; p. 241 Sergio Dorantes/© Corbis; p. 244 Erich Lessing/Art Resource, NY; p. 246 Archive Photos; p. 251 Corbis-Bettmann; p. 252 Corbis-Bettmann; p. 254 Courtesy of the High Commission for South Africa and the South African Tourist Board; p. 257 (top) The Granger Collection, New York, (bottom) *Non Sequitur* 10-12-92 © 1992, Washington Post Writers Group. Reprinted with permission; p. 259 Archive Photos; p. 261 New York Public Library Picture Collection/Corbis; p. 265 Bridgeman/Art Resource, NY; p. 266 The Granger Collection, New York; p. 267 Bridgeman/Art Resource, NY; p. 269 Scala/Art Resource, NY [detail]; p. 276 Scala/Art Resource, NY; p. 279 Corbis-Bettmann; p. 279 Corbis-Bettmann; p. 281 (top) Erich Lessing/Art Resource, NY, (bottom) Michael Cranny; p. 282 (both) Corbis-Bettmann; p. 283 Corbis-Bettmann; p. 285 Giraudon/Art Resource, NY; p. 287 The Granger Collection, New York; p. 288 Jacques

Boissinot/Canapress; p. 289 The Granger Collection, New York; p. 290 Archive Photos; p. 291 Archive Photos; p. 292 (both) The Granger Collection, New York; p. 293 The Granger Collection, New York; p. 294 The Granger Collection, New York; p. 295 Archive Photos; p. 296 The Granger Collection, New York; p. 300 Archive Photos/Srinivas Kuruganti; p. 302 Werner Forman/Art Resource, NY; p. 303 (top) Eric Colquhoun, (middle) Superstock, (bottom) SEF/Art Resource, NY; p. 304 Superstock; p. 311 Giraudon, Paris/Superstock; p. 315 Archive Photo; p. 317 (top) Vanni/Art Resource, NY, (bottom) Tom Bean/Corbis; p. 319 (top) Peter Langer/Trudy Woodcock's Image Network Inc., (bottom) The Granger Collection, New York; p. 321 (top) Adam Lubroth/Art Resource, NY, (bottom) Archive Photos; p. 325 Robert Everts/Tony Stone Images; p. 327 AKG/Superstock; p. 329 (top) Vanni/Art Resource, NY, (bottom) Arthur Thévenart/Corbis; p. 331 Dick Hemingway; p. 333 Victoria & Albert Museum, London/Art Resource, NY; p. 339 Jan Becker; p.341 Reuters/Corbis-Bettmann; p. 344 Karen Taylor; p. 347 The Granger Collection, New York; p. 348 The Granger Collection, New York; p. 350 Superstock; p. 351 (top) SEF/Art Resource, NY, (bottom) UPI/Corbis-Bettmann; p. 352 (top) Ajit Kumar/AP/Canapress, (bottom) UPI/Corbis-Bettmann; p. 353 (top) SEF/Art Resource, NY, (bottom left) Imapress/Pictorial Parade/Archive Photos, (bottom right) Jan Becker; p. 354 Corbis-Bettmann; p. 355 Toronto Star/Tony Bock (July 4/97). By permission of the Toronto Star Syndicate; p. 356 Victoria & Albert Museum, London/Art Resource, NY; p. 357 Dick Hemingway; p. 358 Private collection/Bridgeman Art Library, London/Superstock; p. 360 Bridgeman Art Resource, NY; p. 361 (top) Reuters/Brijesh Singh/Archive Photos, (bottom) Jan Becker; p. 362 Victoria & Albert Museum, London/Art Resource, NY; p. 363 Jan Becker; p. 365 Nicholas DeVore/Tony Stone Images; p. 370 Kente cloth #81.17.433 The Seattle Art Museum, Gift of Katherine White and the Boeing Company. Photo by Paul Macapia; p. 372 Victor Last/Geographical Visual Aids; p. 375 Hulton Getty Collection/Tony Stone Images; p. 376 Werner Forman/Art Resource, NY; p. 379 Holton Collection/Superstock; p. 380 Werner Forman/Art Resource, NY; p. 381 Holton Collection/Superstock; p. 382 Wolfgang Kaehler/Corbis; p. 383 John Beatty/Tony Stone Images; p. 384 Holton Collection/Superstock; p. 385 Hulton-Deutsch Collection/Corbis; p. 389 (all) Werner Forman/Art Resource, NY; p. 390 AKG/Superstock; p. 391 Werner Forman/Art Resource, NY; p. 392 Peter Langer/Trudy Woodcock's Image Network; p. 393 Werner Forman/Art Resource, NY; p. 394 Superstock; p. 396 Frans Lanting/Tony Stone Images; p. 397 Werner Forman/Art Resource, NY; p. 399 Giraudon/Art Resource, NY; p. 404 Asian Art & Archaeology, Inc./Corbis; p. 409 The Granger Collection, New York; p. 410 (top) Granger Collection, New York, (bottom) Pierre Colombel/Corbis; p. 411 "The Lion is Awake!" by Wang Yani from *A Young Painter: The Life of Wang Yani* © 1992 Byron Preiss Visual Publications and New China Pictures Company; p. 412 Archive Photos/Imapress; p. 415 The Granger Collection, New York; p. 418 Archive Photos/Adrian Bradshaw; p. 419 The Granger Collection, New York; p. 421 Scala/Art Resource, NY; p. 422 Courtesy of Spode; p. 423 SEF/Art Resource, NY [detail]; p. 426 Corbis-Bettmann.

Primary Sources

p. 13 Excerpt from the *New JPS Translation of the Holy Scriptures according to the Traditional Hebrew Text*, copyright © 1985, The Jewish Publication Society, Philadelphia. Used by permission; p. 23 Excerpt from pp. 225-226 of THE HISTORY OF THE FRANKS by Gregory of Tours, translated by Lewis Thorpe (Penguin Classics, 1974) copyright © Lewis Thorpe, 1974. Reproduced by permission of Penguin Books Ltd., London; p. 24 Reproduced by authority of the Minister of Industry, 1997. Adapted from Statistics Canada publications: Cat. No. 11-001E page 5, Cat. No. 91-213-XPB Table 2.2. p. 26 From pp. 50-51 of *The Life of Charlemagne* by Einhard, University of Michigan Press, Ann Arbor; p. 28 Excerpt from p. 27 of *Beowulf and the Fight at Finnsburg*, 3e, Fr. Klaeber, ed., © 1950 by D.C. Heath & Co. Reprinted by permission of Houghton Mifflin Company; p. 29 (top) Excerpt from pp. 89-91 of *Beowulf: A Dual Language Edition* by Howell D. Chickering, Jr. © 1977 Doubleday, New York. Used by permission of Bantam Doubleday Dell Publishing Group Inc., (bottom) From pp. 45-46 of BEOWULF by Burton Raffel, translator, Translation © 1963 by Burton Raffel, Afterword © 1963 by New American Library. Used by permission of Dutton Signet; p. 30 From p. 160 of HOW THE IRISH SAVED CIVILIZATION by Thomas Cahill. Copyright © 1995 by Thomas Cahill. Used by permission of Doubleday, a division of Bantam Doubleday Dell Publishing Group, Inc.; p. 31 Excerpt from p. 73 of *The Anglo-Saxon Chronicle*, translated by Anne Savage, © 1995 Colour Library Books Ltd., UK. Used by permission of CLB International; p. 45 (left) Courtesy of Citizenship & Immigration Canada, (right) Excerpt from p. 121 of Weisner, Merry E., Julius R. Ruff, and William Bruce Wheeler, *Discovering the Western Past: A Look at the Evidence, First Edition, Volume I*, page 181. Copyright © 1989 by Houghton Mifflin Company. Reprinted with permission; p. 46 Excerpt from p. 213 of *The Anglo-Saxon Chronicle*, translated by Anne Savage, © 1995 Colour Library Books Ltd., UK. Used by permission of CLB International; p. 51 Poem by William Langland from *The Vision of Piers Plowman*, translated by Terence Tiller, 1981, British Broadcasting Corporation, London; p. 61 Excerpt from pp. 49, 51-52 of *The Travels of Sir John Mandeville* by Norman Denny and Josephine Filmer-Sankey, 1973, HarperCollins Ltd., UK. Used by permission of the author; p. 62 Excerpt from p. 174 of *The Travels of Marco Polo*, © 1987 Dorset Press, New York; p. 64 Excerpt from pp. 35-37 of *Eyewitness to History*, John Carey, ed., © 1987 Avon Books, New York; p. 73, p. 98 Poetry translated by J. R. Hightower in Cyril Birch, *Anthology of Chinese Literature*, Grove Press, New York; p. 84, p. 85, p. 90 Translated excerpts from Patricia B. Ebry, *Chinese Civilization: A Source Book*, Revised Edition, New York, The Free Press; p. 106 Qur'ân 3:195; p. 116 Qur'ân 34:27; p. 122 Translated excerpts by A. J. Arberry quoted in A. Hourani, *A History of the Arab Peoples*, Belknap Harvard, Cambridge, 1991, p. 34; p. 126 (top) Quoted in A. Hourani, *A History of the Arab Peoples*, Belknap Harvard, Cambridge, 1991, p. 120, (bottom) Quoted in W. H. McNeill and Marilyn Robinson, Editors, *The Islamic World*, Oxford, New York, p. 131; p. 127 Quoted in A. Hourani, *A History of the Arab Peoples*, Belknap Harvard, Cambridge, 1991, p. 210; p. 140 Excerpt from pp. 72-73 of *Eyewitness to History*, John Carey, ed., © 1987 Avon Books, New York;

p. 148 Excerpt from pp. 165-166 of *The Trial of Jeanne D'Arc*, translated by W.P. Barrett, © 1931 George Routledge, London. Used by permission of Routledge Ltd.; p. 152 Excerpt from p. 181 of Weisner, Merry E., Julius R. Ruff, and William Bruce Wheeler, *Discovering the Western Past: A Look at the Evidence, First Edition, Volume I*. Copyright © 1989 by Houghton Mifflin Company. Reprinted with permission; p. 157 Excerpt from Letter LVIII of *The Paston Letters*, John Fenn and Archer-Hind, eds., © 1951 J.M. Dent, London. Used by permission of Orion Publishing Group; p. 164 Excerpt from pp. 55-56 of *The Decameron* by Giovanni Boccaccio, translated by G.H. McWilliam, © 1972, Penguin Books Ltd., London; p. 165 Adapted from p. 57 of *Tillage, Trade and Invention* by George Warner, 1912, Blackie and Son, London; p. 170 *Tale of Genji* by Lady Murasaki, translated from the Japanese by E. Seidensticker, Knopf; p. 174, p. 183 Quoted in P. H. Varley, *Japanese Culture: A Short History*, Holt, Reinhardt, Winston, New York, 1977, p. 58; p. 192 Excerpts quoted in *Yukio Mishima on Hagakure*, Penguin, Middlesex, 1986, pp. 57-58; p. 194 (top and middle haiku) Quoted in Lee Sherman, *A History of Far Eastern Art*, fifth edition, Prentice Hall, Englewood Cliffs, 1994, p. 421; (bottom haiku) courtesy Cam Murray; (bottom excerpt) Quoted in L. A. Beck, *The Story of Oriental Philosophy*, Farrar and Reinhardt, New York, 1928, p. 422; p. 219 (top) From *The Family in Renaissance Italy* by David Herlihy. Copyright © 1974 by The Forum Press, Inc./Harlan Davidson Inc., (bottom) Excerpt from p. 28 of *The Bed and the Throne: The Life of Isabella D'Este* by George Marek, © 1976 Harper Row, New York. Used by permission of HarperCollins Publishers Inc.; p. 223 Excerpts from pp. 96-97 and 99-100 of THE PRINCE by Niccolò Machiavelli, translated by George Bull (Penguin Classics 1961, Second revised edition 1981) Copyright © George Bull, 1961, 1975, 1981. Used by permission of Frederick Warne & Co./Penguin Books Ltd., UK; p. 227 Excerpt from pp. 176-177 *of Selections from the Notebooks of Leonardo Da Vinci*, I.A. Richter, ed., © 1952 Oxford University Press, Oxford. Used by permission of Oxford University Press; p. 236-241 Excerpts from pp. 42-43, 46-47, 71-74, 80, 83, 114-115, 137-138, 144-145, 161-162, 175, 193, 197-198, 220-221 from *The Incas: Royal Commentaries of the Inca*, Alain Gheerbrant, ed., © 1961 Avon Books, New York; p. 258 (top) Excerpt from pp. 513-515 of *Christopher Columbus, Volume 1: His Life, His Work, His Remains* by John Boyd Thacher, 1903-1904, G.P. Putnams' Sons, New York, (bottom) Excerpts from p. 83 from *The Incas: Royal Commentaries of the Inca*, Alain Gheerbrant, ed., © 1961 Avon Books, New York; Excerpt from p. 181 of Weisner, Merry E., Julius R. Ruff, and William Bruce Wheeler, *Discovering the Western Past: A Look at the Evidence, First Edition, Volume I*. Copyright © 1989 by Houghton Mifflin Company. Reprinted with permission; p. 259 Excerpt from pp. 236-237 of *The Discoverers* by Daniel Boorstin, © 1985, Vintage Books. Used by permission of Random House, Inc.; p. 262 Excerpt from pp. 47-48, 237 of THE CONQUEST OF NEW SPAIN by Bernal Díaz, translated by J.M. Cohen (Penguin Classics, 1963) Copyright © J.M. Cohen, 1963. Used by permission of Frederick Warne & Co./Penguin Books Ltd.; p. 265 Excerpt from pp. 17-18 of *Hakluyt's Voyages*, I.R. Blacker, ed., (c) 1965, Viking, New York. Used by permission of Penguin USA; p. 273 Edited from the original document, as on p. cxcviii in *Mary Queen of Scots and the Babington Plot* by J.H. Pollen, © 1992 The Scottish History Society, University of Edinburgh; p. 279 Excerpt from p. 103 of *A Popular History of the Reformation* by P. Hughes, © 1960, Image Books; p. 280 Excerpt from Volume 14, p. 457 of *History of the Pope, 14 Volumes* by Ludwig Pastor, (c) 1898, St. Louis; p. 288 Excerpt from Volume I, p. 457, *Epistles in Three Volumes* by Erasmus D., 1901, London; p. 296 Excerpt from p. 24 of *The Rise and Fall of the British Empire* by Lawrence James. © 1994, Little, Brown and Company, London. Used by permission of Little, Brown and Company; p. 297 Excerpt from pp. 23, 24, 25 of *The Life of Olaudah Equiano, or Gustavus Vassa the African* by Olaudah Equiano, edited by Paul Edwards, Introduction ©1988 Paul Edwards, 1989, The Longman Group UK Limited; p. 299 Graphs from *A Popular History of the Reformation* by Philip A. Hughes, 1960, Image Books; p. 311 Qur'ân 25, 5; p. 313 For more information about PMI, see Edward DeBono, *The Use of Lateral Thinking*, London, Cape, 1967. p. 314 Quoted in Jan Read, *The Moors in Spain and Portugal*, London, Faber, 1974, p. 35; p. 318 Poetry of Seville Quoted in Read, pp. 112-15; p. 319 El Cid, quoted in Read, pp. 140-41; pp. 334-338 Adapted from *The Ramayana: A Shortened Prose Version of the Indian Epic* by R. K. Narayan, Viking Press, New York, 1972, pp. 151-60; p. 344 (top) The *Rig-Veda*, 10:90, verses 1-3 and 9-12, (bottom) The *Rig-Veda*; p. 347 Edict on Ashoka's First Pillar of Law in Sinharaja Tammit-Delgoda, *A Traveller's History of India*, Windrush Press, Gloucestershire, 1994, p. 60; p. 349 Quoted in A. Craig et al, *The Heritage of World Civilizations*, third edition, McMillan College, New York, p. 351; p. 350 Quoted in Alistair Shearer, *The Hindu Vision: Forms of the Formless*, Thames and Hudson, 1993, p. 20 ; p. 355 The Toronto Star Syndicate ; p. 357 Quoted in A. Craig et al, *The Heritage of World Civilizations*, third edition, McMillan College, New York, p. 736; pp. 366-69 *Ibn Battuta in Black Africa*, translated from the Arabic and edited by Said Hamdun and Noel King, London, Collings, 1975; p. 370 Poem quoted in *The Horizon History of Africa*, American Heritage Publishing, New York, 1971; p. 376-77 Adapted from "The Revolt Against God," in *The Horizon History of Africa*, American Heritage Publishing, New York, 1971, pp. 37-8; p. 378 From Nila K. Leigh, *Learning to Swim in Swaziland: A Child's-eye View of a Southern African Country*, Scholastic, New York, 1993; p. 390 From Edmund d'Auvergne, *Human Livestock: An Account of the Share of the English-speaking People in the Maintenance of and Abolition of Slavery*, Grayson and Grayson, London, 1933, quoted in *The Horizon History of Africa*, American Heritage Publishing, New York, 1971, p. 335-36; p. 392 From *Periplus of the Erythraean Sea* public domain; pp. 400-403 Excerpted from Cao Xueqin, *The Story of the Stone, Volume 1, The Golden Days*, translated by David Hawkes, Penguin Classics, 1988, pp. 87-92; p. 404 "The Wild Flower Man" by Lu Yu in K. Rexroth, *One Hundred Poems from the Chinese*, New Directions, 1971, p. 103; p. 415 Quoted in W. Marsden, *The Travels of Marco Polo*, Dorset Press, New York, 1987, pp. 123-4; p. 417 Quoted in Louis Untermeyer, *Lives of the Poets*, Simon and Schuster, 1959, p. 353; p. 424 Excerpt translated by Nancy Lee Swan, in Alfred J. Andrea and James Overfield, *The Human Record: Sources in Global History*, Vol. 1, second edition, Boston, Houghton Mifflin, pp. 148-53; p. 426 Matteo Ricci, *The Diary of Matteo Ricci, China in the Sixteenth Century*, translated by Louis Gallagher, Random House, New York, 1970.